INTRODUCTION TO CLINICAL PSYCHOLOGY

Perspectives, Issues, and Contributions to Human Service

Norman D. Sundberg / *University of Oregon*

Julian R. Taplin / *Morrison Center for Youth and Family Service*

Leona E. Tyler / *University of Oregon*

PRENTICE-HALL, INC. Englewood Cliffs, New Jersey 07632

Library of Congress Cataloging in Publication Data

SUNDBERG, NORMAN D.
  Introduction to clinical psychology.

  Bibliography: p.
  Includes index.
  1. Clinical psychology. 2. Psychotherapy. 3. Psychodiagnostics. 4. Community psychology.
I. Taplin, Julian R. II. Tyler, Leona Elizabeth (date). III. Title.
RC469.S93 1983   616.89   82-23069
ISBN 0-13-479451-6

*Editorial/production supervision and
  interior design: Linda Benson
Cover design: Diane Saxe
Manufacturing buyer: Ron Chapman*

Printed in the United States of America

10 9 8 7 6 5 4

ISBN 0-13-479451-6

PRENTICE-HALL INTERNATIONAL, INC., *London*
PRENTICE-HALL OF AUSTRALIA PTY. LIMITED, *Sydney*
EDITORA PRENTICE-HALL DO BRASIL, LTDA., *Rio de Janeiro*
PRENTICE-HALL CANADA INC., *Toronto*
PRENTICE-HALL OF INDIA PRIVATE LIMITED, *New Delhi*
PRENTICE-HALL OF JAPAN, INC., *Tokyo*
PRENTICE-HALL OF SOUTHEAST ASIA PTE. LTD., *Singapore*
WHITEHALL BOOKS LIMITED, *Wellington, New Zealand*

CONTENTS

II PRINCIPLES OF CLINICAL ASSESSMENT

IV THE PLACE OF CLINICAL WORK IN LARGER CONTEXTS

PREFACE

This introduction to clinical psychology is intended to serve as a knowledge base for people whose work involves helping other people. We anticipate that the primary readers will be students taking their first course in clinical psychology, either advanced undergraduates considering careers in the human services or first-year graduate students in clinical, counseling, or community psychology. Another set of readers might be people already working in the human services—nurses, social workers, physicians, the clergy, teachers —who are interested in learning about recent thinking and research in clinical psychology. During the writing of the book we have repeatedly asked ourselves: "What knowledge do all such readers need from the field? What fundamental principles and concepts does psychology have to offer that are useful for work in the human services?"

We recognize that the life stage through which many of these students are passing is a period of continuing search for interesting and rewarding career possibilities. Some are thinking of becoming psychologists. Many with other goals will need to make use of knowledge accumulated in clinical psychology—juvenile counselors, social workers, teachers, nurses, personnel workers, ministers, physicians, lawyers, public administrators, police officers, and volunteers in service programs. Others will simply be seeking a general education in the liberal arts; they will be interested in learning more about ways in which psychology is applied toward improving human lives. Probably only a few will eventually wind up in the professions labeled *clinical, counseling,* or *community* psychology. However, since clinical psychology provides a broad base of knowledge and attitudes, it can contribute importantly to the careers of men and women in all these other fields. A former president of the American Psychological Association, Nicholas Cummings (1982, p. 10) has said "I foresee the day when clinical psychology training will become the generic education for a variety of endeavors, from high school principal to legislative aide, just as law has become the generic education for a broad spectrum of endeavors." In general the human services are likely to become more and more important in the future, as the long-range trend in jobs throughout the world shows decreasing opportunities in direct production (agriculture and manufacturing) and increasing possibilities in services (especially information industries and leisure and helping services in postindustrial societies).

To sum up, as the title suggests, this book is intended to present what will be useful and thought-provoking not only to prospective clinical psychologists, but also to other students of human nature and to people working in the helping services. To emphasize this view, we have used general terms, such as *clinician* or *psychological services* to indicate the broad applicability of the ideas under consideration. Only in the beginning and ending chapters have we specifically emphasized the profession of clinical psychology and the particular concerns of those planning to become clinical psychologists. In other places, where we have described activities of psychologists, the basic information will be of use for work within all helping services.

Along with the fundamental concepts and principles, students need to learn that facts and ideas can be looked at from different perspectives. We have identified four major orientations from which clinical work is approached—the psychopathological, or curative perspective; the learning perspective, both behavioral and cognitive; the growth or developmental view; and the ecological orientation. To these four we have prefaced a fifth—the "natural helping" or every-day perspective which is often overlooked by experts but is important to understand, since much of the success of clinical and community work depends on the way natural systems work. In organizing the material, we have used concepts from systems theory, developmental psychology, and an emerging possibility theory. We have not, however, adhered slavishly to these viewpoints. They all have limitations, and during the near-century that clinical psychology has been in existence, useful concepts, methods, and research findings have turned up in many nooks and crannies of the territory. We have included these even when they did not fit easily into our system.

As we have thought about clinical psychology we have been impressed with how very broad the subject is and how much it has drawn from not only the basic science of psychology but also from medicine, psychiatry, social work, sociology, anthropology, education, and other fields. The sheer amount of what has been written about ways of helping people is overwhelming, impossible even to summarize within the space limitations set for this book. We were forced to select and set priorities. In blazing a trail through this vast and somewhat chaotic territory we have focused on the most prominent historical landmarks in theory and research. We have continually had to resist the temptation to write research reviews, with which we are all well acquainted. If this book is to be useful it must not be a catalog, compendium, or a long list of studies. It needs to be a structure of highly selected, well-organized ideas and research findings. We have done our best to approximate this ideal. But we know, of course, that we have omitted things which some instructors consider important; we hope that those instructors will supplement the book with other readings. For example, we have presented only limited discussions of two areas close to clinical work—psychological testing and abnormal psychology, because of the amount of detail that would have been necessary for a thorough introduction. We assume that readers needing more elaborate coverage will make use of separate courses devoted to those special fields.

This book is not a revision of our previous two books on clinical psychology (Sundberg & Tyler, 1962; Sundberg, Tyler, & Taplin, 1973). It is intended to be different. Compared with those two large volumes, which were often used in graduate classes (or even as review resources for licensing and ABPP examinations) this book is smaller, simpler, more selective, and, of course, more up-to-date. About two-thirds of the reference material was published after the 1973 volume. In a way, however, this book is a descendant of the earlier ones. We have used them as sources of ideas, sorting out those which have stood the test of time and checking the old ideas against recent research and new approaches to therapy.

Though we have focused on students taking their first course in clinical psychology, we believe that the book may also be of interest to many other students and professionals in the diverse array of colleges, universities, and mental health agencies to be found in the English-using world. Some instructors will find the book simple enough to use at a sophomore level along with other early material in psychology; others will assign it as a review and brief introduction to advanced graduate students in counseling or clinical psychology and in other human service fields. Some teachers and professionals in neighboring fields, such as psychiatry, social work, and psychiatric or psychosocial nursing, may find useful this organization of the psychological knowledge and these discussions of issues. We have made rather heavy use of referencing especially in the additional material at the end of chapters in order to provide opportunities for those wanting to pursue a topic in depth. Although our references are mainly to American writings, we have tried to keep in mind a worldwide readership, since we know from personal experience that nations and cultures differ greatly in their assumptions and arrangements for helping services. Clinical principles and research need to be approached with some skepticism when crossing cultures.

At the end of all chapters there are annotated suggestions to facilitate more extensive learning about psychological theory, practice, and research. With most of the chapters, too, we have provided summaries of selected research studies to illustrate the way psychologists and other social scientists go about evaluating practice and testing theory. We trust these will be of considerable value to both instructors and students.

Instructors can exercise considerable flexibility in using the book. There are two major levels at which the book can be used. Those who wish to emphasize only introductory, less complex material may simply assign the main text of the chapters. Those who are interested in more detail or who are working with more advanced students may place emphasis on special topics to be found in the boxes and on research examples at the end of the chapters; they may want to supplement the text with the recommended readings. The critiques at the end of chapters and the issues raised in many boxes could add to lively discussion in classes.

The writing of the book has been a source of great pleasure and intellectual stimulation for the three of us. We have met together at each others' homes over a five-year period, almost on a monthly basis, combing over the chapters as they emerged from their early forms and sharing criticisms and elaborations. These meetings have been interrupted by periods during which we have individually taken trips to Europe, Australia, China, and Southeast Asia and have conducted workshops, carried out clinical and teaching responsibilities, and attended professional meetings. All of these experiences have somehow led us to new thoughts and interesting ideas related to the book. We hope this sense of time and distance has entered into the perspectives that readers take from the book. The field of clinical psychology should provide new vistas for growing and changing and for exploring human landscapes.

We are indebted to many people for help. Our instructors and colleagues who have played important roles in shaping the development of our thinking include Richard Elliott, Donald G. Paterson, Starke Hathaway, William Schofield, Paul Meehl, Robert Leeper, James G. Kelly, Peter Lewinsohn, Lewis Goldberg, and many others. Several, such as Edward Lichtenstein and Carolin Keutzer, have contributed specific suggestions for sections of the book. We appreciate the help from Prentice-Hall and the critical suggestions made by reviewers who read earlier versions of chapters: George J. Allen, University of Connecticut; Anthony R. Ciminero, University of Georgia; Richard P. Halgin, University of Massachusetts; Michael Hirt, Kent State University; Bernard Levy, George Washington University; Joseph Lyons, University of California, Davis; Lizette Peterson, University of Missouri, Columbia; Donald S. Strassberg, University of Utah; and Lee Willerman, University of Texas as Austin. To students who have reviewed parts of this book and contributed suggestions we are also most grateful—David Antonnucio. Greg Clarke, Judith Clements, Lowell Coutant, David Gostnell, Sandra Hamilton, and Gregoire-Jean Hutchings. We are also indebted to many clients, who have not been described exactly in case illustrations, but whose contributions to our ideas have been significant. Finally we are grateful to our families who not only provided our support systems over the years but have given us invaluable opportunities to learn and enlarge our deepest understandings about human relationships.

Norman Sundberg
Julian Taplin
Leona Tyler

PART I

INTRODUCTION AND BASIC CONCEPTS

The first three chapters address three important questions: What is clinical psychology? What are the useful ideas for work in clinical situations? How do we go about setting up programs to help people psychologically and avoid harming them? In these chapters the reader will see that clinical psychology provides a knowledge base useful not only in the practice of clinical psychology but also in many other kinds of human service work such as nursing and law enforcement. That knowledge base is fed with ideas and research results from many areas of effort. Ideas and skills are like tools for working with people which anyone who tries to help people must have. We believe three perspectives are particularly valuable for the potential helper: (1) to consider people as functioning in systems—organismic, personal, familial and small group, organizational, community, and societal; (2) to see people and systems as being in the process of development, moving and evolving their patterned way of life; (3) to emphasize choice and possibilities, to help people think creatively of different ways of spending their allotted 24 hours a day. There are also many other ideas from the broad field of psychology which can be useful for specific clinical problems. Most of these ideas can be grouped under four professional orientations: the curative (or psychopathological), the learning, the growth (or developmental), and the social-ecological. These four together with the kinds of interventions found in everyday living make up the five orientations mentioned throughout this book. Since many community, family, and other helping networks occur naturally in clients' daily lives, human service workers need to become familiar with them so that they will not do damage to these important, already existing sources of support and encouragement.

1 CLINICAL PSYCHOLOGY: What Is It?

What is clinical psychology? As a start, we can say it has to do with the body of psychological knowledge that practitioners use as they attempt to help with behavioral and mental disorders and to promote people's well-being, productivity, and self-expression in their communities. Although clinical psychology is the largest single specialty within psychology that deals with principles and skills applied outside the laboratory, it is by no means all of *applied psychology*, which includes industrial, educational, organizational, military, and several other specialties. The word *clinical*, derived from the Latin and Greek words for *bed*, suggests the treatment of individuals who are ill, but clinical psychology has come to mean a broader area than just mental illness of individuals. Among the ultimate aims of clinical psychology are the psychological well-being and beneficial behavior of persons; therefore, it focuses on internal psychobiological conditions and on external social and physical environments within which individuals function.

SHIFTING VIEWS
OF THE FIELD

The scope and emphasis of clinical psychology have changed over the years. At one time *clinical psychology* and *abnormal psychology* were almost synonymous terms. During another period the clinical specialty was considered to be almost exclusively mental testing. Before World War II most psychological clinics were services for children, not adults. Later on the central emphasis was on individual psychotherapy. Now clinical psychology is all of these things and more. Furthermore, it has come to overlap so much with counseling psychology, which was originally confined to educational and vocational assistance, that it is often difficult to make a distinction. It also overlaps with other professions and disciplines. Any work with human problems and possibilities almost inevitably calls for interdisciplinary cooperation and knowledge of other helping resources.

The main trend in this constantly changing pattern seems to be that more and more kinds of people and more and more settings are included within the purview of clinical psychology. For example, clinics in the 1920s and 1930s were mainly concerned with retarded, maladjusted, and delinquent children. The concern persists, but now the resources for studying and treating such children have greatly expanded, and maladjusted and delinquent adults also receive attention. The clinical psychologist's first role in mental health teams was that of the expert on testing and education. This is still an important function, but now additional roles include psychotherapy, community consultation, and the administration of programs. Research was always a significant aspect of clinical psychology; however, now research efforts have diversified, and increasing emphasis has been placed on evaluation—the evaluation of whole programs and organizations as well as individual improvement under treatment. Clinical psychology is being practiced in schools, factories, and prisons as well as in mental hospitals and clinics, and, like lawyers and physicians, many clinical psychologists are in private practice.

The field of knowledge called *clinical psychology* cannot be defined simply as "what clinical psychologists do." It has broader implications. Individuals who are not trained psychologists have increasingly felt a need for personal growth experiences and voluntary groups of many kinds, with or without psychologists at the helm. They are attempting to apply psychological knowledge in enriching their own lives. Furthermore, since the 1960s a great variety of new mental health workers has come upon the scene, loosely characterized as *paraprofessionals*, who focus on particular groups or special needs—drug abusers, exconvicts, minority clients, potential suicides, for example—without advanced degrees in psychology, or often in any other discipline. The body of knowledge we are talking about is important to them and needs to be included in the training programs they undergo, at school or on the job.

These constant shifts in what is being attempted, who is being served, and who is doing the work naturally create some confusion about the boundaries of clinical psychology. There is conflict as well as confusion in the total picture of the professions in mental health. The closest and most persistent comparison has been between psychiatry and psychology. Psychiatrists—that is, physicians who specialize in the treatment of mental illness—have the legal right to prescribe the drugs widely used in treating mental patients. Historically they have headed the teams, made the final decisions, set the policies. But increasingly since World War II psychologists have been challenging this leadership. Many, perhaps most, of the problems that people bring to mental health clinics do not really seem to be "illnesses" at all but are primarily difficulties that have arisen during the individual's development through the learning processes or are behavior patterns generated in particular social settings and circumstances. It is estimated that two-thirds of the physical complaints that patients bring to medical doctors are partially or primarily psychological. Psychologists and even some psychiatrists contend that much of medical training is irrelevant in such cases and that the professional worker best equipped to deal with them is the one with the most extensive and intensive psychological knowledge. In this continuing struggle psychologists have gained the right to act as therapists, to practice independently, and to act as administrators of hospital wards, agencies, and programs. The shape of clinical psychology today is partly determined by this continuing dynamic interplay in the mental health systems.

Figure 1–1 shows the special emphases and concerns of the four core mental health professions—psychiatric social work, clinical psychology, psychiatry, and mental health nursing. All have traditions as independent professions, and even such names as Florence Nightingale, Jane Addams, Sig-

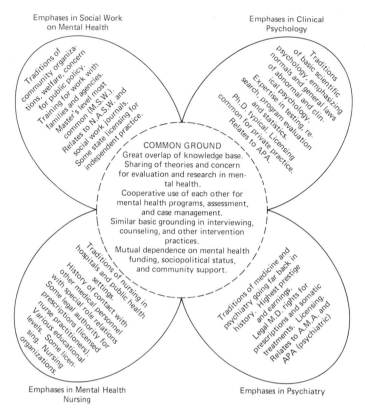

Emphases in Social Work
on Mental Health

Emphases in Clinical
Psychology

Traditions of community organizations, welfare, concern for public policy. Training for work with families and agencies. Master's level most common (M.S.W.). Relates to N.A.S.W. and social work journals. Some state licensing for independent practice.

Traditions of basic scientific psychology, emphasizing normals and general laws of abnormal and clinical psychology. Expertise in testing, research, program evaluation and statistics. Ph.D. typical. Licensing common for private practice. Relates to APA.

COMMON GROUND
Great overlap of knowledge base.
Sharing of theories and concern
for evaluation and research in mental health.
Cooperative use of each other for
mental health programs, assessment,
and case management.
Similar basic grounding in interviewing,
counseling, and other intervention
practices.
Mutual dependence on mental health
funding, sociopolitical status,
and community support.

Traditions of nursing in hospitals and public health settings. History of contact with other medical personnel with special role relations. Some legal authority for nurse practitioners (licensed prescriptions). Various educational levels. Some licensing. Nursing organizations.

Traditions of medicine and psychiatry going far back in history. Highest prestige and earnings. Legal M.D. rights for prescriptions and somatic treatments. Licensing. Relates to A.M.A. and APA (psychiatric).

Emphases in Mental Health
Nursing

Emphases in Psychiatry

Figure 1-1   Commonalities and specialities of the four core mental health professions.

mund Freud, and B. F. Skinner have special connotations to the different professions. Each profession has its own national and local organizations and professional journals toward which its members turn for leadership and support; oftentimes even a well-read person in one profession may not be familiar with research in another field. Each of the four has some form of licensing, registration, or certification in various North American states and provinces. Social work and nursing are much less involved in private practice, have a higher proportion of women in their ranks, tend to be lower paying, and have fewer doctoral-level practitioners than psychology and psychiatry. Prescription of drugs and authority over such physical treatment as electroconvulsive therapy is legally limited to physicians; however, in some states certain kinds of licensed nurses are allowed to prescribe some drugs. Nurses and psychiatrists have a long history of close connection with hospitals, whereas social workers have a long history of a community orientation. Psychology has a history of close relations with colleges and universities, through its connection with liberal arts psychology; psychology has strongly emphasized knowledge of normal development and general psychological principles and laws. Usually psychologists will have the most thorough grounding in research of the four professions, but often they have relatively less practical experience during their training than the others, who make strong use of an apprenticeship model of learning.

Despite the many differences in backgrounds, training, and traditions among the four, there is a great amount of overlap and sharing. All of the four core professionals use theories of learning, psychoanalysis, and basic psychobiology. They are often equally well equipped to conduct assessment interviews, to diagnose abnormality, and to carry out psychotherapy or other interviews. They are all dependent on general public attitudes toward mental health. Within these professions, as in all fields, individuals differ greatly in competency and interests.

Just as psychologists have challenged psychiatrists, they in turn are being challenged by the specialists in the other disciplines, and by the paraprofessionals mentioned earlier. There are those who think that the differentiation into separate professions, each with its own standards, organizations, and skills, has outlived its usefulness. Should the top position in a community mental health clinic, for example, with its prestige and high salary, go to either a psychiatrist with a medical degree or a psychologist with a Ph.D.? In the organization there may be a dedicated nurse or social worker whose skills in working with staff members, knowledge of the community, and administrative competence are greater than those of anyone else. Should insurance payments for mental health services be channeled only to professionals with designated degrees, or should they be available to the paraprofessionals who clients think have been most helpful? Such questions produce a ferment in clinical psychology that anyone who hopes to understand it must recognize.

SOME ILLUSTRATIVE CASES

Oliver

One way to get a feeling for what clinical psychology is all about is to think about some specific persons and situations. For example, 17-year-old Oliver was referred to the Oak Glen Mental Health Center by a physician who treated him in the hospital emergency ward to which his frantic mother had brought him when she found him in a coma on the floor of his room, beside an empty bottle of pills. She had known for some time that he was depressed. He had even talked vaguely about "ending it all" on a number of occasions, but she had not really considered that these were serious threats; she had hoped that he would "snap out of it." It was difficult for her to believe that there could be anything seriously wrong with him. He had always seemed to be a normal child. Although he was perhaps a little quieter than the average, it had only been during the last year or so that his depression had become apparent to his mother. She had asked him what the matter was, but he had nothing to say.

Coming to the mental health center, Oliver looked like most high school students in those days—long hair a little unkempt, jeans, T-shirt, sneakers. After a thorough physical examination had shown that there was nothing organically wrong, Bill Everett, a paraprofessional counselor, was assigned to this case because he was experienced in working with adolescents, was also young, and because Oliver seemed to like him in initial contacts. Without being too formal about it, Bill interviewed the young man, beginning by talking to him in an easy, friendly way in the reception room and walking out to Oliver's car with him.

Although not very communicative, Oliver did tell Bill about some of the circumstances of his life. He was an only child, and his father, a lawyer, and mother had been divorced about five years before. His mother had gone to work as a computer programmer, and she and Oliver moved away from the small town where they had lived since Oliver's birth. In the city they lived in a comfortable apartment in a good neighborhood, but somehow Oliver never managed to make friends with anybody there or at the large high school he attended. Most of his spare time was spent watching television. His mother, on the other hand, had many friends, including one man she was thinking of marrying. None of her friends paid much attention to Oliver. He was just there.

During his last year in high school, the strain on him increased. It was necessary for him to think about what to do after graduation. His father, who had seen Oliver only a few times since the divorce, now reappeared and wanted to send Oliver to the prestigious college from which he had graduated. Oliver was only a mediocre high school student, however; his grades were mostly C's, although some test scores suggested that he might have more ability than he had shown. None of the vocational programs appealed to him. He was not good at sports, and the other boys made fun of his awkward attempts when he tried to play basketball. Without any close friends, he looked down on his fellow students and made no attempt to get to know them.

There were other complications as well. For years he had been doubtful about his own sexuality. Young women seemed not to respond to him with any interest—at least not the ones he found attractive—but he did not think he was a homosexual. His athletic awkwardness seemed to confirm his weak masculinity. Furthermore, he had jettisoned the religious beliefs he had grown up with at the time of his parents' divorce and had become profoundly cynical about life in general. More and more he felt as though there was nothing worth living for. The conjunction of a quarrel with his mother and concern about an important school examination seemed to have triggered his suicide attempt.

What does clinical psychology have to say about a life like Oliver's, and how does a program for changing it take shape? There are several approaches, two of which stand out as most frequently employed—an emphasis on the individual's feelings and ideas (an *intrapsychic* approach) versus an emphasis on the environment and its relation to the person (a *situational* and sometimes a *social learning* approach). The intrapsychic approach, which has been dominant for many years, grew out of the research and practice of Sigmund Freud and his many followers. This approach would attempt to help Oliver to understand his own feelings and motives as they had developed over the years and to enable him to replace unsound attitudes with sound ones through a close relationship with an adult therapist. This is likely to be a time-consuming and expensive business, too expensive for many public services. The situational approach would focus attention on the outer environment and the person's behavior in relation to it. This perspective assumes that Oliver's actions and attitudes are responses to present situational problems and would attempt to change some aspects of the surroundings in ways designed to produce cumulative improvements in the young man's behavior. Some of this latter approach to human problems rests on the research into the learning process that psychologists have been engaged in for decades and to some extent on the work of the social psychologist Kurt Lewin and his successors.

A particular therapist or clinic is likely to emphasize one of these patterns in treating a person, although combinations and variations are common. In a case like Oliver's, the second seemed more feasible to the clinicians in the center. Because his isolation from other human beings appeared to be such a prominent feature of his situation, the first step would be designed to change his social environment. Most clinics sponsor therapy groups. If Oliver were willing to join a group of young people discussing personal problems, he could begin to find a place in a network of human relationships, to understand others, and to allow them to understand him. Other features of the plan worked out in cooperation with Oliver involved leaving high school and getting a job. In order to do this he would need to learn job-seeking skills and social skills he now lacks. The plan also included ways of getting to know some young women through a return to activities in church or other places where young people meet. He needed to learn such simple social skills as how to ask for a date and how not to be too discouraged if he is turned down. These are examples of the concrete kinds of learning that enter into treatment of the second sort. The therapist's skill lies in sensing what steps are actually possible for a particular client, applying what he or she knows about the learning process in devising a plan likely to accomplish them, and monitoring progress so that the plan can be changed as needed.

Bill and Sally

Bill and Sally have been living together, at least off and on, for more than 15 years. In their case it seems to be literally true that they cannot live with each other or without each other. They were married during their college years when Bill was 21 and Sally 19. Bill obtained an engineering degree and joined a consulting firm where he was very successful. Sally dropped out of college when their first child, a son, was born and never went back. Within the next five years they had two other children, a daughter and another son. Conflicts became sharper as the years passed. There were constant arguments over money, over Sally's sloppy housekeeping, over the disciplining of the children. Bill became involved in several not-too-serious affairs with women at the office, affairs that Sally found out about and bitterly resented. After about seven years of constant bickering, they decided that divorce was the only solution. Sally was granted custody of the children and a liberal financial allowance. She tried her hand at various jobs, but without a college degree or any salable skills, she never managed to get into anything that interested her. After a few months on a job she would quit or be fired. The children, as might be expected, showed signs of strain. Since both parents still lived in the same city, they saw their father frequently and became expert in manipulating both parents, playing one against the other.

Bill and Sally found that they missed each other a great deal. Before long they were seeing each other fairly regularly. Their sexual relationship had always been extremely rewarding for both of them. About a year after the divorce, they decided to give marriage another try. Almost immediately the arguments and recriminations started once again, becoming more and more bitter and violent. John, the older son, became involved in some minor delinquencies, and each parent blamed the other for his behavior. Bill harped on Sally's inability to hold a job or manage a household. He thought that if she could only get in some activity of her own, she would get off his back. Sally suspected that Bill was having affairs again, although he was better at concealing them now.

Another divorce seemed inevitable, but this time they decided to try some counseling before they gave up. Ann Farmer, the counselor whom they consulted, following the learning-situational approach, looked at the ongoing family system as a unit rather than attempting to make changes in the personalities of Bill and Sally as individuals. By analyzing the complex functioning system as a whole, Dr. Farmer hoped to locate some crucial aspects of the family situation that, if changed, would produce changes in the way the whole system worked. Clinical psychology, as well as sociology, has developed some knowledge about such interactive systems and some usable techniques for modifying them. The first step in the plan that she worked out with Bill and Sally called for the keeping of detailed daily records of everything that went on at home, including what they did and talked about.

Arrangements were made to have some of their conversations videotaped, so that they and the counselor could watch and listen to the tapes. After about two weeks of this intensive observation, they all agreed on two change points. The first was to help Sally find a job that she would persevere at for at least six months. The second was to arrange for both Bill and Sally to get training at a children's clinic that specialized in teaching parents methods of managing children like eight-year-old Kevin, whose behavior was by now completely out of control. The prescription worked. The family system began to function differently. Bill and Sally had less to argue about and more to talk about without getting upset. Anxiety, guilt, and anger directed at the children were reduced. The plan seemed to be working, as the family found ways to have fun together despite occasional friction. From a follow-up telephone call six months after termination of counseling, Dr. Farmer learned that the family was still together and could give several illustrations of successful problem solving.

Seldom do stories coming out of mental health clinics conclude with "they lived happily ever after." New problems may appear. Old difficulties may reappear. Therapy ends when the client's life is proceeding reasonably smoothly. There is no reason to think that a person who has had worries or job problems will not have some again. Freud wrote that psychotherapy removed neurosis and returned a person to the stresses and strains common to everyday life. One hopes, however, that a therapeutic experience will develop general ways of handling problems that will help the person contend with future adversities.

Ward K

In accordance with modern thinking about the treatment of mental illness, a large state hospital was attempting to discharge as many patients as possible into the communities from which they came. There seemed to be no hope of this for the patients on Ward K, however; family and staff members had given up hope for most of them long ago. Some had been residents of the hospital for 20 years or more. Others had been in and out repeatedly, going out when their behavior became less obviously psychotic, returning a few months later when they were unable to make it on the outside. Most of them had no home or family anymore and could only go to cheap hotels in a run-down part of the city. Some were delusional, muttering unintelligible remarks to passersby. Some were incontinent, others messy with their food. Many were completely passive, responding to nothing and no one.

The administrator of Ward K, a highly competent psychiatric nurse, Ms. Fuller, decided that there was nothing to lose and potentially a good deal to gain by instituting a token economy on the ward. The first step was to make an analysis of what behavioral changes were advisable and possible for each individual patient. Ms. Fuller recognized that it was important that the initial behavior changes sought be small ones. Mary, for example, might be asked to dress herself and make her bed. Henry, mute for years, might be rewarded for saying "good morning" in response to an attendant's greeting. Cynthia would get credit for leaving her room and going to an occupational therapy session. Working with attendants, Ms. Fuller developed these behavioral prescriptions and gave them a supply of colored tokens to be handed out to the patients as soon as they carried out the actions indicated. An exchange system was set up that allowed patients to use these tokens later to purchase canteen items or hospital privileges. As improvement occurred, behavioral prescriptions were revised upward—that is, as a patient made one small improvement in behavior, another, perhaps a little larger, could be attempted. Progress was slow but steady, as Ms. Fuller's records demonstrated. After several months the ward had become a much pleasanter place for both patients and staff. Several of the patients made enough progress so that they thought they could maintain the new habits without the token rewards and were willing to try to get along outside the hospital. They were discharged to a halfway house where former patients lived and helped one another cope with the problems that arose. Such learning through reinforcement, based on extensive laboratory research, is an important part of clinical psychology.

These are only a few of the attempts that are being made to apply psychological knowledge in solving human problems and improving human life. The illustrations have emphasized the learning-situational approach, but there is a great variety of ways in which psychologists and related professionals work with people. Throughout the book there will be many other cases and illustrations of that variety.

A BRIEF HISTORY

Although clinical psychology as a professional specialty is less than 100 years old, its roots go far back in human history, as Figure 1–2 shows. Persons, families, and communities in ancient Greece and India, medieval London, and colonial America faced many of the same problems in adapting to their social environments and internal quandaries that we do now. Accepted ways of dealing with psychological difficulties are worked out in every culture, with particular individuals playing roles similar to those of psychologists and other mental health workers today. The oracle at Delphi, the witch doctor in Central Africa, wise elders of Indian tribes, and priests and pastors down through the centuries have helped men and women to make decisions about what to do, to accept the inexorable realities of their lives, and to change unsatisfactory attitudes and behaviors. Even today many persons still prefer to consult an astrologer or a fortuneteller about their difficulties rather than to bring them to a psychological clinic or other professional service.

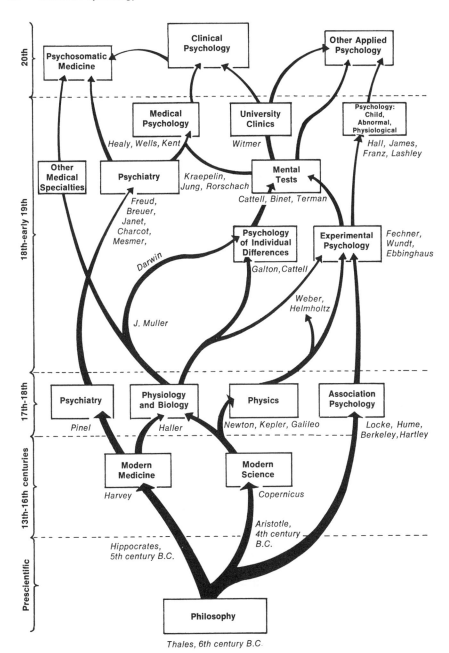

Figure 1-2 Development of clinical psychology—antecedent areas of knowledge and historical persons. From "Clinical Psychology" by Helen D. Sargent and Martin Mayman in *American Handbook of Psychiatry, Volume II* edited by Silvano Arieti. © 1959 by Basic Books, Inc.

The ideas woven into the fabric of clinical psychology also go back to the beginning of recorded history. Greek philosophers developed scientific ways of looking at human beings as well as at nature. Aristotle (born 384 B.C.) is often considered to be the first psychologist, although the word *psychology* did not come into use until centuries later. Hippocrates (born 460 B.C.) initiated the medical approach to abnormal psychological phenomena that gradually replaced the prevailing supernatural or demonological conceptions. Scientific conceptions of human nature waxed and waned as the centuries passed, never disappearing entirely. Even during the fifteenth and sixteenth centuries, the heyday of witchcraft trials, there were always enlightened souls who spoke out against the prevailing views and practices.

The Early Years of Clinical Psychology

It was in Europe and America during the late nineteenth century that psychology emerged as a science. Three social developments made this possible and necessary. The first was the Industrial Revolution, which led to the replacement of family and community ties by bureaucratic and impersonal relationships in many areas of life. The second was the growth of science and the increasing confidence people placed in it as a foundation for human progress. The third was a new view of human nature, adding to the rational and hedonistic assumptions of the eighteenth century an interest in romanticism, the irrational and primitive impulses, and mysteries like hypnosis.

The first psychological laboratory, established by Wilhelm Wundt in Leipzig in 1879, and the early applications of measurement and statistics to human characteristics by Francis Galton in England exemplify the scientific influence. At the same time William James in the United States was exploring other aspects of psychology and framing philosophical concepts to support the science. Sigmund Freud's practice in Vienna and the publication of his first book, *The Interpretation of Dreams,* in 1900 exemplify the interest in analysis of the irrational.

The honor of first using the term *clinical psychology* and of establishing the first psychological clinic goes to Lightner Witmer. The clinic opened at the University of Pennsylvania in 1896. Witmer asserted the importance of careful assessment before treatment and was deeply committed to a broad view of the emerging profession. He urged a concern for prevention in working with children in the Philadelphia slums (Reisman, 1981). Soon other clinics were started, and mental hospitals began to include psychologists and social workers on their staffs.

The early twentieth century was an exciting period of new ideas, new plans, new tools. People held great hopes for human progress and expected psychology to help turn those hopes into reality. Several highly influential thinkers published important books during this period—Freud, James,

BOX 1-1 *FIRST ISSUE OF THE FIRST CLINICAL PSYCHOLOGY JOURNAL*

Below is a reproduction of the title page of *The Psychological Clinic*, which was a journal aimed to present "examinations and treatments of individual mental and moral peculiarities—not necessarily abnormal—associated with developmental phenomena" to psychologists, educators, physicians, and social workers. The yearly subscription price for nine issues in 1907 was $1.00! Witmer continued to edit this journal until 1935 when it ceased publication. In 1937, the *Journal of Consulting Psychology* took over many of the same topics and soon became an official journal of the APA. In 1982 Sol Garfield, the editor of the present *Journal of Consulting and Clinical Psychology*, commemorated the 75th anniversary of Witmer's journal.

Vol. I, No. 1.   March 15, 1907

THE PSYCHOLOGICAL CLINIC

*A Journal for the Study and Treatment
of Mental Retardation and Deviation*

Editor:
LIGHTNER WITMER, Ph. D.,
University of Pennsylvania.

Associate Editor: Associate Editor:
HERBERT STOTESBURY, Ph. D.,   JOSEPH COLLINS, M. D.,
The Temple College,   Post Graduate Medical College,
Philadelphia.   New York.

CONTENTS

THE PSYCHOLOGICAL CLINIC PRESS
WEST PHILADELPHIA STATION, PHILADELPHIA, PA.

Garfield, 1982, p. 168

McDougall, Dewey, Adler, Jung, Watson, to name just a few. Psychologists rallied around one or another of the systems set forth in these books. Psychology became differentiated into separate "schools," in conflict with one another on many points. The sharpest and most persistent of these theoretical conflicts, surviving even today, centers on the question of whether psychology is the science of *mind* or *behavior*. Only after decades of argument did syntheses begin to appear. Today most of us can agree that psychology is the science of both experience (a broader concept than mind) *and* action (a broader concept than behavior). We expect clinical psychology to help people to feel and to act in more satisfactory ways.

From 1900 to 1920 many of the tools that psychologists and other human service workers would use were also being invented. The most important of these new instruments was the intelligence test, important not only because it provided a scientific way of measuring one major aspect of individuality but also because it led to a long series of assessment devices, which are still being perfected. Binet's first scale was published in 1905 in Paris. Almost immediately revisions, translations, and adaptations were undertaken in Europe and the United States. During World War I American psychologists developed group intelligence tests that extended Binet's original ideas in new directions. The Army Alpha made it possible to test adults as

Figure 1-3   Some pioneers in psychology at Clark University meeting in 1909. Front row (left to right) Sigmund Freud, G. Stanley Hall, and Carl Jung. (Mary Evans Picture Library)

well as children and to administer tests to groups as well as to individuals. The Army Beta was a nonverbal test that could be given to illiterates. By 1920, standards for reliability, validity, and norms that were to govern the whole testing enterprise had been formulated.

These years also saw the beginnings of personality testing. As early as 1904 Jung proposed a word association test for probing unconscious meanings. In 1917, while other psychologists worked on intelligence tests, Woodworth produced a questionnaire called the *Personal Data Sheet* to be used in screening military recruits for psychiatric difficulties. It was the first of a long line of personality inventories, to which additions are still being made.

It was during these decades of development that clinical psychology attained a recognizable identity. Although psychologists had organized the American Psychological Association in 1892 (with an initial membership of 30), it was not until 1919 that clinical psychologists set up a special section of the parent organization. A journal called *Psychological Clinic* was started by Witmer in 1907, following the establishment of the *Journal of Abnormal Psychology* in 1906. Now psychologists could belong to an organization and have publication outlets for their ideas.

The Period of Consolidation

The years between the two world wars brought growth in numbers, advances in the science of psychology, and the development of a standard pattern for the organization of psychological services. In the realm of ideas and concepts Freudian psychoanalysis became the dominant orientation, although Adler, Jung, and other dissident members of the original psychoanalytic school also had their adherents. The behaviorist movement, strongly influential in psychological research activity, was not really felt in clinical psychology until later.

Actually what most clinical psychologists were doing during the 1920s and 1930s did not have much to do with theory. Most of the clinics in which they worked were focused on the problems of children, whereas personality theories of the times were concerned mainly with adults. Child guidance clinics, following a pattern used in demonstration clinics organized under the auspices of the Commonwealth Fund, featured the treatment team consisting of psychiatrist, psychologist, and social worker. Each profession was assigned a special role. The psychologist was in charge of testing, some of the interviewing, and school relationships. Psychology was viewed as an educational rather than a medical specialty. Little psychotherapy was being provided by anybody during these decades, except for lengthy psychoanalyses by specially trained practitioners, mainly psychiatrists with patients who could afford the high cost. (Increasingly a medical degree was being required for admission to psychoanalytic training institutes in the United States, even though Freud had opposed this restriction.)

This team organization seemed to work smoothly enough at the time, perhaps partly because many clinical psychologists had only masters' degrees and were content to think of themselves as technicians rather than independent practitioners. But it saddled the emerging profession with problems that were to become increasingly urgent in subsequent decades when the level of training for clinical psychologists was raised and the overlap between the competencies of psychiatrists and psychologists became much greater.

The major shift occurred during and just after World War II. Psychologists became strongly involved in hospital work with military personnel and veterans and with adults, rather than children; they often found themselves responsible for psychotherapy as well as assessment. Clinical psychology was transformed from an educational into a medical specialty. During the war years there was plenty of work for anyone who possessed some psychological knowledge and skill, but psychologists were no longer willing to accept a status lower than that of psychiatrists with the same duties. Conflicts between the professions became sharper during the immediate postwar years and still persist.

During the 1930s another group of applied psychologists was attempting to get counseling services established for students in colleges and universities, the University of Minnesota taking the lead. Here the conflict with medicine was initially not a problem because psychologists were in charge of the whole treatment process. During and after World War II, however, counseling psychologists broadened the scope of their activities, providing service to soldiers, veterans, and other adults, and found it necessary to work with other mental health professionals.

A wide variety of assessment techniques was promulgated during this quarter-century. There were other intelligence tests to supplement the original Binet, tests for particular kinds of people and for special purposes. In addition to the personality inventories mentioned earlier, a new kind of instrument, the *projective technique*, came into use, based on the assumption that what a subject did with ambiguous stimulus material revealed something about the structure of his or her personality. The Rorschach set of inkblots was the most conspicuous and widely used of these techniques. Psychological tests to diagnose the kind and extent of behavioral changes associated with brain damage were invented. The Strong Vocational Interest Blank was developed on a solid basis of research evidence that people in different occupations differed significantly in their likes, dislikes, and preferences for a wide variety of activities and situations.

The Period
of Rapid Professional Growth

During the two decades following World War II clinical psychology really came into its own as a profession. The many psychologists who had been drawn into a wide variety of activities during the war were ready for new ideas, new organizations, new standards for training and practice. The profession had become highly visible, and large numbers of students were attracted to it, so that its numbers increased very rapidly.

What the typical clinical psychologist was doing in the 1950s was very different from what the clinician in the 1930s had been doing. Assessment was still an important responsibility, but the emphasis was on personality characteristics rather than on intelligence. A large number of assessment techniques were available, so that choosing those most appropriate for a given case was an important skill. The interpretation of test results was a major responsibility since scores alone were of little value, especially in the case of projective techniques. In addition to assessment, psychotherapy was now an important activity of psychologists, and many of them regarded it as much more interesting than diagnostic or assessment work. Psychoanalysis and its offshoots were still the predominant theories, but other ideas were circulating, such as Rogers' client-centered therapy, existentialism, and social learning theory.

Probably the most significant accomplishment of the period from 1940 to 1960 was the establishment of a new pattern of training, along with new organizations and ethical standards to govern practice. The American Psychological Association was reorganized in 1944, with clinical psychology as one of the divisions. A committee was appointed to develop a plan for training clinical psychologists, and in 1949 a landmark conference was held in Boulder, Colorado. The principles worked out there have shaped the development of the profession ever since, with minor adjustments and changes coming out of later conferences, in 1956, 1958, 1965, and 1973. The Boulder Plan, along with earlier decisions about job descriptions and hiring by the U.S. Veterans Administration, made the doctoral degree the standard for clinical psychologists. Graduate training was to prepare the student for a threefold role in assessment, in therapy, and in research. The would-be clinician was to be thoroughly grounded in the science of psychology as well as in essential skills. Practicum training was to accompany academic study, and a one-year internship in an established clinical setting was required for graduation. What the Boulder Conference established was the *scientist-practitioner model*. Over the years that followed, the necessary arrangements were worked out for accreditation of programs, certification of individual practitioners, codification and enforcement of ethical standards, and many other matters.

Further Expansion, Doubts, and Reorientations

The early 1960s marked a high point in the development of American clinical psychology. Although the number of clinical psychologists has continued to increase, a period of less certainty and optimism and more diverse views about what clinical psychologists should be doing has set in since then. A significant marker growing out of a massive study of American mental health needs in the late 1950s was the Community Mental Health Act, signed by President John F. Kennedy in 1963. Mental health was then designated as a national concern, and the opportunities facing clinical psychologists appeared limitless. Psychologists since then have become wiser but sadder. Mental health for everyone is not going to be as easy to achieve as we once thought it was.

A number of factors can be identified in the change of attitude. There were, of course, sobering historical developments. The Vietnam War and the increasingly angry protests against it threatened to tear the United States apart. Several of the country's most beloved leaders were assassinated. The cities continued to deteriorate. Crime and delinquency flourished, and drug use increased alarmingly, especially among the young. The Watergate disclosures led to widespread cynicism, and the passivity and apathy of the 1970s were no more encouraging than was the militancy of the 1960s. The economic stagnation and inflation starting in the late 1970s reverberated through the public and private sectors and brought a leveling off, and even decline, in training research and services in mental health. Important positive trends can also be discerned, such as major scientific advances, awareness of, and some progress toward equality, but these were not enough to counteract the general deterioration of confidence in the future.

Within both clinical psychology and the general mental health field, there were also some sobering developments. A growing number of follow-up studies showing mixed results led to doubts about the efficacy of much psychotherapy. Research also proved that paraprofessionals could do many kinds of treatment as well as professionals. It was clearly shown in other studies that many people in the population, especially the poor, were being inadequately served. Furthermore, the complex interpretations that clinicians were making on the basis of test scores were found to be less predictive of what patients would do than were simple statistical combinations of scores on a small number of tests—when those were available. Although mental hospital populations were dropping in the mid-1950s, the result was often a piling up of mentally ill in different locations—such as cheap hotels in run-down areas. Drugs were heavily prescribed in and out of institutions with some negative side effects. Community mental health agencies were never adequately financed and did not accomplish what had been expected of them. As colleges ceased expanding and public funds became scarcer in the late 1970s and early 1980s, new jobs for new clinical psychologists became harder to find.

The clinical psychology of the last few decades of this century is thus assuming a different face from the clinical psychology of the 1960s, although many individuals are still plying their profession much as they did then. In the realm of ideas and theories, the influence of psychoanalysis has declined, and interventions based on learning and environmental change have become

BOX 1–2 *SIGNIFICANT EVENTS IN CLINICAL PSYCHOLOGY*

The following events were chosen by at least three of five textbook authors as significant events for discussions of the historical background of clinical psychology (Bellack & Hersen, 1980; Bernstein & Nietzel, 1980; Kendall & Norton-Ford, 1982; Phares, 1979; and Sundberg, Tyler & Taplin, 1973).

1892   American Psychological Association founded.

1895   Breuer and Freud publish *Studies in Hysteria;* transference in the therapist-client relationship described.

1896   Lightner Witmer founds first psychological clinic at U. of Penn.

1905   First practical test of intelligence produced by Binet and Simon in Paris.

1908   National Committee for Mental Hygiene founded by Beers, author of *The Mind That Found Itself.*

1909   Healy establishes Juvenile Psychopathic Institute in Chicago.

1916   Terman's Stanford-Binet test published; incorporates ratio IQ.

1917   U.S. Army Alpha and Beta tests (for intelligence) and Woodworth's Personal Data Sheet (for personality) developed for screening recruits.

1919   Section on Clinical Psychology formed in APA.

1921   Rorschach publishes his inkblot test in *Psychodiagnostik,* Switzerland.

1922   J. McKeen Cattell founds the Psychological Corporation.

1924   Mary Cover Jones reports early use of behavioral therapy—the case of Peter.

1925   Gesell's *Mental Growth of the Pre-School Child* gives developmental tests.

1935   Christiana Morgan and Henry Murray publish the Thematic Apperception Test (TAT).

1936   Louttit publishes first clinical text, *Clinical Psychology.*

1937   Terman and Merrill publish revision of the Stanford-Binet.

1937   Clinical Section of APA disbanded and American Association for Applied Psychology formed (which was abolished in 1944 as APA reunified).

1938   Lauretta Bender introduces Visual-Motor Gestalt Test.

1939   Wechsler publishes Wechsler-Bellevue Intelligence test incorporating age norms and deviation IQs.

1942   Carl Rogers in *Counseling and Psychotherapy* formulates client-centered therapy.

1943   Hathaway and McKinley publish the MMPI.

1946   U. S. Veterans Administration, National Institute of Mental Health, and U. S. Public Health start supporting doctoral training programs in clinical psychology.

1947   American Board of Professional Psychology established.

1949   APA's Boulder conference on graduate education in clinical psychology affirms the scientist-professional model.

1950   Dollard and Miller in *Personality and Psychotherapy* apply learning principles to therapy.

1953   APA after extensive study and committee work, publishes *Ethical Standards* and a casebook.

1958   Wolpe's *Psychotherapy by Reciprocal Inhibition* helps initiate the behavioral therapy movement.

1973   APA holds Vail Conference which adds the professional training model to the Boulder model.

more common. More patients from mental hospitals and institutions for the retarded are being discharged into the community, so that more mental health workers are needed in community agencies, fewer in hospitals. There has been a marked and steady increase in the number of clinical psychologists going into independent practice, alone or in cooperative partnerships, as well as a marked increase in the treatment of mental difficulties by nonprofessionals. Most clinics employ paraprofessionals, and self-help groups have sprung up everywhere. How to make psychological knowledge available to nonpsychologists is a major challenge.

As time has passed, the time-honored scientist-practitioner model has come under increasing attack. It has been shown that research training does not make researchers out of most clinicians (although it may make them better "consumers" of research). The majority never do more research after their doctoral dissertations. Many clinicians are also dissatisfied with the course work required in graduate training, viewing some of it as irrelevant. Graduate programs not affiliated with universities are springing up. New professional specialties such as community psychology have developed, and it is unclear, as it is with counseling psychology, just where the boundaries with clinical psychology are to be drawn.

While the value of research training is being questioned, a new research specialty has emerged that may play an important part in the training and activities of future clinical psychologists. *Evaluation research* is trying out methods for determining the value of whole programs as well as improvements in individuals.

In short, the closing decades of this century are ones of uncertainty and some anxiety. Perhaps at the end of the last century there was a similar feeling of unease and dismay about the state of human welfare. In the late 1800s the conditions of child labor, the status of women and blacks, the flood of nearly illiterate immigrants into the United States, and many other conditions made for much discontent and ultimately resulted in many social reforms. The world situation now is much different; many countries are very affluent and are struggling with the problems of "over-choice" of possibilities for life styles and also with the emerging realization that the runaway growth of population and use of the earth's resources must slow down. The haunting possibility of nuclear war and total annihilation of all life on earth cannot be forgotten. Such concerns in the *Zeitgeist*, or "spirit of the times," cannot help but contribute to the unease in clinical psychology, involved as it is not only in the greatest intimacies of the human individual but also in the vagaries and politics of the human community.

New integrating theories and methods may be just around the corner, but they are not yet visible. Occasionally statements such as the 1978 Report of the President's Commission on Mental Health have charted some new and promising directions. For instance, that report expressed a strong concern for the unserved and underserved, especially minorities, children, the aged, the

GYN Family Planning
GYN Planificación de Familia

Walk-In Services
Pacientes Sin Cita

Mental Health
Servicios Psicologicos

LABORATORY
LABORATORIO

Figure 1-4
As minority groups increase in the
United States, more services are
multilingual. (Ken Karp)

handicapped, chronic patients, rural people, and people of low income; such concerns can be expressed in policies and administrative procedures about the training in the four core mental health professions (psychiatric or social-psychological nursing, social work, clinical psychology, and psychiatry). Achieving adequate sociopsychological assistance for all and developing the knowledge base for such assistance is a continuing challenge for clinical psychology. We will defer further exposition and speculation about the current and future state of the field until the last chapter.

SUMMARY

Clinical psychology is the body of psychological knowledge that practitioners use as they attempt to deal with mental and behavior problems and to promote people's mental health, well-being, and productivity. Initiated at about the beginning of the twentieth century, it has constantly expanded its scope to include more kinds of people in more kinds of situations. It can no longer be considered applicable only to the treatment of mental illness and of individuals.

During the early years of its history, up to about 1920, the major thrust was toward the generation of new ideas, new tools, new plans. The ideas of

Freud, Adler, Jung, Watson, and others were widely influential. Mental testing techniques were invented and elaborated. Professional organizations and journals made their appearance. The period between the two world wars was one of growth and consolidation. The period from 1945 to about 1960 marked the development of clinical psychology as a highly visible profession, with established standards, training programs, and ethical principles. The numbers of persons going into this new field increased markedly. The Ph.D. became the standard professional qualification, and positions were available for all qualified graduates. Optimism about professional accomplishment was widespread. Since 1970 more clinical psychologists have been trained, but their certainty, optimism, and satisfaction have declined. The period has been marked by considerable skepticism about prospects and by the emergence of a variety of alternative proposals for dealing with personal and social problems, along with new sorts of training programs. This diversity and ferment may very well result in an enriching and strengthening of clinical psychology.

RECOMMENDED READINGS

Sundberg, N. D., Tyler, L. E., & Taplin, J. R. *Clinical psychology: Expanding horizons* (2nd ed.). Englewood Cliffs, N.J.: Prentice-Hall, 1973. Chapters 1 and 2.

    In the more comprehensive chapters in our previous book, a much more detailed account of the nature and development of clinical psychology can be found. The chapters give illustrations of types of settings, clientele, and activities of psychologists and relate the general history of the periods covered as well as landmark books and events. We also strongly recommend Reisman's *A History of Clinical Psychology* (1976); also a chapter by Reisman (1981) is a useful condensation and analysis of later trends. Levine and Levine's *A Social History of Helping Services* (1970) is particularly useful in reviewing the reforms around the turn of the century and later; they suggest the intriguing thesis that intrapsychic modes of help are prominent in times of conservatism, when there is a tendency to "blame the victim" and the environment is assumed to be good, whereas environmental modes are prominent during periods of reform, when the general population is "hurting" in some way.

Shakow, D. Clinical psychology seen some 50 years later. *American Psychologist,* 1978, *33,* 148–158.

    One of the great clinical psychologists, long with the National Institute of Mental Health, reports on the formative events of the young profession, especially the important conferences at the end of World War II. In addition he gives his observations and perspectives on the unity of psychology and the need for standards of training and practice. An earlier book by Shakow (1969) presents his papers over a 40-year period of work in clinical psychology and the influences of the great pioneers such as William James, Freud, and others. Another retrospective view of the field is that of Garfield (1981) who reviewed the developments from 1940 to 1980—the increased activity of psychologists in therapy and its increased popularity; the relative decline of psychoanalysis as behavioral, cognitive, and brief therapies emerged; and the recent concern for accountability and effectiveness in psychotherapy. Garfield concludes that there have been no real breakthroughs and that the many variants of psychotherapy show we are still at an early stage.

Kaplan, B. (Ed.). *The inner world of mental illness.* New York: Harper & Row, 1964.

Kaplan helps readers understand the experience of people who have suffered from psychoses or other mental illnesses. Included are accounts from some of the well-known pioneers in the development of the mental health movement, such as Clifford Beers. Rabkin (1966) has collected interesting literary accounts of psychological disorders. An experienced psychologist, Elton McNeil in *The Quiet Furies* (1967) sympathetically tells what psychological suffering is like through case examples. A patient and therapist both present their separate views of the experience in *Mary Barnes: Two accounts of a journey through madness* (Barnes & Berke, 1971).

JOURNAL RESOURCES FOR KEEPING UP WITH THE GROWING KNOWLEDGE BASE

The journals published by the American Psychological Association are major sources for most recent thinking and research in clinical psychology—the *Journal of Consulting and Clinical Psychology, Journal of Counseling Psychology, Journal of Abnormal Psychology, Professional Psychology, American Psychologist,* and *Psychological Abstracts.* The *APA Monitor* is a monthly news magazine with reports and articles of immediate professional import. There are at least 50 other journals and series publications of relevance to clinical psychology in English, including the following: *American Journal of Community Psychology, American Journal of Orthopsychiatry, British Journal of Clinical Psychology, Clinical Psychology Review, Journal of Applied Behavior Analysis, Journal of Clinical Psychology, Journal of Community Psychology,* and *Journal of Personality Assessment.* An important resource for students in any area of psychology is the *Annual Review of Psychology,* which periodically covers the last three years or so of publications on many clinical topics.

2 USEFUL IDEAS ABOUT PEOPLE:
Theoretical Perspectives

First Fundamental Perspective—The Theory of Living Systems

Second Fundamental Perspective—Development
Stages of development
Deviance and the life cycle

Third Fundamental Perspective—Possibilities-Alternatives-Choices

Usable Concepts from Many Sources
Curative or psychopathological orientation
Learning orientation
Development or growth orientation
Social-ecological orientation

Five-year-old Sarah Billings refuses to go to school—refuses absolutely and unequivocally. On the September day when school opened, Cynthia Billings, her mother, dressed her up in the new outfit bought especially for this occasion and walked with her over to the neighborhood school. The kindergarten room was newly refurbished, bright, cheerful, full of interesting-looking toys and materials. Some 20 other children were there, some of them, like Sarah, clinging to their mothers, a few bolder ones beginning to explore the possibilities of this new place. Having introduced Sarah to the teacher, Mrs. Billings prepared to leave. Sarah set up a howl that could be heard throughout the first floor of the building and began to weep uncontrollably. "Don't worry about it," Miss Phillips said. "Most children cry at first. She'll get over it as soon as you leave."

But Sarah didn't get over it. Her screams got louder and louder. She would have nothing to do with Miss Phillips, the other children, or any of the things in the room. Finally, in desperation, Miss Phillips called her mother to come and get her so the kindergarten activities could begin.

Day after day, for a week, Mrs. Billings attempted to get the girl to school and persuade her to stay there. Sarah would lie down in front of the door at home, kicking and screaming. If she succeeded in getting Sarah to walk down the street with her, the child would suddenly break away and race back toward home like a wild creature threatened with some dreadful danger. In desperation Mrs. Billings made an appointment to discuss the problem with a psychologist at the child guidance clinic.

How is a psychologist to make sense of behavior like this? Clinical psychology presents what might be called an "embarrassment of riches." There are dozens of concepts and theoretical principles that might apply. Is this a case of some unresolved infantile anxiety producing an overdependence of the child on her mother? Is this behavior of crying in a strange situation simply a habit that has been strengthened again and again by the reward it brought—being returned to the safety of home? Is there something in the school situation that is associated in Sarah's mind with an unpleasant incident of the past? Does Miss Phillips, for example, look like someone who has hurt or frightened her? One could go on and on listing possibilities. The clinical worker is faced with the task of narrowing them down, through information obtained from the child, from her mother, and from others who know the family. After this, the clinician must decide which hypothesis provides the best "handle" for getting hold of the problem. What concepts and principles seem most useful in understanding a case and making decisions about how to help? First, let us attempt a theoretical overview of the whole complex picture presented by what we call *human nature*.

FIRST FUNDAMENTAL PERSPECTIVE—THE THEORY OF LIVING SYSTEMS

During the middle decades of the twentieth century, an interdisciplinary approach to scientific thinking about nature in general and the nature of life in particular has been attaining more and more influence. *General systems theory*, proposed in the 1940s by Bertalanffy, has been developed since then by Bertalanffy (1968), Laszlo (1972), and most completely by J. G. Miller (1978).

The essence of systems thinking is that the entity studied is a set of *interacting* units rather than separate entities or cause-effect linkages. The key word is *relationship*. Everything in a system is related to everything else in it, and these relationships are different from any of those outside the system. A change in one part of the system changes the whole pattern of relationships. For example, when a neurotic woman undergoes psychotherapy, her family system will change, for better or worse. Systems have *boundaries* that limit the area in which these relationships occur. A cell is a living system. So is a person, a family, a nation.

Systems are organized into *hierarchies*, or levels, as shown in Figure 2-1. Cells combine into organs, organs into organisms such as persons or animals, individual organisms into families or groups. Theorists such as J. G. Miller (1978) assume that at all levels the organizing principles are the same. Whether this is true in all respects, there are certainly some characteristics that are common to all of them, from the smallest one-celled organism to the largest organization. Higher-order systems select from the outputs of their subsystems what they need to incorporate in their own organization, rejecting the other outputs as waste. *Adaptation*, the basic process in evolution, occurs through this process. Simon (1981) has explained how the hierarchical organization has facilitated evolution, making it possible. Intermediate stable forms serve as subsystems to be incorporated in more complex forms. The development of individuals also involves this hierarchy of levels. To some extent and with many qualifications, ontogeny does recapitulate phylogeny (that is, individual development traces the evolution of the species) with the human embryo passing through stages that resemble ancestral forms, which, when modified, can serve as subsystems in the mature organism.

In some ways, as Simon (1981) has pointed out, the word *hierarchy* is the wrong term. It suggests that the higher-level system exercises some sort of authority over the subsystems. This is not necessarily true. Influence and control extend in *both* directions. Changes made at higher levels change the functioning of lower-level systems, but changes made at the lower levels also affect the functioning of higher-level systems of which they are a part. A disabling illness, for example, in one child changes the structure and functioning of a whole family. Koestler (Hampden-Turner, 1981, pp. 162–165) has pro-

SupraNational System
e.g., Common Market, United
Nations, satellite communications
network

Societal System
e.g., one nation, a large part
of a nation

Organizational System
e.g., industrial concern, social
agency, professional
association

Group System
e.g., family, work team,
recreational group,
animal group

Organismic System
e.g., individual person,
animal or plant

Organ System
e.g., nervous system,
alimentary system

Cell System
e.g., individual cells
within a body

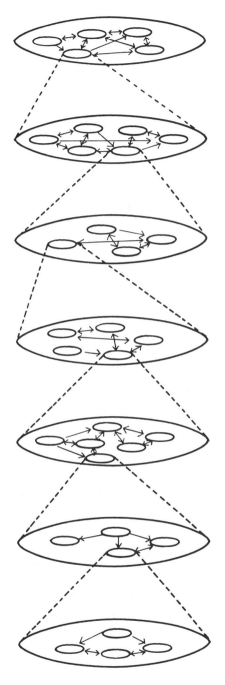

Figure 2-1   Hierarchy of systems. (Sundberg, Tyler, & Taplin, 1973, Figure 4-2, p. 101.
Copyright © 1973 by Prentice-Hall and used by permission.)

posed the term *holon* for the units at all levels and *holarchy* for the relationship between them, a term more neutral about control than *hierarchy*.

J. G. Miller (1978) goes into great detail about the distinguishing
characteristics of living systems. Figure 2–2 depicts a few that need to be
highlighted for our purposes. First, living creatures are *open* systems through
which there is a continuous flow of *matter, energy,* and *information.* One can
observe their *inputs* (everything that penetrates the boundary) and *outputs*
(everything that results from the processing or throughput that occurs within
the system). The input-output concept is similar to the psychologist's familiar
stimulus-response concept, but it is much broader in its scope. Systems are
self-regulating and tend to maintain *steady states.* The concept of *homeo-
stasis,* which physiologists have been studying for many years, is an example of this property, the complex coordinated reactions of glands and nervous system that keep body temperature constant as external temperatures
change markedly or that keep the sugar content of the blood constant no mat-

Figure 2-2   Schematic representation of essential features of a system.

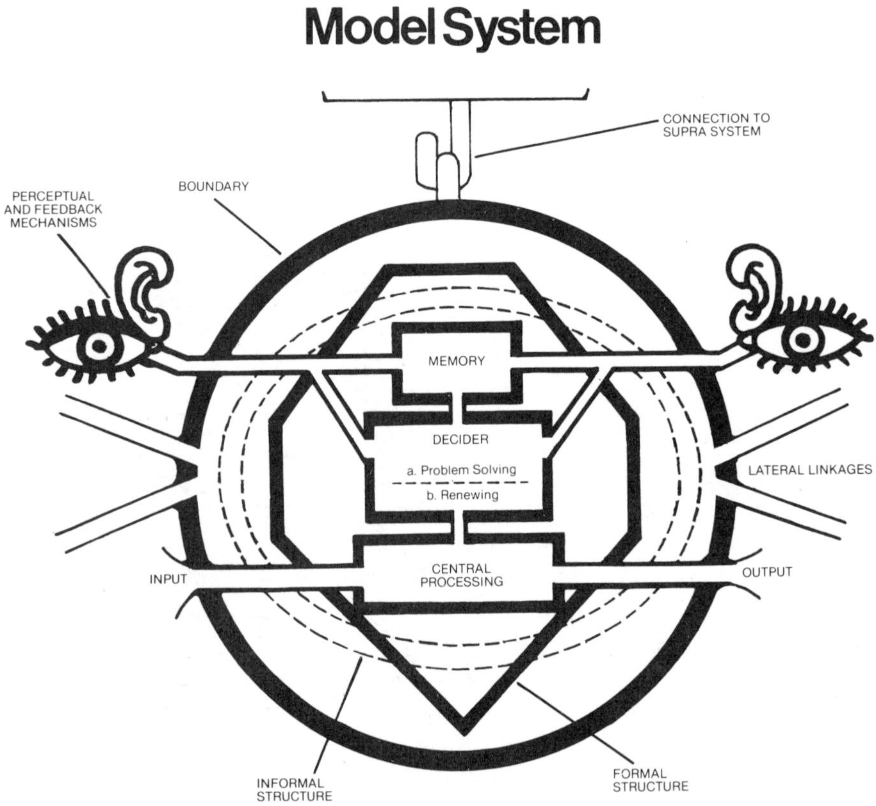

Model System

BOX 2-1   *QUESTIONS FOR ANALYZING SYSTEMS*

The following questions are examples of those that a clinician might ask about major subsystems within any system, whether it be an individual, a family, or an organization.

Decider (including system purposes, priorities, problem-solving)

What is doing the decider task? What general methods are available? What seem to be the system purposes, stated and unstated? Does the system gather information, plan, forecast consequences, view alternatives, have capability to improve choosing process? Is there an understanding of the need for change or review? Are there strategies for self-renewal?

Boundaries

Do the boundaries serve to protect adequately? Do they isolate excessively or allow overclose (enmeshed) relationships? Do they divide into functional subgroups or wall off inappropriately?

Perceptual and feedback functions

Can the system scan and focus adequately? Is there sufficient detection power? What selectivities or inattentions prevail? Is set-breaking ability adequate? Is meaningful feedback information available? How is feedback gathered, evaluated, used?

Input, central processes, output

Is the input healthful and adequately regulated? Do the main processes or transactions have any kind of monitoring, quality control, or review? Is the output or result monitored for change or improvement?

Memory

What performs memory functions? How large is the memory, how durable? What access does the organism have to it? What kinds of things are remembered and in which circumstances?

Formal and informal structure

Is there a formal structure? How does it resemble the informal structure? What are the procedures for resolving conflicts and evaluating harmony?

Linkages

Do the linkages serve to promote new knowledge, skills and experiences, feedback, emotional support/morale, socialization, or provide tangible support? Or are they constraining, draining? How do these linkages with the external environment relate to internal processes?

ter what the person eats. The concept of *steady state* extends even more widely to cover the processes by which a rate of growth programmed in an individual's genes is maintained under varying circumstances during development. Each system, from the smallest one-celled organism to the largest social organization, contains subsystems, the most critical of which is always the *decider*, which receives information from all other subsystems and integrates it into a unified response of some sort. Another essential component is *memory*, in which information can be stored a long or short time.

One of the most pervasive concepts in systems theory is that of *feedback*, the basis of processes for which engineers and computer experts coined the term *cybernetic* (pertaining to self-controlling systems). Information from output channels is continually fed back into input channels to govern the functioning of the system. *Negative feedback* is essential to the maintenance of steady states, operating to eliminate or counteract some ongoing process. For example, an oversupply of sugar in the blood leads to a compensating flow of insulin, or an elevated sense of anxiety leads to a movement away from the source of anxiety. *Positive feedback* serves the opposite purpose, increasing rather than reducing deviations from steady states and thus leading to *change*, change that can be either disastrous or constructive. Living systems are constantly changing, and it is this aspect that provides hope for interventions. Prigogine (1980), a Nobel-prize–winning chemist, has demonstrated that the parts of any system, living or nonliving, are constantly undergoing small-scale change. When some of these small changes are magnified by positive feedback, the old equilibrium may be destroyed and a completely new structure take shape, often more complex than the old one. This is a revolutionary idea of great potential importance for psychology.

System change, of course, underlies all psychological intervention. To adopt the systems perspective means to abandon the assumption that a single cause produces a single effect. The question is always: How will this change in one component of the system affect the functioning of all the others? Many of the useful concepts discussed in the last section of this chapter represent ways that clinicians have found to eliminate, strengthen, or weaken essential components of individual and group systems and to deal with the byproducts of such system change as well as with what were intended as its main effects. For example, a sullen, predelinquent 12-year-old is found to be a nonreader. By the use of special techniques, he is taught to read. His prospects for the future, his attitude toward school, his relationships with his family, his friendships—even his appearance—may change because of this one intervention.

The decision as to what subsystem should be the target for change is one of the most important ones a clinical workers must make. In the emergency room of the local hospital, the mangled hand and bleeding face of an accident victim leave no doubt about which system is the logical target for intervention. Clearly the injuries require physical treatment or, to use systems language, intervention at the biological system level. When we get to "people problems," however, the choice of system level for intervention is often less obvious. Take the case of 8-year-old Billy. His teacher thinks he is so "emotionally disturbed" that he should not be in her class: "He's wild. He won't listen to me. He won't stay at his desk and bothers other kids. He makes fun of the way I talk, and the others laugh at him." She calls him "a hyperactive child." Billy's parents have been unhappy with him for some time because he sasses them, teases his sister, "tortures" the cat, and generally seems out of control at times. The teacher's complaints increase their concern. A worker in a helping agency could choose any of the initial plans shown in Table 2–1.

Billy's situation, like most others, involves problems in several different systems. No clear guidelines yet exist by which we can determine the best system for intervention. What must be done is to brush aside, as far as possible, tradition and bias and to make a step-by-step review of how the various systems are functioning. On the biological level, we can ask questions such as: "When did Billy last have a physical exam?" "How is his hearing?" "Is there any likelihood of a genetic influence, and have his father or other relatives shown behavior like this?" "Was his course of motor development normal? For example, did he walk about on time?" "How are his balance and coordination now?" "Has he had significant accidents or illnesses, especially high fevers?" Answers to such questions will provide clues to how intact or problematic the biological system is. The personal system can be screened by means of interviews, observations, and tests, procedures we take up in detail in later chapters. Screening the family system involves questions such as: How many parenting people are actually in the home? Is a family breakup or

TABLE 2-1 System Levels to Consider with a Child (Billy)

SYSTEM LEVEL	REASONS FOR SELECTING	POSSIBLE INTERVENTION
Physiological	"It's minimal brain damage."	Secure medication and monitor behavior.
Personal		
Intrapsychic	"He's emotionally disturbed."	Individual play.
Behavioral	"He shows deviant behaviors."	Reprogram behavior contingencies in the home and school.
Family	"His behavior is related to a collapsing marriage."	Intensive family or marital therapy.
Small group	"Need to change his role in the class."	Hold meetings with teachers and peers.
Organization	"Those teachers get nervous and refer too much."	Group consultation with teachers.
Community	"This involves problems of interagency communication."	Establish new multiservice coordination; hold training workshop.

Adapted from Sundberg et al., 1973, p. 151.

crisis imminent? What is Billy's role in the family? Is he, for example, being set up by the mother as a rival to his stepfather? What is going on in the classroom that affects Billy's behavior? Similarly all systems in which dysfunction could be leading to the presenting problem must be carefully screened. An accumulation of such indicators of social difficulties in a community suggests that community organizations, attitudes, and resources might be examined.

SECOND FUNDAMENTAL PERSPECTIVE—DEVELOPMENT

As we think about living systems at all levels, we must always remember one thing—they are moving, not static, constantly evolving, changing, growing, aging, constantly on their inexorable path from creation to dissolution. No living system that the clinical worker touches—be it body, psyche, family, or community—fails to change as time passes. Sometimes we speak of periods of rapid cell division, of differentiation of the self from the environment, of the acquisition of an identity, of the choice of a career, of the decline into senescence, or of an organization's successive changes of leadership. All of these are rather routine aspects of the *patterned change processes* that we call *development*. At any time an individual or a family (and to an extent a school, a community, or a society) is at one particular point in a fairly predictable developmental sequence. The importance of development for clinical psychology, then, is that all of our intervention is aimed at a moving target, at a system that will be changing whether we intervene or not.

A child who knew nothing about insects might watch a caterpillar enter the chrysalis phase and conclude that it had become sick and died. Only a clear understanding that normal development of a butterfly involves the early stages of being a caterpillar and chrysalis prevents making false inferences. Humans do not undergo quite such striking changes in the course of their development, but it is important that we do not regard common occurrences, for example, tension and conflict with parents at emancipation time during adolescence, as pathological and thus requiring treatment. Many clinicians are overly ready to classify all troubles as psychopathology.

In 1971 Jones, Bayley, Macfarlane, and Honzik published a set of articles summarizing the major findings from longitudinal research on development. When they looked first at the subjects as children and then as adults, they were in for shock after shock: "Close to 50 percent have turned out to be more stable and effective adults than any of us with our different theoretical biases had predicted; some 20 percent were less substantial than we had predicted, and slightly less than a third turned out as predicted" (p. 408). Rigler (1973), reviewing the book, suggests that such inaccurate predictions resulted from the wrong perspective: "Too often deviance was seen as

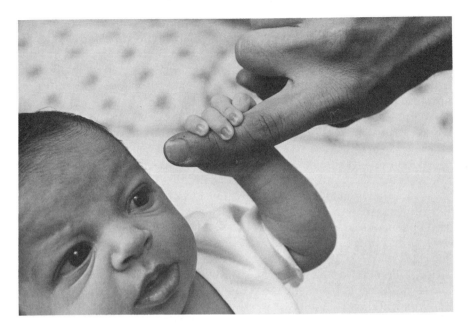

Figure 2-3   An infant will grasp reflexively, helping establish early social bonds. (Ken Karp)

pathognomic, transitional behavior was seen as persistent, stress was mistaken for trauma, and the potential for learning from experience was ignored" (p. 317).

Thus we must make sure that the psychological tools used by a clinician are appropriate for the developmental level of the patient. It makes a great deal of difference whether our patient is one who is learning to stay dry at night or one whose anxiety is about adequacy as president of a company. An approach using immediate feedback, simple rewards, and reassurance may be appropriate for the enuretic. Complex, abstract talk about values, fantasies, life history, and life goals may be necessary for the president.

Courses in developmental psychology are included in the training programs for clinical psychologists, but surprisingly many psychologists and other clinicians in their practice ignore developmental principles. It is time that developmental research workers and clinical workers joined forces.

Stages of Development

It is convenient to postulate stages of development, although they are not fixed, invariant, or tightly scheduled. The rate at which stages are attained varies from person to person, and some even pass particular milestones in the "wrong" order. This variation is particularly true of the social stages as compared with the more physical ones. Ordinarily a person must pass through one stage in order to be "ready" for the next. Babbling precedes talking, toilet training precedes entry into public school, emancipation ordinarily precedes marriage in our culture. When such sequences are short-circuited, trouble often results, as when parents force emancipation before a child has the skills to handle it or when young people get caught in early pregnancies before they have achieved independence.

Knowledge of developmental stages facilitates various kinds of clinical work. Stages during which rapid growth occurs, often more stressful than others, may require skills in crisis intervention. A major approach to the prevention of psychological problems is to intervene at a stage earlier than that at which the problem behavior usually occurs—for example, equipping young people with coping skills before they face the stresses of adolescence or providing preschool programs such as Head Start to enable children to meet the challenges of the school years.

Where there have already been developmental abnormalities, special complications arise. For example, the mother's use of drugs or alcohol during a child's prenatal development may have an irreversible effect. A clinician needs considerable knowledge to evaluate the continuing effects of an early developmental abnormality. Is it one out of which the individual may grow or one which will cause the child to fall even further behind peers? Is there a possibility of a catch-up growth spurt in cases like this? Can an individual adapt to the condition without experiencing a serious handicap?

It is essential to know what stage a person is in. For example, if we are told that Elaine has thrown herself on the floor and is kicking and screaming, that Julie has started to have sex, that George has been driving a racing car, and that John has been making out a will, we are likely to assume that Elaine is perhaps 2½ years old, Julie is about 20, George about 25, and John is 50 to 70. When we are told that, in fact, Elaine is 25, Julie is 9, George 61, and John is 14, it becomes clearer—in this case with a bit of shock—just how much we rely on normal developmental sequences as our yardstick when we form working images of people. One way to conceptualize the problems of these four is that they are behaving in ways wholly uncharacteristic of their ages. Julie and John have apparently leaped ahead. We might well ask the origin of the prematurity; what's behind this rush—is it thrill seeking, high intellectual ability, overstimulation at home, absence of limit setting or appropriate parenting, need for friends, or depression? Obviously several developmental stages, several skills and maturities that most people have by the time they start to have sex or make wills, are not present. What will be the effect of starting a behavior when the normal background is absent? Will an otherwise constructive behavior undertaken without prerequisite skills and experience prove harmful? It well may.

Sixty-one-year-old George and 25-year-old Elaine have apparently slid backward or regressed. With George's reckless, racing car activity, we might ask, "What's in it for George? Is he trying to ward off advancing age, to conquer time? Is he deliberately risking his life? If so, why?" Assuming Elaine's temper tantrums are not related to being drunk or playacting, we might ask, "Has she gone back to such a primitive developmental level because her thought processes and emotions have become disordered (as with psychosis)? Has she sustained terrible grief or been overwhelmed by rage?" In both cases we will ask what's missing for George and Elaine that they are using behavior patterns appropriate to stages so much earlier. Did they miss essential maturational stages? What harm will it do them to ignore age-appropriate behavior? Unless something can be done to help them, people at strong variance from developmental expectations risk being committed to mental hospitals or being ostracized in many societies.

Research and theory about development have accelerated during the last 30 years. Psychologists have extended their concern upward to the adult years and downward to infancy. Cognitive as well as emotional development has been charted. New kinds of psychological services have been established. We can touch here on only the highlights of a continually expanding picture.

Emotional Development.   Freud was the first modern developmental theorist. His complex system is sketched out in some detail in Chapter 8. Here let us look only at the developmental stages his theory postulated, based on the characteristic way in which the individual seeks emotional gratification. The first is the *oral* stage, when the mouth is the main source of gratification. The second is the *anal* stage, when pleasure is related to bowel stimulation and retention of feces. The third, beginning at about four, is the *phallic* stage, with the pleasure focus on genital stimulation. The fourth, lasting from about six to puberty, Freud called *latency* because libidinal energy, the basis of all the pleasure strivings, is being held in abeyance, not producing conflicts or stress. *Adolescence* is, of course, the next stage and a very stressful one. Freud's treatment required that the patient return to the stage in which his or her conflicts originated and, through emotional expression, insight, and emotional reorganization, chart a new developmental course. This theoretical and treatment program has largely been found inadequate by researchers, and the more sophisticated system proposed by Erikson (1950, 1963) has been receiving more attention.

Although derived from Freud's, Erikson's stages are not basically physiological, but psychological and social. Furthermore, they cover the whole life cycle, not just childhood. The basic concern is the nature of the individual's relationship to other people. Each of the eight stages involves a challenge of some sort that must be met, and each is expressed as a polarity: (1) basic trust versus mistrust, (2) autonomy versus shame and doubt, (3) initiative versus guilt, (4) industry versus inferiority, (5) identity versus role confusion, (6) intimacy versus isolation, (7) generativity versus stagnation, and (8) ego integrity versus despair.

Erickson's developmental theory fits well into the general theoretical

Figure 2-4
Achieving and maintaining intimacy
—a major aspect of adulthood. (Teri
Leigh Stratford)

structure we have attempted to build. Each stage is a system of concepts about the self and relationships to surrounding people and things. Each involves possibilities, alternatives, choices. The outcome is never a foregone conclusion. Erikson, a compassionate and creative psychoanalyst, is essentially a realist whose theory finds a place for firmness as well as love in parents and for social structures that facilitate the individual's mastery of the successive challenges. Practitioners of various persuasions utilize these concepts. They make it possible to understand many human problems without labeling or name-calling. They suggest approaches to the solution of the problems, with society helping but the individual still basically responsible. There has been little empirical research on Erickson's theory, perhaps because of its broad, global character, but it has been very influential. The Ericksonian stages present the values and "philosophy" behind social and emotional competence as people pass through life.

Cognitive Development. Most psychologists tend to keep ideas about personality and motivation separate from ideas about perceiving and thinking, and some theorists have proposed cognitive stages rather than the emotional ones we have considered.

By far the most prominent of these theorists is Piaget (1952). (See also Flavell's presentation of Piaget's work, 1977.) He postulates four major stages from infancy to adulthood, each of which includes substages. They are as follows:

1. *Sensory-motor* (0–2 years), in which primitive perceptions and actions are coordinated into cognitive structures called *schemes* (schemas or schemata). Examples are sucking and grasping.
2. *Preoperational* (2–6), in which the child can begin to deal with the world symbolically by talking about objects without manipulating them directly.

3. *Concrete operations* (6–12), in which the child can carry out mental transformations on objects without having to perform them, developing usable concepts in the process.
4. *Formal operations stage* (12 on), in which the child becomes able to handle highly abstract concepts without physical attributes, such as truth or honor.

Piaget postulates two basic processes that characterize the person's interaction with the world: *assimilation,* or the incorporation of new experience into already existing schemes or structures; and *accommodation,* the modification of these structures to fit the new experience. These concepts, compatible with systems thinking, have been valuable tools in clinical as well as developmental psychology. Piaget's ideas have stimulated a great amount of research, much of which is supportive. However, cross-cultural studies suggest that there are variations in timing and the appearance of the last stage, and methodological problems remain (Dasen & Heron, 1981, pp. 295–342).

Cognitive development occurs in several spheres at the same time. Piaget has shown how stages in *social attachment* can be viewed from this perspective. Kohlberg (1964) has proposed a stage theory of *moral* reasoning that has stimulated considerable research.

Stages of Adulthood.   Only recently have many psychologists and other people recognized that change and development do not cease with the attainment of maximum physical growth, although Jung and Erikson made the point some time ago. Gail Sheehy's book *Passages* (1976) turned out to be a best seller. Vaillant's (1977) report on the Grant Study, a follow-up of Harvard graduates first assessed in 1937, and Levinson's (1978) book giving detailed biographies of 40 men, 10 each of biologists, novelists, executives, and workers, have provided some data. Levinson postulates four overlapping stages:

1. Childhood and adolescence (birth to 22)
2. Early adulthood (17 to 45)
3. Middle adulthood (40 to 65)
4. Late adulthood (60 to death)

Each transition period between successive stages poses particular challenges and may involve turmoil and disruption. Such developmental crises are normal, not pathological. Clinical workers dealing with such stages as the so-called mid-life crisis need to use supportive procedures designed to help people negotiate them and enter the next stage with maximum health and autonomy.

BOX 2–2   *DEVELOPMENT IN ADULT LIFE*

Below is a chart from Levinson's book, *The Seasons of a Man's Life* (1978). Levinson's outline of developmental periods and their attendant tasks and challenges is based on intensive, longitudinal research interviews with 40 selected men (10 executives, 10 biologists, 10 factory workers, and 10 novelists).

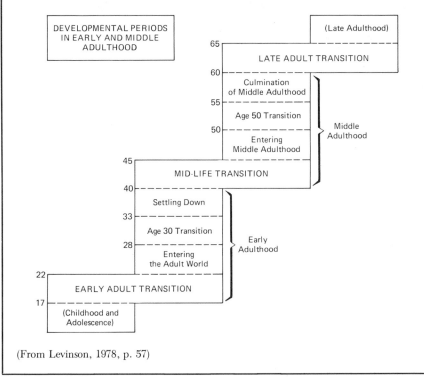

(From Levinson, 1978, p. 57)

Deviance and the Life Cycle

Although attempts to catalog the kinds of breakdowns characteristic of various life stages have not been successful, with some exceptions such as the forms of schizophrenia most likely to appear during adolescence, progress has been made in identifying the *precursors* of many life problems, both genetic and environmental. Poverty, for example, is the single biggest predictor of disordered development for children (Escalona, 1974), but others have also been identified. Research on *vulnerability* to schizophrenia has been especially rewarding (Garmezy, 1975). The intriguing research question is that only some of the children identified as being "at risk" for some sort of mental breakdown actually develop the condition. Why? Research on this question is difficult for many reasons. Longitudinal designs require large investments of time and money and large numbers of subjects if one is to consider many variables. Psychological difficulties have multiple causes, and all must be considered.

Rutter (1979b) has gone far in examining the vulnerability and prevention issue by asking, "What about children who developed well despite horrible situations? How did they differ from those who fell into problems?" His responses to that question, he points out, are somewhat tentative, but they do form a corroboration of other views that bad early experience does not necessarily condemn a child to later troubles. His study definitely contains support for the concept that we can all stand a certain amount of stress but that it can have cumulative and thus overwhelming effects. He tentatively identifies the following factors:

1. The patterning of stresses: A single, even gross stress appears not to raise the risk of psychiatric disorder, whereas any two occurring together raise the risk fourfold.

2. Individual differences due to constitutional and experiential factors: The presence of psychiatric or conduct disorder in one's parents raises the likelihood of disorder.

3. Individual temperament: Personality helps determine how the environment reacts to an individual (e.g., the easygoing child may avoid being scapegoated even in quarrelsome homes, whereas the temperamentally difficult child may attract parental criticism and scapegoating).

4. Compensating experiences outside the home: Some schools have supportive, growth-facilitating effects for children, rather similar to those that a positive work situation may have for an adult.

5. Self-esteem: Self-esteem based on above-average attainment in some phase of school seemed to have a protective effect.

6. Using the scope and range of available opportunities: Assortative mating and self-limitation of opportunity seems to be common among children from unhappy, deprived, or disadvantaged homes. They tend to marry young, to have babies early, and to select a mate from a similarly deprived background. Those, by contrast, who avoid cutting off their opportunities with early marriage or early pregnancy show evidence of being able to use the broader opportunity structure effectively, at least in this culture.

7. Structure and control: There is a link between chaotic, nonsupervising families and delinquency. A study of poverty showed that families who maintained strict supervision of the children's activities were more effective in preventing delinquency than were those that just had a happy family atmosphere. Perhaps, he speculates, structure and control become more important in conditions of deprivation, chaos, and uncertainty.

8. Bonds and relationships: One good relationship with a parent provides a substantial protective effect when the relationship includes personal aspects such as being close and confiding. Children who have a number of caretakers and who have little chance of forming early enduring relationships with an adult are more likely to have enduring, although not always severe, social deficits such as higher rates of attention seeking or disobedience.

9. Coping skills: Children who have had normal separation experiences are able to cope better with hospital stays. Although still specifically unidentified, Rutter

believes that there must be coping skills that can be acquired and that can apply to other forms of stress. There has been some research on the teaching of these coping skills. The work of Spivack and Shure (1978) stands out and will be discussed later on in the book. They show that what they call *Interpersonal Cognitive Problem-Solving Skills*—that is, a child's capacity to think through and reach adaptive conclusions about relations with other people—has a major effect on subsequent social adjustment.

It should be noted that the idea of development can be applied to all systems, not just the organismic or personal level. For instance, the early phases of the formation of an organization can be identified, then later and more mature phases, and finally a terminal phase as it disintegrates. Some writers have delineated the family life cycle and its variations (Carter & McGoldrick, 1979).

THIRD FUNDAMENTAL PERSPECTIVE—POSSIBILITIES-ALTERNATIVES-CHOICES

Marlene was in the doldrums. She did not see what a counselor in the college counseling center could do for her, but she stopped in anyway because a friend had suggested it. She was a junior at the university, majoring in biology. For the past two years she had lived with Trent, a premedical student she had known since high school days. Neither of them had wanted marriage. They had agreed that each of them would be free to leave at any time. But their relationship had lasted for so long that Marlene had somehow come to assume that it was permanent. It was a tremendous shock to her when Trent announced that he wished to live with another woman. She did not argue with him or beg him to stay, but after he left she felt as if her world had fallen apart. Alone in the apartment, too big and too expensive for one person, she brooded over the past. What had she done wrong? How could she go on like this alone? She slept a lot and often did not bother to get up for her morning classes. It was hard to settle down and study, and as she dropped further and further behind in her classes, catching up seemed impossible. She was completely miserable.

After talking to Marlene and thinking about how to help her, the counselor decided that Marlene needed help in finding a situation that would set up a new system of interaction between her and her world. Little by little, the counselor encouraged Marlene to start thinking about alternative futures rather than the unalterable past. Between them they canvassed several alternatives. She could go home to her family, who lived in a large house not far from the university and would be happy to have her back. She could try to find a roommate to share the apartment with her. She could join a communal group, several of whose members she knew and liked. She could take a room in the dormitory for the next term. How to get back on the track academically also was a matter of alternatives. Dropping out for the rest of the term? Dropping some courses and continuing the others? Working out a study program and sticking to it? Each of the alternatives had different ramifications and long-term consequences, the discussion of which involved a searching examination of values. The counselor functioned as a facilitator of this examination of possibilities.

In dealing with situations like Marlene's, two aspects of general systems theory are particularly relevant. One is the fact emphasized earlier that a *decider* is an essential feature of every system. The other is that because of the part the *boundary* plays, only a fraction of the available information is ordinarily used in making decisions. One of the strategies for improving the functioning of a system is to let into it more information than normally enters. This brings us to a consideration of *possibilities* and *choices*. The kind of information most likely to make a difference is information about possibilities.

Moving from an unsatisfactory social system to a productive one requires that one develop some sort of image of the system to which one wishes to move. Any individual's future consists of multiple possibilities, many of which we recognize. The reality we experience in our own lives and see all around us in other people's lives constitutes only a small fraction of the possibilities that once existed. No one has expressed this more vividly than the great early American psychologist and philosopher, William James.

> The mind is at every stage a theater of simultaneous possibilities. Consciousness consists in the comparison of these with each other, the selection of some, and the suppression of the rest by the reinforcing and inhibiting agency of attention. . . . The mind, in short, works on the data it receives very much as the sculptor works on his block of stone. In a sense the statue stood there from eternity. But there were a thousand different ones beside it, and the sculptor alone is to thank for having extricated this one from the rest. . . . the world we feel and live in will be that which our ancestors and we, by slowly cumulative strokes of choice, have extricated out of this, like sculptors, by simply rejecting certain portions of the stuff. Other sculptors, other statues from the same stone! Other minds, other worlds, from the same monotonous and inexpressive chaos. (1890, pp. 288–289)

For any individual or, for that matter, any group, community, or nation, possibilities, although numerous, are not unlimited. The most inexorable limitation is *time*. A person can engage in only a small number of activities simultaneously, and a lifetime is finite. Thus choices of possibilities to be actualized are forced upon us, and selection of some requires renunciation of others. This selection and rejection occurs in many ways besides conscious choice. One's genetic makeup rules out many human possibilities. Only a few children are endowed with the necessary combination of nerves and muscles to become outstanding athletes. Only a few can hope to be corporation presidents or Hollywood stars. The possibility of becoming a great violinist only exists if the person is genetically programmed to develop unusual musical talent. Other limitations on the individual's possibility world arise from early experience. Most readers of this book will never be really fluent in Russian or Mandarin or Swahili because they learned to talk in a family in which English was spoken. Chance happenings also set limits to possibilities. An automobile accident leaves a young girl paralyzed from the waist down, thus ruling out a large number of the lives she might have lived. And finally, our own actions limit the possibilities the future holds. Because a young boy fell in with a social group that carried on delinquent and criminal activities, he comes to possess a prison record that prevents him from getting some of the kinds of jobs for which he would otherwise be qualified.

But with all of these limiting factors, there is still room for conscious *choice*, and most of us have much more choice about the direction our futures will take than we realize. This consideration is important for clinical and counseling work. As we grow up, we develop cognitive structures of many kinds that sort out possibilities automatically. Each of us has values, interests, behavior strategies, and styles of thinking and acting that serve as filters letting in only some of the potential input. Because the human organism is complex and continually learning, we develop alternative cognitive organizations—ways of thinking—that can be applied to the same situation, so that the sorting and filtering process is never completely automatic. We can cultivate the development, awareness, and utilization of alternative "windows on the world" and thus see more possibilities than a first glance in one direction reveals. In the case of Marlene, for example, the hours spent with the counselor may serve to make her aware of some of these alternative organizing structures through which she sees her world—her attitudes toward her family, her expectations about a career, the values she adheres to in the realm of sex, love, and marriage. Being aware of these organizing structures in her own personality can make it easier for her to decide which of the alternative living arrangements sketched initially are genuine possibilities for her. There are always alternatives if we can find them. At any stage of life, each of us always has some choice about the shape the remainder of our life is to take.

In connection with research on creativity, psychologists have devoted considerable attention in recent years to *divergent thinking*. In contrast with the sort of thinking one is asked to carry out on intelligence and achievement tests—that is, thinking that leads to a single correct answer—divergent thinking produces many answers, the more the better. One technique researchers have used extensively is to ask the subject to think of as many uses as possible for some common object, such as a brick, a newspaper, or a tin can. What handicaps those who do poorly in such a task is the imposition of unnecessary restrictions. Those who produce only short lists of uses for a tin can, for example, assume that it must serve only as a container. Cut it open, flatten it out, pound it into a ball, paint it, cut holes in it, and dozens of possible uses come to mind. People can be taught to improve their performance in creativity tests and experiments by looking for and getting rid of unnecessary assumptions that limit their vision. It is this kind of thinking that is needed to deal more adequately with life possibilities.

In this chapter we have at least begun the construction of a theoretical framework for the multitudinous assortment of ideas and practices that make up clinical psychology. Psychology as a whole has only partially assimilated the concepts of general systems theory, and it has made even less progress in coming to terms with multiple possibilities. Because people are embedded in many systems, their behavior is not completely determined by any one of them. Because we possess the mental equipment to conceive of alternatives, to look ahead, to choose and to plan, we need never be completely at the mercy of particular circumstances. The whole enterprise of clinical psychology is permeated by *choice*—choice of theories and concepts to use in understanding persons, choice of a system level at which to intervene, choice of a strategy of intervention, continuing choices about modifying, supplementing, or terminating the treatment a client is receiving. It is a useful basic assumption that alternative possibilities always exist for ourselves and for those we try to help.

Young (1978), in summarizing what a lifetime of research on the brain has taught him, points to *choice* as the most fundamental aspect of all life, from the single cell on up the scale. "Life depends upon choice among various possibilities. All living things *must* choose. Human beings have a greater number of possibilities of action than any other creature and therefore the widest burden or privilege of choice" (p. 20).

USABLE CONCEPTS
FROM MANY SOURCES

Besides these fundamental assumptions that enter into all activities of clinical workers, there are dozens of concepts that they use at one time or another in particular cases. They have been culled from research work carried on in psychological laboratories; from clinics and consulting rooms; from the writings of sociologists, anthropologists, and other students of society; from practical dealings with people in schools and work places; from philosophers and religious leaders. From this rich storehouse each clinician selects and organizes the most helpful repertoire of ideas.

In sampling and organizing these concepts, far too numerous to be cataloged completely, we shall use an outline of the four major approaches to clinical activity, to be discussed in some detail at the beginning of Chapter 3: (1) The *curative* approach, in which psychological difficulties are viewed as symptoms of psychopathology, or mental illness, which one aims to diagnose and cure; this view is essentially a medical model; (2) the *learning* approach, in which difficulties are seen as learned behavior to be modified through educative processes broadly conceived; (3) the *developmental* (or growth) approach, in which difficulties are thought to arise from inadequate or misdirected development which can be corrected by releasing inherent potentialities for growth; and (4) the *ecological* approach, in which psychological difficulties arise from inadequate adaptation to the human and nonhuman environment and can be corrected by making suitable changes in the environment.

Curative or Psychopathological Orientation

The concept of *stress*, first elaborated by Selye (1956) has to do with a complex reaction of the whole organism, involving a sequence of secretions from the adrenal and pituitary glands, delicately coordinated. Pathological symptoms arise both from the attempts made to cope with stress and from the organismic collapse that occurs if they are unsuccessful. Stress may arise from either external stressors or internal physiological or mental ones.

Within the view that disordered processes cause mental illness fall many concepts from psychoanalysis. Earlier we mentioned Freud's emphasis on *early* development and the crucial importance of infancy and childhood. The concept of *infantile sexuality* occupies a prominent place in Freud's thinking, with the idea that at different stages of development, sexual pleasure is derived from the stimulation of different body parts or zones. Basic to all psychic disorder is the concept of the *unconscious*. As Freud showed, this concept explains many sorts of irrational and self-defeating behavior and leads to one objective of treatment—making patients aware of primitive urges and motives now inaccessible to them.

Freud has been responsible for many of the concepts used in following the curative approach. The assumption that neurosis arises from *anxiety* and the *defenses* raised against it is especially important. *Repression* is another postulated property of mental life relating to both unconscious processes and anxiety. It is the defense mechanism by which threatening feelings and impulses are excluded from consciousness, the partial failure of which produces anxiety. The distinction between the *pleasure principle* and the *reality principle* and the conflict between them (later conceptualized as *id* versus *ego*) also fits many cases.

Freud's concept of *transference*, the assumption that emotional attitudes arising in one situation can be transferred to another in later years, underlies much psychotherapy, not only the psychoanalytic varieties. Through this process an adult in his or her relationship to a therapist can relive and "work through," for example, the painful childhood relationship to a parent that still hurts.

BOX 2-3 *STRESS, A BRIDGING CONCEPT*

One of the most important concepts linking the environment and the individual is stress. Ask several different people to name environmental stressors and they will probably name a wide variety of things like final examinations, probation, the break-up of a romance, pregnancy, fatigue, or a car wreck. Each of these is likely to be a stressor to someone. But it was Hans Selye (1974) who recognized that though stressors are diverse, ". . . medical research has shown that in many respects the body responds in a stereotyped manner, with identical biochemical changes, essentially meant to cope with any type of increased demand upon the human machinery" (cited in Spielberger, 1979, p. 6).

Selye called these bodily reactions the General Adaptation Syndrome (GAS) consisting of three major stages: the alarm reaction with fight or flight impulses; resistance or trying to cope; and exhaustion, where coping may have depleted resources, sometimes fatally.

How are environmental or developmental stressors linked to the physical reactions described by Selye? First, how a person perceives the event is critical. Someone who has anticipated a problem and who has planned strategies for coping with it will likely do better than someone who interprets the problem as a disaster and defines him or herself as powerless in it. Second, stressful events can accumulate faster than our capacity to recover from them. The social Readjustment Rating Scale of Holmes and Rahe (1967) assigns Life Change Units to a variety of events, such as death of a spouse (100), divorce (73), jail (63), being fired (47) pregnancy (40). A high total of units in a short time is associated with increased physical illness and mental difficulties.

Adverse stress reaction comes from an excess of environmental demand over an individual's coping capacity. Some limited or modulated stressors are essential for psychological growth and the development of good coping strategies. But when the threat is excessive, the disturbance of the homeostatic balance too great, then excessive anger and anxiety are likely to predominate.

In research on both anxiety and anger, Spielberger (1980, 1982) distinguishes between the state (how intense is anger or anxiety at a particular time) and the trait (how frequently does the person tend to become anxious or angry). His measurement devices, the State-Trait Anxiety Inventory and the State-Trait Anger Scale, have produced promising findings, for example, high STAS scores relate to hypertension and thus to coronary disease.

The area of stress and the management of anger and anxiety have great importance for psychology whether it be for clinical, community, or general research work. It touches biological, personal (emotional, coping skills, and development), interpersonal, and community variables and thus links many branches of helping psychology. But most of all, it has obvious potential for reducing suffering and expense with education and other broad-scope methods in community and workplace. Classes, workshops, and the mass media can be used to tell people about stress and how to control one's reactions and the environment in which one works so as to make stress useful instead of destructive. As Selye has pointed out stress, if it is not extreme, can function to improve performance and enliven lives; he has distinguished the positive and negative aspects by calling one "eustress" and the other "distress."

BOX 2-4 *TYPES AND AMOUNTS OF PSYCHOPATHOLOGY IN THE WORLD*

Below is a table showing the medians and ranges of rates of all types of psychopathology and the major subtypes, compiled by social scientists who have done a great deal of work on *epidemiology*, the study of the occurrence of disorders in large populations. These percentages refer to rates for adults only.

Type of Psychopathology by Geopolitical Area	Number of Studies	Median (%)	Range (%)
All types of psychology*			
N. America and Europe	27	20.85	0.55–69.00
U.S.	8	22.60	0.55–69.00
Non-U.S.	19	20.50	3.67–55.84
Psychoses			
N. America and Europe	24	1.56	0.00– 8.30
U.S.	6	1.72	0.00– 8.30
Non-U.S.	17	1.56	0.36– 5.45
Schizophrenia			
N. America and Europe	14	0.59	0.00– 2.68
U.S.	3	Too few studies	0.00– 2.68
Non-U.S.	11	0.59	0.00– 1.50
Affective			
N. America and Europe	13	0.29	0.00– 1.91
U.S.	3	Too few studies	0.00– 0.41
Non-U.S.	10	0.33	0.00– 1.91
Neuroses			
N. America and Europe	24	9.38	0.28–53.51
U.S.	6	15.06	0.28–40.00
Non-U.S.	18	8.30	1.17–53.51
Personality disorder			
N. America and Europe	20	4.76	0.07–36.00
U.S.	4	7.02	0.07–36.00
Non-U.S.	16	4.76	0.88–14.86

*These rates include psychophysiological disorders for studies which employed mutually exclusive diagnostic categories.

(From B. P. Dohrenwend et al., *Mental Illness in the United States*. Copyright © 1980 by Praeger Publishers and reprinted by permission of Praeger Publishers.)

The concept of *diagnosis* is another offshoot of the curative model of treatment, the assumption that one classifies the patients into specified categories before treating them. Diagnostic systems in common use, such as the DSM III (the third edition of the *Diagnostic and Statistical Manual*, American Psychiatric Association, 1980) fit here.

Learning Orientation

Laboratory research on learning has been an important undertaking in psychology ever since Pavlov's dog first salivated to the sound of a bell, and it has led to a whole new way of looking at psychological problems and how they might be treated or prevented. The first of the important concepts is the *conditioned response*, the attachment of a natural or previously learned response to a new stimulus, which can often explain irrational fears and impulses. But there are also *operant* responses, chance bits of behavior that are strengthened through *reinforcement*. From pigeons pecking at a colored square to fully functioning people putting together chains of complex skills, the same basic principle is applicable—rewarding a particular action and withholding the reward when it fails to occur. Other concepts have branched off from this one: *shaping* behavior by rewarding successively accurate approximations to the action one wishes to produce; *modeling*, or having someone else do what one wishes the subject to do; *extinction*, the elimination of a kind of behavior by not rewarding it; *generalization*, the spread of behavior elicited under special conditions of reinforcement to other situations; and *discrimination*, the process of learning to distinguish between similar stimuli through the reinforcement of one and not the other. More about how these principles are being applied in behavior therapy will be found in Chapter 9.

Not all work on learning that clinicians find useful has behavioralistic origins. Gestalt psychologists emphasized perception and the fact that it is an organized process. Another concept very useful in psychotherapy is *figure and ground*, some features standing out, others receding into the background. By changing figure-ground relationships, clients come out with different perceptions of their past and present lives. Gestalt therapy is also based on the demonstrated mental persistence of uncompleted tasks—the seeking for closure. Also extensively studied are other sorts of *cognitive structures*—the organizations of experience that individuals use to make sense of their worlds. The *personal constructs* proposed as organizing structures by George Kelly (1955) are such entities, classifications that an individual takes for granted of ways in which some people, places, or situations are similar or different. By changing their constructs one may be able to improve one's functioning.

Earlier we mentioned Piaget's concept of *scheme*, a cognitive structure through which ongoing experience is processed. Henry Murray (1938), one of the major personality theorists of our time, also used the concept of *schema* as a basic building block in his theory.

Another cognitive concept that has been used increasingly is that of *cognitive style* (Witkin & Goodenough, 1981), a central adapting, regulating personality structure. Witkin and his associates accumulated a vast amount of information about one of these styles, *field dependence-independence*, and demonstrated its relevance to clinical activities.

The concept of *trait* itself may be seen as related to learning research, as individual differences showed up very clearly in such work and needed to be taken into consideration. What *trait* means is an aspect of an individual personality that can be singled out, a characteristic possessed to some degree by all human beings, thus making possible the *measurement* of its strength in each individual. *Intelligence* is the trait most widely known, and in clinical practice it is assessed more often than any other.

Development or Growth Orientation

The concept of development is an essential component of the thinking of *all* clinical workers, whatever their orientation. Some of them, however, believe that growth itself is the basis for all significant change that occurs in human lives. Jung is probably the first and most notable of these. His emphasis on *creative or constructive unconscious processes* added a new dimension to Freud's formulations. In his concept of *individuation* he expressed the conviction that psychological health consists in developing one's unique self more completely. Related concepts are those of *identity*, explored in depth by Erikson, and *self-actualization*, emphasized by Rogers, Maslow, and other humanistic psychologists. Erikson's theory has also contributed the idea that developmental *crises* constitute the challenges that facilitate growth. Thus a psychotherapist holding this orientation does not view these crises as pathological, regardless of how much turmoil and distress they arouse, and remains confident that the individual can surmount them and emerge at a higher level of development. A growth-oriented psychologist can also utilize Freud's concept of *regression*, or reversion to an earlier stage of development, but tends to think of it as a temporary interlude in the general forward movement of personality.

Students of individual differences have contributed to the pool of growth-oriented concepts by providing trait measurements that assist people to define their own individuality. Also much studied has been creativity, the trait that enables one to produce multiple answers for the same question and original new ways of looking at situations and problems. Among the many personality traits measured, perhaps the most significant are those having to do with Jung's concept of *introversion* versus *extroversion*, the channeling of mental energy and interests in an inward or outward direction.

From philosophy and religion has come Mowrer's (1967) formulation about the part that *sin and guilt* play in constructive personality development. *Authenticity*, a concept much used by existentialists and often taken over by psychologists, stresses the importance of honesty in one's confrontation with the world, of expressing one's real feelings rather than covering them with a layer of deceit. *Meditation* and other techniques often grouped together under transpersonal therapy are derived from oriental religious practices.

Growth-oriented psychologists who deal with children derive usable concepts from many areas of research in child development. *Growth curves and developmental norms* are based on longitudinal studies of hundreds of children. They enable clinical helpers to assess the probabilities that a child referred for troublesome behavior will grow out of it as he or she moves into a later stage.

Social-Ecological Orientation

Many usable concepts are derived from sociological and social-psychological sources. Durkheim contributed the concept of *anomie*, a condition of being without organization or system, of not belonging to society, of not having a "place," often used to explain suicide and behavioral aberrations. Both sociologists and psychologists have talked about *role* to refer to both the function a person has in a group and the behavior expected of the person. Research in small and large groups has helped clinicians become aware of *communication channels*, the paths along which symbols and meanings pass from one member to another.

Ecologically oriented psychologists are interested in the person's adaptation to the nonhuman as well as the human world. To Kurt Lewin we owe the concept of *life space*, the perceived psychological environment, the part of the environment one sees and the way one structures it. This is similar in some respects to *style of life*, a concept that Adler contributed to our understanding of individuals, which is related not only to the perception of the environment but also to the person's characteristic way of responding to it. In our time the concept of life style has become very familiar, and clinicians find it natural to recognize diversity. Barker and his co-workers have given general currency to the concept of *behavior setting*, a place that can be differentiated from others on the basis of the kind of behaviors that occur there. The ideas of *community* and of *organizational development* add great breadth to the ecological orientation.

In recent years biological concepts related to ecology have been adapted for psychological uses, but because they are much less familiar to most psychologists, we shall not discuss them here. The ecological orientation is much newer than the others, and the curative orientation is much older. The number of concepts that are familiar and widely used is to some extent dependent on how long they have been available, but clinicians of any orientation can use concepts from all orientations as tools of their trade. Because of the value of possessing such an assortment of conceptual tools, basic education in psychology is stressed in the training of helping persons. The list included here is just a sampling from many and is intended as only a first introduction.

SUMMARY

General systems theory is an interdisciplinary approach to the biological and social sciences. The basic entity is a set of interrelated parts rather than the single variable, and systems at all levels from the single cell to the large organization show certain common features. Clinical workers can see their task as that of improving the functioning of a system rather than of eliminating or modifying particular symptoms or problems. The first essential is always to decide at what system level to intervene—for example, the individual's attitudes, the family relationships, or the community.

The second basic component of our clinical conceptual framework is development. Clinical psychology's subjects are human beings in motion, moving through fairly predictable sequences from birth to death. Working with them *must* be in the context of their developmental attainments. Intervening to help people can partly be seen as a way of clearing the track for their further development—setting new contexts, remediating skills, teaching adaptive behavior, or getting people ready to profit from natural support systems. It has been useful to delineate several stages. Freud proposed that this be done by identifying the parts of the body from which greatest pleasure is obtained. Erikson redefined the stages in terms of personal-social crises that arise at successive ages. More recently Levinson has differentiated four adult stages. Piaget outlined a sequence of stages based on cognitive development. Developmental concepts are particularly important when the aim of clinical intervention is to prevent later difficulties. Work is in progress to identify children "at risk" and reduce their vulnerability through training.

Our third basic element for viewing clinical work emphasizes alternatives and decisions. An individual faces multiple possibilities for developing in different directions, and choice, whether conscious or unconscious, plays a part in setting the pattern.

Besides these broad perspectives from which all clinical work can be viewed, workers have at their disposal a rich variety of concepts drawn from many sources that they can use in understanding the personalities with whom they deal. For each of the four major orientations—curative, learning, growth, and social-ecological—there are many such ideas.

RECOMMENDED READINGS

Tyler, L. E. *Individuality: Human possibilities and personal choice in the psychological development of men and women.* San Francisco: Jossey-Bass, 1978.
This book explores the concepts of possibility, choice, and cognitive structures in detail. It reviews and relates these concepts to research in the areas of creativity, values, interests, competencies, and development.

Simon, H. A. *The sciences of the artificial (2nd ed.).* Cambridge, Mass.: MIT Press, 1981.

Short as it is (247 pages), this collection of lectures by a Nobel-prize–winning economist and psychologist contains some profound insights about psychological structure and functioning, backed up or at least suggested by computer research on artificial intelligence. His discussions of systems in the last three chapters are especially valuable.

Miller, J. G., & Miller, J. L. Systems science: An emerging interdisciplinary field. *The Center Magazine*, 1981, *14*(5), 44–55.

This short article in the magazine of the Center for the Study of Democratic Institutions explains general systems theory quite simply as well as comprehensively. At each of the seven levels of living systems, the authors outline 19 critical subsystems, such as memory, boundary, and decider, mentioned in this chapter. For a clear explanation in simple language of the systems view, the way it differs from the prevailing atomistic view, and the significance of this way of thinking, see Laszlo (1972); also the edited collection of papers by Emery (1969). Anderson and Carter (1978) present an introductory social systems approach to human behavior at different levels. Egan and Cowan (1979) integrate systems with a life-stage development orientation and discuss ways of changing systems. Chin and O'Brien (1970) also cover systems theory and applications, and Taplin (1980) in a short article outlines how systems theory applies to assessment and intervention.

Hampden-Turner, C. *Maps of the mind.* New York: Macmillan, 1981.

Sixty different theories describing the organization of the human mind are presented briefly, and for each a sketch, or "map," shows its salient features. Biologists, linguists, sociologists, religious and political thinkers as well as psychologists are represented. At the end the author attempts a synthesis. The writing style and the makeup of the book are unusually attractive.

Wolman, B. B., & Stricker, G. (Eds.). *Handbook of developmental psychology.* Englewood Cliffs, N.J.: Prentice-Hall, 1982.

The editors offer a comprehensive overview—some 960 pages in 50 chapters—of developmental psychology, described in six parts. "Research Methods and Theories" lays groundwork and gives basic perspectives. "Infancy" brings together such recent work as infant attachment and the prenatal effects of smoking. "Childhood" covers aspects such as cognitive skills, memory, language, and moral development. "Adolescence" looks at several biological, personal, and social changes, including vocational development. "Adulthood" includes material on life cycles, mid-life development, divorce, and the impact of children on parents. Finally, "Aging" reviews changes in ability, social behavior, and physiology among others. The handbook's emphasis on research, its breadth of topics, and its attention to practical issues make it a valuable source book.

Another important book on development is that by Cairns, *Social Development: The Origins and Plasticity of Interchanges* (1979). Chapters 1 and 2 are particularly relevant. Since about 1970 striking changes have occurred in theoretical concepts about how individuals develop. The theory presented here is a synthesis of ideas from biology, ethology, sociobiology, and psychology. The basic unit is a reciprocal interchange between the child and other people and things rather than a response the child makes to a stimulating situation. At every stage biological and social influences are so completely merged in the total pattern that any attempt to disentangle "nature" from "nurture" is futile. Development at all stages is plastic, malleable, and reversible, so that no unfavorable experience, such as deprivation in infancy, must be accepted as a permanent handicap.

Birren, J. E., & Schaie, W. K. (Eds.). *Handbook of the psychology of aging.* New York: Van Nostrand Reinhold, 1977.

This *Handbook* and its companion volume, the *Handbook of Aging and the Social Sciences* (Binstock & Shanas, 1976), are major resources for information about the later half of life. Of particular importance here are the last several chapters on problem solving (by Rabbitt), personality (Neugarten), psychopathology (Pfeiffer), morale (Chown), clinical assessment (Schaie & Schaie), and intervention and rehabilitation with psychiatric disorders (Eisdorfer & Stotsky). Smelser and Erikson (1980) edited a collection of reports by some of the most prominent theorists and researchers on the later half of the life span, particularly examining the relation between the individual and society.

Bronfenbrenner, U. *The ecology of human development: Experiments by nature and design.* Cambridge, Mass.: Harvard University Press, 1979.

A distinguished developmental psychologist synthesizes a great many findings and principles and proposes a theoretical system consisting of a long and generative series of propositions and hypotheses. He is particularly impressed with the importance of familial and social environments in children's lives and asserts that subjective perceptions of situations influence behavior. He sees the need for "ecological validity" in research—the accurate representation in design of settings to which the researcher wishes to generalize. He advocates a reciprocal relation between policy making and research. Masterpasqua (1981) also argues for attention to natural settings and a close relation between developmental and clinical psychology; he particularly focuses on the fostering of *competence* in children. Using concepts akin to ecology and development, Gilmore (1980) synthesizes many clinical ideas and procedures into a comprehensive theory for eclectic intervention. Counseling and psychotherapy deal with the spheres of relationship, work, and aloneness in human lives with three possible purposes: choice, change, and coherence.

3 HELPING WITHOUT HARMING:

Designs and Decisions for Intervening in Human Lives

"Hello. This is John Howard. I'm a social worker in a hospital in Grand Forks. We're discharging a patient, and he's moving to your city. He wants to continue to work on his drinking problem. Is there any place I can refer him to?"

"I've got to talk to someone. My husband is trying to kill me. This morning there was funny white stuff in the cereal box."

"We've brought Karen here to get her straightened out. She's been messing around with this punk twice her age. Don't you think a girl of 13 should stay home nights? We can't do anything with her."

"The court requires an evaluation of competency to stand trial. Have Harry Samuelson's case worked up by Monday."

"Can you work with anorexia nervosa? My daughter vomits everything she eats."

"At the school, we have a lot of Mexican-American kids now. The tests are not good, and the counselors can't seem to relate to the kids. Could you give us a workshop?"

"I'm flunking out of mathematics. I hate it. But I still want to be an engineer, and my mom and dad are expecting it. What'll I do?"

"My mother is 86 now, and she lives alone in an old house. She refuses to leave, but the other day when we came in, the burner was red hot, and the teakettle was almost dry. She could start a fire. We've got to do something."

"This therapy group is a mess. We never talk about anything important. We're just sitting around and gossiping."

"At the County Clinic, we want to set up a new program for educating teenagers about drug abuse. There has been an upsurge of overdoses lately. How could we go about it?"

"The state hospital is spewing all these patients into the community. They don't have anything to do, and some of them are so doped up that they sleep all day in their rooming houses. Something should be done."

"I've been coming to your office for 10 weeks now. I think I've settled most of my problems. Should I come next week?"

"The only way to get money for our free clinic is from the United Community Appeal, but they insist we give them a long statement about goals and objectives, community needs, nonduplication of services, involvement of volunteers, and community participation. Can you help us obtain the information and organize the report?"

These requests are samples of the kinds that come to working clinicians. They all relate to the knowledge and skills accumulated by practicing psychologists and others over the years. How are clinicians to use their psychological "know-how" in meeting these requests? What are the fundamentals of clinical work? This chapter is an overview and introduction to the basic processes in dealing with such human problems. In searching for principles underlying assessment and therapy, we will be trying to understand the processing of information in clinical systems, "service environments," particularly what goes into *decisions and designs for action.*

We use the word *design* here to indicate that the planning of a program dealing with people's concerns is an art as well as a science. Like an architect or a composer, the clinician develops an appreciation for style (or way of life) and makes use of materials and techniques to help construct new ways of perceiving and behaving in the world. The clinician is involved in creatively restructuring "programs of living." However, unlike many artists, the clinician does not work alone but achieves the resulting "product" (or program) through the life activities of others, somewhat like a consultant director or playwright helping to refashion a continuing drama. The clinician only enters clients' ongoing stream of development temporarily, using all scientific background and skill available, but remaining continually sensitive to the needs and purposes of these people who are designing their own lives.

In early times medical practitioners adopted a rule or motto for their efforts: *primum non nocere* (first, do no harm). They recognized implicitly that, in the absence of clear knowledge, harming the patient was a distinct possibility. Human service workers have been less emphatic about adopting the same rule, but increasingly they are realizing that poorly conceived interventions, misguided forays into someone's life, can also result in harm. The word *intervention* in describing any kind of case management or therapy truly suggests that clinicians are "coming between" or "entering into" elements of the system of natural interaction. To intervene is to interfere—either for better or for worse.

Making decisions and interventions to produce clear benefit is a difficult task. No easy guidelines or quick recipes exist; varying degrees of controversy surround almost every assertion one makes. As the title of the chapter suggests, we will try always to keep the possibility of nonintervention—that is, doing nothing—in mind. As the catchy phrase "Don't just do something, stand there" implies, a considerable quantity of human service, mental health, and social service activity may have only been "doing something," keeping our image of action intact, rather than thinking through the situation carefully and working toward a clear goal. Physicians also often sense pressures to do something—for instance, prescribe drugs—when doing nothing might actually be better for the patient.

In Chapter 2 we discussed hierarchies of systems and confronted the first decision to be made—choosing the system level or levels we may hope to change. As an example we cited the case of Billy, who seemed to be emotionally disturbed, and showed how all system levels from the physiological to the community might be considered as targets for change (Table 2–1). At each of these levels intervention would consist of altering inputs (e.g., perceptions) or outputs (e.g., behaviors) or changing internal processing of information. Some psychologists would choose to intervene at the personal system level. Those who are behaviorally oriented would work out a plan for reinforcing constructive behavior and eliminating stimuli that lead to negative output. Those who follow psychoanalytic guidelines would encourage Billy to communicate inner feelings and resolve interpsychic conflicts, so that the pattern of internal processing might be changed. Other workers electing to intervene at the biological level using medication, or at the family level using parent education techniques, would also be attempting to modify important subsystems.

Because psychology has been so largely concerned with individual functioning, only recently has the possibility of intervention at other system levels taken on the importance it deserves. Deciding which system to enter may well be the most crucial decision to be made. When, for example, the police apprehended Jerry, a 14-year-old caught smashing furniture and throwing plates and glasses in an unoccupied vacation cabin, the juvenile court judge had to decide at the outset what the goal was to be. It may be simply to attempt by means of an appropriate punishment to eliminate acts of vandalism from Jerry's behavior repertoire. But if Jerry belongs to a gang of boys believed to be responsible for vandalism on a large scale, the decision may be to direct the intervention to this group rather than to Jerry personally. Furthermore, the two plans may be so combined so that both Jerry and his group become intervention targets.

In this chapter most of the emphasis is on intervention designed to alter the functioning of individuals rather than larger systems, but many of the principles apply at all levels. In later sections the special characteristics of intervention at the higher system levels are considered in more detail.

FACTORS INFLUENCING
DECISIONS ABOUT INTERVENTIONS

Client Attitudes and Expectations
about Intervention

Candidates for psychological assistance are either *voluntary* or *involuntary*. The former comprise most of the patients to be found in outpatient clinics and in private therapists' offices. The latter comprise many of the patients in locked wards of mental hospitals, institutions for the criminally insane, and some services for children and juveniles. People who are committed to mental hospitals and prisons against their will are clearly involuntary, but there are many others who come under some form of duress. The person may have to attend group sessions or seek individual therapy as a condition of the judge's sentence after conviction for driving under the influence of drugs or alcohol or some other offense. Children are often brought in unwillingly as "identified patients" by their parents. Many exhospital patients are ambivalent about the recommended continued follow-up. Many people go to clinics or hospitals or other psychological services with mixed feelings about whether they want to have their lives scrutinized or altered and whether they will trust the agency workers to know them or help them sufficiently.

Figure 3-1 Waiting rooms for public services may be crowded and impersonal. (What could be done to improve this?) (David Krasnor, Photo Researchers, Inc.)

A major issue in many countries is inequity—some sets of people have many more behavioral problems than others. Many studies have indicated that the poor, those with little education, the less accepted minorities, and those living in crowded, dilapidated inner cities or in isolated rural settings often have more than their proportion of behavioral problems (e.g., Lorion, 1978). Many of these people need many services—help with housing, food, employment, and physical health as well as mental and behavioral problems. They are *multiproblem* families and persons. They contribute more than their share to prison populations and welfare roles, but many of them do not know about mental health services or do not see how those services could help them. These sectors of the population often need psychological services but much more than the typical clinics and private offices can provide. In addition to what services psychologists can give to individuals and groups, they and other professionals need to be concerned about larger public policies and the human services they promote.

In any case whether the clients come voluntarily or are sought out by the service, they need to be seen as varying greatly in their attitudes and expectations about help. Of course, it is much better for the success of the intervention if the client is interested, cooperative, and positive in expectations. Part of the mixed assessment-intervention approach of the clinician early in the contact is then centered on how favorably the client sees the service and what he or she expects to gain from it.

Figure 3-2 Middle-class services are often approachable and accommodating—if one can pay.

Five Orientations of Clinicans toward Interventions

In thinking about how to help others psychologically, most clinicians would emphasize three general sets of notions or models: the medical or curative orientation, the learning orientation, and the growth, or self-development, orientation. To these core three, we have added two possibilities less often recognized: the "natural," or everyday, processes and the ecological orientation. These five, outlined in Table 3–1, are as follows:

1. The *natural helping orientation*. At any time, in any culture or part of society, there are thousands of psychological problems in various stages of solution. The vast majority of troublesome psychological conditions do not come to the attention of professional experts. They are handled, well or poorly, either by the person, by consultation with family members or friends, or by changes in the natural course of events. Also within any culture there are folk experts to whom people go with physical and psychological symptoms. These "experts" may be folk healers, village elders, or in many industrialized societies, professionals who are not specialists in psychological problems. Understanding the culture-based beliefs and folkways about human difficulties is fundamental to the other orientations to designing intervention.

2. The *curative orientation*, often called the *medical model*, holds that mental difficulties result from sickness or pathology analogous to physical pathology and often caused by physical pathology. The objective is to diagnose the source of the pathology and to eliminate or neutralize it. This orientation has a long and useful history, but it also has its weaknesses.

3. The *learning orientation* is based on the premise that behavior and thought are acquired through conditioning or perceptual-attentional mechanisms. This model asserts that deviant behavior that causes people anguish and discomfort can be changed. What was learned can be unlearned or replaced. Skills such as self-control and problem-solving strategies can be learned. The intervention procedures are educative and rely heavily on psychological research.

4. The *growth (or developmental) orientation*, allied closely with the *humanistic approach* and *self-development*, is based on the premise that exploratory forces in personality lead toward self-actualization and fulfillment. However, blockages in this natural growth process can occur, causing one to lose touch with one's values. Intervention involves removing the blockages, getting in touch with one's values (and sometimes spiritual beliefs), and permitting growth and skill development to resume.

5. The *ecological orientation* is based on the premise that all behavior and thought is a function of interaction with the environment; any system can only be understood in terms of its communications, relations, and interchanges with its surroundings, both physical and social. Particular emphasis is placed on resources for help in families, organizations, and communities. An individual would not be treated in isolation. Intervention would involve consultation and participative manipulation of the selected behavior setting. This last approach depends strongly on information about the natural environment. Both the natural helping and ecological orientations are less well formulated and researched than the other three.

This division into five orientations is like most organizational schemes, somewhat oversimplified. For instance, the broad and variegated realm of thought called *psychoanalysis* does not fit well only in the curative mode, where we have placed it. Many individual therapists will see elements of the last four approaches within their practice; most practitioners think of themselves as having mixed or eclectic orientations. Still the five orientations can be useful guides to understanding the different ways that people have tried to deal with psychological problems and possibilities over the years, and they will be referred to frequently in later chapters.

Possible Side Effects—
The Case for Nonintervention

The inclusion in Table 3–1 of the first orientation—the reliance on natural helping mechanisms—suggests a further elaboration of a point raised earlier in this chapter—the dangers of professional interference. Intervening in human lives all too often brings unforeseen consequences or negative effects. Because of pitfalls the decisions to change intervention procedures or not to intervene at all must be considered as possible ways of dealing with an unsatisfactory situation. There are many possible considerations, of which we will illustrate a few.

Intervention may be harmful when people are insensitive to cultural or social standards. Through ignorance one can behave in ways that offend particular cultural groups. In some Native American (Indian) cultures, for

TABLE 3-1 Basic Orientations for Designing Interventions

	NATURAL HELPING (Folk-Nonprofessional)	CURATIVE (Pathology-oriented)	LEARNING (Behavioral-Cognitive)	GROWTH (Self-Development)	ECOLOGICAL (Interactive-Environmental)
Typical View of Problem	Depending on culture, client may be "in trouble," "immature," "sick," "possessed"	Client is sick, distressed, mentally or physically	Client has learned maladaptive habits or thoughts	Client not functioning at own optimum level of development	Client interacting in a malfunctioning system, not using resources
Emphasis for Intervention	On believed problem in self or environment	On psychological pain and underlying "causes"	On specific behaviors or ideas that are identified as problems	On release of inherent growth potential	On physical and social situations, supports, relations
Nature of Assessment	Everyday, common-sense impressions, folk beliefs of causes	Diagnosis of pathology and assignment to psychiatric categories	Pinpointing precise behaviors and thoughts and their reinforcers	Awareness of self; recognition of developmental influences over time	Analysis of systems, environments, interaction, and social structures
Nature of Intervention	Daily problem solving; talk and activities from helpful friends and family; folk healers; advice of "wise" people; self-help groups	Medication or psychotherapy; psychoanalysis and related therapy	Designed program to replace maladaptive problem with adaptive behavior and thinking	Creation of climate to encourage self-exploration, confrontation, and openness	Reorganization of system or environment; consultation for resource development

View of Prevention	Proper observance of family and community folkways, religion; proper child rearing	Seen as public health problem; search for "immunization" for people "at risk"	Parent education and community efforts to teach competent behavior	Growth groups and centers to facilitate development, especially at turning points in life	Improvements in schools; encouragement of citizen participation in community betterment
Strengths	Fits the culture; little stigma; inexpensive; encourages self-help	Uses biological and medical aids; has medical prestige and financing; important for somatic and psychotic cases	Links with psychological research; self-evaluating; starts where client is and builds own learning	Active participation of clients in process; discourages dependence; interested in spiritual values	Benefits whole system, not just client; identifies and uses community resources
Weaknesses	Great variety in resources and effectiveness; poor with uncommon problems; tends to confuse nonconformity with abnormality	Tends to focus on individual; dependence on experts; little concern with assets and larger environment	Emphasis on problems, symptoms, not total personality; new habits may not generalize to new situations	Usually not useful with serious disorders and less verbal people; little research underpinning	Inadequate research base; techniques poorly developed; complexity of large systems

example, looking straight into people's faces for direct communication is considered effrontery. Anyone with reasonable manners looks respectfully downward or away while speaking. Furthermore, it is an offense to lead children's games in a setting normally reserved for tribal ceremonies. An inappropriate approach of a mental health worker in inner city or rural environments may also violate local understandings, not only ruining the current attempt at intervention but also making future attempts much more difficult. Knowing the community's norms and expectations is important for making the intervention decision.

Poorly planned interventions may harm existing community assets. For example, natural support groups may be harmed by well-meaning professional intervention. *Informal natural networks*, consisting of grandmothers, concerned neighbors, members of a religious congregation, and *self-help groups*, such as Alcoholics Anonymous, Recovery Incorporated, and Parents Anonymous, all have substantial skills which deserve attention from the professional. In some communities *curanderos*, or other native healers, perform important services. To establish a clinical program that disregards or belittles these contributions may make matters worse.

The existence of a poorly conceived intervention can redefine problems in living or social changes as needs for professional help, and two problems result: First, needless intervention can detract from people's ability to solve their own problems. It can promote dependency or teach people to "play pa-

BOX 3-1   *MORE IS NOT ALWAYS BETTER*

Nicholas Cummings (1977) reviews a series of his studies which show that when psychotherapy is included in the offerings of a prepaid medical insurance plan, outpatient medical usage is reduced. Patients with emotional complaints and problems in living were treated immediately with psychotherapy without preselection criteria. For 85 percent, what Cummings describes as active, innovative short-term psychotherapy was more effective than long-term psychotherapy in reducing medical utilization.

That result is striking enough. But a small subgroup of patients, 5.3 percent of the total, had a mean of 47.9 psychotherapy sessions per year and appeared simply to have switched from frequent medical visits to frequent psychotherapy visits. With the idea that even more intensive psychotherapy might in some way cure the dependency of these patients, the 5.3 percent group was divided into matched subgroups. These groups were given one, two, and three sessions of psychotherapy per week.

Briefly, the three times per week patients *increased* the concomitant outpatient medical utilization so much that the intervention was changed. When psychotherapy frequency was drastically reduced, concomitant outpatient medical visits dropped off dramatically. The issues here are complex, but those who plan interventions must be clear that more is not necessarily better.

tient" for an extended time. Second, it can create a weighty body of helpers who naturally form a professional (or paraprofessional) alliance to propagate their kind and guarantee their security. Such groups become a costly item for tax- or feepayers. Compared with some less developed societies, there is a potential to make Western, industrialized societies top-heavy with paid helpers. For example, in one center smoking marijuana was seen as clear evidence of emotional disturbance. The clinic's rolls became swollen with young smokers, and there were cries for more staff. Only the happy fact that money could not be found for the staff prevented the spread of smoker therapizing. (Lest we be misunderstood here, we want to make it clear that we do not favor a wanton abandonment of the mental health system that exists now, rather we favor a skeptical attitude accompanied by extensive evaluation and research to identify what is useful in particular societies.)

Nonintervention in a natural, continuously evolving ecosystem may have more long-term benefit than would intervention if we examine later degrees of stability, maturity, survival skills, and problem solving. Evaluating past interventions can have a sobering effect. The huge facilities built for the retarded, mental patients, delinquents, and prisoners did not provide the "treatment" they promised but instead taught communities to have an attitude toward inmates of being "out of sight, out of mind."

We should be especially skeptical about interventions that bypass natural systems. If, for example, the Jones family isn't coping well with 14-year-old John and a clinician recommends foster care, it is more likely that other Jones children will be pushed into foster care as problem behavior occurs. The basic societal system—the family—may never acquire the strength to deal with its tasks, and the bypass—foster care—will soon become hopelessly overloaded. We must always be cautious about recommending a certain kind of intervention simply because facilities are available. A wealth of resources can be a mixed blessing. Patients who can afford it must not be channeled into private residential sanitoria in preference to community clinics just on financial grounds. Old persons should not be placed in nursing homes just because Medicaid funds can be obtained for this. Juveniles should not be processed through elaborate diagnostic facilities just because such a service exists. Fortunately psychologists and others doing research are becoming more aware of the need for evaluation, as references and research summaries at the end of many chapters will illustrate. Chapter 13 will bring together the major ideas and methods for evaluation.

Diagnosis—
The Problem of Classification

Throughout the development of clinical psychology, the first step in decisions about intervention has often been classification or diagnosis. This is, of course, a medical concept, and there has been considerable controversy about how useful it is in psychology and the other helping professions. Rogers (1942) was one of the first to argue that categorizing people dehumanizes and deindividualizes them and prevents proper attention to therapy. Some (e.g., Hobbs et al., 1975) decry the dangers of labeling, by which they mean the attachment of a name that stays with the person and leads to images and decisions that are detrimental, just as stereotyping a person as a "nigger" or "homosexual" creates prejudice. But to the extent that diagnosis facilitates at least preliminary decisions about intervention plans and provides a means by which persons involved in them can communicate with one another, classification is generally held to be useful.

As would be expected in view of the medical origin of the concept of diagnosis, the system related to the curative model in Table 3–1 is the most widely used. Kraepelin, the German psychiatrist, in the late nineteenth century gathered together the mental illnesses then named and organized a classification system which is the basis for the current official psychiatric nomenclature throughout the world. In a series of *Diagnostic and Statistical Manuals*—DSM I in 1952, DSM II in 1968, and DSM III in 1980, the American Psychiatric Association has provided the terms for describing mental disorders and has given official sanction to such labels as schizophrenia, paranoia, and depression. These classifications are influenced by scientific progress and by prevailing opinions in international psychiatry and society at large; an example of change is that the American Psychiatric Association at one time classified all homosexuality as a mental illness but later dropped it.

Table 3–2 provides a list of the major clinical diagnostic categories in DMS-III (American Psychiatric Association, 1980), covering the major familiar titles, such as mental retardation, organic disorders, psychoses, and neuroses (now indirectly named). The diagnostician uses much finer classifications, however; all of these are fairly carefully defined in DSM–III. For instance, in order to be diagnosed schizophrenic, a patient must have deterioration from a previous level of function, must have continuous signs of the illness for at least six months, must have an onset before age 45, must not have these symptoms because of organic disorders, and must have at least delusions, hallucinations, or incoherent associations, which are described in detail. Although not fully indicated in Table 3–2, this diagnostic system provides for five axes of classification. Axis I covers clinical syndromes; Axis II, personality disorders and specific developmental disorders; Axis III, concomitant physical disorders; Axis IV, ratings of the severity of psychosocial stressors; and Axis V, ratings of the highest level of adaptive functioning in the past year.

This multiaxial system can result in a statement for each axis and thus is a five-part diagnosis when fully used. The multiaxial approach is intended to make sure that diagnosticians attend to certain types of disorder, to aspects of the patient's environment, and to areas of functioning that might not be noticed if only a single label were used. Routine usage requires completion of

TABLE 3-2   Major Categories of DSM-III Classification

Axis I: Clinical Syndromes

DISORDERS USUALLY FIRST EVIDENT IN INFANCY, CHILDHOOD, OR ADOLESCENCE:
   Mental retardation: Mild, moderate, severe, or profound
   Attention deficit disorder: With or without hyperactivity
   Conduct disorder, e.g., undersocialized, aggressive
   Anxiety disorders of childhood and adolescence, e.g., separation anxiety
   Other disorders of infancy, childhood, or adolescence, e.g., reactive attachment
   Eating disorders, e.g., anorexia nervosa
   Stereotyped movement disorders, e.g., chronic motor tic
   Other disorders with physical manifestations, e.g., functional encopresis
   Pervasive developmental disorders, e.g., infant autism
ORGANIC MENTAL DISORDERS
   Dementias arising in the senium (old age) and presenium
   Substance-induced
SUBSTANCE USE DISORDERS (alcohol, barbiturate, opioid, amphetamine, etc.)
SCHIZOPHRENIC DISORDERS (e.g., paranoid)
PARANOID DISORDERS
PSYCHOTIC DISORDERS NOT ELSEWHERE CLASSIFIED
AFFECTIVE DISORDERS
   Bipolar disorder: Mixed, manic depressed
   Major depression: Single episode, recurrent
   Other specific affective disorders, e.g., cyclothymic
   Atypical affective disorders
PSYCHOSEXUAL DISORDERS
   Gender identity disorders
   Paraphilias, e.g., transvestism
   Psychosexual dysfunctions, e.g., inhibited sexual desire
   Other psychosexual disorders, e.g., ego-dystonic homosexuality
FACTITIOUS DISORDERS
DISORDERS OF IMPULSE CONTROL NOT ELSEWHERE CLASSIFIED, e.g., pyromania
ADJUSTMENT DISORDERS, e.g., with depressed mood
PSYCHOLOGICAL FACTORS AFFECTING PHYSICAL CONDITION
ANXIETY DISORDERS
   Phobic disorders (or phobic neuroses), e.g., agoraphobia
   Anxiety states (or anxiety neuroses), e.g., panic disorder
   Posttraumatic stress disorder: acute, chronic, or delayed, atypical
SOMATOFORM DISORDERS, e.g., psychogenic pain
DISSOCIATIVE DISORDERS, e.g., psychogenic amnesia

Axis II: Personality Disorders and Specific Developmental Disorders

PERSONALITY DISORDERS
   Schizoid, schizotypal, histrionic, narcissistic, antisocial, borderline, avoidant, depen-
   dent, compulsive, passive-aggressive, atypical, mixed, or other
SPECIFIC DEVELOPMENTAL DISORDERS
   Developmental reading, arithmetic, language, articulation disorder, mixed specific or
   atypical specific developmental disorder

---

at least Axes I and II rather than all five, and clinicians may record "no diagnosis or condition noted" if that happens to be the case with either axis. Table 3–2 lists the clinical syndromes of Axis I and the personality disorders and specific developmental disorders of Axis 2. The system has been worked out over many years and has been subject to studies of reliability, until a high level of interclinician agreement has been reached. However, note that there are miscellaneous or atypical categories liberally sprinkled through the list. Familiarity with psychiatric situations and training in the system are needed to use it accurately.

For many decades a great deal of professional time has been devoted to *differential diagnosis* (identifying and determining the appropriate label among several possible ones) of each patient coming to a clinic or hospital. This is still true in many psychiatric services and private offices. In medical settings the psychiatrist is usually the final authority on whether a person is called a *schizophrenic*, an *antisocial personality*, or a *social phobic*. The label goes into the formal record (often referred to as the patient's *chart*) and becomes a part of the statistics reported to state authorities and probably to health insurance carriers. The diagnosis may be passed on to staffs of other hospitals having contact with the patient, thus providing a powerful part of the "working image" of the person. Massive record keeping on individuals by insurance companies and governmental bureaucracies provides both for assistance in future efforts to help people and for perpetuation of inappropriate or damaging labels in charts and data banks. It also raises questions about personal privacy.

Because of the widespread usage and acceptance of terms such as *schizophrenia, depression*, and *paranoia*, it would be difficult to stop using them, and there are many advantages to a common parlance. The classification system facilitates discussion of important differences among people and makes for some degree of comparability between different cases, but there is widespread demand for a better diagnostic system. The categories in DSM III, although an improvement in many ways over previous systems, are still not clear and independent of each other. Some are based on overt behavior (e.g., disturbances of speech); others have known etiology or causation (e.g., organic brain syndromes and certain forms of mental retardation); and others are vague general descriptions (e.g., anxiety disorders of childhood). Most patients have mixtures of the symptoms described—this is, a patient may have both neurotic and psychotic features.

One major criticism has been the questionable degree of agreement between diagnosticians. Many studies of reliability (a concept to be discussed in the next chapter) have reported a variety of results when two or more psychiatrists or psychologists are asked to diagnose the same patient. Studies in the United States and Europe using judgments of the same videotaped patients show that American psychiatrists tend to use the label *schizophrenic* more frequently than European psychiatrists do and Europeans use the *manic-depressive* label more (Kendell, Pichot, & von Cranach, 1974).

Diagnoses of many patients may also be changed when they are readmitted to hospitals even though their symptoms are the same. Rosenhan (1973), in a provocative article entitled "On Being Sane in Insane Places," showed how normal persons reporting only initial symptoms of anxiety and a hallucinatory experience were readily diagnosed as psychotic and had drugs prescribed by unsuspecting mental hospital professionals. After an extensive review Frank (1975) concluded that the behavioral and test correlates of psychiatric diagnoses were inconsistent and of little use for predictive purposes. More recently some highly structured interview procedures along with clear standards and criteria for classification, such as those used with the SADS (Schedule for Affective Disorders and Schizophrenia) (Endicott & Spitzer, 1978; Spitzer & Endicott, 1978), have provided impressive reliability. In spite of many flaws the system continues to be useful, and the widespread requirements for official and insurance records as well as for a common language for practitioners and researchers makes it important for all clinicians to know this classification system well.

What are some of the alternatives? One is an attempt to find the common dimensions used in the *natural language terms* for describing personality (e.g., Goldberg, 1982). Factor analyses of the many terms used in natural language to describe persons (as found in dictionaries) have repeatedly produced five categories which might be called *surgency* (active forcefulness, extraversion), *agreeableness* (friendliness-hostility), *conscientiousness* (achievement orientation), *emotional stability*, and *intelligence* (or cultural sophistication) (Digman & Takemoto-Chock, 1981; Norman, 1963). A second approach is to classify *responses* or *behaviors*. For example, Adams and his colleagues (1977, pp. 47–48) are developing the Psychological Response Classification System (PRCS) which categorizes behaviors by response systems: motor, perceptual, biological, cognitive, emotional, and social. A third and well-developed system is that of specifying the *interpersonal characteristics* of cases—e.g., their tendencies to be dominant or submissive, friendly or hostile to each other (McLemore & Benjamin, 1979). A fourth approach emphasizes the measurement of positive characteristics and *competencies* as well as negative or pathological ones (Sundberg, Snowden, & Reynolds, 1978). A fifth direction may involve new possibilities for depicting *individuality* (Tyler, 1978). Other directions might involve trying to classify environments or interactive styles and roles people play in different settings. The coming years may bring classification systems more satisfactory than the currently dominant psychiatric one, for the issue is a persistent and important one in daily clinical tasks of describing people and making decisions.

Differences in Interveners

Suppose that grant funds have become available to study the problem of adolescent suicides. Three cities compete. Proposal A suggests subsidizing psychiatrists and psychologists in private offices who see suicidal adolescents. Proposal B offers to start a clinic staffed by volunteers and have a big advertising campaign to attract distressed adolescents. Proposal C recommends that grant funds be used to train personnel at the state hospital to treat potential suicides. You are asked to critique these proposals.

What you note is that type of intervener and setting interact significantly. Proposal A has an unacceptably low capacity for *outreach*. Almost no disturbed adolescents contemplating suicide will be likely to know of the scheme, confront the problems of transportation, and face the anxiety of going alone to a strange place. A troubled boy's fantasies may deter him. "Do you have insurance, young man?" "No, I thought the doctor would see me on that federal program." "Oh yes, you want to be subsidized by the suicidal kid program." By focusing on *affordability* alone, the writers of the first proposal have failed to meet other equally important requirements.

Proposal B is strong where Proposal A is weak. This combination of intervener and setting promises to be *client-responsive*. Young people can be reached in familiar places, such as hamburger joints or ball parks. The weakness of this proposal is in the staffing of the project, but this may be corrected by provisions for selection, training, and supervision of volunteers.

Proposal C is probably the least acceptable. The combination of intervener and setting proposed is likely to communicate *stigma*, a quality which any ideal intervention should avoid. It not only makes the intervention less acceptable and accessible, but it also gives clients something negative to carry with them afterwards. Having been a "state hospital mental patient" may lead to an acute sense of failure, worthlessness, and self-disappointment—enduring handicaps. Considering these various factors, enlightened officials would probably award the grant to Proposal B.

Decision Making about Cases

Even *within* any one mental health service there is a complexity of organization that must be considered throughout the contact with the client. As Figure 3–3 shows, a sequence of decisions typically takes place in determining the approach to the clinic, the acceptance, assessment procedures, interventions, and termination. The figure shows how subsequent feedback may affect the subsystem in making assessments and the whole agency in its policies about admissions and treatments.

The various sections of the decision-making sequence may also be broken down rationally into specific parts. For instance, a university psychology clinic might handle its telephone inquiries and referrals as shown in Figure 3–4. A series of decisions and their various alternative steps must be known by all clinic staff who receive calls. In practice, clinic staff would have telephone numbers and, it is hoped, names of contact persons.

In addition to the analysis in terms of rational decisions, one needs to recognize the differences in socioemotional climate created by such decisions.

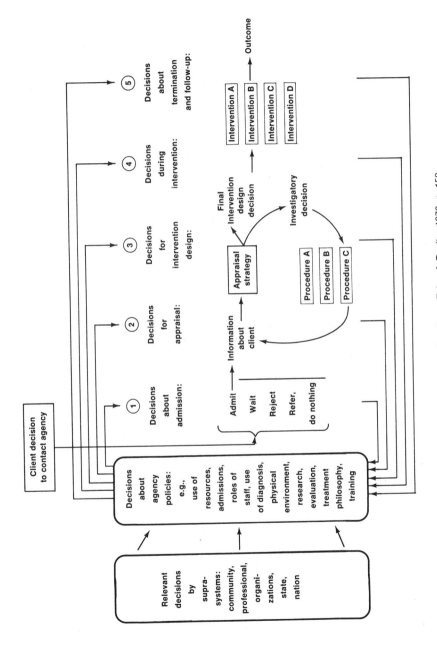

Figure 3-3 Decisions surrounding a clinical case. (From Sundberg, Tyler, & Taplin, 1973, p. 158. Copyright © 1973 by Prentice-Hall and used by permission.)

Different service environments suggest different feelings to clients. A large hospital setting may give patients a sense of depersonalization that a small office in an old house in which two psychologists conduct their private practice does not. A walk-in center for low-income people on a 24-hour emergency basis located in an old store creates still a different atmosphere.

Each continuing psychological service fills an ecological niche in the community, providing certain services and serving a particular clientele; it will tend to resist taking certain cases and program requests, while welcoming and even recruiting others. The resources of a center for helping others will depend not only on the internal character of the organization and the abilities and interests of the staff but also on the support from the community and financial status of the organization. Leadership styles will also provide emphases and guidance and establish a climate. These things must be taken into consideration as decisions about intervention are made.

GOALS IN INTERVENTION: PLANS AND CONTRACTS

Designing a Plan

Working out a plan for intervention in any particular case is essentially a problem of *design*. Using many kinds of information, the designer makes a series of decisions fitting into an overall "package" custom-made for a particular person or persons in a particular situation. We can differentiate several stages in this design process:

Ascertaining what the current situation is now—the system of focus, the main influences, and actors.

Clarifying what is desirable—as seen from several viewpoints, most often the primary client, the primary system of the client, and the influential parts of the larger society.

Examining resources and feasibility—who can work with the client or program, and what they can do.

Formulating the plan for the case or program that will move the person or persons from the present situation to a more desirable one.

Evaluating the ongoing development and reformulating treatment plans if needed.

Following up on a case or program after completion to develop improved design capabilities for the future.

In order to be effective, most clinical designing must involve the client intimately in the process. Participative designing is necessary in order to lead to personal commitment in the next step—the contract.

Psychological functions of the clinician include *contracting* the treatment plan, either explicitly or implicitly. A *contract* is an agreement between people to do certain things for and with each other. It implies an ex-

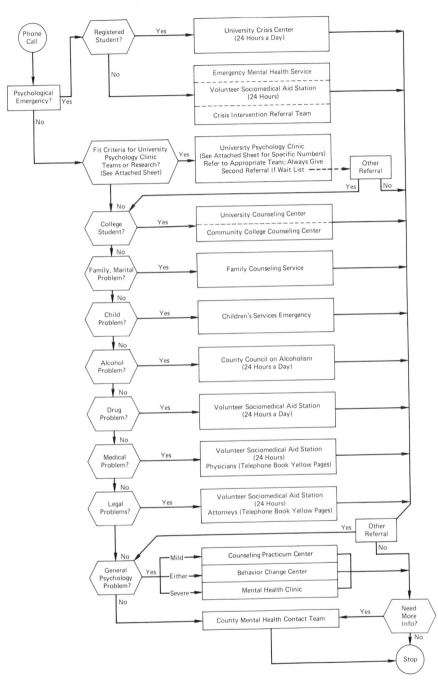

Figure 3-4 Decision chart for handling clinical inquiries and referrals in a university psychology clinic.

change—You do something, I'll do something in return—an agreement, which is common in all social systems explicitly or implicitly. Different people perform different roles fitting into the pattern of the system. The contract sets up *expectations;* it also has consequences for breaking the contract and opportunities to renegotiate the contract. Contracting requires considerable communication skill on the part of the clinician or counselor. In the process there is often an adjustment of the "working images" that the client and clinician hold of each other. Revisions and new joint decision making are common. The contract should set the stage for action—namely, implementation of intervention plans. The immediate measures of a good contract are understanding and commitment; the ultimate measure is satisfactory action bringing about new and more desirable possibilities.

Gilmore (1973) advises making an explicit contract with clients, even a written one in some instances. She sees several objectives being served by contracts: The purposes of the psychological assistance become the mutual concern of the clinician and client, and there is an attitude of joint responsibility—especially if the plan has been formulated carefully together. The purposes need to be clearly understood by both parties and their mutual expectations of each other clarified. Furthermore, with a clear contract each can evaluate the degree of success attained.

Confusion about Goals

The design process is greatly complicated by confusion about just what the goals of a plan or program are. If the client is well informed and has a clear understanding of how to use psychological services beneficially the goal of intervention is provided by the patient—the patient sets the goals. In the majority of cases, however, someone else besides the patient is involved in the goal setting.

"Who sets the goals for those who set the goals?" This is like the old Roman puzzle, "Who will be the custodian of the custodians?" Besides client and therapist, the family, the community, and the larger society may have goals they seek: "John has to have good treatment like in a hospital, doctor—and besides, our family's cracking up while he's around." "This young man has frightened so many children in our neighborhood he's simply got to be sent to the state hospital for treatment. Our neighborhood association demands it, and we'll go to our senator if he isn't." "Any person having knowledge of child abuse shall report it so that the victim may be protected and the offender dealt with according to law."

Not infrequently the goals that different groups want differ greatly, and conflict ensues. An adolescent runaway's mother may want Susie to be helped by psychotherapy to stay home and obey her stepfather. Susie may want to go to live with her father and have her stepfather and mother go to psychotherapy. A neighborhood mother may want to keep Susie and be willing to go to counseling with her. Other neighbors want the girl sent to an institution because she is corrupting their children, but the juvenile court gets some incentive money from the state for *not* sending status offenders to the institutions and therefore presses for intervention in the community.

Reaching attainable goals in a situation like Susie's—and it is not particularly far-fetched—demands, first, careful synthesis of the facts, for example:

Who is the client?	The girl, Susie
Who has custody (and therefore legal power)?	The mother
Are there any special legal demands or issues?	Yes, if child abuse occurs it must be reported; change in custody will require court proceedings
What are the possibilities?	Living with the mother, the neighbor, the father
What must be ruled out now?	Institutionalization

Goals must be thrashed out with the parties involved—and often that working-out process may take a long time. *Goals often evolve.* The first sessions with Susie, her mother, and stepfather may be hostile and result in decisions to leave each other as soon as possible. The decision may free the parties to change their focus to the girl's relationship with the stepfather; perhaps she has been hoping for a much closer relationship and has found him cold. (Understanding may become the next goal.) Perhaps he has been making frightening suggestions or demands. (Barrier setting or separating may become the next goal.)

The role of the clinical worker is simply to help the clients establish goals (in all cases except the most incompetent clients). The clinician is a facilitator rather than a goal setter. Happy endings do not always occur. Sometimes when discussion brings no resolution, the clinician, recognizing the potential harm involved in the only courses open, may simply have to say, "I'm sorry, but I'm not able to work with you toward any of those goals." Happily such endings are infrequent.

CARRYING OUT THE CONTRACT— CASE MANAGEMENT

Once a plan has been agreed upon, the task still remains of carrying it out. This task, in general, is often called *case management,* but the label suggests activity on the part of the clinician that is more impersonal and directive than it actually is. Responsibility for the important decisions and arrangements rests with psychologists, social workers, nurses, and others along with the psychiatrist who in times past was the person solely responsible for case management. (In some places there seems to be an emerging occupation or paraprofession called a *case manager*—a person who is responsible for the arrangements for a patient, usually a chronic mental patient or a mentally retarded person who has been placed in the community.) In large clinics and hospitals responsibilities for working with a family and others will be split among several professionals, but a clinician working alone or in a small group must handle all aspects of a case. Here are several brief accounts of case management to illustrate some of the variety:

Sharon Poe.   Sharon came to the counseling center very depressed over a breakup with a lover. After exploration of her willingness to review her feelings, the counselor offered continued appointments for one hour a week for the rest of the college term, at the end of which they would evaluate where things stood. Sharon was eager to do this, and after seven sessions she decided that she felt much better and had more understanding of herself; therapy was terminated with the provision that she might come back later if she wished. This was a simple contract calling for the client to commit herself to a certain amount of sharing of feelings and ideas.

Jim Archer.   Jim, a 22-year-old bricklayer, was picked up for drunken driving and put in jail when he resisted the officer. Given a choice of a jail sentence or going to a clinic, he chose the latter. At the clinic the interviewer found that Jim seemed to want sincerely to get over his drinking and assigned him to an evening class called "Drinking Decisions." After eight weeks of lectures and discussions about alcoholism, Jim continued voluntarily in another eight-week series of group counseling. We see here a set of agreements—the choice of the treatment program, the commitment to participate, and the plan to continue further.

The Williams Family.   Mrs. Williams called the clinic about Robbie, an 11-year-old, who was doing poorly in school, fought with his younger sister, and refused to do what he was told. The clinician with major responsibility for the case asked the whole family to come in and with a colleague saw each of the four individually and also together. It looked as if the mother was near a panic state. She was interviewed and tested in an additional session. So was the boy. One clinician also made a home visit after school hours. On the basis of information gathered, clinicians presented a plan for the Williams family in a joint meeting of the whole family and the two clinicians involved. The contract involved a set of positive and negative reinforcements for specified things Robbie did, to which father and mother both agreed. Records were to be kept of certain behaviors. In addition the mother was to come for individual sessions and was to take tranquilizing medication prescribed for her by a physician. The contract was to be reviewed after one month of operation. The therapists made home visits occasionally to evaluate and facilitate progress. After one month the family group came back to the clinic. It had become quite clear that there were marital problems. Mr. Williams was not following the reinforcement plan. At this meeting he clarified some of the difficulties, and as a result the plan was modified. Meanwhile Mrs. Williams did not seem to be improving, and Robbie was still a great source of irritation and anger. A vacation for Mrs. Williams was added to the plan. She took their daughter for a visit to her sister in a distant city. Upon her return Mrs. Williams was much better and started working with one of the counselors to formulate plans for parttime work. Repeated attempts to get Mr. Williams to go along with the reinforcement program for Robbie met with only partial success, but with a change of classes Robbie's school work improved. After a year, during which the mother became much better, the family and the clinician decided that they had gone as far as they could at this time. On follow-up six months later the mother reported conditions were not ideal but were livable. The contracting in this complex case involved renegotiation and reevaluation of goals.

Mary Adams.   Mary Adams had spent 15 years on the "back ward" of a state hospital, when a new program was developed in one of the other wards. The program had arisen after careful staff assessment of patient needs and staff training. It involved a series of graded steps in which certain privileges were added, such as the privilege of having cigarettes (if the person smoked) or being allowed to go outside with groups. Decisions on improvement in behavior were made at staff meetings based on the daily records they kept. The program planned for Mary involved, among other things, getting her to stop shouting out when she hallucinated. The nurse patiently explained to Mary that if she heard voices saying insulting things to her, she was to ignore them as much as possible, and if she had to say something, she should whisper. Mary seemed to understand the instructions, although for the first month she still shouted occasionally and did not show much progress. Over a period of a year, however, Mary's behavior in the hospital improved markedly, and staff members decided to allow her occasional supervised visits to nearby shops, although it was believed that she would never live independently. In this case the patient may not have understood the explanation of the contract at first, but she did learn the expected behavior by continuing experience in the structure set up by the staff.

Many more illustrations might be given, but these are perhaps sufficient to show what a variety of decisions must be made in the course of any intervention program, both before and after a plan is put into effect. Decision making is fundamental to all clinical work.

AVOIDING DISTORTIONS AND BIAS

All through this process of information gathering, goal setting, contract development, and case management, there is a continuing hazard—that the clinician's own circumstances, attitudes, and assumptions will have more influence than they should on the decisions that are made. Let us look at some of the origins of such biases.

Origins of Biases

Money.   Some therapists practice in settings in which their salary remains constant. For them the clients they see and the goals they set are more likely to be influenced by supervisor's policies than by money. But others, notably those in private practice, have the financial incentive to make each hour bring in the maximum amount possible. Few studies have been done in this sensitive area, although the pressures for profit making seem to make more likely such decisions and actions as the following:

> Selecting a richer rather than a poorer client
> Selecting full-fee clients rather than welfare clients
> Setting more distant goals with private clients who pay promptly
> Spending little time in nonrevenue activities such as outcome research or follow-up
> Setting goals that can be reached within the benefit coverage of insurance or welfare
> Terminating clients after their insurance or welfare benefits are exhausted.

Workload.   Pressure to maintain a caseload of a given number of clients is usually applied to salaried therapists. If a clinician is responsible for, say, 35 active cases, naturally, although perhaps unconsciously, the clinician will prefer to have quieter, more peaceable cases, in which evening or weekend emergencies or other demands on the therapist are minimized. Decisions in such situations can show a slant toward the following:

> Avoiding confrontation in therapy and referring out to crisis service.
> Minimal therapy for awkward patients so goals can be reached quickly and such patients can be terminated.
> Long-term supportive therapy for quiescent dependent patients.

Therapist's personality problems.   Some people who have rather clear psychological difficulties seek entry into helping professions almost as if they expected that healing others would secure for them the changes they want for themselves. Naturally such therapists tend to pay attention to the issues that trouble, fascinate, or preoccupy them. Some therapists try to make clients emotionally dependent, attempt to secure praise or power, or try to become a psychological parent to child patients. As an example, Janice Harvey's treatment plans always included the goal of having her adolescent clients focus at great length on their relationship with their fathers. She had had a close relationship with her father and at age 15 had experienced some ambiguous behavior from him which might have been a sign of improper sexual advance, and then again might have been nothing of the kind. Before there was any clarification, the father was killed in an accident. Other clinicians, knowing Ms. Harvey's background, might conclude that she was dealing with unresolved personal problems—unfinished developmental tasks—in the way she solicitously but ambivalently clung to some male clients. Clinical workers have learned that the ancient maxim "Know thyself" is an important guideline for their work.

The theoretical orientation or model of the clinical worker also influences decisions. Any human life is complex enough so that quite different accounts of it are possible. Imagine, for example, that three counselors are asked to consider the case of George, an overly anxious college student. We'll imagine that all three see George's problem as basically a personal system problem and that his biological system and family system seem intact. Counselor A has been trained to see such problems as signs of mental sickness —the pathology-curative perspective mentioned earlier—and believes that anxiety comes about when defenses against primitive impulses are about to be breached. Counselor A asks what kind of impulses are troubling George, how will they be manifest, and what went wrong in George's childhood—in his psychological development—what defenses didn't become adequately developed? Counselor A decides on a method of treatment that will help George to explore his feelings about his childhood and uncover the point where his development became blocked by conflict. George has very little input into the type or direction of his treatment—and he may be called "unmotivated" or "resistive" if he asks many questions about it. A more organically oriented counselor would refer for tranquilizers.

Counselor B, who comes from a "problems are learned" presumption, assumes that George has acquired excessive, inappropriate anxiety responses. Counselor B's puzzle is to understand what keeps the problem going and then to design ways that George can unlearn the response of becoming anxious and learn new, more adaptive responses. The learning of new skills may also be emphasized. The specific goals of his treatment will probably be worked out with George in some detail. The counselor will probably also ask him to keep daily counts or records of problem behaviors. In the event that the treatment does not work well, George's part in keeping the contract can be examined, but learning therapists are willing to blame themselves, rather than the client, for not having designed an optimally effective set of retraining contingencies.

Counselor C, working with a growth and self-optimization model, may expect George's feelings of depression to decrease as the treatment proceeds, but the aims of treatment will be broader. George will be encouraged to review all of his assets and strengths; to become more closely aware of his own wishes, preferences, and needs; and to reach a point where he takes charge of his own further growth and development.

None of these approaches is wrong. Any one of them may help George.

But it is important that the persons using them recognize their own predilections so that they do not try to fit all clients into the same mold and will understand alternative possibilities.

Overestimating One's Predictive Ability

One other source of bias in clinical workers has been the focus of considerable research. It has been shown that clinicians are not as good at predicting what clients will do as they believe they are. In 1954 a book appeared that was to create a great disturbance in the clinical world—Paul Meehl's *Clinical versus Statistical Prediction.* Earlier the accepted theory was that expert judgment was superior to mechanical ways of using data in working with people. The clinician, after all, could talk with the person and get a great deal more information on which to base a judgment than could be revealed by a statistic or test result. Even before Meehl, Sarbin (1943) had shown that through a simple statistical procedure combining test scores with high school average grade, a more accurate prediction of how well students would do in the university could be made than counselors could produce using much more information. What Meehl did in his 1954 book was to collect several such studies of various sorts of predictions indicating that in almost every case the clinician was a poorer predictor than the calculating machine was. A great deal of controversy and many other studies followed, all pointing in the same direction.

In the designing of plans and contracts, predictions must be made. No one, after all, wishes to enter upon a course of action for which the chances of success are very low. What the research in statistical versus clinical prediction means is that if there are already prepared statistical tables, as in the case of scholarship prediction, one should rely on them rather than cling to the fallacy that "the doctor knows best." In areas in which no statistical formulas are available, which is true in most cases, one should predict with caution and check frequently as a planned program proceeds. Accurate prediction is only part of the broader quality, good judgment.

Good judgment is essential for working intimately with people and for making important decisions in people's lives. What is good judgment? There is no easy answer. The differences in theories about personality and psychotherapy attest to the fact that there is no agreement about the best way to understand and assist others. We believe that good clinical judgment grows out of a deep interest and respect for individuals, an understanding and respect for the communities in which one works, a high sense of ethical values, an understanding of the developmental nature of life, a perspective on the place of people in larger systems, and a continual willingness to learn more and evaluate one's competence.

BOX 3-2 *THREE APOCRYPHAL STORIES*

Joanne, 30, had had a bout of illness, culminating in a hysterectomy. Just after that, her favorite sister was suddenly killed in a car accident. Joanne became anxious and depressed. The family doctor referred her to a local private hospital where she was admitted to the psychiatric ward. After several weeks, the treatment team told Joanne's rather large family, "When she comes home, don't burden her. Make things very easy, and don't have her do any work. She needs rest." After about a week at home, Joanne was found dead. A suicide note said, "First, can't be a mother any more. Then I lose Sis. Then I'm a mental patient. Then I lose my family—they won't let me do anything anymore—I'm not fit to belong anywhere. . . ."

George was 10 when he was first suspected of having some learning difficulties. In the rather well-to-do school district various specialists added a wide variety of different labels. These ranged from parental influence, through emotional problems, to a number of labels about learning disability and brain dysfunction. George's parents were confused and frustrated. George slowly became the odd and special one in the family, an identity which was confirmed when one helper said, "If we can qualify George as Learning Disabled with Dyslexia and Emotional Overlay, he can go to Faraway School's classroom for that group." The new placement sealed George's rejection by neighborhood children who called him "Spastic" and "Retard." George's parents would have felt better about the situation if they had been able to see any improvement. . . .

Paul, 18, had had difficulty for several years with bouts of confusion and rather strange speech. When he was 17, at one clearly bad episode, his parents were counseled to try a private psychiatric hospital to get to the heart of Paul's problems. "That superficial therapy at the mental health center is just not enough," they were told. Costs at the long established and quite prestigious institution were exorbitant. They had, in fact, completely ended Paul's sister's hopes for college and had cut deeply into vacations and ordinary spending. When the parents asked for progress reports, hoping for an end to the financial drain, the responses were remarkably similar: "We're getting really close to some very important deep unconscious material in the psychotherapy. Don't take him out now or you'll ruin his relationship with the therapist and end Paul's chances of ever dealing successfully with that deep material. Surely Paul is worth another loan. . . ."

GENERAL DISCUSSION—
UNRESOLVED ISSUES

In this chapter we have covered the broad fundamental decisions that relate to the whole clinical enterprise. These are decisions involving whether to intervene in a situation, at which system level to intervene, which model to employ, and in which diagnostic category, if any, a case should be placed. There are many decisions about the goals of intervention in particular cases and about how contracts are to be implemented.

One broad classification into which all such intervention decisions fall is decisions about *disposition* and decisions about *understanding—what* is to be done about a person or group, and by *whom*, and *how* to proceed to enlarge our understanding of the person with whom we are working.

We must emphasize that we never know whether the decisions we make are the right ones. Because this is true, a number of as-yet-unresolved issues have arisen. One involves the *evaluation* of what the programs we design are accomplishing. For many years this concern has given rise to research on outcomes of psychotherapy with individuals. In recent times there has been increasing interest in *program evaluation*, meaning attempts to find out what large-scale efforts at social betterment, such as Head Start, are accomplishing. There is a growing concern that mental health agencies and psychological services be accountable to the public, to the "consumers." Program evaluation and accountability present interesting dilemmas: how to reconcile conflicting goals of different interested parties, how to make evaluations that are not threatening to staff members but give them a genuine opportunity for self-study and development, and how to evaluate the usefulness and expense of evaluation itself. Where is the point at which evaluation is too much and "documentitis" or overgrowth of information sets in? Also is there a danger that in our concern for accountability we become like shortsighted accountants who attempt to translate human values into dollars and cents? Program evaluation must be given great attention, but it can be overemphasized. Evaluation will be covered more thoroughly in Chapter 13.

Another issue requiring increasing attention is that of cultural differences, which influence a great many of the decisions we make about intervention. Psychologists are realizing that the principles their research has revealed may not be general laws of human behavior at all, but apply to only a small fraction of the human race. What clinical workers see as deviant behavior may be perfectly normal in some cultures. Designs for living acceptable to a middle-class psychologist may be completely unworkable in a different subculture. Sensitivity to cultural differences and interest in cross-cultural research is growing in all the areas of human life with which we are concerned.

One of the results of past "culture blindness" is that many subcultural groups in the United States and Europe have been "underserved"—to use a currently popular term. This is partly because of their inability to pay for service but also because of differences in attitudes, communication techniques, values, and expectations. We must endeavor to counteract this deficiency in our vision.

More broadly still, issues about ethics and morality are being raised in our time that were never considered before. The professional groups have created ethical codes and procedures for making sure they are complied with, but larger ethical questions remain. Is it right to enable a person to function better in an unsound or even corrupt work situation, or should all of our efforts go into abolishing or drastically changing it? Are the activities in which psychologists and social workers have been engaged simply bandages applied to infected tissues? These are troubling questions and will also be considered in some detail in our final chapter.

SUMMARY

A steady stream of requests for assistance flows into clinics and service centers. To deal with them involves repeated decisions by clinical workers. Decisions about whether and how to intervene in individual lives rest partly on whether one understands and allows a natural process to continue or whether one is oriented toward the curing of pathology, the learning of better habits, the facilitating of growth and development, or to improving the interactive setting (the natural helping, curative, learning, growth and sociological orientations). Work done in accordance with the curative, or medical, model usually involves a diagnosis of the person's difficulties in the terms used in successive psychiatric *Diagnostic and Statistical Manuals.* Other systems of classification are being developed but have been less widely used.

Simply doing something for people in distress without careful analysis of their situation may result in no progress, or worse, in harmful effects or side effects. Simply doing what has been done for other cases, likewise, reflects inadequate forethought. Clinicians must consider both the immediate and the longe-range effects of what they do. They must also be wary of possible biases or predilections in their own thinking.

The goal of intervention is a plan or a contract agreed to by the client and the professional worker. Confusion often occurs in a complex situation about whose goals are to prevail. Once a contract has been agreed upon, decisions must be made repeatedly in the course of carrying it out, as circumstances change. There are many sources of distortion and bias in clinicians' thinking, and these must be recognized in order to be avoided or counteracted. A variety of general issues remain in the conduct of interventions. Progress must constantly be evaluated, and ethical questions repeatedly considered.

RECOMMENDED READINGS

Garfield, S. L., & Bergin, A. E. *Handbook of psychotherapy and behavior change: An empirical analysis* (2nd ed.). New York: John Wiley, 1978.
This large book is an important resource for anyone wishing to read about research on psychotherapy. It comprehensively covers the methods and findings of

research and evaluation in a wide variety of individual and group therapies. It covers such special topics as placebo effects, comparisons of drug therapy and psychotherapy, individual differences in clients and therapists that relate to therapy, behavioral approaches with children, marital and family therapy, applications to low-income and minority groups, and training for therapy skills. Another book that is of special relevance to this chapter is *Psychotherapy for Better or Worse* by Strupp, Hadley, and Gomes-Schwartz (1977). They review all studies to date that report negative effects and discuss the opinions of expert therapists. Their conclusions are summarized in an article (Strupp & Hadley, 1977). Mays and Franks (1980) also discuss deterioration in psychotherapy patients and decide the research is not conclusive.

Lichtenstein, E. *Psychotherapy: Approaches and applications.* Monterey, Calif.: Brooks/Cole, 1980.
This excellent introduction to the field of psychotherapy describes not only the nature and history of the three major streams of therapy—psychoanalytic, humanistic, and behavioral—but also the kinds of therapy settings and the sociopolitical and economic influences. It also analyzes the problems of evaluation. One interesting feature is some reference to cultural influences on the field of psychotherapy, including the description of a case treated by a native healer in Borneo. For a well-written and more extensive coverage of the question of cultural factors in therapy and commonalities across cultures, see Torrey's *The Mind Game: Witchdoctors and Psychiatrists* (1972).

Salzinger, S., Antrobus, J., & Glick, J. (Eds.). *The ecosystem of the "sick" child: Implications for classification and intervention for disturbed and mentally retarded children.* New York: Academic Press, 1980.
The three editors of this book intend to stimulate practitioners, researchers, and policy makers to think in ecosystem terms—to be aware of environments and interactions when dealing with children with problems. They are critical of the usual classification procedures because they are insensitive to situations and overly individualistic. The editors recognize the ambiguities and lack of organized procedures for ecological analysis but argue for the necessity of moving in this direction. Another extensive coverage of problems in professional coverage of children is *Issues in the Classification of Children*, edited by Hobbs (1975); the chapter by Rains, Kitsuse, Duster, and Friedson, among others, points out how helping can miscarry when diagnostic labels have a bad effect. They assert that labels create new roles and expectations for identity, which then have serious social consequences. Both the social environment and the individual use labels to coerce or excuse behavior. For instance, a child may say: "I don't have to sit still; I'm hyperactive," or "I don't have to be responsible; I'm a delinquent." One of the greatest problems is the medical model and the psychiatric diagnostic system required by the medical and insurance industry. Miller, Bergstrom, Cross, and Grube (1981) show in a survey that many psychologists are highly critical of the DSM system. One of the problems with DSM III is that it identifies and labels scores of sociobehavioral difficulties and brings them into the psychiatric orbit. Although psychologists may object, there is no viable alternative, and the current system is tied to the economics of fee-for-service treatment.

Robins, L. N. *Deviant children grown up.* Baltimore, Md.: Williams & Wilkins, 1966.
To be effective, intervention must be appropriate to the problem at hand. In this famous study Robins examined the records of a child guidance clinic. With follow-up she established that the children who had come to the clinic with problems of antisocial behavior or other forms of conduct disorder (as contrasted with those who showed

fears, phobias, depression, withdrawal, and so on) had a posttreatment life adjustment virtually indistinguishable from similar children not treated at all. Although her data make such youth appear unsuited to and unresponsive to conventional one-to-one relationship and insight-oriented therapy, alternatives for this group are scarce, and many practitioners continue to offer a helping method shown not to be effective. Zigler (1981) in a passionate article gives an illustration of the continued use of a poorly validated but vigorously defended program for retarded children; the program requires a great deal of parental work with the child, which often is very time consuming, disruptive of family life, and productive of guilt when the child does not improve. A philosophy of helping without harming requires attention to both the validity of the procedures and the overall effect on people's lives.

Ryan, W. (Ed.). *Distress in the city*. Cleveland, Ohio: Case Western Reserve, 1969.

Ryan reports an extensive study of mental health services in Boston. The survey clearly documents the conclusion that helpers are not working at the center of the problem. Epidemiological studies indicated that more than 150 out of every 1,000 Bostonians were handicapped by emotional disturbance, but only 10 were receiving help in mental health settings. What of the other 140? The report outlines subsidiary resources such as family doctors, social agencies, and churches which may provide some form of service. The survey's striking finding is that people seeing psychiatrists are relatively young (half between the ages of 22 and 36), female (two-thirds), college-educated (four out of five) and not psychotic (four out of five). A tiny group of 3,000 young college-educated women in their twenties and thirties made up one-fourth of the patients in private treatment. Despite the richness of mental health resources in Boston (ten times greater per capita than in the state of Mississippi), only half of Boston's emotionally disturbed persons received any help at all. Nonpsychiatric physicians provide care for about twice as many emotionally disturbed persons as all other resources combined, and clergy counseled twice as many Bostonians as those in private psychotherapy. Another study of urban mental health with somewhat similar results was the well-known Midtown Manhattan study carried out in the 1950s (reported in a revised and enlarged book by Srole & Fischer, 1978). It is very likely that more up-to-date studies would reveal somewhat similar findings, although the much greater emphasis of the 1960s and 1970s on bringing treatment to the underserved and unserved has made a difference. Lorion (1978), for instance, stated that he is cautiously optimistic that significant progress has been made to provide for mental needs of the disadvantaged; he also states that there is an unfortunate lack of interest in research on life styles and mental health expectations of the poor and minority groups.

Whitmer, G. E. From hospitals to jails: The fate of California's deinstitutionalized mentally ill. *American Journal of Orthopsychiatry*, 1980, 50, 65–75.

Whitmer, a social worker, looks at the consequences of a change in the law. In 1968 California shifted the criteria for involuntary hospitalization to focus, not on diagnosis, but on the concept of dangerousness. The Lanterman-Petris-Short Act also limited the duration of involuntary confinement and provided a financial impetus to put the locus of treatment in communities rather than state hospitals. All of these moves appear laudable or reasonable, but an undesired effect soon became apparent. Ghettos of former state hospital patients sprang up in the inner urban areas, where the discharged patients, lost to local treatment programs, lived without appropriate care. Another result was that former patients entered the criminal justice system when they were apprehended for crimes or nuisances committed while disoriented or delusional. The debate continues about patient rights, involuntary commitment, and the locus of custody.

Estroff (1981) and Felton and Shinn (1981) also analyze the deinstitutionalization movement and conclude that it has failed to provide adequate community alternatives, especially for the most needy. Many programs, often rightly viewed as promising better conditions, are not adequately financed or planned, and experimental trials and evaluation are not carried out first.

PART II

PRINCIPLES
OF
CLINICAL ASSESSMENT

After setting out a general background of the field in the first part, we are moving on to a more specific area of clinical activity.

Chapters 4, 5, and 6 will cover a very important function of clinical psychology—assessment. Assessment is an activity, not limited to psychology, that describes the gathering, organizing, and communicating of information about a client. Using this information, those working with the client can then make decisions about or with the client, gather impressions (or "working images"), and check on clinical or research hypotheses. Each of the five orientations—"natural," pathological, learning, growth, and ecological—has its own particular view of assessment and sometimes its own particular techniques and language. The most common assessment procedure is interviewing. Although others do assessment, psychologists are particularly notable for their attention to tests and to research and theory about assessment. The major tests are discussed along with the standards for evaluating them. Tests generally fall in two major divisions answering the simple questions: "What can the person do?" and "What characteristics does the person have?" In addition to the well-established tests on intelligence and personality, recently many new procedures have been devised for assessing the moment-to-moment behavior of people. Interviews, observations, and test results are of no value unless they are communicated well to those working with the client and unless they lead to helpful decisions and programs. The pitfalls in the final stages of assessment include poor interpretation of the results and reporting overly generalized or misleading information about clients. Well-done assessment promotes effective intervention.

4 OBTAINING USEFUL INFORMATION: The Assessing Process

If you listened to psychologists talking to clients, you would hear questions and comments such as the following:

"Tell me, what brings you to the clinic?"

"When did you first start feeling this way?"

"You seem to be saying you are confused and angry and don't know what to do."

"Describe what an ordinary day is like for you. When do you get up and what do you do first, and so on?"

"After I say some numbers, repeat them to me backwards: 7–2–3–8–1–6."

"How are a house and an airplane alike?"

"Here is a booklet with lots of statements in it. For each, you should mark 'True' or 'False' on the answer sheet to show how the statement applies to you. The first one is 'I like to go to dances and parties.' "

"Now, I'd like you to make up some stories about a set of pictures. I'll show them to you one at a time. Tell what is going on and what will happen."

"Here are a bunch of cards with occupations or activities on them. Sort them into groups that are alike in some way."

"You have this awful choking sensation at times. Tell me about the last time it happened. Exactly where were you and what was going on?"

"Here is a worksheet for you to keep a record each day of the times Johnny doesn't do what you tell him to do. There are places to put the time it happened, whether others were present, what you asked him to do, and how he responded. Think you can do that?"

In each case the clinician is trying to understand the client's actions, feelings, and thinking processes and to decide where to focus the investigation of the complex picture any human life presents. What one needs is a "working image" of the client and the situation that will suggest how to proceed. In the last chapter decisions regarding intervention and nonintervention were discussed. In this chapter and the next two, we will focus on how one gathers, organizes, and communicates information entering into such decisions and plans for treatment and case management. Many of these assessment processes are used in schools and employment offices, but here our interest is in clinical settings.

THE PURPOSES
OF ASSESSMENT

Assessment, the information-processing part of clinical work, has three functions: *decision making*, *image forming*, and *hypothesis checking*. In our view clinical work always involves assessment at some point—often at several points. Even if the contact is very short, such as a ten-minute interview ending in referral elsewhere, the clinicians must gather some information that leads to a decision; they inevitably form some impression or picture of the person; and frequently they test hypotheses or guesses about the client's purposes, interests, or situation.

Every client contact involves the potential for intervention or influence, however small. The assessment activities with the client are themselves a form of intervention, and the decision to interview or administer a test should take into account the possible influence the action will have on the client. The early interviews, tests, and other procedures may start the person's self-examination, may produce a new view of the details of the life situation, and may suggest certain kinds of relationships with the clinic or agency. As Craddick (1975, p. 282) has stated, "The telling of the story very often is the beginning of the therapeutic process and suggests that one cannot clearly demarcate where assessment ends and therapy begins."

This intermixture of assessment and intervention is easy to recognize when the same clinician continues with the case through both phases, but in large agencies or hospitals it is often necessary to involve several clinicians. The assessment process may be assigned to several specialists. For example, a social worker may obtain family information, a psychologist may select and administer tests, and a psychiatrist may conduct a mental status interview. Not too long ago in the history of clinical psychology, the psychiatric team was the prevailing pattern of organization for mental health clinics. One or more psychiatrists, psychologists, and social workers constituted one of these teams, and each professional played a different role. Appealing as this clear division of labor is, it no longer meets today's increased demands. Psychologists, psychiatric nurses, social workers, and psychiatrists conduct assessment interviews and therapy. Who does what depends on the needs of the agency, the availability of personnel, and the special skills of the staff. Normally the psychologist is most knowledgeable about specialized psychological tests.

Assessment may be managed by one agency and intervention carried out by another. For example, a juvenile court may contract with a psychologist in private practice to conduct a personality assessment and write a report on a 16-year-old boy. The court will use the report in making a decision between probation or commitment to an institution. The nature of the larger system in which the assessor operates affects the assessment process. The psychologist is likely under these circumstances to select different tests and to write a different sort of report from those designed for use entirely within one agency. In the report the psychologist will try to prevent errors and misunderstandings since it will be difficult to correct them once the report is in the hands of the court.

Decision making occurs in initial contacts with a client. One must know what kinds of facilities and competencies are available in the agency in order to decide whether the client can be appropriately served. If not, the person should probably be referred to another person or agency. For instance, if a woman comes to the clinic telling about excruciating back pain and the interviewing clinician knows that this clinic cannot handle such problems as well as can a pain clinic in the community, then a quick referral is appropriate. In making decisions in early interviews, the clinician evaluates the client's willingness to explore life situations and life history. There are great individual differences in client openness and in expectations about what a person should reveal to a strange clinician, especially at the beginning. The psychologist or other clinician must consider the feelings of the person and judge when it is beneficial to press for more information and expression of feelings and when it might be detrimental to progress. At the beginning the client is the major determiner of what is to be revealed. Illustrations of research on client openness and self-disclosure are discussed at the end of this chapter.

The second important purpose of assessment is to provide the clinician and others with a *working image* of the person seeking assistance, one that can be communicated to all who are involved in case management or therapy. There has been some research on how such images are formed. Meehl (1960) demonstrated that impressions of a person are formed quite quickly. He obtained ratings of patients from therapists after each of the many interviews they conducted. He found that by the third interview, the personality ratings that the therapist made of the patient correlated very highly with the final ratings made after as many as 30 interviews. Experiments in social psychology have also shown that early impressions (especially unfavorable ones) are quite difficult to change. Paralleling each person's process of impression-formation is what social psychologists call *impression management*. Each person in the assessment process wants to project an image to the other, especially if important decisions ride on the assessment, such as being confined to jail or being offered a job. Another "person-perception" process of clinical importance involves the impression of what causes a person's behavior, the causal *attributions* one makes. Social psychologists have shown that people tend to attribute environmental causation to their own problematic behavior and personal causation to others' behavior. The dangers of labeling, stereotyping, or failing to change one's image as new information comes in are obvious. The clinician must always attempt to keep the working image tentative and open to modification.

The third function of assessment, *hypothesis checking*, primarily refers to the use of assessment for research; all research with people uses some kind of assessment procedure. In a less formal way hypothesis checking also occurs when the clinician develops informed guesses or diagnoses and then attempts to confirm and disconfirm them. Such checking keeps the other two functions on the right track, preventing snap decisions and distorted images.

Tests play an important part in assessment, especially in its hypothesis-testing function. Assessment is much more inclusive than is psychological testing, however, and uses many other techniques for obtaining information, such as interviewing, observing, examining records, and analyzing products such as school reports or diaries. The final task in assessment is to combine data from these many sources into an organized whole.

DIFFERING ORIENTATIONS

Table 3–1 in the last chapter illustrated "natural helping" and four major professional orientations to clinical psychology that suggest different goals, procedures, and standards of effectiveness. People taking these approaches have different ideas about assessment—how much is necessary or desirable, when in the sequence of clinical tasks it should come, and what techniques should be used. Table 4–1 summarizes these differences. As with intervention we have preceded the four professional approaches by an extra column showing assessment processes of everyday life. Everyone collects information, forms images of the persons with whom he or she associates, makes decisions, and checks up on hypotheses about them all the time. These are not strange or esoteric activities. They are essential to social systems, and they play a large part in mental health services, especially those not using formal testing, as is usually the case in storefront clinics, crisis centers, and street work by paraprofessionals. This kind of informal, natural functioning poses many intriguing research problems almost never tackled by psychologists remaining in their laboratories and clinic offices.

In the past the most common formal model has been the *pathology (or curative) orientation.* Assessment is seen as a clinical laboratory procedure analogous to medical laboratory procedures for ascertaining the normality or pathology of the blood and urine, measuring neural transmission and muscle potentials, or scanning internal structures by X-rays. With this approach clinical psychology is viewed as an adjunct to medicine. The patient's psychological functions, like physiological functions, should be ascertained by tests, interviews, and other procedures for deviation from the normal. The concern is to diagnose interfering emotional and thinking problems in order to provide a prognosis about the course of the disorder and to set up plans for treatment.

The *learning orientation* also emphasizes assessment, but of a different sort. It concentrates on the actions and thoughts that might be learned, changed, or unlearned to improve adjustment. The task for assessment is to find what particular functions of the person need to be modified and to check progress at every stage of the learning process. Such assessment is sometimes called *functional analysis.* One is concerned with habits that are lacking, excessive, or inappropriate. Many assessment procedures are tailored to individual clients—for example, counting the number of times a child disobeys a parent's command or the number of cigarettes a person smokes in an hour. Traditional psychiatric diagnosis is usually considered irrelevant. Personality is seen as a set of abilities and habits, including both behavior and thought patterns.

Of all the approaches the *growth orientation* places least emphasis on formal assessment, at least with adult clients. This is the orientation congenial to humanistic psychology. Such psychologists deny the value of diagnosis. They often use only interviewing. They assume that the client will

TABLE 4-1 Orientations toward Clinical Assessment

	EVERYDAY (Informal, "Natural")	PSYCHOPATHOLOGY (Diagnostic, Curative)	LEARNING (Behavioral, Cognitive)	GROWTH (Developmental, Experimental)	ECOLOGY (Interactive, Environmental)
Aims	To use simple, usually untutored, "folk" ways of understanding people.	To diagnose. To describe and predict psychopathology, dynamics and course of disorder.	To pinpoint problems and their antecedents and consequences, to monitor change.	To help clients experience and understand self, to clarify directions of development.	To identify and modify interactions and settings for improvement of social systems.
Typical Settings	Ordinary life situations, and nonoffice clinical work. Much of out-reach, hot line, and storefront services.	Psychiatric and medical clinics, hospitals, and offices.	Behavioral programs. Psychoeducational services.	Many counseling centers. Personal growth workshops. Encounter groups.	Community programs. Some health maintenance organizations.
Typical Procedures	Observations, conversations, unstructured interviews; little or no recording of information.	Psychological and medical tests. Records of diagnoses, and so forth.	Observation. Tailormade checklists. Frequency counts. A few tests.	For children, some tests and observations. For adults, interviews and self-reports.	Observation and interviews in systems. Behavior-setting analysis. No individually oriented tests.
Formality of Assessment	No formal assessment period.	High, mainly at early diagnostic stage.	Moderate, throughout all stages.	For children, moderate. For adults, low.	Moderate. Continual system feedback.

	EVERYDAY (Informal, "Natural")	PSYCHOPATHOLOGY (Diagnostic, Curative)	LEARNING (Behavioral, Cognitive)	GROWTH (Developmental, Experimental)	ECOLOGY (Interactive, Environmental)
Focus on Internal vs. External Factors	Mixed, with attention to both personal and environmental concerns.	Strongly internal (inferred states). Emphasis on individual client.	Mixed. Attention to both individual and social environment.	Mainly internal. Stress on personal phenomenology, self-assessment.	External. Interactive. Persons are parts of larger systems.
Origins and Traditions	Practices and beliefs in the culture. Folk language.	Medicine, psychiatry, psychometrics, psychodynamics. "Medical model."	Psychological research and educational practice. "Training model."	Counseling, life-span, developmental, and humanistic psychology. Spiritual aspects. "Experiential model."	Ecology. Community and environmental psychology. General systems theory. "Systems model."
Personality Ideal	Well-adjusted, self-reliant person, valuing cultural ideals.	Normal person, free of pathological disorders	Competent person, possessing skills needed for self-maintenance.	Self-actualized, aware person, growing throughout life.	Socially interested person, facilitating community improvement and the "common good."
Criticisms and Dangers	Possibility of prejudice, labeling, stereotyping, naivety.	Overemphasis on negative pathological characteristics.	Narrow and short-range view of person's goals and needs.	Overly verbal. Some unclear and occult theories.	Complex. Over-inclusive. Vague theories. Questions of practicality.
Primary Role of Assessor	Participant observer.	Laboratory technician.	Researcher and teacher.	Codiscoverer with client.	Consultant, facilitator of social systems.

improve with increased self-experience and knowledge. In some growth-oriented counseling centers, interest and ability tests are used to assist in self-assessment and to help the person formulate career plans. In the spirit of coassessment, psychologists discuss questionnaire, test, and checklist results openly with the client (Dana & Leech, 1974). All decision making is done *with* the client, not *about* the client—which may be the case in the two previous orientations. Personality is seen as a matter of perceptual processes and choices.

Since this orientation emphasizes development, special note should be taken of children. Young people will be seen in clinics with all of the several orientations discussed. When the client is a child, several special techniques are available for assessing what level of development has been reached. Individual intelligence tests can be used as indicators of the level of cognitive development. There are similar standardized methods for assessing social development and motor skill. With active research now going on about the course of development throughout the adult years, it is likely that useful aids to assessment of adult life stages will eventually become available. Almost any tests and other assessment procedures are tools that can be used to diagnose pathology, to expose learning needs, to encourage self-development, or to facilitate systemwide improvements.

The fourth assessment model is the *ecological* one. With this approach the task of assessment is to provide a picture not just of the individual but also of the systems within which the individual operates. Because this is a newer theoretical approach, assessment procedures are less well worked out than in the others. They generally focus on organizations and environments. The concepts deal with interactions in settings over time. Personality is seen as interactional or transactional and strongly related to context. We shall have a limited amount to say about ecological assessment techniques in this and the two following chapters, but they will be also discussed in chapters on the family, groups, organizations, and community.

As noted in the last chapter, these four professional orientations are not always distinctly separate in the practical activities of clinicians. Any given clinical operation may combine two or more approaches or may use other variations. However, the four perspectives do provide a good way to simplify and clarify much of the thinking of clinicians—a good entry into the complexity of the clinical world.

TASKS AND RELATIONSHIPS IN ASSESSMENT

Like the common, everyday processes of "sizing up" and understanding other people, assessment has two major aspects—*task* and *relationship*, or *content* and *process*. The first involves obtaining the information that one seeks. The second is the social-emotional aspect—empathy, feelings, interests, friendliness, and willingness to cooperate; there must be good rapport among the people involved. Both components are important. The first is usually easier to teach and learn; the second can be described but must be felt or experienced in order to master it. That is why clinical training always requires supervised practice directly with people.

The tasks of clinical assessment have been discussed in the previous section—the description and planning for clients, be they individuals or groups. The four different orientations suggest the content of the search in assessment. Although our emphasis in this book is on clinical settings, we should recognize that assessment is used in a variety of situations for a variety of purposes. It may involve work with large groups of persons, as in mass testing programs in schools, employment offices, or military installations. The purpose is either *selection*, as when students are chosen for a graduate program, or *classification*, when children are assigned to accelerated, normal, or remedial classes. Clinicians might sometimes participate in mass selection and classification activities, but they are peripheral rather than central to the clinical work discussed here.

Individualized assessment—focusing on a particular person or set of persons—has traditionally been the clinician's major responsibility. Sometimes the procedures are the same as those used in mass or group testing, and the clinician may administer a routine battery of tests, but always there is an individualized result—a decision, a report, or other action—focused on an individual person or situation. Sometimes selection and classification enter into individualized assessment, as for instance, when following an interview, a patient is selected for a new therapy group, or when in psychiatric settings each new patient's diagnostic category is determined. However, in most cases, clinical assessment does much more than select or classify; it produces ideas about how to treat clients or change their living situation. The working image it provides takes into consideration the individual's unique history, habits, fears, liabilities, and assets, thus facilitating therapy or case management. It delineates the person's unique living situation and the resources provided by family and community.

In addition to the task or content component of assessment, there is the *socioemotional*, or process, component. What kind of relationship have we established? How open does the client feel about revealing intimate thoughts and feelings? How does she or he perceive the patient or client role to be played? As mentioned before, the process of assessment itself has a therapeutic or antitherapeutic impact. Dynamics of the relationship are as important in assessment as they are in therapy or counseling.

One word for the kind of relationship that should be established even in the first interview or testing session is *rapport*. Some illustrations will show how difficult this may be to achieve and what creative clinicians have done to develop rapport.

Working in a diagnostic center for delinquents, Jim Aronson meets the newly incarcerated Billy Reed. Outside the center Billy is a talkative youngster; with his friends he is always playing around and joking. However, here he is angry and confused, and Billy figures that the best chance he has for getting out and protecting his friends is to say as little as possible. He answers Jim's beginning question, "How's it going for you here?" with a short "Okay." When Jim asks Billy to tell about his family, he says, "Aw, you know, like anybody else's." Try as he may, Jim cannot get Billy to open up. Even on an intelligence test Billy answers questions with short responses, copies block designs, and makes drawings in an offhand, perfunctory manner. When finished, Jim is sure that the results underestimate Billy's true ability. Jim decides to learn how Billy behaves in other situations so he joins an informal basketball session in the recreation room with several of the boys. During a break Billy finds it easy to tell Jim about what other sports he likes and what he used to do in school; the way is open for more fruitful assessment.

Sarah Simpson is in the locked ward of a psychiatric hospital in a private room. She is disheveled, paces continually during the day, and does not talk except a little to herself. She was brought yesterday by the police, whom her husband had called when he came home from work and found her pacing in the backyard in her bathrobe. Inside he found a gruesome sight: Their six-month-old daughter strangled in her crib. At first the clinicians working with Sarah tried to talk with her but could get no reaction. After a few days, however, during which Sarah is taking relaxing sedatives and getting used to the hospital, she becomes less rigidly resistive. In an informal chat in her room Sarah begins to talk about her beliefs that evil forces have seized her husband. It was necessary to destroy the baby because it was formed from an "evil seed." Ultimately this freer talking allows the clinicians to obtain the full story of Sarah's psychotic delusions and to plan treatment.

In a university counseling center Joe Chun comes to see a counselor about his trouble in the premedical program. The counselor, Mary Samuelson, finds it easy to get a superficial picture of Joe's formal status in school; he has received a card saying he is on probation because of continuing poor grades. Mary believes that his troubles may be related to his family's expectations about what he is studying. She asks him to tell her about his father and mother in Hong Kong and what they feel about his life plans. Joe will not say much about his family and answers in very brief sentences. She also wants to know more about his daily study routine; about that he talks more freely and in some detail. But whenever she brings the conversation around to the family, he will not say much. Mary realizes that some Chinese students feel that one must not reveal family matters to strangers; she decides to start dealing directly with study habits, and Joe is pleased to get some direct advice.

These three examples illustrate several kinds of difficulty one may have in establishing a cooperative relationship for assessment. There are many others. Clients may present only a small part of their "story." They may interpret the situation as a very hostile one and may avoid any self-disclosure. They may be so confused or handicapped that they cannot give the clinician the information needed. There may be client-clinician differences in background, language, and culture that make it difficult for certain kinds of things to be communicated. In most assessment situations people are willing and interested, especially if they come as volunteers with some realistic expectations about psychological service. But in any situation, a clinician can assume that what the client is saying is naturally filtered through perceptions of the situation and the role to be played. Part of the initial assessment job, in preparation for later interpretation, is to determine the client's attitude and manner of approaching the assessment task itself.

Research of relevance falls into two categories—the detection of *test-taking attitudes* and the factors influencing *self-disclosure*. On several tests, such as the Minnesota Multiphasic Personality Inventory (MMPI), counts are made of very infrequent responses, or of answers to overly "nice" and proper items; these test-taking attitude measures will be discussed again in the next chapter. To illustrate the research on self-disclosure, we will look at a study by Higlen and Gillis (1978). They used an *analog procedure*, an experiment similar to an interview, in which their 20 male and 20 female undergraduate subjects were asked to imagine themselves in the situation and to give a response. The subjects listened to the description of a situation—for example, a surprisingly pleasant time with someone of the same sex. Their verbal responses were audiotaped and rated by people trained to detect expressions of feelings and the use of feeling-type words. In certain situations students revealed more feelings to persons of their own sex than to those of the opposite sex. Other studies of disclosure suggest that people will tell more about themselves if the interviewer appears to be more involved in the conversation and is willing to reveal his or her own feelings (McCarthy & Betz, 1978), and if the room environment is pleasant (Chaikin et al., 1976). Studies (Goodstein & Russell, 1977; Hoffman-Graff, 1977) also show that there is a discrepancy between subjects' reported self-disclosure of behavior and the same behavior as reported by informants. Showing videotapes of people expressing feelings prior to interviews seems to facilitate self-expression in viewers (Annis & Perry, 1977). In several studies females were more self-disclosing than were males. Although these studies are suggestive, they should be taken with some skepticism since most of them used analog procedures rather than real interviews; they should be used mainly to provide hypotheses for further assessment research.

THE BASIC METHODS—
INTERVIEWING
AND OBSERVATION

The first and most important skill that the new clinician must learn is to interview. The interview has been defined as "a conversation with a purpose" (Bingham & Moore, 1924); it is used to obtain information and to establish a relationship that will be appropriate and helpful. Because all of us naturally engage in conversation, we tend to assume that interviewing is simple. Actually skilled clinical interviewing is a great art, and people differ markedly in their styles.

One aspect that makes interviewing different from friendly conversation is the setting in which it occurs; the setting always implies particular goals and limitations. An interviewer would find it very different if the same interview were carried on in a jail or in a private practice office. In any setting the role of the interviewer is to exert some kind of control over the conversation, a control that is often nonobvious, nonjudgmental, and congruent with the client's need to relax and feel accepted. The good interviewer, while establishing a friendly, easy exchange, controls the interview for timing (its beginning and ending), its content (covering all important topics and questions), the manner of response (open-ended questions or questions with yes-no answers), and closeness of the relationship. The perceived closeness will depend on the degree of self-revelation and warmth that the interviewer shows the interviewee and how much reciprocal closeness the interviewer encourages in the client.

Interviewing Skills

Interviewing skills obviously involve both listening and talking. For the person seeking to acquire interviewing skills, the question "How should I listen?" is often more important than the question "What should I say?" It is through

Figure 4-1   Interviewing a child in school. (Courtesy of Elizabeth Hamlin, Stock, Boston)

listening skills that clients are encouraged to tell about the important things in their lives. The client is likely to come to the first interview with a great deal of emotional apprehension. In fact, it is usually extraordinary emotionality that motivates a person to come to a clinic, hospital, or psychologist's office. The voluntary client has somehow found the courage to walk in and talk about a fear, a failure, or an unmanageable problem. The client who has been coerced to come about some problem, such as a crime or paranoid behavior, is likely to be angry, fearful, or frustrated. A child client may be afraid of the stranger in the clinic and does not want to come at all. The interviewer therefore needs to observe the signs of emotional turmoil and be prepared to listen for what the person is ready to reveal at the pace she or he finds comfortable. If the interviewer interrupts frequently and appears to be determined only to follow a rigid agenda, the client may soon become passive and uncommunicative. Early introductions and light comments about the weather or the occasion can express an openness, warmth, willingness to hear the client's story, and an interest in the client's world and its problems. Continuing through open-ended questions, occasional comments, and active attentiveness to what the client says, the clinician communicates an attitude of listening and understanding. Carl Rogers, the well-known founder of the client-centered (or person-centered) approach to therapy, describes his own feelings about listening:

> I want to share with you my enjoyment when I can really *hear* someone. . . . I can remember this in my early grammar school days. A child would ask the teacher a question and the teacher would give a perfectly good answer to a completely different question. A feeling of pain and distress would always strike me. My reaction was, "But you didn't hear him!". . . . I believe I know why it is satisfying to me to hear someone. When I can really hear someone, it puts me in touch with him; it enriches my life. It is through hearing people that I have learned all that I know about individuals, about personality, about interpersonal relations. . . . When I say that I enjoy hearing someone, I mean, of course, hearing deeply. I mean that I hear the words, the thoughts, the feeling tones, the personal meaning, even the meaning that is below the conscious intent of the speaker.
>
> I think, for example, of an interview I had with an adolescent boy. Like many an adolescent today he was saying at the outset of the interview that he had no goals. When I questioned him on this, he insisted even more strongly that he had no goals whatsoever, not even one. I said, "There isn't anything you want to do?" "Nothing. . . . Well, yeah, I want to keep on living." I remember distinctly my feeling at that moment. I resonated very deeply to this phrase. He might simply be telling me that, like everyone else, he wanted to live. On the other hand, he might be telling me . . . that at some point the question of whether or not to live had been a real issue with him. So I tried to resonate to him at all levels. I didn't know for certain what the message was. I simply wanted to be open to any of the meanings that this statement might have. . . . My being willing and able to listen to all levels is perhaps one of the things that made it possible for him to tell me, before the end of the interview, that not long before he had been on the point of blowing his brains out. (1980, pp. 7-9)

One of the important characteristics that contributes to the interviewer's ability to listen and the client's ability to open up is a *nonjudgmental attitude*. Rogers tells what this means to him. He compares appreciating a person to appreciating a sunset:

> People are just as wonderful as sunsets if I can let them *be*. . . . When I look at a sunset. . . , I don't find myself saying, "soften the orange a little on the right-hand corner, and put a bit more purple along the base, and use a little more pink in the cloud color." I don't do that. I don't *try* to control a sunset. I watch it with awe as it unfolds. (1980, p. 22)

As mentioned before, the interviewer does have to control some of the features of the interview. Time is limited, and certain topics must be covered. Yet within the limits that must be set, the attitude of real listening in an attempt to understand the person encourages the communication of more information and an increased willingness to participate in therapy, if this is indicated.

There are some special techniques that can be used to facilitate communication. One is *paraphrasing*, which is simply a restatement summarizing what the person has said. The clinician says something like this: "You mentioned that your mother gave you a birthday present and then said you should be more grateful." Going a little further, the clinician may use *reflection of feeling:* "You love your mother but you get really mad at her." The clinician may use *perception checking:* "I get the impression that you have very mixed feelings about your mother; sometimes you love her and sometimes you dislike what she does; is this right?"

A caution is in order here. Although most of these procedures are harmless and are in fact useful in everyday life, some of these interview techniques, especially those encouraging intense expression of feeling, are best left to therapy interviews, where the clinician can follow up on any problems that arise. Interviews having limited assessment purposes generally allow for indications of underlying emotional conflicts but do not encourage expression of emotions that can more properly be dealt with after a therapy plan is devised and a contract is clear. Still the clinical assessor should be aware of such procedures and be able to use them appropriately. Another skill an interviewer needs is to be able to move the interview to new topics, particularly when a client is repetitive or overly talkative.

The interviewer must remember some important distinctions, such as that between behavior and feeling—actions as opposed to emotional reactions, attitudes, impressions, and evaluations. For significant events the interviewer will want to get both descriptions of behavior and descriptions of feelings. In order to help clients distinguish behaviors from feelings, the interviewer might encourage them to pursue one single event in considerable detail attending to what they *did* and how they *felt* at that time, and afterwards.

BOX 4-1   *BASIC DIMENSIONS OF COMMUNICATIONS*

Communication is such a basic requirement of human (and animal) survival and effectiveness that we often ignore or take for granted the complex processes involved. These processes are as much nonverbal as they are verbal, occurring in a reciprocal system of perception and behaviors. Gilmore (1973, p. 232), in discussing training for interviewing, gives examples of the verbal and nonverbal aspects of sending and receiving messages:

	Sending	Receiving
Verbal	Asking a question	Hearing exactly what client has said
	Restating what client has said	Imagining what an experience was like for client
	Describing your own feelings	Sorting and organizing a jumbled story
	Explaining the implications of a test score	Placing a choice or problem in context
	Summarizing a session	Listening for the feelings accompanying an episode
	Assigning a task to be completed by next session	
Nonverbal	Gesturing toward chair in which you expect client to sit	Hearing client's voice quality change, i.e., become husky, shrill, choked, etc.
	Nodding and smiling	Seeing a client squirm, wring hands, flush, perspire, etc.
	Frowning and looking away	Smelling scent of heavy perfume worn by 13-year-old girl
	Tapping your fingers on the chair arm	Watching client choose to sit in chair further away
	Touching arm of weeping client	Noting that client never takes his eyes off you, until you speak
	Wearing a white coat; a white shirt and tie; a colorful polo shirt; a dirty sweatshirt	

Another common distinction the clinician may want to make is between personal perception of events and what actually occurred. The clinician may attempt to uncover this distinction by asking clients to tell about events from the viewpoint of other people or inquire whether others saw it the same way as the clients did. One cannot expect exact reporting of events. Research on testimony that witnesses give at staged or actual crime scenes has shown that what people report seeing or hearing may be quite different from documented happenings (Yarmey, 1979). The clinician must continually remember both the client's perceptions of a situation and the fact that "reality" may be different. Reports from family members or others may also help to complete the assessment picture.

Developing an understanding of the client's perception may take time and persistence. Morganstern and Tevlin (1981, p. 87) give an interesting illustration of how a clinician progressively checks with the client and corrects what could have been a misleading impression of what the client was saying (C = Client; I = Interviewer):

C: Whenever my boss asks to see me, I almost start shaking, wondering what I've done wrong.

I: The anticipation of criticism really makes you anxious?

C: Well, it's not really that. I'm scared of what might happen.

I: What might happen?

C: I don't know what will happen; that's it.

I: So it's the suspense that makes you feel uncomfortable.

C: No, not the suspense—I keep saying to myself that if he starts chewing me out I'm just going to let him have it.

I: How would you let him have it?

C: Well, what I *think* I'm going to do is argue right back at him—or even quit right there.

I: And what *do* you do?

C: Nothing!

I: Nothing?

C: I never do anything. I just stand there while he's talking and never say a word.

I: So what really makes you shake, as you say, is feeling a great deal of anger and not being able to express it?

C: Yeah. And the one I'm really mad at is myself for being such a patsy all the time.

I: What do you think would happen if you really did argue back with your boss?

C: He probably would respect me a lot more than someone who's too scared to defend himself.

I: What you're saying is that you're really afraid to challenge you boss's criticism. But when you think about it, you become angry at yourself for not being assertive.

C: Yes.

Kinds of Interviews

Interviews are used in many ways with many different goals. Those frequently used in clinical work are *intake* interviews to obtain initial information about the client's reasons for coming and background data; *case history* interviews, which go into details about health, work, family of origin, current family relations, and so on; *testing orientation* interviews preceding, or sometimes following, the administration of clinical tests; *mental status* interviews and *behavior problem* interviews, which are used to develop a diagnosis or functional analysis; and *psychotherapy* and *counseling* interviews. Other less common kinds of interviews used by clinicians are *crisis* interviews, often conducted by paraprofessionals over telephone "hot lines" for rape, suicide, child abuse, and other traumatic events; *selection* interviews for hiring employees or choosing paraprofessional volunteers; and *research* interviews used in a wide variety of investigations of clinical and community problems. Here we will describe only a few common assessment interviews.

Probably the most widely used clinical interview is the *history-taking interview*, or case history. Be the interview short or long, the clinician must get some kind of history in order to work with a client. Some points of view— e.g., the person-centered or Rogerian orientation—deemphasize history and concentrate on whatever the client wishes to bring up. Other orientations require quite extensive interviews covering the client's background. Typically a history comes out in bits and pieces. A thought about the present problem may remind the client of future worries or past events, and the story does not unfold in the organized way ideal for the written report. The interviewer has to be prepared for meanderings but still keep in mind a set of topics that need to be covered. One quite comprehensive set of topics for a case history interview is listed in Table 4–2. Such a list might take several hours to cover, especially with a talkative client, so the clinician will have to judge what is most important for the decisions to be made. Of course with a child, a speech-disabled person, or a psychotic, such an extensive list of topics would have to be modified. In addition it would be desirable to confirm and supplement findings from the client by interviewing a family member who knew the client's situation very well.

Conducting a *mental status examination* of new patients is a common practice among psychiatrists and some psychologists who work in psychiatric outpatient and inpatient settings. The interviewer is usually meeting the patient for the first time, and the examination results will be placed in the patient's medical chart. In many psychiatric services this examination and the case history are the only assessment provided a patient, and they lead directly to the psychiatric diagnosis. Sometimes, however, this sample of current psychological functioning will uncover the need for more detailed examination by means of psychological tests before the diagnosis and treatment plans are fixed. The mental status examination is an important feature of what we have called the *psychopathological*, or *curative*, orientation.

Different guidelines for mental status interviews list varying numbers of topics to be covered. Maloney and Ward (1976) give 12 topics, based on a

TABLE 4-2 Outline for a Case History Interview

1. *Identifying data,* including name, sex, occupation, income (of self or family), marital status, address, date and place of birth, religion, education, cultural identity.
2. *Reason for coming* to the agency, expectations for service.
3. *Present and recent situation,* including dwelling place, principal settings, daily round of activities, number and kind of life changes over several months, impending changes.
4. *Family constellation* (family of orientation) including descriptions of parents, siblings, other significant family figures, and respondent's role growing up.
5. *Early recollections,* descriptions of earliest clear happenings and the situation surrounding them.
6. *Birth and development,* including age of walking and talking, problems compared with other children, view of effects of early experiences.
7. *Health and physical condition,* including childhood and later diseases and injuries, current prescribed medications, current use of unprescribed drugs, cigarettes, or alcohol, comparison of own body with others, habits of eating and exercising.
8. *Education and training,* including subjects of special interest and achievement, out-of-school learning, areas of difficulty and pride, any cultural problems.
9. *Work record,* including reasons for changing jobs, attitudes toward work.
10. *Recreation, interests, and pleasures,* including volunteer work, reading, respondent's view of adequacy of self-expression and pleasures.
11. *Sexual development,* covering first awareness, kinds of sexual activities, and view of adequacy of current sexual expressions.
12. *Marital and family data,* covering major events and what led to them, and comparison of present family with family of origin, ethnic or cultural factors.
13. *Social supports, communication network, and social interests,* including people talked with most frequently, people available for various kinds of help, amount and quality of interactions, sense of contribution to others and interest in community.
14. *Self-description,* including strengths, weaknesses, ability to use imagery, creativity, values, and ideals.
15. *Choices and turning points in life,* a review of the respondent's most important decisions and changes, including the single most important happening.
16. *Personal goals and view of the future,* including what the subject would like to see happen next year and in five or ten years, and what is necessary for these events to happen, realism in time orientation, ability to set priorities.
17. Any further material the respondent may see as omitted from the history.

(Adapted from Sundberg, 1977, pp. 97–98)

presentation by Crary. Most others use fewer topics. In general the following headings and questions cover the mental status examination well:

1. *Appearance and behavior.* This section is based mostly on observation and covers such questions as the following: How does the patient present himself or herself? What are the patient's general looks? How neat and clean? How appropriate are the clothes for the person's background and current situation? Are there any special adornments? Any apparent physical handicaps? How did the patient act during the interview or other recent observations? Were there any bizarre gestures or actions? Any repetitive "nervous" movements? What was the posture of the patient? Was eye contact avoided? Is activity slow or restless? The interviewer may also record impressions of wariness, submissiveness, attentiveness, or friendliness. Deviation in appearance and behavior from what is ex-

pected are useful baseline data for later comparison. Bizarre posturing or extreme motor retardation are suggestive of psychotic disorders.

2. *Speech and communication process.* What is the patient's general flow of speech? Is it rapid, carefully controlled, or hesitant? Are there speech impediments? Are there evidences of cultural or ethnic dialect or content? Is there over- or underproductivity of speech? A flight of ideas? Loose associations? Blocking on certain content? Rambling and irrelevancy? Unexpected grammar or terminology? Do nonverbal communications (smiling, frowning, gestures, posture) express the same feelings as the verbal? Does the content say one thing and the tone of voice another? How interested is the person in communicating well? The interviewer will record clinical impressions here as well as observations of behavior. Deviations, such as loose associations or inability to keep to a topic, may signal severe disorders.

3. *Content of thought.* What does the individual talk about, especially topics that are brought up spontaneously? Are there recurrent complaints, persistent themes or problems, distracting ideas? Is there evidence of delusions (bizarre beliefs), hallucinations, phobias, obsessions, or compulsions?

4. *Sensory and cognitive functioning.* How intact are the senses of the person: hearing, sight, touch, and so on? Can the person concentrate on the task at hand? How oriented is the person to time, place, and person? Is the person aware of where she or he is? Knowledgeable about the date and year? Able to give his or her name and other identification? (Disorientation may be found with severe organic or psychotic disorders.) How good is the person's memory for immediate, recent, and remote events? (If one tells the patient to remember a word or sentence and then asks for it ten minutes later, does he or she remember it? Does the person remember what he or she did yesterday? Or important events such as the year of marriage long ago?) Does the person's vocabulary and general fund of information reflect his or her occupatonal and educational background? Can the patient do simple arithmetic? Read? Write? Severe cognitive problems suggest organic, psychotic, or dissociative disorders. If there is no history of previous higher level functioning, mental retardation is a possibility.

5. *Emotional functioning.* What is the general mood, or apparent emotionality, of the patient during the interview—sad, elated, indifferent, angry, irritable, changeable, anxious? Does the patient react to the examiner in a flat, cold, or friendly way? Is the emotional display congruent with what the person is talking about? What does the person say about his or her mood and feelings, and is this self-report congruent with the interviewer's observations or impressions? It is common for neurotic people to display signs of anxiety but to be attuned to reality, whereas psychotic people are likely to show inappropriate or excessively deviant emotionality.

6. *Insight and judgment.* What is the person's belief about why she or he is coming to the psychiatric service, and is this belief appropriate and realistic? How psychologically minded is the patient? Is she or he aware and observant of problematic behavior and feelings? Does the person have ideas about what might be the problem or alternative notions about causes? If so, do they seem appropriate to the person's condition? Are there ethnic or cultural elements in the beliefs about causes? How good is the person's judgment about carrying out practical activities? How does she or he solve problems of living—impulsively, independently, responsibly, by trial and error? Does he or she make appropriate use of advice or assistance? How interested is the person in understanding and improving his or her situation? Impressions about these topics are relevant to therapy planning and case management.

As an illustration of an assessment interview with a different purpose, we will look at an outline for a behaviorally oriented interview. The intent is to pinpoint the client's problem in preparation for plans to assist the client in a behavioral or social learning therapy program. Peterson (1968, pp. 121–122) presents such an outline:

A.   Definition of problem behavior
1.   Nature of the problem as defined by client
As I understand it, you came here because . . . (discuss reasons for contact as stated by referral agency or other source of information). *I would like you to tell me more about this. What is the problem as you see it?* (Probe as needed to determine client's view of . . . problem behavior, . . .)
2.   Severity of the problem
a.   *How serious a problem is this as far as you are concerned?* (Probe to determine perceived severity of problem.)
b.   *How often do you . . .* (exhibit problem behavior if a disorder of commission, or have occasion to exhibit desired behavior if a problem of omission. The goal is to obtain information regarding frequency of response.)
3.   Generality of the problem
a.   Duration
How long has this been going on?
b.   Extent
Where does the problem usually come up? (Probe to determine situations in which problem behavior occurs, e.g., Do you feel that way at work? How about at home?)
B.   Determinants of problem behavior
1.   Conditions that intensify problem behavior
Now I want you to think about the times when. . .(the problem) *is worst. What sort of things are going on then?*
2.   Conditions that alleviate problem behavior
What about the times when. . .(the problem) *gets better? What sorts of things are going on then?*
3.   Perceived origins
What do you think is causing. . .(the problem)?
4.   Specific antecedents
Think back to the last time. . .(the problem occurred). *What was going on at that time?*
As needed:
a.   Social influences
Were any other people around? Who? What were they doing?
b.   Personal influences
What were you thinking about at the time? How did you feel?
5.   Specific consequences
What happened after. . .(the problem behavior occurred)?
As needed:
a.   Social consequences
What did. . .(significant others identified above) *do?*

b.   Personal consequences
How did that make you feel?
6.   Suggested changes
You have thought a lot about. . .(the problem). What do you think might be done to. . .(improve the situation)?
7.   Suggested leads for further inquiry
What else do you think I should find out about to help you with this problem?

(D. R. Peterson, *The Clinical Study of Social Behavior,* © 1968, pp. 121–122. Reprinted by permission of Prentice-Hall, Inc., Englewood Cliffs, N.J.)

On the other end of the scale from planned and extensive interviews is the *crisis interview.* This typically occurs in a crisis center in response to telephone calls from people who are very emotionally upset. The crisis may be related to suicide, rape, a fight with a live-in partner, a drug episode, or child abuse. Here is an example (from Phares, 1979, p. 175) of a call received by a volunteer telephone worker from a mother who during the absence of her husband became terrified that she would hurt her little boy:

MOTHER: My God, help me. Is this the place . . . that . . . I mean, I need somebody. Tell me.
VOLUNTEER: Yes, it is. Tell me what it is. Go ahead and talk.
M: I'm so nervous. I feel like I'll bust. Danny is crying, and my husband isn't here, and I've got to stop him. I can't stand it any longer.
V: OK. I think I understand. Are you alone?
M: Yes, but I can't handle it.
V: I know. And you're very upset. But I think we can talk it over.
M: I wish John would come home. I feel better when he's here. I just can't handle it. Nobody thought I should get married. . . .
V: What do you think is wrong? Are you afraid of hurting Danny?
M: He won't stop crying. He's always crying. John doesn't know what it's like. I suppose he blames me—I know Mother does. (Starts crying uncontrollably.)
V: Look, that's all right. Take it easy. Where is John?
M: He's. . .He drives a truck. He won't be back till Thursday.
V: I think I understand. . .and I know how you feel. Have you talked with anybody about your feelings on these things?
M: No. Well, with Marge next door a little bit. She said she felt like that a few times. But. . .I don't know.

The volunteer kept talking and encouraging the woman to do something about the situation by coming to the center the following day. Finally she agreed to come and bring her son with her.

BOX 4-2 *A DIAGNOSTIC INTERVIEW—THE SADS*

In moving toward clearer delineation of psychiatric diagnoses, Spitzer and Endicott have made several important contributions. One of them is a set of structured rating scales that is used in conjunction with a quite clearly specified description of information needed for the diagnosis and prognosis of affective and schizophrenic disorders. They supplement the interview and rating scales with a related procedure for using diagnostic criteria. Thus they are trying to reduce the two major sources of unreliability in clinical diagnosis—the variation in information obtained and the variation in the diagnostic standards. Endicott and Spitzer (1978) describe the Schedule for Affective Disorders and Schizophrenia (SADS)—the interview and rating guide. For instance (p. 839), they spell out how to probe for maniclike behavior. If the person has already described a depressed mood, the interviewer is to say something like this: "I know you have been feeling depressed. However, many people have other feelings mixed in or at different times so it is important that I ask you about those feelings also . . . have there been times when you felt very good or too cheerful or high—not just your normal self? . . . (If unclear) . . . when you felt on top of the world or as if there was nothing you couldn't do? . . . If people saw you, would they think you were just in a good mood or something more than that?" The interview schedule then calls for a rating on degree of mania from "1, Not at all, normal or depressed" to "6, Extreme, e.g., clearly elated, exalted expression and says, 'Everything is beautiful, I feel so good.' " The authors want to be careful to exclude behavior that is clearly explicable from alcoholic or drug intoxication. The schedule goes on to require questions about the need for sleep and the amount of energy and activity in the past week, with ratings being given for both sleep and energy. A scoring system is specified and good inter-rater reliability is reported. Training is required for administering the SADS interview and using the Research Diagnostic Criteria. The SADS and variations on it are becoming widely accepted as more exact ways to diagnose psychopathology than previous ones. In the long run such systems will contribute a great deal to research and to shorter, more practical forms useful for routine clinical practice.

How Good Is the Interview for Assessment?

This question can only be answered by "It depends." There can be no simple research answers since the variables involved are so various and complex—the many kinds and purposes, the assortment of settings, the variety of clients, and the different personalities and abilities of interviewers. Research reports are often surprising or conflicting. For instance, some suggest that self-disclosure may be enhanced by a reserved kind of behavior by interviewers and that interviewer "warmth" does not necessarily help clients express themselves (Heller, 1971, 1972; Heller, Davis, & Myers, 1966; Wiens, 1976). Reports differ on whether blacks or other ethnic groups prefer interviewers to be from their own ethnic background (Sundberg & Gonzales,

1981). Apparently there are wide individual differences in the importance interviewees attach to race, ethnicity, and gender. As might be expected, long utterances by the interviewer lead to shorter answers by the client, and closed, or "yes-no," questions lead to less talk by the client (Matarazzo & Wiens, 1972; Wiens, 1976). Structured interviews produce more agreement between several interviewers' ratings or diagnoses than do *laissez-faire*, or nondirected, interviews. Interviews have been found to add little or nothing to prediction of academic success (Meehl, 1954; Sarbin, 1943). There are enough serious questions about the reliability and validity of interviews to make them suspect for many assessment purposes (see reviews by Matarazzo, 1978; Wiens, 1976). In assessment it is useful to check interview findings against tests and other procedures and records, but interviewing will probably continue to be the major form of clinical assessment. It is hard to conceive of an efficient substitute that will provide as much flexibility, observability of interpersonal behavior, sense of "knowing" the client, and opportunity to orient the client to clinical services. It behooves all people who will be working with others to develop their interviewing skills and at the same time to understand their limitations.

Observations

The second most common clinical assessment procedure is observation. Interviews provide, of course, for observation. The appearance of the person, the manner of dress and conduct, may provide clues to important aspects of personality, cultural influences, self-control, attitudes, and relationships with others. Throughout history and in all cultures, when people wish to take on a distinctly different identity—to become a nun or a guru-follower, to be a member of a gang, to be a grown-up, or to assert status—they put on certain clothes or adornments, cut their hair, or perform certain rituals. Probably everybody displays some symbols of personal identity and role, if one is keen enough to observe them. Astute observers, such as the mythical Sherlock Holmes, pick up such clues in an amazing manner.

Besides using informal, everyday kinds of observation, clinicians learn to look for signs of abnormality, personal concerns, and kinds of interpersonal relations. For instance, a certain gait, a kind of "floating" walk, is characteristic of some schizophrenics. The effects of some cerebral-vascular accidents (strokes) are revealed by one-sided muscular problems. Eye contact or its avoidance helps in assessing interpersonal relations. Wiens (1976) notes that eye movements play an important role in signaling verbal interaction. The listener usually is looking at the speaker's eyes or mouth, and the speaker tends to look away from the other person. When a time comes to change speakers, the one who is talking will look to the listener, who will often glance away momentarily. Eye contact is also related to culture. It is expected, for instance, that girls or young women in many cultures, such as the traditional Japanese, are not supposed to look a man directly in the eyes.

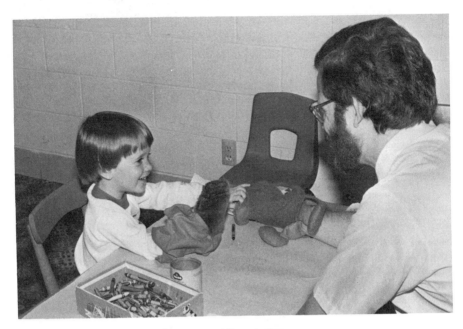

Figure 4-2 Young children are often assessed through play.

One particular problem with observations is *reactivity*. The observation itself has an effect on the behavior of the client. A number of studies and reviews (e.g., Johnson & Bolstad, 1973, 1975) have shown that such effects can be reduced if the observers are as unobtrusive as possible. Some psychologists have urged that greater use be made of unobtrusive indicators of behavior, such as cigarette butts left by a person or number of pieces of mail received (Palmer & McGuire, 1973; Webb et al., 1981).

Psychologists, especially those with the learning orientation, have developed elaborate coding systems for recording observations from televised tapes, observations in the home, or a one-way observation window in the clinic. Behaviorally oriented psychologists frequently require home visits as part of treatment. They also often ask clients to do self-observations. Clients keep their own records, such as kind and amount of food eaten while on a weight-reduction program or time and place when an unwanted gesture (or tic) occurs.

TESTS AND TESTING

Another major variety of assessment techniques is testing, and nearly everyone knows that clinical psychologists give tests. In fact, for many years testing has been the major activity of clinical psychologists, and even those psychologists who work only as therapists are expected to be knowledgeable about tests and testing (Levy & Fox, 1975).

Tests may be seen as structured and standardized interviews or observations. A paper-and-pencil personality inventory may have questions on it similar to those asked in an interview. An individual intelligence test during which the client copies designs using blocks or traces a path through a maze provides opportunities for observation of behavior. However, there are differences. Tests structure or restrict the interpersonal interaction, especially in the case of group tests, and a client is likely to have a different attitude toward the answering process from that characterizing the freer interview situation. The advantages of testing over the individual interview or observation are that information may be obtained faster with less use of costly professional time and that tests can be used for comparisons between people and for checking performance in a systematic way. Tests also lend themselves to statistical development and research more readily than do unstandardized procedures.

A test is a method for acquiring a sample of a person's behavior in a standard situation. It is a recorded specimen of activity in the presence of at least partially specified stimuli and instructions. Because testing always takes place in a particular setting and obtains its behavioral sample at a particular time in the person's life, the assessor in interpreting scores must always ask if the setting had any unusual qualities or if the testee was sick or disturbed in some way.

Norms

An important aspect of standardized testing is the use of *norms* and *norm-referencing.* In preparing a test for publication, a psychologist will administer it to a large and representative sample of the sector of the population in which it is to be used, such as 10-year-old schoolchildren, entering college students, or employment service clients. These subjects' scores are then arranged in a norm table, thus making it possible to ascertain the degree to which another person's score is above or below average.

Another less common way of making test scores meaningful is called *criterion referencing.* Instead of comparisons with a norm, comparisons are made against a standard set by judgments or previous research. In this procedure items may be arranged in order of difficulty or, in case of symptoms, of seriousness. An individual taking the test works up this ladder, as it were, as far as he or she can. The score represents the height reached and does not require group norms to make it meaningful. Particularly for persons following the learning or growth orientations, such tests, when available, fit into improvement plans better than norm-referenced tests do.

Reliability

The basic standards that tests are expected to meet are called reliability and validity. *Reliability* essentially means consistency or accuracy. Different parts or forms of the same test should not lead to markedly different evaluations of individuals, and repetition of the test after a short interval should produce scores that are similar to the original ones. Because chance factors, such as the particular sampling of items or fluctuations of attention in the test taker, affect scores, no test is ever completely reliable, but the good ones are accurate enough so that scores are meaningful. Correlation coefficients of around .80 or more are needed for reasonable accuracy in individual work.

Validity

Validity concerns what the test measures. To what extent does an intelligence test, for example, really evaluate intelligence? The determination of how valid tests are has turned out to be a highly complex matter. There are several techniques used to study it, involving correlating sets of scores with scores on other tests or current real-life conditions (*concurrent* validity), correlating scores with outcomes or later achievements (*predictive* validity), analyzing the nature and sampling of items in the test (*content* validity), and ascertaining how scores link up with many variables that theory suggests should be related to them (*construct* validity). In carrying out assessments, the psychologist should be aware that validity is a primary factor in interpreting the results of tests, especially if the studies are similar populations with similar prediction problems. Validity coefficients are typically much lower than are reliability coefficients; few attain a correlation figure as high as .50 or .60. Even such a figure leaves much of the variation in outcomes unexplained.

Evaluation Applied
to Other Assessment Procedures

The standards that have come to be generally accepted for tests should also apply to the other techniques of assessment. Interviews and observations should be reliable and valid if we are to place confidence in the soundness of the information they produce; however, the methods for determining how reliable or how valid they are will be somewhat different from the methods used in the construction of tests. For validity, some of the information that interviews reveal can be checked against records to determine how accurate it is. The validity of observational ratings of children's aggressiveness can be ascertained by relating the frequency of hitting and toy snatching in preschool, for example, or against ratings for aggressiveness made by teachers who know the children well. The most common way of determining reliability of an observation or interview techniques is to compare ratings of two or more interviewers or observers—interrater agreement.

The standards for evaluating interviewing and other assessment techniques are especially important when the main purpose of the assessment is the making of life decisions, such as commitment to an institution or placement in a foster home. The problem is that few techniques have been carefully studied against relevant criteria. Techniques that do not meet high standards may be of some value when there is ample opportunity to check hypotheses against other data, as is the case in continued therapy.

Other practical matters to consider are costs, time taken to administer and interpret the procedure, whether there are alternative procedures that are less costly and time consuming, the amount of training required for using it, whether a procedure can be adequately administered by personnel other than highly paid professionals, how appropriate it is to the prospective testees in features such as readability and difficulty, and how acceptable the procedure would be to the agency. Concerning acceptability, although direct relevance to the decisions and concerns of client or staff helps to "sell" the test or procedure to them, a more subtle and less obvious procedure may actually be more valid. Psychologists have to use good judgment and perhaps consult with experts before selecting the battery of procedures to be used for making decisions, forming useful images, and testing hypotheses about people.

PERSONAL PRODUCTS
AND RECORDS

Along with interviewing, observing, and testing, the assessing psychologist will often have available various records and products that will tell a great deal about the client. One obvious place to look for information about a child or adolescent is in the school. With the permission of the parent and the child, the psychologist may obtain the record of grades and tests and begin to construct a picture of the achievements or failures of the child over several years of schooling. In medical settings physicians and nurses keep hospital charts and reports of laboratory tests and medical problems. Other settings keep other records. Surprisingly the sheer weight of a record may tell one that the person had many problems which were not easy to solve. Pankratz (1981) reports that the medical record of one patient weighed 9.8 kilograms; it was full of excessively repeated laboratory tests on this "professional patient" who went from hospital to hospital with dramatic symptoms.

Another kind of information about a person may be found in personal documents or products. Allport (1965) provided a fascinating report on a series of letters from an elderly woman to her son revealing her paranoid feelings and her attempts to cope with loneliness. Letters, diaries, artwork, poetry, and work samples are examples of other things that tell a lot about a person's competencies, interests, and personal concerns. Gilmore (see Sundberg, 1977, pp. 99–101) has made an innovative use of photographs from family albums, asking the client to arrange them chronologically and examining the client's attitudes toward the self and others at various times in life.

Gathering information with a client can be a creative and interesting task. The assessor may think of new procedures that fit the particular client's situation and needs. Sharing the same purposes, clients may work with the psychologist to devise ways to tell the assessor more fully what life means to them and what they want it to be.

CRITIQUE

In each of these three assessment chapters and in other chapters, we will ask three fundamental questions. Later assessment chapters will cover testing and final stages. Here we will emphasize theoretical and early aspects.

How adequate is assessment conceptually?   Early in this discussion we identified four major clinical orientations toward assessment in addition to the informal, everyday form. Each of the four leads to a different emphasis in the attitudes, procedures, and conclusions about human beings and their situations. The dominant one in clinical work historically has been the concern for psychopathology, based on assumptions that disordered processes are within the person and that one needs to obtain a label, a diagnosis. Each of the other three has moved away from the psychopathological orientation. The behavioral, or social learning, approach avoids the labels of the psychopathological orientation and attends to well-defined problems and the processes of change. The growth orientation also avoids labeling and emphasizes the assets and the development of personal awareness rather than judgments of disorders by experts. The ecological one puts the problems in context and says that disorder is a problem of the functioning of systems. Each of these approaches has strengths and weaknesses.

There have been few attempts, none of them really successful, to put all of these concerns together into a theory of practice. To what should the clinician attend, and what is the overall assessment strategy? The mental status exam is one partial attempt at bringing together many functional aspects of the person, but it does not rest on coherent theory. Leary (1957) and McLemore and Benjamin (1979) have developed a promising combination of interpersonal theory (using the two major dimensions of dominance-submission and love-hostility) with levels or kinds of perceptions of a person (the person as viewed from outside, the person's stated self-concept, and the unconscious aspects of the personality). They have shown how each of these different dimensions and levels might be measured by different tests. Another attempt to bring together a diverse set of assessment inquiries is the multimodal approach of Lazarus (1973, 1976), further elaborated by Nay (1979). The different areas of the person to be assessed are summarized by the acronym *BASIC ID* which stands for the following: *B*ehavior; *A*ffects, such as anxiety, anger, or job; *S*ensations, such as muscle tensions; *I*magery; *C*ognitions, such as ideals and insights; *I*nterpersonal relations; and finally, *D*rugs, if medication is a concern. The relevant theory is behavioral and cognitive, and a set of assessment techniques accompanies each BASIC ID function. However useful these attempts to systematize the variety of information-seeking modes, they are very limited in theory and do not cover the four orientations we have discussed nor the several systems levels (Taplin, 1980) that form the basis for the review of clinical work in this book.

The people who are active in the large domain called *assessment* come from diverse professional orientations and speak different languages. Language itself is one of the problems. Each of the four core professional orientations has different preferences for concepts. The diagnostic categories from psychiatry do not jibe with systems theory or the many terms from personality theory, social psychology, and sociology. To complicate matters, the assessing clinician must use both the language of everyday life in conversations with clients and the professional languages of colleagues and written reports. Among the clients' ethnic and cultural groups, there are differences in the meanings of terms describing basic human emotions and conditions (Marsella, 1980). A few psychologists have tried to develop a basic terminology for describing personality by deriving a small set of terms from the thousands of words used to describe people in the English language, as mentioned in the last chapter (e.g., Goldberg, 1982). Even if we had a widely accepted set of terms for describing persons, we still would have the problem of describing situations and interacting systems in which they participate. Mischel (1968, 1973) has issued a well-known challenge to trait psychology, showing that environmental events must be acknowledged in assessing behavior and pointing to a set of cognitive processes that mediate between environmental stimulation and behavior. If there were a theory of practice using a universal language for describing people and situations, communication would be much easier; the research and conceptualization have a long way to go.

How practical are the basic assessment procedures? How much information is useful to obtain on a client and the situation? There is, of course, no cut-and-dried answer. Peterson (1968, p. 119) has estimated that three-fourths of the usual psychiatric and psychological interview information is of no use in treatment. Morganstern and Tevlin (1981, p. 72) answer the question of how much information is needed as follows: "Everything that is relevant to the development of effective, efficient and durable treatment interventions . . . and no more." They point out that ethical considerations as well as economical ones argue for focus and conciseness. To pursue sexual adventures unnecessarily in an interview or to give tests just because they are interesting to the assessor is a waste of time and perhaps an undue invasion of the client's privacy. The costs of assessment for the private patient (or the taxpayer in the case of public clinics) need to be considered. The clinician needs to know what is practical to do in the clinical situation and to limit inquiry to what is relevant. On the other hand, important information must not be overlooked.

A long-range perspective on data gathering is necessary for research. It is important for university clinics and many others to collect data for studies of assessment and treatment that may not be used in actual work with a particular client. Routine administration of tests, for instance, provides local norms and predictive statistics which can be of considerable value for subsequent patient assessment.

Clinical services use interviewing as the primary and often sole assessment procedure. How practical is it? We have noted that structured tests may provide more exact information than do unstructured interviews, and if the tests are self-administered, they will require less use of expensive professional time. Some assessment studies (e.g., Kelly, 1954; Kelly & Fiske, 1951) show that the interview adds little to assessment results. However, social scientists have done very little research in analyzing the practicality and efficiency of various assessment procedures in actual clinical operations. Matarazzo's extensive review (1978) of the use of the interview in psychiatric diagnosis concludes that with well-trained people, interviews show "adequate reliability and beginning validity" (p. 93).

Another seldom-investigated practical aspect of assessment is the question of how interesting and rewarding it is for the clinicians. If clinicians must be like assembly-line workers or lab technicians doing boring tasks that provide little satisfaction, then their boredom and burnout are likely to reflect adversely on their clinical work (Edelwich, 1980; Pines, Aronson, & Kafry, 1980). Interviewing, unless it is very structured, is likely to be interesting to people who choose to do clinical work with people. Observing may also be rewarding. But some workers have to carry a heavy caseload, and they feel their work is not being useful or recognized. Dissatisfaction is likely to be communicated to clients. Repetitious testing or administration of behavioral assessment and treatment procedures do raise questions for personnel of clinical organizations. Possible solutions lie in having variety in the working situation, assigning some work to paraprofessional helpers, and developing computerized automation of some routine aspects of assessment.

How socially worthwhile is assessment?   Does assessment do more harm than good? In recent decades there have been many objections raised to mass testing and to testing that is unfair to minorities. Some object to testing as an invasion of privacy when questions cover such matters as sexual and religious attitudes. We will discuss these questions in more detail in the next chapter. Here we can say that most of these objections apply to nonclinical situations in schools, industries, government, and the military, where mass testing is often used. There has been little criticism of clinical use of tests, partly because they are usually administered individually and the psychologist can check on problems of anxiety and misunderstanding about testing. However, the clinician must also be aware of the criticisms. In using norm tables derived from large samples, she or he may be misled by their lack of relation to the client's cultural background. In using interviews and tests, clinicians need to be sensitive to possible ethical violations of privacy and informed consent. A key word in choosing what to do in assessing clients is *relevance*. Is the procedure relevant to the important questions about the case and the goals of the service?

We have repeatedly said that some amount and some form of assessment is necessary; the clinician must obtain and organize information about clients and their situations. How worthwhile are different amounts and forms of assessment? The basic four orientations differ in this regard. Traditional clinicians oriented toward diagnosis of pathology and behavioral clinicians both place a heavy emphasis on assessment as the first step in making decisions about a case. Ecologically oriented assessors also collect considerable data, but less from the individual and more from the social and physical environment. Growth or humanistically oriented counselors generally place little emphasis on formal assessment (except perhaps for research) and even believe that the explicit concern for history, testing, and evaluation sets the wrong tone for therapy and establishes the wrong relationship with the client. In the course of therapy, personal history may be revealed, of course, and some humanistic counselors make use of self-assessment procedures. There is little research on the effect of the assessment orientation on relationships or therapy.

Other questions in early assessment are the following: "To whom is the problem disturbing?" "Who is the client?" There are many instances of people being brought to clinics who are only the "identified" client, whereas the major problem actually lies elsewhere—the aggressive "bad" child in a family in which another child is obviously being heavily favored by the parents, old people whom others wish to be rid of, a person who is entangled in a damaging relationship. A systems approach with a decision to scan the significant relationships in the presented client's life situation can help to alleviate problems of misplaced emphasis on the individual.

For assessment processes to be worthwhile, the agency or other clinical setting must be analyzed. Does psychological interviewing, observation, and testing add anything beyond what the agency must do anyway? How does psychological assessment fit into the ultimate outcomes of the service—whether it be treatment, case management, recommendations to courts or other outside agencies, or referral to other community services? What kinds of systems interventions and treatment perspectives does the agency have available? The role of the assessing psychologist must be recognized in the process—whether she or he is only giving opinions and recommendations for others to decide about a case or is actually making the decisions in the organization. The role of the assessor in follow-through treatment must also affect the worthwhileness of the assessment. How assessment might contribute to proper matching of client problems with both the system levels of intervention and the perspectives of the helping professionals needs to be clarified (Pankratz & Taplin, 1982; Taplin, 1980). This larger view of the assessment in context is a challenge for the future.

SUMMARY

Psychological assessment is concerned with obtaining useful information about persons and their situations. The three clinical purposes are decision making, image forming, and hypothesis checking. The working image is a set of hypotheses about the client and the client's situations that develops rather rapidly as impressions form on first contact and as hypotheses are checked by further information coming from the assessment process; ultimately the clinician transmits this working image to others who work with the person. There are several orientations of assessment—an everyday, natural assessment procedure that is common in the lives of everyone and four professional orientations. The four, similar to those of interventions mentioned in the last chapter, are the psychopathological or curative orientation (based on the medical model), the learning orientation (emphasizing behavioral or cognitive change), the growth orientation (emphasizing inherent potential for development and value of self-experiencing), and the ecological orientation (seeing individuals as part of larger environments and interacting systems). Many clinicians use a combination of these four orientations and still retain much of the "everyday" assessment approach. Clinicians conducting assessment have both a task to perform (obtaining certain information, certain content) and a socioemotional relation to consider (establishing a trusting, helpful, credible exchange with the client). The basic methods for assessment are interviewing and observation. Interviewing skills depend on development of listening and such techniques as paraphrasing and perception checking. There are many kinds of interviews, including case histories, mental status examinations, elicitation of problem behaviors, and crisis interviews. Observations occur during interviews or may be specifically arranged, especially for behaviorally oriented assessment. Tests are another major kind of assessment—a sampling of behavior in a standard situation. Tests make use of norms and information on reliability and validity. Validity, particularly as it relates to clinical outcomes, is most important. Assessment may also make use of records and personal products. Assessment, although probably the most highly developed scientifically of clinical tasks, is still far from adequate for the complex job of understanding persons and their situations; much research is needed. Questions must continue to be asked about the conceptual development of assessment, its clinical practicality, and its social worth.

RECOMMENDED READINGS

McReynolds, P. (Ed.). *Advances in psychological assessment* (Vols. 3, 4, & 5). San Francisco: Jossey-Bass, 1975, 1978, 1981.

This series, which also includes two earlier volumes (McReynolds, 1968, 1971), contains many chapters of value to instructors and students. For instance, there are discussions of observation, assessment of memory and cognitive style, environmental assessment, and cross-cultural issues. Another useful source is *Advances in Personality Assessment*, edited by Spielberger and Butcher (1982); of particular interest for this chapter is a comprehensive discussion of the use of observations, life history information and tests in assessing individuals in crisis. Another important reference is Woody's *Encyclopedia of Clinical Assessment* (1980) which covers a wide range of topics, such as interviewing, observation, role playing, psychophysiological measures, and information processing, as well as assessment of certain disorders, such as schizophrenia, and certain functions, such as imagery. Wolman's *Clinical Diagnosis of Mental Disorders* (1978) is another useful resource. No survey of assessment approaches would be complete without attention to the burgeoning area of behavioral and social learning assessment. Among several books are the *Handbook of Behavioral Assessment* by Ciminero, Calhoun, and Adams (1977) and *Behavioral Assessment: A Practical Handbook* by Hersen and Bellack (1981). Kleinmuntz (1982) and Sundberg (1977) provide general introductions to personality assessment.

Gilmore, S. K. *The counselor-in-training.* Englewood Cliffs, N.J.: Prentice-Hall, 1973.

Gilmore introduces the purposes and processes of counseling for choice, change, and confusion-reduction, but the most relevant parts for this chapter are the sections on processes of communication and discussions and examples of such fundamental interviewing techniques as paraphrasing and perception checking. She also provides illustrative practicum exercises for students and instructors. Another introductory book for human service workers is Benjamin's *The Helping Interview* (1969). Matarazzo (1978) gives a good review of reliability and validity of interviews for the purposes of psychiatric diagnosis. Pope (1979) in *The Mental Health Interview* sees the interview as dyadic communication and relationship, reviews the research, and gives numerous examples to aid beginning students.

Patterson, G. R. Naturalistic observation in clinical assessment. *Journal of Abnormal Child Psychology*, 1977, 5, 309–322.

Patterson and his colleagues at the Oregon Social Learning Center worked for many years to develop a recording and coding system useful for observations of children and parents interacting in the home or elsewhere. Here he describes the result, the Behavior Coding System (BCS). The BCS has 28 categories of verbal and nonverbal behaviors, such as Command, Cry, Yell, Ignore, Tease, Work, and Play, which the observer checks at prescribed intervals. Patterson discusses the uses for BCS, interobserver reliability, effects of observation, and validity. As one illustration of validity, the rates per minutes of total deviant behavior of three samples of boys were as follows: .30 (normals), .57 (stealers), and .75 (aggressives). Robinson and Eyberg (1981) present the Dyadic Parent-Child Interaction Coding System, a promising observational procedure, which they use while observing child-directed and parent-directed play.

Korchin, S. J., & Schuldberg, D. The future of clinical assessment. *American Psychologist*, 1981, 36, 1147–1158.

This article is an excellent condensation of many of the issues and trends in assessment. Korchin and Schuldberg define assessment as "the process by which clinicians gain understanding of the patient necessary for making informed decisions" (p. 1147). They identify four models of assessment, slightly different from the four in this chapter: the dominant psychodiagnostic or psychodynamic approach, the psychometric orientation, behavioral assessment, and humanistic assessment. The authors identify several reasons for the decline of clinical testing over the past 20 years and point to new trends. They conclude that clinical assessment is showing a renewed vitality as new techniques and research develop. For an elaboration of Korchin's views, see his introduction to *Clinical Psychology* (1976). For other overviews of clinical assessment strategies, see other texts, such as those by Phares (1979) and Bernstein and Nietzel (1980), and Kendall and Norton-Ford (1982).

Adinolfi, A. A. Relevance of person perception research to clinical psychology. *Journal of Consulting and Clinical Psychology,* 1971, *37,* 167–176.

Adinolfi reviews some of the leading research on such topics as stereotype accuracy, the study of the perceiver, differential accuracy, perceiver-perceived relations, and labeling. He notes possible conflicts between the clinician's orientation toward a person's past life and the orientation toward empathic understanding in the immediate clinical situation. Most accuracy in perception is achieved by those most similar to the target person or client or by those most familiar with the situation and the person. Adinolfi mentions the possibility that white, middle-class people who compose the vast majority of clinicians will have problems perceiving nonwhite, lower-class clients accurately. Wills (1978) reviews the research on perceptions of clients by professional helpers, concluding that there is a tendency for attitudes to be negative because of lack of similarity, overemphasis on the individual, client's resistance to change, and tendencies to sample negative aspects of a client's behavior. Also see Weary & Mirels (1982).

RESEARCH EXAMPLES

Introductory Note: Here and at the end of most of the following chapters, we are presenting brief reports of studies to illustrate how research is carried out on clinical questions. Since the amount of publication is enormous, these few selections only show a little bit of the whole research effort; there are many other possible research directions to take. Readers are encouraged to read the original articles which we summarize here. Each example should raise questions in the mind of the reader about how to extend and improve the area of study.

Chapman, L. J., & Chapman, J. P. Genesis of popular but erroneous psychodiagnostic observations. *Journal of Abnormal Psychology,* 1967, *72,* 193–204.

This study is one of a series showing the fallibility of clinical thought and the difficulty in training for greater accuracy. Many clinicians use drawings, such as the Draw-A-Person test, to diagnose personality. Chapman and Chapman obtained from practicing clinicians a set of beliefs about how to interpret such drawings—for instance, the hypothesis that suspicious people would give special attention to the eyes of the person drawn, that men who worried about their manliness would overemphasize shoulders and a manly build, or that those who worried about their intelligence would draw large heads. The researchers hypothesized that such beliefs may be due to *illusory correlations* held by many people in the culture. They presented 45 drawings to 108 undergraduates, each drawing paired randomly with one of six symptoms such as those mentioned. The students were then asked to list the characteristics of the drawings that went with each of the six symptoms. Despite the random experience they had received, their answers were highly systematic; in every case the most frequent student response was the same as the most frequent clinician belief.

In other studies Chapman and Chapman confirmed these studies. They also showed that repeated experience did not reduce errors and that the illusory correlations were very resistant to change. Apparently both clinicians and students make use of widely shared stereotypic thinking. Golding and Rorer (1972) obtained similar findings regarding assumptions about signs of homosexuality on the Rorschach inkblot test and also found these beliefs resistant to change using various training methods. Wampold, Casas, and Atkinson (1981) applied the illusory correlation research model to graduate students in a psychology program using stereotypic characteristics often attributed to American minority groups and Anglo-Americans. After viewing different sets of cards on which characteristics were paired randomly with various ethnic groups, the graduate students (some of whom were from minority groups and others Anglo) were asked to indicate what information was given on the cards. It was found that the Anglos made fewer errors when the correct answer corresponded with a widely held stereotype. These findings suggested to the researchers that stereotyping did affect information processing. These studies point to the importance of being skeptical of stereotypes and assumptions in one's thinking (some of which may be correct, of course) and to make use of verified facts whenever possible.

Stokes, J., Childs, L., & Fuehrer, A. Gender and sex roles as predictors of self-disclosure. *Journal of Counseling Psychology*, 1981, *28*, 510–514.
Self-disclosure is important in interviewing and therapy, and there is some evidence that greater willingness to tell about one's feelings and ideas is associated with better adjustment in general. Several kinds of self-disclosure questionnaires have been developed (Chelune, 1978). In this study Stokes and his colleagues used a questionnaire asking subjects about their willingness to talk about 14 topics of different degrees of intimacy (such as the school one has attended, fluctuations in one's weight, and feelings about one's sexual performance) with six different kinds of persons (strangers, acquaintances, and intimates of the same or opposite sex). Subjects also completed the Bem Sex Role Inventory (BSRI) which separately measures masculinity and feminity, so that a person can be high on one or the other or both; when a person is high on both masculine and feminine interests and characteristics, that person is called androgynous. Subjects were 109 male and 107 female undergraduates. It was found that androgynous subjects reported more self-disclosure than did all other subjects. The authors concluded that intimate self-disclosure required both assertiveness associated with the masculine role and the expressiveness and sensitivity associated with the traditional feminine role.

LeVine and Franco (1981) in a somewhat similar study relating self-disclosure to sex and ethnicity found that females reported significantly more disclosure than did males and Anglo-Americans reported more than did Hispanics. Hispanic males were particularly low in self-disclosure. However, Hispanics reported high self-disclosure under some conditions, especially with females. Both of these studies suffer from being self-reports by students. It would be desirable to collect data on self-disclosure in actual clinical assessment or therapy situations.

Harder, D. W., Gift, T. E., Strauss, J. S., Ritzler, B. A., & Kokes, R. F. Life events and two-year outcome in schizophrenia. *Journal of Consulting and Clinical Psychology*, 1981, *49*, 619–626.
Since the early research in the mid-1960s by Holmes and others, it has become apparent that breakdown, both physical and mental, is related to frequency and kind of stressful life events. In this study the authors hypothesize that new hospital admissions diagnosed as schizophrenic would recover more rapidly if their breakdown was preceded by high and recent stress. Recognizing that the diagnosis of schizophrenia is variable, they used three methods and an intensive interview process. At the end of the interview they administered the scale designed to measure degree of life changes and

stress during the previous year. Subjects were drawn from over 200 new admissions to a psychiatric facility. Excluding those who didn't meet the criteria or could not complete testing, the research team found between 31 and 41 subjects two years later and repeated the procedures. The general findings confirmed the hypothesis with the two more rigorous methods of diagnosing schizophrenia. High levels of stress in the year previous to first admission significantly related to a better outcome two years later. Recently stressed patients, it appears, are likely to have less chronic, more situationally related problems. This kind of finding, although it needs to be checked with other samples, suggests that life-events assessment of recent life changes is useful in predicting the future course of a disorder.

Jacobson, S., & Moore, D. Spouses as observers of the events in their relationship. *Journal of Consulting and Clinical Psychology*, 1981, *49*, 269–277.

Direct observation is the ideal way to assess behavioral problems and changes as therapy takes place. Spouses would seem to offer important possibilities for observation of problem behavior, such as overeating, smoking, and other activities. The question is how good spouses would be as observers. In this study Jacobson and Moore gained the cooperation of 36 couples (some distressed and some nondistressed) to collect data in the home for 12 days. Once a day they independently completed the Weiss Spouse Observation Checklist according to whether an activity had happened during the previous 24 hours—for instance, "We watched TV," "We held each other," "We engaged in sexual intercourse," "Spouse said he (or she) was glad to see me," and "We talked about personal feelings."

Consensus was measured by percentage agreement and statistical procedures. The average agreement for all couples was 48 percent. Nondistressed couples showed somewhat greater agreement than did distressed ones. It appeared that items on the checklist requiring some inference about intent or feeling produced less agreement than did other items. Jacobson and Moore discuss the rather small amount of agreement they found as an opportunity for theoretical speculation and more research. They conclude that two spouses living in the same environment live in quite different worlds. A spouse is limited as an exact observer of the other person, but it is important to know the kinds of perceptions that both partners have of each other.

Lorber (1981), in a doctoral dissertation research project, applied somewhat similar questioning to the perceptions of parents in observing their children. Using standard videotapes of parent-child interaction, he found that mothers of children with conduct problems did not identify problem behaviors as well as did those with nondisturbed children. His findings raise problems about psychological treatment which depends on selecting certain kinds of behavior for reinforcement and ignoring other behavior. In using observations for assessment, we need to know the adequacy of the training and reliability of the observer.

5 USING PSYCHOLOGICAL TOOLS:

Testing for Ability, Personality, and Behavior

The Nature and Use of Tests—General Considerations

Testing of Abilities and Cognitive Functioning
> Intelligence tests
> Intellectual deficit and cerebral dysfunction
> General achievement and ability tests
> Learning potential testing

Tests of Personality or Socioemotional Functioning
> Inventories for personality, values, and interests
> Projective techniques
> Behavioral assessment
> Other tests and procedures

Testing in Larger Systems

Critique

The previous chapter described the tasks that psychologists undertake in making assessments of persons. The tools they often like to use are tests, because tests usually provide fairly exact ways of gathering information about people and their situations and of making comparisons among people and are usually less affected by bias and subjective impressions than is information obtained solely from interviews. Thousands of tests have been developed since the first major one by Parisian scientist Alfred Binet in 1905. Millions of test administrations occur every year, mainly in educational, business, military, and governmental settings in which many people are screened for jobs, promotions, or admissions to training. The majority of that kind of testing is oriented to mass administration and scoring, whereas the majority of testing in clinical settings takes place on an individual basis, allowing for much closer scrutiny of the persons involved.

It would be satisfying to report that the hundreds of published tests provide the psychologist with a tool kit of reliable and valid instruments for answering all the questions that arise in assessing individuals according to the four major orientations indicated in Tables 4–1 and 5–1. We would like to be able to give clean demonstrations of helpful ways of identifying a person's psychopathological tendencies, learning competencies and needs, potentials and possibilities for development, and the ecological demands, resources, and opportunities in life situations. However, as prolific as test inventors and developers have been, their efforts still have been far from adequate in meeting many of the practical needs for clinical information and understanding. It is important to know both the possibilities and the limitations of testing.

A few illustrations will show the differences between what clinical questions and what tests can provide. Consider, for example, a fairly typical case referred to a psychologist working with a school district. The third-grade teacher reports that Billy is not doing well in school; he turns in messy papers, is far behind the others in reading and arithmetic, and seems distracted or "dreamy" much of the time. The teacher wonders what the psychologist would recommend. The psychologist's tool kit includes intelligence tests, such as the WISC-R (Wechsler Intelligence Scale for Children-Revised). That test would give a useful indication of how Billy compares with others his age in general abstract thinking ability, but the scores and the IQ would not say much about his style of doing his schoolwork, why his papers are messy, and why he seems distracted and dreamy. Some other tests might be of limited help, but they would not automatically give recommendations about what the teacher should do in the classroom to help Billy. It would be important to supplement the test scores with such activities as clinical observations during testing and in school situations and clinical interviews with Billy and others.

Another illustration is a counseling case. Maria, a new community college student, cannot decide what occupation to prepare for and what courses to take. Interest and ability tests help her and the counseling psychologist focus on various areas of work, but what about the degree of independence Maria feels from her family and her mild depression about a breakup with an intimate partner? These questions may get entangled in counseling, and tests can contribute only a little.

A complex set of questions also faces a psychologist brought in as a consultant on a murder case, that of Virginia Steele who shot her husband. The psychologist, if the patient is cooperative, may give the Minnesota Multiphasic Personality Inventory and several other tests useful in detecting psychopathology, but the major legal questions are not directly answered by these psychological instruments: Did Mrs. Steele know right from wrong at the time of the murder? Did she act under an irresistible compulsion? Was she acting in self-defense? Was it her intention to obtain insurance money? How much collusion, if any, was there in the crime between her and her alleged lover? To some extent each psychological case is like the mystery implied by these questions—questions that go far beyond what a particular test can offer. Still tests can be very helpful in answering these larger questions—questions derived from the larger case analysis. We need to know the potentialities for contributions and the limitations of these tools.

In this chapter we will concentrate on the published tests that are widely used by psychologists and on the concepts and knowledge base surrounding them. Space given to any one test is limited here; readers who continue in clinical psychology will study tests in much more detail in special courses, practica, and workshops; those who are reading this book for general knowledge about clinical psychology need not know about them in such detail. At the end of this chapter we list many of the major tests used by clinicians which readers might like to examine further. Suggested readings at the end of this and other assessment chapters are also helpful.

THE NATURE AND USE OF TESTS— GENERAL CONSIDERATIONS

A *test* is a standard method for obtaining a sample of behavior. To be standard, the method must be in a form that can be repeated by different people with different subjects; the same stimuli, instructions, methods of recording responses, and scoring rules are always used. In practice this means that most tests are printed and are accompanied by a test manual telling what instructions to give the subject, how to obtain answers or responses, and how to score and interpret the responses. Such manuals should adhere to the high standards with regard to norms, reliability, validity, and interpretation aids, which are spelled out in guidelines formulated by professional organizations, e.g., *Standards for Educational and Psychological Tests*, (APA, 1974). In actual practice many test manuals fall short of the ideal or even the minimal requirements, especially regarding evidence for validity.

A person trying to learn something about a common test will go to various sources for information. There are a number of textbooks that describe a wide array of tests (e.g., Anastasi, 1982). The several editions of Buros's *Mental Measurements Yearbooks* (e.g., 1972, 1978) present careful reviews of the test's psychometric properties and its applications. Some tests can be obtained from local agencies or by writing to the publisher. Some that are administered nationally to large groups for selection purposes, such as the Graduate Record Examination or the Scholastic Aptitude Test, are kept confidential, but recent legislation in some states requires testing companies to show subjects how their answers were scored. Many intelligence and personality tests are also available only to persons with professional qualifications to use them. Persons trying to develop their knowledge and skills often find it useful to take a test themselves, to get a "subject's eye view" before reading about the test in the manual or elsewhere.

Tests use many sorts of stimuli, such as verbal questions, blocks, pictures, or a blank sheet of paper. For any given client the stimulating situation is not just the printed page or the objects presented but also the instructions and the whole physical and social context in which the testing takes place. This context means that no clinical testing situation is exactly like another, but the aim is to make them as much alike, as *standard*, as possible. A number of studies and reviews of research (Masling, 1960; Sattler, 1970; Sattler & Theye, 1967) have shown that situational and examiner variables can affect the outcomes of tests. For instance, a noisy room may distract the test-taker, or the degree of warmth and personal interest shown by the tester may affect the number of responses given on an open-ended test. Even the way a test question is asked can make a difference. On a task of repeating digits, a person who hears a pause in the middle of the numbers—for instance, "865–2918"—can remember better than can the person hearing each digit said in an equally spaced manner—"8–6–5–2–9–1–8."

Tests also vary a great deal on the response side. The person may be instructed to mark "Yes" or "No" on a mechanically scored answer sheet, to sort a set of mixed-up cards so that they make a story, or to make a drawing of his or her family. If responses are to be made in a standardized form, the subject should have a clear idea of what to do. Some tests provide practice items to insure that the person understands the instructions.

The examiner tries to facilitate honest, nonanxious, interested behavior. With clinical subjects, many of whom start out anxious or defensive, it may require considerable time and effort on the part of the assessor to develop *rapport*—that is, a cooperative, harmonious relationship. The client will naturally want to know what the testing is about and how it will be used. In the early part of the interview the clinician will explain the general intent of the tests and answer questions that the client has. For testing, as for other clinical activity, the ethical assessor should obtain the client's *informed consent* and explain to the client that he or she may stop the process at any time. With young children the parent or guardian must be involved in the explanation and informed consent procedures.

With anyone, mild apprehension about testing is to be expected, but certain subjects have an extraordinarily high level of *test anxiety.* Psychologists have found that there are great individual differences among children and college students in this regard. High test-anxiety scores tend to go with lower scores on intelligence and achievement tests (Gaudry & Spielberger, 1974; Sarason, 1961, 1978). In general, however, studies seem to show that grades in school are related more closely to past performance and academic skills than to anxiety level (Galassi, Frierson, & Sharer, 1981). In clinical assessment one should evaluate the level of anxiety at least informally and consider it in interpreting results.

If tests are well administered and rapport is good, they provide an efficient way to compare the performance of a person with others or with a relevant criterion. Although there has been considerable opposition during recent years to the whole testing enterprise, clinical testing has encountered less of it than educational and industrial testing have. Clinicians testing persons individually can adapt to the special needs the person may have. Clinicians are also likely to know their clients much better than group testers do and so can interpret the results with greater attention to individual problems and test-taking styles.

TESTS OF ABILITIES
AND COGNITIVE FUNCTIONING

Cronbach (1960) distinguishes between *maximum performance* and *typical,* or *characteristic, performance.* The first kind requires subjects to do the best that they can and has right and wrong answers. This approach applies generally to tests of intelligence (or general ability), tests of specific abilities, tests of aptitude (or potentiality for developing an ability or performance), and tests of achievement (knowledge or past learning).

The second general kind of test does not require the subject to do his or her best and has no right and wrong answers. Tests of characteristic performance cover personality, attitudes, interests, values, and life styles—the socioemotional functioning of the person. These tests represent the *manner* with which one expresses one's abilities. In other words, the first kind concerns the question "What *can* the person do?" and the second addresses the question "How *does* the person do or like to do things?" This second kind will be discussed in the next section after we cover tests of maximum performance.

Intelligence Tests

Why can't Jenny, a new child in third grade read like the others in her class? Why can't she follow instructions given for games at recess? One of the tests people would consider for her would be one of *intelligence*. The question is less concerned with the problem of learning particular classroom work than with the more encompassing problem of general ability in many different aspects of life. Perhaps Jenny needs a special school situation or training program. The school psychologist, Ms. Brady, is likely to give the WISC-R or one of the other intelligence tests for children.

The *Wechsler Intelligence Scale for Children (Revised)* is a set of graded tasks. Figure 5–1 shows the kit and the record sheets used by psychologists, and Figure 5–2 shows a child taking the WISC-R. The first half of the test includes several verbal parts, such as words to be defined, arithmetic tasks, questions about information that is ordinarily picked up in daily living. The other half of the test, the performance scale, has tasks such as copying designs by putting together blocks, assembling cut-up figures, and arranging a set of pictures so that they tell a story. From the administration of these tasks, Ms. Brady obtains a verbal IQ, a performance IQ, and a full-scale IQ for Jenny, based on comparisons with others Jenny's age. Since the valid-

Figure 5-1 The WISC-R testing kit. (The Psychological Corporation)

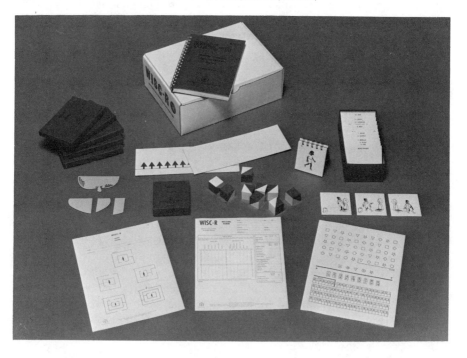

Figure 5-2
Psychologist and girl in testing situation. (Mimi Forsyth, Monkmeyer)

ity studies show that, for children from the main culture who have no special handicaps, the IQ is fairly predictive of school success, Ms. Brady can identify part of the difficulty that Jenny will have with ordinary schooling and make some recommendations. If in the course of assessing Jenny she discovers that Jenny's language at home is not English, or finds some indicators of abnormal brain function, or observes that she seems excessively preoccupied and worried, Ms. Brady may make other interpretations and give other tests.

Besides the WISC-R and the WISC (its earlier form) there are other intelligence tests. Ms. Brady could have used the *Stanford-Binet* with Jenny. For younger children the *Wechsler Preschool and Primary Scale of Intelligence* is appropriate. For adults a psychologist might use *Weschler Adult Intelligence Scale* in its original and revised forms (WAIS and WAIS-R) or one of several group tests. For handicapped people there are tests especially adapted for blind, deaf, or crippled persons. Mercer (1979; Mercer & Lewis, 1978) has developed an elaborate set of procedures to cover problems of evaluating schoolchildren with special ethnic backgrounds, called the *System of Multicultural Pluralistic Assessment* (SOMPA). This procedure for 5- to 11-year-olds of American black, Hispanic, and white background uses the WISC, parent interviews, and some other tests. The SOMPA provides comparisons with samples from both the dominant and minority cultures.

Intellectual Deficit
and Cerebral Dysfunction

When abnormality in brain function of adults is suspected, practitioners often use a quick screening procedure, the *Bender Visual-Motor Gestalt Test*, but it is very limited. A longer and widely used procedure is the *Halstead-Reitan Neuropsychological Test Battery*, aimed at evaluating various brain functions such as memory for designs, tapping speed, remembering a sequential set of numbers or letters while tracing a path, and reporting shapes by feeling objects. Chapter 8 will explore neuropsychological assessment in more detail.

General Achievement
and Ability Tests

Another test that a psychologist might use in a school problem situation is a measure of school learning, such as the *Wide Range Achievement Test* (WRAT) to assess knowledge of common school subjects. Many other tests based on national norms for schoolchildren cover school subjects commonly tested by schools themselves. Records on such tests are usually available to the clinician working with a child.

A widely used set of aptitude tests helpful in employment, vocational, and rehabilitation counseling is the *General Aptitude Test Battery* (GATB). Developed by the U.S. Employment Service, the GATB is routinely used throughout the United States in state employment offices. It measures such traits as clerical perception, spatial aptitude, finger dexterity, motor coordination, and verbal aptitude. Other batteries of aptitude tests are also available from publishers.

Learning Potential Testing

Before we leave intelligence and ability testing, we should mention a relatively new development—that of testing for *learning potential*. This approach derives either from an interest in the Piagetian stages of cognitive development or from behavioral methods of training and has been applied most successfully with retarded children. Such testing aims to sample performance on tasks important for education or training. As Anderson (1980) states in his review of assessment of mental retardation, the traditional IQ test makes only a gross differentiation between levels of assignment to special educational services; the clinician needs more detailed knowledge of what the person can do to be able to set up a learning program. Often the task involves measurement before and after initial training to examine differences in performance and responsiveness to the particular intervention tried. For instance, the psychologist presents the child with a task of assembling some wooden pieces to make a figure. After giving the child a fair amount of time to solve the puzzle, the psychologist shows how certain pieces fit together. The measure of learning is how quickly the child masters the task with added clues and demonstrations. Reviews of such procedures are presented by several people (Feuerstein 1979; Haywood, Filler, Shifman, & Chatelanat, 1975; Irvin & Halpern, 1979). Such tests move toward the ideal of measuring what a person can do—the person's *competencies*—in coping with life situations.

There are many other tests and many other factors beside tests to be considered in evaluating intelligence, abilities, aptitude, and intellectual deficit. Clinical judgment is often needed. One may observe, for example, during the assessment of cognitive functions that the person has other problems, such as emotional and personality difficulties, intermixed with the intellectual ones.

TESTS OF PERSONALITY
OR SOCIOEMOTIONAL
FUNCTIONING

Tom Michaels is a 43-year-old construction worker who has been laid off from his job and has had his license suspended for drunken driving. The state has a program that judges may offer people with severe driving problems as an alternative to jail sentences. Tom was routinely interviewed for that program, but the interviewer noticed that he seemed to be inattentive, uncertain about dates and events, and somewhat defensive and suspicious. A referral to the county clinic for psychological evaluation seemed in order. Should Tom have special clinical attention in addition to or instead of the regular group program for alcoholic driving offenders? After she considered what kinds of questions and alternative possibilities there might be for his condition and his treatment, Dr. Ramirez of the county clinic interviewed Tom. Does he show some brain dysfunction common in long-time alcoholics? To check this she certainly would include some quick measures of intellectual deficit—part of the WAIS and the Wechsler Memory Scale. If there seemed to be serious signs, she would refer to a neurologist and probably arrange for the Halstead-Reitan battery. Is he suffering from a serious socioemotional disturbance of some sort? Are there paranoid tendencies? Dr. Ramirez had been reading about different patterns of alcoholics on a personality inventory (Conley, 1981; Eshbaugh, Tosi, & Hoyt, 1978; Svanum & Dallas, 1981). Does Tom fit any of these types? If so, she would get some clues for suggesting a special program. Also, how supportive would his wife be, and what is his social life like? With only an hour and a half at this time to devote to him, Dr. Ramirez decided to use much of it for interviewing, to take about a half hour for a quick exploration of intellectual deficit, and then to ask Tom to answer the personality test by himself. If necessary, she would schedule another appointment after the test was scored, but she realized that with her heavy schedule that might prove impossible.

Inventories for Personality, Values, and Interests

Personality inventories such as the *Minnesota Multiphasic Personality Inventory* (MMPI) offer one important alternative to direct clinical interviewing. Personality inventories are *objective*, in the sense that they do not require the interjection of clinical judgment between the subject's response and the scores and profiles that are obtained. (However, subjectivity enters in the later use of the results.) In some cases even the test profiles are interpreted automatically, but usually the profiles are interpreted clinically. Even when computerized interpretations are provided, the clinician must decide to what degree the interpretations apply to this particular person's situation and consider alternative actions that might be taken. Because of its objectivity and the availability of aids to interpretation, the MMPI is a very widely used clinical instrument. In the early 1980s, there were about 7000 publications on the MMPI, most of which report research with the test.

The MMPI was developed by Hathaway, a psychologist, and McKinley, a psychiatrist, in the late 1930s and 1940s. In constructing the test they used *group contrast* procedures. These procedures compared two groups' answers to each item from a large pool of items. One group had a clearly identified psychiatric disorder, such as depression or schizophrenia, and the other was a large normal group. The true-false items were derived from questions typically asked on psychiatric interviews and from older personality tests. Those items for which there were statistically significant differences between patients and normals made up the initial scales. These were

Figure 5-3
Paul Meehl and Starke Hathaway in 1952 at the time of the publication of the first book giving MMPI patterns and associated case descriptions. (The Department of University Relations, University of Minnesota, 1952 photo)

refined in further studies. Ultimately ten clinical scales and four scales for test-making attitudes were constructed. These scales are illustrated in Table 5-1.

TABLE 5-1   Scales of the MMPI with Simulated Items

VALIDITY (OR TEST-TAKING ATTITUDE) SCALES

? (Cannot Say) Number of items left unanswered.

L (Lie) Fifteen items of overly good self report, such as "I smile at everyone I meet." (Answered True).

F (Frequency or Infrequency) Sixty-four items answered in the scored direction by 10 percent or less of normals, such as "There is an international plot against me." (True)

K (Correction) Thirty items reflecting defensiveness in admitting to problems, such as "I feel bad when others criticize me." (False)

CLINICAL SCALES

1 or Hs (Hypochondriasis). Thirty-three items derived from patients showing abnormal concern with bodily functions, such as "I have chest pains several times a week." (True)

2 or D (Depression) Sixty items derived from patients showing extreme pessimism, feelings of hopelessness, and slowing of thought and action, such as "I usually feel that life is interesting and worthwhile." (False)

3 or Hy (Conversion Hysteria) Sixty items from neurotic patients using physical or mental symptoms as a way of unconsciously avoiding difficult conflicts and responsibilities, such as "My heart frequently pounds so hard I can feel it." (True)

4 or Pd (Psychopathic Deviate) Fifty items from patients who show a repeated and flagrant disregard for social customs, an emotional shallowness, and an inability to learn from punishing experiences, such as "My activities and interests are often criticized by others." (True)

5 or Mf (Masculinity-Femininity) Sixty items from patients showing homoeroticism and items differentiating between men and women, such as "I like to arrange flowers." (True, scored for femininity).

6 or Pa (Paranoia) Forty items from patients showing abnormal suspiciousness and delusions of grandeur or persecution, such as "There are evil people trying to influence my mind." (True)

7 or Pt (Psychasthenia) Forty-eight items based on neurotic patients showing obsessions, compulsions, abnormal fears, and guilt and indecisiveness, such as "I save nearly everything I buy, even after I have no use for it." (True)

8 or Sc (Schizophrenia) Seventy-eight items from patients showing bizarre or unusual thoughts or behavior, who are often withdrawn and experiencing delusions and hallucinations, such as "Things around me do not seem real" (True) and "It makes me uncomfortable to have people close to me." (True)

9 or Ma (Hypomania) Forty-six items from patients characterized by emotional excitement, overactivity, and flight of ideas, such as "At times I feel very 'high' and excited for no apparent reason." (True)

0 or Si (Social Introversion) Seventy items from persons showing shyness, little interest in people, and insecurity, such as "I have the time of my life at parties." (False)

One important and interesting feature of the MMPI is the emphasis on *test-taking attitudes*. These scales aid in discovering attempts to "fake bad" or "fake good." Defensiveness and different ways of self-presentation are revealed. These procedures do not completely eliminate the possibility of faking, but they do help.

In addition to the 14 original scales, there are hundreds of additional scales and indexes developed by different research workers over the years. There are actually more scales than items on the inventory, most of them constructed by the contrasting group method—scales for anxiety, ego strength, alcoholism, laterality (of brain damage), hostility, and many other characteristics. The volumes by Dahlstrom, Welsh, and Dahlstrom (1972, 1975) summarize research on the MMPI. The availability of the extra scales besides those based on pathological groups make the MMPI applicable for assessing a wide variety of people.

In her assessment of Tom Michaels, Dr. Ramirez might very well have seen a profile like one of those shown in Figure 5-4. Knowing if the profile is fairly typical of the neurotic type of alocholic rather than the others would suggest certain kinds of treatment. She might have had the MMPI scored for the special MacAndrew alcoholism scale, on which a certain score is characteristic of people who show serious and prolonged alcoholism. On the basis of this kind of profile and collaborative information from the interview and history, Dr. Ramirez could recommend that Tom be encouraged to seek individual psychotherapy at the clinic in addition to the group counseling sessions being offered, or perhaps she would encourage him to join Alcoholics Anonymous or some other helpful group.

In addition to the MMPI, there are many other personality inventories useful for various special purposes. A rather new one with some features that improve on the MMPI is the *Millon Clinical Multiaxial Inventory* (Millon, 1977), designed to facilitate psychiatric diagnosis. A prominent nonpathology-oriented inventory, constructed like the MMPI, is the *California Psychological Inventory* (Gough, 1968). The CPI has been found useful in counseling and research with adolescents and adults because it measures characteristics such as dominance, social poise, responsibility, achievement, and flexibility. Another promising nonpsychiatric instrument is the *Jackson Personality Inventory* (Jackson, 1978), carefully developed over many years to assess such characteristics as anxiety, complexity, and energy. The *Personality Inventory for Children* (PIC) has a large number of items to be answered by the child's mother or other knowledgeable adult (Wirt & Lachar, 1981); thus, it is a report of observations and impressions, not a self-report. The scales cover academic achievement as well as emotional and interpersonal problems.

Factor analysis, a statistical procedure for identifying clusters of items that go together, has been widely used in personality inventory construction. The most prominent of these instruments is the *Sixteen Personality Factor Questionnaire* developed by Cattell (Cattell, Eber, & Tatsuoko, 1970; Kar-

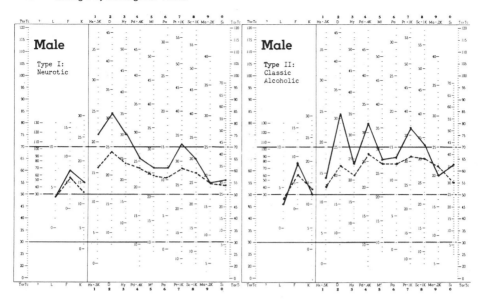

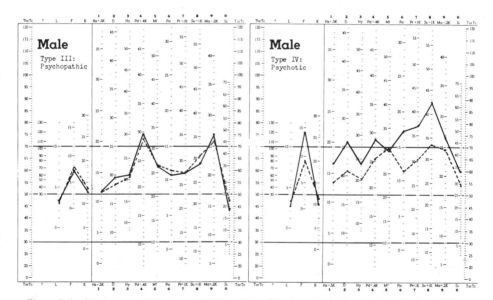

Figure 5-4 Admission and discharge MMPI profiles of the four alcoholic types (admission profile: solid line; discharge profile: broken line). (From Conley, J. J. An MMPI typology of male alcoholics: Admission, discharge and outcome comparisons. *Journal of Personality Assessment*, 1981, 45, 33–39. Copyright 1981 by the Society for Personality Assessment and used by permission)

son & O'Dell, 1976), from a long series of studies of basic personality dimensions. Other personality scales have been constructed using a rational or theory-based approach which starts with a set of concepts about personality. Items are written to fit the theory and grouped into scales on the basis of these theoretical concepts. The *Allport-Vernon-Lindzey Study of Values*, for example, was developed from Spranger's theory about the six types of human value orientation—economic, political, social, theoretical, esthetic, and religious. The test is written in such a way that respondents must choose among items that express these various values.

We have mentioned the three different methods of constructing personality inventories—group contrast, factor analysis, and the rational-theoretical approach. Goldberg and his colleagues (Ashton & Goldberg, 1973; Hase & Goldberg, 1967) have shown that each method can be useful. The best way to construct a personality inventory probably combines all three methods. For theoretical purposes, scales need to relate to a larger conceptual system, and items need to measure one characteristic clearly. For practical purposes, the scales need to relate to important outcomes, distinctions, or decisions to be made about people.

One particular aspect of personality that has been of great importance in counseling is vocational interests. Using group contrast procedures, Strong in 1927 constructed the Strong Vocational Interest Blank. It has gone through many revisions, the most recent being the *Strong-Campbell Interest Inventory* (SCII) (Campbell, 1977). Strong compared groups of successful men in various professions and occupations with men in general to develop scales with such names as "Lawyer," "Accountant," "Physician," "Psychologist," "Printer," and "Farmer." Subsequently a women's form was produced. The most recent revision combines both men's and women's forms and gives norms for both sexes. Longitudinal studies (Campbell, 1968) have shown that after about age 25, most people's interests have crystallized, and their early scores correlate well with scores achieved later in life.

Projective Techniques

We now shift to a very different way of getting at personality and socioemotional functioning—*projective techniques*. These require more skill to administer, record, and score than do the objective inventories. The stimuli are not printed statements and questions but unstructured or ambiguous material, and the purposes of the tests are likely to be unclear to the subject. George Kelly's quip (1958, p. 332) is an appropriate comment comparing the two approaches to personality: "When the subject is asked to guess what the examiner is thinking, we call it an objective test; when the examiner tries to guess what the subject is thinking, we call it a projective device." Lindzey describes such assessment devices this way:

> A projective technique is an instrument that is considered especially sensitive to covert or unconscious aspects of behavior; it permits or encourages a wide variety of subject responses, is highly multidimensional, and it evokes unusually rich or profuse response data with a minimum of subject awareness concerning the purpose of the test. (1961, p. 45)

The *projective hypothesis* is that the responses of the person to a relatively unstructured situation reveal the private world of inner predispositions, dynamics, and conflicts. Because the emphasis is on the unconscious and on conflicts between primitive impulses and the task of getting along in a world of reality where these impulses cannot be directly expressed, projective techniques have been adopted enthusiastically by psychoanalytically oriented psychiatrists and psychologists.

The major personality test of this sort was invented by Swiss psychiatrist Rorschach and published in 1921. The *Rorschach* consists of ten inkblots, to each of which the subject responds by saying what he or she perceives it might be. Various scoring systems for the responses and various systems for interpreting them have been worked out.

A rather typical referral to a psychologist who is oriented toward projective techniques would be as follows: "Dr. Meier, Mrs. Pelto has just been admitted to our ward and is showing signs of schizoid thinking. Please evaluate her and give a recommendation for diagnosis at the next staff meeting." The psychologist, Dr. Meier, checks the chart and learns something of the patient's background, perhaps talks further with psychiatrists and nurses on the ward, and then arranges an interview with Mrs. Pelto. During the interview, after some conversation and perhaps other tests, Dr. Meier shows her the Rorschach blots, one at a time, and asks Mrs. Pelto to tell what she sees. After writing down her responses to the ten blots, Dr. Meier presents each of them again and asks her where in the blot she saw each object and what it was about the blot that made it look like that. Afterwards Dr. Meier may score the answers according to the comprehensive system developed by Exner (1974; Wiener-Levy & Exner, 1981) or some other system. An example of an inkblot something like those found in the Rorschach and two scored responses can be seen in Figure 5–5. The scores reflect whether the person uses the whole card or a detail, uses space, reports movement, attributes the perception to the form of the blot and the content (human or human detail); many other scores than those shown are used in full scoring.

Rorschach responses can be viewed as a sample of a person's perceptions and thought. They can also be viewed as symbols representing complex personality processes and problems. In Mrs. Pelto's case, Dr. Meier would not base the diagnosis and interpretations on this test alone, but would also check the clinic record, the behavior on the interview, and the results of other tests, such as the MMPI, before coming to a conclusion.

There are many other projective techniques, and many books have been written about them. The most commonly used ones, in addition to the Rorschach, are the *Thematic Apperception Test* (TAT), a series of pictures about which the person is asked to tell stories; the *Draw-A-Person* and the *House-Tree-Person* techniques, which require the subject to make drawings that the examiner can interpret; and *sentence completion* tests, which simply ask the person to finish sentences such as "The trouble with my body now is

Figure 5-5   Inkblot. (From Sundberg, 1977, p. 207. Copyright© 1977 by Prentice-Hall and used by permission)

1. A flying man—A vampire

    Inquiry: Here's the evil face (in the middle). He's spread his coat. He's got spindly legs.   WS   M—   (H)

2. An elf (holding the card sideways)   D   F +   (Hd)

    Inquiry: This part (pointing to a profile on one side). Just the head. It's just like one of the little dwarfs that played with Snow White—probably it's Sleepy. Here's the nose and eyelashes.

_____," or "My mother _____." There are many other ingenious ways for psychologists to encourage people to reveal their inner thoughts. Lindzey (1961) has classified projective techniques into five main types on the basis of the behavior they are intended to evoke: *associations* (such as Rorschach or word association tests), *construction* (such as story telling on the TAT or building a scene using little dolls and blocks), *completions* (such as the sentence completion tests), *choice* or *ordering* (such as ranking pictures according to preference or placing objects in categories), and *self-expression* (such as drawings, play with certain objects, or finger painting).

Projective techniques have been much criticized on psychometric grounds. Each test may have its own scoring system, the reliability and validity of which is open to question. Many experienced psychologists do not score the Rorschach at all, even though it has the most elaborately developed system of all projective techniques, but instead use it to analyze qualitatively the characteristics of the person. There have been some notable attempts to apply psychometric development procedures to projective techniques, the most successful of which is the *Holtzman Inkblot Technique* (HIT) (Holtzman, 1975). The HIT consists of two equivalent sets of 45 blots to each of which the subject is asked to give one response. Scoring for such characteristics as hostility and anxiety is quite unambiguous and reliable, and the validity of some scores has been demonstrated through research.

After excessive enthusiasm for projective techniques during the heyday of psychoanalytic approaches in the 1940s and 1950s, there was a decline in interest, although many psychologists are still their staunch advocates. The reasons for the decline were vagueness and complexity of interpretation, lack of evidence for reliability and validity, and the amount of clinical time they take for administration and interpretation. Psychoanalysis as a personality theory became less popular among psychologists during the 1960s and 1970s, and there was increasing interest in the behavioral approach to assessment and therapy.

Behavioral Assessment

The behavioral, or social learning, approach to intervention has generated several books on behavioral assessment (Barlow, 1981; Ciminero, Calhoun, & Adams, 1977; Cone & Hawkins, 1977; Hersen & Bellack, 1976; Mash & Terdal, 1981) and a new journal, the *Journal of Behavioral Assessment.*

Assessment of behavior is closely related to therapy and case management. The plan is to obtain baseline measures of behavioral problems at the start and to repeat these assessments as therapy progresses to see if changes have occurred. If they do not occur, the clinician can modify the treatment plan. The purpose of behavioral assessment is to produce evidence of what is wrong and suggest procedures to be used in changing the behavior. This demand for evidence leads to much record keeping and a healthy regard for research. Behaviorists look upon personality as a set of skills or abilities that can be acquired or modified through learning.

Thus the aims and concepts of the behavioral approach are quite different from those of the objective and projective procedures. Table 5–2 presents a comparison of the three approaches. It is important to note that behavioral assessors look at whatever they obtain from the client as a *sample;* the clinician may generalize from the sample to describe the likelihood of similar behavior in similar situations, but sweeping generalizations are not encouraged. For instance, if little Rickie hits his mother several times while she is talking with the psychologist in the office, the behavioral clinician may conclude that hitting is characteristic of Rickie, perhaps especially when he is with his mother. A clinician using the objective approach would, in contrast, be trying to establish what the *correlates*, or the features associated with the behavior, are or to what they relate. Mother-hitting might be classified with other attack behavior on an aggressiveness scale and correlated with school problems or child abuse in the home. A clinician using the projective approach looks at behavior as a *sign* of inner problems or conflicts. Such a clinician might infer from Rickie's frequent hitting of his mother that he feels she has not given him enough affection or that he suffers from an unresolved

TABLE 5-2   Comparisons of the Three Major Assessment Approaches

	BEHAVIORAL TECHNIQUES	OBJECTIVE TECHNIQUES	PROJECTIVE TECHNIQUES
Primary Aim:	To determine antecedents and consequents of problem behavior (S-R)	To develop test scores that relate to criteria of problem or solution (R-R)	To elicit material of importance for inferring inner dynamics of person (R-O)
Construction methods:	Individually tailored data collection on problem behavior, counting, recording	Theoretical or empirical scale construction, norms, validity, reliability	Theoretical or impressionistic selection of ambiguous stimuli and classification of signs
Typical stimulus format:	Natural or contrived situations, interviews, report form for own behavior	Paper-and-pencil, self-reporting, verbal personality inventories, attitude scales	Ambiguous, open-ended stimuli, both verbal and nonverbal.
Typical data produced:	Observational reports, coded records, behavior counts	Choices on verbal items, scores, profiles	Perceptual reports, verbal narratives, observations, scores
Obtained data treated as:	Sample	Correlate	Sign
Level of subjective interpretation:	Low	Medium	High
Time scale:	Here and now, baseline plus follow-up of problems; little use of history	Mixed; predictive	Concerned with childhood history, long-range dynamics
Classifications and "language" used:	Behavioral excesses, deficits, and inappropriateness; functional analysis; learning terms. Specific language.	Traits, diagnostic categories, psychometric terms, social-psychological terms.	Psychodynamic terms; psychiatric categories; perceptual-cognitive terms. Global language.
Principal theoretical underpinning:	Behavioral learning theory, functional analysis. Assumption that actions maintained by current reinforcement.	Trait and factor theories, attitude theories, psychometrics. Few assumptions; empirical search for connections.	Psychoanalysis, perceptual-cognitive theories. Assumption that people primarily motivated by unconscious forces.
Examples of assessment instruments:	Few standard devices; Behavioral Coding System, Fear Survey Schedules	Many standardized inventories and scales, MMPI, CPI, Strong, EPPS, PIC, A-V-L, F scale	Great variety, Rorschach, TAT, sentence completion, Draw-A-Person, Bender, World Test, play situations

Adapted from Sundberg 1977, pp. 154–155.

Oedipus complex. The projectivist tends to make theoretical assumptions about psychosexual development and unconscious motivation, which both objective and behavioral approaches would avoid.

The variety of behavioral assessment techniques is very great, as the books mentioned will testify. Although the ideal is to observe behavior directly, behaviorally oriented people use almost all the procedures that other assessors employ, including even some projective procedures, such as asking a person for three wishes or imaginary stories (Lazarus, 1971). They use the results, however, as behavior samples, not correlates or symbols of "deeper" characteristics. Cognitive behaviorists who include thinking as an aspect of behavior, such as problem solving, and imagining, have broadened the range of these assessment techniques, which will be discussed in Chapter 9 in connection with therapy.

Two commonly used self-report procedures can serve here as examples of behavioral assessment. The *Fear Survey Schedule* (Tasto, Hickson, & Rubin, 1971; Wolpe & Lang, 1964, 1969) lists situations, objects, and people which the client rates for fearfulness on a scale of 1 to 5, or 1 to 7. Topics such as the following are listed: strange dogs, snakes, cemeteries, roller coasters, being alone, failing a test, hypodermic needles, or seeing a fight. This inventory is usually used with individuals to identify problems and it can also detect which respondents in a large group would be good subjects for research on fears and phobias. It can be used repeatedly to chart changes in fears, as treatment proceeds.

The *Pleasant Events Schedule* and its companion, the *Unpleasant Events Schedule* (Lewinsohn & Amenson, 1978; Lewinsohn & Lee, 1981; Lewinsohn & Talkington, 1979; MacPhillamy & Lewinsohn, 1982), are used in treatment of depressed persons and research on depression. The items were obtained by having people keep track of events that please them or make them feel unhappy. Examples of pleasant events are "having a warm bath" or "quietly reading a book." Examples of unpleasant events are "having to tell someone I don't agree with them" or "catching a cold." The person checks these items and receives a score which can be compared with others for the total number of pleasant and unpleasant experiences checked. In work with individuals the schedules can assist in planning and monitoring therapy. The therapist can review the list of events and help the client increase pleasant experiences and decrease the number of unpleasant ones.

Other Tests and Procedures

We have mentioned only a few of the tests available. There are many other tests, some of which are listed at the end of this chapter. There are tests that cannot be classified with either the ability or the personality tests but share features of both, such as the procedures for assessing *cognitive style* (Witkin & Goodenough, 1981). There are techniques for revealing an individual's *per-*

sonal constructs, the mental structures controlling how the individual's world of values and personal relationships is perceived (Landfield & Leitner, 1980). Little (1977; Palys & Little, in press) has developed an important variation called *personal projects* whereby the goal-oriented efforts of individuals may be analyzed. There are ways of finding out how *creative* a child or adult is likely to be in dealing with problems (Nappe, 1980). There are *biographical data banks* designed to identify the directions in which the circumstances of one's life have channeled one's development (Owens & Shoenfeldt, 1979). There are ways of assessing psychological states and traits by measuring the functioning of physiological systems such as blood pressure, heart rates, or galvanic skin responses. These will be discussed in Chapter 7.

Finally, in discussing testing procedures we should note that *ratings*, *codings*, and *checklists* are methods for quantifying observations and impressions of judges and constitute an important part of assessment. Some of them have been standardized and are widely used. For instance, the *California Q-sort* (Block, 1961) is a method for sorting a set of cards with descriptive phrases to picture a person's psychological characteristics and psychodynamics. Another example is the 75-item *Inpatient Multidimensional Psychiatric Scale* (IMPS) described by Lorr (1971) to be used by professional interviewers with individual patients to provide ratings on such characteristics as hostile belligerence, disorientation, and anxious depression. Gough's widely used *Adjective Check List* (ACL) lists 300 adjectives, such as "helpful," "conceited," and "interests narrow," that subjects or observers can use to describe themselves or others in a few minutes. The ACL has been used to develop descriptions of high- and low-scoring people on the MMPI and CPI, descriptions which can later be used as an aid to interpretation of scales or profiles. Masterson (1975) describes the ACL and other such lists. For suggestions about getting acquainted with a wide array of tests, see the end of this chapter.

TESTING IN LARGER SYSTEMS

The great majority of tests that have been published are designed for the assessment of individuals, not larger systems. Yet, as we have pointed out in earlier chapters, the possibility of planning interventions at system levels larger than the individual has become important for clinical workers; the assessment of how a family, a schoolroom group, a department, or a whole community is functioning becomes a major challenge. The assessment question may also be seen as the way that a system, at any level from the individual person to the community, adapts to its environment—its ecological competence. Here we shall point to only a few of the attempts to standardize testing procedures for these purposes. Others will be discussed in the special chapters on larger systems. There are three major methods to quantify these larger assessment problems: (1) by collecting, summing, and organizing individual's perceptions pertinent to the larger system, (2) by observing the interaction of people in a group or other situation and by coding and organizing the observations, and (3) by compiling and analyzing recorded data about the system, such as records or ratings of objects or products. Examples of the last method would be the work of demographers with the statistics on a city or of a procedure such as a checklist of objects in a home (e.g., Gough's Home Index, 1971). The first two are the most common in the psychological literature.

One set of procedures building on individual preferences is *sociometric* measures—that is, the assessment of attractions or repulsions within a specified group. A graphic portrayal of these is called a *sociogram*, which is derived from asking a set of people who know each other well to indicate others with whom they would like to do something. For instance, Figure 5–6 is a result of preferences for roommates in a college dormitory. A group of young women well acquainted with each other were asked to give their first two choices for a roommate in a two-person room. Their choices are indicated by arrows. As can be seen immediately, one person, Andrea, is chosen by many; she is called a *star*. Other women, Mary and Doris, are not chosen by anyone; they are called *isolates*. Studies of sociometric choices show that they compare very well in reliability and validity with psychological tests and that they seem very relevant to daily choices and activities (Byrd, 1951; Fiske, 1971; Lindzey & Byrne, 1968). At first glance, it is rather surprising that sociometrics have been used very little in clinical work;

Figure 5-6 Sociogram of choices for roommates in a college dormitory. (From Sundberg, 1977, p. 123. Copyright © 1977 by Prentice-Hall and used by permission)

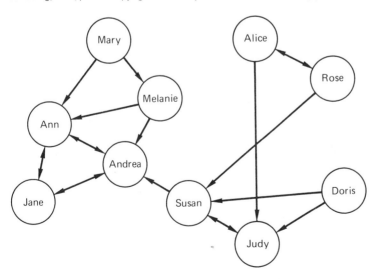

however, there are many practical problems in getting groups together to rate an individual client or set of clients.

An alternative approach is to ask a client to list or rate people they know who do or would provide social support; from such a rating a clinician can develop an understanding of the person's *social network*, or *support system*. The amount and quality of help from others is an important element in work with individuals or larger systems. The *buffering hypothesis* states that a person's (or system's) ability to withstand stress and cope with life crises is related to the available support system—that is, the circle of friends and helpers. On closer investigation this hypothesis seems to be true for the certain kinds of help that match the client's needs; having a confidante with whom to talk problems over is particularly important (Cohen & McKay, 1983; Heller, 1979).

A simple graphic way of showing an individual's social network may be used to illustrate how clinicians may innovate to develop their own informal testlike procedures. A clinician who is interested in the client's perception of his or her "circle of friends" may use a blank piece of paper to do what is shown in Figure 5–7. While discussing the social life and needs of a client, the psychologist would ask the person to write the first names or initials of people that she or he meets and talks with fairly frequently, placing them at various

Figure 5-7 Perceived social network of a 63-year-old woman client, Mrs. Y.

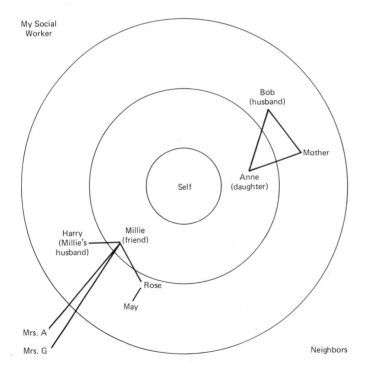

distances to show feelings of closeness. The innermost circle represents the self; the next circle is for the most intimate relationships; less close ones are in the next circle and occasional but still important people are in the outermost spaces. The psychologist may ask the client to draw connecting lines between the names of people who frequently communicate with each other, thus showing graphically how small groups are formed around the client. In the example in Figure 5-7, Mrs. Y sees her daughter, Anne, and her friend, Millie, as the only people with whom she is close. Her husband is more distant, as is her mother and other people. She perceives Millie as having many more friends than she does. The clinician can use such a procedure to lead into many questions, such as the age of people, the forms of help exchanged, and possibilities for changing the picture, thus exploring the client's social world. Individuals in families or other groups can be asked to make similar drawings and answer questions for comparisons between members of the group. With such a group, a larger network of social and helping outreach could be revealed. Although this technique is not a test as such, it can be a useful assessment exercise, and it would be possible through research to make it a more rigorous procedure.

Another kind of assessment technique involves interaction, *role playing*, or improvisation (McReynolds, 1978). Role playing is used fairly frequently in treatment, but it can also be used for assessment if it is formulated as a regularized procedure to be repeated with different people. Then it may be called a *situational test*. Probably the best-known tests of this sort are those employed in World War II by the Office of Strategic Services (1948) to screen people for espionage and sabotage under the stressful conditions of working in enemy territory. One role-playing situation involved instruction to two candidates, A and B; A had borrowed B's car and had an accident while driving through an overlooked stop sign. The two had just met when the improvisation began; as A and B interacted, observers rated their performance on such dimensions as interpersonal tact and sensitivity and dominance or submission. Another situational test required the candidate to construct a small bridge with the help of uncooperative assistants who were really stooges. Observers in such improvisations judge the persons' abilities to act out a role, their comfort in dealing with the situation, and other personal and interpersonal characteristics. Other forms of situational tests simply ask a group of subjects to discuss some topic—e.g., the Leaderless Group Discussion (Bass, 1954). Situational tests can be quantified in much the same way that an interview can—through rating scales, checklists, and even quantitative counts of words on a transcript of the interaction. McReynolds (1978) reviews a number of such approaches and indicates that considerable reality and validity can be obtained with trained stooges and judges using standardized situations designed to bring out specific behavior. These situational tests are usually seen as meaningful and interesting to subjects, and some could be well integrated into clinical therapy or counseling. They are, however, time consuming and usually cannot be managed by an assessor working alone.

The assessment of *family interaction* and *family environment* is an important aspect of clinical work, still in its early stages. One of the rather common ways to get an understanding of a family is called the *revealed differences technique* (Bodin, 1968). Each member of the family fills out a questionnaire or takes a test alone; then the family group is brought together and asked to resolve their differences in front of observers. (Sometimes they are told what differences they have, and sometimes they are not; in the latter case the procedure is called the *unrevealed differences technique.*) The cooperativeness or obstinancy of family members in arriving at a joint decision and the relative dominance of particular members in different areas of family functioning can be observed. The observations can be rated or coded by judges. Another technique by Moos (1975) is the *Family Environment*

BOX 5-1 *THE PREPOSTEROUS PSEUDO-PSYCHOLOGICAL PERSONALITY PROCEDURE*

Making up items like those on the MMPI can be fun. In an unusually clever review of objective tests, Goldberg (1974) lists several fictitious items devised by the noted humorist Art Buchwald and others. Below are some of them along with others we have concocted:

1. I twirl at least once a day.
2. I hate television, radio, and other forms of commun.cation.
3. When I was a child, I was an imaginary playmate.
4. Frantic screams make me nervous.
5. Animals often try to tease me.
6. I have often met people who are copies of myself.
7. One of my fears is that someone will cut off my nose.
8. I would like to drink blood.
9. Killing flies gives me great pleasure.
10. There was never a time when I was not completely happy and content.
11. Some people never look at anyone.
12. I use shoe polish to excess.
13. It is hard to concentrate in a room full of mice.
14. I am someone else.
15. I can seldom tell the sex of people on the street.
16. As a child I was deprived of ice cream.
17. If I had power, I would turn night into day.
18. The future will never come.
19. I cannot read.
20. When in trouble it is best to look dumb.
21. My father and mother were the same.
22. Those who sing in the bathroom should be shot.
23. I would like to be baked in a pie.
24. Round buttons turn me on.
25. This questionnaire has given me great pain.

Scale (FES). This instrument has ten subscales covering such topics as family cohesiveness, conflict, achievement orientation, moral-religious emphasis, and control. The answers of all the members in the family can be averaged to get a family profile, or differences among family members in their perceptions of the family can be studied. These measures will be discussed again in Chapter 11.

Some ingenious ways of assessing still larger systems such as organizations and communities will be covered in later chapters. Social climates of schools, industries, and organizations can be studied by obtaining reports from participants on the characteristics of the system of which they are parts. Often public records are helpful for such assessments as case records, office memos, and census data (Mikawa, 1975). Several environmental psychologists have developed promising methods for assessing behavior settings and the physical environment that might be applied in some clinical work (Craik, 1971; McKechnie, 1978; Wicker, 1981).

CRITIQUE

How adequate is the conceptualization of tests and testing?   As in many areas of psychology, a great deal of work has been done, but a great deal remains. Many clinical tests have "grown up like Topsy" without much connection with theory. Just as physicians use aspirin or other medications because they work even though they do not know how, clinical psychologists find many tests useful, even though they have not developed a full-fledged theory connecting them to the origins of behavioral disorders or the course of improvement. In an ideal world, tests should dovetail with theories about human abilities and performance, personality, psychopathology, psychotherapy, and behavior change. These theories should guide researchers to the important test dimensions and the criteria for their studies, but at present many of the most useful clinical procedures are quite atheoretical. Of course, arguments can be made that the Wechsler tests and the MMPI, for instance, have implicit hypotheses or low-level theory. Certainly there are assumptions about the importance of including the given items in the tests, and there are general ideas about the scope of coverage of such tests. However, the tests are not derived from explicit systems of information processing or personality. On the other hand, not many theory-based tests have made much of an impact in clinical work; they are a long way from the popularity and utility of the Wechsler tests and the MMPI.

On one side of the questions about the theoretical status of tests is what we have just mentioned about personality and psychopathology. On the other side are the questions about the adequacy for clinical purposes of psychometrics and test theory. Concepts of validity and reliability are interwoven into the thinking of every clinical psychology student and are certainly important and useful in considering individual tests. However, in clinical practice we are not collecting psychometric data on large groups under controlled conditions. The actual usage of tests must relate to conceptualizations about how agencies make decisions in the real world and how people use information about other people and their situations. This larger view of testing should incorporate not just traditional psychometric theory but also ideas about decision making, impression formation, information processing, and organizational and systems theory in general. Cronbach and Gleser (1965) have begun to address parts of the problem, particularly the use of tests in institutional decision making about personnel. However, so far we have only a limited coverage of decision making about or with individuals, especially as decisions relate to actions taken in therapy and case management. The implicit theory in most articles in clinical journals is a low-level empirical one: Find out how test results relate to other tests and to outcomes.

As we noted at the beginning, there are few clear links between clinical assessment problems and the tests available. The psychologist must perform the intermediate step of conceptualizing the major questions and choosing the instruments that come closest to answering those questions. Tests have primarily been developed to fit the individual system level and the psychopathological orientation. We have a limited number of tests for other levels and orientations. A full-scale matrix of levels and kinds of assessment approaches could be an intermediate step in moving toward conceptual clarity (Sundberg, 1977). Psychologists do not have the gaps clearly in mind and use only the tests that are available. If they could see the broad range of needs, perhaps they would invent other tools and more clearly choose methods of value. In developing such a conceptual framework, it seems particularly likely that computerized processes will be of help in handling the complexity of possibilities for assessment of human functions.

How practical are tests?   This chapter has touched only briefly on a small sample of the wide variety of tests, each with different histories, purposes, and psychometric properties. The field of testing has produced an array of tools, as if on a workshop wall—an axe for chopping down a tree, a spade for digging up the soil, a clipper for trimming a hedge. Each of these differs from the others in sharpness, size, and ease of usage. One would not use a clipper for cutting down a tree or digging up the soil. Likewise one has to know how suitable a test is for the clinical task at hand. One cannot say that all testing is bad, or all good. One must always consider the situation and the alternative tools available for collecting, organizing, and interpreting information about a person or larger system. A client is almost never assessed on the basis of one test. The broader assessment task involves interviewing, observing, obtaining information from family or other clinical workers, and, when tests are used, combining findings from several tests or a battery of tests. But clearly, testing plays an important part in clinical psychology as surveys have shown (Levy & Fox, 1975; Wade & Baker, 1977).

In evaluating the usefulness of tests, we need first of all to examine their psychometric status. A few general impressions about classes of tests can be summarized from sources such as the *Mental Measurements Yearbooks*. In general, the reliability of tests, especially ability and objective tests, is high. The reliability coefficients of most achievement and intelligence tests are at least .80, which means that they are accurate enough to be used for individual predictions. The reliability of personality measures varies a great deal. Some of the MMPI scales have satisfactory reliability (over .75), but others are quite low. It is difficult even to measure reliability of projective techniques. Many of the projective techniques suffer in reliability because they have too few "items"—that is, they do not have enough nearly equivalent stimuli to check whether the same behavior is elicited repeatedly. Reliability is important because it indicates how accurate the score is. Any test score must be viewed not as an exact point, but as a band of possible scores. Because of their low reliability, this band or range of scores is much higher around most personality test scores than around most ability test scores. Thus we have to be more skeptical of personality interpretations and check them repeatedly against other test findings and life history.

Validity is even more important than reliability, especially when it relates to prediction of clinical outcomes or future behavior or when it shows whether a test gives a useful portrayal of the person's possibilities in the life situation. We cannot expect extremely high correlations between test behavior and behavior in life situations because life situations are very complex, and accidents and unpredictable events do occur. As with reliability, tests of maximum performance (tests of achievement, ability, and intelligence) tend to rank higher in validity than do tests of characteristic performance (personality inventories or projective techniques). College entrance examinations, for example, are often found to correlate at about the .50 level with scholastic performance. Many intelligence tests correlate to about the same degree with school performance and teachers' ratings.

Validity coefficients of personality tests average considerably lower. Society does not provide handy external criteria for personality comparable to school grades recorded over several years, and personal behavior of the kind that personality measurements attempt to capture may be quite situation oriented and variable. Many objective personality scales will show correlations of around .30 with criteria such as psychiatric diagnoses or peer ratings of such characteristics as dominance or aggressiveness. Such a correlation allows an assessor to predict better than chance how a large group of people will score on a criterion—but not much better. About 90 percent of the variance (the variation among individuals) is due to other sources. With projective techniques the validity coefficients are likely to be even lower, if they are available at all.

The many "slips 'twixt the cup and the lip" to be found in validity studies include the limited sampling of behavior that a test provides, the clients' test-taking attitudes or subsequent attitudes toward situations in which they are being observed and rated, and intervening experiences, both in therapy and outside. It is understandable why a few responses to questions or inkblots do not correlate well with later behavior. Interviews and behavioral assessment techniques have many of the same validity limitations and some additional ones. An advantage of behavioral assessment is that the strictly behavioral measures are often concrete and readily observable and are directly related to desired therapy changes. However, behaviorally oriented psychologists need to remember that clients vary in their accuracy in observing behavioral problems (Lorber, 1981) and that the observation process itself can create unwanted reactions in clients.

Norms constitute another psychometric problem for many tests, as they may not be appropriate to the group with which the clinician wants to make a comparison. Clinical comparisons should be made against *relevant* groups. For instance, a Stanford-Binet intelligence test on a first-grader who speaks only Spanish will not measure the child's real ability to handle school tasks after she or he learns English. There may be some useful indication of reasoning and spatial ability on a task of drawing or block manipulation, but even with these nonverbal tasks, the content of a strange language situation is not likely to call out a representative effort from the youngster. On the other hand, although a set of norms for an equivalent test in the Spanish language will tell more about real ability, it may not provide comparisons with children in a typical first-grade English language school. As mentioned before, the SOMPA procedure (Mercer, 1979) is one attempt to overcome cross-cultural comparison problems. Similar problems obtain for personality tests; there is still controversy about whether one can use MMPI norms for American blacks although it seems they score higher on certain scales (Gynther, 1979; Sundberg & Gonzales, 1981). Another problem with norms is that they are often based on a national sample or on one taken many years ago, and the local situation may be quite different. It is important for the clinician to recognize these differences in interpreting test results and to develop local norms for special uses.

In addition to these psychometric qualities there are many practical factors that are just as important—factors such as the cost of the test, the amount of training required to give it, the amount of time required to administer it, its appearance and interest for clients, its acceptability and reputation with the staff, and the amount of assistance with interpretation that the publisher or others provide. In a given situation there is a cost-benefit ratio for each test that the clinician must consider.

How socially worthwhile is testing? In recent decades psychological testing of all kinds, but especially educational and industrial testing, has been sharply criticized. Clinicians themselves vary a great deal in their attitudes. Some see testing as being unfavorable to the therapy process and refrain from any testing at all. Some assert that testing leads to mechanical labeling and the formation of misleading impressions based on comparisons that are not necessary. A few criticize testing as a kind of ritual in the clinical culture that may someday seem as quaint as phrenology does to us now, or as unscientific as tea leaf reading or astrological characterization. Others are ardent devotees of particular procedures such as the Rorschach, the Halstead-Reitan, or the MMPI, and nearly every clinical worker knows a psychological "ace" who can do remarkably accurate characterizations or predictions with a favorite test. Some psychologists like testing so much that they devote most of their professional time to it. All, or nearly all, psychologists would agree, however, that tests are limited and must be used with other information for clinical decisions and image making, and they also recognize that some knowledge about tests is important for anyone wishing to understand and evaluate the past, present, and future of clinical psychology.

Looking at the full testing task, there are many nonpsychometric considerations that relate to the social context and purposes that make the job worthwhile. The psychologist must come up with a description of the person and the person's life situation and with recommendations about important decisions—such as incarceration, psychotherapy, or ways of dealing with family relationships. The clinician has to use ways of collecting information that are reasonably familiar and reasonably relevant to the clinical purposes. Often the clinician feels that previous experience and training with a particular test, even if it is not very good psychometrically, are important for understanding the task. The survey by Wade and Baker (1977) has shown that most clinicians rate personal experience as more important than anything else in choice of tests. People who are highly trained on projective techniques or the MMPI tend to persist in using these techniques; undoubtedly they mean more to such clinicians than other, unfamiliar tests would, facilitating observation of the manner in which the person talks or handles test materials, not just the test scores. The problem is one of overreliance on one's intuition and half-checked impressions. Responsible clinicians are continually attempting to improve their knowledge and skills. The utility of tests is highly dependent on the clinician who does the interpretations and writes the report, as we shall see in the next chapter. In the hands of a clinician who has the client's interests firmly in mind and is competent and responsible, tests can be very helpful.

The major social objections to tests have centered around selection procedures which tend to shut out minority groups from jobs or shunt minority children into special education classes. Several American states have passed laws prohibiting group intelligence tests. The U.S. government has set up guidelines for insuring equal opportunity in hiring. Also, some people see tests as an invasion of privacy. Despite some very vocal opposition to standardized testing, public opinion polls show that the public in general is not greatly concerned. Some psychologists are alarmed by legislative attempts to overregulate testing (Lerner, 1981). Limitations on testing may work against

BOX 5-2 *QUALITY AND EQUALITY—BASIC ISSUES IN TESTING*

Should the basic applied purpose in developing tests be the promotion of psychometric quality—that is the reliability and validity of tests in predicting social criteria such as success in school or at work? Or should the purpose of testing and assessment in general be to facilitate the promotion of such societal goals as equality and social justice? In the later half of the twentieth century, tests have become part of the great debate about how to achieve greater social development in such countries as the United States. The debate between quality and equality relates to the context in which testing is to be judged—a context which has changed over time (Gordon & Terrell, 1981). Psychometric testing developed in the early part of the century in a context of selection. Intelligence tests in France and elsewhere were developed to pick out children who could profit from regular schooling, and intelligence and personality tests were developed during the two world wars to select people for the military services and especially those who could do well in expensive officer training or flight training. Much of the civil service selection was based on the notion of meritocracy—that is, only those who had superior knowledge or skills should be offered government jobs. Industry selected workers for similar reasons. Most psychometric devices were primarily used to select those most likely to succeed, thus eliminating all but the highest scoring persons. Strong arguments can be made to continue that practice—a search for talent.

On the other side, people challenge the purposes of testing. When education is compulsory for all children in many countries and the kind of schooling is limited mainly by the imagination and the willingness of citizens to allocate resources, then testing may be used to deny opportunity and assistance. Similarly with employment, most countries are able to provide work for all if people are willing to use their resources for that purpose. If the commitment is to social justice, the criteria for assessment would not be merit or talent alone, but fairness, sensitivity to diversity in skills and backgrounds, and appropriateness to social context. "Under such a commitment the purpose of assessment can no longer be to sort, to predict or to select with a view to identifying and rewarding a chosen few who are most likely to succeed" (Gordon & Terrell, 1981, p. 1168). Technical characteristics of tests are subsidiary to purposes of testing, which determine the standards and criteria to be used. These need to relate to differences in culture, language, social class, gender, and conditions of handicap and development. People would not be categorized in terms of current functioning alone, but in terms of potentiality for learning and for occupying positions in a relevant community.

Can these two goals—psychometric quality and human equality—be brought into harmony? Many of the arguments for the democratization of testing are in line with the clinical approach, wherein an individual and relevant contexts are studied intensively, but clinical attention is limited to a very small proportion of the population. Mass testing for schools or industries does not typically have this individual clinical concern, but individuals are nevertheless affected. Is it possible for testing, whether in a mass or individual procedure, to be responsive to the functional characteristics of persons as well as their particular environments? Can we apply psychometric rigor to testing used in the promotion of greater opportunity for neglected sectors of society?

the identification of talent and other positive benefits. Those interested in this complex controversy will find the references at the end of this chapter useful.

There is a ferment in the testing field, stimulated by public criticisms and the advent of the behavioral and cognitive movements. It is likely that the coming years will see many new kinds of tests, especially those concerned with learning potentials, information processing, neuropsychological functioning, behavioral recording, and environmental or situational assessment. It also seems likely that there will be improvements in relating individual tests to other tests and other information. It would not be surprising to see computerized analyses based on multidimensional procedures for studying a wide variety of functions of individuals as well as various kinds of settings. Testing, although it is properly criticized, still holds much promise for the future.

SUMMARY

There are thousands of psychological tests, many of which could be used in clinical practice. The clinician chooses particular tests to elicit the information needed for decisions and descriptions about or with the client and the relevant situations. In testing it is important to maintain standard conditions but at the same time to establish a cooperative relationship and to be sensitive to the ways in which clients vary. These matters must be considered in interpreting results.

In a broad and general way tests can be divided into those that attempt to elicit maximum performance, such as intelligence, ability, and achievement tests, and those that aim to elicit characteristic performance, such as personality and behavioral procedures. Under the first category come the widely used Wechsler intelligence tests for children and adults as well as many other intelligence tests. Tests of intellectual deficit or cerebral functioning also fit into this category. An important trend is toward the measurement of learning potential—that is, the testing of the ability of a subject to improve through successive trials in response to demonstrations or instructions.

Tests of personality and socioemotional functioning include a wide variety of objective techniques, such as the Minnesota Multiphasic Personality Inventory; projective techniques, such as the Rorschach; and behavioral assessment, such as surveys of fears, reinforcements, and pleasant or unpleasant events. One important difference among these three techniques is the way in which they treat the test results. The behavioral procedures treat the results as samples; the objective ones predominantly as correlates of something else; and the projective techniques, as signs of underlying or unconscious conditions in the person. In this section we also discussed the three ways in which the scales of tests (especially inventories) can be constructed—that is, test developers select and put items together by group contrast methods (by using items significantly differentiating between normal and abnormal samples), by factor analysis, and by rational-theoretical judgments. Supplementing ordinary tests is a set of procedures used to record impressions such as ratings, adjective checklists, and so on.

Most psychological tests are for individuals, but some procedures have been developed for assessing larger systems. Examples are sociometric procedures that produce sociograms, ways of reporting support systems, role playing or situational tests, family interaction or environment tests, and some attempts to get at organizational climates.

In the critique we noted that theoretical development of tests leaves much to be done both on personality and psychopathology and on psychometrics. We reviewed the practical nature of tests and noted that reliabilities of well-established tests tend to be high but validity figures are only moderate at best, especially with personality measures. Norms and other psychometric qualities need to be studied with the groups of most relevance to the setting in which the clinician works; clinicians especially need to be aware of cross-cultural problems in using tests. We also noted that the use of tests has been criticized in regard to several social problems, especially on matters of confidentiality and minority group disadvantage in the United States. Tests need to be seen as tools that if properly used can help clients achieve their highest potentials.

RECOMMENDED READINGS

Important Clinical Tests

What are the most important tests for students to know about in order to understand testing that clinicians do and become familiar with procedures often mentioned in the clinical publications? The following list emphasizes 20 primary tests frequently used in clinical work, supplemented at the end of each section by additional tests. The 20 primary tests, each of which is in dark print, were based on surveys of test usage (Brown & McGuire, 1976; Goh, Teslow, & Fuller, 1981; Lubin, Wallis, & Paine, 1971; Wade, Baker, Morton, & Baker, 1978) and on tabulations of frequent mentions in recent major books on assessment and clinical psychology (Anastasi, 1982; Bellack & Hersen, 1980; Bernstein & Nietzel, 1980; Golden, 1979; Kaplan & Saccuzzo, 1982; Kendall & Norton-Ford, 1982; Phares, 1979; Walker, 1981). In a recent survey of APA counseling psychologists, Fee, Elkins, and Boyd (1982) report that the following, all of which are included among the 20 listed below, be learned by students (in order of preference): MMPI, WAIS, Strong-Campbell Interest Inventory, WISC-R, TAT, Bender-Gestalt, Rorschach, and Stanford-Binet. Secondary tests, in each paragraph, were selected from among additional mentions in the foregoing books in order to round out the picture of the clinical tools available. If students know about the primary 20 tests, they will be able to appreciate most of what they find in the testing literature and in clinical practice. All these tests are described in Anastasi (1982) and most in the various *Mental Measurements Yearbooks* (Buros, 1972, 1978).

Intelligence Tests:
Stanford-Binet Intelligence Scale, Wechsler Adult Intelligence Scale (WAIS and
WAIS-R) Wechsler Intelligence Scale for Children (WISC and WISC-R),
Wechsler Preschool and Primary Scale of Intelligence (WPPSI), and Progressive
Matrices.

The first four are widely used, individually administered tests, appropriate for different age levels, the WAIS being solely for adults. The Progressive Matrices, developed by Raven in Great Britain, can be given as a group test and consists entirely of sets of figures that require discrimination and reasoning and little verbal understanding; it is widely used in Europe and "has received growing recognition in America" (Anastasi, 1982, p. 291). Supplementing these five are many additional tests of intelligence; among them, McCarthy Scales of Children's Abilities, Peabody Picture Vocabulary Test, Bayley Scales of Infant Development, Porteus Maze Test, the Quick Test, and the Goodenough-Harris Drawing Test (formerly the Draw-A-Man) are widely used.

Adaptation, Achievement, and Special Ability Tests:
Adaptive Behavior Scale (ABS), Wide Range Achievement Test (WRAT).

The ABS was developed by the American Association on Mental Deficiency; it is to be answered by parents or teachers and covers development of personal care, use of language, responsibility, socialization, and other aspects of daily life that are often impaired with mentally retarded or emotionally disturbed children. The WRAT is frequently used by clincians to provide a quick screening for learning problems at the preschool to adult levels. Other general and well-known tests are the Vineland Social Maturity Scale, the Illinois Test of Psycholinguistic Abilities, the Porch Index of Communicative Ability, and a large number of educational tests. Of value for clinicial rehabilitative settings are some occupational ability measures such as the Bennett Mechanical Comprehension Test, the Minnesota Clerical Test, and the General Aptitude Test Battery.

Tests of Cerebral Function:
Bender Visual-Motor Gestalt Test, Halstead-Reitan Neuropsychological Battery,
Luria-Nebraska Neuropsychobiological Battery (Golden, 1981).

One of the most popular clinical procedures is the copying task commonly known as the Bender. It is, however, a very limited indicator of "organicity" (Bigler & Ehrfurth, 1981). The other two are extensive sets of different kinds of tasks. In addition to the Bender, other widely used short tests are the Memory for Designs and the Wechsler Memory Scale.

Tests of Interests and Personal Orientations:
Strong-Campbell Interest Inventory.

Other widely used tests are the Kuder Occupational Interest Survey; Kuder Preference Record-Vocational; Personal Orientation Inventory and the Personal Orientation Dimensions Inventory, reviewed by Forest and Sicz (1981); Self-Directed Search; and Study of Values.

Personality—Inventories:
California Psychological Inventory (CPI), Minnesota Multiphasic Personality Inventory (MMPI), Sixteen Personality Factor Questionnaire (16 PF), Personality Inventory for Children (PIC).

Other personality inventories of importance in the literature are the Edwards Personal Preference Schedule, Eysenck Personality Questionnaire, Jackson Personality Inventory (Jackson, 1978), Millon Clinical Multiaxial Inventory, Myers-Briggs Type Indicator, State-Trait Anxiety Inventory.

Personality—Projective Techniques:
Draw-A-Person (D-A-P, Machover), House-Tree-Person (HTP), Rorschach, Rotter Incomplete Sentence Blank (ISB), Thematic Apperception Test (TAT).

The first two are drawing tests, the validities of which have been sharply questioned by reviewers (e.g., Falk, 1981; Swenson 1968) but which are still high on test usage surveys. The Rotter ISB is the best known of many sentence completion tests, a form of projective procedure that has been considered by some as the most valid (P. Goldberg, 1965). There are many other widely known projective procedures, including the Children's Apperception Test, Hand Test (reviewed by Hoover, 1978), Holtzman Inkblot Techniques, and Rosenzweig Picture-Frustration Study.

Miscellaneous Tests and Techniques:
Many other tests listed in Anastasi (1982, pp. 670–682), the Buros Yearbooks, and Sundberg, Tyler, and Taplin (1973, pp. 561–569) are of value to clinical situations (such as the Adjective Check List and observational coding systems mentioned in this book). Many other procedures are not formally published by commercial companies and are found only in journal articles and books and in compendia as those by Chun, Cobb, and French (1975), Comrey, Backer, and Glaser (1973), and Goldman and Busch (1978). Behavioral assessment techniques have not been covered here, since few of them have been commercially published and most of them are quite new; interested readers are advised to see books on behavioral assessment (e.g., Ciminero, Calhoun, & Adams, 1977; Hersen & Bellack, 1981).

American Psychological Association. Special Issue—Testing: Concepts, policy, practice and research. *American Psychologist*, 1981, *36*, 997–1189.

This special issue of the main professional journal of the American Psychological Association particularly takes up such topics as the problem of testing minorities and the relation of testing to federal guidelines for equal opportunity, but it also covers problems of testing for giftedness, intelligence, college admissions, and effects of coaching. A good historical supplement to these readings is the article by Cronbach (1975) entitled "Five Decades of Public Controversy over Mental Testing." Anastasi's *Psychological Testing*, now in its fifth edition (1982), also has extensive discussions of testing issues.

RESEARCH EXAMPLES

Golden, C. J., Kane, R., Sweet, J., Moses, J. A., Cardellino, J. P., Templeton, R., Vicente, P., & Garber, B. Relationship of the Halstead-Reitan Neuropsychological Battery to the Luria-Nebraska Neuropsychological Battery. *Journal of Consulting and Clinical Psychology*, 1981, *49*, 410–417.

When a new test is introduced to the psychology audience, it is important to examine its role relative to older "stars on the stage." The Halstead-Reitan grew out of many years of work by Halstead with people who have intellectual impairment related to brain damage and the combining of many tasks into a long battery. The battery includes copying figures, drawing lines between numbers in a given order, perceiving sounds, tapping a finger, categorizing objects, reporting locations of touch and the WAIS test and produces an Impairment Index. The Luria-Nebraska, inspired by qualitative observations of the Russian neurologist Luria, has been developed in recent years into a quantitative set of scales derived from over 200 items; the scales provide standardized scores on such areas as motor function, receptive speech, writing, arithmetic, and memory—tasks quite similar to those on the Halstead-Reitan and

WAIS. The questions addressed by this research study concern the effectiveness, or relative validity, of the two tests and to what extent the major 14 scores on the Halstead correlate with the 14 summary scores on the Luria.

The many authors of this study arranged for both tests to be given to 108 patients in three medical centers for chronic patients. The patients were mainly male, and their average age was in the late thirties. The group included 48 clearly diagnosed brain-damaged people, 30 schizophrenic people, and 30 normal controls. Statistical procedures (discriminant analysis) with the Luria-Nebraska correctly identified 87 percent of the neurological group and 88 percent of the control group; the Halstead-Reitan discriminated at almost the same percentages. Hit scores for the schizophrenics likewise did not differ significantly between the two test batteries. Other statistical procedures (multiple regression) were used to predict Halstead scores from the Luria ones and vice versa. The correlation figures were high, most exceeding .85. The authors conclude that as far as this study of validity went, there is no statistical superiority for either battery. (They discuss a number of small differences in parts of the tests.) It should also be noted that the Luria-Nebraska can be administered in two or three hours, whereas the Halstead-Reitan may take six. In another study, some of the same authors (Golden, Moses, Fishburne, Engum, Lewis, Wisniewski, Conley, & Berg, 1981) demonstrated the utility of the Luria in detecting the area of brain damage found by computerized scans. Much effort is going into development and validation of neuropsychiatric tests, and undoubtedly further research will identify the best kinds of behavioral indicators of cerebral functioning.

Rose, D., & Bitter, E. J. The Palo Alto Destructive Content Scale as a predictor of physical assaultiveness in men. *Journal of Personality Assessment*, 1980, *44*, 228–233.

This study is a sample of considerable work in trying to detect potential dangerousness, which is one of the most important characteristics to consider when courts make legal decisions about incarceration and commitment to a mental hospital or when boards decide to place a prisoner on parole or in an outside work situation. Psychologists are often asked to help with such decisions. The study also illustrates how a projective technique can be coded to produce a quantitative score.

Making use of earlier Rorschach research and clinical impressions, the authors developed a way of scoring the content of a subject's response to the Rorschach inkblots. The Palo Alto Destructive Content Scale (PADCS) describes five categories, from nondestructive to active or violent destructive content. For instance, a score in the middle, a 3, would be applied if the person reports perceiving a victim of destructive action or a character warding off anticipated harm, such as "a man holding up his hands to protect himself." A score of 5 would be reserved for such content as stabbing, shooting, or "a tiger stalking his prey." Subjects for the study included 12 former offenders, 11 repeat offenders, 20 child molesters, 20 rapists, and 12 murderers who produced at least nine Rorschach responses when given the test at a state hospital for mentally ill criminals. This statistical analysis (Mann Whitney U test for differences between groups) showed that the former offenders (who had not been in trouble for at least three years) had the lowest PADCS scores, significantly lower than those for all the other groups except the child molesters. Rapists and murderers were highest and did not show a significant difference from each other. The findings are consistent with earlier studies indicating that assaultive male offenders produce more hostile and destructive content on the Rorschach. It is particularly interesting if the findings hold up with further work on predicting success of parolees. The numbers of subjects in these groups are small. Obviously further work needs to be done on this procedure, in relating destructive content scores to other tests, case history data, and subsequent behavior. Attempts are also being made to identify MMPI patterns and other information related to violence (e.g., Lothstein & Jones, 1978).

Lachar, D., Butkus, M., & Hryhorczuk, L. Objective personality assessment of children: An exploratory study of the Personality Inventory for Children (PIC) in a child psychiatric setting. *Journal of Personality Assessment*, 1978, *42*, 529–537.

The Personality Inventory for Children (PIC) is a well developed but new instrument for use with a primary informant, usually the mother. The informant answers 600 items about the child, and the scored result is similar to the MMPI with 16 profile scales covering test taking and clinical and social topics. In this study the authors set out to relate PIC scores and patterns to case findings about children, a form of validation. The subjects (described by mothers) were 79 preadolescent, nonpsychotic children seen in an outpatient clinic with symptoms such as hyperactivity, aggressiveness, learning disturbance, and depression. Without knowing the PIC results, two trained raters used a 94-item checklist to record information and behavior reported in the clinic records. Then each PIC scale was correlated with the items on the checklist. Each PIC scale obtained an average of 12 significant correlates. These case study correlates were substantially in the predicted direction for 14 of the 16 scales. The Delinquency Scale received the strongest support in the form of checklist items about impulsivity, aggressivity, and uncooperative behavior. Correlates of scales named Hyperactivity, Depression, Anxiety and Withdrawal, and Social Skills were also clearly related to relevant case history information. The authors conclude that the test is promising for use at this preadolescent age. Its results, obtained fairly straightforwardly from mothers and other informants, suggest highly probable behaviors and characteristics which can be used by clinicians with a variety of theoretical persuasions. At the end of this article two cases illustrate the use of the PIC. In a later article the authors (Lachar & Wirt, 1981) respond to some criticisms, such as the effects of obtaining information from informants, and show that there is still strong evidence for validity.

Sattler, J. M., Avila, V., Houston, W. B., & Toney, D. H. Performance of bilingual Mexican-American children on Spanish and English versions of the Peabody Picture Vocabulary Test. *Journal of Consulting and Clinical Psychology*, 1980, *48*, 782–784.

This study illustrates the need for research on the use of tests with special populations. A question in testing children of a different language background is whether translations of a test are equivalent to the English version. The Peabody Picture Vocabulary Test (PPVT) is a widely used and researched procedure for quickly estimating vocabulary which is a major component of intelligence tests and educational achievement. It consists of a series of cards with four pictures on them; the subject is asked to point to the picture best representing the meaning of the word or concept the examiner provides. It takes only about 10 to 20 minutes and can be used with children who are handicapped in speech or motor abilities. In this study Sattler and his colleagues administered the test in Spanish and English to 33 boys and 42 girls (between 3 and 12 years of age) who were of Mexican-American background and showed equal proficiency on a test of bilingualism (Spanish and English). The results showed that the children obtained higher scores on the Spanish than on the English version but that they scored low in both as compared with norms. The authors conclude from their study and from a review of the literature that the PPVT should not be used to assess the intellectual capabilities of Hispanic children or be used alone to make decisions about educational classification. Before testing, the preferred language of the child should be determined and used in administering the tests, which should include nonverbal as well as verbal tasks. Sattler and Gwynne (1982), from a review of research, found that there is no evidence that the examiner's race affects black children's intelligence test results.

Lah, M. I., & Rotter, J. B. Changing college student norms on the Rotter Incomplete Sentences Blank. *Journal of Consulting and Clinical Psychology*, 1981, *49*, 985.

This brief article illustrates the need to be concerned about the shifting of norms over time. The Rotter Incomplete Sentences Blank (ISB) is a widely used projective technique consisting of a list of 40 beginnings of sentences, such as "My mother _____" or "My greatest fear is _____," followed by sufficient space to write a complete sentence. The authors randomly selected 100 protocols (50 male and 50 female) obtained in introductory psychology for each of the years 1965, 1970, 1977. Trained raters made ratings on a seven-point scale according to degree of adjustment using the standard illustrative responses. Interscorer reliabilities were high. The results showed significant differences from the 1950 means in nearly all groups and subgroups by sex. The differences were in the direction of greater conflict and maladjustment than in 1950. Another widely used and theoretically interesting technique of this kind is the Washington University Sentence Completion Test, the scoring of which is based on Loevinger's constructs of ego development (Loevinger, Wessler, & Redmore, 1970).

6

THE USES
OF INFORMATION:

Interpreting and Communicating Findings

In the course of getting to know persons and situations for clinical purposes, the psychologist has collected a great amount of information. Now what? This chapter will examine the processes of putting information together, selecting the most relevant aspects, making useful sense of the findings, and communicating in ways that help the client and the agency as much as possible.

**FACTORS INFLUENCING
THE FINAL PHASES
OF ASSESSMENT**

Up to now we have been considering the early stages of the assessment process—particularly the preparation, or planning, stage and the input, or data collection, stage. Now we are looking at the processing and output stages. Figure 6–1 shows the course of clinical assessment as it occurs in various agencies and institutions. In ovals on the right side are subjective judgments that clinicians must make along the way. The processing stage often includes both statistical and judgmental processing. It leads to decisions about organizing and transmitting information to others in oral or written form, and finally to clinical actions, such as psychotherapy, assignments to particular programs, and so on.

Among the factors influencing the final phase of assessment, certainly one of the most important is the context in which the assessment takes place—especially the setting and the role of the psychologist in the setting. It makes a great deal of difference whether the assessor is working in a large Veterans Administration hospital with many resources and many regulations or in a small health clinic in a remote rural area where there are no other mental health professionals and few formalities. Private practice differs in many ways from public service. Circumstances determine how much responsibility the assessor takes for follow-through with the client and how a report is written and used.

Another factor influencing what one looks for and how one organizes a report is the orientation of the clinician and his or her colleagues—whether they are behavioral, humanistic, or psychoanalytic. The assessor must "speak the language" of the professional "minicultures" of the clinic, hospital, or community team. If the report goes to someone outside the agency, such as a judge or a rehabilitation counselor, another set of considerations come into play.

Certainly the purposes of the assessment will influence the handling of the final stages. The purposes are determined partly by the nature of the admission or referral and partly by the clinician as the assessment picture emerges. The referral questions may be such as the following: "What is the patient's intellectual functioning?" or "What is the diagnosis?" or "Give me a

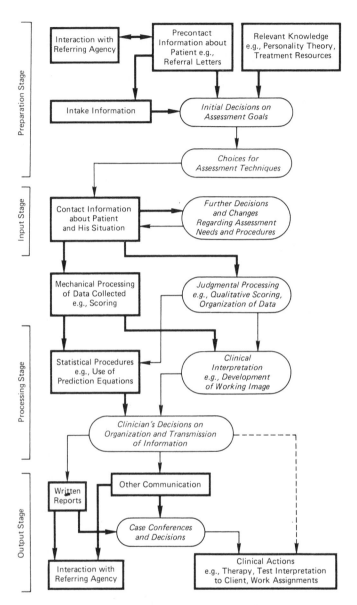

Figure 6-1   The course of clinical assessment. (From Sundberg & Tyler, 1962, p. 87. Copyright 1962 by Prentice-Hall and used by permission)

picture of the patient's psychodynamics for use in therapy," or "What cerebral functions remain useful, after the accident, so that we can plan occupational training?" Many referrals are nonspecific. Early in the process the psychologist must clarify the questions with the person making the referral and then must keep in mind those questions, as revised by the process of assessment, when he or she comes to writing a report.

Most practical clinical purposes fall within the two general objectives of assessment mentioned earlier: decision making and image forming. Similarly Levy (1963) and Levine (1981) have distinguished between bounded and unbounded assessment problems: "The bounded problem is one involving a discrete prediction or decision, usually circumscribed in time and most often concerned with the classification or disposition of a case, whereas the unbounded case involves problems of case management such as in psychotherapy, where the therapist requires . . . a formulation that will serve as a continuing guide in his moment-to-moment and day-to-day decision making" (Levy, 1963, p. 194). The assessor's task, then, involves either (1) weighing the advantages and disadvantages of alternatives for action by or for the client or (2) developing a picture or model of the client and his or her world to use in further work. The third purpose of assessment—hypothesis checking—enters into the preceding functions but is most clearly displayed when assessment instruments are used in research.

A related consideration for the assessor is whether the case formulation will be used for actions and decisions *about* the client or *with* the client. The nature of the report, the language used in discussing the client, and the level of assumed knowledge about client and context will be affected by whether the report is to be discussed openly and directly with the client or used only by a professional person as background for treatment or as a basis for decisions about placement or assignment.

Finally, there are certain practical factors that influence the final stages of assessment in any given situation. These include such mundane but important matters as the time allowed for thinking about the information collected and for writing up a report and talking with people about it. Time is a precious commodity in mental health centers as well as in many other situations. Another practical problem is cost; in times of reduced budgets, referrals for psychological testing may be curtailed. Agencies must balance costs against benefits. Other practical questions are whether automated and statistical assessment processing equipment and procedures are available, whether the case can be discussed with consultants and colleagues, and whether the client is available for follow-up.

SKETCHES OF CASES
FORMULATED FROM DIFFERENT
PERSPECTIVES

Figure 4–1 identified five different orientations to the assessment task. The choice of orientation influences how the last stages of assessment are handled. As mentioned before, we assume that there is always some form of assessment, no matter what the situation. The following cases give two brief illustrations of each of these perspectives, with comments.

Informal Assessment

(Case A)   Mrs. Anders, a mother of a one-year-old baby, is wondering if her child is retarded; he doesn't seem to smile and respond like other babies she knows of that age. She bought a baby book and read that most children a year old can walk by themselves and imitate a few words. She decided that something was wrong and went to a clinic.

(Case B)   A trained volunteer, Bob Fitz, working at a community telephone service, received a call from a man who sounded very depressed. Bob thought the man was depressed because he talked slowly and was choked up. Bob asked him a number of questions about his situation, his mood, and ultimately his thoughts about suicide. Bob decided that the man was "at risk" for suicide and encouraged him to come to the mental health center. Bob wrote a brief report of the conversation for the worker scheduled to interview the man.

Comment: In many ways Mrs. Anders and Bob Fitz are behaving like professional clinical psychologists. They gather information about the person of concern; they organize the information into a picture of the person, a picture that at least raises questions about an informal diagnostic label; they come to a conclusion or decision to act; and they communicate about the person to others. This kind of assessment goes on daily in millions of situations. The most obvious way in which it differs from professional assessment is that special theory and techniques are absent. It is also likely that the high emotional involvement in the case, especially with Mrs. Anders, makes her less objective about image formation and decision making than a psychologist would be. Nevertheless, the point is that professional and informal assessment share a great deal in common.

Assessment for Pathology

(Case C)   Tom Celotta, a 34-year-old veteran, was referred to the neuropsychologist for evaluation of an apparent cognitive deficit and for suggestions about which areas of brain function were affected. The psychologist, Dr. Margaret Mills, working in a veterans hospital, interviewed Mr. Celotta and gave him intellectual and personality tests. As expected since Mr. Celotta had been an Air Force technician and later a foreman in an electronics industry, he performed at average to high-average levels on almost all intellectual tasks, except those involving organization, reproduction, and memory for complex visual designs. His personality tests reflected more preoccupation with physical problems than is common in men of his age. Because the

psychological tests showed impaired visual organization and Dr. Mills observed during the interview slightly slurred speech and a barely perceptible flattening of the muscles on the left side of the nose and mouth, she sent Mr. Celotta to the neurologist with an urgent recommendation that he look into the possibility of a right hemisphere lesion. Brain scan and radiographic studies of cerebral blood vessels revealed a tumor in the front part of the right hemisphere, and an operation was immediately scheduled (case adapted and summarized from Lezak, 1976, pp. 11–12).

(Case D) Sharon Dickman, a 45-year-old housewife and mother of two teenage children, has been drinking heavily in recent months since her husband left her. She decided to come to the nearby community mental health clinic. The intake worker after a brief interview referred Mrs. Dickman to Dr. Ricardo Ruiz for further evaluation a few days later. As Dr. Ruiz thought about the case, he decided that several questions were important: What diagnosis should be entered in the clinic's record? Will Mrs. Dickman profit from drug therapy? If so, a psychiatrist must be brought in. What are her major areas of concern and conflict of which a therapist in the psychoanalytically oriented clinic needs to be aware? During his appointment time with Mrs. Dickman, Dr. Ruiz administered a brief intelligence test, a drawing test, and the Rorschach, and he asked her to take the MMPI. A few days later, when the tests were scored and profiled, Dr. Ruiz wrote a report for the record and for therapists who would work with her. He concluded from the history, the greatly elevated score for depression on the MMPI, and the use of dark features and depressive content on the Rorschach that Mrs. Dickman was suffering from a minor depression, situationally related. Her verbal abilities and general intelligence were above average. He advised that she be given temporary relief by antidepressant drugs and that she start psychotherapy immediately. He described some of the suggestions from the Rorschach that she might have oral-dependency problems and certain conflicts over her diminishing sexual role. At the regular weekly case conference, he reviewed Mrs. Dickman's case, and the head of the clinic assigned a social worker to work with her.

Comment: These cases show many aspects of the most common and traditional approach to clinical assessment. In the last phases of the assessment sequence, the pathology-oriented psychologist reviews data from many sources and produces diagnoses and recommendations leading to decisions about the case. In Levy's terms (1963) the first case was a bounded one, and the second had bounded aspects, since it called for decisions and recommendations. The second case also had "unbounded" aspects—that is, the psychologist's task was to provide a description of the client and suggestions for general directions in therapy, a *working image*.

BOX 6-1 *CONTROVERSY IN DIAGNOSIS—THE BORDERLINE PERSONALITY*

A psychopathological condition receiving much attention recently is the borderline personality—a personality that borders on psychosis, called latent schizophrenia earlier. This popular diagnosis remains very unclear. It would seem that psychological tests would be valuable in clarifying the term.

The *Diagnostic and Statistical Manual III* of the American Psychiatric Association (1980, pp. 321–323) describes the term. Borderline is one of several adjectives associated with the personality disorders (to be coded on Axis II). These disorders are generally characterized by inflexible and maladaptive personality traits that impair social or occupational functioning or cause severe subjective distress, generally recognizable in adolescence and continuing into adulthood. The essential feature of the borderline variety is instability in mood, self-image, and interpersonal relations. Quite often there is social contrariness, pessimistic outlook, and profound identity disturbance. The DSM III requires for the diagnosis of borderline personality at least five of the following: (1) impulsivity and unpredictability in potentially self-damaging behavior, such as substance abuse, sexual acting out, gambling, or shoplifting, (2) a pattern of unstable and intense interpersonal relationships, (3) inappropriate or uncontrolled anger, (4) uncertainty about several issues related to identity such as self-image, gender identity, or long-term goals, (5) affective (mood) instability, (6) intolerance of being alone, (7) physical self-damaging acts, such as suicidal gestures, and (8) chronic feelings of emptiness and boredom. Psychiatrists and psychologists often find it difficult to distinguish borderline personality from schizophrenia, schizoid, and schizotypal personality. The term schizoid personality disorder emphasizes defect and indifference in social relationships—being a "loner." The term schizotypal personality stresses oddities of thought or behavior, such as magical thinking, loose associations in speech, and minor depersonalization.

How would borderline personality disorder show up on psychological tests? The major proposition is that borderlines would show a good performance on structured tests, especially intelligence tests, and poor performance on unstructured tests, especially the Rorschach. Some psychologists assert that borderlines will show more bizarre and unusual Rorschach responses than openly schizophrenic persons. In addition there have been general structured assessment procedures developed (Diagnostic Interview for Borderlines [Kolb & Gunderson, 1980]). Carr and Goldstein (1981) present a case chosen by using the DIB and illustrating different approaches to diagnosis; the case shows ordinary reasoning on the WAIS but thought-disordered associations on projective techniques.

In contrast, Widiger (1982) reviews the literature and finds no support for optimistic claims that the Rorschachs of borderlines are more disturbed than schizophrenics or that they present much more disturbance on unstructured than structured tests. Borderlines do present disturbance of thought on intelligence tests. Widiger also reviews the history of the term and points out that interpretation of the research is confused by the vague and variable criteria used for the borderline diagnosis. He recommends much more careful specification of the diagnosis, and he points out the necessity for studying base rates of incidence in different populations and the study of test patterns that differentiate the borderline personality from other diagnostic categories with which it might be confused. It seems that the term "borderline" has filled a need among diagnosticians for a label to cover the confusing meeting ground between psychosis and other conditions, but it may have only added to the confusion.

Assessment for Learning

(Case E)   Eight-year-old Eddie Pierce is an only child of parents in their mid-thirties. An interview with the parents and an observation during another clinic visit confirms the initial impressions of a child out of control. Bill Henderson, the psychologist, noted that Eddie refused to obey requests and made inappropriate demands on his parents and schoolmates. At home he yelled, slammed doors, and threw things until his demands were granted. The Pierces scolded him and sometimes spanked him in anger, but they felt guilty about their anger and gave in to him often when he had temper outbursts. Bill Henderson concluded that the child and the parents were unintentionally training each other to maintain negative, or aversive, control strategies. What the assessment period did was to pinpoint Eddie's behavior and its antecedents and consequences. The next step was for the parents to keep careful records of the occurrences of problem behaviors. (Home observation, using trained observers, was not used here because the procedure was too costly.) Henderson drew up a treatment plan and discussed it with the parents; it involved continued parental observations, training sessions with the parents, the use of "time out"—a temporary removal of the child to a quiet part of the house—and other ways of changing the parents' behavior to modify Eddie's.

(Case F)   Frank is a college student who appeared for the intake interview in jeans and sandals and spoke softly with occasional minor speech blocks. He identified his problem as anxiety in public speaking and in situations in which he is being evaluated. He reported that his family continually compared him with his more successful younger brother, that his father was very critical of his school work, and that he had had an ulcer operation at age 15. The interviewer noticed that he perspired excessively. Frank said that "nervousness" interfered with his ability to perform on examinations and that he was shy with others, especially young women. The interviewer, Sally Norris, asked Frank to fill out a form listing fears. She identified his major problems as speech anxiety and lack of assertiveness. She saw his assets as moderate brightness, warmth, and sensitivity. Together they identified the targets for change: unrealistic self-statements of devaluation in social-evaluative situations and skills associated with assertiveness. Dr. Norris asked Frank to recapitulate as clearly as possible several problem situations and what went on before and after. She recommended relaxation training, after which he would work at rational restructuring of the self-devaluating statements and at role playing of speech making and other evaluative situations. (A full presentation of a similar case along with assessment formulations from other viewpoints can be found in Bernstein & Nietzel, 1980, pp. 143–150.)

Comment: These behavioral, or learning-oriented, cases illustrate an assessment emphasis on specifying the problem as exactly as possible. In an actual case, the details of the problem behavior or thought patterns would have to be much more explicit than can be reported in these brief sketches. The ABC's of such assessments are specific problem behaviors, along with their antecedents and consequences. The treatment recommendations consist of plans to alter reinforcement patterns in the situations in which the problem behavior occurs.

Assessment for Personal Development

(Case G)   Ginger is a high school senior. Her parents suggested that she see a counselor or clinician about planning for her future. In talking with the psychologist, Dr. Mays, Ginger said that she agreed to see him partly because of what her parents said about her needing to decide about going to college. She had not told her parents that she also came because she was afraid she was pregnant and she didn't know what to do. The more Ginger talked, the more it became apparent that she was a very confused adolescent—not knowing what she wanted to do in life, feeling great pressures on her from her family and boyfriends. She needed to have a sense of direction and to understand herself. First, she needed to find out whether she was pregnant. A referral to a physician established that she was. Second she needed information about her interests and abilities. She reported moderately high grades and a lack of any specific interests except possibly having a home and family. The Strong-Campbell Interest Inventory showed high scores on social service. These, along with school reports, were discussed in counseling sessions to help Ginger become aware of her interests and abilities. Counseling focused on enabling Ginger to understand herself, exploring feelings and relationships, alternative possibilities for what to do about her pregnancy, communication with friends and family, and her self-concept as she projected her future. She needed to be encouraged to move through the developmental sequences characteristic of this time of life as well as to make decisions about current problems.

(Case H)   Harry Hoover is a 28-year-old mental hospital patient, one of many chosen randomly to participate in a research project about the application of person-centered therapy with schizophrenics. (See Meador & Rogers, 1979, for a full description of this case, including transcripts of parts of interviews.) Harry was hospitalized several times in the past. He completed high school and some college work. (The therapist, Dr. Rogers, intentionally did not look at Harry's case history because of his belief that therapy takes place in the immediate moment-by-moment interaction. He also did not examine the extensive set of tests and research records which were obtained separately from the therapy interviews.) Although Harry said almost nothing in the beginning, the therapist concluded that the patient attached some meaning to the encounters, since he was always on time and

rarely forgot to come. The therapist liked Harry and believed the feeling was reciprocated. Harry muttered something to his ward physician about finally meeting someone who understood him. In early interviews, if the therapist waited patiently and expressed impressions of the way the patient might be feeling, ultimately Harry talked. Most importantly, Harry revealed that he felt entirely rejected by his family. Therapy continued in the way it had begun, building on initial feelings of relationship as the patient expressed himself more openly.

Comment: As mentioned before, the developmental, or growth, orientation does not typically use much testing or formal assessment. With vocational and some personal problems, people of this persuasion use test findings *with* the client as an adjunct to *self-assessment.* In humanistic assessment the client is a coevaluator (Petzelt & Craddick, 1978). The other use of formal assessment procedures is for research, and almost alone among people of a humanistic orientation, Carl Rogers and his colleagues have led the field in research. The tests are administered by other people, however, and are simply for research, not for use in therapy. Still, early in the therapy itself, there are, we believe, many aspects that construct a working image and lead to certain decisions; this process could very well be called *assessment,* assessment based on assumptions about the centrality of the self-concept and self-awareness as they are built up over the years of development. The assumption is that as a child grows and discriminates between self and others, she or he assigns "ownership" of life responsibilities to self or others. The client's inner view is essential to further work in therapy, and the assessor-therapist examines and encourages this self-awareness in the various ways in which the client is willing to share experiences. Since the assumption is that growing self-awareness within a relationship is the crucial factor in therapy, the growth-oriented psychologist gives minimal attention to tests, case history, and outside behavior.

Assessment Emphasizing the Ecology

(Case I)   Fifteen-year-old Iris is the only child of Mr. and Mrs. Baker, who are about 50 years of age. Mrs. Baker works as a social worker in a large hospital, and Mr. Baker is a manager in a computer industry. When the three of them came to the clinic, they reported that Iris in recent months had become moody and depressed and had dropped out of school. After one initial joint interview in the clinic, the clinician, Dr. Roberta Orr, arranged for two two-hour sessions with the family in their home, a pleasant place in a wealthy suburb. Dr. Orr interviewed each of them individually while the others worked on questionnaires in adjoining rooms. She used four short questionnaires, three concerning classroom, family, and work environments and one concerning health and daily living, in which the person is asked to describe both the actual and the ideal environment. The semistructured interview ex-

plored how Iris spent her time and used her environmental resources. The interview showed that Iris spent a great deal of time alone and in passive pursuits, such as reading and watching television. It was also clear from her questionnaire descriptions of her favorite class (history) that she felt little friendliness, organization, or involvement in that environment. Her problems lay more in the social than the academic arena. Comparing answers on the family questionnaires, Dr. Orr saw several distinct differences in the way the parents and Iris perceived the family environment. Iris saw much more conflict and less cohesion than her parents did; she gave the family a low score on recreation. The parents did not view their relationship as conflictive. It appeared that Iris's lack of involvement in social activities might reflect a lack of opportunity to learn warm, expressive interpersonal skills and casual activities at home. The parents' descriptions of their work settings also told more of the story; they both sensed considerable job pressure, especially the father. Further attention to the history of the family and the work systems showed that the parents had been so involved in their own careers that they had waited until their thirties to have a child; they recognized early that their baby daughter would need attention from them, but as she grew older they spent less and less time with her and were often tired at the end of their work days. At the same time financial retrenchment in Iris's school eliminated the music and art programs she enjoyed. The parents had not thought much about all of these external changes and influences and were unaware of the depth of Iris's feelings. The questionnaires did show a large amount of agreement in some areas—for example, intellectual and recreational preferences around which some family togetherness and social skill building might develop. The plan for family therapy involved considerable use of feedback from the environmental questionnaires. (For more information on the case and procedures described here, see Fuhr, Moos, & Dishotsky, 1981; Moos & Fuhr, 1982.)

(Case J)   Jack, a 31-year-old businessman, came to the center saying he was at the end of his rope; he could not go on with his work and his confused life situation. To the psychologist, Tony Angelo, who saw Jack initially, he did not seem on the brink of drastic action, and the vocational problem seemed a good way to start an exploration of Jack's situation and his feelings about himself and his competencies in interaction with the environment. In addition to the informational booklet asking about education, family, work, recreational interests, and self-definition of problems and strengths that all clients filled out, Dr. Angelo asked Jack to answer the MMPI (to check severity of the anxiety and other disorders), the Strong-Campbell Interest Inventory, and a new test of communicative styles in work and intimate relations developed by Angelo and his colleagues. On the second interview a few days later, Dr. Angelo discussed with Jack many items on the informational form, filling in a picture of his family and employment history. Jack had completed a bachelor's degree in Spanish with a minor in art and had worked mostly in retail sales. He had participated in two management training programs and had learned about his current jewelry business through on-the-job training. What appealed to him about his work were customer contact and organizing and displaying the finely crafted articles; what repelled him were incompetent superiors and the boredom of day-to-day sales routine. The Strong-Campbell showed Jack to have interests similar to those of social scientists, artists, and writers. He was drawn to the world of ideas and wanted to be located in a "learning community" near a university. Dr. Angelo asked Jack to assemble a portfolio of his artwork that he might use in approaching museums, libraries, and other possible places of work. Meanwhile Dr. Angelo encouraged him to seek another job in jewelry to keep "bread on the table" until more interesting work could be found. In the second interview Jack revealed another aspect of his overall search for a less damaging pattern of life. He said that within the last year he had become intimate with a clergyman named Jim, somewhat older than he, and now the town in which they lived together was making their situation intolerable. He and Jim wanted to be free to express their relationship without fears of censure. Where could they go? Since the understanding and planning for the relationship now involved another, Dr. Angelo requested Jack to bring his partner to the next meeting. At that meeting it became clear that the two were indeed warmly attached to each other and that Jim was also unhappy about the living and working situation. Through similar assessment procedures and through joint discussions of their preferences for living and working styles, Dr. Angelo helped them to work out a plan to explore opportunities in other places during a two-week vacation. They discussed what to look for in communities. Dr. Angelo also prepared to discuss the varied needs and style differences in the way the two men thought about their future lives. Jack was more adventurous and quick paced, needing less assurance of success in order to move into new things, whereas Jim was more cautious and wanted a lot of information before abandoning current situations. (This report is modified from a presentation by Fraleigh, 1980.)

Comment: These cases illustrate primary assumptions of an ecological approach: People are embedded in their environments, and a clinician cannot assess the individual or recommend treatment without understanding the significant interactions. This approach, although it may start with the individual, moves on to an assessment of larger systems—the family and its outside connections in the case of Iris, and with work environment, partnership, and potential community in the case of Jack and Jim. One of the first questions an ecologically minded psychologist asks concerns *where* important interactions of life take place. This concern for situations or settings then leads to questions about roles, role expectations, behavioral supports, and preferences for styles of working and relating with others. Almost as if trying to understand a play, the assessor looks at the various scenes in which the person plays a part and sees if the person's competencies and preferences match the expectations of the other participants. This approach also emphasizes assessment for feedback into the personal and interpersonal systems. (For further discussion see Gilmore, 1980; Moos & Fuhr, 1982; Sundberg et al., 1978.)

Any given assessment orientation may overlap with another. For instance, Dr. Angelo, in the last case, used the MMPI and the interviews to decide whether psychopathology was present. He might also have helped Jack and Jim set up learning situations to develop new competencies. Dr. Angelo used the tests to promote self-awareness as in growth-oriented therapies, but he did not restrict the treatment plan to this orientation. In many ways the ecological approach promotes a synthesis of the other three orientations, but it also has a distinct quality of its own. Later chapters on family, group, organizational, and community intervention will exemplify further ecological principles.

THE MAKING OF MEANING—
CLINICAL INTERPRETATION
AND INTEGRATION

After all information on a person and situation has been collected, the clinical work of interpreting and integrating the diverse set of data comes to a focal point. Impressions that the clinician has been developing must now be assembled to create a coherent view of the person and situation. Recommendations and plans must be made. This task has both subjective and objective aspects. The subjective, or impressionistic, aspects of the task are the less clear but usually the more important.

Figure 6-2 portrays some of the information available to the psychologist for interpretation. Many data are impinging on the clinician even in a simple assessment case, although the information may vary according to amount and nature. Figure 6-2 groups the information on a 43-year-old woman under three broad categories: (1) information about the client—her biological and personal systems, including physiological functioning, behavioral characteristics, self-report, self-presentation, and self-concept; (2) information about larger systems—the client's environment, especially the significant other people in her life, her work situation, the physical aspects of the environment such as housing and transportation, and her opportunities for relaxation and stimulation; and (3) information from the relevant professional agency, including people's impressions of the client and knowledge of therapeutic resources of the agency. All this information is combined with the clinician's own observations and "naive" feelings. In evaluating results of the intervention decided upon, these same three sources of information will be used (Strupp & Hadley, 1977).

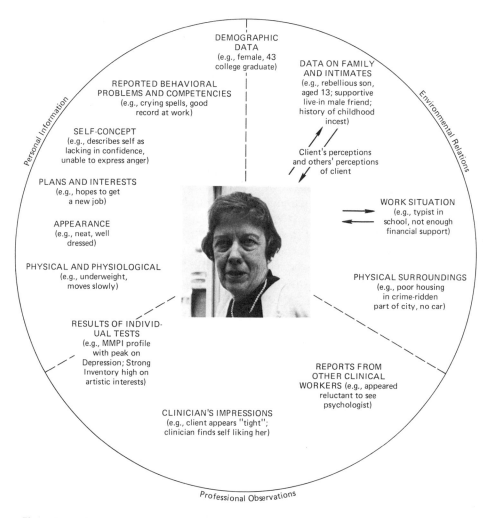

Figure 6-2   "Collage" of information for interpretation and integration.

Selecting What Is Important

In this jumble of information, what stands out as most important? One of the first things to consider is *relevance* of the information to the assessment task of developing a diagnosis or treatment plan. The clinician, acting in the psychopathological tradition in assessing the woman shown in Figure 6-2, whom we will call Mrs. Wilson, sees the slowness of movements and the self-reports of crying and lack of confidence as evidence of depression. Implicitly the clinician may be matching Mrs. Wilson's characteristics against several possible models or stereotypes used in psychiatric diagnosis to see which one produces the best fit.

A second consideration is *deviation from norms*. According to either objective or subjective norms, some feature may stand out as especially different from what one expects of normal people, usually good or poor memory, for instance. (Deviation may be positive as well as negative.)

A third consideration in selection of information is *prominence*, or salience; just as with a landscape dominated by a peak or a town clustered around a lake, some aspects of personality stand out—a particular way of speaking or signs of withdrawal and shyness. Anything that happens repeatedly may also indicate salience. The clinician may be struck by a single part of the case history, such as the episode of childhood incest reported by Mrs. Wilson.

Still another element in selection is *multisource confirmation*. When a clinician notes evidence for some particular problem or asset in several sources of information—the client's self-report, interviews with family members, or clinical observations—this bit of information gains added significance. With Mrs. Wilson the MMPI as well as several observations and her self-report point to depression.

Clinical interviewers learn to take the client's report of events for what it actually is—the *reported perceptions* of the world and the self that the client is willing to share. It is obvious that some criminals will lie or avoid telling about their activities, as clinicians dealing with psychopaths recognize. However, such overt avoidance and unconscious defensiveness is present to some extent in most people. Furthermore, some people are poor self-observers and are unable to make accurate comparisons of themselves with others. For instance, Nietzel and Bernstein (1976) showed that there may be considerable discrepancy between students' reports about their social assertiveness and their actual assertive responses.

Discrepancies as well as agreements between different sources of data are important. One way of viewing the different sources was developed by Leary (1957) and further expanded by Klopfer (1981, 1982), taking various sources as levels or kinds of communication. Inquiry about a person or with a person can answer such questions as these: (1) How is the person perceived by significant others? (Public communication) How does the person perceive his or her public image? The sources of such information are usually interviews with others or with the client. (2) How does the person perceive the self? (Conscious self-presentation) The source of such information may be an interview with the person or an assessment procedure such as the TAT or sentence completion. (3) What does the person reveal about himself or herself indirectly and symbolically? (Private symbolization) The source of such information is not direct and conscious but must be inferred from the self-report or projective techniques. Agreements and disagreements among these three kinds of data are important for the clinician to note.

Sample, Correlate, and Sign

Until now we have been emphasizing how to select items or a set of items from diverse sources of information. The next question is how to treat the selected information. The raw data do not have meaning until we give it to them. There are three ways in which we may view each item of information—as a sample, a correlate, or a sign. The assessor or judge can look at a life event, a test result, or a direct observation of a person and ask these questions: (1) "What can one reasonably infer about general behavior and situations from this sample?" (2) "With what other important characteristics is this information correlated or associated?" (3) "Is this information a sign or symbol of some underlying condition?" The fundamental distinction between sample or sign was first pointed out by Goodenough (1949) and has often been noted by others (e.g., Sundberg, Tyler, & Taplin, 1973). Earlier we noted that the three assessment techniques—behavioral, objective, and projective—emphasize the sample correlate, and sign respectively in interpretation. Actually any item of assessment information can be used with any of the three approaches. Using an example from Bernstein and Nietzel (1980, pp. 121–122) we will illustrate the three approaches to the following brief news item:

> A man took 16 sleeping pills before going to bed at the hotel last night but was saved when discovered by a maid and rushed to the intensive care unit of a hospital.

This apparent suicide attempt can be viewed as a sample of the client's behavior—an example of what the person could and might do under certain circumstances, without attempting to speculate about reasons or underlying motives. A sample-oriented assessor might make these interpretations: (1) The person has access to potentially lethal medications. (2) The person did not want to be saved (if there is no evidence that he told someone else or knew about the maid coming to the room). (3) Under similar circumstances the man might attempt the same suicidal actions again.

From a correlate orientation, experience or research may have shown that suicide attempts are associated with other characteristics, and the following inferences might be made: (1) The man probably is single or divorced and lives alone. (2) The person has little emotional support from intimates. (3) He is likely to have warned someone or to have attempted suicide before. (4) His MMPI profile is likely to show a high score on the Depression scale. We know that statistical correlations are not perfect relationships, and we must remember that these guesses about related conditions always need to be checked. Little theory of any sort is needed for interpretations based on correlates.

In the sign approach, inferences based on theory about problems, conditions, and stresses are drawn from the suicide attempt. Psychoanalytic theory is most often used in this way, but other orientations may be used as well. Sign-oriented psychological interpretation might include the following: (1) The man has turned his intense hostilities about others toward himself. (2) He wants to show others how bad they are and make them feel guilty. (3) The attempt to kill himself was an unconscious cry for help. (4) The person has extreme intrapsychic conflicts and taking pills may be an effort to return to infantile dependence, in which conflicts are avoided.

Note there is another particular usage of the word *sign*. *Pathognomic signs* are often mentioned in medical settings. They are almost certain indicators that a particular disorder or disease exists. For instance, seeing a patient's paralyzed left side and face, the clinician may infer with high probability that the person has right hemisphere cerebral damage. Likewise, inappropriate emotional behavior while the patient seems to be talking to an absent person strongly suggests schizophrenic thinking. In these instances, the observed symptoms are treated as correlates of other conditions, and the distinction between correlate and sign becomes blurred.

One should note that all these interpretations are probabilistic, hypotheses to be checked by other data. As more information from various sources confirms the interpretation, the probabilities become higher, and one becomes more confident in them.

**Taxonomic Sorting
versus Emerging Synthesis:
Variations in Clinical Style**

Clinicians use different methods to reach their final conclusions about people. Some lean toward a logical procedure similar to what Sarbin, Taft, and Bailey (1960) call *taxonomic sorting*, the assignment of individuals to carefully defined classes. Such clinical thinking is fundamentally a process of syllogistic reasoning: The clinician uses a major premise, based on his or her experience and theoretical orientation, such as "People who do well in psychotherapy have considerable anxiety and an intact ego." From the assessment work-up, the clinician finds evidence of anxiety and some ego strength in the client, Mr. Jones, and concludes that Mr. Jones is an instance of the class of persons who will improve readily in therapy.

On the other hand, some clinicians may be described as using a process of *emerging synthesis* (Sundberg & Tyler, 1962). Their tendency is more like that of the artist painting a picture; an element here and there, a chance remark by the client, some "soft signs" on the psychometrics ultimately coalesce to form an image of the person and the situation. Such clinicians use empathy a great deal; they attempt to experience themselves in the situation of the client as the client would. The taxonomic approach is analytical and verbal, whereas the emerging approach is holistic and Gestalt-like.

There are probably many other assessment styles besides these two. Perhaps future research will find similarities between general cognitive styles and clinical cognitive activity. At this point it seems reasonable to advise people to use a variety of ways of thinking about a case and to look for congruence among these ways and for confirmation of the various hypotheses that emerge.

Like creative research, interpretation is a combination of the getting of ideas (perhaps by intuition, guesses, or logical extensions) and the testing of those ideas against the full set of facts one has and against future "experimentation" in the interactive ecology of daily life. The clinician interpreting information also needs to be concerned with the ecological validity (Brunswick, 1947) of the original data and the final recommendations for action—how representative these are of past and potential actions in the environment.

QUANTITATIVE AND STATISTICAL AIDS TO INTERPRETATION

One of the distinctive features of psychological work with people is the attempt to apply some rigor to the process—that is, to define characteristics carefully enough so that they can be recorded and counted, to collect data from appropriate comparison groups for use when a person is to be compared with others, and to develop statistical ways of predicting likely outcomes. Tests and other procedures vary a great deal in the amount of statistical information that is available about them and the number of interpretive aids they provide.

Quantitative Information

Perhaps the simplest quantitative technique for the clinician to use is one employed by psychologists with the behavioral and social learning orientation—namely, a simple *recording of occurrences* of a defined behavior. With the client (or the parent of a young client) the clinician works out a way to keep a record of each occurrence of a problematic behavior, such as nail biting, cigarette smoking, temper tantrums, or attacks of tension. Only simple counting and descriptive statistics may be applied to charts of these occurrences—daily counting and noting of any trends following natural environmental changes or interventions. If enough observations are obtained, one can compute means and standard deviations and use standard significance tests. If others have tried the same treatment, one can compare counts.

Another simple statistical aid is the *norm table*. Test manufacturers, especially those constructing objective personality and ability tests, usually provide norms based on the general population. Often it is also useful to have norms on special populations, such as women, men, people in different age groups, prison inmates, people with certain handicaps—in short, any defined subgroup of the population that is likely to differ from others in test scores. Norm tables can tell the clinician where the person stands in relation to comparable others, whether the person's score is average, different from the mean, or extremely deviant. Figure 6–3 shows the familiar bell-shaped normal curve and the various ways in which scores may be represented. With the Wechsler IQs, for instance, the mean is set at 100, and the standard deviation is 15 IQ points. Thus a person obtaining an IQ of 140 is between two and three standard deviations above the average of the general population, or in approximately the top one percent. It should be noted, of course, that knowing the relative position of the score does not in and of itself tell one anything

Figure 6–3 The normal curve and derived scores. (From Sundberg, 1977, p. 50. Copyright © 1977 by Prentice-Hall and used by permission)

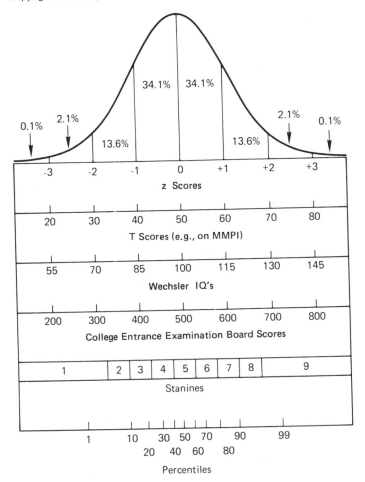

about its reliability or relevance. Reliability and validity as well as norms are necessary. All that norms do is to provide *comparisons* with a defined group. Therefore the appropriateness of the norms must be scrutinized carefully, especially if the person has an unusual background, such as language difficulties, physical handicaps, or an ethnic origin different from the mainstream population.

A somewhat related concept is that of the *base rate*—the prevalence of a characteristic in a specified population. In a clinical setting base rates are tabulations of cases, decisions, events, or other characteristics that are of interest. For instance, a clinician working in a hospital admissions ward would find it particularly helpful to check the files to see the number of cases that have been diagnosed in different psychiatric categories and their dispositions. If almost all cases coming to the hospital ward are released within eight days, that is simple but useful information. If 90 percent of those diagnosed as anxiety neurotics are sent home and 60 percent of those diagnosed as schizophrenic are sent to the state hospital, the clinician can make some predictions about the likely dispositions of new cases coming in. In some hospitals in which almost all admissions are diagnosed as schizophrenic and are of low socioeconomic background, one can predict with a high degree of certainty that the next person to be admitted will be schizophrenic and poor. Base rates become important when one tries to check the value of tests or other information. The important question becomes "Will this new information improve our prediction above that of the base rates?" Meehl and Rosen (1955) identified the base rate problem and noted that it is very difficult for additional assessment data to improve on extreme base rates. For instance, if 95 percent of the people coming to a hospital for the "criminally insane" are going to be called dangerous anyway, a new test to identify nondangerous people is not likely to be successful. The test might work much better in a mental hospital in which about 50 percent of those admitted are found to be dangerous; then the test could be useful in making the distinction. This question of improvement in predictability over base rates or over other information routinely obtained is called *incremental validity* or *utility* (Meehl, 1959; Sechrest, 1963).

Similar kinds of statistical aids are *expectancy tables* and *expectancy formulas*. These provide information about the probable success or outcomes for people based on their test scores. For instance, it would be feasible to develop a table, or formula, showing how a test of personality (or a record of behavior) in a youth correctional facility relates to subsequent delinquent activity or its absence. Expectancy tables and formulas are used by many colleges to determine cut off scores on college entrance examinations for admissions of new students, in order to avoid having people come who are almost certain to fail. In Chapter 10 there is an example of an expectancy table.

Another statistical adjunct to interpretative activities is a set of *descriptive terms significantly associated with scores or profiles.* Gough (1968) has been particularly interested in providing this assistance with the California

Psychological Inventory. He usually asks judges to describe people who come through an assessment center program. (An assessment center is a place where selected samples of people such as army officers, students, architects, or writers are studied intensively over several days, using interviews, tests, situational exercises, and other techniques; typically there are many observers who rate each participant on many variables. See Bray, 1982; MacKinnon, 1975; Office of Strategic Services Staff, 1948.) These descriptions, which might be obtained by using the Adjective Check List (Masterson, 1975) are then correlated with high or low scores on the CPI or with certain patterns on the test. When significant results are obtained and cross-validated, these are then reported for people to use in the future in interpretation of the CPI. For instance, people who score high on the So (Socialization) scale of the CPI are frequently described by others as "organized" and "reasonable."

Test pattern, coding, and *profile comparisons* provide another way in which the clinician can receive interpretative assistance. The MMPI has generated an especially rich assortment of studies and resource materials along these lines (e.g., Hathaway & Meehl, 1951; Marks, Seeman, & Haller, 1974). The technique can be applied to any test or set of tests on which there is normative data for a number of scales. The pattern is summarized by a code such as 13"2' on the MMPI. This code means that Scale 1 (Hypochondriasis) is the highest and 3 (Hysteria) is the second highest and they are both over the 80 T-score level, with 2 (Depression) not quite so high but over a T-score of 70. The clinician can then look up in a reference book the incidence of this three-point code in a large sample of psychiatric patients and the psychiatric diagnoses and personality and outcome characteristics most frequently associated with it.

Automated Interpretations

The most comprehensive statistical aid of all is the *automated interpretation system.* Several widely used tests have accumulated enough data of the sort mentioned previously—norms, associated descriptions, and expectancy tables—so that enterprising experts have been able to develop computerized printed interpretations of individual score profiles. There are several systems for the MMPI (see reviews in Buros, 1972, 1978). Through linking scores obtained on the many scales developed for this inventory, using indexes of patterns on profiles, and adding some systematic clinical interpretations, these commercial ventures produce written descriptions. Here are some excerpts from an MMPI interpretation by Caldwell's system of a young soldier involved in drug activities. On the MMPI profile most of his scores were much higher than average.

> He was probably overstating the severity of his disturbance. . . .The pattern is often seen with an acute identity crisis. . . .Chronic worrying, nervousness, fears

and anxieties are apt to have become overwhelming. He appears markedly self-preoccupied and prone to ruminate about his feelings of inferiority and inadequacy. Disturbances of sleep are common with this pattern. . . .He may have been deeply hurt in past close relationships and be distrustful and questioning of the motives of others. . . .Lacking in longterm goals, he is apt to tolerate frustrations poorly. . . .Schizo-affective and psychotic depressive diagnoses are common with this pattern. . . .The profile suggests a mild suicide risk. . . .The profile recommends a relatively cautious and "here-now" handling of his anger since deeper interpretations could be disorganizing of his controls. Discovery of his personal ways of keeping others at a distance—perhaps especially as he uses them on the therapist—is apt to be of direct benefit in treatment. (Sundberg, Tyler, & Taplin, 1973, pp. 555–558)

The psychologist who worked with the case judged the report to be particularly apt in most places but irrelevant in others. Needless to say, these automated interpretations need to be handled with caution and only by qualified personnel. Green (1982) found clinicians rated certain automated report services quite favorably on utility and accuracy.

Clinical versus Statistical Contributions

As mentioned elsewhere, the 1954 book by Meehl on clinical versus statistical prediction precipitated a storm of comment and many research projects. To date there has been no refutation of the basic claim by Meehl that, where appropriate statistical information exists, clinicians using the same information cannot improve on the predictive performance of the formulas. The catch is the phrase "where appropriate statistical information exists." It is very rare that formulas are available for what the clinican needs to do, and often the data on which the statistical predictions are based were developed in a context quite foreign to the hospital, clinic, or office where the clinician works. The consensus among many clinical psychologists (e.g., Bernstein & Nietzel, 1980; Holt, 1978; Phares, 1979; Sawyer, 1966) now seems to be the following: (1) If statistical procedures are available for assisting in interpretation, the clinician should know them and use them appropriately. (2) Clinicians should be involved in quantifying and improving the accuracy of their clinical judgments. (3) Some clinicians are much better at predictions and other clinical judgments than are others, but we do not know yet what makes for better clinical skills. (4) The statistics and computerization of clinical assessment depend on the input of good clinical observations and data, and the clinician is well equipped to generate such data even though the human organism cannot match the accuracy and exact memory of the computer. In general it seems important for clinicians to use *both* statistical and clinical approaches to understanding and predicting human behavior, not argue for one to the exclusion of the other.

COMMUNICATION
OF ASSESSMENT FINDINGS

After the clinician has interpreted the findings, she or he comes to the last and very important stage in the process—the transmission of impressions and recommendations to others. Written reports are often required, short notes or long analyses to be put in a patient's chart, letters to a defense attorney or a judge, an outline of a treatment plan to be discussed with a client or family. A common report for a patient's record is one to three pages long. In most situations a written report is not the only communication; the assessing clinician also talks directly with the nurse, psychiatrist, or social worker who is dealing with the patient or the family. Obviously the assessment work is wasted if the findings are not used. Many long reports have gathered dust in hospital records, having had little or no impact. When compiling a report, the competent psychologist considers who will be using the information and for what purposes it will be used.

BOX 6-2 *COMPLETELY BLIND ASSESSMENT*

Psychologists often do what is called "blind assessment"; that is, they do diagnoses or predictions based only on limited information, such as age, sex, and the results of one test. In actual clinical situations, such a blind assessment must not be the final one; that must include full information on a case to see if the test results are confirmed or disconfirmed by other data. In the following instance the writer only knew that the person was a patient in a veterans hospital scheduled to be discussed at a convention session entitled "A Case Study of Schizophrenia." The report, written without seeing anything else, was as follows (Sundberg et al., 1973, p. 578):

> This veteran approached the testing situation with some reluctance. He was cooperative with the clinician, but mildly evasive on some of the material. Both the tests and the past history suggest considerable inadequacy in interpersonal relations, particularly with members of his family. It is doubtful whether he has ever had very many close relationships with anyone. Those few that he has had were tinged with a great deal of ambivalence. He has never been able to sink his roots deeply. He is immature, egocentric, and irritable, and often he misperceives the good intentions of the people around him. Projection is one of his prominent defense mechanisms. He tends to be basically passive and dependent, though there are occasional periods of resistance and rebellion against others. Although he shows some seclusiveness and autistic trends, he is in fair contact with reality. Vocationally, his adjustment has been very poor. Mostly he has drifted from one job to another. His interests are shallow and he tends to have poor motivation for his work. Also he has had a hard time keeping his jobs because of difficulty in getting along with fellow employees. Although he has had some relations with women, his sex life has been unsatisfactory to him. At present he is mildly depressed, although a great deal of affect is not shown. What physical complaints he has appear mainly to have a func-

tional origin. His intelligence is close to average, but he is functioning below his potential. In summary, this is a long-time inadequate or borderline adjustment pattern. Test results and case history, although they do not give a strong clear-cut diagnostic picture, suggest the diagnosis of schizophrenic reaction, chronic undifferentiated type. Prognosis for response to treatment appears to be poor.

This completely blind report was judged by other participants to be very much on the mark. The writer assumed several things in developing the report: (1) Cases referred for testing often are not clear-cut, so some hedging is expected in a report. (2) There are some modal characteristics, or base rates, common to patients coming to veterans hospitals. Most of them are unsuccessful at jobs and personal relationships, for instance. (3) The best guess on intelligence is average if the population from which the person comes is close to the general population. (4) Staff reports contain certain jargon, and there are preferences for certain diagnoses, such as schizophrenic reaction, chronic, undifferentiated type, which was frequently used in the veterans hospital from which the patient came— another base rate. (5) Since it was known that the case is of a schizophrenic, some common characteristics of such cases can be mentioned. (6) Some "universally valid" adjectives may be safely used, such as "immature." (7) In less clear areas, a vague statement or a "double-barrelled" one, mentioning both sides of the condition, is best to use. Readers can be counted on to overlook a few vague misses and to select the descriptions which go with their own preconceptions.

The possibility of doing such a completely blind analysis has many implications for the portrayal of "working images." It points out the way that the Barnum Effect and knowledge of base rates can be used even unintentionally to gain acceptance. Clever astrologers, magicians, and palm readers may use many of these assumptions. This illustration also raises questions about developing truly individualized case reports for clinical work.

Written Reports

In writing a report the psychologist faces such questions as these: What are the main points and how should I organize them? What kinds of language should I use in writing the report for this particular recipient? How detailed should the report be?

A number of psychologists have pointed out pitfalls. Meehl (1956) coined the term *Barnum Effect* to characterize descriptions that are a mixture of stereotypes, vagueness, and evasion, reports that include *universally valid statements*, such as "The patient is anxious," or "The mother has mixed feelings about her child's behavior; sometimes she is angry and sometimes she is pleased." The problem of individualizing a psychological report is not an easy one. Research has shown that people will readily accept Barnum, or fake personality, descriptions as true of themselves (Forer, 1949; Snyder, Shenkel, & Lowery, 1977; Sundberg, 1955). To avoid these vague, generalized communications, the psychologist should report the incidence of targeted behavioral problems or examples from the individual's own statements or from the case history. These help to individualize and make the meanings of interpretations clear and concrete.

Direct Communication
with the Client

In most counseling situations and in many clinical situations, the assessment report should be appropriate for discussion with the client. (With most psychotic and severely disturbed people, it may not be possible or therapeutically advisable to discuss the results in any detailed way.) At this point assessment clearly merges with therapy. The psychologist, knowing the treatment plan, can show how the findings relate to the "contract" being developed with the client. Reports designed for discussion with clients need to avoid the jargon that psychologists often use, especially pathological-sounding psychiatric terms that may be disturbing.

Ethical Aspects of Communication

The gathering and transmission of personal data bring up many questions about confidentiality and social responsibility. Hospitals and clinics keep personal materials in locked files and do not allow people other than authorized staff professionals to read them except by permission of the patient or the patient's guardian. The same rules apply to psychologists in private practice. Clients must also be informed in advance about the psychological tests and procedures to be employed and must give their informed consent to such procedures. They should be informed if they are to be observed by people, or if video or audio records are to be made. Generally any client who wishes to should be able to examine his or her case records. Ethical issues will be discussed again in a later chapter.

Case Illustration

The following reports show how one psychologist, Dr. Harry James, communicates with professional staff members and with the patient in his work in a hospital outpatient clinic. A young man, Ray Bircher, in a coma after a motorcycle accident, had been brought to the emergency room of the hospital. A year later he had recovered from the immediate physical injuries but still had problems that required rehabilitative treatment. Dr. James made use of the earlier record and conferred extensively with the social worker who had also interviewed Ray and his family. Both of the following reports were originally longer; excerpts are used to illustrate main points.

REPORT OF NEUROPSYCHOLOGICAL
AND PERSONALITY EVALUATION

Patient: Ray Bircher, Age 17

Date: _____

Place: _____

Reason for Referral: Information for planning a vocation and for independent living.

Tests Administered: Wechsler Adult Intelligence Scale, Wechsler Memory Scale, Wide Range Achievement Test, Minnesota Multiphasic Personality Inventory, Halstead-Reitan Neuropsychological Battery.

Behavioral Observations: Ray was cooperative and interested in the tests, but quiet and subdued. He was dressed neatly in typical high school garb. There were occasional signs of carelessness and willingness to say, "I'm done," early in the testing process. He seemed to have poor recall for testing done six months ago.

Intellectual Abilities: Ray obtained an above-average WAIS Full Scale IQ, with Verbal and Performance IQs only slightly different. The pattern of subscales showed an average amount of scatter. All subscales showed at least a few points' improvement from those obtained six months ago; the largest gains were in those performance tasks requiring visual spatial analysis (Block Design, Picture Arrangement, and Object Assembly). His progress has been gratifying, but recovery tends to slow down with time. The encouraging "normal" picture on the WAIS must be tempered with the realization that many essential functions, such as memory and social judgment, are not well measured by this test.

Academic Achievement: The Wide Range Achievement Test samples the level of attainment in reading, spelling, and arithmetic. Ray was in the tenth grade at the time of the accident, and schooling since that time has been interrupted occasionally. Although he had been average for the ninth grade on school records, the current testing shows him to be well below average, falling at the seventh-grade level in reading and the eighth grade in spelling and arithmetic. Progress may be expected if special remedial assistance can be made available.

Neuropsychological Functioning: The Halstead-Reitan covers a wide variety of tasks related to the integrity and efficiency of cerebral function. These tasks, along with allied tests and observations, provide the basis for the following summary of each major area: (1) *Sensory-motor abilities.* The left hand does not show the expected grip strength, and there is a decrement in finger tapping and left-handed performance in general. These findings reflect inadequate right cerebral hemisphere functioning. Basic sensory-perceptual abilities are intact. (2) *Language skills.* Ray performed well on parts of the aphasia screening test but was unable to name a simple item (dysnomia) and, most seriously, produced several irrelevant and ill-formed letters in writing (dysgraphia). (3) *Memory.* Tests show a significant impairment in memory, especially for short-term verbal functions; he was unable to recall ten simple words after ten promptings. He was also poor at remembering elements of a simple verbal passage. (4) *Complex Problem Solving.* Ray did creditably well on these tasks, although one can detect a slight insufficiency in visuospatial function related to right hemisphere damage.

Personality: The MMPI results were compared with both adult and adolescent norms. The results suggest a cooperative, nondefensive attitude and willingness to admit to problems. The most significant feature was impulsiveness. His energy level may outrun his judgment. Young people of his age tend to show high energy levels and some impulsivity and lack of prudence, but Ray is above his age-mates in this regard; it seems likely from the history given by the parents that these personality characteristics were present before the accident. These present levels do cause concern for Ray's capacity for self-managment and judgment.

Summary: This young man shows problem solving and intellectual skills at or just above the normal level. Academically, however, he is three or more years behind average. His memory functions poorly, especially when distractions are present. Clear left motor problems and some specific language problems are found. His major difficulties in functioning will relate to the use of good judgment in regulating his activities, maintaining attention on tasks, and achieving stability over time. Impulsiveness is an important problem.

Recommendations: Ray's parents will need to reevaluate some of their hopes for their cherished son. A process of designing new hopes and goals will need to be started. A counselor may help by using the following two suggestions: (1) Recognize that there are two competing goals of (a) safeguarding him when his impulsiveness and inadequate memory may lead him to harm, and (b) giving him as much freedom as possible to develop himself. (2) Plan a series of activities with these two goals in mind; in general, trying things should be encouraged, and where he shows competence, foresight, and maturity, more opportunity may be granted. Perhaps the parents should consider a trusteeship or other way of safeguarding the considerable amount of money he will receive as a result of the accident. More specifically, three areas of developmental activities should be considered: possibilities for jobs and community college training, visiting and living away from home on a trial basis, and having fun, even thrills, without the risks of alcohol, drugs, or fast motor vehicles. Community resources for these activities include several sports clubs, church groups, and the community college.

Ray asked for a copy of the report. The formal one would not be meaningful, thought Dr. James, noting Ray's tenuous adjustment. Ray was often drawn into teenage drinking episodes and had trouble finding his way home after alcohol or marijuana use. Nevertheless, he deserved to be "in the picture" as much as possible. Dr. James decided to write Ray a less technical letter, discussing the findings and opening the topic of dealing with limitations and impulsiveness. The following letter served as a focus for discussion and provided Ray with a document of his own:

Dear Ray:

As I mentioned to you the other day, I am sending this letter to you to summarize the results of all the testing you have had. Your cooperation and willingness to carry out many tasks was excellent and help give a picture of your thinking processes and abilities at the present time. You have made fine progress since the accident. You deserve a lot of praise for sticking at tasks when they haven't been easy. This letter shows that you have several good strengths to build on as you think about what you will do next in your life.

The intellectual ability tests measured how much you know and how well you solve certain problems as compared with others of your age as of this time. You did well, with scores falling at the average or a little above average on most of the tests. It is particularly gratifying to see that you have improved over the test results of six months ago, especially in your short-term memory (such as repeating numbers back to me).

The test of school subjects showed that you have forgotten some of the material you learned years ago, as you suspected. Quite understandably, your accident has interfered both with your progress in school and in your memory for things you learned earlier. The tests show you to be at a level of students who are a few years back in school in reading, writing, and arithmetic.

The neuropsychological tests you took involved a great variety of tasks such as copying figures, tapping with your finger, and seeing how strong a hand grip you have. Our brains have to do a lot of different things such as working out what to say, controlling our muscles, solving problems, and remembering how to get from one place to another. The tests show that your left hand is not quite as strong and fast as your right, which is okay. You did very well when it came to recognizing things, and your solving of complicated problems was good, too. (Remember the slides on the screen with the bell and the blocks you put in the board while blindfolded?) One area that wasn't strong, which we talked about a bit the other day, was trying to remember details when there are things around to distract you. You will find it useful to practice your memory and to notice how to improve your concentration.

The personality tests tell about your attitudes and feelings. They don't have any right or wrong answers; they just show how people think about things. Your report about yourself in responding to the many statements by marking "true" or "false" suggests several ideas. You seem to be overly optimistic and impulsive about what you might do at times. So it would be good to be careful about getting thoughts anything like these, "Rules don't matter," "Everything is going so fast I don't have time to think," or "Nothing should get in my way." If such ideas come, just slow down and start over, because thoughts such as these are probably not correct, and they often get people into difficulties. The test says that sometimes you are quite impatient and impulsive. However, in general you are in pretty good spirits, which is a real asset.

Where to go from here? In a nutshell you have some really good strengths according to the test results. With those strengths you can build a life for yourself doing something you enjoy and living in a place that's pleasant.

First, the job: The work needs to be difficult enough to challenge you, but not so difficult that you are swamped and unhappy. It is important that you sample different kinds of jobs and job training until you find something you like that will fit in with your abilities and needs. Vocational counselors in the rehabilitation office can help you learn about work and training.

Now, about the living situation: As we discussed, living on your own can give you a good deal of freedom and independence, but there are several risks. After a severe injury to the head, brains need the very best care they can get. That means good food, good rest, and avoidance of the use of alcohol and drugs which damage the way the injured brain does its work. I hope you can discuss with your parents where you might move to and when, so that you all have good plans laid and feel happy about the decision.

Finally, about having fun: We talked about the importance of having a good time, too. It is really important for you to be able to enjoy yourself while at the same time taking good care of your head. Finding other people who will not get you into fast driving and a lot of alcohol and drugs are things to consider seriously. There are lots of things going on in this town that are a lot of fun for young people and fit your interests and your needs to avoid risks to your brain. So do look around and find friendly places and friendly people to enjoy yourself.

If you have any questions about this letter, please give me a call. I will try to stay in touch with a telephone call or two in the next few months at least.

Sincerely,
Harry James, Ph.D.

This letter to Ray was only part of a long process with several agencies working with the client. Some readers may perceive the letter as somewhat "preachy," but given the serious nature of the problems and the amenability of the client to direct advice, the psychologist found it to be useful. It is important, whether a letter is sent or not, to communicate clearly with clients about the results of the findings and to answer questions they may have.

CRITIQUE

Chapters 4 and 5 have already covered a number of criticisms about assessment—especially those dealing with the initial stages of the process and with testing. Here we will concern ourselves with the final stages of interpreting and communicating findings and with general strategies.

How adequate is the assessment process conceptually? In introducing the four major clinical orientations in Chapter 4, we commented on the lack of overall unification of their different approaches. Furthermore, little connection is ordinarily made between formal assessment processes and the informal day-to-day processes of making decisions and understanding others. This task is one of synthesizing contributions from the cognitive, social, and personality branches of psychology as well as from practical clinical work.

Some progress has been made in exploring the cognitive activity of the clinician. One approach is called *thinking aloud*. The investigator presents the clinician with a set of data and asks for a step-by-step report of how he or she attends to the information, organizes it, forms impressions, and comes to decisions and recommendations. Sometimes *stimulated recall* is used in replaying an interview or some other recorded clinical situation, and the clinician is asked to recall his or her thoughts. Elstein, Shulman, and Sprafka (1978), working with expert medical diagnosticians, found that they immediately focused on problematic cues in cases and entertained three to five diagnostic possibilities. Kleinmuntz (1970) has applied this technique to develop a sequence of steps to be used by a computer in interpreting the MMPI—a decisional flow chart. A second major approach has been to develop a model of a clinician's judgments by having him or her sort a large number of profiles of a test such as the MMPI. Because each profile varies on different scales, it is possible to ascertain the weight that the clinician places on each of the scales in making the judgments and to develop a statistical model of the clinician's thinking. Goldberg (1970) derived models from a group of clinicians sorting MMPI profiles into neurotic or psychotic categories and demonstrated the superiority of a combined formula over individual clinical judges. The large amount of research on clinical versus statistical prediction has already been mentioned. These studies are interesting technical exercises, but they still have not led to comprehensive

BOX 6-3   *TABULATING OUTCOMES OF ASSESSMENT—*
HIT RATES AND BASE RATES

In any assessment situation, if the assessor takes enough care to define descriptions and predictions, it would be possible to check on their accuracy. Doing the simple procedure outlined below would help assessors learn a great deal about the quality of their assessment procedures and their own assessing behavior. In each of the four boxes the assessor should tabulate in two ways—whether the assessment procedure or judgment is positive or negative and whether the actual condition (as judged by someone else or as found out on follow-up) is positive or negative. As an illustration, let us say that a clinician was interested in how effective she (or he) is in predicting the ultimate diagnosis of schizophrenia on the basis of the sentence completion test alone. She would read only the sentence completion test (obtained by someone else) and decide whether the new patient is schizophrenic or not, perhaps based on unusual associations and peculiar expression of thoughts. After she had done 50 of these, she would check on the agency charts to see what diagnoses the patients were given on the basis of the whole psychiatric work-up (which had preferably omitted the sentence completion). A possible result (with numbers in parentheses) is shown below:

	Positive	False Negatives (5)	True Positives (30)
ACTUAL OUTCOME	Negative	True Negatives (10)	False Positives (5)
		Negative	Positive

JUDGMENT FROM ASSESSMENT

The hypothetical success rate of the psychologist turned out to be very high. She had a high rate for true positives and true negatives combined of 80 percent, which a chi square statistic would show to be significant. Among various things the psychologist could learn from such a table is whether she had tendencies toward overusing or underusing the diagnosis.

The picture becomes a bit more complicated, however, when we consider the base rates for schizophrenia in this particular facility. If the actual percentage of people entering the agency were high—say 80 or 90 percent—the psychologist could have done as well by calling all of them schizophrenics without reading the sentence completions. However, if the proportion of schizophrenics were about 50-50, then the psychologist's use of the sentence completion did add something beyond the base rates. When base rates are extremely lop-sided, either very high or very low, it is difficult to find a procedure that will add incremental utility beyond the base rates. One has to take into account also the dangers of making a wrong decision. Within a hospital setting, it might be advantageous to overselect for schizophrenic or suicidal tendencies so that more careful attention can be given to the patient. In a sample of people from off the street where the base rates are very low, calling someone schizophrenic or suicidal on the basis of limited information may lead to many misleading and even damaging errors. For a full discussion of hit rates and base rates, see Wiggins (1973).

theories of clinical information processing. Ultimately one can expect that such research will produce many helpful statistical aids. Dawes (1979) has shown the utility even of "improper" models—that is, a formula based on intuition and other nonoptimal methods. He notes that people seem to be better at selecting and coding information than at integrating it. Determining what is relevant in a case requires good clinical sense and experience. Snyder and White (1981) have shown that the strategies people use in looking for evidence for a hypothesis affect the results. Those instructed to confirm a hypothesis performed differently from those told to disconfirm it. Just how clinicians develop working images, arrive at decisions, and test hypotheses needs much more investigation, allied with a theory of practice.

The third purpose of assessment—hypothesis checking—has previously been mentioned. It is implicit in all research, other than that limited simply to description. Some clinical theoreticians, following George Kelly (1955), view all people as "scientists" seeking to make sense of their experience through continually testing hypotheses. Psychologists use assessment procedures, such as structured interviews, tests, and analyses of records, to investigate theoretical propositions or predictions. Nearly all measures used in clinical work are also used for research. There is an interdependency between the methods and the theories, since the theories cannot be tested empirically without some means for gathering information, and the methods derive their meaning, their construct validity, from the use of theoretical propositions. Thus a *nomological network* (a set of case-tested or empirically tested general laws) is built up around the primary assessment concepts (Cronbach & Meehl, 1955; Wiggins, 1973).

The criterion problem in the broad sense is the major stumbling block in the development of a theory of assessment practice. Cronbach (1970, pp. 677–678), reviewing a number of assessment programs, states, "The most important requirement for valid assessment is that the assessors understand the psychological requirements of the criterion task." Some of the most successful assessment research efforts (e.g., Holmen et al., 1956; Vernon, 1950) have been those that have made a careful criterion analysis; in some cases the individuals making the assessment ratings were familiar with the eventual work situation of the assessees. The implication is that clinical work needs to be ecological—that is, it should use information about the situations in which people will be judged and in which they judge themselves. Competencies and life-style characteristics that fit the present and potential ecological niches of the person's daily interactions promise to be major elements in successful assessment.

How practical are the final stages of the assessment process?
The question of the usefulness of various approaches to interpretation, of statistical aids, and of reports at the end of assessment has been seldom studied, considering that the "proof of the pudding" should be in practical ac-

tions. Affleck and Strider (1971) investigated 340 psychological reports in a large psychiatric institute. The referral source (usually psychiatrists in training) regarded the reports as generally very valuable and stated that 52 percent of the reports had altered management in some way and only 22 percent had no effect; 2 percent were seen as detrimental. Smyth and Reznikoff (1971) also obtained a generally favorable report from referral sources, but Moore, Bobbitt, and Wildman (1968) found that referring psychiatrists said they made use of the psychological reports only 20 percent of the time. Ladd (1967) studied record keeping in psychiatric and psychological clinics and noted that, although generally useful and helpful, records that contain damaging views can be a continuing source of prejudice. Tallent's book (1983) presents a comprehensive survey of the many pitfalls of report writing. In general, studies and practical experience suggest that reports should have a clearly understood purpose and use methods designed to achieve that purpose.

Another practical question is whether assessment is useful for treatment or therapy. Some surveys (e.g., Kelly, 1961) suggested that at least a few decades ago, few psychologists made use of test results in providing treatment. We have frequently pointed out here that some assessment must go on, but its thoroughness and formality varies with the orientation of the therapist. Recently the behavioral orientation has led to much more assessment, although not of the traditional testing kind. Rogers and other person-centered therapists have intentionally not used tests or traditional intake interviews in direct clinical work, but they have used them extensively for research purposes. The question to be raised is whether systematic assessment information of various sorts adds to treatment effectiveness, and very little has been done to research this question.

Another practical question regards the time and effort put into various kinds of testing and assessment. The question is one of costs and benefits of aspects of the assessment process against criteria of usefulness and acceptability. Does the Rorschach, which may take several hours of clinical time to administer, score, and interpret, contribute more than would several hours spent doing something else? Which among several sets of neuropsychological tests provides the most return for the least time? Does an interview obtain as much information for practical decision making as do certain tests? Do any assessment procedures add much to the conclusion about a person obtained from the basic identifying data or a short case history, which have to be collected anyway? The questions touch on the idea of the *incremental utility* of a procedure, which was mentioned earlier in connection with base rates. To date, there are few research data on this complex topic, but what there are suggest that the case history and basic identifying data are very important in their contribution to the final picture about a person (Golden, 1964; Horowitz, 1962; Little & Shneidman, 1959). Kostlan (1954) varied systematically the way in which he gave 20 clinicians data from the

Rorschach, MMPI, sentence completions, or the case history on several patients. He found that clinicians' descriptions were no better than those based on minimal descriptive data such as age, occupation, and marital status, unless they also had access to the case history. Potkay (1973), in a review of such studies, concluded that "personal history data as a source of clinically descriptive or predictive information is at least as effective as information derived from psychological test scores" (p. 208). Further research needs to demonstrate where the strengths of various tests and other psychological information lie *in addition to* the base rates and other basic data.

A related question is about the extent to which assessment procedures add to the *confidence* of clinical decision makers. Frequently referrals for testing are made because the psychiatrist or other person responsible for the care is unsure of his or her own judgment. Aside from accuracy the question is how much the report adds to the perceived correctness of decisions reached. This confidence is an important ingredient in psychological aspects of treatment, which is after all a process of social influence.

How worthwhile and effective is the assessment process? The whole assessment process is a combination of client, clinician, methods (tests, interviews, and so forth), and situation (the agency and the external systems) in interaction. Studies of incremental utility of various procedures get at part of this process but not the whole thing. There is very little research evidence now to suggest which of these elements can be improved and made more worthwhile. Sadly, most of the research studies on improving clinical judgment through training have not yet discovered how to make training more effective (Crow, 1957; Danet, 1965; Goldberg, 1959, 1968). Chapman and Chapman (1967) have shown that clinicians sometimes interpret data in terms of stereotyped beliefs or "illusory correlations"; these are very difficult to shake even with training (Golding & Rorer, 1972; Kurtz & Garfield, 1978; Nisbett & Ross, 1980). Many clinicians are apt to overlook base rates, to overgeneralize from a small sample of behavior, to overpathologize, to "blame" individual predispositions rather than situational variables, and to be ethnocentric. In sum, research suggests decided limitations in assessment and human judgment.

Certainly we need much more understanding of how to select, nurture, and educate people who are to be making important judgments about others. Assessment remains a very important enterprise—a necessary part of clinical work. Lazarus (1973, p. 407) concludes concerning behavioral work that "faulty problem identification (inadequate assessment) is probably the greatest impediment to successful therapy," and Levy (1963, p. viii) asserts "interpretation is the most important single activity engaged in by the clinician."

There is considerable social responsibility in making the necessary decisions about and with people and in developing the psychological working images that are used as guides in therapy and case management. The whole assessment process is a form of social influence. In the absence of well-documented knowledge about what is worthwhile in improving clinical judgment, we can, however, conclude that we must avoid some of the problems that have been identified—such as failure to take base rates into account, tendencies to use Barnum statements and not to individualize reports, over emphasis on the negative and pathological, and overlooking relevant information at several systems levels. The clinical assessor is bombarded with a great amount of information and needs to be tolerant of ambiguity and lack of closure; decisions must be made, but they should not be based on over-simplified, unrepresentative, or irrelevant data. Finally the clinician certainly needs to keep firmly in mind the welfare of the client and the significant other people in the situation. An ethical, well-informed, and balanced advocacy of the interests of the client and the relevant social systems will facilitate the making of good assessment decisions.

SUMMARY

In this chapter we have been concerned with tying together the loose ends of the assessment process and reporting the results. These final phases include the quantitative processing of data as well as the judgmental processing leading to decisions about organization and transmission of information through written and oral reports. Through examining cases, we looked at how the orientation of the clinician and his or her colleagues affects this final processing, whether the assessment orientation be toward everyday, pathological, learning, growth, or ecological considerations.

Using personal information, environmental relations, and professional observations, the clinical psychologist selects what is important. Importance depends on what is relevant to the assessment questions, what is deviant from normal, what has prominence, and what is congruent or discrepant across different sources of data. The selected information may be treated as a sample, correlate, or sign of conditions, depending on the orientation of the psychologist. Sometimes pathognomic signs are used—that is, highly probable indicators of psychopathology. The psychologist's way of combining information to arrive at a final picture of the person for the report may be viewed as an analytic, logical procedure (taxonomic sorting) or an empathic formation of a picture or "Gestalt" (emerging synthesis); clinicians have different cognitive styles in approaching this task.

Quantitative aids to interpretation include the recording of behavior or other occurrences, use of norm tables to compare with other people's scores, comparisons with base rates of incidence of a disorder or problem in the relevant population, use of expectancy tables or formulas, descriptive terms that research has shown to be related to scores or profiles, and codebooks for comparing results with previous cases. A growing area of assistance to interpretation is the automated or computerized report. Tests, such as the MMPI, can be sent to centers where they are scored and interpreted by means of previously developed norms and formulas to provide a description of the client and probable diagnosis and prognosis. The research contrasting clinical with statistical prediction shows that, where formulas exist, they can equal or improve on the predictions made by clinicians. However, clinicians still must make many judgments, since formulas are seldom available or appropriate to local conditions. Clinicians are also important for the many basic observations on which formulas may be based. A reasonable combination of statistical and clinical processing seems best in most instances.

The communication of assessment findings usually involves oral as well as written reports. The Barnum Effect applies to personality descriptions that are accepted by people as being written particularly for them, whereas the reports are actually made up of universally valid or vague statements that apply to almost anyone. A good report conveys information of use for that particular person. Sometimes the psychologist discusses the report of assessment results directly with the client, but most often it goes to the referring person or agency. A case example of a report to an agency and to the client was given.

In critically reviewing interpretation, reporting, and assessment in general, we found much need for improvement. Much more theory-related research is needed on the cognitive activities of clinicians and on ways of making decisions and facilitating clear and useful communications about clients. Understanding the ultimate criteria of success or failure of client-related activities is a major objective; this involves knowing the ecology of the clients' living situations. Studies of the usefulness of reports indicate a generally positive attitude, but there are many pitfalls. One practical question is about the worth in terms of professional time and cost of the various tests and other procedures that are used in assessment—does a given procedure provide enough incremental utility beyond the basic case data that has to be gathered anyway? Frequently cases are referred because of the uncertainty of the psychiatrist or other responsible person about what to do—does the report add to the confidence in decisions that must be taken? Despite the many criticisms the importance of assessment seems assured; the development of better ways to collect, organize, and interpret data about persons and situations is a continuing challenge.

RECOMMENDED READINGS

Arkes, H. R. Impediments to accurate clinical judgments and possible ways to minimize their impact. *Journal of Consulting and Clinical Psychology,* 1981, *49,* 323–330.

    In an excellent summary of research in cognitive psychology, Arkes identifies five problems: inability of people to estimate or use covariation properly, the influence of preconceived notions, lack of awareness of one's judgmental processes, overconfidence, and the tendency to find reasons for judgments by hindsight. Arkes suggests that clinicians should counter these judgmental problems by considering alternatives, thinking statistically, and decreasing their reliance on memory. In *Human Inference* Nisbett and Ross (1980) recognize both the rational and irrational aspects of judgments. They discuss many problems in assigning weights to data (such as the tendency to overemphasize vivid events), in generalizing from a small sample of observations, in judging correlations, in attributing causes, and in predicting. People usually try to confirm the beliefs and theories they already hold. The authors end by suggesting ways to improve inferential strategies, including early teaching of statistical reasoning. Another book from social psychologists relevant to other aspects of the last phases of assessment is *Decision Making*, by Janis and Mann (1977). Berger (1979) applies a decision-making model to assessment in school situations. Among the many interesting areas of research in social psychology that are relevant to clinical assessment are strategies that people use to test hypotheses about others (e.g., research by Snyder & White, 1981, showing that people tend to preferentially select information in line with their prior orientations).

Pankratz, L. D., & Taplin, J. R. Issues in psychological assessment. In J. R. McNamara & A. G. Barclay (Eds.), *Critical issues in professional psychology*. New York: Praeger, 1982.

Using a general systems theoretical perspective, the authors discuss the curative, learning, and growth or developmental perspectives. They identify areas in which assessment sometimes falls short—missing information about the self, about the context, about biological and neuropsychological bases of the person's condition, and about psychosocial bases. They argue that assessment and adequate evidence about the nature of problems is absolutely necessary for interventions and that there are profound legal and ethical implications with inadequate assessment.

Meehl, P. E. *Psychodiagnosis: Selected papers*. Minneapolis: University of Minnesota Press, 1973.

Meehl, an eminent clinical psychologist, presents a series of papers on testing, diagnosis, and the thinking processes of clinicians. Some of the chapters of particular interest are these: "The Cognitive Activity of the Clinician," "When Shall We Use Our Heads Instead of the Formula?," and "Why I Do Not Attend Case Conferences." In other chapters Meehl discusses some of the most important concepts in clinical assessment, such as base rates, the Barnum Effect, validity, and genetic questions about schizophrenia. Other important sources for discussions of the clinician's cognitive activities are *Psychological Interpretation* by Leon Levy (1963) and *Clinical Inference and Cognitive Theory* by Sarbin, Taft, and Bailey (1960).

Wiggins, J. S. Clinical and statistical prediction: Where are we and where do we go from here? *Clinical Psychology Review*, 1981, *1*, 3–18.

This is an excellent review of the developments since Meehl's classic inauguration (1954) of the debate over clinical and statistical prediction. Wiggins concludes that prediction models are now fairly clear and simple, and what we need now is the development of better assessment procedures and more useful criterion measures. He states that clinical judges should not be treated as second-rate computers but should be studied to see what rules and guidelines they use in decision making and predictions. One of the important landmarks in improving prediction is Goldberg's demonstration (1970) that models of clinical judgment can outperform the original judges.

Tallent, N. *Psychological report writing* (2nd ed.). Englewood Cliffs, N.J.: Prentice-Hall, 1983.

Tallent, who has done considerable research on psychological reports over the years, gathers together a great deal of information about the most effective ways to communicate about cases. Guided by earlier surveys of reporting problems, he covers problems of content, interpretation, orientation, communication, and professional background and role. He warns about Barnum-type reports and heavy use of jargon. He advocates a case-focused report and gives many illustrations of different kinds of reports. Klopfer (1982), who also has been studying this topic for many years, presents a chapter entitled "Writing Psychological Reports" in which he reviews the literature and presents examples.

RESEARCH EXAMPLES

Little, K. B., & Shneidman, E. S. Congruencies among interpretations of psychological test and anamnestic data. *Psychological Monographs*, 1959, 73(6), 1–42 (Whole No. 476).

This major study examines the value of combinations of assessment information. Little and Schneidman used 48 psychologists who were experts in the particular tests. Twelve each interpreted the MMPI, Rorschach, TAT, and the Make-A-Picture-Story (a projective test involving choosing among several possible figures for a scene and making up a relevant story). The authors had obtained the test results from 12 men equally divided among psychotic, psychophysiological, neurotic, and normal categories. In addition to the tests, a case history was made available to some judges. Each judge answered with five kinds of interpretive measures: diagnosis, rating of maladjustment, a 76-item Q-sort of adjustment and social behavioral items, a 117-item true-false questionnaire of statements like those in psychological reports, and another questionnaire on facts about the person's past and present life. Judges based their answers on tests and history data that were given them in a balanced design. The criterion against which their answers were judged were the responses of 24 psychiatrists and psychologists who read the case histories. When the experimental judge's answers were compared with the criteria, a great deal of data emerged through correlational procedures. In general the results were not impressive. Judges who were experts on particular tests produced only a small increase over chance variation. The MMPI fared somewhat better than did the projective techniques. There are criticisms of the study—for instance, the clinicians who produced the criterion answers did not interview the subjects and may have been selective in their judgments according to the predominant psychoanalytic orientation.

In another frequently cited study Kostlan (1954) systematically presented clinicians with test scores and social history and asked them to make inferences on a checklist. These inferences were compared with those made by a panel of experts. Kostlan's finding was that minimal data (the identifying data alone) produced inferences that were better than chance, and without the case histories clinicians did not improve over the success rate of that based on the minimal data. There were large individual differences in success rates among the clinicians. The point of these two studies and others is that the utilities of individual tests, case history, and interview data need to be carefully checked. Clinicians are limited, indeed, in their ability to combine information from various sources, but the case history and basic identifying data are important parts of the picture.

Snyder, C. R., & Newberg, C. L. The Barnum Effect in a group setting. *Journal of Personality Assessment*, 1981, 45, 622–629.

This study is one of a series by Snyder exploring the circumstances under which people will accept personality descriptions of themselves. For an excellent review of the concept and the research over many years, see Snyder, Shenkel, and Lowery (1977). The Barnum Effect was given that label by Meehl and seems to have been clearly identified first by D. G. Paterson, who demonstrated the gullibility of students, business executives, and others by giving the groups a description of each person's personality that was purportedly based on individual tests or observations but that was actually the same set of statements for everyone. The statements that people accept readily as pertaining to their individual personality are generally vague or widely shared in common (i.e., universally valid). The two earliest experiments reported in the literature were by Forer (1949) and Sundberg (1955). Despite the common stereotype of greater female suggestibility, both of these found no sex differences, and in these and later studies subjects often judged the fake descriptions to be better than the true descriptions based on actual psychological assessment. A large number of studies followed, some confirming that astrologers' descriptions were readily accepted, too. The review by Snyder et al. (1977) concluded that statements are more likely to be accepted as true if they are alleged to be interpreted by a high-status clinician, are brief and ambiguous, and do not point out distinct differences from the majority of human beings. Snyder and his colleagues point out that such acceptability is likely to be greater from clients who are in an insecure situation and that acceptance of interpretations by clients in no way proves the validity of psychological tests.

In this particular study Snyder and Newberg experimented with bogus feedback to individuals participating in small groups of eight in situations somewhat analogous to a group counseling session. The volunteer subjects were 96 female undergraduates, who after an hour of personal discussion led by a psychologist wrote descriptions of other group members. A little later each group member received a bogus description by another group member or by the psychologist leader. In addition to this manipulation of the status of the alleged writer of the description, the favorability of the statements was manipulated (half negative and half positive) as were the expectations that the subject would meet with the person describing her for further discussions (the answerability manipulation). All subjects rated the descriptions they received as to accuracy and acceptability and were later asked to recall the descriptions. They were, of course, debriefed afterward as to the deception.

One result, as expected, was that favorable descriptions were more readily accepted and judged accurate than were unfavorable ones. Differences in answerability (whether the person was to discuss the description with the writer of it or not) did not have a significant effect. The status of the alleged writer had a strong effect; the psychologist leader's descriptions, even if they were negative, were significantly more readily accepted, seen as accurate, and recalled. The authors point out that although this was an analog situation, there are many similarities with therapy and training groups in which members and leaders give feedback to participants about their personal characteristics. They caution that the leaders, because of their status and influence, bear special professional responsibilities.

PART III

INTERVENTION AT DIFFERENT SYSTEMS LEVELS

As one of several basic concepts, the first part of this book emphasized that living systems can be seen as nested inside one another, with the smaller ones being components of larger ones. The hierarchy we suggest includes organismic (or biological), personal, family, small group, organization, and community.

Part III presents an overview of psychology's intervention or treatment strategies with this group of systems, arranged in order of size. The individual system remains centrally important, and so there are three chapters on aspects of working with individuals. But psychologists have been active— and psychological knowledge has been expanding rapidly—in work with other systems. The three chapters dealing with all the other systems are necessarily chockfull. Throughout this section, but perhaps especially in biological, cognitive, and family areas, there are many fascinating oppportunities for new professional roles and research. Part III also mentions some assessment techniques from Part II, this time in the context of psychotherapy and case management.

This section draws primarily from clinical psychology, although contributions from counseling, industrial-organizational, community, and other branches of psychology as well as psychiatry and social work are clear in places. The great diversity of approaches, of work settings, and of ultimate goals has the common element of seeking to improve the human condition through the ethical application of scientifically derived psychological knowledge.

7

TAKING THE BODY INTO ACCOUNT:

The Integration of Biological and Psychological Knowledge

Psychologists must have a clear understanding of many bodily processes and problems. This chapter emphasizes that psychologists encounter body-related issues often and in a wide variety of guises. In each instance the psychologist needs to know a good deal about the phenomenon in order to perform good psychological service and to relate effectively to other professionals.

In earlier times philosophers and psychologists debated over what has come to be called the *mind-body problem*, the problems of relating concepts about the mind to concepts about the body. We need not go into the complex history of the problem because this issue is not as important today. Psychologists tend to assume interaction of psychological and physical processes, and findings in developmental, cognitive, and neuropsychology are slowly filling in pieces of the puzzle of brain-behavior relationships.

Many areas of professional work engage the psychologist in biological issues. Grouped roughly, they include:

—Biological aspects in the life cycle, covering sexuality, birth, feeding, sleeping, growing, mating, aging, dying, all of which have great psychological importance.

—Situations in which physical problems result in psychological symptoms—e.g., genetic problems, birth injuries or defects, neurological damage, and many illnesses.

—Situations in which psychological and behavioral phenomena interact with the body. For example, external stress with people so predisposed may cause ulcers, headaches, or other symptoms. Note that many problems such as alcoholism or obesity are not easily classified because they arise from incompletely understood interactions of genetic, metabolic, or other physical factors with environmental factors.

—Several of the body therapies, therapies whose system includes the view that psychological change takes place through physical activities such as exercise, powerful massage, correct and complete orgasm, primal screaming episodes, or movement awareness.

Some writers in biology (Wilson, 1978; Young, 1978) raise the possibility that some complex human behaviors we have felt to be "civilized" or learned—for example, altruism—may in fact be innate or instinctual. If their suggestions receive continued scientific support, psychology may be paying even more attention to biological variables—in this case instinctual or inherent characteristics—revising its notions of how particular behaviors come into being, and taking a rather more nativist and less environmentalist position than in the past.

SOME ILLUSTRATIVE CASES

Jody, 18, and Jim, 21, were going for an afternoon ride on Jim's motorcycle. On their way home, they had a serious accident when a car braked sharply in front of them. Jim wasn't hurt badly, but Jody was thrown clear and sustained a serious head injury. After the emergency surgery she remained unconscious for some days but by the end of a week became progressively more alert. A variety of therapies were begun. Her parents, finally becoming convinced that she could not continue in college, began to press her physician for a clear prognosis. Dr. Sims, the neuropsychologist, was asked to administer the Halstead-Reitan Neuropsychological Battery. With the several measurements she obtained, Dr. Sims was able to get a clear picture of the severity of Jody's loss of function and to make some inferences about the location of the site of damage. She made plans with Jody and the Department of Vocational Rehabilitation for some job training. Her report, which was written to emphasize Jody's remaining strengths and skills as well as to point to deficits, also took careful note of the fact that disappointment, grief, and anger were issues with which Jody and her parents needed help.

Dr. Sims's next referral was a 54-year-old man, Mr. Mills. A local psychiatrist asked, "Do you think Mr. Mills is functional or organic?" meaning, did Dr. Sims think there was clear psychopathology or a problem with an identifiable organic component. Mr. Mills had held a responsible position in his company for several years, but lately the quality of his work had fallen off and co-workers had begun to notice occasional, rather bizarre behavior. Even when asked simple questions, Mr. Mills used meaningless verbalisms, such as "Yes, sir, you really caught me short on that one, you sure did." Occasionally when someone would press for answers, Mr. Mills burst into tears. After hearing of two such episodes, his manager contacted his wife, who called a psychiatrist, who in turn asked Dr. Sims for her opinions. After helping Mr. Mills feel comfortable in her office, Dr. Sims asked him to copy some geometric designs. This he did with so many inaccuracies, reversals, rotations, and failures that Dr. Sims elected to administer the WAIS next. On the WAIS-R, an intelligence test having eleven subtests each sampling a different function, Mr. Mills produced a pattern of results seen in patients with organic damage. A call to the referring psychiatrist resulted in Mr. Mills being scheduled for a CAT (computerized axial tomography, a very sophisticated X-ray development) scan. Subsequent diagnostic findings reported the presence of a cerebral degenerative disease.

Comment: In both examples the psychologist was asked to evaluate brain function. Both cases called for advanced and specialized knowledge of relationships between brain function and the signs by which it can be measured. In the first case psychological functions are returning after an accident. Jody's interaction with the environment has to be programmed to capitalize on what strengths she has and to remediate as far as possible those that have been lost. In Mr. Mills's case he has formed some primitive defense and coping mechanisms but will be in a steady decline for the rest of his life. Both cases need sensitive counseling services to help them accept their condition and maintain maximum dignity in their new circumstances. Jody, because of her higher functioning, will probably need help in dealing with fears and fantasies about incompetence and estrangement. Reality-based information about her condition and prognosis will probably help.

John complained to his friend over a beer, "I thought being assistant manager would be better—but it's all the more pressured. My belly is rumbling and squeaking so bad that I wonder if even customers will hear it and be put off. Then I'll be in even worse shape." As the pain got worse and as John's trips to the bathroom became more frequent, he decided he ought to do something. However, he kept putting it off until a set of particularly poor sales figures was posted, and he felt so bad that he went home sick. His wife persuaded him to see the family physician who referred him to a gastroenterologist. The specialist's finding of mucous colitis resulted in a referral to a psychologist, Dr. March. Dr. March identified early in the interview that John's sales job was a problem and also that his wife's parents exerted a heavy pressure on him to keep economic pace with his older brother-in-law. In the next interview to which he asked John to bring his wife, Betsy, he discovered that their relationship was clouded by memories that they hadn't intended to marry but had "had to" when Betsy became pregnant. Dr. March saw his task as (1) helping the couple evaluate whether they wanted to be a couple, (2) helping clarify their financial values and goals, and (3) helping them manage emancipation from the parents and parents-in-law.

The nurse called Philip's name and took him to an examining room in the student health service. When the physician came in and said cheerily, "And what's your problem, Philip?" Philip looked desperately around the room, flushed deeply, and then, looking resolutely at the floor, mumbled at last, "I can't get it up." The physician asked gently but thoroughly about the erection problem. No pain, no other symptoms of any kind, an occasional erection when awakening, and fairly frequent masturbation. One really unsatisfactory episode with a girlfriend appeared to be a critical incident. After more discussion and a general physical examination, the physician referred Philip to Dr. Paul at the counseling center. Dr. Paul's work with Philip helped Philip begin to view intercourse as a way of expressing feelings, to evaluate his views of sex in relationships, and to be more relaxed. Bit by bit he let go of the unrealistic expectations that had caused the crippling anxiety.

Comment: Neither of the last two examples is concerned directly with neuropsychological (brain) function. Each has a physiological reaction to some part of the psychological condition. Note that both cases came to a physician for help—that is, they came through formal medical channels. Much of the subsequent quality of psychological service depends on the physician's knowledge of and prior experience with psychological service. In all four examples the psychologist has to consider the full realm of client functioning—biological, personal, family, job setting, and so on. In the next four sections we will consider several of the major functions performed by psychologists that relate to or interact directly with the biological system. We have chosen to emphasize these particular areas—neuropsychological assessments, biofeedback, pain, sexual dysfunction, and genetically influenced problems—because of their current importance for psychologists, but in later sections we will present a quick inventory of many other important but less frequently encountered problems in applied biopsychology.

CLINICAL NEUROPSYCHOLOGY

Neuropsychology, says Lezak, "is an applied science concerned with the behavioral expression of brain dysfunction" (1976, p. 3). The field occupies a fascinating position somewhere between neurology and various branches of psychology and education. Figure 7-1 shows how assessment techniques of neuropsychology meet and overlap with those of the neighboring areas.

The essence of neuropsychology is that a series of procedures has been shown in prior research to give different results for persons with damaged brains (or parts of brains) than it does for persons with intact, normally efficient brains. The neuropsychologist may then entertain two basic types of questions: (1) Is there reason to think that this patient's difficulties have an organic basis? (2) Given that this patient has some organically related difficulties, which functions are impaired most, which least, and what remediation should be pursued? Our discussion elaborates these two questions and outlines sequences of clinical work after referral.

Brain function.   Although it would be presumptuous indeed to attempt to summarize in just a few lines how the brain works, certain ideas are essential to the understanding of the neuropsychological endeavor. Earlier investigators thought that they could localize particular functions to par-

Figure 7-1
Neuropsychological   assessment   and   its neighbors.

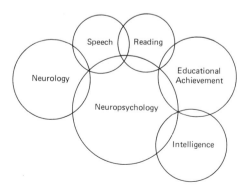

ticular places in the brain. Some theorists, for example, thought there were separate centers for cautiousness, agreeableness, and a variety of other qualities. These people were called *localizationists*. Their position was made difficult by a series of investigations disconfirming a number of their assertions and by evidence supporting the notion that for some functions (notably memory) the brain seems to act as a whole.

The Russian neuropsychologist Luria opened a new era in the understanding of brain function by offering the idea of functional systems. The three systems he proposed are " . . . a unit for *regulating tone or waking*, a unit for *obtaining*, *processing*, and *storing* information arriving from the outside world and a unit for *programming, regulating, and verifying mental activity*. A man's mental process in general, and his conscious activity in particular, always take place with the participation of all three units, each of which has its role to play in mental processes, and makes its contribution to their performance" (Luria, 1973, p. 43). System one is considered to involve low or brain stem centers; system two, some low centers, the posterior parts of the cortex, and the brain's top layer; and system three, a few low centers and the anterior or frontal parts of the cortex. Luria's notions are elegantly elaborated in *Higher Cortical Functions in Man* (1980). They represent some of the most important theorizing and observational data which has been done to date.

It has been long established that each side of the brain receives from and sends to (that is, controls) the opposite side of the body. Thus a person with a serious lesion in the motor areas of the right cerebral hemisphere is likely to have left-sided paralysis. Neuropsychologists use this finding. They measure right and left side performances and, by reference to normal right-left differences, can make inferences about the efficiency or inefficiency of the left and right hemispheres.

Then came the observation that the hemispheres perform different functions: The normal right-handed person probably has most of the language function in the left hemisphere, which also mediates logical information processing, particularly activities of a serial or sequential nature. The right cerebral hemisphere is probably more involved in spatial relations and holistic problem solving. The use of *probably* denotes that this division of activities is not invariant—left-handed people often have the pattern reversed. Just as localizationists invented "centers" for a variety of qualities, enthusiastic speculators have apparently gone too far in specifying what takes place in each hemisphere. Notions such as "logic is in the left hemisphere" or "religion is a right hemisphere activity" appear to have seriously outrun the data, and caution must be used before particular complex behaviors are labeled *right hemisphere* or *left hemisphere*.

Consistent with Luria's three systems, data have been offered on the differential functions of the brain as we advance from back to front of the cerebral cortex (see Figure 7–2). Neuropsychological sourcebooks such as

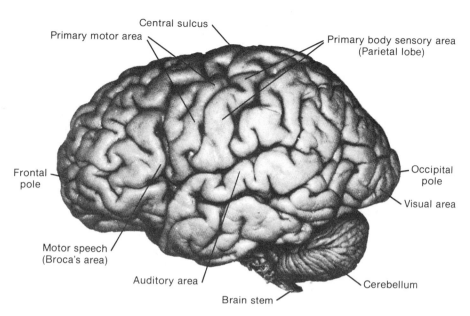

Figure 7-2 Side view of the human brain, including the cerebrum, cerebellum, and part of the brain stem. (From *Neuropsychological Assessment* (p. 34) by Muriel Deutsch Lezak. Copyright © 1976 by Oxford University Press, Inc. Reprinted by permission.)

Walsh (1978) or Filskov and Boll (1981) generally present a picture of differing functions for the major areas: visual reception and interpretation in the occipital (posterior) lobes; hearing and language functions in the temporal lobes; motor speech and other motor functions along the central sulcus (fissure), multisensory integration in the parietal lobes, and capacity for abstract thinking and self-regulatory behavior, or self-control, in the frontal lobes. The control functions are perhaps the hardest to evaluate. "Among the more readily observable signs of impaired control are emotional lability, a heightened tendency to excitability, impulsivity, erratic carelessness, rigidity, and difficulty in making shifts in attention and ongoing behavior . . . and decreased tolerance for alcohol" (Lezak, 1976, p. 30). Brain organization has remarkable complexity because various centers must work together in complex tasks—for example, reading involves spatial as well as linguistic skills.

Neuropsychological assessment. Even the brief review of brain functions just presented suggesting a complicated set of interrelated functions—many of which must work together to produce a particular observable behavior—makes psychologists' early efforts to produce a single test for brain damage, or "organicity," look misdirected. Many of the single tests were tests of visual memory and visuomotor and spatial abilities, sampled by showing patients particular figures and, after a pause, asking that the figures be

BOX 7-1 *SINGLE TESTS MAY MISS MAJOR ASPECTS OF BRAIN CONDITION*

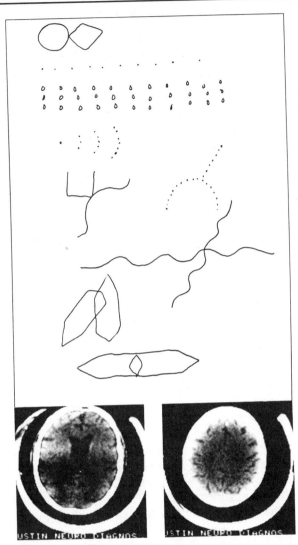

The Bender Visual Motor Gestalt Test is a simple copying test, widely used to get at *organicity*. However, it tests only a few functions and may produce many false negatives. Here are results with a 64-year-old man with poor memory and job performance. The Bender has been quite reasonably executed but the patient's CAT scan shows obvious pathology. Ventricular enlargement and presence of sulci widening indicate brain atrophy.

From E. D. Bigler & J. W. Ehrfurth, The continued inappropriate singular use of the Bender Visual Motor Gestalt Test. *Professional Psychology*, 1981, *12*, 562–569. Copyright by the American Psychological Association and reprinted by permission of the author.

drawn. Such tests do sample the integrity of *certain* functions but omit the critically important functions of language, speech, reading, other types of memory, and complex problem solving, to name just a few.

Neuropsychological assessment strives to evaluate a wide variety of cerebral functions for efficiency or decrement, for localization and progressiveness of lesions, and chiefly for designing remediation and rehabilitation activities. Thus most neuropsychologists recognize that, especially in initial assessment of a patient, a broad range of functions must be systematically sampled before areas of organic efficiency or decrement can be inferred or described. The need to assess across a broad range of functions has led to the development of standard batteries, briefly mentioned in Chapter 5.

Reitan's batteries. Perhaps foremost among these standard batteries is the work of Ralph Reitan and co-workers (e.g., Reitan & Davison, 1974), who, building on the early work of Ward Halstead, developed three batteries, one each for adults, older children, and younger children. Each battery contains roughly ten procedures, many of which yield several results or indicators. The validation of Reitan's procedures on adults and older children must be called impressive. Not only is there a rich history of formal studies, but also the case examples of, say, the neuropsychologist correctly predicting tumor location before post mortem or finding lesions overlooked by CAT scan (x-ray) procedures are impressive. Reitan's strategy has been basically empirical: Retain procedures that distinguish persons without impairment from persons with independently established impairments, and reject those that do not.

Reitan insists that neuropsychological results must be evaluated by *four methods of inference:*

1. Level of performance. How well did this person do compared to the normal unimpaired person of his or her age? Level of performance is the normative concept very familiar to most psychologists.

2. Patterns of performance. Does the patient have particular areas of clear decrement or inefficiency not easily explained? Similar to the scatter of scores on the Wechsler sub-tests, pattern of performance analysis draws conclusions from the nature of the low and high points.

3. Right-left comparisons. Are right-side performance and left-side performance in normal relationship to each other? The relative performance of right and left hand, reflecting relative performances of left and right cerebral hemispheres respectively, is known from experience. Inferences may be drawn from abnormal results.

4. Pathognomonic signs. Are there any signs in the record that are pathognomonic, or strongly indicative, of organic troubles? Such signs are numerous and include making clear mistakes in easy verbal tasks, writing one's name, or copying simple figures. Perseveration (repeating unnecessarily) and forgetting instructions partway through a task are also significant signs.

Other approaches.   Among the other batteries, the approaches of Golden and Lezak are noteworthy. Golden's strategy has been to design a battery of quantified tasks to reflect Luria's conceptual scheme of the brain and then to set about validating it. Some data produced so far for the Luria-Nebraska Neuropsychological Battery appear supportive (Golden, 1981).

Lezak's strategy is to do only a relatively few standard procedures and then, on the basis of the initial results, to make clinical judgments in selecting additional, more specialized measures. Questions about standardization and validation are less easy to answer with this method, but her books (Lezak, 1976, 1983) give excellent comprehensive overviews of specialized neuropsychological measures.

When clinicians are concerned about missing something, the widespread coverage from a battery of tests seems to be the most suitable procedure. Reitan's batteries are based on extensive data and have much clinical versatility. Some neuropsychologists supplement them with others for memory evaluation. Golden's Luria-Nebraska Battery, with Luria's system as its theoretical base, has inspired argument and competition along empirical and theoretical lines (Adams, 1980; Spiers, 1981). Some experts argue that the original theory does not lend itself to standard battery format; yet there is some evidence that both the Reitan and Golden batteries give similar results (Golden et al., 1981). Rather than seeking to demonstrate that battery A is better than battery B, it seems best to direct one's energy to continual refinement of theory and procedures. For example, are the different forms of memory well enough evaluated? What about self-control, judgment, and initiative—are they measured well enough anywhere?

Neuropsychology's role in diagnosis or detection of cerebral pathology has not been eliminated. However, the new biophysical technologies such as CAT scans, which provide computer-aided pictures of "slices" through the brain, make the location of cerebral lesions more clear and psychological tests less necessary than before. Still, the CAT scans cannot tell how behavioral functions are impaired or how easily a person may learn new skills. So rehabilitation provides exciting opportunities for neuropsychological assessment. Postinjury, postillness, developmental delay, and learning disability patients can all benefit from neuropsychological evaluation to determine their strengths and decrements. Such findings are directly applicable to the construction of remedial programs in conjunction with other disciplines, such as occupational therapy, physical therapy, special education, and speech therapy. Repeated testing can be useful to determine progress and review the programs.

The field of neuropsychology has well demonstrated its ability to use psychological measures to make inferences about the state of the brain. The new strategy of linking such diagnoses to remedial efforts is especially promising.

BIOFEEDBACK AND PAIN

Biofeedback

Psychology has contributed prominently to the areas of biofeedback, essentially a kind of applied psychology of perception. If we stand on tiptoe for a long time, we will feel the calves of our legs start to quiver—that is, we will get signals from the muscle that it is in a state of tension. In obvious situations, then, feedback from our body lets us know about its condition. Our bodies normally give us a wide variety of informational feedback about our internal states, but that feedback is usually quite crude. We are not used to paying much attention to it and, furthermore, the signals are sometimes hard to interpret. (For example, accustom one hand to water at 38° and the other to water at 110°. Then put both into water at 58°. One hand will send the message "warm water," and the other, "cool water.")

The central purpose of biofeedback is simply to detect any one of several bodily states or processes of which we are unaware or only dimly aware and transform it into some more obvious sensory input. For example, tension in the frontalis muscle in the forehead may be detected through electrodes placed on the skin. The resulting signal may be amplified and shown to us on a meter. As soon as the equipment is in place on our forehead and we see the meter, if we frown mightily or clench our teeth, the meter jumps. The therapist says, "Now see how *low* you can make it go." We relax the frown, and the meter reading falls at once. After working for a while we achieve much lower meter readings than we could at first. Thus we have the main therapeutic rationale of biofeedback: With the increased feedback given by the equipment, patients are able to gain clearer control over several body functions by learning to change their bodies to produce the desired feedback.

What types of bodily function are detected in biofeedback? Basically they are as follows:

EMG (Electromyography). High conductance electrodes with electronic equipment detect and amplify the very small electrical activity involved in muscle firing and contraction.

Temperature. Sensitive thermistors with electronic equipment detect and amplify changes in temperature of the body part in question.

EEG (Electroencephalography). High conductance electrodes with electronic equipment detect and amplify the naturally occurring electrical brain waves. Normally only one of the wave patterns, the alpha rhythm, is of concern in biofeedback.

GSR (Galvanic Skin Response). High conductance electrodes with electronic equipment detect the natural electrical resistance of the skin, which relates to the amount of perspiration present (usually on the hand).

We have been careful so far to separate *what is detected* from *how it is presented to the patient*. In the example, we mentioned a simple meter with a needle that went up with tension and down with relaxation, but couldn't we have used a tone that got louder and softer or lights that got brighter and dimmer? Here we leave physiology and come to the inventiveness of technology. A few of the many available presentation modes are visual (meters, dials, lights, and so on) and auditory (varieties of tones, turning music on and off). The application of biofeedback in clinical practice has increased quite rapidly. Psychologists, psychiatrists, nurses, and others have become "biofeedbackers," some with their own staff assistants who actually do a majority of the training of the patient. What does the technology actually have to offer patients? EMG work can move patients toward muscle control and relaxation, especially when the patient has been unaware of chronic muscle tension. Temperature work changes blood flow rates and so is useful in problems of vasodilation and vasoconstriction, such as cold hands or feet. It has been used in efforts to treat migraine headaches. EEG detection of alpha rhythm is used to promote alpha wave occurrence because alpha rhythm is associated with a subjective sense of well-being. Finally, because GSR fluctuates with anxiety, GSR-based procedures usually aim at reduction of anxiety.

No reputable biofeedback treatment is done without a current physical examination or medical collaboration. Several possible problems, although of low probability, could have serious consequences. For example, increasing temperature and thus blood flow in the vicinity of a tumor may promote its growth.

The basic assumption—that with moment-to-moment direct information about bodily functions the patient can *learn* to control that process—appears sound and clinically valuable. At the same time, however, it is probable that not many human problems are solvable just by learning about the state of the body. For that reason a clinician's full assessment of the problem is irreplaceable. To use a biofeedback approach first as a treatment for Debbie, who complains of anxiety about a boyfriend's beatings, clearly shows the wrong priorities.

Research in biofeedback has not kept pace with the expansion of practice. Why? Three factors have pushed the expansion: (1) Procedures are easily accepted and understood. They have the trappings of science—lights, boxes, wires, and so forth—and require little in the way of self-examination. (2) The equipment is commercially sold. Practitioners face advertising pressure to buy and use biofeedback equipment. (3) Clinicians who need a sense of doing something concrete and scientifically definite find biofeedback appealing. There are some tensions among psychology, psychiatry, and other disciplines over who "owns" biofeedback. It is time, says Neal Miller (1978), for researchers to concentrate on the production of controlled studies and to leave uncontrolled demonstrations behind. In general, biofeedback research yields promising results, but occasional studies (e.g., Chesney & Shelton, 1976) hint that equivalent results can be produced without all the biofeedback technology. As with all tests and treatments, clinical researchers need to determine the utilities or costs and benefits of biofeedback in comparison with other procedures such as relaxation training.

The *polygraph*, or *"lie detector,"* deserves mention in a section on biofeedback, because like biofeedback, it detects and amplifies a person's physiologic responses. Instead of doing that so a patient can achieve greater self-control, the polygraph does it so an operator may view a subject's responses and make inferences about truthfulness. Making such inferences plainly involves a great deal of psychological knowledge and understanding, but, interestingly enough, psychologists have not shown great interest in the field to date. Szucko and Kleinmuntz (1981) have enlivened matters by arguing that statistical analysis of polygraph results yields more accurate conclusions than does the trained operator's clinical judgment. Despite the great complexity, the area deserves psychologists' broader interest and study because of its profound social importance. As with biofeedback, the polygraph has been used and abused by people with a wide range of training (Lykken, 1981).

Pain

Psychology makes major contributions in another area involving the body and its sensations—pain research and pain treatment. Many of us have the primitive notion that pain accompanies a definable injury or disease, ending when the condition clears up, that there are a few people who suffer real, chronic pain, and that there are "crocks" and hypochondriacs who complain of pain when there really is none. With the latter, one hears "It's all in your head." Sternbach (1974) proposes a more analytical and less pejorative perspective. He suggests describing pain phenomena in neurological, physiological, behavioral, and affective terms. Pain of unknown origin may, of course, cover a variety of types of problems and may involve several other system levels. For example, a guilty person may engage in self-punishment by suffering pain (interaction with personal system); grandpa may maintain control of the entire family with his attacks of pain (interaction with family system); some veterans or Social Security beneficiaries must continue to experience pain in order to retain pensions or benefits (interaction with social-bureaucratic system).

Not only are the origins of pain and the role of pain for the patient complex issues, but *what* is measured (e.g., pain threshold, tolerance, or magnitude) and *how* it is measured (e.g., reaction time, verbal rating) tend to be very difficult to objectify.

A variety of assessment techniques have been used on pain. Sternbach (1974), for instance, has employed a technique in which the patient is asked to vary the pain of an applied tourniquet until the pain subjectively balances the chronic pain intensity. Other investigators have developed paper-and-pencil procedures, such as the McGill Pain Questionnaire (Melzak, 1975). The MPQ provides information on the sensory, affective, and evaluative dimensions of pain. Besides specific pain-related measures, the psychologist will assess the apparent role of pain in the patients' lives and its effect on them and their families, their work, and daily lives.

Treatment methods being quite new and somewhat experimental require continuous monitoring and the highest levels of quality control. Actual procedures involved in a case may include one or more of the following: (1) prescribing of medication—often relaxants or a psychoactive agent (see the following section on medications); (2) using neurosurgical procedures of several types; (3) structuring expectancies for benefit—such interventions may include hypnosis or the construction of a ward social milieu in which pain reduction, even to the point of giving placebo pain medication "cocktails," occurs through the impact of the unit's total conviction that improvement can occur; (4) training in relaxation therapy, which may follow a verbal instruction method or may be assisted by biofeedback; (5) promoting self-control—that is, the ability to voluntarily influence somatic activity, which brings biofeedback and hypnosis into importance in antipain treatment. Teaching patients to make muscles relax to increase blood flow in certain areas, to reduce general anxiety, and so on, forms a major portion of the psychologist's treatment effort. Also helpful are peripheral stimulation—e.g., acupuncture—to cause competing or blocking stimulation and psychotherapy—e.g., focusing on finding alternatives to pain as a life style or on finding alternative things to pay attention to besides pain.

What notions guide the therapeutic team in selecting among procedures? Basic efforts of the team generally seek *to remove possible contributing factors and to block pain perceptions.* Once they have studied the psychological and medical assessment material, the treatment is constructed with these two concepts as guides.

SEXUAL DYSFUNCTION

Only recently have psychologists begun to participate in the assessment and treatment of sexual dysfunction as the perspective about such problems has changed. The psychoanalytic perspective, dominant in much of mental health in earlier years, had labeled sexual dysfunctions as signs of deep-seated personality conflict and faulty psychological development. The direct and successful approaches of Masters and Johnson (1970), however, opened the door to several entirely new ways of conceptualizing problems such as woman's failure to experience orgasm or a man's inability to maintain an erection.

Treatment Concepts

LoPiccolo (1978) cites several basic principles for treating sexual dysfunction. Sexual dysfunctions within a couple are seen as shared disorders, thus there is *mutual responsibility*. *Responsibility*, naturally, differs from *blame*. The mutual responsibility principle means the involvement of both spouses in treatment, a procedure usually made easier by a male-female cotherapy team. *Information* and *education* form a basic step in procedures, with the therapists making sure that patients have clear, accurate information about their (and their partner's) physiologies and sexual response cycles. Procedures generally involve some attempts to *change attitudes*, perhaps by enabling patients to value overt sexual behavior more positively.

Most persons with sexual dysfunctions are continually anxious about their performance, straining to reach an often unrealistic goal or being overly attentive to minor problems. It is important, then, to *eliminate performance anxiety* by helping the patients focus on process rather than outcome. Partners are taught how to help each other increase effective sexual techniques by using positive and guiding statements rather than negative or directionless ones. Therapeutic efforts focus on *changing destructive life styles and sex roles* contributing to the problem. LoPiccolo notes that people with one typical life style value sexual activity highly but schedule it for late night times when tiredness and tension almost guarantee difficulties or disappointments. Finally, current approaches *prescribe changes in behavior*. "Try" or "do" or, often, "don't"—that is, prescriptions and proscriptions—are frequently related to a reporting or incentive system.

What are the more common types of sexual dysfunction? Premature ejaculation and erectile failure in coitus are the major problems in men; orgasmic dysfunction and vaginismus (involuntary spastic contraction of the vagina so that intromission is either painful or impossible) constitute the major presenting problems in women.

Assessment

Psychologists have also made notable contributions to assessment procedures. The importance of accurate and complete history-taking interviews is stressed by Lobitz and Lobitz (1978), who point out that although treatments tend to be "here and now," historical information can profoundly influence a therapist's formulation of a case. They assess specific habitual behaviors and thoughts. For example, the male patient with a problem of premature ejaculation may say to himself:

> Uh-oh! I'm pretty excited, I'm going to ejaculate too soon. Quick, don't think of sex. Shut your eyes. Count backwards by sevens. 93—86—79—72—uh—let's see, 65, uh. Oh, no! I'm going to come now!—Damn it. I did it again. I'll bet she's angry with me. I feel so awful. I'm such a failure. (Lobitz & Lobitz, 1978, p. 95)

The clinician must recognize such a cycle of internalized self-defeating behavior and plan interventions designed to break it, thus decreasing the anxiety which supports it.

Inventories have been constructed to obtain comprehensive, reliable, and valid data. LoPiccolo and Steger (1974) have introduced the Sexual Interaction Inventory consisting of 17 heterosexual behaviors (examples: female seeing the male when he is nude; male caressing the female's breasts with his hands; male and female having intercourse). For each of the 17 behaviors husband and wife separately answer six questions about the behavior, using a six-point rating scale—e.g., this behavior currently occurs never, rarely, occasionally, fairly often, usually, always. The results form a profile.

The field has produced a profusion of literature, most of it building on the well-respected Masters and Johnson (1970) work. Evidence accumulates that several procedures and groups of procedures—that is, treatment programs—do produce change. Some researchers, appropriately, are pursuing the questions "How durable are the effects?" and "What are the essential components of intervention for different types of problems?"

Great controversy surrounds the field because only some of its practitioners, possibly even a minority, are professionals with recognized training and qualifications. Some sex therapy clinics offer package prices at as much as five times standard psychotherapy rates. The training of sex therapists is of uneven quality, and licensing or other quality controls are inadequate. A second source of controversy surrounds the use of surrogates—that is, persons who will actually participate in genital activity with patients, for example, helping the impotent man toward potent performance. Such activities have been generally abandoned (or were never used) by the more reputable therapists, and they frequently offend community standards. As an added caution Wolfe (1978) notes instances of surrogates separating from their mentor and "going into private practice"!

GENETIC PROBLEMS

The potential psychologist or human service worker must have an appreciation of the profound importance of genetic factors in the areas of assessment, intervention, research, and policy making. "If it is true that genes influence behavior (in the sense that they are the instrumentalities that lead to differences in the organization, structure, and chemistry of all systems in the body that mediate behavior), *it is equally likely that they influence much behavior we call abnormal*" (Rosenthal, 1970, p. 7, emphasis added). Genetic problems are of two basic types: those that occur as the result of an error in the synthesis of the offspring's chromosomes from those of the parents, and those that are transmitted from parents to offspring. For more details consult a behavior genetics sourcebook such as Rosenthal (1970) or Plomin, DeFries, and McClearn (1980).

Problems in chromosomal synthesis and physical defects. Three examples of errors in the joining and organization of chromosomes in the embryo are the following:

1. *Klinefelter's Syndrome.* An XXY sex chromosome formation occurs in one out of 400 to 500 males. Klinefelter's is the most common cause of underdeveloped gonads and infertility in men. It usually comes to the attention of a child psychologist in a tall, effeminate boy, perhaps with some breast development, who may be of below-normal IQ and who may show some combination of behavior problems, such as insecurity, poor judgment, and body image concern. It is diagnosed by genetic study, and if positive, medical as well as psychological treatment is indicated.

2. *XYY Syndrome.* This syndrome becomes important in studies of antisocial behavior. Smith (1978) notes that institutionalized juvenile delinquents have been found to have an XYY occurrence rate 24 times greater than that in the population at large. In a careful and extensive study Witkin et al. (1976) substantiated the association between XYY and criminality, although the picture is far from clear because the lower intelligence of XYY males may be an intervening factor.

3. *Down's Syndrome or Trisomy 21.* Children with this syndrome used to be called *mongoloid* because their eyes have a characteristic appearance somewhat like those of East Asians. Down's babies are born more frequently to older than to younger women. If a sample of amniotic fluid is taken from a pregnant woman, a test can determine the presence of Down's Syndrome and other disorders in the fetus; the family may then make some decisions about having the child. When a Down's child is born, the psychologist may help the family adjust to and plan for the child, who will probably be too handicapped to function very independently. Much can be done with special education and parental assistance to optimize the child's learning. Some remarkable gains have been made in research and training, many of them related to the programs stimulated by the U.S. federal government in the 1960s.

The three chromosomal conditions just mentioned generally do not appear in the parents' genetic makeup. Some other rare conditions are definitely inherited—that is, the problems existed in the parents'phenotype (their obvious characteristics) or genotype (the genetic material they pass on). Huntington's Chorea provides an example of a condition with high heritability. Writhing, dancelike movements become uncontrollable as the nervous system degenerates. Psychologists often become involved since sufferers usually undergo changes of personality and require residential care during their long decline.

Genetic counseling is another relatively new development. For instance, couples who know of an inherited disorder in one or both parents often want to think through whether they wish to have a baby themselves or adopt one.

Figure 7-3 As more research comes, genetic counseling is likely to become prominent. (Catherine Ursillo, Photo Researchers, Inc.)

Inheritance of psychopathology. Are there genetic components of schizophrenia, manic-depressive illness, crime and delinquency, hyperactivity? The problem of teasing apart hereditary and environmental contributions has been addressed by a quite powerful design which compares outcomes for the four relevant groups: children of schizophrenic mothers who were (1) raised by their own mothers or (2) adopted by normal parents, and children of normals who were (3) raised by their own mothers or (4) adopted by schizophrenic mothers. Such studies, be they for schizophrenia or other problems, require that researchers have access to comprehensive longitudinal records. Because of that requirement, much of the major work has been done in Denmark, where the *Folkeregister*, or social register, provides a treasury for genetic research. For many years it was popular in psychology to assert that schizophrenia was caused by factors in the environment—the so-called schizophrenogenic mother, or some early psychic trauma, or being put in a "double bind" in family communications. But by 1971, with the first good crop of Denmark studies completed, Lindzey et al. (1971, p. 63) stated, "The presence of genetic predisposition to schizophrenia-like disorders may now be regarded as firmly established."

Studies have since concentrated on methodological improvements, such as refining the quality of control groups, refining diagnostic criteria, and looking at outcomes in siblings. Studies indicate a clear genetic influence in schizophrenia, although it is not overwhelmingly large. For example, prevalence of schizophrenia among the biological relatives of schizophrenics is usually close to 13 percent, some eight times the control rate. At least one adoption study (Wender et al., 1977) has suggested that being reared by a seriously deviant parent is not a necessary condition for the development of schizophrenia.

Although a hereditary component in schizophrenia has been established, the weakness of the factor forces additional explanatory mechanisms. These lie in two basic directions: (1) The incomplete or partial heritability is explained by yet-undiscovered genetic or biochemical mechanisms; and (2) the incomplete or partial heritability is explained by psychological mechanisms.

According to the *diathesis-stress hypothesis,* the predisposition or diathesis does not by itself cause anything but has enabling properties. However, in the presence of stress, those who have a genetic predisposition (the diathesis carriers) will exhibit schizophrenic symptoms. It is fair to say that there has not been overwhelming research progress in specifying the nature, conditions, or parameters of the stress component.

What are the implications for psychologists and other human service workers? First, the evidence for heritability of schizophrenia makes obsolete all theories asserting that the causes of schizophrenia are wholly environmental. The genetic evidence shifts the focus of intervention toward strategies of case management (e.g., reducing stress, putting together support systems), constructive accommodation (e.g., teaching needed skills, self-management, and self-protection techniques and helping the patient adjust self-concept), and prevention, rather than toward attempts to cure or eliminate the condition.

The experimental design of following adoptees in different categories has produced studies in the areas of criminal behavior, alcoholism, and hyperactivity. Studies such as that by Hutchings and Mednick (1975) show heritability effects in criminality, although, again, other factors also enter in. Studies also strongly suggest that alcoholism and hyperactivity similarly have genetic components.

What are the implications of these findings for our thinking and our practice? First, we must keep clearly in mind that a demonstration of heritability with the low correlation coefficients found here does *not* mean that crime, for instance, is destined, foreordained, or inevitable in the offspring of criminals. Second, we must remain wary of polemics or emotional arguments that might dissuade us from thinking scientifically about methods and findings. Recognizing the ideal of objectivity in scientific knowledge, psychologists can take a more analytical direction. It is society, not genes, that defines the meaning of *criminal* or *criminal behavior.* Genes control such aspects as temperament, body build, aspects of intelligence, and attentional deficits. It could be, to pick a hypothetical example, that deficits in attention to social cues or deficits in anxiety and intelligence may make a person particularly vulnerable to influences producing behaviors that society calls *crime*. The task of the behavioral sciences is to advance the status of such crude hypotheses and then to mount preventive programs. Third, we must be wary of committing ourselves to treatment or preventive programs based on notions for which there is little or no evidence. Blaming mothers or others in the family or blaming ethnic or racial origins may be particularly harmful.

HEALTH PSYCHOLOGY AND OTHER TOPICS

The area of health psychology commands increasing interest. The contributions of Matarazzo (1980, 1982) and other sources—for example, Stone, Cohen, and Adler (1979) and the August 1979 issue of *Professional Psychology*, edited by Budman and Wertlieb, have focused on the psychological aspects of generating, restoring, and maintaining human health. Health psychology includes the study of psychological aspects of various illnesses and types of patient care, as well as the study of how the care delivery system influences those services. Our final section briefly reviews several topics generally included in health psychology.

BOX 7-2   *THE POTENTIAL OF HEALTH PSYCHOLOGY*

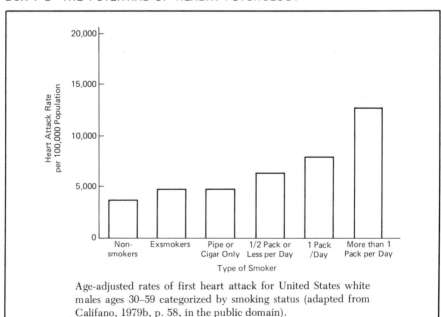

Age-adjusted rates of first heart attack for United States white males ages 30–59 categorized by smoking status (adapted from Califano, 1979b, p. 58, in the public domain).

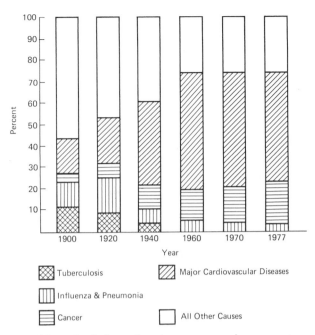

United States deaths from selected causes expressed as a percentage of all deaths (adapted from Califano, 1979b, p. 4, in the public domain).

"Over 99 percent of us are born healthy and made sick as a result of personal misbehavior and environmental conditions. The solution to the problems of ill health . . . involves individual responsibility . . . and social responsibility through public legislature and private volunteer efforts . . " Knowles, 1977, p. 58.

"Although it has been a leader in . . . *mental health* . . . psychology has been curiously slow to recognize opportunities . . . as they relate to the *physical* health of our nation" Matarazzo, 1982, p. 12.

We stress again that our sampling of topics is not exhaustive. The interaction of soma with psyche is exceptionally complex and occurs in a most diversified group of settings and phenomena. We hope here to give some sense of that diversity and to invite prospective psychologists and human service workers to develop an open, inquiring posture toward the involvement of bodily systems. Because we live in, because to some extent we *are* our bodies, somatic influence cannot be escaped. We hope that the fascinating, complicated area of body and behavior interaction will attract more attention. As we briefly enumerate the various issues we have selected, ponder these questions: "What role can the psychologist or human service worker play in preventive or in educational programs?" "What specific psychological activities are appropriate (or inadvisable) here?" What areas of psychological research into the behavioral-developmental-personality aspects of the problem are most needed?"

Prescribed Medications

As our society becomes more reflective about its chemical intake, it becomes painfully clear that the system of medical care in many countries, the profit-making drug industry, and the belief that chemicals will help solve life dilemmas contribute a great deal to the acceptance of chemical dependency. Sedatives, stimulants, and minor tranquilizers are liberally dispensed by physicians caught between a variety of pressures and incentives. The result—the "overmedicated society," as Muller (1972) calls it—has become a social problem and a challenge for psychology.

Are these various agents actually helping patients with their thought and behavior problems? Psychologists' skills in experimental design and in the measurement of change play a key role in breaking up this huge question into smaller, more manageable questions about types of patient, types of measurement, and types of situation (in hospital, in community, and so on). Interestingly, in a survey of research, Smith, Glass, and Miller (1980) question the old assumption that medication helps patients respond better to psychotherapy by suggesting that groups receiving both drugs and therapy show little or no special advantage over medication or psychotherapy alone. In at least one important case, that of lithium carbonate, the medication seems to have highly positive effects for some (generally manic or manic-depressive) patients, but the medication is not perfectly risk free and requires close medical monitoring.

Psychoactive medications form a special subgroup of prescriptions. They may be roughly grouped into (1) major tranquilizers usually used for psychosis, (2) antidepressants, (3) minor tranquilizers, usually used for anxiety and agitation, (4) lithium carbonate, specific for forms of manic-depressive illness, and (5) stimulants, used in hyperactivity with children. Appleton's (1976) abbreviated guide or Levenson's (1981) book provide excellent overviews and list further resources. Psychologists have an interest in developing ways to predict which patients will respond positively to lithium and other medications. Most work to date centers on analysis of MMPI scores and shows some promise.

Prenatal Hazards

Maternal malnutrition.   Poor nutrition is not only a problem of poor countries; many expectant mothers in affluent countries do not eat properly. The effects of malnutrition on human physical and psychological development, however, are remarkably elusive. In clinical malnutrition, the more severe type, reduced growth and delayed development are easily shown. However, in subclinical malnutrition, where there is chronic subnutrition resulting in generalized stunting or wasting, clear-cut results have been harder to demonstrate. Malnutrition never occurs alone but is always accompanied by other factors, such as family disorganization, poor housing, and a psychological climate of apathy and despair. For those reasons retrospective studies are weak. Not all prospective studies have demonstrated positive findings for nutritional supplements.

Fetal alcohol.   In 1973 Jones and co-workers reported common disorders in children born to alcoholic mothers. Later work (Jones et al., 1974) has elaborated on the developmental outcome of the children. They tend to have multiple serious physical defects such as cardiac, skeletal, and facial abnormalities. Jones's group had an average IQ of 63, fine motor dysfunction (weak grasp), poor eye-hand coordination, or tremulousness. Autopsy results have shown clear structural malformation of the brain (Smith, 1978).

Obviously such effects are not limited to alcohol but can occur with a wide variety of other poisons, drugs, and prescribed medications. Problems resulting from those identified to date are, in theory, preventable. Psychologists have a great deal of work to do with the varying types of congenital brain damage. We do not yet know how they differ or what particular developmental deficits or remaining strengths each type may show. Some research has suggested that the fetus goes through periods of vulnerability to particular agents. Psychologists need to assist such research in order that we may understand the long-term developmental aspects of the problems.

Birth defects.   We began the chapter by noting how accidents that impair the functioning of the central nervous system impose profound limits on psychological functioning, limits which can be assessed using psychological procedures. Similarly a variety of birth defects and neurological diseases involve assessment and rehabilitation skills of the psychologist who understands normal development. Hydrocephalus (fluid pressure on the brain), incomplete formation of the spinal column, and a variety of inborn errors of metabolism such as phenylketonuria are just a few of the many birth defects that may harm the nervous system and hence limit psychological development.

Autism

The condition of early infantile autism merits mention in a chapter on somatic problems. The condition itself, originally described by Kanner (1943), is manifested as children, starting as "good" babies, showing more and more conclusively that they are unaware of or uninterested in people. Speech usually fails to develop normally, and there is much repetitive and fetishlike behavior. Older views assumed that the parents' own psychopathology caused the child's psychic withdrawal, an accusation which was hard to disprove but which has not been supported by data. Recent studies have shown clear biochemical abnormalities in autistic children, and other lines of research hint that autism may be the result of a viral infection of the fetus at one particular developmental stage.

The etiology issue is important for obvious reasons. If notions of somatic etiology continue to be supported, part of the psychologist's job is to optimize the affected child's learning of social and self-care skills and emotional attachment. Another part is to help the parents work through the emotional impact of such a problem and to give them information, planning, and coping skills to aid in constructive decisions about the child's life and about their own. Such an approach contrasts sharply with trying to cure the child's psychic injury and probing the parents' unconscious needs to reject their child. Rimland (1974) and Rutter and Schopler (1978) offer good summaries of autism.

Mental Retardation

Retarded persons in the United States number roughly two million, although of course the figure depends to a great extent on definition. Retarded people are not all the same. Some 75 percent of mental retardation is classified by some authorities as related to *psychosocial disadvantage*, but in 25 percent of cases, *clinical* (biological) phenomena can be found.

The problems of the clinical group come from multiple origins, such as genetic defects, and neurological diseases as well as from many other nonheritable somatic conditions. Examples are gross malnutrition, very early pregnancy, poor prenatal care, various infections, close spacing (less than one year) of pregnancies, asphyxiation in delivery, various toxins such as lead, illicit drugs, some prescription drugs, insecticides, and so on, and, of course, damage from fevers, disease, or physical trauma. The clinical types of retardation are generally more severe than are those connected with psychosocial disadvantage. Often some physical deformity or incapacity will occur in the clinical patient, too.

The families of the clinically retarded often experience residual rage, shock, guilt, or denial at the occurrence and, not infrequently, a repetitive searching for complete cure. Quite often, also, parents of clinically retarded children oppose forms of "mainstreaming" in school and take a not inappropriately protective stance toward their child. Active psychologist-physician and psychologist-teacher liaison is required. With a clear knowledge of cognitive and emotional development and with accurate evaluation, the psychologist can make valuable contributions to the education and habilitation of the clinically retarded.

Body Image

For some people the shape, size, or regularity of noses, jaws, teeth, hair patterns, breasts, genitals, and many other features can cause acute personal embarrassment or distress. Sometimes a person's body has perfect features but looks like that of a much older or much younger person. Psychologists must be aware of the basic pervasive influence that noticeable physical abnormalities in combination with social attitudes can exercise on the formation of self-concepts. In working with such people we need to know what medical procedures can offer and to be aware that sudden profound changes (such as by surgery) may require a great deal of sensitive support in the readjustment phase.

Excesses

Alcoholism.   As one of America's three largest health problems, the degree of involvement of alcoholism in a wide range of social problems is amazing. The number of deaths, divorces, rape and incest events, absences from work, suicides, road accidents, and physician visits that are alcohol related all have profound implications for personal well-being and for that of the community and nation.

Early notions that alcoholics lacked willpower were supplanted by psychodynamic notions (e.g., alcoholics drink because of oral craving coming from early development problems) and by behavioral notions (e.g., alcohol had unfortunately become associated with pleasure, relief, or escape). But researchers soon found that the etiology was much more complex. Issues of family system emerged: Many alcoholics have some type of "collaborator," usually a spouse, whose earnest efforts end up making the continuation of drinking patterns possible. Issues of the biological system emerged, too, with findings of genetic involvement in alcoholism, as we mentioned earlier. And again, questions of developmental predisposition have come up with Jones's (1968) finding of stable premorbid personality types.

Formalized psychological assessment with alcoholics has not shown striking utility. There have been problems in the extent to which toxicity may influence results and some antipathy toward any kind of professional input by many workers in the field. A good deal of work has been done with the MMPI, delineating profile characteristics of alcoholics. One MMPI specialty scale (MacAndrew, 1965) has shown ability to differentiate alcoholic from nonalcoholic psychiatric patients. The work of Hoffman et al. (1974) suggests that the MacAndrew scale may be effective in identifying prealcoholic persons who later become alcoholic.

The basic competing approaches to treatment are (1) *the disease model,* which posits a definite disease and prescribes detoxification, vitamin and other medical supplementation, social supports, family changes, and continued sobriety. It teaches alcoholics that they have a disease which makes further drinking lethal. Although the evidence is far from specific, alcoholism is sometimes considered to be a metabolic problem and likened to diabetes. (2) *The learning, or psychological, model,* seeks to apply principles of aversion therapy (including antabuse and shock), counterconditioning, or systematic desensitization to alcohol. Taken singly, none of the treatments appears to show durable efficacy (Nathan, 1976); in general, behavioral approaches are moving toward multimodal treatment. In their occasional suggestions that continued but controlled drinking may be a viable goal for some drinkers, they incur the wrath of both the disease treaters and the self-help people. (3) *Self-help groups,* such as Alcoholics Anonymous, with its companion groups, Al Anon for spouses and Alateen for teenagers, depend primarily on social group phenomena for their effect. AA helps its members learn to live constructively "one step at a time," constantly guarding their sobriety. Members are encouraged to receive and give to the group's substantial support and outreach.

The field of alcoholism, as the largest of the substance abuse or addiction areas, needs far more psychological study and service than it has had heretofore. Psychology is beginning to make useful contributions, especially in areas of outcome evaluation and program design. The multimodal, learning-based work shows clear promise, and AA has such remarkable outreach to a population rarely seen elsewhere that it, too, deserves support and study. The time may not be far off when the common elements of the three approaches begin to overshadow their differences.

Nonprescribed drugs.   The forces promoting the use of nonprescribed (usually illegal) drugs appear to resemble those involved in alcohol. Subcultural values, economic incentives, the need to belong, the desire to escape from boredom, and alienation, or a search for a psychic anaesthetic all may be involved. Furthermore, the various agents used have different properties and varying capacities for physical and psychological addiction. Psychologists need to be aware that users of nonprescribed drugs may simply be honoring a subcultural practice and may not have harmed themselves measurably nor have clear psychopathology. However, many compounds are clearly harmful and have a variety of frequently irreversible effects on the nervous system. People with such drug problems go to clinics with such gross symptoms as trembling, acute suspiciousness, and hunger, or perhaps more subtle signs such as urgent need for money, inability to function up to par, or severe problems of studying or of getting up or going to sleep. If the problem is acute, the person may go to a medical facility. Intervention minimally involves medical care, counseling, and often changes in the support or reference groups of the person.

Smoking.   Some important work has been done in helping people to stop smoking, although having people perform rapid smoking, a technique which showed clear promise, has been generally dropped because of the health hazard it may represent. Levenberg and Wagner (1976) found a clear regression toward pretreatment rates of smoking on follow-up and noted no clear differences among particular treatment modes. Research by Condiotte and Lichtenstein (1981) shows that perceived self-efficacy is important; it rises during training to control smoking and is predictive of success. Relapses after cessation are accompanied by a lowered sense of competence.

Eating disorders.   Overuse of food—that is, obesity—has attracted considerable attention from psychologists and has resulted in several different treatment approaches. Again the obesity shows some clear, but not strong, genetic linkage and gives identifiable subtypes. Some obesity may be traced to endocrine disorders. Here as elsewhere the psychologist must be in close and effective communication with the patient's physician. Further, obesity in childhood tends to predict a less favorable course of treatment and is more related to the presence of emotional disorders than is obesity only in adulthood.

Ruling out other physical causes, generally calorie intake in excess of need and low physical activity or idleness account for the excess fat. Although psychoanalytic approaches offered comprehensive explanations of obesity and sometimes treatment attempts, the behavioral approaches have contributed the most and best-documented work in the area. After a classic study by Stuart (1967), stimulus control became the dominant method of treatment. Ferster, Nurnberger, and Levitt (1962), the architects of stimulus control, recommended strategies to control the stimuli associated with eating by separating eating from all other activities so that those other activities do not "suggest" or "require" food—for example, eating in a specified room at designated times, not doing anything else while eating, and limiting the times and places for eating. Exactly *what* procedures are necessary and sufficient has not yet been clarified, although treatment of obesity by psychological techniques now rests on solid ground.

Some attention has been given to the clinical condition called *anorexia nervosa*, a problem of underuse of food, even to the point of starvation. Most often seen in adolescent girls and young women, the inability to eat or vomiting after eating was long explained in psychoanalytic terms. Behaviorally based treatments have been successful in the in-hospital life-saving phase of treatment, but much more work remains to be done. *Bulimia*, or binge eating, often followed by self-induced vomiting, is another eating disorder.

Obviously many more specific problems of the body involve psychologists than we can mention here. Asthma, disorders of sleep, sex-change counseling—the list could be much enlarged. Although our list is not comprehensive, we have tried to give a feel for the complexity, the variety, and the exciting progress being made in psychological work involving bodily systems.

Body Therapies

Body therapies range from psychotherapy to programs of exercise designed to promote heightened awareness and enjoyment. Green (1981) identifies four current major divisions of body therapy: (1) physical manipulation systems—e.g., Rolf's methods of deep (and often painful) massage designed to alter connective tissue and facilitate energy flow by postural reintegration and realignment of the body; (2) energy-balancing systems—e.g., a polarity therapy which seeks to balance and harmonize the flow of energy by helping areas of the body to promote a natural flow or circuit; (3) movement awareness systems—e.g., that of Feldenkrais which teaches various movements and exercises so that a client may experience release from old physical and emotional patterns and replace them with right functioning of body and psyche; (4) emotional release systems—e.g., primal therapy, rebirthing, and bioenergetics. Primal therapy uses basic or primal screaming as its major mode of promoting emotional release. Rebirthing uses immersion in water to simulate the womb and to lead toward a primitive emotional experience. Bioenergetics, with the longest and fullest history, can be traced to Wilhelm Reich, who observed through studying failures of psychoanalysis that emotional disturbance and postural distortion appeared to be related. Reich's view was that the muscular holding patterns were a form of character armor which occurred in rings or layers and blocked the flow of the vital energy. Therapists use the control of breathing and direct work on muscles to release emotion and overcome energy blockages. They also use methods of character analysis to bring resistances into the open and to deal with them. Besides its debt to the works of Reich (1970, 1971), bioenergetics owes much to Lowen (1975a, 1975b). These therapies seriously need evaluation.

CRITIQUE

How adequate is clinical biopsychology conceptually?   In trying to give a feel for the breadth and diversity of the ways in which biological variables are important in clinical psychology, we have covered the waterfront, so to speak. The wealth of material has been difficult to organize into simple classes or groups. After trying several inadequate organizations, we realized that the way in which the body interacts with behavior and thinking cannot be simply organized. The very fact of this difficulty indicates how far psychology has to go to attain a coherent and comprehensive way of conceptualizing the relationship between the biological system and the personal system. Nonetheless, although there is no simple big picture, the various areas are contributing to exciting conceptual progress. As one of many examples neuropsychology promises to yield better ideas about how the brain works and to become a linkage between cognitive development, educational psychology, neurology, and rehabilitation.

How practical is the field?   The general topic has the potential for being intensely practical for three major reasons. First, it has a profound effect on the type of therapies that psychologists design. Where genetic or other physical conditions underlie psychological problems, psychology should no longer design psychological therapies to cure the condition or to blame others for it. Second, some psychological interventions can reduce utilization of physical treatments and health care networks. Third, many parts of biopsychology hold promise as a basis for the design and monitoring of remediation and prevention programs. For instance, neuropsychological testing of mental and behavioral functioning has direct implications for training and vocational rehabilitation. The preventive aspects of health psychology—helping people to wear motorcycle helmets and seatbelts, to brush their teeth better, to secure immunizations more reliably, and so on—promise clear social benefit.

How socially relevant and worthwhile is this area of knowledge?   There is no lack of examples of the social importance of clinical biopsychology. Biofeedback has begotten an industry eager to sell equipment, but there is little regulation of user qualifications. Some enthusiasts of "pop" neuropsychology have grossly outrun not only their data but neurology as well when we find workshops with titles like "Dancing with Your Right Brain." In the past some psychologists have not recognized the worth of self-help groups such as Alcoholics Anonymous. In popularizing some biopsychological knowledge, such as treatments for sexual problems, psychologists and others run into social criticisms from many conservative groups. Some biopsychological procedures have been inappropriately commercialized.

Social and ethical issues remain poorly addressed. Large families, close birth spacing, and young motherhood all are associated with decreased opportunities or capacities in the offspring. Should a profession take an official position? Start education programs? Ignore the data? Difficult as those questions are, they are only a warm-up exercise for questions that come from the genetics findings. If the heritability of criminality should be further substantiated—or if any other antisocial characteristics are confirmed as hereditary—what position should the profession take? None of the alternatives—sterilization, ignoring the data, or attempting to design environments in which diathesis carriers (those with genetic vulnerability) will be better socialized and less stressed—appears appealing as we race toward overpopulation, scarcity, and pollution in a world where civil liberties are already dangerously weakened.

Because the biopsychological field is split into many subareas, general evidence for efficacy cannot be produced. Nonetheless, many encouraging signs are appearing. Researchers continue to refine their questions. Some areas, such as neuropsychology and biofeedback, produce a good deal of relatively high-quality research—research which often links psychology with allied disciplines and fields. Other important areas, such as polygraph usage, have made less progress in attracting research interest. High need and good opportunities exist, but with so many areas, making clinicians aware of current research remains a slow process. Nonetheless, research-trained psychologists have greater likelihood of helping avoid a wrong therapy or assessment (e.g., insight therapy for a child with grossly impaired verbal capacity) and more likelihood of correctly evaluating specific need (e.g., work to increase the child's language development and verbal capacity). A second contribution is helping medical therapies address their target more accurately and accountably. A third is that of contributing substantially to public health and preventive programs, not only for stress management, but for conditions such as alcoholism, obesity, and smoking. Psychology, in short, appears to be on the threshold of a vital and important role as a link between the "study of the mind" and the "study of the body."

SUMMARY

Both from a theoretical and practical standpoint, paying attention to biological or physical issues makes sense for psychology. The interaction of behavior, thoughts, and feelings on the one hand, with biological variables on the other, proves to be complex; although the vast continent remains basically unsettled, some significant and vigorous colonies do exist.

Neuropsychology expands psychology's boundaries with neurology, rehabilitation, and special education by studying how brain dysfunction is expressed in behavior. Reitan's pioneering work has been joined by other approaches. The field is now at the stage of competition between perspectives.

Biofeedback, giving patients information about otherwise unknown states of their body such as the tension of muscles, has aroused a great deal of interest, both in application and in the manufacture and sale of equipment. The area has produced some promising research as well as findings that question the need for equipment. Lie detection, a relative of biofeedback, deserves more study by psychologists.

Psychologists also work with chronic pain sufferers and with sexual dysfunction sufferers, using ideas and procedures especially developed for these problems. Genetic influences on behavior must be better understood and considered by psychologists. Genetic involvement in the etiology of certain conditions presses us to change ideas of intrapsychic or environmental causation. Health psychology, the special psychological skills for promoting physical health and for helping people when they are sick or handicapped, continues to expand in its importance.

Although the general area does not organize easily, its importance is clear. In time, a major part of applied psychology may well be concerned with taking the body into account.

RECOMMENDED READINGS

Springer, S. P., & Deutsch, G. *Left brain, right brain.* San Francisco: W. H. Freeman & Company Publishers, 1981.
Springer and Deutsch offer a useful overview of research in hemispheric asymmetry. Their chapters include split-brain research, asymmetries of the normal brain, and the puzzle of left-handedness. They cover findings in sex and asymmetry and the development of asymmetry. The section on asymmetry in animals begins, provocatively, with "which paw does your dog shake hands with?" They end with a review of asymmetry and psychopathology and some speculation about future discoveries.

Lindemann, J. E. (Ed.). *Psychological and behavioral aspects of physical disability: A manual for health practitioners.* New York: Plenum, 1981.
The relationship between psychology and medicine and the application of psychology to the care and rehabilitation of disabled people are prominent parts of the general field of clinical psychology. It is becoming quite clear that the *behavior* of people has a great deal to do with their state of physical health. This eclectic book presents a variety of experts writing about such topics as the stigma of disability and problems of adjustment; particular physical problems such as hemophilia, diabetes, genetic disorders, cerebral palsy, epilepsy, and heart malfunction; and mental retardation and sensory handicaps.

Pikoff, H. Biofeedback: A resource directory and outline of the literature. *Professional Psychology,* 1981, *12,* 261–270.
Pikoff provides good access to major elements of the area of biofeedback. His outline of the literature includes a list of frequently cited research papers, research reviews and bibliographies, introductions and overviews, articles on questions and professional issues, and a resource directory which includes training, instrumentation, multimedia aids, and professional organizations.

Budman, S. H., & Wertlieb, D. (Guest editors). Special issue: Psychologists in health care settings. *Professional Psychology,* 1979, *10* (4), 397–644.
A "must" for those interested in health care psychology, this special issue contains 16 articles on health care psychologists at work. It also has sections on conceptual issues in health care psychology, becoming a health care psychologist, and legal and political perspectives for health care psychology. For those who would like a wide-ranging understanding of health psychology and references to major publications, other good

resources are *Health Psychology—a Handbook*, by Stone, Cohen, Adler, and Associates (1979), and the *Handbook of Clinical Health Psychology* by Millon, Green, and Meagher (1982), and an excellent overview of the use of drugs in psychiatry is provided in *Mind, Mood and Medicine* by Wender and Klein (1981).

Lykken, D. T. *A tremor in the blood: Uses and abuses of the lie detector.* New York: McGraw-Hill, 1981.

David Lykken, in this highly readable book, describes the use of the polygraph in a wide variety of situations. There are several thousand people who use it, many of them poorly trained; a common use is in preemployment selection, about which Lykken says there is no evidence of validity for preventing thefts. He does approve of its use by well-trained police. The so-called lie detector does not actually tell if a person lies; it simply indicates if a person gives an emotional response to questions or statements. The reader who would like a shorter version may see an article by Lykken (1974).

RESEARCH EXAMPLES

Pearce, J. W., LeBow, M. D., & Orchard, J. Role of spouse involvement in the behavioral treatment of overweight women. *Journal of Consulting and Clinical Psychology*, 1981, *49*, 236–244.

This study examines the interesting interaction between physiological variables and social variables. Previous studies had noted that weight-loss candidates who underwent treatment by themselves had lost significantly more weight at a six-month follow-up than had those who participated with partners, who apparently reinforced each other for deviating from newly learned eating patterns. But other studies have shown that where spouses participated by reinforcing appropriate eating and exercise behaviors and refraining from punishing or criticizing partners' weight-loss efforts, spectacular results had been obtained. The question, then, was whether the facilitative effect of spouse training was attributable to the active training of spouses or merely to preventing spouses from sabotaging their partners' weight-loss efforts.

Some 68 overweight married women were assigned to one of five groups: (1) with a cooperative spouse, in which spouses were trained in modeling, monitoring, and reinforcement techniques, (2) women alone, in which they underwent the basic behavioral program by themselves, (3) nonparticipating spouse, in which spouses were told not to participate in their wives' programs, (4) alternative treatment, which took a historical and insight-based approach to find underlying causes, and finally, (5) a delayed treatment control.

The women underwent a ten-week treatment phase after which, although all groups lost weight, there were no significant differences among any of the groups. At a three-month follow-up all groups had continued to lose weight. At six months some had gained. By 12 months alternative and women alone groups had continued to gain (alternatives showing no overall loss) but cooperative-spouse and nonparticipating-spouse groups returned to losing. Although the cooperative-spouse group had lost more weight than did the nonparticipating-spouse group, differences were not significant. The authors suggest that instructing spouses not to sabotage their wives' efforts may be as effective for long-term maintenance as actively training them to aid their wives. (Some family theorists might speculate that the nonparticipating-spouse group might do better than the cooperative-spouse group on longer follow-up, because a cooperating spouse may seem to be the wife's disciplinarian, an inherently destabilizing role.)

Bell, A. P., Weinberg, M. S., & Hammersmith, S. K. *Sexual preference: Its development in men and women.* Bloomington: Indiana University Press, 1981.

The authors report on a major study of sexual preference in which some 1,500 individuals were systematically interviewed. The interview schedule covered issues usually thought critical to sexual preference, such as the relations which interviewees had with their parents and siblings, the relationship between the parents, and the degree to which the respondents conformed to stereotypic roles of males and females in childhood. The data were examined by path analysis, a procedure which permits tracing the relationships between variables. The findings are somewhat startling in their clarity: There was no support for the popular notion that parents or early childhood events are responsible for the development of sexual preference, an idea particularly central to psychoanalytic theory. The findings suggest a strong correlation between early and deeply ingrained patterns of gender identity and adult sexual orientation. The study points toward biological variables—for example, the hormonal climate of the developing brain. If these findings are replicated, they prompt us to rethink entirely our approaches to working with sexual preference minorities and their parents.

Townes, B. D., Trupin, E. W., Martin, D. C., & Goldstein, D. Neuropsychological correlates of academic success among elementary school children. *Journal of Consulting and Clinical Psychology,* 1980, *48,* 675–684.

Reitan and his associates have assembled batteries of tests that are sensitive to the presence of a wide variety of brain impairments. The procedures have differentiated between brain-damaged and nonbrain-damaged children, between lesions in the right versus the left cerebral hemisphere, and between children identified as having minimal brain damage versus those having a learning disability. These authors sought to move beyond questions dealing with the battery's ability to detect or discriminate to see if the battery had the capacity to identify specific patterns of adaptive abilities which would predict academic success.

The investigators studied 456 kindergarten (116 males, 114 females) and second-grade children (123 males, 103 females) after their parents had given permission. All subjects except two were white and predominantly middle class. Mean WISC IQs were in the bright normal range. The WISC and the Reitan-Indiana Neuropsychological Battery were administered to all subjects with appropriate precautions for reliability among psychometrists. Classroom teachers administered the appropriate level of the Stanford achievement tests. Verbal IQs and performance IQs were calculated from the WAIS, and 19 variables were obtained from the Reitan-Indiana. Percentile scores were also computed for each subject on the available subtests of the Stanford test.

The first analysis showed possible significant age and sex differences. Results showed that second graders were significantly more efficient than were kindergarteners on all neuropsychological variables except VIQ (verbal IQ); PIQ (performance IQ); a measure of eye, hand, and foot preference; and degree of motor dominance. Thus for children five through eight, these findings suggest that within that age group, separate age norms on the Reitan are required. The sex differences favored girls on tests of verbal reasoning, language skills, and serial perceptual matching. Boys were superior on tests of spatial memory and motor skills.

The second question asked whether boys and girls differ in academic achievement level by the end of kindergarten or second grade. A comparison of the Stanford scores showed that there were no significant differences in kindergartners but second-grade girls showed superior reading skills. If that finding is replicated, the difference may be due to differences in the rate of development of spatial and language-related abilities.

The third question asked was: Can a subset of the most cost-effective neuropsychological tests adequately distinguish between normal and low-achieving subjects? It was found that a group of ten of the brief and easily administered neuropsychological subtests could correctly classify over 75 percent of the subjects into high-achievement and low-achievement groups. Also, the addition of VIQ and PIQ scores did not increase predictive accuracy substantially.

The results document the developmental advantage of girls over boys in the early acquisition of abstract verbal reasoning and pattern matching skills. Results suggest that boys are at a developmental disadvantage with respect to academic achievement during the early elementary school years.

This study, as well as other more specific reading work, suggests that spatial and linguistic skills develop at different rates in boys and girls and therefore that boys are at substantially higher risk of being called dyslexic when reading instruction relies entirely on linguistic strategies. The authors say that teaching methods are needed that rely in part on spatial abilities and not only on phonetic analysis. Such methods should be used with children who have either greater spatial skills or an innate preference for cognitive processing through spatial modalities. Finally, they note that using the selection of neuropsychological measures, the clinician can make a very informed forecast about a child's potential academic success, a matter of great importance when advising parents about the early placement of a child in kindergarten.

8 WORKING WITH INDIVIDUALS:

Psychoanalysis and Psychodynamic Approaches

Psychoanalysis did not spring fullblown from the brow of Freud, notes Thompson (1950/1957, p. 3). Concepts and practices that Freud initially explored have undergone marked evolution and change, both in his time and subsequently. Freud's arrival in the arena where people struggle with abnormal behavior and troubling emotions has resulted in permanent contributions to that struggle. When unintended words pop out of someone's mouth, almost certainly a listener will say something about a "Freudian slip." Much more profoundly, though, when disturbed persons with frightening, perhaps grossly antisocial thoughts or behavior present themselves in our communities, few are likely to declare that they are possessed of demons and demand their punishment, ridicule, or rejection. The notions that irrational behavior should be understandable and that persons showing it are worthy of dignified consideration and treatment form a large part of the legacy of Sigmund Freud. To be sure, Freud was quite specific in what he thought had gone wrong and in what ought to be done to correct it—and he frequently had to revise what he had proposed because earlier notions failed to fit later data. Those revisions, of course, show his integrity as a scientist and demonstrate his commitment to providing a science of mind and behavior that would make obsolete the moralistic, primitive, or demonological explanations so often in vogue.

His work has had a profound impact on the psychiatric and mental health establishments of the Western world, not to mention its effect on philosophy and literature. Freudian concepts and applications have found enduring fertile ground in psychiatry, especially child psychiatry, and in social work. Geographically perhaps the East Coast of the United States represents the area where Freudian concepts and their descendants have enjoyed the most widespread recognition in several helping professions, although, as we shall see, some reappraisal is taking place.

Sigmund Freud was born in Moravia in 1856, the first child of his father's second marriage. His intellectual talent was recognized early, and his childhood environment—in Vienna—seems generally to have been nurturant and supportive. Perhaps from that childhood he developed a reservoir of endurance which stood him in good stead during the decade of his professional life when he received little, if any, positive recognition or support. Freud specialized in the sciences and took a medical degree in Vienna. After six years of working in a research institute, he began private practice in neurology. Many of his patients were psychoneurotic—that is, they were neurologically intact but seemed to have psychological problems. Thus began his search for answers to questions about psychological problems, a search which was to take him to study the methods being used by Charcot and Bernheim in France. At last he began work with Josef Breuer in Vienna, using basically a cathartic method—the "talking cure." Their 1895 book, *Studies on Hysteria*, was the first great milestone in a career of stellar productivity in which Freud examined a wide variety of questions and began a revolution of

BOX 8-1 *HYPNOSIS: ITS NATURE AND ISSUES*

Hypnosis is as fascinating to psychologists as it is to lay people. It is usually considered an artificial state in which a person is highly responsive to suggestions from another, the hypnotist. It is often induced by the hypnotist asking the subject to relax thoroughly and at the same time to focus attention sharply—to look at a spot or object and to listen only to the hypnotist's voice. Sometimes the hypnotist challenges the subject to make some movement, such as opening the eyes or letting a hand float, which seems to the subject to be happening automatically. In the hypnotic condition, the subject may be encouraged to have vivid recall of early experiences, to experience illusions, to ignore usually painful stimuli, to learn new ideas or connections between stimuli, and to accept plans for future behaviors but later "forget" what was discussed under hypnosis.

This important psychological phenomenon has waxed and waned in professional and public interest for centuries. Its use is not confined to psychoanalysis, though it was important to the early discoveries of Freud, who had studied Charcot's hypnotic investigations of hysteria. Freud ultimately gave up hypnosis, preferring the more passive role of the psychoanalyst behind the couch; but many psychoanalytically oriented psychologists and psychiatrists have made much of hypnotherapy. Hypnosis is widely used now by professionals of behavioral, cognitive, and other orientations.

Opinions differ with regard to the meaning and value of the hypnotic experience. Some people assert that it is as widespread as social communication and suggestion; others even deny its existence. Research is clarifying many of the basic problems. The key issues center around the following (Fromm & Shor, 1979): the role and importance of unconscious processes in hypnosis; the importance of the behavior versus the personal experience (especially the existence of altered states of consciousness); continuity versus discontinuity between the hypnotic and waking state (and the importance of role playing); and the possibility of extraordinary physiological changes and behaviors during the hypnotic state. There is also a difference in what people include within the meaning of the term. Some use the term to refer only to situations of formal induction by a hypnotist; others use it to refer to naturally occurring "trance states" involving limited attention, such as what occurs when one is so absorbed in reading a story that one does not hear someone calling.

A variety of specific uses has been reported (Bowers, 1982; Fromm & Shor, 1979). Hypnosis helps to secure rapid catharis of painful experiences; to desensitize people about feared situations; to improve control of intractable pain; to provide relaxation and painlessness during childbirth, surgery, or dental work without anesthetics; to probe for remembered observations during criminal events; to change unwanted habits; and to deal with a host of other clinical problems. Even though quite painful operations may be going on, many subjects report feeling as if they were "detached observers." Research on hypnosis is assisted by the development of several standardized scales for assessing individual differences in suggestibility and hypnotic responsiveness (Hilgard, 1975), of which the best known are the Stanford Hypnotic Susceptibility Scales. Those interested in reading further about hypnosis will find good summaries and reports on research in Bowers (1982), Fromm and Shor (1979), and Hilgard (1975). For a semipopular presentation, using an inclusive view of altered states of consciousness in the context of neuro-linguistic programming, see *Tranceformations* by Grinder and Bandler (1981).

thought. He died in London in 1939, after fleeing the Nazi takeover in Austria.

CONCEPTS
AND THEIR EVOLUTION

When we speak of psychoanalysis and psychodynamics there are three things to which we could be referring: the personality theory, the modes of psychotherapy, and the professional guild. In this chapter we will try to distinguish clearly among these three aspects. The personality theory—that is, the Freudian view of how behavior and feelings arise—has undergone continual change and evolution so that our consideration of it will take a historical or developmental course. The modes of intervention, the actual performance of psychoanalytic therapy, have evolved less; our focus there will be on the major methods used. The professional guild issues require mention because of the way in which the followers, as disciples often do, have sought to retain the purity of their movement by imposing various restrictions.

Freud's psychoanalytic writings cannot be generally compared to the books of the Bible, but in one important respect, there is indeed similarity. Both collections present ideas. The details or supporting notions change rather rapidly but the central concepts endure, evolving and becoming reshaped by the passage of time, but still recognizable. Freud wrote prolifically and not systematically. Our task must be to establish at least a beginning point from which we can familiarize ourselves with the concepts that Freud presented.

Two Fundamental Concepts

The most basic of these ideas is that of the *unconscious*. Figuratively speaking, it is a reservoir of wishes and impulses that have been repressed. Fundamental to therapy is the idea that because of the anxiety they generate, some wishes, thoughts, and feelings have been "pushed down" into the unconscious and are thus not available to the patient unless some means can be found to weaken the repressing influence. What one experiences as neurotic symptoms are indirect effects of the conflict between impulses struggling for expression and the repressing forces. Personality difficulties appear baffling and incomprehensible when we do not see their source in this struggle. From the beginning of Freud's work to the present, a major aim of psychoanalytic therapy has been to open up some of the areas of the unconscious to conscious scrutiny.

Another basic Freudian idea is that the roots of a person's behavior go back to the earliest years of life—to *origins in childhood*. All behaviors and feelings are in theory determined to some extent by the person's experience, and the basic patterns for this experience were set early in life. This assumption accounts for the concern in Freudian therapy for tracing emotional or peculiar experiences back to their source in a person's life history. It also leads the analyst to expect that the patient will revive during therapy the same kind of emotional relationship with parents that played such a decisive part in the early shaping of personality.

Freud's Evolving Thought

The evolution of Freud's psychoanalytic thought is not easily simplified. It is the story of a brilliant thinker breaking new ground. As he does so, various forces, such as the disapproval of society or the emergence of rival theorists, influence him. Some of his ideas appear to be confirmed by available evidence whereas others are disconfirmed and must be changed. He is handicapped by being alone, therefore making it difficult for him to be aware of the biases or limitations to which we are all subject.

Because of the isolation and pain Freud first endured, we can under-

Figure 8-1
Sigmund Freud, founder of psychoanalysis. (Bildarchiv d. Ost. Nationalbibliothek)

stand his later satisfaction in his role and status of leader of *his* group. Throughout it all, his prodigious energy and dedication remained. Some of his followers became rigid and orthodox, some made brilliant progress as the movement diversified and became immensely complex. In the following few pages we will try to convey some of the flavor of those years. Readers should not agonize about terminology or incomplete explanation but attend instead to the ebb and flow of concepts, thus developing an appreciation of the evolving nature of the system and its profound diversity and comprehensiveness.

Following the lucid outline of Thompson (1950/1957), the course of Freud's work can be divided into four rather clearly demarcated states. From 1885 until about 1900 he took his initial steps, focusing on the treatment of hysteria. (The term is used here in its classical sense, in which a hysterical symptom might involve a minor paralysis or loss of feeling.) Freud and his co-worker, Josef Breuer, began by using hypnosis to suggest to a patient that a particular symptom would disappear. They observed that under hypnosis a patient would begin to talk of painful past events—events which were simply not remembered in the waking state. After talking of the experiences, the patient's symptoms often disappeared. To Breuer and Freud it seemed as if the act of pouring out the past painfulness had been therapeutic, and thus the first therapeutic activity—helping the patient achieve *catharsis*—was proposed.

Freud began to theorize about underlying causes and hypothesized that an early sexual event noxious to the patient—such as a molestation or a seduction—caused a great deal of anxiety which eventually resulted in symptoms. This first theory of anxiety became an early casualty when Freud found that his patients' histories did not always support the idea that their symptoms came from psychic trauma caused by an early sexual experience. Nonetheless, the early period of theorizing did result in several important conceptual milestones which have shown amazing durability. Freud began to pay attention to unconscious forces, believing that dreams, symptoms, slips of the tongue, and even humor gave evidence of processes taking place outside a person's awareness. The concepts of *repression* (making an experience unconscious) and *resistance* (the way it is kept unconscious) were products of this era, and the concept of transference, later to play a large role in psychoanalytic thinking, made its initial, simplified appearance. *Transference* means that a patient begins to feel about the analyst as he or she has in the past about someone with whom he or she has intense unresolved fantasies.

Another important development of this early era was that as Freud became more interested in pursuing the role of sexual forces as the basis for neurotic problems, Breuer and others withdrew. Thompson (1950/1957, p.7) quotes Freud from his *Collected Papers* as saying, "When I later began more and more resolutely to put forward the significance of sexuality in the etiology of neurosis, he [referring to Breuer] was the first to show that reaction of distaste and repudiation which was later to become so familiar to me, but which at that time I had not learned to recognize as my inevitable fate."

The second major period brought active and courageous revision of theories to fit the data. Freud elaborated the ideas about unacceptable wishes becoming repressed and formulated the notion of an inevitable *Oedipus complex*, the struggle in which the young boy wishes to dispose of the father so he does not have to share the mother and, since he cannot, ends up essentially by joining the father and trying to become like him. His theory of infantile sexuality and the Oedipus complex (together with a sketchier Electra complex for girls) were carefully elaborated in this period.

We should notice that at this point Freud turned from the notion of environmental causation (the assumption that externally imposed sexual experience causes psychic trauma) to a notion of *constitutional causation* (the belief that the sexual development of the child followed clear patterns, patterns which influenced the child's later life). Of this shift Thompson (1950/1957) says "... the impression grew on Freud that the patient fell ill primarily because of the strength of his own instinctual drives. This shift of emphasis had certain unfortunate results. It tended to close his mind to the significance of environment and led him to pay too little attention to the role of the emotional problems of parents in contributing to the difficulties of their children" (p. 9). It did, however, focus attention on the great importance of childhood for subsequent personality development.

Toward the end of this second period, an almost inevitable development occurred. Two of Freud's followers became critical of the heavy, dogmatic emphasis on sex as the root of psychological difficulties. Their theorizing took them in different directions. Alfred Adler felt that the root of problems lay in the fact that people struggled for power in an attempt to overcome basic feelings of inferiority. Adler thus came to emphasize social and interpersonal causes and laid the foundation for an important way of looking at personality. At the present time, besides the group calling themselves *Adlerians*, other workers also emphasize styles and patterns of interpersonal behavior, calling their approach *transactional analysis*. The second pupil to break openly with Freud was Carl Jung. He, too, opposed the emphasis on sexuality and proposed that human beings are influenced by other forces, such as cultural symbols and the interplay between one's higher spiritual nature and one's animal nature.

During the third period Freud proposed several new definitions and new relationships. First was a three-part structure of personality, consisting of *ego*, *superego*, and *id*. This brought new ideas about the origin of anxiety. During this period Freud formulated a new theory of instincts, in which he postulated aggression as well as sex as a basic drive and held that both instinctual sex and instinctual aggression in the id must be socialized by the ego in order for people to be able to function in society. Basic methods of psychoanalytic treatment during this period changed very little. Patients still produced free associations, experienced catharsis, and were given interpretations designed to increase their insight. By 1920 Thompson says psychoanalysis as a method of therapy was at its lowest ebb. Cures had been found not to be permanent, and it was becoming clear that if a therapy for neurosis were to be effective, it would have to consider the fact that neurosis involved the total personality.

At this point Freud's followers Otto Rank and Sandor Ferenczi pressed on energetically and clarified an old issue in a new way. The earlier goal of therapy had been to bring back past experiences into consciousness and thus produce a cure. The method had been, as we mentioned, to have the patient continue to produce free associations about his or her childhood. The newer view held that the patient did not suffer as much from the past as from the way the past was influencing present behavior. With that shift of emphasis from past to present, an important focus on the doctor-patient relationship came into being.

In the fourth period, approximately from 1925 on, the psychoanalytic movement turned more attention to the *method* of therapy, and the concept of *transference* in the doctor-patient relationship became central to treatment. The idea here was that the patient would transfer neurotic tendencies about, say, her or his father, to the therapist, who could then provide interpretations. The interpretations would, in turn, give the patient insight into why problems had come about, and after a period of *working through* or adjusting to the insights, the patient would be better. Although Ferenczi, Reich, and Freud's daughter, Anna, did not question Freud's instinct theories, other neo-Freudians, active followers of Freud who modified his notions, such as Rank, Horney, Fromm, and Sullivan, discarded the instinct theories in favor of other key concepts. Horney and Fromm developed theories about the shaping of character through cultural and interpersonal influences, whereas Sullivan made interpersonal relations the core of his approach.

Late in the fourth era, after about 1933, a group called the *ego psychologists* because of their emphasis on the development of a *conflict-free ego* (that is, an ego not wholly concerned with controlling id impulses) also reacted against the idea of all-powerful unsocial instincts. Hartman (1964) for example, became interested in ideas about how certain kinds of skills and strengths develop. The stress on biologically innate sources of behavior was reduced. More recently psychological thinking about the interaction of biological and social influences has become more sophisticated because of research findings in genetics and physiology. It is clear that both kinds of factors must be considered.

PSYCHOANALYSIS AS TREATMENT

Related to the personality theory is a standard method of treatment for psychological ills which will be described briefly. (The remainder of the section is adopted from Sundberg & Tyler, 1962, pp. 377-379.) The physical features of standard psychoanalytic treatment have become familiar to us through hundreds of novels, movies, television programs, quips, and cartoons. The patient lies on a couch with the analyst sitting behind her or him taking notes, occasionally commenting on what she or he says. In a typical analysis both participants work at this task for an hour, five days a week, for two or more years. The tools they use are primarily *free association* and the *analysis of dreams*. During this period the analysis becomes the center of the patient's life. It is an intense, profoundly moving experience.

When we analyze the process that occurs and try to explain why it does constitute so vital an experience, several aspects of it are apparent. First, the release through free association of emotions that have long been repressed constitutes *catharsis*, a purging of the system of feelings that have been poisoning it. In some variations of analytic treatment, such as the narcotherapy used for treatment of war or traumatic neuroses, this emotional release seems to constitute the "cure" itself. More typically, however, it is not sufficient to free the patient from his or her difficulties. Most psychoanalysts do not consider it to be a major therapeutic influence

The second feature of analytic treatment consists of *interpretation* by the therapist, contributing to *insight* by the patient. If the patient is really able to obey the basic rule and verbalize her or his every thought, even if it seems silly or shocking, parts of the total picture that have previously been inaccessible to conscious awareness begin to emerge. The analyst helps the patient to put these together and make what could be called *psychoanalytic sense* of them. In this the analyst must always proceed cautiously and tentatively, trying never to confront the patient with interpretations that the patient will repudiate entirely.

No matter how cautious the analyst's interpretations are, *resistance* always develops in the patient. It shows itself in many ways—by long periods of silence, by hostile remarks, by unpunctuality or failure to keep the appointments. This resistance itself becomes something to be interpreted and diminished. The ability to handle this resistance to the task is an important part of the analyst's skill. Resistance is the form that repression takes in the psychoanalytic situation. Thus the analyst's principal task in interpreting the patient's thoughts is to weaken this repression, not simply to clarify some psychological point suggested by what the patient has said or to lead to a purely intellectual understanding of experience. Thus the timing of the analyst's interpretive statements and the verbal form they take may be as important as their soundness in assisting the patient to express these repressed feelings.

Another phenomenon fundamental to psychoanalytic work is *transference*. Freud discovered that a patient whose analysis proceeds to a successful outcome always developed for a time an intense personal attachment to the therapist. Because of the way the whole situation is structured, the patient cannot, of course, know the therapist in any of the ways in which we know our friends in ordinary social life. As patients lie on the couch they do not see the therapist during the session itself. Between analytic sessions they have no social or professional contact with the therapist. With such an unstructured and socially blank screen on which to picture the therapist, it is natural that the patients react during therapy in the way they have reacted to similar and significant persons in their past life. They may *transfer* to the therapist their whole relationship, perhaps, to their father, reenacting even painful early struggles of which they have no clear memory. According to Freudians it is this experience wherein lies the possibility for profound personality reorganization. It is as if the patient in a sense *relives* the developmental periods in which the basic personality patterns were laid down and modifies these patterns through this new emotional experience. This experience is what analysts mean by the *transference neurosis*. The resolution of this neurotic attachment to the therapist is of major importance in the patient's recovery.

The transference must of course be understood at all times by analysts so that they can make sure that it constitutes for the patient this kind of corrective emotional experience. Lately there has been increasing attention directed to *countertransference*, or the emotional relationship of the analyst to the patient. Analysts must understand their own reactions if these powerful forces are to be channeled wisely.

Along with these processes there is another that becomes increasingly prominent as the analysis proceeds toward its close. This is called *working through*. The new insights achieved do not automatically transfer to every area of life. Emotional relationships to spouse, to child, to colleague may all need to be reshaped as basic attitudes change. There is much to discuss even after most of the significant unconscious material has been brought to light, and considerable time is needed to resolve a deep transference—to free the patient from dependence on the analyst. Thus a complete psychoanalysis is very time consuming and, as a consequence, very expensive. It is likely to require several years and to cost several thousand dollars.

Reading Freud

It is necessary to put flesh on these dry bones of notions and concepts. What in fact did Freud do, how did he assess and treat his patients? What was the process like, viewed through his eyes? How did his mind work as he thought about a particular case? We shall read excerpts from one of his famous cases in sufficient length to acquire some of the flavor of both the case and Freud's lucid prose. (He did, after all, win a Goethe Prize for literature.) But clearly, he did not write with our current society in mind; as we read his words, we must be aware that he wrote from a background vastly different from our own. He did not know or have access to much of modern science or technology. Conversely we have no direct contact with the burning issues of his time.

Although Freud's works are scattered and poorly summarized, any student of psychoanalysis will do well to seek the primary source. Many apologists and systematizers have attempted the job, but all too often they have added their own colorations. The following excerpts from the delightful decalogue by Holt (1973) give valuable reinforcement to the sense of yeasty evolution which permeated Freud's thought. It cautions us to heed his context in interpreting his work.

> Don't expect rigorous definitions; look rather for the meanings of his terms in the ways they are used over a period of time. And don't be dismayed if you find a word being used at one place in its ordinary, literary meaning, at another in a special technical sense which changes with the developmental status of the theory. An enterprise like the Dictionary of Psychoanalysis, put together by a couple of industrious but misguided analysts who lifted definition-like sentences from many of Freud's works, is completely mistaken in conception and betrays a total misunderstanding of Freud's style of thinking and working.
>
> Finally, be particularly cautious not to gravitate toward either of two extreme and equally untenable positions; that is, don't take Freud's every sentence as a profound truth. This may present difficulties but only because of our own inadequacies, our pedestrian difficulty in keeping up with the soaring mind of a genius who did not always bother to explicate steps that were obvious to him. This is the temptation of the scholars working from within the psychoanalytic institutes, those earnest Freudians who, to Freud's annoyance, had already begun to emerge during his lifetime. For most of us in the universities, the corresponding temptation is the more dangerous one: Don't let yourself get so offended by Freud's lapses from methodological purity that you dismiss him altogether. Almost any reader can learn an enormous lot from Freud if he will listen carefully and sympathetically and not take his pronouncements too seriously. (R.R. Holt, On reading Freud, pp. 70, 71. Copyright © 1973 by Jason Aronson, Inc. Used by permission.)

Freud's Account of a Short Case History (1895)

The following excerpt from Freud's writings is a short vignette from the 1895 book *Studies on Hysteria* (J. Breuer & S. Freud [trans. by James Strachey]. Excerpts from pp. 125–134 used by permission of Basic Books, Hogarth Press Ltd., Sigmund Freud Copyrights Ltd., and The Institute of Psychoanalysis). We see clearly the clinical application of his early notions about the sexual etiology of the neuroses, specifically that the impressions from a presexual period, which seem to produce no effect on the child, attain traumatic power at a later date as memories. The vignette is one of five from a lengthy book on hysteria. It allows a glimpse of Freud as a clinician and a flexible one at that. Many of his followers might have refused to talk to the girl because she was outside the structure of analysis agreement, couch, and fee, but not Freud. Note that he recognizes clearly the limitations of the brief contact.

In the summer vacation of the year 189__ I made an excursion into the Hohe Tauern so that for a while I might forget medicine and more particularly the neuroses. I had almost succeeded in this when one day I turned aside from the main road to climb a mountain which lay somewhat apart and which was renowned for its views and for its well-run refuge hut. I reached the top after a strenuous climb and, feeling refreshed and rested, was sitting deep in contemplation of the charm of the distant prospect. I was so lost in thought that at first I did not connect it with myself when these words reached my ears: "Are you a doctor, sir?" But the question was addressed to me, and by the rather sulky-looking girl of perhaps eighteen who had served my meal and had been spoken to by the landlady as "Katharina". To judge by her dress and bearing, she could not be a servant, but must no doubt be a daughter or relative of the landlady's.

Coming to myself I replied: "Yes, I'm a doctor; but how did you know that?"

"You wrote your name in the Visitors' Book, sir. And I thought if you had a few moments to spare. . . . The truth is, sir, my nerves are bad. I went to see a doctor in L____ about them and he gave me something for them; but I'm not well yet."

So there I was with the neuroses once again—for nothing else could very well be the matter with this strong, well-built girl with her unhappy look. I was interested to find that neuroses could flourish in this way at a height of over 6,000 feet; I questioned her further therefore. I report the conversation that followed between us just as it is impressed on my memory and I have not altered the patient's dialect.

"Well, what is it you suffer from?"

"I get so out of breath. Not always. But sometimes it catches me so that I think I shall suffocate."

This did not, at first sight, sound like a nervous symptom. But soon it occurred to me that probably it was only a description that stood for an anxiety attack; she was choosing shortness of breath out of the complex of sensations arising from anxiety and laying undue stress on that single factor.

"Sit down here. What is it like when you get 'out of breath'?"

"It comes over me all at once. First of all it's like something pressing on my eyes. My head gets so heavy, there's dreadful buzzing, and I feel so giddy that I almost fall over. Then there's something crushing my chest so that I can't get my breath."

"And you don't notice anything in your throat?"

"My throat's squeezed together as though I were going to choke."

"Does anything else happen in your head?"

"Yes, there's a hammering, enough to burst it."

"And don't you feel at all frightened while this is going on?"

"I always think I'm going to die. I'm brave as a rule and go about everywhere by myself—into the cellar and all over the mountain. But on a day when that happens I don't dare to go anywhere; I think all the time someone's standing behind me and going to catch hold of me all at once."

[Convinced that it was indeed an anxiety attack the girl was describing, Freud proceeded to inquire about its content, asking her to tell him when and how the first one occurred. She described an intensely embarrassing scene in which she had come upon her uncle making love to her cousin, Franziska. She blamed herself for the divorce that occurred when the aunt found out about the affair with Franziska.]

"One day two years ago some gentlemen had climbed the mountain and asked for something to eat. My aunt wasn't at home, and Franziska, who always did the cooking, was nowhere to be found. And my uncle was not to be found either.

We looked everywhere, and at last Alois, the little boy, my cousin, said, 'Why, Franziska must be in Father's room!' And we both laughed; but we weren't thinking anything bad. Then we went to my uncle's room but found it locked. That seemed strange to me. Then Alois said: 'There's a window in the passage where you can look into the room.' We went into the passage; but Alois wouldn't go to the window and said he was afraid. So I said: 'You silly boy! I'll go. I'm not a bit afraid.' And I had nothing bad in my mind. I looked in. The room was rather dark, but I saw my uncle and Franziska; he was lying on her."

"Well?"

"I came away from the window at once, and leant up against the wall and couldn't get my breath—just what happens to me since. Everything went blank, my eyelids were forced together and there was a hammering and buzzing in my head."

'Did you tell your aunt that very same day?"

"Oh, no, I said nothing."

"Then why were you so frightened when you found them together? Did you understand it? Did you know what was going on?"

"Oh no. I didn't understand anything at that time. I was only sixteen. I don't know what I was frightened about."

"Fraulein Katharina, if you could remember now what was happening in you at that time, when you had your first attack, what you thought about it—it would help you."

"Yes, if I could. But I was so frightened that I've forgotten everything."

[Katharina went on to describe what happened later when her symptoms recurred, especially the vomiting.]

We (Breuer and I) had often compared the symptomatology of hysteria with a pictographic script which has become intelligible after the discovery of a few bilingual inscriptions. In that alphabet being sick means disgust. So I said: "If you were sick three days later, I believe that means that when you looked into the room you felt disgusted."

"Yes, I'm sure I felt disgusted," she said reflectively, "but disgust at what?"

"Perhaps you saw something naked? What sort of state were they in?"

"It was too dark to see anything; besides they both of them had their clothes on. Oh, if only I knew what it was I felt disgusted at!"

I had no idea, either. But I told her to go on and tell me whatever occurred to her, in the confident expectation that she would think of precisely what I needed to explain the case.

[Katharina continued her story about what happened when she told her aunt what she had seen. Then she suddenly changed the subject.]

After this, however, to my astonishment she dropped these threads and began to tell me two sets of older stories, which went back two or three years earlier than the traumatic moment. The first set related to occasions on which the same uncle had made sexual advances to her herself, when she was only fourteen years old. She described how she had once gone with him on an expedition down into the valley in the winter and had spent the night in the inn there. He sat in the bar drinking and playing cards, but she felt sleepy and went up to bed early in the room they were to share on the upper floor. She was not quite asleep when he came up; then she fell asleep again and woke up suddenly 'feeling his body' in the bed. She jumped up and remonstrated with him: "What are you up to, Uncle? Why don't you stay in your own bed?" He tried to pacify her: "Go on, you silly girl, keep still. You don't know how nice it is."—"I don't like your 'nice' things; you don't even let one sleep in peace." She remained standing by the door, ready to take refuge outside in the passage, till at last he gave up and went to sleep himself. Then she went back to her own bed and slept till morning. From the way in which she reported having defended herself it seems to follow that she did not clearly recognize the attack as a sexual one. When I asked her if she knew what he was trying to do to her, she replied: "Not at the time." It had become clear to her much later on, she said; she had resisted because it was unpleasant to be disturbed in one's sleep and "because it wasn't nice."

[She also remembered some other occasions when her uncle behaved strangely toward her or toward Franziska.]

At the end of these two sets of memories she came to a stop. She was like someone transformed. The sulky, unhappy face had grown lively, her eyes were bright, she was lightened and exalted. Meanwhile the understanding of her case had become clear to me. The later part of what she had told me, in an apparently aimless fashion, provided an admirable explanation of her behavior at the scene of the discovery. At that time she had carried about with her two sets of experiences which she remembered but did not understand, and from which she drew no inferences. When she caught sight of the couple in intercourse, she at once established a connection between the new impression and these two sets of recollections, she began to understand them and at the same time to fend them off. There then followed a short period of working-out, of "incubation," after which the symptoms of conversion set in, the vomiting as a substitute for moral and physical disgust. This solved the riddle. She had not been disgusted by the sight of the two people but by the memory which that sight had stirred up in her. And, taking everything into account, this could only be the memory of the attempt on her at night when she had "felt her uncle's body."

So when she had finished her confession I said to her: "I know now what it was you thought when you looked into the room. You thought: 'Now he's doing with her what he wanted to do with me that night and those other times.' That was what you were disgusted at, because you remembered the feeling when you woke up in the night and felt his body."

"It may well be," she replied, "that that was what I was disgusted at and that that was what I thought."

"Tell me just one thing more. You're a grown-up girl now and know all sorts of things . . ."

"Yes, now I am."

"Tell me just one thing. What part of his body was it that you felt that night?"

But she gave me no more definite answer. She smiled in an embarrassed way, as though she had been found out, like someone who is obliged to admit that a fundamental position has been reached where there is not much more to be said. I could imagine what the tactile sensation was which she had later learnt to interpret. Her facial expression seemed to me to be saying that she supposed that I was right in my conjecture. But I could not penetrate further, and in any case I owed her a debt of gratitude for having made it so much easier for me to talk to her than to the prudish ladies of my city practice, who regard whatever is natural as shameful."

[Freud goes on to conclude the case and offers a discussion.]

I hope this girl, whose sexual sensibility had been injured at such an early age, derived some benefit from our conversation. I have not seen her since.

If someone were to assert that the present case history is not so much an analysed case of hysteria as a case solved by guessing, I should have nothing to say against him. It is true that the patient agreed that what I interpolated into her story was probably true; but she was not in a position to recognize it as something she had experienced. In this respect the case of Katharina is typical. In every analysis of a case of hysteria based on sexual traumas we find that impressions from the presexual period which produced no effect on the child attain traumatic power at a later date as memories, when the girl or married woman has acquired an understanding of sexual life. The splitting-off of psychical groups may be said to be a normal process in adolescent development; and it is easy to see that their later reception into the ego affords frequent opportunities for psychical disturbances. Moreover, I should like at this point to express doubt as to whether a splitting of consciousness due to ignorance is really different from one due to conscious rejection, and whether even adolescents do not possess sexual knowledge far oftener than is supposed or than they themselves believe.

A further distinction in the psychical mechanism of this case lies in the fact that the scene of discovery, which we have described as "auxiliary," deserves equally to be called "traumatic." It was operative on account of its own content and not merely as something that revived previous traumatic experience. It combined the characteristics of an "auxiliary" and a "traumatic" moment. There seems no reason, however, why this coincidence should lead us to abandon a conceptual separation which in other cases corresponds also to a separation in time. Another peculiarity of Katharina's case, which, incidentally, has long been familiar to us, is seen in the circumstance that the conversion, the production of the hysterical phenomena, did not occur immediately after the trauma but after an interval of incubation. Charcot liked to describe this interval as the "period of psychical working-out."

The anxiety from which Katharina suffered in her attacks was a hysterical one; that is, it was a reproduction of the anxiety which had appeared in connection with each of the sexual traumata. I shall not here comment on the fact which I have found regularly present in a very large number of cases—namely that a mere suspicion of sexual relations calls up the affect of anxiety in virginal individuals.

[In a 1924 footnote, Freud tells us that Katharina was not the niece actually but the *daughter* of the landlady. The lifting of Freud's veil of discretion, then, indicates that the girl fell ill as the result of sexual attempts on the part of her own father.]

This case, from the first period of Freud's development, illustrates the kind of theoretical thinking he was doing at that time, as well as his general style and attitude. During subsequent stages of his career, the concepts were modified, but the style and therapeutic approach persisted.

CURRENT PSYCHOANALYTIC PSYCHOTHERAPY

We have dwelt at length on the foundations of psychoanalytic thought and treatment because it is difficult for anyone to make sense out of current efforts without a clear feeling for the roots of the movement. What modifications have taken place in the intervening years? Orthodox psychoanalysis, the strict two-or-three-times-a-week on-the-couch procedure emphasizing free association, the out-of-sight analyst, and transference was typically of about four years' duration. Quite quickly therapists discovered that many patients did better with briefer therapy, and so the distinction between psychoanalysis and psychoanalytically oriented psychotherapy was born. Psychoanalytically oriented therapy is often called "psychodynamic" and we will use the terms interchangeably.

Techniques in Briefer Therapy

In its mechanics psychoanalytically oriented psychotherapy appears similar to other talking therapies. Both patient and therapist sit in chairs and look at each other. Not all therapists, however, use the same parts of the theory. Some emphasize earlier parts of Freud's work, looking for sexual traumata, and base interpretations on this first theory of anxiety. Others work with later concepts such as defenses against the instinctual impulses of the id or transference as a form of resistance. In briefer psychotherapy the therapist does not aim to develop a complete transference. He or she will be sensitive to what it represents, however, because what the patient projects onto the neutral therapist (e.g., "You're just like my father") clearly points to emotional issues vital to the patient. Such issues are dealt with verbally, without the formation of the intense regressive, preoccupying, or "neurotic" feelings that patients often experience during long analysis.

Dealing with Resistance

Resistance in therapy is seen as having a defensive function. Therapists are careful in interpreting defenses. Getting "inside" has no value if the patient experiences terror or damage. Judy, a college student whose long-time partner, George, has just taken up with someone else, says to her therapist, "I'm really so happy George is experiencing such deep meaning with Lucinda—he'll be able to grow interpersonally and deepen his awareness of other women." The therapist surmises that Judy experiences loss and damage to her sense of self and that she may be in a kind of psychological crisis. Judy could be told, "Be realistic, Judy. George is looking out for himself. Face it, you've been dumped because you're clingy and stifling." Such an assaultive, frightening, dignity-stripping confrontation, even though it may have a seed of truth, would probably cause Judy to withdraw further and defend more vehemently. The therapist realizes that Judy is probably focusing on George in order to master the anxiety of being rejected. This way she can appear caring, mature—and stay centered on George. So the therapist uses the common and valuable approach of *going with the resistance*—rather than against it—and starts asking about how Judy has cared for George. The therapist establishes at length that Judy has shown nurturance and sensitivity toward George. With trust beginning to grow, the therapist asks, "And Judy, you've cared so well for George—who's caring for you?" At this point the tears begin, and Judy's inner suffering can become the focus of therapeutic work.

A common modification, especially relating to some theories of therapy in social work, is to focus on promoting a *therapeutic relationship* which is felt to have some aspects of transference but also some supportive nurturant aspects.

The Function of Interpretation

Psychoanalytically oriented psychotherapy relies on *interpretation*, the process in which the therapist suggests an alternative meaning or relationship. Several kinds of things can be interpreted, for example:

"I told my mother—I mean my wife—that . . ." may represent how the patient unconsciously thinks about his wife;

"I got right up to the point of kissing her and then I seemed to freeze" may represent uncertainties or insecurities about masculinity;

"I just love to collect money" or "I'm going to keep the stuff he needs" may represent fixations (being stuck) at the anal stage of psychosexual development.

In short, the interpreter translates behavior and experience into psychoanalytic terms so that, translated, they make sense in the psychoanalytic system, whereas untranslated they do not. Take, for example, a freshman's statement: "I just don't know why I always take my girlfriend home with me, when it makes my mother so furious." Uninterpreted the statement makes no clear sense. An interpretation, "Perhaps you have an unconscious wish to hurt your mother after you failed to win her away from your father," an interpretation coming from the concept of the Oedipus complex, supplies something many of us hunger for—a way of seeing the apparently unfathomable as part of a logical process. Other interpretations are, of course, possible such as "You want your folks to be impressed that you have such a pretty girlfriend" or "You're trying to tell them you're grown up and ready to leave." The therapist may choose which one to suggest or may not interpret at all for the time being.

Rules for interpretation in psychoanalytic psychotherapy are not clearly stated. It is clear, however, that therapists must not interpret too soon, nor must they interpret too much at once, or the patient is more likely to refuse or deny the interpretation. Many patients find the ubiquitous sexual symbolism revealed in interpretations disgusting; the disgust itself is grist for the interpreter's mill. Psychoanalysts attempt to avoid overly shocking or threatening interpretations by interpreting only material of which the patient has preconscious awareness. For all the controversy and inexactitude surrounding it, interpretation gently and sensitively presented has an enduring place in dynamic psychotherapy.

After issues dealing with transference, resistance, and the like have been interpreted, briefer therapy, like psychoanalysis, usually involves *working through* or assimilating the insights and learning to use them as vehicles of emotional change. Finally, just as in classical analysis, termination is seen as a tension-filled time in which angers, disappointments, and dependencies on the therapist are likely to emerge. Consideration of termination begins early. The therapist brings the subject up frequently in gentle attempts to deliver the patient back to his or her life with maximum autonomy.

Learning and Practicing
Psychodynamic Psychotherapy

Training in psychoanalytically oriented or psychodynamic psychotherapy occurs in many settings. Many departments of psychology, most schools of social work, psychiatric residency programs, and some graduate psychiatric nursing programs train students in various forms of psychodynamic psychotherapy. Specialized psychoanalytic institutes generally train only those with an M.D. degree (although Freud opposed such discrimination). Training courses understandably vary greatly in length, prerequisites, and intensity of supervision.

Partly because of the early Freudian notion that the therapist would present a psychologically neutral slate to which the patient would project his internal dynamics and partly because of the tradition of the psychoanalytic institutes, personal psychotherapy for student therapists has always been seen as highly desirable or mandatory. Such requirements also vary greatly. The requirements of some institutes are rigid and may call for four years of personal therapy even before the four years of didactic therapy can begin. Whatever the requirements, there seems little doubt that *personal work*, as it is called, has real utility for helping a therapist explore his or her own motives as a therapist and as a person.

All therapeutic systems can be misused. In psychodynamic psychotherapy recent writers have laid increasing stress on the maturity, openness, and understanding of the therapist, rather than on possession of appropriate jargon. Bruch (1974) says of the immature practitioner, "Instead of sympathetically observing and responding to his patient's behavior and utterances, he will label him with accusing, punitive and invalidating epitaphs—'passive aggressive,' 'masochistic,' 'compulsive,' 'latent homosexual,' and so on. . . . Sooner or later a student must come to terms with the plain unalterable fact that there are no definite complexes or psychodynamics to be recognized in all his cases, no definite rules, which, if rigidly applied, will turn him into an effective therapist" (p. 25).

Psychotherapy rarely provides a support network for the therapist. Doing psychotherapy, as Bruch (1974) says, is basically a lonely business. It means the therapist must suspend concern about personal needs and inadequacies and attend only to those of the other person. Therefore some supportive relationship, normally through *supervision, case conferences*, informal or special contacts, becomes very important. Despite theoretical differences it is helpful to have someone with whom to share concerns and anxieties. Professional growth and maturity depend to some extent on the effectiveness of the professional sharing and reviewing.

OFFSHOOTS OF FREUDIAN PSYCHOANALYSIS: JUNG, ADLER, AND NEO-ANALYTIC THOUGHT

As we have mentioned, Freud's thinking spurred creative efforts in others. These efforts demand study because of the tacit messages they contain about Freud's original work. Which concepts stimulated objection and alternatives? Which ones begat elaborations? We can become clearer about Freud's limitations and strengths, as well as his basic intentions, by studying the followers and reactors. Jung and Adler both made proposals that have had enduring impact on theory and practice and that resulted in their separation from Freud's circle. Major second-generation workers such as Horney, Sullivan, and Fromm have also had profound influence. Their ideas have been seen as extensions of some of Freud's ideas, not, as with Adler and Jung, as challenging alternative formulations, so that Horney, Sullivan, and Fromm have retained key positions in the developing psychoanalytic movement.

Figure 8-2
Carl G. Jung. (The Bettman Archive, Inc.)

Jung.   Carl Gustav Jung was for many years thought to have been excessively given to mysticism. His principal axiom—that a person's conduct is governed by inborn archetypes—is translatable into a system for helping disturbed people. Jungian analysts have particularly emphasized the latter half of life. Jung's work did not attract many workers in the mainstream of American psychology or psychiatry, but it has received some attention, especially from pastors and religiously oriented counselors. Jung's insistence on the concepts of destiny or purpose in human development, the search for wholeness and completion, and the yearning for rebirth have particularly seemed appropriate in group counseling and group retreats often under religious auspices. Jung's interest in other cultures and their symbols have also profoundly affected interpretations of art and ideas about creativity. His ideas about personality types and styles have been reflected in the acceptance of his concepts of introversion and extraversion, and in a well-known test, the Myers-Briggs Type Indicator (McCaulley, 1981).

Adler.   Alfred Adler's ideas, rather in contrast to Jung's, have found wider use in clinical work, engaging the interest of several notable "post-Adlerians"; they constitute a particular approach to treating children and their families. We must note clearly that Adler, because of the sharp differences in basic concepts, does not belong in the psychoanalytic camp but could well be called a *social psychologist;* he will also be referred to in our

Figure 8-3
Alfred Adler. (The Bettman Archive, Inc.)

later chapter on cognitive therapies. Adler was perhaps the first of several followers and students of Freud to stress the significance of social conditions in shaping personality, as opposed to the Freudian emphasis on constitutional, sexual, and instinctual energies. Erich Fromm has acknowledged that Adler was the first analyst to emphasize the fundamental social nature of human beings.

What, then, were Adler's specific contributions? First, Adler assumed that people are motivated mainly by social urges. Hall and Lindzey (1978) point out that where Freud emphasized sexual drives, Adler stressed an inherent *social interest (Gemeinschaftsgefühl)* which makes possible such phenomena as interpersonal relationships, cooperative activities, placing social welfare above selfish interests, and acquiring a predominantly social style of life. A second major contribution was Adler's emphasis on a *creative self*—as contrasted with Freud's *ego*, a group of processes serving or defending against inborn instincts. Adler's creative self interprets and makes meaning out of experience and searches for ways to fill out the person's unique *style of life;* if such experiences are unavailable, the creative self will try to synthesize them. Finally, Adler stressed *personal uniqueness*—that each person has a special combination of motives, traits, interests, and values. One especially important source of motivation in Adler's system is motivation coming from a sense of inferiority and efforts to overcome that inferiority and powerlessness.

First among Adlerian working concepts is one rather confusingly known as *fictional finalism*. As Freud had laid great stress on constitutional factors, such as instincts, and on early childhood experiences as determiners of personality, Adler postulated that people are motivated by expectations of the future. A central difference between Adler and Freud is that Freud believed in causality (behavior is the way it is because something has caused it) and Adler believed in a guiding final fiction or image (behavior is the way it is because the person is trying to attain a goal).

> Individual Psychology insists absolutely on the indispensability of finalism for the understanding of all psychological phenomena. Causes, powers, instincts, impulses, and the like cannot serve as explanatory principles. The final goal alone can explain man's behavior. Experiences, traumata, sexual development mechanisms cannot yield an explanation, but the perspective in which these are regarded, the individual way of seeing them, which subordinates all life to the final goal, can do so. (Adler, 1930, p. 400)

Inferiority feelings and efforts to compensate for them were proposed early in Adler's work. Such concepts, once fused with the notion of striving toward a goal, suggested an innate, overreaching need within people to "make it to the top" which Adler called *striving for superiority. Social interest*, again seen as an inherent quality, contrasts with Freud's concept of self-interest. Finally, in notions of *style of life*, Adler rounds out the basic components of his system. Today we might use a computer analogy and view

BOX 8-2   *EARLY MEMORIES*

Among the different schools of therapy, the one putting the most emphasis on early memories is that of Adler. Fundamental to Adlerian understanding is a person's life style. Assessing this requires that the therapist obtain from the client reports on the earliest events clearly remembered. These early recollections are considered along with the early family constellation (especially the client's birth order and role vis-a-vis siblings), evidence of unrealistic assumptions called "basic mistakes," and personal assets in formulating the life-style analysis, which is the basis for therapy (Mosak, 1979). The reason early recollections are important in understanding the client is that they serve (in the words of Adler, quoted by Bruhn & Last, 1982, p. 120) as "the reminders he carries about with him of his own limits and of the meaning of circumstances. . . . [They serve as] a story he repeats to himself to warn him or comfort him, to keep him concentrated on his goal, to prepare him, by means of past experiences, to meet the future with an already tested style of action."

Adlerian theory about early memories differs from Freudian theory in several ways. Freud saw these reports as superficial "screen memories" covering important events, usually sexual, not available to consciousness; the latent content underlying the manifest report described events which had caused later pathological symptoms. Adler, however, viewed such reports as information about the person's current perceptions and projected goals; early memories are selectively retained to help keep the person on track to carry out a chosen life style, be it neurotic or normal. As a client improves in therapy, other memories will be chosen or a new interpretation of events will appear.

Considering the importance of childhood and life history, it is surprising that there is little research and little connection made with the extensive work on memory by experimental cognitive psychologists. Theoretical ideas that would seem to be relevant to research on early memories are the "schema" concept proposed by Bartlett (1932) and developed by Piaget and Bruner and the "cognitive styles" concept (Witkin & Goodenough, 1981). Hedvig (1963) found that reported early memories were more stable over time than TAT stories. Ferguson (1964) found that clinicians could match early recollections with longer descriptions of personality. Below is an illustration of an Adlerian interpretation of early recollections of an adult male suffering from depression (abbreviated from Forgus & Schulman, 1979, p. 319):

Memory 1, age 5: "It was a long distance home from school. One day, . . . I had to move my bowels. I couldn't hold it any longer so I did it in my trousers. I felt ashamed."

Memory 2, age 7: "I was left in a car while mother and father went to visit somebody. I tried to follow them but I didn't know the way. I went back to the car and felt they deserted me and I should hurt myself to make them feel sorry."

Memory 3, age 8: "I had a fight with a boy and I gave him a bloody nose. Later I was afraid he would get his gang to beat me up."

Interpretation: "Life is difficult . . . and the patient suffers. . . . He accuses others of not caring for him properly and demonstrates suffering in order to punish them. He is an angry and frustrated person with little trust either in others or in his own capabilities."

life style as the master program controlling the selection of all other programs.

Horney.   Karen Horney took issue with a number of Freud's concepts, but she retained a sufficient number, such as psychic determinism, unconscious motivation, and emotional nonrational motives, so that she may still be counted in the vanguard of latter-day psychoanalytic thinkers. Her conviction was that psychoanalysis should outgrow the limitations set by its being an instinctivistic and genetic psychology. For her, disturbed human relationships, particularly those occurring early in a child's life, are likely to promote *basic anxiety.* Various strategies to deal with basic anxiety, isolation, or helplessness may emerge in the form of neurotic needs—called *neurotic* because they are irrational solutions to the basic problems. In Horney's view, neurotic needs—for example, the excessive need for a partner who will take over one's life—are usually found in someone who is afraid of being deserted and left alone.

In later work Horney grouped her ten neurotic needs into three basic orientations: (1) moving toward people—e.g., needing love; (2) moving away from people—e.g., needing independence; and (3) moving against people—e.g., needing power. In her view the inner conflicts stemming from the neurotic needs are avoidable or resolvable if the person is raised with security, love, and trust. Unlike Freud and Jung, Horney does not see conflict as built into human nature.

Sullivan.   Sullivan, a contemporary of Horney's, had medical and psychoanalytic training, but he also drew influence from the Chicago School of Sociology where he acquired a strongly interpersonal and interactional view of human behavior and human problems. Personality, for Sullivan, was a reflection of the sum total of interpersonal behaviors, not a distinct entity.

Sullivan followed Freud in postulating a clear and rather fixed series of developmental stages, but he showed greater attention to social variables and far less to constitutional or instinctual ones. His stages take in a greater portion of the life span, placing him midway between Freud and Erikson (mentioned in Chapter 2). For Western society he posited (1) infancy, (2) childhood, (3) juvenile period, (4) preadolescence, and (5) late adolescence, to be followed by (6) maturity. He offers a clear set of tasks for each stage, with attention given to the role of deep intimate relationships among young people (same sex first, then opposite sex) in the developmental process. Sullivan, as a practicing clinician, did a great deal of work on the interview, taught actively, and stimulated a considerable amount of research.

In summary then, Adler, Fromm, Horney, and Sullivan have required or added vitally important social dimensions. Although these latter four are clearly opposed to Freud's doctrines of instinct and the fixity of human nature, they have not proposed a pure environmentalist position—that an individual personality is only the creation of the social and physical environment. All four seek a balance between the purely psychological and the purely social.

CRITIQUE

How adequate is psychoanalysis conceptually?   Psychoanalysis as an approach to personality and to psychotherapy has several serious vulnerabilities not offset by its venerable age and status. Because at its core it espouses a thoroughgoing personal determinism, psychoanalysis shows little sensitivity to other higher systems, such as family, small group, organizational, or community variables. However, its narrowness of focus should be appreciated for the pioneering effort it was in its time—an effort to explain behavior at the personal-system level rather than relying solely on either the biological system or extraneous demons and spirits.

Psychoanalysis uses so many models—dynamic, topographic, economic, and developmental—that any thought or behavior can be explained on a post hoc basis, but almost nothing can be predicted. Furthermore, many of its concepts are difficult to observe or quantify. The id, the ego, and the superego are uncomfortably akin to members of the Greek pantheon, and scientific observations and tests of hypothesis have been difficult.

As a final defense of Freud, it must be stressed that he also was a researcher and scientist, not afraid to make major revisions when findings seemed to demand them. Much of the subsequent conceptual ossification and creation of orthodoxy would probably have been scorned by Freud.

How practical is psychoanalysis?   The psychoanalytic goal of cure through insight must be criticized on two grounds. First, from the standpoint of social acceptability, the widespread dissemination of notions such as castration anxiety, penis envy, or Oedipus complex strains the system's credibility and acceptability in the community. Second, the success of such interpretations appears to be a complex social psychological process, perhaps less related to the content of the interpretation and more to the variables of situation, such as client trust and interpreter investment in believing.

Because the most influential membership in the movement in the United States has restricted itself—contrary to Freud's advice—to holders of the M.D. degree, its outreach potential, or potential for paraprofessional or community involvement, has been limited. With most psychoanalysts in private practice, there is also a tendency to avoid the poor and the seriously disturbed and to work with verbal, intelligent adults. Ryan's *Distress in the City* (1969) reports that in Boston, where psychoanalysis is strong, "slightly over half of all Boston residents in private psychiatric treatment live in four . . . census tracts . . . out of Boston's 156 census tracts" (p. 15); a "tiny group of approximately 3,000 young, college educated women in their twenties and early thirties furnishes about one quarter of Boston patients in private psychiatric treatment" (p. 16). Critics note that such treatment frequently promotes dependency and, especially in the private residential institutions, can be financially ruinous to whole families. Also, psychoanalytic approaches seldom encourage preventive work or recognize the importance of other systems such as the family or the community.

Although psychoanalytically oriented therapies can be as effective as most others (Smith, Glass, & Miller, 1980), their proponents have not kept up a research productivity to support any extra costs or extra time needed by their procedures or to justify the great degree of training they need. Some psychoanalytic concepts may survive in eclectic approaches, but unless the proponents attend more seriously to the problems of expense, length of treatment, lack of research, and the elitism and orthodoxy of practitioners, the future of the psychoanalytic movement would not seem bright.

How socially worthwhile is psychoanalysis? A central strength of orthodox analysis appears to be willingness to look at the darker side of human nature—at aggressive, sexual, and bizarre phenomena—and to view such things as realities of the human condition. But having sounded that note well and effectively, the movement needs other notes to play.

Psychoanalysis, concerned as it is with psychopathology and the interplay of inner forces, has had some general tendency to teach people to "blame the pathology" instead of examining and changing themselves or other systems such as family or community. However, some psychoanalysts have shown broader awareness by joining with legal scholars in clearly worthwhile attempts to influence how courts treat children in custody and termination of rights cases.

Psychoanalysis served effectively in bringing humanitarian concepts through hostile times. The Christian church in the Renaissance had to reluctantly give up being the authority in astronomy because scientists developed a superior astronomy. Similarly psychoanalysis must find ways to acknowledge the well-validated findings from sciences with stronger methodologies, such as behavior, genetics, cognitive development, and family systems. However, its guild aspects and its economic stature offer its adherents ample reason to preserve the status quo.

Chapter 13 reviews the outcome literature on psychotherapy into which many empirical efforts of psychoanalysis fall. Several other important efforts have attempted to break through the problems of the testability of concepts, especially in the developmental area. Santostefano's (1978) work has attempted to add developmental concepts from psychoanalysis to cognitive developmental concepts. The resulting developmental assessment model has received some empirical support, but difficulty in quantifying Freud's ideas has generally meant that psychoanalysis has begotten little research, very little when compared to, say, nondirective or Rogerian psychotherapy and behavioral approaches. Luborsky and Spence (1978, p. 331) wryly conclude a review of research on psychoanalysis as follows: "Quantitative psychoanalytic research remains little known. Rare is the psychoanalyst who knows of any of these studies and even rarer is the psychoanalyst whose practice has been altered by them."

SUMMARY

Psychoanalysis is the product of Sigmund Freud, a towering genius who continued to modify, change, and even reject parts of his earlier work until his death in 1939. His thinking, more open to data than that of many of his followers, has had profound effects on Western society. Psychoanalysis can refer to a personality theory, a mode of psychotherapy, or a professional guild.

Psychoanalytic personality theory comes from several sources among Freud's prolific writings. The concept of the unconscious, the notion that individuals have unacceptable thoughts and feelings of which they are generally unaware, holds a key position. Another major notion asserts that early experiences, especially if unsatisfactorily resolved, form the basic roots of a person's behavior. Freudian interventions thus often emphasize bringing the unconscious up to awareness and tracing back in a person's history to uncover significant early events.

In the beginning of his work Freud attempted to treat classical hysteria and found catharsis, or outpouring of feelings, useful. Much catharsis involved sexual content, and although Freud later abandoned early sexual trauma as the cause of anxiety or hysteria, he continued to give sexuality a prominent place in his thinking. Freud noted the struggle of the young boy to be solely important to the mother and thus began his work on the Oedipus complex. The heavy emphasis on instinctual drives prompted Adler's and then Jung's break from Freud's circle. Further work brought Freud to assert the notion of a three-part structure of personality—id, ego, and superego—and to see the doctor-patient relationship (transference) as highly significant.

The method of treatment, then, came to involve the patient's free associating, to which the analyst would make interpretations in order to foster insights. It was found that resistance in the patient must be diminished so that the more important associations could emerge. Also, transference—the idea that a patient would transfer neurotic attitudes about, say, a parent, to the therapist—offered a way to understand the intensity of the doctor-patient relationship and to ameliorate the neurosis. Working through the transference became another major therapeutic goal.

Current psychoanalytic or psychodynamic psychotherapy has de-emphasized Freud's focus on the id and on determinism. Ego psychologists have sought to place more weight on cognitive functions. They emphasize going with resistances, the importance of the broad therapeutic relationship, and avoiding doctrinaire interpretations.

Offshoots of the psychoanalytic movement, Adler, Jung, and other neo-Freudians have also contributed greatly to clinical psychology. Adler's social and cognitive psychology continues to be broadly influential. His concepts of social interest, creative self, and inferiority as motives provide a counterpoint to Freud's constitutional determinism. Horney and Sullivan have also emphasized social dimensions in etiology and treatment.

In criticism of the psychoanalytic approach, we have noted limitations in application and research. Despite these faults psychoanalysis has had a profound effect in the history of human thought.

RECOMMENDED READINGS

Arlow, A. Psychoanalysis. In R. J. Corsini & contributors, *Current Psychotherapies* (2nd ed.). Itasca, Ill.; Peacock, 1979, pp. 1-43.

Arlow provides a clear account of Sigmund Freud's ideas and psychoanalysis. He gives examples of therapy cases and methods. For an excellent presentation of psychoanalytic contributions to personality theory, see the relevant chapter in Hall and Lindzey (1978).

Strupp, H. H. Psychotherapy, research and practice: An overview. In S. Garfield & A. E. Bergin (Eds.), *Handbook of psychotherapy and behavior change* (2nd ed.). New York: John Wiley, 1978, pp. 3-22.

In an important chapter in an important book, Strupp brings together most of the current major issues in research and practice in psychotherapy. He considers verbal psychotherapies in general and then compares and contrasts psychoanalytic therapy in several ways. He examines patient and therapist variables, problems of measuring psychotherapy outcome, problems in comparing techniques, and issues in future directions in psychotherapy. Also directly related to this chapter is the review in the same book by Luborsky and Spence (1978).

Buttenweiser, P. *Free association.* Boston: Little, Brown, 1981.

This novel about the life and work of a practicing psychoanalyst provides an inside view of this sort of therapy—its satisfactions, its anxieties, its problems, and the feelings of the therapist about what he is doing. The people are real, and the psychiatrist, the central figure, is a likable and very human character.

Thomas, A. Current trends in developmental theory. *American Journal of Orthopsychiatry*, 1981, *51*, 580-609.

Long a leading figure in psychodynamic views of child development, Thomas has summarized and integrated developmental findings from a variety of sources. He uses recent evidence to argue that developmental psychology must be *human* and that animal or mechanical models are by themselves insufficient. He points out that neonates have a biological inheritance of capacities for social interaction and task mastery, a unique plasticity of brain function, unique capacity for learning and an extra genetic cultural inheritance. He supports an ongoing interactionist view of development in which goodness of fit between infant and environment is a key concept. Several cherished psychodynamic concepts such as the primacy of early experience are seriously questioned; ". . . simple linear prediction from early childhood to later childhood adolescence and early adult life is not possible" (p.594). Also, Thomas feels it unlikely that stable sequences of development (except those going from the cognitively simple to complex) can be identified. It is likely, he says, that Freud's and Erikson's stages represent sequences of demands and expectations of a specific environment rather than any preprogrammed maturational sequence.

Along with cognitivists, Thomas now gives a prominent place to task mastery and social competence. His notion of goodness of fit does not imply absence of stress. Stress and the development of skills to handle it are important, too. Thomas concludes with a plea for us to see the full scope of human diversity and to continue to evolve developmental theory which is constructively open to the huge breadth of human diversity. Thomas's work typifies the best of the psychodynamic tradition, a gentle humane concern for the individual, together with an openness to findings from many sources.

RESEARCH EXAMPLES

Speisman, J. C. Depth of interpretation and verbal resistance in psychotherapy. *Journal of Consulting Psychology,* 1959, *23,* 93–99.

Speisman's research grew out of a difference that he noted between psychoanalytic and nondirective procedures. Fenichel, a psychoanalytic theorist, advised therapists to use interpretations that were just beyond the preconscious. Rogers advised that therapists should clarify or reflect the feelings of what the client has already said. Speisman's study investigated the effect of interpretations of different depth on the subsequent resistance on the client in ongoing psychotherapy. This study, therefore, is one of process, not outcome of therapy.

Speisman developed rating scales for depth of interpretation and resistance. Raters listened to recordings of interviews and judged whether what the therapist said was simply a repetition of what the client said at one end of the rating scale or if it was an inference completely outside the client's awareness at the other. The resistance scale was applied by other judges to the statements following that of the therapist and indicated the degree to which the client explored his or her own feelings and perceptions further or "closed up" by giving rejecting or superficial remarks. Judges rated transcripts from interviews with 22 neurotic clients seen by a variety of therapists.

The results showed that deep interpretations led to most resistance, moderate ones to the least, and superficial ones in between. The connections were statistically significant but not large. The author concluded along with Fenichel that "moderate interpretations encourage free expression by producing a new frame of reference or by making new connections for materials which are close to consciousness" (p. 99). However, Speisman's study does not prove that Fenichel was right and Rogers wrong. Rogerian reflection of feeling can be seen as a moderate level of interpretation.

Litt, C. J. Children's attachment to transitional objects: A study of two pediatric populations. *American Journal of Orthopsychiatry,* 1981, *51,* 131–139.

In psychoanalytic literature a transitional object has been considered to be the first "not-me" possession. In general a transitional object is some soft toy, blanket, or other possession to which an infant becomes attached sometime in the first two years. It serves the unique function of reducing distress and being a source of comfort or consolation. The observation that such objects can seem more important to an anxious child than the mother herself has made psychoanalysts very interested in the phenomenon. Although many writers have seen transitional objects as a pathological fetish, a major group of psychoanalytic thinkers has felt the presence of a transitional object to be a healthy psychological sign. Some writers consider it to be a psychological universal.

In this study Litt attempts to provide empirical answers to such questions as "Is the transitional object truly a universal phenomenon?" and "Should children who fail to develop transitional objects be considered to have had inadequate mothering?" Two groups of families were selected for the investigation. The first group, the private clinic group, consisted mainly of white middle- and upper-income patients, whereas the second group, the clinic group, consisted of black lower-middle and low-income patients seen in the outpatient department at a major children's hospital. The clinic group contained 166 subjects—78 boys and 88 girls—and the private group contained 119 subjects—50 boys and 69 girls. In some ways the groups were comparable, but there was a significant difference in numbers of adults living in the home; 98 percent of children in the private group lived with two parents, whereas 41 percent of the clinic group lived in single-parent homes, and 17 percent lived in homes that included adults other than the parents. Children's ages ranged from two to five years. Trying to cover a relatively large number of subjects, the authors used a detailed questionnaire method.

Some 77 percent of the private subjects developed an attachment to an inanimate object, whereas only 46 percent of the clinic subjects did so, a significant difference. Children in the private group formed their attachments at a mean age of 1.03 years, whereas clinic children formed theirs at a mean age of 1.31 years, a significant difference. Also, children differed in the manner with which they used their objects. Children in the private group showed a greater oral and tactile involvement with their objects and more frequently stroked or fingered them. They more frequently rubbed them against their faces and sucked their thumbs while using the object. Children in the private group used these objects more consistently and in a wider variety of stressful situations. They were universally used at bedtime and often at naptime.

The two groups differed significantly in sleeping location before and after 12 months of age and in the methods by which they were fed as infants. In their comments some private mothers were aware of how important and how soothing the object was for the child, and three mothers expressed a wish to have such a soothing object for themselves. Some were sensitive to their displacement by the object at times. In general the comments suggested that the private mothers were more supportive and accepting of transitional objects than were the clinic mothers who were somewhat more likely to see the object as a sign of weakness or immaturity.

The results suggest that the transitional object phenomenon is far from a universal event in normal child development. Middle-class children developed such an attachment 1.5 times more frequently than did black lower-SES children. Although cultural, SES, and racial factors are confounded in this study, Litt speculates about the development of the noted differences. Children who sleep in their own beds in their own rooms from infancy on are more likely to develop an attachment. Such a factor is primarily a socioeconomic one. Other factors may play their part in these differences. For example, among the higher SES, babysitters are more accessible, and thus children may be more subject to strange caretakers and so seek object permanence through the transitional object.

9 WORKING WITH INDIVIDUALS:
Behavioral and Cognitive Approaches

Sometimes we hear it said that learning the first elements of German is easy—it's learning the rest that is terribly complicated. Something of the same is true for behavioral and cognitive approaches to working with people. In this chapter we will try to explain a few clearly related concepts and findings and avoid a welter of confusing detail. First, the very title of the chapter suggests that we will discuss two lines of theory and application. Are behavioral and cognitive approaches separate, or have they merged? Here already there is disagreement. Key early behavioral figures and key early cognitive figures each tend to say, "Hold fast to our early principles," whereas more recent workers are saying, "Let's try whatever works, and if a new hybrid cognitive-behavioral approach holds promise, let's investigate it." Thus some believe there has been a potentially productive marriage, whereas others wait for a poorly conceived romance to fail.

Pure behaviorists have taken as an article of faith that only observable behavior and observable consequences are to be studied. Sometimes they have said that the person should be seen as a "black box"; we are properly concerned, they say, with the relationship between what goes in and what comes out, but not with speculations about what goes on within the box. Cognitivists, by contrast, seek to understand what goes on inside the person; they are willing to use concepts such as perception, attention, mental sets, and imagery. They pay more attention to verbalizations. They see all behaviors as signs of cerebral activity. Rather than focusing on overt behavior, cognitivists stress information processing and study memory, problem solving, and self-regulation. We will review the behavioral origins and contributions in some detail, then take up origins and contributions of cognitivists, and finally examine samples of current cognitive behaviorism.

BEHAVIORAL APPROACHES

Pavlov and Classical Conditioning

The Russian scientist Pavlov (1849–1936) discovered important relationships among stimuli and their responses. In his classic dog experiments, he noticed first that the presence of meat powder made the dog salivate (technically, the unconditioned stimulus caused the unconditioned response). Next, he rang a bell whenever he presented the meat powder—that is, he paired the unconditioned stimulus with the bell several times. Finally, he rang the bell alone—with no meat powder present—and it elicited the salivation. An unrelated neutral stimulus—in this case, the bell—could be made to elicit an unconditioned or reflex response—the salivation.

Classical conditioning, also sometimes called *respondent conditioning,* has had notable clinical impact. Most students become familiar with Little Albert, an 11-month-old boy (who lived well before the properly stringent regulations on human subjects experimentation!). Watson and Raynor (1920) noted that a loud noise (the unconditioned stimulus) elicited a startle and fear reaction from Little Albert. After pairing the noise with a white rat, soon the white rat and other furry objects, all conditioned stimuli, elicited fear and startle reaction. Happily Albert was successfully deconditioned afterwards. (In passing, it might be noted that there is controversy over the accuracy of Watson's oft-cited study; see Samelson, 1980.)

Because in classical conditioning, events or stimuli that *precede* the response come to elicit or control that response, the model has been used in treatment of enuresis. The beginning reflex here is that a loud bell elicits waking. A loud bell rung while the person sleeps becomes paired with bladder distention and urinating. Behavioral clinicians have attempted with notable success to condition bladder distention and urinating to waking (Schaefer & Milliman, 1977).

Probably the major clinical work using classical conditioning has come from Joseph Wolpe (1958). Wolpe's *systematic desensitization*, an approach to the treatment of fears, anxieties, or phobias, begins with the construction of a hierarchy of fear-eliciting stimuli—for example, "Taking off in an airplane is worst, say a 10. Getting in one would be a 6, seeing one on the ground a 4, and talking about going for a flight only a 1." Wolpe then has the patient systematically and deeply relax (sometimes with the aid of hypnosis) while imagining the lowest of the fear-producing stimuli. Once the patient has desensitized—that is, once the fear-producing stimulus is no longer paired with fear, but with relaxation—Wolpe goes on to desensitize the stimulus next up the hierarchy. Technically each of the former fear-producing stimuli is conditioned to produce relaxation, a response incompatible with fear. (In passing we should note what the cognitive therapists later pointed out—namely that the Wolpe technique depends on imagining the feared situations, which is a thinking process, not an external, observed behavior.)

Systematic desensitization has held an important place in behaviorally based interventions for some time, not only in popularity but in its ability to produce results comparable to or superior to other methods. For example, Paul (1967) compared a desensitization with a more traditional insight therapy in treating college students who suffered from acute public-speaking anxiety. The results in a two-year follow-up study showed the superiority of the desensitization approach.

Skinner and Operant Conditioning

B. F. Skinner receives credit for the clarification and rather extensive development of *operant conditioning*. As he observed rats and pigeons, he noticed that many behaviors simply occurred randomly. However, those particular ones that were followed by a pleasant consequence tended to occur more often. In behavioral language, a freely emitted behavior is called an *operant* and the pleasant event a *reinforcer*, so the operant conditioning concept says that operants that are reinforced tend to be emitted with greater frequency.

The importance of operant conditioning as a conceptual tool for working with people lies in the fact that most behaviors that people emit can be seen as operants whereas relatively few are construed as respondents for classical conditioning approaches. Arranging the conditions that follow them can, then, influence the course of talking, smiling, working, reading, and so on. We will look briefly at two ways in which conditions can be arranged: changing reinforcement schedules and changing type or time of consequence.

What is a reinforcer?   A reinforcer's definition has the subject at the core, not the observer. That means that a reinforcer raises or maintains the rate of a certain behavior for a certain subject. If it does not, it simply was not a reinforcer for that subject in that situation. It does not matter what we as observers think *ought* to be reinforcing for someone—only those things that do raise or maintain the rate of responding are reinforcers. Reinforcers thus differ greatly by subject and by situation.

Figure 9-1
B. F. Skinner. (Harvard University)

TABLE 9-1   **Classes of Reinforcers**

CLASS	EXAMPLES
Philosophical/ Spiritual	Sense of having attained a set of values, goals, or developmental criteria
	Promise of going to heaven
Social	Sense of being able to help others grow—e.g., one's children
	Sense of being esteemed
	Sense of being accepted or at ease
	Having power over others
Developmental	Knowledge of results—feedback about performance
	Sense of intellectual attainment
	Physical skills
	Curiosity
	Many forms of entertainment
Acquisitive	Symbolic things—money
	Real things for play, status, and amusement
Sustenance	Food
	Drink

There are, of course, many different kinds of reinforcers, and there have been several attempts to classify them. Table 9-1 shows one way to view them, ranging from the tangible (at the bottom) to the less defined inner feelings.

Sometimes professionals in human service work lack both imagination and vision when they think of selecting reinforcers for a clinical setting. Our classification in Table 9-1 suggests Maslow's (1968, 1971) hierarchy of needs and contains clear developmental inferences. After old Mr. Evans was hospitalized for a slight stroke, he didn't want to go anywhere or work on his therapy. Staff members found, however, that for afternoon tea and scones (Mr. Evans still had a trace of his Welsh ancestry), he would begin to do his exercises. Pleased as Miss James, the speech therapist, was, she knew that food rewards are developmentally rather primitive so she tried to find others. Even though his progress was good, knowledge of results was not reinforcing to Mr. Evans because he said "shouldn't 'a happened anyway." But at last she found another man, rather more handicapped, in whom Mr. Evans began to take a fraternal interest. In behavioral language we would say that Mr. Evans went from an externally administered food reinforcer to a self-administered social reinforcer.

Reinforcement schedules.   Imagine for a moment a situation in which a child is reading a series of words to a parent who is patting the child.

Logically the parent may pat the child after every word, a continuous reinforcement schedule, or after groups of words, an intermittent reinforcement schedule. Within the latter category there are four subtypes: fixed ratio—say, one pat every four words; variable ratio—one pat for a variable number of words; fixed interval—one pat every two minutes; or variable interval—one pat after a varying length of time.

These schedules must be carefully studied by clinicians because each one has special characteristics. For example, the variable ratio schedule produces responses which are very, very durable. Like the gambler at the slot machine, the person responds over and over, hardly tiring, as if he or she cannot believe that nothing will be forthcoming. If a clinician is asked to help a parent whose child has frequent temper tantrums and observes that about every sixth tantrum the parent capitulates to the child, the hypothesis is that tantrum behavior has a variable ratio reinforcement schedule of parental capitulation. The clinician should avoid having the parent stop capitulating as the only strategy because (1) the tantrum behavior is likely to go on a long time anyway, and (2) if the parent should even inadvertently capitulate after 15 tantrums the situation will still be variable ratio reinforcement, with the child being reinforced for its greater persistence.

Types and uses of consequences   Consequences may be broadly classified into two types: (1) positive ones, the reinforcers we have just discussed, and (2) negative ones, such as punishment. At the same time consequences can be used in two ways: (1) The consequences may be presented after a behavior has occurred; and (2) it may be withdrawn after a behavior has occurred. We then have four possible conditions, as Figure 9–2 shows.

1.   When a positive reinforcement is presented following a particular behavior, rates of that behavior maintain or increase. A parent may, for example, give a child a social approval reinforcer for correct use of the toilet; a child may reinforce a parent by being delightfully pleased at being taken for an outing; or an employer may reinforce employees with bonuses when they bring in new customers. In general, most behaviorists urge that socially appropriate behaviors should

Figure 9–2
Type and use of consequence.

Type of Consequence	Use of Consequence	
	APPLIED	REMOVED
Positive, a Reinforcer	a) Learning (increase of rate)	b) Extinction (time out)
Negative, a Punishment	c) Punishment	d) Negative reinforcement (a response terminates a negative event)

receive positive consequences; they believe that society has too many mechanisms set up to pounce on negative behaviors.

2. When a positive reinforcer is removed or is absent after the behavior, rates of that behavior are likely to decrease and perhaps to disappear. When, for instance, a parent who has been positively reinforcing a child's whining by paying attention to the child for whining completely removes the positive reinforcement, the whining is likely to decrease or drop out altogether. As we mentioned earlier, absolute removal of some positive reinforcers may not be easy. Patterson's approach (1971) to the problem, removing the child temporarily from all social reinforcers by placing him or her in a neutral, isolated (reinforcer-free) place, such as an empty closet, has given us the term "time out."

3. When a punishment follows a particular behavior, rates of that behavior decrease or drop out altogether. Punishment, like reinforcement, may take a variety of forms. In our contexts perhaps social disapproval, withholding, or forms of deprivation are the most commonly applied. Fines, incarceration, and occasionally corporal punishment also occur. Punishment usually requires someone to administer it—often an emotionally laden task. This approach also sensitizes both punisher and "punishee" to a punitive view of the world. Finally, such approaches lend themselves easily to polarization or politicization, through which it becomes easy for some groups to band together to classify groups of human beings as alien and rightful objects of punishment. These problems must caution us to use punishment sparingly and appropriately. A sharp swat on the behind may be lifesaving for a toddler with a penchant for running into the road; punishment approaches may be among the only available techniques in facing certain classes of problems. To be effective, both the timing and the context of punishment must be carefully controlled.

4. When a punishment or noxious happening is removed after a particular event, we say that the event has had negative reinforcement. Such events are likely to continue or increase in frequency. The old saw about hitting oneself with a hammer because "it feels so good when I stop" belongs here. Typical examples often occur without our awareness. For example, children build compliance or passivity in their parents by making some obnoxious, noisy, or bratty demands. When the parent becomes compliant or passive and acquiesces to the demand, the obnoxiousness temporarily ends, and so compliance has been reinforced by the removal of the negative event. (When we look at this sequence from the child's side, we see that demanding behaviors have been reinforced by parental acquiescence; that is the first category, the applied positive reinforcer situation. No one should be surprised to find the child's demand frequency going up and probably, to get "peace," the parent's passivity.) Notice how clearly these concepts apply in the adult world in cases such as gang-land "protection," extortion and blackmail rackets, and some forms of geopolitical aggression.

The Evolution of Behavioral
Thought and Practice

During the 1960s and 1970s the number and kinds of behavioral interventions multiplied. In 1969 Krumboltz and Thoresen listed ten methods in addition to reinforcement and punishment, but in 1976 they named 30 additional methods. Methods such as guided practice, instruction, modeling, and role playing appeared in both lists and are self-evident. Token systems or token economies have played an important role in behavioral approaches, too.

BOX 9-1 *DEFINITIONS OF BEHAVIOR THERAPY*

As Applied Learning Theory

"Behavior therapy may be defined as the attempt to alter human behavior and emotion in a beneficial manner according to the laws of modern learning theory" (Eysenck, 1964, p. 1).

"Behavior therapy, or conditioning therapy, is the use of the experimentally established principles of learning for the purpose of changing unadaptive behavior" (Wolpe, 1969, p. vii).

As Application of Results and Methods of Experimental Behavioral Science

". . . treatment deducible from the sociopsychological model that seems to alter a person's behavior directly through application of general psychological principles" (Ullmann & Krasner, 1969, p. 244).

"Behavior therapy is seen in broader terms as an approach to clinical problems which relies on the methods and the results of experimental behavioral science" (Brady, 1977, p. 249).

". . . a way of formulating cases and using a series of specific techniques derived from the experimental laboratory, usually but not exclusively based on learning theory, and applied in a social influence situation . . . a technology built upon a base of behavior influence" (Krasner & Ullman, 1973, p. 279).

As Experimental Study of Change Processes

"By requiring clear specification of treatment conditions and objective assessment of outcomes, the social learning approach contains a self-corrective feature that distinguishes it from change enterprises in which interventions remain ill-defined and their psychological effects are seldom objectively evaluated" (Bandura, 1969, p. v).

As Controlled Experimental Studies of the Single Case

". . . the attempt to utilize systematically the body of empirical and theoretical knowledge which has resulted from the application of the experimental method in psychology and its closely related disciplines in order to explain the genesis and maintenance of abnormal patterns of behavior, and to apply that knowledge to the treatment or prevention of those abnormalities by means of controlled experimental studies of the single case" (Yates, 1970, p. 18).

As Technical Eclecticism

". . . approach which can be developed into a science . . . It is an approach which urges therapists to experiment with empirically useful methods instead of using their theories as *a priori* predictors of what will and will not succeed in therapy" (Lazarus, 1971, p. 29).

From C. E. Thoresen & T. J. Coates, What does it mean to be a behavior therapist? *The Counseling Psychology*, 1978, *1*, 3–21. Copyright © 1978 by the American Psychological Corporation and used by permission of the author.

When Mr. and Mrs. McAllister came to the Mental Health Clinic for help with their 9-year-old boy, Stanley, they complained that he did only bad, difficult, or bothersome things and that there was almost nothing they enjoyed or liked about him except when he was asleep. Their therapist, Arthur Haynes, asked the McAllisters to collect data on some of the specifics of Stanley's life. It was soon clear that Stanley lived in an environment in which little pleasantness ever came his way, and to which he contributed little that was pleasant, either. Dr. Haynes asked the parents to write down entries in two categories: (1) For what can Stanley earn points? (2) For what should Stanley lose points? He asked Stanley to write down what special events or good things he'd like to spend points on. Despite Haynes's warnings and encouragements, however, the classic problems appeared. The parents could think of almost nothing for which Stanley could earn points, and their second list could have been subtitled "Angry Parents' Revenge" because of its length, detail, and severity. Stanley's list, typically, was a bit unrealistic. However, after much negotiation, the lists were simplified so Stanley was more likely to earn points, so he would not lose them at every turn, and so realistic spending plans were possible. Stanley's father suggested one idea which was attractive: Points could be exchanged for spending money (Stanley didn't get an allowance) at the rate of one small coin apiece.

When Dr. Haynes went over the McAllister case with his students, he stressed that goals must be chosen or agreed to by the family members. Any system like this becomes really a way for each family member to write down its particular values and assign numbers or weights to them. Second, the system has to be worth everyone's time or someone simply won't play. The token approach has strength because it forces parents to look for positive behavior and provide responses, not just punishments for their child. Finally, a token approach requires writing things down. Examining those records lets child, parents, and therapist see and appreciate change or presses them to redesign their system of interaction.

Token economies are used frequently in residential facilities where several aspects of a resident's or patient's day can be monitored. A facility for seriously delinquent youngsters might have income possibilities from, say, basic daily tasks, school, appropriate use of time, peer interaction, staff interaction, and bonus (caught being good). As Figure 9–3 shows, data can be continuously plotted and monitored for good treatment planning. It is clear that although Jimmy B's average performance remains roughly the same, his school performance, peer interaction, and appropriate use of time are in decline, but his bonus points ("caught being good") are up sharply. A program analyst might well worry: What is causing J.B.'s three declines? Has J.B. become the favorite of one or two staff members? The data prompt investigation and action.

We have considered token economies as an example of a behavioral method of real historic durability. Kazdin (1977) has summarized the very

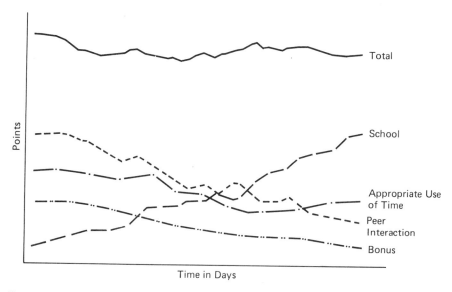

Figure 9-3 Token economy income J. B., aged 10.

considerable literature on token economies, and readers are directed to him for further reading. What about some of the 20 methods mentioned by Krumboltz and Thoresen in 1976 which were not listed earlier? In this book we cannot be concerned with the definitions and technical meanings of terms such as *covert reinforcement, covert sensitization, self-instruction, self-monitoring, self-punishment, self-reinforcement,* or *thought stopping,* to list only a few. Each requires some internal process, something to go on inside the head. Put another way, no longer is the person a "black box." Behaviorists are recognizing internal processes and are attempting to deal with those processes in some way.

Toward the beginning of this section we gave a simplified view of reinforcement which was true early in the behavioral movement. Just as the number of interventions or methods proliferated, so did the ways in which reinforcement could be viewed. The same trends toward assuming internal processes can be seen in Table 9-2.

We have briefly traced behavior therapy from its roots in classical conditioning and operant conditioning through periods of elaboration and expansion. Other examples of the powerful ideas of behaviorism will be found in Chapter 11, where the often-used technique of observation in family interaction is exemplified. Observation depends on perception and coding, or categorizing, observations. Other "behavioral" techniques require imagery. We will note that this approach is busy with ideas which most people would say plainly include aspects of thinking, remembering, perceiving, deciding, and so on—in short, many of the notions central to cognitive psychology.

TABLE 9-2 Four Conceptualizations of Reinforcement

1. Reinforcement alters behavior automatically and unconsciously
   Unilateral control from external environment
   Reinforcement presented immediately and sometimes intrusively when behavior
   is performed
   Participants not informed of reasons for reinforcement

2. Reinforcement designates appropriate conduct
   Informs person about what must be done to gain beneficial external outcomes
   Provides incentive for appropriate conduct
   Instructions about contingencies enhance effects

3. Reinforcement acts as social contracting
   A social exchange practice; conditioning social agreements
   Depends upon preferences of person being reinforced
   Can be presented symbolically
   Need not occur instantly because persons can bridge gap between action and
   reinforcement

4. Reinforcement is self-regulation
   Persons set personal standards to evaluate actions
   Both overt (e.g., material) and covert (e.g., self-congratulatory statements)
   May be consistent with or antagonistic to external reinforcement
   Personal self-reinforcement can override external environmental contingencies

(Thoresen & Coates, 1978; adapted from Bandura, 1974)

COGNITIVE APPROACHES

Having been on the behavioral bank of the river and having seen the raising of bridge foundations on that side, let us visit the cognitive bank and review some history, gain a sense of the major ideas, and then look at the bridge building on that bank. Finally, we will survey the possibilities, the pitfalls, and the progress of the joining of cognitive psychology and behaviorism.

Cognitive psychology has to do with thinking. It begins by recognizing explicitly that a great deal goes on inside people's heads, and it asks what, how, and when questions about those processes. The questions are psychological: e.g., What cues must be there for Joe to grasp a relationship? How long can Sandy remember something under particular conditions? How can Gloria be taught to look for problem solutions rather than to cry and become emotional? Why is it that Mark stays focused on irrelevant issues whereas Julie can dismiss the irrelevant and go on to things which make a difference? There are psychological concerns about activities in the head. They differ from psychological questions about electrical activity or chemical changes. Cognitive psychology encompasses a wide area, including classical academic psychologies such as perception and motivation, some approaches to psychopathology, some personality theories, neuropsychology, neuropsychologists, and developmental psychology. The common thread remains an interest in some aspect of what can generally be called *thought processes*.

Origins

Cognitive psychology does not trace itself back to two or three specific founders or focal authors, as does behavioral psychology, although in academic psychology the landmark book outlining the full implications of the cognitive approach was *Plans and the Structure of Behavior* (Miller, Galanter, & Pribram, 1960). Many psychologists began to see the possibility of a scientific model of people that did justice to the complexity of human thought, feeling, and behavior. The computer model provided a palpable basis for mental phenomena; the idea of *programming* made purposiveness concrete. Hierarchical organization and reorganization suggested new ways of looking at learning and problem solving. Finally, the central role of language in all aspects of human life was dramatized.

Information-processing concepts are also applied to brain functioning, perception, memory, language, learning, cognitive development, problem solving, decision making, social interaction, and motivation. Information processing is not just another topic in psychology; it is a new way of looking at the entire spectrum of human functioning (Murray & Jacobson, 1978, p. 667). Another major force in the emergence of cognition was the developmental work of Piaget (Flavell, 1963). His methods provided ways of studying the interaction between the organism and the environment affecting intellectual, moral, and social development. Piaget suggested mental structures as a way of organizing experience and regulating behavior. Finally, the developing child was viewed as an active, information-seeking and -processing organism instead of as a passive receptacle for environmental inputs.

Historically the Greek philosopher Epictetus is cited by some as having first proposed one of the notions central to bringing cognitive concepts into the study of personality: that people act not so much on the facts as on what they believe the facts to be. Beck et al. (1979, pp. 8–9) cite Adler: "Alfred Adler's Individual Psychology emphasized the importance of understanding the patient within the framework of his own conscious experience. For Adler, therapy consisted of attempting to unravel how the person perceived and experienced the world." Adler (1931/1958) stated:

> We do not suffer from the shock of our experiences—the so called *trauma*—but we make out of them just what suits our purposes. We are *self-determined* by the meaning we give to our experiences; and there is probably something of a mistake always involved when we take particular experiences as the basis for our future life. Meanings are not determined by situations, but we determine ourselves by the meanings we give to situations. (p. 14)

"What we believe the facts to be" has implications for several different processes. Cognitivists recognize perception, learning, memory, language development, and motivation as important areas in addition to thinking styles and strategies. In perception, for example, we do not just open our eyes and see what is there; instead what we see depends greatly on our experience, on our current information, and on the state of our motivation. Early Gestalt psychologists taught us that we could see the central element in a picture as figure and the rest as ground and then that we have power to change ground to figure.

When complex perceptual processes fail to work well, serious situations develop. Each of us has probably been around a person who perceives far too many ordinary happenings as a deliberate personal slight, insult, or challenge. Child abusers typically have a cognitive organization that is set to perceive relatively normal behavior by the victim as a deadly, insulting, personalized challenge or affront, willfully designed to make maximum difficulty for the abusing parent. Similarly some families develop their perceptual processes to detect any and all negative behaviors on anyone's part, with the result that positive behaviors go unnoticed and tend to decrease in their frequency. Some therapists, for example Haley (1976), may use strategies to press a patient to consider forming a new percept out of the old data, for example, "It really infuriates you when your husband does that to you, but he may not be doing it because he's hostile—perhaps he's doing it because he cares so deeply about you—has a real need for you—and doesn't want his weakness to show." Many call this therapeutic tactic *reframing*.

Cognitive Structure and Thinking Styles

Thinking and thought processes occupy center stage in cognitive theories. Clearly thoughts do not occur randomly. We each have certain fixed notions and stored information guiding or structuring how we think. Meichenbaum (1977) approaches cognitive structure this way:

> By *cognitive structure* I mean to point to that organizing aspect of thinking that seems to monitor and direct the strategy, route, and choice of thoughts. I mean to imply a kind of "executive processor" which "holds the blueprints of thinking" and which determines when to interrupt, change, or continue thought. By cognitive structure I mean to imply that which is *unchanged* by learning a new word but which *is* changed by learning a new word-skill, such as the skill of listening to one's own internal dialogue. The cognitive structure I refer to is, by definition the source of all the scripts from which all such dialogues borrow. (pp. 212–213)

A variety of words such as *schema*, *image*, and *belief* have been used to describe cognitive structures. Ellis (1970), for example, in a more clinical than experimental model, views people who suffer from, say, an anxiety neurosis as having adopted an erroneous, mistaken, or illogical belief, such as, "I must be loved and approved of by everyone, and if I'm not, it will be an awful, unspeakably painful tragedy." He approaches therapy by teaching clients to identify and actively challenge the irrational belief and to substitute a rational one for it—for example, "It will be uncomfortable and unpleasant if Susan doesn't love me, and I will feel bad, but there are constructive things I can do."

No one good classification of thinking styles has appeared, but several theorists and researchers have given us a variety of important concepts. We will discuss several briefly.

Means-end thinking occurs when a person works to fill in the intermediate steps needed to achieve a particular end. It is an advanced skill, critically important in life planning and use of personal resources.

Alternative-solution thinking simply relates to the mental behavior of generating several alternative solutions to a single problem. The alternative-solution thinker has the advantage of several possibilities to pick from, and, as we will discuss later, the skill seems highly related to prosocial behavior in young children.

Consequential thinking allows persons to move forward in time to forecast the outcome or consequences of their actions. Conventional wisdom often holds that if young delinquents could only use consequential thinking skills, they would not do what they do. It seems likely, however, that most of them already have consequential thinking skills, and these skills alone may not be the single key to prosocial behavior.

Causal-thinking skills, in which answers can be given to questions such as "Why did you do that?" have been shown almost unrelated to prosocial skills or reduction of aggressive and impulsive behavior in young children despite the fact that parents almost universally demand to know "Why did you do that?" whenever a child emits a problem behavior.

Other ways in which thinking styles have been described are as follows:

Field independent versus field dependent. Some people tend to be able to think well almost regardless of the field or context, do well with logic, and may disregard surroundings. Others, mindful of the field or context or dependent on it, may be not as analytical but are more socially aware and perhaps more easily influenced.

Convergent versus divergent. Convergent thinking requires reasoning correctly toward a correct answer. It is more scientific but less creative than is *divergent thinking,* which more readily produces originality, novelty, and alternative possibilities.

Scanning versus focusing. Scanning thinking involves evaluating all details uniformly and going from one detail to the next. *Focusing thinking* involves attending more to those details that seem to be central and ignoring the others. Scanners are slower at some tasks and surer at others.

Egocentrism versus role taking. Role-taking skills allow persons to think their way into another's shoes, to set themselves in another's place, asking, "What might it be like to be that person?" The more primitive *egocentric pattern*, the inability to imagine another's viewpoint or predicament, has been described as a frequent component of delinquent and antisocial behavior.

Yet a third view of thinking styles, this one with a clear developmental flavor, comes from Beck et al. (1979, p. 15):

"Primitive" Thinking	*"Mature" Thinking*
1. *Nondimensional and global:* I am fearful.	*Multidimensional:* I am moderately fearful, quite generous, and fairly intelligent.
2. *Absolutistic and moralistic:* I am a despicable coward.	*Relativistic and nonjudgmental:* I am more fearful than most people I know.
3. *Invariant:* I always have been and always will be a coward.	*Variable:* My fears vary from time to time and from situation to situation.
4. *"Character diagnosis":* I have a defect in my character.	*"Behavioral diagnosis":* I avoid situations too much, and I have many fears.
5. *Irreversibility:* Since I am basically weak, there's nothing than can be done.	*Reversibility:* I can learn ways of facing situations and fighting my fears.

Emotions in a Cognitive Perspective

We should ask about emotions at this point. Many cognitive psychologists conceptualize emotions quite differently from their psychodynamic colleagues. Psychodynamic thinkers view emotions as the major psychological issue and thinking as a secondary process. Cognitivists, not surprisingly, tend to believe that emotions *follow* thought. For example, a person with an incorrect belief or thought that something will be catastrophic may experience anxiety or depression when it occurs; a person who failed to learn good problem-solving skills and means-end thinking may feel inferior to those whose skills have carried them well clear of the frustrations and bitterness of insecurity, poverty, or unsatisfactory interpersonal relationships.

Cognitive Therapies

As we have mentioned, Albert Ellis, perhaps the major modern pioneer in cognitive therapy, saw the therapist's job as uncovering the client's mistaken notion, challenging it, and helping the client to substitute a correct or adaptive idea. (After that, of course, clients are taught to do the process for themselves.) An example illustrates: Ellis is working with a man who had reported unhappiness because a group of men with whom he had played golf had not liked him:

T: You think you were unhappy because these men didn't like you?

C: I certainly was!

T: But you weren't unhappy for the reason you think you were.

C: I wasn't? But I was!

T: No, I insist: You only think you were unhappy for that reason.

C: Well, why was I unhappy then?

T: It's very simple—as simple as A, B, C, I might say. A, in this case is the fact that these men didn't like you. Let's assume that you observed their attitude correctly and were not merely imagining they didn't like you.

C: I assure you that they didn't. I could see that very clearly.

T: Very well, let's assume they didn't like you and call that A. Now, C is your unhappiness—which we'll definitely have to assume is a fact, since you felt it.

C: Damn right I did!

T: All right, then: A is the fact that the men didn't like you, C is your unhappiness. You see A and C and you assume that A, their not liking you, caused your unhappiness. But it didn't.

C: It didn't? What did, then?

T: B did.

C: What's B?

T: B is *what you said to yourself* while you were playing golf with those men.

C: What I said to myself? But I didn't say anything.

T: You did. You couldn't possibly be unhappy if you didn't. The only thing that could possibly make you unhappy that occurs from without is a brick falling on your head, or some such equivalent. But no brick fell. Obviously, therefore, you must have told *yourself* something to make you unhappy. (Ellis, 1962, p. 126)

Beck and his associates (1979) provide a recent and detailed elaboration of the themes of cognitive therapy. They define it in this way:

> Cognitive therapy is an active, directive, time limited, structured approach used to treat a variety of psychiatric disorders (for example, depression, anxiety, phobias, pain problems, etc.) It is based on an underlying theoretical rationale that an individual's affect and behavior are largely determined by the way in which he structures the world (Beck, 1967, 1976). His cognitions (verbal or pictorial "events" in his stream of consciousness) are based on attitudes or assumptions (schemas), developed from previous experiences. For example, if a person interprets all his experiences in terms of whether he is competent and adequate, his thinking may be dominated by the schema, "Unless I do everything perfectly, I'm a failure." Consequently, he reacts to situations in terms of adequacy even when they are unrelated to whether or not he is personally competent. (p. 3)

They give a sequence of steps which are involved and outline some of the techniques:

> A variety of cognitive and behavioral strategies are utilized in cognitive therapy. Cognitive techniques are aimed at delineating and testing the patient's specific misconceptions and maladaptive assumptions. This approach consists of highly

BOX 9-2 *ELEVEN IRRATIONAL BELIEFS*

All cultures and societies indoctrinate their young with a set of assumptions on which the accepted ways of life are based. These are often unverbalized and unanalyzed. In addition, groups, families, and individuals learn special beliefs that dominate the way they think about their choices and interpretations of life events. Sometimes these beliefs get in the way of successful living.

The psychologist Albert Ellis has taken these unrecognized and often damaging beliefs as the cornerstone of his therapeutic approach. Around 1950 he was finding that his clients, after gaining "insight" into traumatic events in childhood, did not get better but were reindoctrinating themselves with the original taboos, superstitions, and irrationalities they had picked up or invented in their early lives (Ellis, 1979). Ellis recognizes that this aspect of his approach, Rational-Emotive Therapy, overlaps with Adler's concern for detecting the client's "basic mistakes," but RET does not stress early childhood memories or social interest and is much more specific than the Adlerian approach in attacking the concrete, internalized, and defeating beliefs that clients keep telling themselves. Ellis (1962) identifies eleven beliefs that are frequently found in American culture and probably in many others as well. We have summarized these as what clients may be telling themselves repeatedly at some level:

1. It is absolutely necessary for me to be loved and approved of by nearly every person with whom I have close contact.
2. I must be thoroughly competent and adequate in all respects or I am worthless.
3. Certain people are bad or wicked and must be blamed and punished. (The person fails to recognize that badness is in the eye of the beholder and that punishment for its sake alone is irrational.)
4. If things are not the way I like them to be, it is a terrible catastrophe.
5. Unhappiness is caused by external events over which I have almost no control.
6. Some things are terribly dangerous and life-threatening; so I must keep thinking about them most of the time.
7. It is easier to avoid difficulties and responsibilities than to face them.
8. I am not able to do things myself; I must find someone stronger on whom I can rely.
9. What happened to me in the past determines what I do and think now, and because some event was traumatic in the past it will be traumatic now.
10. I should be very upset over other people's problems and disturbances.
11. There is always a right and precise solution to human problems, and if that is not found, I must be very upset.

On the surface, most people would say that it is silly to expect to be perfect all the time or to be loved by everyone. However, these damaging beliefs are largely unconscious; yet the person's self-talk and behavior is based on them. Some clients may have learned only one of these beliefs really well; others have taken several as assumptions; others will have produced irrational beliefs different from any of these. Ellis's approach to therapy is to expose these beliefs often in a direct, confrontative way. He insists that the person take responsibility for self-talk and behavior. Kranzler (1974) in an easy-to-read book called *You Can Change How You Feel* explains the rational-emotive approach. Ellis (1979) discusses the background, assumptions and processes of this kind of therapy and presents a case.

specific learning experiences designed to teach the patient the following operations: (1) to monitor his negative, automatic thoughts (cognitions); (2) to recognize the connections between cognition, affect, and behavior; (3) to examine the evidence for and against his distorted automatic thought; (4) to substitute more reality-oriented interpretations for these biased cognitions; and (5) to learn to identify and alter the dysfunctional beliefs which predispose him to distort his experiences.

Various verbal techniques are used to explore the logic behind and basis for specific cognitions and assumptions. The patient is initally given an explanation of the rationale for cognitive therapy. Next, he learns to recognize, monitor, and record his negative thoughts on the Daily Record of Dysfunctional Thoughts . . . The cognitions and underlying assumptions are discussed and examined for logic, validity, adaptiveness, and enhancement of positive behavior versus maintenance of pathology. For example, the depressed person's tendency to feel responsible for negative outcomes while consistently failing to take credit for his own success is identified and discussed. The therapy focuses on specific "target symptoms" (for example, suicidal impulses). The cognitions supporting these symptoms are identified (for example, "My life is worthless and I can't change it.") and then subjected to logical and empirical investigation. (p. 4; this and preceding quote from Beck, A. T., Rush, A. J., Shaw, B. F., & Emery, G. D. *Cognitve therapy of depression*. New York: The Guilford Press, 1979. Used by permission.)

The following is an illustration of Beck's approach:

A thirty-five-year old wholesale frozen-food distributor has experienced chronic depression since his divorce six years earlier. He had been raising his two daughters and did not know the whereabouts of his wife and only son. A tragic historical event was the suicide of his father when he was fifteen years old. His father died in his arms.

In the past year the patient's depression had intensified, and he found it increasingly difficult to go to work or to call on customers. He would spend his time doing errands around the house saying, "Tomorrow I must get started calling on customers." He felt in danger of being fired, and each day of avoidance made it more difficult for him to go to work and face his boss. The avoidance led to shame. He was convinced that he was not suffering from depression but from laziness. He shared with his therapist his conviction that it would be preferable for him to commit suicide as this was his only "realistic solution." The therapist inquired what problems he had that would be realistically solved by suicide. "First, I have lost face with my boss. He pays me a salary and I haven't made any sales or calls on customers for over a month. I couldn't stand to face him or any of my clients. I'm sure I've lost my job and all self-respect. Second, in the absence of commissions, I'm not making enough money to support my daughters adequately. One of these days they'll want to go to college and I won't have any money. Third, I'm constantly depressed, and I'm not the kind of father I should be. Lately, they've been asking me, "Daddy, why are you acting differently?"

The therapist pointed out the illogic of his position. First, he had no real evidence that he had lost his job or had lost face. In order to find out, he would have to contact his employer, explain his situation frankly, and get some information. And if he had lost the employer's respect and/or job—which seemed unlikely in light of the fact that the employer had suggested and helped to underwrite the therapy—suicide would not correct the situation. Nor would suicide help his daughters go to college or obtain good fathering. Suicide would, in fact, add further to their burden by removing the only parent who had been willing to raise them following the divorce.

It was painful to this patient to realize that suicide simply involved further avoidance of his problems, but did not represent a solution. He had no real evidence that his problems were in any way insoluble, since he had not attempted any solutions. He had overlooked the fact that prior to his depression he had been an energetic successful salesman and was not, in fact, lazy or incompetent.

Although not entirely convinced by the therapist's appraisal, he did agree to call his boss and to call on one customer. The employer expressed support and empathy and assured him that his job was not in danger. When he called on the customer, he did receive some ribbing about "being on vacation" for the past six weeks, but also landed a small order. He later reported with surprise that the discomfort from being teased was actually quite small in comparison with the intense depression he experienced every day at home avoiding work. This discovery gave him courage to call on other customers, and over a two-week period he built back up to a normal working schedule and began making plans for the future. As he began to see the future, the past, and the present more objectively and learned to view himself and his external environment with more perspective, there was a corresponding improvement in the rest of his symptomatology. (D. D. Burns & A. T. Beck, pp. 124–126 in J. P. Foreyt & D. Rathjen, *Cognitive behavior modification.* Copyright © 1978 by Plenum Press. Used by permission.)

COGNITIVE BEHAVIORISM

Synthesis

The late 1970s saw a major swing toward acceptance of a combination, or synthesis, of cognitive and behavioral approaches, both by theorists (e.g., Mischel, 1979) and by practitioners (e.g., Mahoney & Arnkoff, 1978; Meichenbaum, 1977). No sudden discoveries kicked off the change; it seems instead to have been more of a collective readiness on the part of behaviorists to admit that they had been dealing with inner cognitive processes such as thoughts, perceptions, and covert speech. Some landmarks, however, can be identified. Bandura (1969) broadened the field of behavior modification to include attention to modeling and observational learning, and he, together with Kanfer and Goldstein (1975), took another clear step toward recognizing internal processes when they began to focus on self-regulation and self-control. Cautela (1973) had for some time recognized internal events in his covert conditioning—the use of conditioning principles to influence the occurrence of thoughts or reactions which he called *covert events*. In a variety of other situations, a more cognitive translation of behavioral procedures took place, so that as the 1980s began, cognitive behaviorism had become almost a fad in its sudden rise to prominence.

Another factor pressing the change has been the acceptability of psychologists in the broad field of human services, mental health, and social welfare. Psychiatrists and social workers, predominantly psychodynamically trained, never really welcomed strict behaviorists. Behaviorists' apparent disregard for underlying motives, contexts, and feelings was frequently taken as being inhumane and "scientistic," a type of accusation which enabled many critics to sidestep or disregard the behaviorists' usually excellent fund of data and high standards of accountability. Some critics sought to limit applications of behavior modification by talking about patients' rights—that is, by taking a legal perspective (Wexler, 1973).

But with an open synthesis of the two traditions, cognitive behaviorists can speak a language and attend to phenomena that other disciplines and the public are likely to find more common-sensical and humane than straight, count-the-externals, behavioral approaches. At the same time the rapidly increasing fund of knowledge about perceptual processes, thinking styles, and information processing which cognitivists are producing can be far better applied using many of the quantification and observation techniques from behavioral work. Furthermore, the burgeoning area of neuropsychology promises to have exciting compatibility with cognitive-behavioral approaches. Some critics say, though, with apparent justification, that the lion's share of cognitive behavioral work is really pure cognitive work because conditioning and reinforcement concepts are so little used.

Many different types and styles of cognitive behavioral therapy have sprung up. Mahoney and Arnkoff (1978) have made an important, if rather pithy, effort to distill out the common features of the new breed:

1. Humans develop adaptive and maladaptive behavior and affective patterns via cognitive processes (e.g., selective attention, symbolic coding, etc.).
2. These cognitive *processes* are functionally activated by *procedures* which are generally isomorphic with those of the human learning laboratory . . .
3. The resultant task of the therapist is that of a diagnostician-educator who assesses maladaptive cognitive processes and subsequently arranges learning experiences which will alter cognitions and, in turn, the behavior-affect patterns with which they correlate. (p. 692)

There seem to be, these authors feel, three major forms of cognitive behavior therapy: rational therapies, coping-skills therapies, and problem-solving therapies. The latter two types, as their names imply, stress careful and elaborate ways of learning or improving adaptive and assertive skills and of broadening problem-solving ability.

Skill Training

One frequent criticism of strict behavioral consequence or reinforcement approaches has been that they make people excessively dependent on the environment. If the environment will not provide reinforcement for sitting still and getting on with work, and if the child in question knows it will not, then the program may not work, runs the frequent criticism. Meichenbaum (1977) is one of several workers who has investigated self-instructional training—that is, teaching hyperactive youngsters ways to instruct themselves to be more appropriate and effective in their classroom. One view of self-control is that we first learn to "talk ourselves through" a situation, perhaps not aloud, but at least in words. Later, with practice, many of the components become automatic. In young aggressive boys, however, several findings have established that their covert speech either doesn't occur, is not consequential, or is self-stimulating or irrelevant.

Meichenbaum selected a variety of tasks ranging from simple sensory-motor abilities to more complex problem solving and used the following sequence:

1. An adult model performed a task while talking to himself out loud (cognitive modeling);
2. The child performed the same task under the direction of the model's instructions (overt, external guidance);
3. The child performed the task while instructing himself aloud (overt self guidance);
4. The child whispered the instructions to himself as he went through the task (faded, overt self guidance); and finally
5. The child performed the task while guiding his performance via private speech (covert self instruction). (p. 32)

The first step incorporates components so often seen in cognitive approaches: defining the problem, focusing attention, getting the response performed correctly, teaching self-reinforcement and self-evaluation.

Problem Solving

Spivack and Shure and their colleagues (1974, 1978) have been responsible for an exciting line of research and practice which has essentially broken new ground both in cognitive behavioral therapy and in parent-staffed prevention techniques. Their research has shown that however children acquire interpersonal cognitive problem-solving (ICPS) skills, the level of those skills best predicts the school behavior of both boys and girls. They have designed an instructional program for the teaching of ICPS skills to the teachers and parents of young children. The program, conducted with games and exercises, aims to develop the two crucial components of ICPS: *alternative-solution thinking* (the ability to generate a wide variety of possible solutions to a problem) and *consequential thinking* (the ability to foresee what may happen if a solution is carried out).

First, prerequisite basic concepts are taught, such as same-different, if-then, why-because, fairness, individual preferences, and some names for common emotions. Next, games and play situations are designed to elicit from the child (not to give to the child) alternative solutions, consequences, and solution-consequences pairing. No values are placed on the quality of what the child produces because the research has shown that the number of alternative solutions, rather than their quality, is the potent variable.

Dialoging is Shure and Spivack's term for the basic activity done by teachers and parents to reach ICPS goals. This dialoging around interpersonal problems involves:

Clarifying the problem, both for adult and child

Noticing that the presenting problem may be the child's effort to solve an earlier problem

Problem solving by the child; stimulation and encouragement, but not solutions or suggestions, by the adult

Focusing on *how* the child thinks, not on the particular solutions produced. Even praising a solution may inhibit the further flow of solutions, warn the authors.

To keep parents working at helping thinking to develop, Spivack and Shure (1978) offer dialoging instructions such as the following:

1. Elicit the child's view of the problem in a nonaccusatory way.
2. Ask matter-of-factly why he acted as he did.
3. Guide the child to talk about how he feels and how he thinks others feel.
4. Ask how he can find out how the other child feels or thinks.
5. Ask the child to give his idea about how to solve the problem, "What can you do if you want him to do that?"
6. Ask the child to think about what might happen next. "If you do that what might happen next?"
7. Guide the child to evaluate whether or not his idea is a good one. "Is hitting back a good idea? Is throwing a toy a good idea?"
8. Encourage the child to think of different solutions. "Is there a second way?"

Interestingly Spivack and Shure report that the quality of a child's proposed solutions is less related to effective ICPS skills than is the quantity or sheer number of alternatives generated. Notice also how the methods relate to our earlier discussion of possibilities and choice. Although many questions remain to be answered, the ICPS method seems to produce clearer behavioral improvement than does, say, spending an equivalent amount of time with a child or giving him or her an equivalent quantity of parental attention. The ICPS work appears to be a good example of solid progress using developmental as well as cognitive concepts. It would also seem to have high potential for prevention programs (Shure & Spivack, 1982).

CRITIQUE

How adequate is the topic conceptually?   Because behaviorism and cognitive behaviorism evolve at such a great rate and because they contain such diversity, conceptual adequacy has several facets. The strict behaviorist side of the house has been under attack for years for presenting human beings as too mechanistic and oversimplified. The famous debate of

Rogers and Skinner (Rogers, 1955) typified the issue. Despite telling blows by the opposition, Skinner's point that an operant paradigm can account for and predict a great deal of highly complex behavior remains strong. Using ideas of system levels and token economies, psychologists have built bridges to ecological treatment and therapeutic community treatment, and notions such as self-control have been carefully elaborated at various system levels by cognitive behaviorists. The concepts of cognitively oriented branches have greater adequacy than the behaviorists when dealing with perceptual processes, thinking styles, or choice-making strategies, but present more difficulty with some clinical applications because measurement is less specific. The cognitive aspects have exciting potential links with developmental psychology, information-processing research, neuropsychology, rehabilitation, and educational psychology.

Both wings of the party have shown sensitivity to other systems larger than the individual—for example, Patterson (1971) in work in family interaction, and Janis and Mann (1977) in work in decision making applicable at organizational and community levels. In emphasizing behavior and thinking, these approaches have been weak in handling emotions. Only recently cognitive behaviorism in various forms has shown itself capable of addressing perhaps the widest variety of human problems addressed by any general perspective, including depression, family and parenting problems, child behavior, delinquency, and community adaptation of chronically mentally ill and retarded. It tends not to offer a great deal to those seeking personal growth through intense introspection or group experiences.

How practical is the approach? The earlier, more purely behavioral aspects are easily applicable in many situations. Moreover, they are free from problems of union cards or professional qualifications. They present a range of tasks which can be broken down to simple components and administered or supervised by paraprofessional or lay persons. The tasks are generally face-valid and sensible. However, the time and cost of observing in the home and school, the training of observers, and the work of keeping records present practical problems for many clinics and private practitioners.

For behavioral services a number of important cautions must be noted. Many *ethical concerns* are raised when deprivation or punishment are used. The public and press seem to insist on *misunderstanding* behavior modification, often attributing to it bizarre use of drugs and fascist thought-reform tactics. Many people *dislike* it—members of psychotherapy professions because it ignores the emotions and demystifies treatment, and many parents because they confuse reinforcers with bribery. (Perhaps, of course, many dislike it because of the high levels of accountability it requires; it is clear whether treatment is succeeding if one counts behaviors.) Finally, the field is far more complex than it seems at first, so there is danger of *oversimplification* by the partially trained.

Operant behaviorism has contributed several techniques which have been taken over or absorbed into other therapies. Observing and coding behavior, counting rates, and analyzing sequences of behavior all have been used by therapists of several persuasions in efforts to improve their accountability.

The more purely cognitive therapies occupy a slightly more conservative position. Although giving opportunity for some nonprofessional and lay participation, they rely rather more on the trained leader. They take more note of emotions (directly addressing, say, depression), rarely involve aversion or punishment, and excite few charges of bribery when they ask adult patients to be good to themselves after a particular attainment.

How socially worthwhile is the topic? Early behavioral approaches seemed ethically neutral—that is, they could be used for good or ill depending on the user. More recent developments, such as self-control therapies, seem less likely to be misused and more likely to be socially worthwhile. Cognitive approaches, with their developmental roots and their focus on making decisions and choices, show high potential to be compatible with our social values and clearly helpful to society. Although critics of Skinnerian behaviorism often accuse it of being overly narrow, simple, and atheoretical, it should be noted that Skinner himself has a deep concern for society. His book *Walden Two* (1948) imaginatively applied behavior principles to develop an ideal community.

At this point cognitive behaviorism appears to be a major thrust of psychology. It appears to offer the potential for an integration of thinking and practice, bringing together diverse areas around the central core of thinking and behavior. The potential for conceptually better-grounded intellectual, developmental, and problem-solving assessment and diagnosis and for more conceptually solid and accountable therapies is a prospect of both social and professional importance.

SUMMARY

Behavioral and cognitive approaches comprise two separate but increasingly overlapping areas. Behaviorism generally is concerned with the relationships between observable events and happenings in the environment. Cognitive psychology, on the other hand, studies internal processes such as thinking styles and perceptual and memory capabilities.

Behaviorism has two major roots: Pavlov and classical conditioning, and Skinner and operant conditioning. Classical conditioning showed that a neutral stimulus can be made to elicit a reflex response by earlier pairing. Applications of the classical conditioning paradigm have been made in treatment of enuresis and in systematic desensitization. Operant conditioning showed that behaviors that were reinforced tended to be emitted more often. Reinforcers are defined by their effect—that is, by raising a behavior's frequency. Reinforcers may be classified or grouped in many ways. Useful groupings distinguish basic or primal reinforcers such as food from those that relate to higher human functioning.

The relationship that the reinforcer has to the behavior is the reinforcement schedule. Schedules may be random, fixed or variable interval, fixed or variable ratio. Each has particular properties and effects, as well as variable ratio-shaping behavior which keeps going very persistently. Time out, a consequence used in many social learning programs with children, means a period of isolation, or removal from social reinforcement.

To these ideas theorists and practitioners have added other ideas such as modeling, imitation, and token economies. In the token economy, tokens are first earned for positive behaviors, lost for negative ones, and the balance traded for reinforcers.

As behaviorism has developed, it has begun undeniably to involve internal or cognitive processes, as examples of self-instruction, self-monitoring, imagery, and thought stopping make plain. Cognitive psychology, too, has historic roots, having used ideas such as plans, programs, erroneous beliefs, and guiding fictions in its clinical work. Cognitivists have studied perception and memory and thinking processes and styles. Recent work uses direct training in such adaptive and necessary skills as means-end thinking and alternative-solution thinking to help children reduce antisocial behavior. Other cognitive therapies seek to supplant the basic beliefs or assumptions through which a patient construes the world to be unpleasant, anxiety provoking, or depressing. Still others seek to internalize self-control and self-regulation mechanisms.

Many writers currently use the joint title *cognitive-behaviorism* for their area. Early battles to keep the purity of behaviorism appear to have given way to a productive synthesis.

RECOMMENDED READINGS

Kazdin, A. E. *Behavior modification in applied settings.* Homewood, Ill.: Dorsey Press, 1975.
Kazdin's little book gives an excellent overview of behavior modification principles and examples of practical application. Although dated in the sense that few cognitive concepts are presented, the book sets out principles, straightforwardly discusses misconceptions of behavior modifications, and then discusses applications. It concludes with ethical considerations and has a glossary and formidable list of references.

Lewinsohn, P. M., Muñoz, R. F., Youngren, M. A., & Zeiss, A. M. *Control your depression.* Englewood Cliffs, N.J.: Prentice-Hall, 1979.
This book is an example of many books in what is becoming a behavioral-cognitive tradition—books that are intended for reading by laypeople as well as for use

in training and therapy by professionals. The basic idea is to help people to develop control of their unwanted behaviors and thoughts. This book is based on many years of research on depression by Lewinsohn and his colleagues. It shows in detail how to record and make use of pleasant and unpleasant experiences and how to relax and develop social skills and positive attitudes.

Merluzzi, T. V., Glass, C. R., & Genest, M. (Eds.). *Cognitive assessment.* New York: Guilford Press, 1981.

This book is wide ranging, covering not only the assessment of thinking, but also information-processing theory, imagery, and electrophysiological relations to cognition. Clinical implications include discussions of depression, anxiety, problem solving, and applications to sports psychology. A related review is "Assessment of Cognitive Style" by Goldstein and Blackman (1978). Assessment is also prominent in behavioral approaches, and a number of important books have already been referred to (e.g., Ciminero et al., 1977; Hersen & Bellack, 1981). Kendall and Braswell (1982) give a thoughtful review of the rapidly expanding array of cognitive-behavioral assessment measures and discuss such important concepts as *expectancies* and *attributions.*

Meichenbaum, D. *Cognitive-behavior modification: An integrative approach.* New York: Plenum, 1977.

Meichenbaum's book provides one of the first major attempts to integrate cognitive concepts and behavioral procedures. Meichenbaum was exposed early in his training to both the orthodox operant behaviorists and a number of what he calls cognitive-semantic therapists—workers such as Ellis and Beck, who seek to uncover and supplant incorrect and troublesome self-statements. The book ranges over several clinical aspects of the integration of the two views, introducing self-instructional training procedures and then discussing cognitive factors involved in common behavioral approaches. Meichenbaum presents stress inoculation training, procedures to help people to withstand stress by prior cognitive preparation, and cognitive restructuring techniques. He emphasizes the importance of internal dialogue in his views of behavior change and concludes with ways of assessing changes.

Argyris, C., & Schön, D. A. *Theory in practice.* San Francisco: Jossey-Bass, 1974.

The book presents a comprehensive theory about the determination of human actions that is potentially very useful to psychologists and others who undertake to intervene in human lives. According to this theory, the actions a person carries out are not just collections of responses that have been reinforced during the past but expressions of a cognitive theory of action the person holds. The authors distinguish between the espoused theory, which is what the person reports that he does in various situations, and the theory-in-use, which may be different from the espoused theory and which can only be understood by observing the actions themselves. It is the therapist's task to construct from such observations a model of the client's theory-in-use and design learning experiences that can modify it.

RESEARCH EXAMPLES

Weissberg, R. P., Gesten, E. L., Rapkin, B. D., Cowen, E. L., Davidson, E., Flores de Apodaca, R., & McKim, B. J. The evaluation of a social-problem-solving training program for suburban and inner-city third grade children. *Journal of Consulting and Clinical Psychology,* 1981, 49, 251–261.

Many authors have understood the immense importance of ability to deal constructively with interpersonal conflicts and the immense disadvantage endured by those who cannot do so. Early attempts by Spivack and Shure to teach social-problem-solving (SPS) skills to young children as a preventive intervention have been largely successful and offer exciting prospects. Specifically for inner-city children they showed that gains in SPS skills resulted in better teacher-rated adjustment, gains in alternative-solution thinking, and consequence thinking related to improved adjustment, and that SPS training endured. However, efforts to replicate these findings with suburban children have not been consistently successful.

This study sought to assess the differential effectiveness of SPS training for both low SES, black, inner-city children and for middle SES, white, suburban third graders. The subjects included 243 third graders from 12 classes in three schools—two in white, suburban, middle SES neighborhoods and one in a low-income, black, urban area. Each school had two experimental classes and two nonprogram classes. There were 122 trained children (89 suburban, 33 urban) and 121 controls (81 suburban, 38 urban). The treatment groups were comparable on key demographic variables such as age, sex, race, and SES (socio-economic status).

The training procedures centered on curriculum materials in five units: (1) recognizing feelings, (2) problem sensing and identifying, (3) generating alternative solutions to problems, (4) considering consequences, (5) integrating problem-solving behavior. Small-group role play was the most important and extensively used training technique. The problem-solving skills were assessed by measuring means-end thinking, alternative-solutions thinking, social–role-taking ability, and problem identification and consequential thinking. Additionally behavioral adjustment was rated by teachers on four standardized inventories.

Results showed that program children improved more than did controls on several cognitive skills, including problem identification, alternative-solution thinking, consequential thinking, and behavioral problem-solving performance. The intervention positively affected the behavioral adjustment of suburban, but not urban, youngsters. However, relationships between problem-solving skill improvements and adjustment gains were not found.

It seems clear that directly favorable results in behavioral adjustment from the teaching of specific cognitive and interpersonal skills cannot be obtained and that there are complex and yet-not-understood interactions among program curriculum, age, and sociodemographic characteristics which intervene between SPS training and the appearance of prosocial behavior. Aspects of the study do not support the link between SPS training and adjustment change, a link critical in presenting SPS as an effective primary prevention approach.

Robinson, E. A., & Eyberg, S. M. The Dyadic Parent-Child Interaction Coding System: Standardization and validation. *Journal of Clinical and Consulting Psychology*, 1981, *49*, 245–250.

Beginning with the pioneering work of Patterson, Ray, Shaw, and Cobb, psychologists of a behavioral persuasion have sought to define and record behavior accurately through observational coding systems. Patterson defined a vocabulary of codes (for instance, CM, command; CO, compliance; PN, physical negative contact; and YE, Yell), and after training observers to record accurately which categories they saw, was able to produce reliable rate and behavior sequence data for his clients. The present study attempts to validate a development of such a system.

The subjects were 20 families referred for treatment of a conduct problem child (2 to 7 years of age) and 22 normal families observed in the laboratory in child-directed and parent-directed interaction. The observers were experienced in behavioral coding and appropriately trained, but did not know to which group the family being observed belonged.

A number of components of the coding system come from earlier work such as command, indirect command, labeled praise, unlabeled praise, negative physical contact, and so on. Additonal categories were included to enable coding of every parent sentence or phrase, and child behaviors were selected from earlier research. The interaction coding system consists of 22 parent-and-child behavior categories in parent-directed interaction and 19 categories in child-directed interaction. Observations were continuous and resulted in the total frequency of each behavior or behavioral sequence for a five-minute interval.

Variables created from the categories include total praise, total deviant, total commands, command ratio, no opportunity ratio, compliance ratio, noncompliance ratio. The results showed that conduct problem children displayed higher rates of non-compliance than did normal children and that their parents were more critical and more directive than were normal parents. Both the referred child and the sibling exhibited behavior problems in conduct problem families, but the referred child was deviant in a greater variety of situations than were the siblings. The coding system proved statistically reliable and correctly classified 94 percent of families and predicted 61 percent of the variance of parent report of home behavior problems.

An instrument such as this provides useful diagnostic information. The normative data provides a basis against which to evaluate treatment outcome, and because it is sensitive to interaction, the system yields characteristics of the parent, as well as those of the child, that contribute to the diagnosis of the conduct problem. For an important development in social learning theory and research about parent-child interaction applied to families with out-of-control children see Patterson's *Coercive Family Process* (1982).

Munford, P. R., Reardon, D., Liberman, R. P., & Allen, L. Behavioral treatment of hysterical coughing and mutism: A case study. *Journal of Consulting and Clinical Psychology,* 1976, *44,*1008–1014.

This case study illustrates single-subject research design—a useful procedure often used by behavioral therapists. The authors conceptualize functional somatic disorders as operants—that is, as behaviors subject to predictable changes as reinforcement is used.

Jennifer, the 17-year-old subject, complained of incessant coughing except during sleep. She coughed about 40 to 50 times per minute and had had the problem for four years. Also, some two years earlier, her speech had become unintelligible, and she had gradually fallen into complete mutism and communicated only in writing.

As a child she had had frequent colds and sore throats. As the coughing problem and mutism evolved, she underwent three hospitalizations, a wide variety of large-scale diagnostic procedures, allergy therapy, two years of psychotherapy, acupuncture, and many other therapies, all without result.

The Munford team began their treatment with a three-month series of outpatient visits in which information was gathered on which inpatient treatment strategies were to be based, and a therapeutic relationship was developed. The team's hypothesis was that the coughing was being maintained by the medical and social attention it brought and by the way it helped her to avoid the anxiety of having to deal with the world outside her home.

To test the first hypothesis Jennifer was hospitalized in a setting where her coughing rates could be studied under different conditions of social reinforcement. Data showed that she emitted a mean of 14.2 coughs per minute when sitting alone doing a task and 51.5 coughs per minute when she was aware of being observed. The hypothesis was clearly confirmed. An extinction procedure was started, in which everyone was to ignore the cough but otherwise to interact normally with Jennifer. The average coughs per minute varied around 44 for the first seven weeks; then they dropped off sharply to about 20 per minute by week 22.

Because the symptom also seemed useful in helping Jennifer to avoid anxiety, she was started on a desensitization program. In her case she was assisted to feel comfortable in increasingly more complicated real-life situations, culminating with socializing at the university and starting driving lessons. Her mutism was treated by a shaping and reinforcing of speech components and speech, using home visits as a reinforcer. Because speech is incompatible with coughing, the coughing and residual sounds disappeared as fluency returned.

Follow-ups at 20 months and at 41 months after discharge showed that she remained symptom free. The authors suggest that their method of using unobtrusive observation and obtrusive observation may be useful in distinguishing functional—at least environmentally maintained disorders—from organic ones. They emphasize the utility of viewing functional symptoms as operants and wonder if perhaps the lengthy prior search for organic and psychodynamic explanations may have even intensified her symptoms.

10 GETTING ONE'S BEARINGS:

Choosing, Planning, Growing, through Counseling

Workers in human service organizations are concerned not only with changing habits or with the diagnosis and treatment of psychological ills. What many clients seem to need is help in "finding themselves," deciding what to do with their lives, involving themselves in experiences that enable them to grow and achieve what they are capable of achieving. In facilitating these efforts the clinical worker draws upon a background in developmental, social, and differential psychology and functions more as a consultant than as a therapist. The following case illustrates this sort of challenge.

May Lathrop is troubled by a vague discontent, a feeling that she ought to do something different with her life. A woman of 38, she appears to have everything a woman would want—a husband with a successful automobile business, a large, well-furnished home in the best part of town, two children with whom she is on the best of terms. Her son, Bill, is just entering college, and her daughter, Diana, is in her third year of high school. May leads a fairly active social life, participates in church and community organizations, gardens, and plays the piano. She has always enjoyed good health and has never shown any neurotic symptoms. She wonders if it is perhaps the feminist movement that is unsettling her life. She has never taken an active part in it, but she cannot completely ignore what its proponents are saying.

Her best friend, Sharon, with whom she discusses this feeling, tells her about a counseling center run by some psychologists where one can get help in surveying possibilities and deciding what one really wants to do. At first May reacts negatively to the idea, protesting that she is not the sort of person who needs to see a "shrink." "There's nothing wrong with me," she insists. Her friend explains, "This is a different sort of place. It's like going to a lawyer or a realtor for advice. Why don't you give it a try?" So after thinking it over for a while, May calls the Jefferson Square Counseling Center for an appointment.

In this chapter we will cover several psychological ways of helping others to develop and more fully approach their potentials. First we will discuss counseling in general, then assisting psychological growth in children, and finally humanistic psychology, including encounter groups and transpersonal ideas and methods.

HOW COUNSELING DIFFERS
FROM THERAPY

The word *counseling* is often used as a label for such service, but the word itself is plagued by ambiguity. It has been in our language for a long time and has been used in many ways. We have camp counselors, investment counselors, counselors-at-law, and many other quite different kinds of people using the title. However, for want of a better label we will call this approach *developmental counseling*. It has some things in common with other intervention techniques, but it also has defining characteristics of its own.

What distinguishes this kind of psychological activity most clearly from other things that clinicians do is its emphasis on *growth*. Referring back to Table 3–1, we would find it concentrated in column 4. The basic assumption is that life from beginning to end involves developmental change and that the psychologist can facilitate development in desirable directions. One way that developmental counseling differs from the psychotherapies we have been considering is that it is for everyone, not just abnormal people. It deals with clients, not patients. All of us encounter situations in which it is hard to decide what to do; all of us get caught up in complex relationships with other persons. Each of us must decide on a career, get established in it, and change it if circumstances change. Each of us faces the challenge of fashioning or finding an adequate philosophy of life, within or outside organized religious groups. In all of these areas the direction that our society seems to be moving toward is more and more complexity. Not only young people, but the middle-aged and elderly as well, often feel lost, not sure what they want or what direction they should take. Developmental counseling can help people cope with their increasingly complex worlds.

Another characteristic that distinguishes counseling of this sort from many kinds of therapy is that clients maintain full responsibility for the decisions they make. The psychologist does not advise, suggest, or plan for clients, although possible kinds of action may be mentioned during interviews. This is true even when counseling goes on, as it often does, as part of the treatment that patients receive in hospitals, mental health clinics, and medical rehabilitation agencies. Even though psychotics or neurotics may be patients at the same time under a doctor's care with regard to their anxiety or phobias, they are clients making decisions about their own lives in their dealings with the developmental counselor. In keeping with this characteristic is the fact that counseling arrangements are always of limited duration. The client comes to the counselor with some purpose in mind, however vague, and enough sessions are scheduled to accomplish this purpose (or in some cases comes to the conclusion that it cannot be accomplished).

Counselors of this sort utilize many more kinds of factual information and many more specialized community services than therapists typically do. To do a good job, one needs to know where the dependable sources of information are, for example, for trends in the job market in one's own or some other area, ways of financing a college education, and special programs for veterans or disabled individuals. One needs to be familiar with the social agencies and educational institutions in the community, its childcare facilities, and its bus lines. It helps to be able to recommend a good divorce lawyer or pediatrician. One needs to know something about the client's housing conditions, family situation, and neighborhoods past and present as well as about abilities and personality traits. Helping with challenges of adaptation requires attention to the world to be adapted to as well as to the adapter.

Counseling psychology, defined broadly as we have been defining it, grew out of a narrower undertaking that was first called *vocational guidance*, and the career aspect of life still gets considerable emphasis in its practice. Its scope has now been extended, however. One such extension is the realization that besides paid jobs, there are many other useful and satisfying activities, and counselors can help people find them. May Lathrop, with whom we began this chapter, may not need to get a job or enter professional training in order to find herself. She may decide instead to run for the city council or the school board, or even for the legislature. She may plan to devote her time to promoting the new art museum or fighting environmental pollution. Work is essential to a full life, but it need not be *paid* work.

Another direction in which this kind of psychological activity has been extended is downward into the lives of young children. People do not choose the directions in which their lives will develop all at once at a particular time or occasion. As research has produced more and more understanding of the growth process, it has become clear to psychologists that *early intervention* can often pay large dividends. Many kinds of special education for children with special needs are now available. To inform children and their parents about these and to help each child find an appropriate growth situation is an undertaking similar in many ways to the work done by vocational counselors in bringing individuals and careers into alignment.

A third direction in which developmental counseling has been extended is the *human potential* movement. In recent years thousands of persons have begun searching for a richer, more satisfying life. They have come to feel that success is not enough, that status and recognition are not really rewarding, and that the quest for happiness through an accumulation of material things is essentially futile. What they seek is growth of a general rather than a particular kind. Psychologists, along with philosophers, artists, writers, and representatives of the world's religions, have played an active part in the movement.

FINDING ONE'S PLACE— STEPS IN THE DEVELOPMENTAL COUNSELING PROCESS

As in all sorts of psychological intervention, the first and most fundamental step is the establishment of a good working relationship. The client must feel accepted, liked, and respected. He or she must have some confidence in the counselor's competence and active goodwill. This is a complex matter resting partly on the circumstances of the referral, partly on how the client feels about the counselor's profession (which may, of course, be social work, the ministry, or something else rather than psychology). But such confidence also involves the subtle "chemistry" of attraction and repulsion. Not all clients can work productively with all counselors. Counseling relationships must have this positive quality, but it must also be recognized that they are *limited* in duration, in closeness, and in responsibility. The good counselor does not allow clients to become dependent.

Early in the counseling process, usually during the first interview, it is advisable that counselor and client together reach a conclusion about the purpose of the undertaking and agree upon a plan for procedure. Sometimes this takes the form of a formal or informal contract covering such matters as the number and frequency of interviews, supplementary techniques to be included, such as participation in a group, and contacts to be made with other persons or agencies. If there is a charge for the service, the client should be informed at the outset.

A part of the plan from the beginning should be how its effectiveness is to be evaluated. Some evaluation is continuous, facilitating decisions about changing or continuing the plan as it proceeds. Other kinds of evaluation occur at the end of the series of interviews to enable the participants to decide whether the relationship should be terminated or a new plan initiated, and to stimulate professional thinking about what is useful and what is not. Follow-up evaluations at specified times in the future are also a rich source of theoretical and practical knowledge, although they cannot usually be planned for at the outset of counseling. Evaluation and continuous control through joint planning has not always characterized counseling services in years past, but leaders in the field are increasingly emphasizing its importance.

The heart of the counseling enterprise is the *exploration of possibilities.* What kinds of action might this person in this situation conceivably take? What directions of movement are now open? What assets does the person possess? What opportunities present themselves? What obstacles block some or all of these paths? What, if anything, can be done about them? What facilitating services are available for various courses of action?

This kind of appraisal with the person requires assessment of person, situation, and the interaction between them. One must consider factors actually present and factors to be encountered if changes are made or if the person moves to a different situation. One must guard against being satisfied with too limited a survey. In the past, standard practice in career counseling has been to examine a client's record; to administer a battery of aptitude, achievement, and interest tests; and to send him or her to the vocational information files to read up on occupations that the test profile suggests as possibilities. But this is not enough. One needs to find out not just how the individuals score on ability tests but also what specific competencies have been developed through experience. Can May Lathrop ride horses, train dogs, play the guitar, bake bread, grow vegetables, repair electric wiring, drive a truck? There are innumerable skills that people pick up during their lives, and until some attempt is made to inventory them, there is no possibility of generating decisions and plans based on them. This is particularly important in cases like May Lathrop's. Because she has had no professional training or experience in the world of work, she and the persons interviewing her may easily underestimate her actual competencies.

Similarly the assessment of interests, motivation, and personality assets by means of tests alone is not adequate. A counselor must be very sensitive to feelings about the experiences that clients recount. Resourceful counselors make special efforts to elicit these feelings. In one center, for example, a photohistory is put together (Sundberg, 1977). The client collects and mounts old snapshots from successive periods of his or her life, and the discussion of these during interviews produces a life history that includes feelings as well as facts. Sorting techniques constitute another useful interview aid. A client can be handed a set of cards on which occupational titles have been written and asked to sort them on the basis of positive or negative feelings toward each and then to group them on the basis of similarity, analyzing the basis of the positive or negative feelings toward each group (Tyler, Sundberg, Rohila, & Greene, 1968). Other items can be used instead of occupational titles—leisure activities, kinds of people, places to live, for example. An individual's unique personal constructs that delineate the framework through which the person views the world can be elicited by the use of an individually designed version of the Role Construct Repertory (Rep) Test invented by Kelly (1955). The client considers parts of his or her environment (most often the significant people in it) three at a time, in each instance telling how two of them are alike in some respect and how the third is different. The criteria by means of which the person classifies people soon become apparent. Again the items judged need not be people. Scenes, books, tasks, objects to own, and a great many other things can be presented in the same way.

These exploratory techniques and others that creative counselors may think of are ways of identifying *situational* possibilities for individuals with their own unique patterns of motivation. It is almost always important to consider the important people in clients' worlds—spouses, children, parents, friends, work associates, and others—and how they help or hinder the clients' search for productive, meaningful lives. Limiting factors must also be considered—financial responsibilities, the feasibility of moving, the scarcity of openings in some fields, and the difficulty in getting into some training programs. It is important, however, not to *overemphasize* limiting factors in either person or situation. Too often young women have been told that it is impossible for them to get into physical sciences or skilled trades. Too often black and Latino clients have been discouraged from applying or training for high-level positions. However, attitudes and employment trends may change drastically. Similarly persons with severe physical and mental handicaps may now find useful and rewarding roles to play in society.

More important than the acceptance of limits is the identification of assets and opportunities in the client's present or near-future situation. There are people one can talk to about what the life of a meteorologist, a male nurse, or a female auto mechanic is like, and how one prepares for it. There are specialized social agencies to help one deal with abusive husbands, retarded children, or senile parents. There are sometimes governmental or private funds available for some educational and training purposes. There are opportunities in some cities and sections of the country that are not available in others. Considering all of these matters can lead to numerous possibilities.

The best way for a counselor to understand a client's situation and feelings about it may be to visit the person's home, neighborhood, or work place. This has not been common practice in the past, but it is coming into more frequent use. The system of interactions in which a client is enmeshed is very difficult to describe adequately in words. One visit to a family during the dinner hour may give a counselor some sense of what the family system is like. We need no longer assume that professional work is done only in an office.

The outcome of such a wide-ranging appraisal process is the emergence of a limited number of real alternatives for action. Not all possibilities turn out to be genuine alternatives. Once this appraisal has occurred, the task of the client is to make a choice or decision, and the task of the counselor is to facilitate this. Some persons have considerable difficulty in making decisions, and for them this may be the hardest part of the whole counseling experience.

Fortunately psychologists have done a considerable amount of research on decision making, and some of the findings are useful in this connection. The models constructed by researchers have two main components: *utility* (the chooser's values and desires) and *expectancy* (the probability of attaining each of the alternative goals). Counseling can serve to clarify both. The appraisal process we have described should have produced some clarity about what the individual really wants from life. Thus the utility of each of the alternative courses of action should not be too hard to estimate. Expectancy is more of a problem, but for at least some alternatives, information is available linking measured characteristics of the person to measurable outcomes in a probabilistic way. This is most likely to be true for occupational decisions. The relationship between test scores and outcomes can be cast in the form of an *expectancy table* such as the following:

TEST SCORE	SUCCESS RATINGS		
	C	B	A
High	16%	45%	39%
Medium	43%	50%	7%
Low	80%	19%	1%

If the table represents the probabilities that college students with different levels of aptitude scores will be admitted to masters programs in psychology after they graduate from college, Stanley, with medium SAT scores of 450–Verbal and 525–Quantitative can see at a glance that only 7 percent of the students with scores like his get A ratings (sure acceptance), 50 percent get B ratings (possible acceptance), and 43 percent get C ratings (rejection). He

BOX 10-1   *POSSIBILITY PROCESSING STRUCTURES*

In helping confused people to find themselves, a useful set of theoretical ideas is centered on the concept of *possibility processing structures* (PPS). The concept rests on several basic premises so obvious that they generate no argument. The first is that a society, especially the complex one in which we live, can maintain itself only if individuals contribute to it in different ways. Each person must find his or her special place or particular role. The second premise is that developmental possibilities for any individual are very numerous. The third is that an individual's time is strictly limited so that one can develop simultaneously or successively only a fraction of those possibilities. The rest must be closed out in order for that fraction to be actualized. What this means is that a developing individual is constantly choosing from the possibilities facing her or him and choices are constantly being made—not only among alternative occupations and careers but also among alternate life styles, values, and kinds of personal relations.

If in each new situation one faces one had to analyze all the possibilities, the choice process would be impossibly difficult. What a person naturally does is to organize experience into mental *structures*. Cognitive psychologists have been accumulating evidence for the existence of information-processing structures in various areas of research such as perception, memory, and intelligence. They are thought of as analogous to computer programs that control the processing of data. Piaget (1970) has provided a comprehensive discussion of the whole concept of structure as it is taking shape in psychological research. He characterizes a structure as a system of self-regulated transformations never observed directly but inferred from its effects.

Tyler (1978) uses the term *possibility processing structures* to characterize the particular kinds of structures that govern choices of activities or paths of life. Terms that psychologists have used for independent fields of research are included under this one label. Interest patterns, moral codes, values, ideologies, self-concepts—these all operate as structures that control choices. Different individuals utilize different combinations of them. During the course of development the individual acquires a *repertoire* of possibility processing structures.

Such structures are not rigid or immutable. Occasionally one of them is discarded completely and replaced by another, as in the case of religious conversion when a structure organized around money and power is replaced by a structure that allows possibilities for service to God and humanity to become visible. More often a structure is transformed gradually through the processes Piaget has analyzed so well—*assimilation* (incorporation of new content into the structure) and *accommodation* (modifying its shape to fit the enlarged scope).

The understanding of possibility processing structures through developing a theory synthesizing principles from research in information-processing, cognitive styles, developmental psychology and personality assessment holds promise for providing a close relation between practice and theory in counseling and psychotherapy. For a more complete discussion of these ideas and a review of relevant research, see Tyler's *Individuality* (1978).

would see that although there is a fair probability associated with the psychology career alternative, he cannot be certain of attaining this goal and perhaps should have a second choice in mind. On the other hand, he might be confident that he has enough of the other characteristics that a psychological career demands, such as high motivation and the willingness to work hard and long, and rate his individual expectancy of being accepted by a good graduate school much higher than the table indicates that it is for students in general. The expectancies that count in decision making are these subjective ones.

One of the major personality theorists of our time has been focusing attention on *self-efficacy* as a factor in decisions (Bandura, 1977, 1982)). He distinguishes between *outcome expectations*, which are what one gets from expectancy tables or other objective observations of what has actually happened to others in similar situations and *efficacy expectations*, which are "convictions that one can successfully execute the behavior required to produce the outcomes" (1977, p. 193). He has been exploring the dimensions and sources of self-efficacy expectations and analyzing research results indicating how they can be changed. These ideas and the research growing out of them should be useful both to psychologists helping adults to make decisions and psychologists planning interventions in children's lives to facilitate development.

Once a decision has been made, there is still one more step in the counseling process—the making and monitoring of a concrete *plan*. This often involves an educational or training program, but in some cases it may consist of a job-seeking strategy. For rehabilitation clients, medical or surgical treatment may be part of the plan, and it may include obtaining and learning to use a prosthesis of some sort. For women without employment experience who wish or need to get jobs but lack confidence in their ability to handle them, a brief assertiveness workshop may be a first step. An individual plan must consider financial demands and resources, family responsibilities, and many other aspects of the client's life. The counselor needs to maintain contact with the person for a time after the plan goes into effect, to see whether it is going to work and to help the person to make any necessary changes.

COUNSELING INTERVIEWS—
THEIR SHAPE AND CONTENT

There is no standardized procedure for counseling interviews. Meetings between client and counselor are used for a variety of purposes. At the beginning they are likely to be "get acquainted" sessions in which the participants begin to reveal who they are and in which the foundations for a good working relationship are laid. At this stage the conversation might appear somewhat superficial to an observer, but even if a man is only talking about his disappointment that rainy weather has canceled a tennis game he was anticipating, his enthusiasm for horses and dogs, or the small town in which he grew up, he may be beginning to open up his essential self to the counselor. Communication of information about the self is a continuing part of the counseling process. As interviews proceed, many other kinds of information are also communicated. For a client who is attempting to map out a satisfying career, both participants may concern themselves with detailed information about the advantages and disadvantages of different lines of work. If a person has taken standardized tests, accurate information about what scores mean must be communicated and understood. If a person is contemplating a divorce, legal information must be obtained and may well be a major topic of discussion in some interviews. Other clients need information about mental health, child rearing, or psychological development in mid-life. An essential function of a counselor is communicating information, but obviously no one person is likely to know everything. What a counselor can do is to put the client in touch with dependable sources and then help him or her incorporate what has been learned into the "apperceptive mass" upon which thinking and planning rest.

Homework assignments are often a part of counseling, activities such as talking to a lawyer, reading an article or book about an occupation, or applying for a civil service job. Interview time is spent setting up these assignments and discussing them after they are carried out. They can be as varied as are the clients themselves. In one case the prescription may be to stop work and give attention, praise, and reward to one's ten-year-old son every day when he comes directly home from school. In another a student's assignment is to look over the posted list of college organizations and activities, choose one in which to participate, and go to a meeting. In still another a client may be asked to read a "How to Study" manual and be prepared to discuss it.

Much interview time is used to talk about relationships with people— parents, spouse, children, neighbors, roommates, boss. Even when these are not the main focus of the counseling, they affect the individual's life in a multitude of ways. Interview time is also utilized in what might be called "brainstorming," trying to bring to light possibilities for action and personal growth that are not seen at the outset. People tend to assume that they have less freedom than they actually have, that their present circumstances are more restrictive than they actually are. Just how this discovery of new possibilities occurs during the counseling interchange is difficult to specify. Any of the items of information that have been mentioned may touch off an association in client or counselor that leads to a "What if . . .?" question. "What if I could move to San Francisco?" "What if I could get my rich aunt to lend me the money for pilot training?" "What if we sold our big house and moved to a smaller one so that we wouldn't be under this pressure to make more money all the time?"

Throughout all of the diverse sorts of interview sessions we have been considering, there is one characteristic that is constant—the attention to feeling as well as facts and thoughts. It is the principal way that counseling differs from ordinary conversation. The most essential quality that a counselor must have and continue to cultivate is sensitivity to feeling. One must be able to read between the lines, so to speak, to pick up the ambivalence in a client's attitude toward his wife, to sense resistance to what seems to be a perfectly reasonable homework assignment, to recognize that a career possibility is distasteful to a woman even though no reason for negative feeling is apparent. In some sorts of therapy such feelings are analyzed and interpreted. In the kind of counseling we are talking about, they need not be, but their presence must be recognized and accepted as part of the total situation being dealt with.

Our discussion so far has suggested that the process of obtaining information, exploring possibilities, and making decisions and plans is a transaction involving only two people in conference with one another. This is indeed the way it began. But increasingly, as the years have passed, much of this activity occurs in groups. The appraisal process can often be carried on more economically that way. The communication of essential information is also more efficient if the group consists of participants all of whom need some of the same information. In the discussion of possibilities, the ideas of some of the group members may well be as stimulating as those that occur to the counselor. From the counselor's point of view, leading such a group calls for the same sensitivity to feelings and skill in communication as interviewing does, and something more besides. The many complex interactions in even a small group require a special alertness to keep abreast of what is going on. Making sure that all members are participating and that the less aggressive are not being silenced by the others may require tactful intervention. However, many counselors are convinced that the benefits of group work outweigh the difficulties.

In this particular connection we are not talking about a change of focus to a group rather than an individual system. The purpose is the same as in one-to-one counseling—to enable each *individual* to attain clarity about what he or she wants from life and to work out a plan for achieving it. Group work of different kinds will be considered in later chapters. Where the purpose of the intervention is to improve the functioning of the group system itself, as in the case of family therapy, the process is somewhat different.

It should be pointed out that the whole foregoing account of the counseling process is simpler and more clear-cut than it usually turns out to be in practice. Furthermore, because of the ambiguity in what the word *counseling* means to different people, many other kinds of psychological treatment bearing little resemblance to the one described here occur under the same label. The purpose of the exposition is to point to a kind of service different from the interventions with which many clinical psychologists and the public are most familiar. Whether it is called counseling or something else is of less importance than whether it is recognized and used.

EARLY INTERVENTION WITH CHILDREN TO PROMOTE OPTIMUM PSYCHOLOGICAL GROWTH

Early intervention with children deserves a place in a chapter on optimizing human growth. Although the methods are often somewhat different from those used in adult counseling, the goal is essentially the same: to help individuals acquire the skills to deal with their environment in ways that will give them new competencies, broader horizons, or increased potentials. In some cases the issue is one of helping groups of children negotiate the ordinary hurdles of growing up, whereas in others the task is to help individuals who have lost some living skills to minimize the impact of that loss on their autonomy. In each case early intervention aims to foster basic skills and attitudes which will in turn permit other levels of more complicated or advanced skills to be added on top of them, as it were.

The chapter in which development was discussed (Chapter 2) outlined some developmental theories, notably that of Piaget, which stress stages of development. Certain component skills must first be present before the new level of development can appear. Although there is controversy between those who think that the appearance of certain skills can be accelerated by instruction and enrichment and those, including Piaget, who hold that it cannot, there is little disagreement that practice in the age-appropriate component skills—sometimes called *readiness skills*—is useful for children.

The federally supported Headstart program in the United States sought to redress the cognitive social and emotional deprivations experienced by many children in our society. From a more academic background, the work of Maria Montessori, an Italian educator and developmentalist, spread into a network of preschools which give their children tasks and opportunities designed for optimal cognitive development. A wide variety of programs and materials issuing from many publishers of educational and pyschological aids is available. Research on the outcomes of these programs has produced mixed results, but on the whole the effects have been shown to be positive (Lazar, Hubbell, Murray, Rosch, & Royce, 1977). The Spivack and Shure (1974, 1978) procedures, discussed in the last chapter, for teaching interpersonal problem solving appear especially promising.

COUNSELING FOR OVERALL
PERSONAL GROWTH—
THE HUMAN POTENTIAL
MOVEMENT

During the 1960s and 1970s increasing numbers of people have been asking not so much for assistance in solving particular problems, making particular decisions, or overcoming particular handicaps, as for direction in their search for higher levels of conscious experience. They have become aware that they are using only a small fraction of the rich resources provided by the indescribably complex human brain. What they seek is some means of releasing this flood of potential psychological energy so that they can move into a new realm of rich and rewarding living. The *human potential* movement is diffuse and many faceted, encompassing an area much broader than psychology, but clinical and counseling psychologists have become involved in it. The label that covers the variegated complex of psychological ideas and practices that have resulted is *humanistic psychology*.

The human potential movement has several identifiable roots, and probably many others that have not been identified. One can see how the attempt to develop clarity about direction, values, and plans which we have been discussing in this chapter is easily widened into a search for nonspecific personal growth. One predecessor is the sensitivity training movement initiated by Kurt Lewin and his students in the 1940s and 1950s, the purpose of which was to enable business organizations, school faculties, civic groups, and other existing social entities to improve communication, create closer personal relationships, and make social systems function more smoothly. These T-groups (training groups) taught normal persons, not "patients," to pay attention to what is being communicated, feelings as well as thoughts, and to realize some of their potential for growth.

During the 1960s the widespread use of drugs, especially LSD, gave others a glimpse of varieties of consciousness very different from their everyday experience. Many of these people graduated from drugs to meditation and mystical disciplines. Psychologists began to make use of some of these disciplines in their theories and practice.

The work of Carl Rogers has been especially important in the development of the human potential movement (Rogers, 1980). Beginning with "nondirective counseling" in the 1940s, the "client-centered" therapy of the 1950s assimilated ideas from existentialism and Oriental philosophies, extended itself into more and more areas where the focus was on *change* rather than on *therapy*, and became the highly influential "person-centered" theory and practice that it is now. Rogers is considered one of the leaders of the human potential movement.

Advanced developments in neuroscience, also coming to stress the im-

Figure 10-1   Carl R. Rogers. (The Bettmann Archive, Inc.)

portance of consciousness, are contributing increasingly to the search for "transcendence" (Ferguson, 1980). Analogies between the human brain and computers, with individuals having different information-processing programs, also help skeptical people to accept possibilities for complex human potentials.

Besides Carl Rogers, major spokespeople for humanistic psychology have been William James, who was perhaps the first psychologist to call attention to the enormous unused potential in human consciousness, and Abraham Maslow, who emphasized *peak experiences* in life when this potential is suddenly made actual. It was Maslow who made *self-actualization* almost a household word. In summary, the one idea holding this amorphous movement together is that there is vastly more to human life than normal, everyday consciousness, and if such human potential can be released, life can be tremendously enriched.

The encounter group became for a time the major technique for the release of human potential. The fuel for its fires seems to have been the "highs" or "turn-ons" experienced by some participants, the social readiness for convention breaking and growth, and, of course, the economic incentives for the group leaders.

Although the fad has apparently crested and several garish variants have run their course, the idea of groups for all kinds of people, as opposed to just teachers, executives, or psychiatric patients, has great merit. But in their heyday such groups were often characterized by too much flamboyance and gimmickry. Yalom (1975) provides some clear and specific correctives to common misconceptions, using findings from the Lieberman, Yalom, and Miles

Figure 10-2
Abraham Maslow. (Brandeis University)

(1973) study of encounter groups. He has reformulated some common maxims often expressed by encounter group participants, as follows:

1. "Feelings not thought" should be altered to "feelings, only with thought."
2. "Let it all hang out" is best revised to "let more of it hang out than usual, if it feels right in the group, and if you can give some thought to what it means." Self-disclosure and positive or negative emotional expressiveness in themselves are not sufficient for change.
3. "Getting out the anger is essential" to "getting out the anger may be okay, but keeping it out there steadily isn't." High expression of anger is not associated with high learning; it generally increases the risk of damage to oneself and the group.
4. "Stay with the here and now" to "here and now is not enough, add the personal there and then." The more productive groups are those with enough flexibility to talk about things outside the present feelings and perceptions within the group setting. Though some here and now orientation is essential, groups which are flexible and permit other personal material (sexual concerns, dream material, feelings of pride, happiness, etc.) are more productive.
5. "There is no group, only person" to "group processes make a difference in learning, whether or not the leader pays attention to them." Learning is heavily influenced by the group's cohesiveness and climate and the role an individual takes in the group.
6. "High yield requires high risk" to "the risk in encounter groups is considerable, and unrelated to positive gain." In the research studies high risk groups were those that produced large numbers of casualties, and they did not at the same

time produce high learners. The productive groups were safe ones. The high-yield, high-risk group is, according to our study, a myth.

7.   "You may not know what you've learned now, but when you put it all together. . ." to "bloom now, don't count on later." Some allege that being un-frozen or shaken up during the group experience is good, since later, after the group is over, a person integrates the experience and comes out stronger than ever. In the studies, individuals who had a negative outcome at termination *never* moved to the positive when contacted six months later. (Yalom, 1975, pp. 489–490)

BOX 10-2   *THE GESTALT WANTS TO BE COMPLETED NOW*

Gestalt psychology originated in Germany early in the twentieth century; its progenitors asserted that psychological phenomena are organized wholes, not separated pieces as suggested by earlier systems. Gestalt therapy originated with Fritz Perls (1893–1970) in the middle of the century and spread widely from its primary seat in northern California. Gestalt therapists focus the client's awareness on the here-and-now and encourage the taking of responsibility for what is thought and done. Perls says the essence is in "now" and "how":

The gestalt wants to be completed. If the gestalt is not completed, we are left with unfinished situations, and these unfinished situations press and press and press and want to be completed. Let's say if you had a fight, you really got angry at that guy, and you want to take revenge. This need for revenge will nag and nag and nag until you have become even with him. So there are thousands of unfinished gestalts. How to get rid of these gestalten is very simple. These gestalts will emerge. They will come to the surface. Always the most important gestalt will emerge first. We don't have to dig, à la Freud, into the deepest unconscious. We have to become aware of the obvious. If we understand the obvious, everything is there. Every neurotic is a person who doesn't see the obvious. So what we're trying to do in Gestalt therapy is to understand the word 'now,' the present, the awareness and see what happens in the now. . . .

In previous centuries, we asked 'why.' We tried to find causes, reasons, excuses, rationalizations. And we thought if we could change the causes we could change the effect. In our electronic age, we don't ask why anymore, we ask how. We investigate the structure, and when we understand the structure, then we can *change* the structure. And a structure in which we are most interested is the structure of our lifescript. The structure of our lifescript—often called karma or fate—is mostly taken up with self-torture, futile self-improvement games, achievements, and so on. And then two people meet, and they have some different lifescripts, and then they try to force the other person to your lifescript or you're willing to please the other person and efface your needs and become part of his script—and then there is involvement, confusion, fighting. . . . (1973, pp. 119–120)

Polster and Polster (1973, p. 7) in presenting Gestalt therapy say the follow-ing: "Some of the most pervasive of the new perspectives which are the founda-tions for gestalt therapy—and indeed for a large part of the humanistic move-ment—are the following: (1) power is in the present; (2) experience counts most; (3) the therapist is his own instrument; and (4) therapy is too good to be limited to the sick."

Techniques used in growth-stimulation groups have been borrowed from many sources—for example, from Gestalt therapy, in which each person in turn occupies a "hot seat" and discusses problems with the therapist while others listen; from psychodrama, in which participants try out new roles; or from primal therapy, in which primitive emotional expression, the so-called primal scream, is encouraged. Different varieties of yoga and meditative disciplines may be taught. As one writer puts it, the human potential movement is "wildly eclectic." In a book presenting innovative approaches, Corsini (1981) lists 250 different kinds of psychotherapy, 12 of which he considers prominent or mainstream and about 60 of which he selected as truly innovative. Although a number of these can be said to be related to the psychoanalytic or behavioral (or behavioral-cognitive) traditions, many are covered by the wide umbrella of the so-called humanist therapies. The variety of possibilities for exploring human development is very great, and efforts to study them lag far behind efforts to create them.

TRANSPERSONAL PSYCHOTHERAPIES

In the decades of the 1960s and 1970s a strain of psychology has been gaining some prominence which is sometimes seen as part of the humanist movement and sometimes seen as a fourth force. It is concerned with the study of ultimate human potentialities as exemplified by mysticism, ecstasy, altered states of consciousness, transcendence of self, and spiritual experience—a cosmic connection. The high states of being and consciousness and the methods involved in achieving inspiration or release had been recognized by early Western psychologists such as William James and Carl Jung, but only in the later part of the twentieth century have they become rather large movements associated with groups and organizational publications. Many of the ideas behind the transpersonal movement arose from non-Western sources, especially in India and Japan.

A spokesperson for transpersonal psychology, Tart (1975) calls these the *spiritual* psychologies and presents a large number of ways in which their assumptions differ from those of mainstream Western scientific psychology. For instance, he notes the "scientific" assumption that all knowledge derives from reason based on observation of physical events. Spiritual psychologies claim instead that there is direct intuitive knowledge, revelation, and enlightenment, which is more profound and influential than is the mundane acquisition of "empirical" knowledge. The transpersonal psychologies emphasize ways of obtaining altered states of consciousness whereby one can obtain direct understandings. They believe that certain truths can be apprehended only through certain emotions and can never be understood intellectually. They also emphasize the potency of symbols and the various procedures for concentrating thoughts on them and evoking their power. They place the motivations for spiritual experience (transcendence) beyond the motives for hunger, sex, and creature comforts which are assumed to be the only basic motives by some scientific psychologists. Among the many therapeutic approaches advocated are meditation (including transcendental meditation), repetitive sound, exercises (such as those of certain kinds of yoga), fasting, Sufi dancing, and study of Christian and Eastern mysticism.

The most widely known and used transpersonal therapeutic technique in Western countries is *meditation*. Walsh (1981) reviews the literature and advocates it as an inexpensive, self-regulated, and effective procedure, which may result in the deepest transformation of identity, life style, and relationship to the world. Walsh describes a variety of ways to induce the meditative state. An individual needs a quiet situation where one can sit comfortably, close one's eyes, and attend to inner experience in short daily sessions of 20 or 30 minutes once or twice a day. Meditative practices emphasize either *concentration*, which is the ability to focus attention on a specified object or experience, such as breathing, or *awareness*, which aims at examining one's own consciousness or experience. Typically beginning meditators find it very difficult to concentrate; their minds wander off into fantasy or concerns about immediate problems. Persons trying to meditate soon learn that they have much less control over their attention than they thought, but they are told not to worry too much about such wanderings, simply when noticed to bring the mind back to the object of concentration. With continued practice most meditators report increased ability to clear the mind and concentrate; there comes a sense of calm and equanimity and a greater openness to experiences. They report that they feel themselves generally to become calm observers of experiences, and they achieve a certain detachment that rises above the stresses and strains of daily life.

Meditation has been incorporated as only one of several techniques in larger systems of psychotherapy. Reynolds (1980) reviews several Japanese approaches in his book *The Quiet Therapies*. The best known of these are Morita therapy (named after the Japanese psychiatrist who started it early in this century) and Naikan therapy (literally meaning "inner-observation" and coming from a sect of Buddhism). Morita therapy involves an initial period of rest and removal from the world and then a gradual reentry; patients are required to keep diaries and to write reactions to events that occur in their lives, which are reviewed with the therapist. The therapist instructs the patient in recognizing purposes, accepting feelings, and controlling behavior. There is no direct attempt to reduce symptoms, such as anxiety; these troubles are simply accepted, while the person goes on doing what he or she should do. Behind the therapy is the Buddhist conviction that the way out of suffering is to give up selfish attachments (pleasures as "trophies for the ego") and shift attention to work that needs to be done, to service (K. Smith, 1981, p. 64).

Naikan therapy also emphasizes guided self-reflection, but the signifi-

BOX 10-3   *MEDITATION—ADVICE FROM AN INDIAN GURU*

Meditation, an activity long prominent in many religious and spiritual movements, may be viewed as a psychological activity. As such, this phenomenon, which many have found helpful, needs to be investigated scientifically.

Meditation customarily has a rationale or place in the philosophy or theology of the movement concerned. One prominent advocate, Swami Muktananda (1980) held that the inner self is both good and complete and that God is the essence of the complete inner self. The individual's task, then, is to honor the inner self and to meditate on the inner self because God exists within each person. In Muktananda's view, the tasks for effective meditation are not particularly complicated but require sustained practice and respectful concentration.

The inner energy and calm is best found by meditating on the inner self, a task which requires establishing a clear focus. One way to establish and keep the focus is to meditate regularly and to use a mantra. "Mantra is the very life of meditation, the greatest of all techniques. Mantra is a cosmic word or sound vibration. It is the vibration of the Self, the true speech of the Self, and when we immerse ourselves in it, it leads us to the place of the Self" (Muktananda, 1980, p. 37).

Well known mantras, *Om Namah Shivaya* (I bow to the Lord, who is the inner Self) or *So'ham* (I am That) are repeated over and over so that the individuals may lose themselves in the meditation and be at one with the inner Self. Meditation's purpose, says Muktananda, is inner happiness, inner peace. "Meditate on your Self. Honor your Self. Understand your Self. God dwells within you as you" (p. 53).

What about the effects of meditation? Kempton in an Afterword in Muktananda (1980) quotes the testimony of a considerable number of practitioners who have found it beneficial in stress reduction and in achieving a more positive view of daily life. (Testimony itself is, of course, not scientific proof.) She sees meditation and science as having the common goal of expanding our knowledge of reality and removing the barriers to our fuller perception of ourselves and the world. Meditation attempts the task from the inside out, and science from the outside in, she believes.

Meditation does in fact seem to have many close relatives or neighbors in psychology. Common elements of goals and practice appear to exist, for instance, with hypnosis (especially self-hypnosis), with relaxation training, with programs for self-renewal and avoidance of burnout, with aspects of biofeedback like induction of resting alpha wave EEG, and with cognitive behavioral therapies which seek to have people believe and act on positive self-statements. These various approaches need to be brought together by systematic theorizing and research.

cant aim is to produce a guilt about what one has done and at the same time a sense of being cared for despite one's inadequacies. The object is to move the client from obsessive selfishness to a gratitude for daily supports and a willingness to help others—a shift from self-concern to concern for others. Neuroses and other psychological problems are seen as evidences of immaturity. The therapist may present the initial meditation task as one of reflecting on behavior and feelings about one's mother in childhood—the things she did and the troubles the client caused her. In the interview the therapist mostly listens nondirectively and then assigns another task, to meditate on another period in life. Interviews are taped and, with permission, are sometimes played to other Naikan patients for instructive purposes; lectures are also given at the Naikan center where therapy takes place. After a week of intensive therapy, patients are discharged and are encouraged to continue Naikan reflection on a daily basis. Naikan treatment is often an impactful assault on one's self-image, leading to a new way of viewing and evaluating oneself.

Japanese proponents of Morita and Naikan therapy do not see them as mystical, and evaluation of them should be possible. However, little evaluation exists. They do seem to be importantly related to cultural assumptions and aims. Some Western psychologists (e.g., Reynolds, 1980) believe that they are of potential value in America and Europe. These transpersonal and Eastern-inspired therapies provide interesting examples of the variety of possibilities for personal growth besides those that are common in Western culture.

CRITIQUE

How adequate are these approaches conceptually? How useful are these concepts about growth and development of potential to the task of psychological intervention? How well do these approaches fit in with what we know about the functioning of living systems at all levels? The answer to these questions is generally positive. At a general level the idea of developmental counseling, namely that the best way to help people is to do whatever is necessary to channel their growth in desirable directions, rests on a firm research foundation at several system levels. The concepts have proved flexible and expandable. We have seen how efforts to assist people to find appropriate jobs have branched out into efforts to facilitate children's growth and to release growth potential at all age levels. Techniques for working with individuals have been transformed into techniques appropriate for small groups such as families and larger groups such as school classes and adult workshops.

The one serious criticism of the general conceptual framework of developmental intervention that might be voiced is that it tends to become overly optimistic. In this regard it contrasts sharply with the psychoanalytic belief in irrational, childish motivation and emotions. If there are people with pathological mental states, uncontrollable hatreds, and tenacious fears —and we know that there are—it is unrealistic to expect that their own growth processes can solve their problems and the social problems they present. For some psychologists, faith in the efficacy of growth is almost religious in its nature. It needs to be tempered by skepticism, and a place must be made for different approaches to treatment in different situations.

Turning from the general level of comment, one finds a wide variety of approaches within the three major categories of developmental intervention put together in this chapter. The specific conceptual bases for career counseling, early intervention, and growth groups are too varied to discuss here. Suffice it to say that there is limited theoretical development, except for the system proposed by Rogers, which is widely recognized as adequately testable.

How practical are these approaches?   Is there evidence that people working in these developmental approaches achieve the objectives they set for themselves? Over the years there have been many outcome studies in which the school achievement and vocational adjustment of equivalent groups of counseled and noncounseled students have been compared (Tyler, 1969, Chap. 14). In general the differences have favored the counseled groups, but they are not large, and the longer the interval between counseling and follow-up, the harder it is to demonstrate such differences. Since most students who receive counseling are those who asked for it, there is always the possibility that motivational differences between the groups existed at the beginning and accounted for the differences found at the end. In one study attempting to check up on this, however (Campbell, 1963), it was shown that motivational differences were not the decisive factors. One study (Meadows, 1975) indicated that differences in motivation and achievement that at the beginning favored the *noncounseled* group were decreased or eliminated by the time of the seven-year follow-up. The tendency in more recent years is to use more limited criteria of benefit. Did the client make a decision? Is the student getting along better with others in the dormitory?

Setting limited goals and checking repeatedly to find out whether they have been attained have been emphasized particularly by counseling psychologists who have incorporated techniques of behavior modification into the counseling tasks (Thoresen & Anton, 1974). Behavioral techniques of intervention have been examined in more detail in the previous chapter. They advocate a procedure called *intensive design* in which for each client a baseline is established for the problem behavior under treatment, to be compared with measurements of the same behavior at different stages of counseling. One distinguishing feature of this kind of evaluation research is that its data are not means or other *group* averages. Results are examined separately for each individual case. Krumboltz, Becker-Haven, and Burnett (1979) have reviewed counseling research of this intensive sort as it has been carried out with a wide variety of problems.

One result usually found is that persons who have had counseling experience speak well of it and state that it helped them. (This of course is true for fortunetellers and astrologers as well.) There is also some evidence that counseling enables participants to organize their concepts about themselves and bring the "ideal self" and "real self" concepts into closer alignment (Tyler, 1969, p. 229).

Outcome studies of early interventions in children's lives have also shown positive but not very large effects. For the most part they have used IQ increases and improvement in subsequent school work as criteria to evaluate the success of the interventions. Clarke and Clarke (1976) have assembled most of what we know about the attempts to stimulate growth by enriching children's experience at an early stage of development, documenting the dramatic IQ increases and the gradual "fade-out" as children progress through elementary school. Ramey and Haskins (1981) report a study in which enrichment began at a very early age (6 to 12 weeks) demonstrating that by the age of three years, children in the experimental group were significantly higher in IQ than were the control children who had not had the daycare experience and that the scores of the experimental children correlated less closely with those of their mildly retarded mothers. (A more complete account of this study is given as an example of evaluation at the end of Chapter 13.) Jensen (1981), commenting on this and other similar reports, questions whether IQ increases are really changes in intelligence itself or only in specific skills in answering the kinds of questions asked on tests. At present there seems to be no way of resolving this issue, but in general we can say that the evidence points to the possibility of stimulating intellectual growth in young children.

As already mentioned, there are some indications that the popularity of encounter groups, the principal vehicle of the human potential movement, may be decreasing. There have been some attempts to evaluate the effects of group participation, and these have turned out to be hardly spectacular although mainly positive. Smith (1975) reviewed 100 studies of sensitivity groups in which participants were compared with control subjects. Statistically significant positive changes in areas such as self-awareness, self-esteem, and personal relationships were reported in 78 of the studies. In 31 investigations in which follow-up contacts were made some time after the end of training, positive effects persisted in 21. There have been fewer evaluations of the more drastic encounter groups, and some concern has been expressed about the possibility of psychological damage to some participants. Bebout and Gordon (1972) collected data on what might be called "run-of-the-mill' encounter groups organized especially for their research project. They found moderately positive changes, especially in self-attitudes, and few negative changes. There were no real casualties attributable to the group experience. In this project no control subjects were available for comparison purposes.

Lieberman and others (1973), in the study which generated the recommendations about encounter groups we mentioned earlier in this chapter, did provide a better design than did most including control subjects. Participants were selected at random from a pool of applicants to be members of groups with differing theoretical orientations led by persons with quite diverse styles. Assessments focused in some detail on the effects of these style differences. On the average, participants manifested statistically significant positive changes, but for about 9 percent the changes were negative. There were a few serious psychological casualties. As was anticipated, changes were related to leader style. Exciting, charismatic leaders tend to produce positive changes, but they also produce more casualties than do quieter, more supportive leaders.

Of course, encounter groups are only one of the sorts of experiences that make up the human potential movement, but they are the part of it with which psychologists are most likely to be concerned. Persons seeking to learn meditation, yoga, or the practice of a new religion are likely to turn to some other sort of guru. Thus we have even less evidence about the effects of these experiences than we have for the groups. The technique of meditation has received some research. Walsh (1981) reports a number of studies that show a reduction of anxiety and positive effects with people having drug addictions or psychosomatic disorders. Nidich, Seeman, and Dreshin (1973) report that normal meditators change more than do control subjects in the direction of enhanced self-control and confidence. At least one study (Walsh & Benson, 1972) shows that particular brain waves appear during meditation that are different from those shown in the normal waking state or under hypnosis. Walsh (1981) concludes that meditation clearly demonstrates psychological and physiological effects, but it is not yet clear whether it is more effective than similar self-regulation strategies such as relaxation training and self-hypnosis.

Although psychologists with the growth orientation, with the possible exception of Carl Rogers, have not produced comprehensive personality theories, those in the vocational wing of counseling have come up with important tests, such as the Strong Vocational Interest Blank and other interest inventories, and many practical techniques suitable for use in schools, personnel offices, and social agencies. The human potential people have also invented many experiential exercises that have been widely used in other settings.

How socially worthwhile are these approaches?   Developmental counseling seems less likely to harm participants or leave them worse off than they were initially than are some other interventions because of the basic principle that responsibility rests always with the client, not the counselor. Occasionally perhaps a person whose career plan does not work out may be more discouraged and depressed than he or she was at the outset, but such occasions are rare. People who fail to benefit from a counseling experience are likely to speak of it slightingly but not bitterly.

Like the more prosaic counseling programs designed to help people with specific problems and situations, the human potential movement is considered to be for everybody, not for the distressed alone, to be *growth*, not *therapy*. However, it may well be that it often attracts troubled persons who really need personality alteration rather than enhancement and who may be especially vulnerable to some of the unpleasant things said during confrontations. Often there is little or no preliminary screening. In fact, screening is out of harmony with the philosophical principles on which many growth centers rest, assumptions that every human being is fundamentally good and able to grow under favorable circumstances. There are still unresolved issues in the human potential movement.

However, even if some of the wilder aspects are gradually eliminated, it seems likely that the search for personal growth and the liberation of human potential will continue, with or without psychological leadership and research. It is an important current in the stream of human aspiration of our time. The movement has been criticized as overly narcissistic, emphasizing individual experience and neglecting urgent practical concerns and social problems. At present this criticism is somewhat less applicable than it has been in the past. In *The Aquarian Conspiracy* (1980), Ferguson has assembled a considerable amount of evidence about the ways in which the discovery of higher levels of consciousness is beginning to transform education, working conditions, environmental policies, and many other aspects of our common life. Rogers (1980) has much to say about the workshops that now constitute one of the most important activities of the Institute for the Study of Persons, which he heads. Groups of persons, very diverse in age, background, values, even nationality, are brought together for a few days or weeks under circumstances in which no external structure is imposed. There is no agenda and no leader. Although there is often considerable chaos at the beginning, in a relatively short time genuine communication is initiated, and a strong feeling of community develops. Participants find it an intense and very moving experience. Many find it exciting to contemplate what the widespread adoption of this way of dealing with barriers, differences, and conflicts might contribute to labor relations, diplomacy, and many other troubled areas of our complex society.

In conclusion it should be noted that the practices of the human potential movement, whether individual or group, are not really parallel with the other varieties of intervention discussed in this book. They do not belong exclusively to psychology or the other psychological helping professions, but clinical psychologists such as Rogers have contributed much to their development and are still participating in an active way in the movement. Techniques widely used in growth centers, such as Gestalt therapy and transactional analysis, are employed by clinical psychologists in the treatment of persons suffering from a variety of psychological ills, as indeed are the less esoteric counseling techniques to facilitate choosing and planning. Psychologists and other human service workers need to be aware of the many-faceted human potential movement, which to some observers appears to be the wave of the future.

In a complex society such as ours in which natural primary groups cannot provide the support, advice, and assistance that individuals need, it is perhaps essential that there be places where people can talk about their confusions, uncertainties, and decisions. By listening to clients' stories, psychologists and others can become aware of places in the social fabric that need mending and of changes in the way things are organized that might be beneficial. This and the other kinds of intervention we consider in these chapters may well serve this larger social purpose.

SUMMARY

One kind of service that clinical workers are often asked to provide is assistance to clients in examining and planning their lives. It differs from most psychotherapy in emphasizing normal growth processes rather than psychological problems, leaving to clients the full responsibility for their decisions and actions, and utilizing a wide variety of informational sources. Career counseling is the earliest counseling specialty to emerge and is still very much in demand. Developmental counseling has now been extended to include early intervention in the lives of young children to help them find promising channels for growth, the burgeoning *human potential* movement, and even the search for spiritual development now being labeled *transpersonal psychology*.

In efforts of this sort it is essential that good working relationships with clients be established and maintained. Possibilities are explored and discussed, using a variety of appraisal techniques. Information is provided to clarify alternatives and facilitate decisions. Plans are made, monitored, and changed as necessary. Clinicians may use interviews for many purposes, but throughout their course must maintain a sensitivity to clients' feelings as well as thoughts.

Efforts to facilitate the development of children involve the teaching of basic skills necessary for coping with complex environments to be encountered later. Such efforts have increasingly been focused on very young children, especially those whose circumstances are less stimulating than the average, or who are biologically "at risk." The Headstart program is by far the largest and best known, but there have been many others, some of them designed for children in the earliest months of life.

The human potential movement gave rise to numerous growth centers and programs, in which groups of people get together, with or without a formal leader, and attempt through self-expression to stimulate each other to higher levels of consciousness and self-actualization. Such encounter groups differ from one another in many ways, but they all encourage participants to experience their true feelings more deeply and express them more openly. The emerging transpersonal psychology makes extensive use of techniques practiced in mystical religions.

RECOMMENDED READINGS

Holland, J. C., Magoon, T. M., & Spokane, A. R. Counseling psychology: Career interventions, research, and theory. *Annual Review of Psychology*, 1981, 32, 279–305.
　　This chapter summarizes current thinking about career counseling and can serve to bring the reader up to date on available materials, techniques, and research findings. The earlier review by Krumboltz, Becker-Haven, and Burnett (1979) covers research on the replacement of maladaptive responses and the prevention of family and school problems through counseling and training in appropriate skills, as well as research on career decision making.

Tyler, L. E. *The work of the counselor* (3rd ed.). Englewood Cliffs, N.J.: Prentice-Hall, 1969.
　　Although this book is somewhat out of date, it can still serve to introduce students and practicing clinicians to the counseling approach. The principles on which it rests are elaborated in some detail. Separate chapters show how test results and information from various sources can be incorporated in the counseling process.

Gendlin, E. T. Experiential psychotherapy. In R. J. Corsini (Ed.), *Current psychotherapies* (2nd ed.). Itasca, Ill.: Peacock, 1979, pp. 340–373.
　　Gendlin's approach to therapy is existential and experiential; he views anxiety not as sickness, but as avoided possibilities. His therapy involves working with a felt or body sense of one's problems and with authenticity in interactions with others. Gendlin's lay book, Focusing (1978) contains exercises for focusing on feelings and listening. Lichtenstein's chapter entitled "Humanistic Psychotherapy" (1980) particularly attends to client-centered and Gestalt psychotherapies, giving examples and reviewing studies. The rest of the book will also be valuable to the reader as an introduction and critique of behavioral and psychoanalytic therapies and comparative evaluation of them and of the general system of delivery of therapy in the United States. Otto's book *Human Potentialities* (1968) explores a wide variety of ways of increasing experience and self-development. *Turning On* by Gustaitis (1969) is an account of the programs and therapies of the founder of Gestalt therapy, Fritz Perls, and of the Esalen center at its height. For a scholarly contribution to the development of humanistic theory of personality, see Mahrer (1978).

Walsh, R. N., & Vaughan, F. (Eds.). *Beyond ego: Transpersonal dimensions in psychology*. Los Angeles: Tarcher, 1980.
　　Walsh and Vaughan have been some of the most active people in the development of transpersonal psychology. They are both clinicians in background. In this book they have assembled writing from a variety of writers including Maslow, Ram Dass, Caora, and others. Tart's *Transpersonal Psychologies* (1975) also is a good resource for a variety of Eastern and mystical ways of thought as well as a reasoned analysis of traditional scientific versus transpersonal assumptions. Noted psychiatrist Jerome Frank (1977) suggests that communicating about transcendental experiences relates to the difficulty in translating a nonverbal, right-hemisphere experience into words. Corsini's *Handbook of Innovative Psychotherapies* (1981) has several chapters of relevance to

humanistic approaches—e.g., Walsh's chapter entitled "Meditation" and Reynolds's chapters on Morita and Naikan therapy. Shapiro (1980), in a book entitled *Meditation*, reviews the scientific evidence and gives instructions about learning to meditate as well as some of his clinical approach, using it as a self-control strategy in a social learning model.

Finkelstein, P., Wenegrat, B., & Yalom, I. Large group awareness training. *Annual Review of Psychology*, 1982, *33*, 515–540.

The authors note that the large-group awareness training movement had largely supplanted the encounter group as an extension of the human potential movement. These training sessions are put on by commercial groups such as "Lifespring" and "est" (Erhard Seminars Training), usually over a few weekends for the cost of several hundred dollars per person. The nature of these groups is described by the authors, and the scanty amount of evaluation is surveyed. Despite much personal testimony for some of these groups, the authors conclude that most of the results come not from specific training offered, but from effects of expectations and response sets. Reports of psychological harm are nonconclusive.

RESEARCH EXAMPLES

Meadows, M. E. Assessment of college counseling: A follow-up study. *Journal of Counseling Psychology*, 1975, *22*, 463–470.

Some 100 students who had sought counseling at Georgia Tech were compared on a number of criteria seven years later. Groups at the outset did not differ in aptitude, but the noncounseled group was getting significantly better grades and was more involved in campus activities.

The difference in GPA was considerably narrowed by graduation. Three years after graduation, the two groups did not differ in job satisfaction, and there was some evidence (inadequate) of greater job success in the counseled. They had shifted to more appropriate majors (SVIB) and were generally more successful in postcollege than in college life.

Truax, C. B., & Carkhuff, R. R. The experimental manipulation of therapeutic conditions. *Journal of Consulting Psychology*, 1965, *29*, 119–124.

Carl Rogers theorized that the necessary and sufficient conditions for therapeutic change were to be found in a relationship in which the therapist showed unconditional positive regard, accurate empathy, and genuineness. In an unusual experimental test of this theory, Truax and Carkhuff used an ABA design—that is, they arranged for the therapist to spend a certain period using characteristic A in the therapeutic interaction, then change to B for a while, and finally return to the A condition with the client. Over the three periods, observers made ratings of the amount of self-exploration which the client did. Truax and Carkhuff had the therapist, during the first A period, offer high levels of unconditional positive regard, empathy, and genuineness for 20 minutes. Then a knock on the door would interrupt the therapist, who would step out for a minute to receive a message. Coming back, the therapist would change to condition B, during which genuineness was maintained but the other characteristics were not emphasized. After another 20 minutes there would be another knock on the door and a message, to which the therapist would respond "I'm relieved to hear that." For the last 20 minutes, the therapist would resume the high level of all three conditions. This article reports the findings with three subjects and demonstrates that the clients' levels of self-exploration definitely dropped during the middle phase and went back up when condition A was restored. Truax and Mitchell (1971) have presented a much more extensive review of research on the effect of therapist characteristics on therapy outcome, much of it supporting the Rogerian theory. Other reviewers (e.g., Parloff, Waskow, & Wolfe, 1978) have been less optimistic about the theory.

DiNardo, P. A., & Raymond, J. N. Locus of control and attention during meditation. *Journal of Consulting and Clinical Psychology,* 1979, *47,* 1136–1137.

Locus of control investigations (Rotter, 1966) have indicated that people differ in the degree to which they ascribe controls to internal or to external factors. The researchers in this study reasoned that since a meditation task involves focused attention, internals would show greater ability to maintain attention.

Twenty undergraduates completed the locus of control scale and then were trained to meditate. In the experiment they were alternated between meditating on an actual stimulus—a candle flame—and an imagined one—the visualization of a candle flame. Subjects were asked to record intrusive thoughts by pressing a button on a counter.

The sample of subjects was split at the median locus of control score, externals being the upper half and internals the lower half. Results showed that, as hypothesized, the internals showed significantly fewer intrusions than did externals. The work suggests a useful way of assessing attentional control and relating meditational capability to a well-studied personality variable.

11 WORKING WITH COUPLES AND FAMILIES:
Marital and Family Therapies

As Chapter 1 made clear, until quite recently clinical psychology and other helping disciplines have shown little concern for the family as a separate system in its own right. To start our chapter we will look briefly at current tasks and dilemmas of the family and why clinicians find such fundamental interpersonal relations to be very interesting challenges. Although family work has been in focus for only a relatively short time, substantial specialization has already occurred. Later in the chapter we will consider three aspects: Couple therapy, alternately titled *marriage counseling;* behavioral and structural approaches to family therapy; and the special areas of work with child-abusing families, incestuous families, and proceedings for termination of parental rights.

CURRENT TASKS AND DILEMMAS OF THE FAMILY

Like other living things, the family continues to evolve. Books such as Murstein's (1974) *Love, Sex, and Marriage through the Ages* or Bell and Vogel's (1968) *A Modern Introduction to the Family* give a useful synthesis of historical evolution of the family. They challenge us to remember that the family's task differs by era, culture, and social and economic position. Some families have had the task of producing males fit to rule, or at least wily enough to retain power. Others have existed to produce a maximum number of new adherents for a religious faith, high-quality soldiers for wars, slaves for plantations, sons to light funeral pyres, workers for family farms, or progeny to care for parents in old age. The family, as a living system, occupies the uncertain terrain between the goals of the larger social system and the goals of the individual family members. At the same time it possesses goals for its own comfort, security, and development. Often, however, community, family, and individual goals differ. This is when clinical psychology has contributions to make.

A book written not many years ago might have given an account of typical family tasks and dilemmas as follows: In high school and perhaps in college, people learn the approved patterns for meeting and getting acquainted which, after graduation and after the male starts his first job, result in marriage. Just as mates, in their adolescence, work on emancipation and individuation, after marriage their psychological task is to create a unique couplehood. Each mate draws on his or her experience—and that normally means that they think of the family they are creating in terms of their family of origin. Familiar assertions, sometimes the source of substantial conflict, arise, such as "That's how my family celebrated Christmas and that's how we want it, too," or "I always swore I would do the opposite of what my family did once I had my own." Next, of course, rules regarding the status and participation of the in-laws and parents must be made. Shall the husband permit his father-in-law to donate large gifts so that his daughter can live as she did before marriage? Here again, separation and individuation, this time of the couplehood, presents the major developmental task.

The arrival of children forces a psychological crisis. The couple's mobility, free time, finances, and sleeping patterns are drastically altered, but so are the questions of basic identity and role relations. The task now is to be parent, as well as mate and as individual. Many couples find that the blissful closeness they enjoyed in early years undergoes a sudden disruption. After a period of settling down, the couple may face other kinds of predictable crises, such as household moves, children's entrance into school, job layoffs, or hospitalizations. After about two decades, the children have emancipation struggles of their own, choosing various ways to leave their family of origin, setting up homes of their own, and producing grandchildren for their parents. About this time the original couple must confront the crises of death of their own parents, in many ways another step in the lifelong emancipation and individuation process, and finally their own physical decline and imminent death. Thus the cycle of one family closes, while others have started.

Although there is nothing especially misleading about our quick sketch, we find that as we move through the last part of the twentieth century, much more diversity and new, sometimes alarming patterns begin to emerge. The mores of Western culture affecting the family and the raising of children have shown accelerating rates of change. Many of the changes do not appear to bode well for the psychological state of the family. Increases in rates of divorce, pregnant adolescents, single parents, unmarried parents, and blended families may well be related to the increasing rates of reported child abuse and incest. (However, the greater frequencies may arise partly from more accurate reporting of such activities.) Additionally families or parents find themselves in dilemmas about fulfillment. To whom *does* a single parent turn for nurturance and intimacy? What skills are needed to avoid the depression and instability of unsatisfactory serial liaisons?

Just having a mate, of course, doesn't solve these problems either. The two people forming the couple progress toward maturity at different rates. Sometimes one becomes wrapped up in career issues at a time when the other focuses more on companionship. Some careers—for example, law enforcement—seem especially hard on family life. In such circumstances husband and wife may engage in external love affairs, which may signify that their relationship is temporarily out of phase or that it needs to enter a new era for reexamining old assumptions. The question of closeness to acquaintances of the opposite sex involves many thorny issues, as this example suggests:

> The prominent lawyer and his wife settled into their chairs at the psychologist's office. Although he didn't really want to, Dr. Furness reflected that it took him a year to earn what this man earned in two months. Few in the community knew, it turned out, but the lawyer was living in a newly purchased lakeside condominium with his mistress while his wife and children still occupied the grand

family home. He and his wife had met in college; she supported him through law school, and for six or eight years afterward their lives were reasonably happy. He had a couple of affairs—both, he said, quite casual—and she started working again as the children became older. Resentments apparently smoldered. He felt she just wasn't interesting any more, and she felt that he had become ashamed of her humble beginnings and lower level of education. He said, "I'm not sure I want to go back, but I promised her I'd come to these sessions to find out if there's anything left. Tell me, Doctor, is there?" Dr. Furness knew he was being challenged; he also knew there was a great deal more for the couple to learn about each other before a final decision would be made.

Recent years have seen the emergence of another source of stress on families, the more overt emergence of homosexual relationships. Joan is an example of one such person who came in seeking help.

Always shy and convinced of her unattractiveness as a child, Joan had become pregnant at 16, and although the boy disappeared, as her father predicted, she decided to quit school and raise the infant. She married another dropout who had seemed pleasant at first, but he spent her welfare money and began to beat her when he was drunk. After two more informal liaisons, both amazingly similar in their exploitive violence, Joan moved in with Rae. In an atmosphere free of violence and drunkenness, she was introduced to lesbianism. Rae was active in a branch of the women's movement, and it provided Joan with a cause and a substantial support network. But there was no father figure for her son, Richard, who was by now eight. "I'm not leaving the movement," she explained to the psychologist. "It's been the only place I've had dignity, but Richard . . . he's a bit *too* shy . . . doesn't play with other children . . . doesn't know what men are like . . . What can I do for him?"

In short, changes in our culture and in the way individuals conduct themselves have added immensely to the tasks and dilemmas facing marriage (or mating) and families in recent years. The rapid changes make it difficult to rely on systematic knowledge, but the development of assessment and intervention techniques continues apace. First we will review work with couples.

COUPLE THERAPY— MARRIAGE COUNSELING

Assessment

Although many, perhaps most, couple therapists or marriage counselors assess their client couples informally—that is, without formalized assessment tools—clinical psychology does offer a growing range of possibilities for more uniform and systematic assessment. The available tools fall into three rough classifications: marital surveys, interpersonal measures, and measures of couplehood functioning. We will discuss each in turn.

The marital survey, usually a questionnaire form, provides an inventory of history and present functioning. Such devices are strong only when their authors have been comprehensive and have used a consistent theoretical perspective. Typically the therapist evaluates such surveys simply by comparison; they normally do not yield quantified results that can be placed on a known statistical distribution. But good questionnaires can be sensitive to the idea that couplehood evolves. They can help a clinician achieve the broader perspective of developmental milestones, phases, and crises.

Interpersonal measures—that is, instruments measuring how people get along with others or how they affect others—are occasionally used with couples; one which has commendable brevity and flexibility is the Interpersonal Checklist (ICL) by LaForge and Suczek (Clark & Taulbee, 1981). It has a list of terms for all manner of relations with others, such as "tends to dominate" and "often expresses affection." Typically a couple may be asked to fill out two such checklists: one for the presently perceived reality ("How does your mate seem to you now?") and one for perceived need ("Ideally how would your mate be?").

Special inventories form a third type of assessment device. They seek to measure or assess specifics of couplehood; for example, which different style of relating to each other does a couple have, or how mature is each person's regard for the other? A final type of measure involves *observing couples* perform a game, task, or other interaction and comparing their performance against that of others. Such procedures have great strength in producing specific analyses but, of course, at the expense of breadth. The quantified

Figure 11-1 Couple and therapist. (Ken Karp)

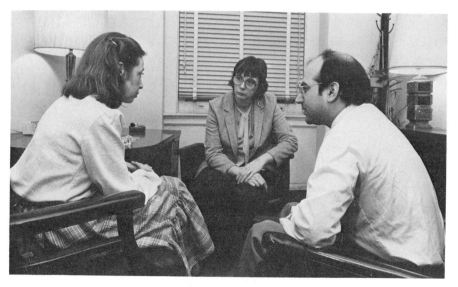

observation of behavior (e.g., how many approvals per minute, how often does Joe interrupt his wife?) provides opportunities for research as well as graphic demonstrations of how they communicate, especially if they witness themselves on videotape. Assessment and feedback form important central methods for behavioral approaches in work with couples (Stuart, 1972). Weiss and Margolin (1977) review ways of specifying problematic marital interaction.

Intervention with Couples

We stressed in Chapter 3 that identifying the best system for intervention is an early crucial decision. Sometimes couples who come for help are best assisted by intervening in biological or personal systems. For example, a wife's concern over her husband's "depression and lack of energy" may stem from a physical problem rather than from any marital problem. We also need to be aware that some clinicians continue to treat couples as if they were only two separate individuals and did not represent a system of their own. Such approaches are actually individual therapy, usually undertaken separately or sequentially with each partner. Several writers have suggested that doing psychotherapy with one spouse may actually facilitate the breakdown of the marital relationship.

The couple system normally represents adults who are in the "family of generation" phase of their lives, who do breadwinning, who have an approved sexual relationship of great importance, and who normally lead or set standards for work, recreation, self-esteem roles, and relations with the outside world. The couple system represents the core of the family system, as shown in Figure 11–2.

Figure 11-2   Locating the couple in a family.

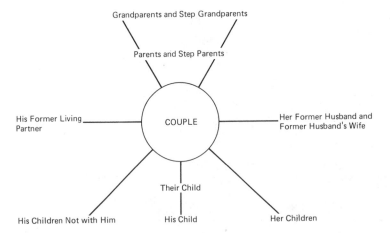

In any discussion of couple and family therapy, it is worth noting that frequently one person will want to come while the other or others resist. The naive therapist often falls into the trap of assuming that the requester is "good" and "open" and the resister "bad" or "uncaring." More experienced therapists are cautious. Sometimes one spouse seeks couple therapy or marriage counseling as one more maneuver in a series of manipulative or controlling ploys. A wife, for instance, may resist involvement because she knows that her husband will try to pull the therapist into a position of alliance or blame and that she will face the remark, "Dr. Clarke agrees with me, dear. If you didn't act like your mother acts, we'd simply be better off."

It is by no means impossible to involve a reluctant spouse. Generally the therapist must communicate directly to that spouse—not using the "willing" one as a message carrier—and let her or him know that the "willing" one is not in charge of judgment or of therapy. Sometimes only one spouse will come, however, and intervention must then focus on that spouse's capacity for coping, changing, and decision making.

Some marriage counselors have said that prime problems with couples occur in three areas: money, sex, and in-laws. That distinction can be useful if we think of money as representing the broad area of role division and resource allocation; sex, issues of closeness and emotional nurturance; and in-laws, issues of dependency and emancipation.

We can identify three rather distinct approaches to working with couples—and must stress that they rarely occur in pure form: approaches promoting development and awareness, approaches promoting communication and the clarification of roles, and approaches designed to change behavior.

The *developmental approaches* take many forms. The therapist attempts to help the two persons to share each other's perspective and to grasp the concept that their union is an evolving, changing entity which may have reached the end of one of its phases and be shifting to another.

> The Johnsons, for example, found themselves in one common variant of that situation. After ten years of marriage, a marriage which had all of the small-town cheerleader–football hero backdrop, both were depressed. Suzy complained tearfully that she was working herself to the bone keeping an immaculate house, getting the children to ballet, flute, and religious lessons, cooking special food for Jim, gardening, and "trying to make it so he'll want to come home—so we'll have what we used to have." Jim was embarrassed. He didn't like counseling, didn't like Suzy's energetic perfection, wasn't sure of his professional direction, and felt acutely guilty about all of these areas. "I'm supposed to like it, and I don't. She's perfect, and I'm a failure." Their therapist helped them to explore their expectations and their development. Using drawings, questions, stories each of them told, and expectations they revealed, the psychologist helped the Johnsons to realize that they had established a marriage of which they *thought* their parents and community would approve and that they did things which they *thought* the other would enjoy. First, she explained that they had reached the end of a phase in which covert assumptions were useful, such as guessing "how it's

supposed to be," and holding in inner distress. Next, couple therapy focused on helping them to design their next phase. The therapist tried to help them to accept the need for continued evolution and change in the marriage and for different phases and stages in their personal growth. Using role playing she helped them to practice more direct communication patterns, especially in the area of expressing personal wants and needs.

Communications approaches involve formulating, sending, receiving, and decoding messages. Although the verbal mode remains primary, the communications therapists have sensitized us to other types of messages, such as the shaking head or the frown, and to the notion of congruity or incongruity of simultaneous messages. Satir (cited in Bandler, Grinder, & Satir, 1976) has formulated a useful way of thinking about communication in therapy with a couple (and a family). Her approach lets the therapist make diagnostic inferences and suggests immediately some basic directions for restorative therapy.

Communications therapists such as Bandler, Grinder, and Satir (1976) are especially alert for occurrences of two pathologic patterns: *Mind reading* involves one-sided presumptions (e.g., "I know Marcy's depending on me" or "I know you want me to do something else") which have the effect of stopping accurate communication and causing pain. *Calibrated communication loops* involve two-sided presumptions in which the sender and receiver have built a loop, or sequence of messages, which they exchange with inevitable misunderstanding and hurt. Therapy takes the basic form of challenging assumptions in detail so that the sender can become aware of what he or she is actually sending and the receiver can reply to what is sent rather than to what he or she is afraid might have been sent.

The third kind of couple therapy is the *behavioral approach*. There are two basic types: the *quid pro quo* (this for that), or contracting, styles and the *learning theory*, or reinforcement-based, procedures. Lederer and Jackson (1968) and Sager (1976) are two proponents of the contracting approach. Sager, for instance, asks partners to consider a lengthy, encompassing list of categories and then asks each one to write down a statement. "Include what you want and what you will give in exchange, and what, if any, problems these items cause between you." (p. 320). The contracting approach, like the behavior analysis approach next discussed, involves stretching a simple notion to cover a wide variety of complex situations—and that demands a high level of therapist training.

Behavioral interventions based on learning theory involve applying the standard notions of behavioral observation or counting to discover what problem behaviors occur, and at what rates, then deciding with the clients which behaviors should be the targets for change, and finally, rearranging the reinforcement contingencies so that the hurtful or unconstructive behaviors are decreased and the frequency of desired areas is increased. We will give greater detail about learning theory and behavioral approaches when we take up their application to family intervention in a later section.

FAMILY THERAPIES

Family therapy burst on the scene almost as a great tidal wave. To be sure, the pioneer Nathan Ackerman had said in 1958 in his *Psychodynamics of Family Life* that the presenting patient could be seen as the emissary of a sick family, and workers such as John Bell, Haley, and Satir had long advocated a family perspective. However, it was the mid-1970s before the community of professionals began to take family perspectives and therapies seriously, and there occurrred a great outpouring of books and articles along with numerous workshops and a number of specialized family therapy training programs.

Although we cannot be certain, several factors seem to account for the rapid rise of family therapy. First, the traditional assumption of psychodynamic workers that behavior is the surface manifestation of the working of the individual's inner psyche had resulted not in new, innovative, and cost-effective programs, but in an orthodoxy—frequently described as elitist—which has little supporting research. At the same time awareness of general system concepts (which we discussed in Chapter 2) made people believe that a malfunctioning family could be both a cause and sustainer of problem behavior. Finally, increasing numbers of children with psychological problems made it clear that parents must be involved if their behavior was to be changed.

Indications
and Contraindications
for Family Therapy

> "Doctor, our nine-year-old, Terry, misbehaves at home and at school. We'd like you to see him for therapy. . . . I'll pick him up after you've seen him. What he needs to be told is that his mother is dead, but his stepmother *does* love him and he simply has to get on with his schoolwork. The marriage? Well, it's true the stepmother and I have been wondering about divorce and we're in counseling, but that's just between us as parents. When can I bring Terry in to see you?"

Any alert human service worker would immediately suspect this father's request. The likelihood is great that this family is a profoundly disturbed entity, each of whose members is deeply affected. Why do the problems seem artificially separated? And why does this father need the therapist to give messages to his child? If the child has lost one parent, isn't it likely that the prospect of losing another will be profoundly disturbing? These and a host of other questions can only be answered by assessing how this family deals with itself as a unit.

> "Doctor, we have an autistic child and we've been told that the kind of relationships my husband and I had with each other and the kind of early relations we formed with our child all contained an unconscious desire to reject him and that's why he's autistic. We'd like to be seen for family therapy so we can make up for those early problems and help our boy become normal."

Here the request for family therapy has unrealistic expectations but of a different kind. Of course, it would be useful to have the couple meet so the therapist could explain that the idea of the child being damaged to the point of severe autism by some unconscious desires in the parents is an old notion, used in a period before evidence supported the current thinking about organic causes for autism. Some couple work may also well be in order, focusing on how the parents have coped with the ensuing disappointment of bearing a handicapped child and on how they plan to manage to have lives of their own.

It should be clear, however, that what people actually ask for rarely indicates whether family therapy is needed. The first question should be "To what extent does the presenting issue reflect malfunction within the family system?" Clinicians with a feel for that question tend to include issues which might at first not seem related to the family system. Minuchin (1974) for example, has reported in detail on successful family therapy where an asthmatic child stimulates the family to seek help. His work has shown that medical symptoms can persist because they are embedded in the family system. In Chapter 2 the question was posed about the system level at which to intervene. For some psychosomatic children, the family system rather than the biological system is the target for intervention.

Family therapy should not be used where it shows no reasonable promise of success or, of course, where it may do harm. Clinicians often feel that when an adolescent is in the process of emancipating himself or herself, goals for family therapy must be cautiously chosen in order to safeguard the youth's growing sense that he or she is legitimately progressing toward independence and responsibility, but they are divided on the advisability of family therapy if the family has a prepsychotic or borderline member. Although the data are far from clear, the first wave of enthusiasm about family therapy for almost everything has passed, and a climate of greater selectivity now prevails.

An Example of Family Therapy

In a book of this length, capturing the flavor of any course of therapy becomes difficult. The task is like that of a car driver who faces the immediate bumps in the road while constantly remembering larger-scale features such as mountain ranges, passes, and valleys. In choosing an excerpt from the case book by

Papp (1977), we have tried to convey the flavor of the therapist negotiating the bumps in the road while still keeping an eye firmly on more distant goals.

In this excerpt the therapist, Harry Aponte, is meeting with a mother and her three sons, the last three children of a large family and the last three at home. Notice Aponte's acute awareness of the family structure and whether it will let him in. Notice also that the major outcome is older brother Bruce's corrective presence in the family structure, not prolonged therapy for the identified patient.

> The family was sitting clockwise: the oldest son, Raymond, mother, an empty chair, Stanley and Daniel. I addressed the mother first. She had been the principal voice of the family's objection to being there. By asking her to introduce her children, I asked her permission to speak to them. In the midst of our tug of war, I was trying to gain her acceptance by acknowledging her power and position. After she introduced them I addressed the oldest son, Raymond. He was sitting immediately to her right, was conspicuously mirroring her attitude of disdain and impassiveness. I wanted to acknowledge Raymond's position as the oldest. I would proceed to the younger ones only after having touched base with him. The gesture of deference to Raymond reflected a very preliminary hypothesis that was later borne out that the protection of the family's borders against outside intruders in the present context was, in a special way, this son's function.

MRS. J.:	This is Raymond, Stanley and Daniel (she points to each).
THERAPIST:	Okay . . . how old are you, Raymond?
RAYMOND:	Seventeen.
THERAPIST:	You're seventeen. You're at home?
RAYMOND:	Uh-huh.
THERAPIST:	And Stanley, you're eleven, right?
MRS. J.:	Will be in May.
THERAPIST:	Will be in May? (when turning to Daniel)
DANIEL:	Fourteen.

Mrs. Jeffrey gave me an opening when she accused Raymond of teasing Stanley. I snatched the opportunity to move toward Raymond. It was a chance to connect with Raymond and approach Mrs. Jeffrey's protectiveness through Raymond. I moved carefully as we were all quite tense and tried to make bridges to Raymond—to his work, school, and other interests.

THERAPIST:	What's your name again?
RAYMOND:	Raymond.
THERAPIST:	Raymond? I would think you'd be the one who'd take care of him.
MRS. J.:	Uh-uh (indicating no).
RAYMOND:	What do you mean by take care of him?
THERAPIST:	Well, you are the oldest brother. I would expect that you would be the one that he would listen to.
RAYMOND:	(laughing) . . . listen . . .
THERAPIST:	They don't listen to you?
MRS. J.:	No, they don't.

(Therapist asks Raymond about his school, his work and his interests. Raymond's interest in boxing emerges . . .)

THERAPIST: Have you been in any kind of amateur bouts or are you just training?
RAYMOND: Just training.
THERAPIST: Uh, huh . . . how much do you weigh?
RAYMOND: About 195 . . . light heavyweight.
THERAPIST: Oh, no . . . you would be a heavyweight.
RAYMOND: Light heavyweight.
THERAPIST: Light heavyweight.

Raymond and I, here, find ground on which we can both meet and compete. I, too, am interested in boxing and we dispute each other about whether or not he is a light heavyweight (the light heavyweight limit is 175 pounds). I engage him on this issue. I want him to like me and so we will continue to talk about boxing, but, I want him to respect me, so I am reluctant to back down in our disagreement. This discussion is a metaphor of the struggle between Raymond and myself as I believe he attempts to protect the family. If I can gain ground with Raymond the odds improve to win the family, but while I try to join him, I must not shrink from him. If I do, I will lose status in my own eyes and possibly his. If I do not feel in control of the situation, I will become inhibited. The tension in me heightens at this point. I struggle between being accommodating and striking back. Being aware of that helped. Did he feel similarly? . . .

THERAPIST: Yeah, that's the camera (addressing Stanley and Daniel who are distracted by the moving video camera) . . . Daniel, where do you go to school?
DANIEL: Collins Junior High.
THERAPIST: Collins? What grade are you in now?
DANIEL: Eighth.
THERAPIST: You are in the eighth grade? Are you doing alright in school? Do you have any problems in school?
DANIEL: I got no problems.
THERAPIST: You got no problems in school or at home or any place else . . . the only one who has problems is him (pointing to Stanley) . . . are you saying yes or no? I said the only one who has problems is Stanley.
DANIEL: I don't know.
THERAPIST: Oh, you don't know anything about it. Okay, well . . . 'cause your mother was saying that Stanley had some kids picking on him in the neighborhood. You don't know anything about that?
DANIEL: I don't consider that a problem. I mean, if they're going to pick on him and he don't stop them from picking on him . . . what else you gonna do.

I had hoped that the contact that I had with Raymond would allow me to reach Stanley through Daniel. But, I was getting too close to Stanley and Raymond cut off my move. Tension was up again.

RAYMOND: I mean, I don't know why they send him to a psychiatrist!
THERAPIST: Stanley, your brother said it's not a problem. You should be able to take care of it yourself.

Raymond was staring right at me, challenging me. I tightened up, but attempted to deflect his jab and make it an issue between Stanley and me.

STANLEY: How?
THERAPIST: Right?
STANLEY: Uh, huh.
THERAPIST: Is it a problem?
STANLEY: Yeah.

I had been leaning forward in my chair and for the first time sat back with some feeling of relief as I finally got Stanley to acknowledge a problem. Raymond countered quickly.

THERAPIST: It is a problem . . . how is it a problem?
STANLEY: (barely audible) They just keep bothering me.
THERAPIST: What?
STANLEY: They just keep bothering me.
RAYMOND: He's at an early age now, I mean he don't know how to just ignore it and walk away from it . . . he can't do that at the moment.
THERAPIST: (to Stanley) He says you should ignore it and walk away.
STANLEY: What happens is they come back.
THERAPIST: Raymond, he says they come back . . . what should he do?
RAYMOND: Are you trying to teach us how to talk, how to communicate . . . what we should do at home, or what?

Raymond is too clever. He saw through my strategy and undid it. I felt caught but not defeated. I had already breached the family's defenses and did not experience myself as a total outsider as before. I leaned forward again in my chair and moved in with more confidence.

By the end of the interview, Mrs. Jeffrey acknowledged the need for an older male to help wean Stanley away from her but she suggested Bruce, another son, who was living outside the home. Daniel and Stanley volunteered agreement with the mother about the desirability of Bruce, who had a good government job and was a popular athlete in the neighborhood basketball league. All three viewed Bruce as reliable and available. (H. Aponte, pp. 104–111 in P. Papp (Ed.), Family therapy: Full length case studies. Copyright © 1977 by Gardner Press. Used by permission.)

Assessment of Families

The therapist in the preceding example did not use formalized paper-and-pencil or counting assessment techniques. Neither the structural nor the communications approaches really lend themselves to an "assess first, then treat" sequence. For them, assessment and intervention occur simultaneously. Every therapist must understand a family's natural history, the who-married-whom-when-and-who-begat-whom-when questions, especially because the increasing fluidity and informality of many families makes the answers less and less obvious. Although assessment of families is fairly new, some work is promising.

There have been few systematic attempts to generate assessment devices that follow psychometric principles—that is, that produce similar results for each family and have known standards of reliability and validity. One instrument which does deserve mention is the Family Environment Scale by Moos and Moos (1981). The FES is one of several scales by Moos (1975) that measure particular social climates. It consists of 90 items comprising three relationship scales (cohesiveness, expressiveness, conflict), five personal development scales (independence, achievement orientation, intellectual orientation, active recreational orientation, moral-religious emphasis), and two system maintenance scales (organization, control). The profiles for each family member can be drawn on the same profile sheet, allowing the clinician to see who agrees and disagrees with whom in which particular areas of family life. Findings from this and other family reports can be used to supplement the family therapist's working image. Behavioral and structural workers build those images differently, and we will examine each in turn.

BOX 11-1 *PERCEPTIONS OF ENVIRONMENTS*

One question which comes up in family therapy is whether family members see their living situation and other situations in the same way. Whether the perceptions of the environment are the same or different, a therapist can make use of them in discussions with the family and in bringing out areas of living on which they might work together. The following charts are taken from a case of an adolescent girl (which was briefly presented as Case I at the beginning of Chapter 6) reported by Moos and Fuhr (1982, pp. 115–116). The first chart shows the scores on the Family Environment Scale of the 15-year-old girl and the average of her parents' scores, both plotted by using the norms derived from giving the FES to 1125 families. There is pretty close agreement on the conditions in the family with the exception that the girl reports much less cohesion and more conflict than the parents do; they all agree that the family is low on recreational activities.

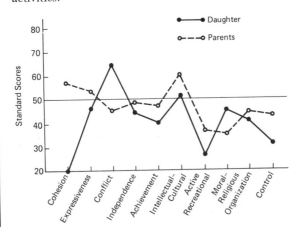

The same sort of assessment procedure can be applied to other environments. Moos and Fuhr in this case asked the adolescent girl to report how she perceived her school environment on the Classroom Environment Scale. This time they asked her to answer the test twice—once for the actual situation and secondly for her ideal or preferred classroom. The results are presented in the second chart plotted on norms for 382 classrooms. There are many discrepancies, especially in the areas of affiliation with peers, involvement, classroom order, and innovation. Such results could be used for discussions with the girl and with school people.

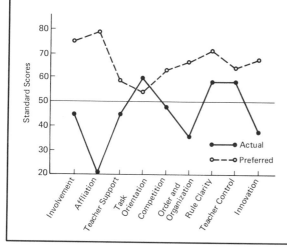

Behavioral Family Therapy

Behavioral observation forms the basis of perhaps the most thoroughly developed approach to family assessment. To gather such data, an observer who has been trained to a high reliability in watching behavior and coding it may enter a home each evening for a week and encode behavior. The observer has committed to memory a variety of codes and their definitions in order to be able to summarize behavior in code form with great accuracy and reliability. The observer may, for instance, record in the Atkinson home:

EVENT	OBSERVER CODES
Mrs. A. asks John to sit down at the table	CM (command)
John does not do as asked	CM-NC (noncompliance)
Mrs. A ignores the noncompliance	CM-NC-IG (ignores)
Mrs. A begins verbal remonstrance	TA (talk)
John begins back talk	TA-TA
There are more such exchanges	TA-TA
Finally John says insulting words	HU (humiliate)
Mother slaps him	HU-PN (phys. negative)
John yells	HU-PN-YE (yell)
(Codes after Jones, Reid, & Patterson, 1975)	

Several advantages of this type of approach become clear: The resulting quantified record that may indicate that the stated problem differs from the observed one—or even that the presented child is not the most deviant in the family. Actual rates of events can be established—for example, average noncompliances per minute or yells per minute—and can be compared with data on normal families. Furthermore, the system produces sequences or chains of typical behavior so that therapists can answer questions about the consequences that keep a behavior going or the antecedent conditions that seem to initiate it. Finally, it makes sense to parents and is relatively easy for them to learn and use. Although coding techniques have been developed by researchers on behavior modification through changing reinforcement contingencies, they are not *necessarily* tied to this or any other particular theory.

One possible disadvantage is that in the process of reducing the complicated outpouring of a family's behavior to an understandable record, some nonobservable factors may be missed. It makes a tremendous difference, for instance, if the youngest child in a family is the offspring of the teenage "sister" or if the wife is the recent exwife of her husband's older brother. The cost of furnishing a trained observer (training, transportation, and supervision, as well as pay) also constitutes a deterrent to the use of this technique.

Behavioral assessment techniques produce data revealing the rates of occurrence of particular behaviors and the sequences in which the behaviors occur. Therapists use the data to attack questions such as "What is maintaining the undesired behavior?" and "What is keeping desirable behavior from taking its place?" Take, for example, the case of Sandra and Bob and their five-year-old son, George. Sandra complains about George's behavior, describing how he yells and howls at the table until she allows him to eat his dessert and then wanders away from the table. She is hurt, depressed, and baffled. A behavioral analysis might go along these lines: The child emits a noxious, deviant behavior and is rewarded for doing so by his mother who uses a food reinforcer, dessert, for the purpose. We could say that the mother is teaching the unwanted behavior, using a food reward. At the same time the child stops being noxious when the mother complies with his demands. We could say that the child is teaching the mother to comply with his demands, using shutting off of punishment as a reward. This little vignette illustrates two most important principles in behavioral approaches: First, learning is *reciprocal*. If a parent trains a child, the parent is at the same time being trained by the child. Second, behavior may be seen as *inadvertent* rather than as the result of sinister forces seeping out of the id or some other source. Most people who have trouble training children do not mean them harm. The behavioral approach has the advantage of not questioning motives or creating guilt.

Typically in social learning therapy parents receive detailed and careful training in the principles and procedures. Often this kind of training occurs over several meetings of a group of parents using a text such as Patterson's (1971) *Living with Children.* After they understand the principles, parents work with a therapist to pick a target for change and then begin to carry out new routines to produce the change.

In Sandra and Bob's case they may have two programs for George: first, to reinforce him with praise when he eats, a behavior incompatible with screaming and yelling; and second, to transplant him briefly to a "time out from social interaction" area, such as a small uninteresting room, every time he emits the noxious behavior. They keep records of events and times and are contacted by phone every few days. Therapists monitor progress by graphing such things as the number of screaming episodes per meal and the number of positive statements Sandra and Bob make to George each meal. After a while if George's behavior improves sufficiently, another goal may be set, such as helping Sandra and Bob to increase the frequency of pleasant events in their own lives. The therapist will help Sandra and Bob to learn new ways of understanding behavior, to actually behave differently, and to report on the data they have agreed to collect. Good results are frequently obtained with these methods, but they are not always lasting, especially when older children are involved.

Structural Family Therapy

We mentioned earlier that structural family therapists use no formalized testing in assessment; they do, however, have an increasingly popular set of concepts for conceptualizing families. Systems theorists, thinking in terms of boundaries, inputs and outputs, and subsystems, will feel at home with this view.

Roles in the family are maintained by two sets of givens: the universal or cultural constraints and the idiosyncratic mutual expectations and historic patterns of the particular family. Each family has subsystems arising from interactions of the spouses (assuming two parents), the parents with children, the siblings, and, of course, others, such as children from either spouse's first marriage, or the wife's premarital or postmarital children. Minuchin (1974) stresses that the type of boundary that the subsystems have relates to the kind of involvement that the subsystems have with each other:

BOUNDARY	INVOLVEMENT
Rigid	Disengaged (distant, separated)
Clear	Normal (conventional role interactions)
Diffuse	Enmeshed (overconcerned, overinvolved)

In structural family therapy, the therapist often functions as a boundary redesigner, clarifying and strengthening diffuse boundaries and opening rigid ones. Besides examining the condition of the boundaries of family and its subsystems, Minuchin (1974) looks to see how the subsystems are doing their various jobs.

The *spouse subsystem* must handle the differences between spouses. It should permit occasional giving in without giving up and should bring out the best in each person. It may have potentially pathological patterns, such as strong good parent protects weak bad child or various forms of mutual rescue games. The *parental subsystem* must have a boundary that allows a child to relate to both parents, without interfering in the spouse subsystem. It should provide nurturance, protection, guidance, and control for the children and must be able to withstand their rejecting and attacking behavior which is essential if children are to become individuated. The *sibling subsystem* should provide a laboratory for experimenting with and for learning peer relations, as well as interpersonal styles and strategies.

Pathology can be observed in many families, but Minuchin (1974) believes that much of what looks like pathology is the stress of readjustment to new structure, of accommodation to change. He reserves the pathology level for those few families who, in the face of stress, increase the rigidity of their boundaries and resist any exploration of alternatives.

Families do not come to therapy with their structure mapped out. The mapping process does not involve asking questions as much as it involves actually trying out various tasks, exercises, or therapist-imposed restrictions (Minuchin calls them *probes*) to see how the system actually reacts. Probes to investigate family structure are not prescribed or standardized but are made up by the therapist to test hunches and observations. An example of a frequently useful probe is "No one is to speak for anyone else, and no one is to guess anyone else's thoughts or feelings." Other probes may involve asking for particular separations or pairings and assessing what the effects are on the family structure.

In brief, to change a family the therapist joins the family in a position of leadership, reveals its structure, and then tries to create circumstances to transform that structure. Minuchin (1974) believes that patients change psychologically in three ways: First, they are challenged in their perception of reality; second, they are given alternative possibilities that make sense to them; and third, once they have tried out some alternative transaction patterns, they become aware of new relationships which are self-reinforcing.

There is a wide variety of ways to approach the restructuring of a family. For example, the therapist may do the following:

Have the family actually live out its transactional patterns by having them enact problem situations, answer questions aimed at the therapist, or react to geographical shifting around in the room.

Mark boundaries, by perhaps sending an enmeshed parent behind a one-way mirror or by emphasizing and legitimizing differences.

Escalate stress by temporarily joining an alliance or coalition, blocking usual patterns that the family uses, or helping an implicit conflict to develop.

Assign tasks, perhaps asking a dependent husband to buy his own clothing taking only his own tastes into account. The nagging wife is asked to continue and even exaggerate her criticism of the husband because he needs to help her by challenging her irrational authority.

Utilize symptoms, perhaps exaggerating a symptom—for example, telling a child, "I want to see if you are skillful enough to steal from your father," thus mobilizing the father's parental controlling functions, or deemphasizing a symptom by relabeling it to change its effect.

Minuchin and Fishman (1981) offer a useful book that elaborates on and gives examples of the techniques of structural family therapy.

Evaluation of Family Therapy

Family therapy is an attractive activity, enjoying a crest of popularity. Furthermore, the logic that something can be wrong with a family or with a couple compels us to think that working with the problem system rather than with the individuals involved makes good sense. But because psychology always faces the task of testing apparent good sense against actual data, we must ask about the state of outcome research in couple and family therapy. Unfortunately outcome studies are very scarce and are usually accompanied by the usual platitudes about complexity and the need for more studies.

The problems of outcome research on family and couple therapy are like those confronted in the evaluation of individual psychotherapy: first, the need for matched controls to prove that the procedures are better than no in-

Figure 11-3 Working with the single parent family is increasingly important.

tervention or simple attention; and second, the difficulties of specifying exactly what the problems of the presenting patient, the characteristics of the therapist, and the type of therapy are. In work with families the type of couple or family also needs to be clearly specified.

It comes as no surprise, then, that DeWitt (1978) located a substantial number of studies but had trouble drawing clear conclusions because of their variability in subjects, procedures, and design. She concluded that full-family approaches are used most often with families in which a child or adolescent is manifesting disordered or delinquent behavior and perhaps next most often with families in which a child or adolescent is schizophrenic. The clear majority of treatment falls either into durations of one to three months (1 to 12 sessions) or three to six (13 to 24 sessions). DeWitt estimated the general success rate of conjoint family therapy was 72 percent if one included those called "slight improvement" and 64 percent without such cases. She concluded these results compared favorably with the figure of 65 percent reported by Bergin (1971) for individual treatment of adults.

Gurman and Kniskern (1978) have provided one of the most comprehensive reviews of the entire field of research on family and marital therapy. These authors have examined a huge number of studies which differ in many crucial dimensions, such as "Who is the IP (identified patient)?" "What was the setting?" "What kind of therapy?" "How long was it?" and have synthesized an important overview of the present state of knowledge.

Looking at gross improvement rates in nonbehavioral family therapy, Gurman and Kniskern found that with child and adolescent identified patients (IPs), 71 percent were rated improved and 29 percent not improved. With adult IPs, 65 percent were rated improved and 35 percent not improved. When these data are examined by setting, 76 percent were found improved in outpatient settings and 24 percent not improved; 59 percent improved in day hospital settings, 41 percent not improved; and 74 percent improved in inpatient settings, 26 percent not improved. Such findings are not unexpected because of the severely chronic nature of day hospital patients. As with recent findings in individual psychotherapy research, 5 to 10 percent of patients (or marital or family relationships) *worsened* as the result of treatment.

In the behavioral family therapies, results tended to be more specific because criteria were clearer and studies more comparable. Treatment was superior to no treatment and to alternative treatments in five out of six studies. When the stimulus conditions can be well controlled, operant methods do change behavior. But it is more difficult to produce evidence that effects endure or that change generalizes across settings. As with nonbehavioral approaches, there is evidence that behavioral family therapy has a negative effect in some instances.

Among the implications and conclusions which Gurman and Kniskern (1978) state are the following:

1. Family therapy appears to be at least as effective as individual therapy and possibly more effective for a wide variety of problems, both apparent "individual" difficulties and more obvious family conflicts.

2. Short-term and time-limited therapies appear to be at least as effective as treatment of longer duration. Where time limits were not set, most of the positive results were achieved in five months or less.

3. The father plays a major role in the efficacy of family therapy when there is a child or adolescent IP. The wisdom of the traditional mother and child model used in child guidance clinics should be questioned.

4. Deterioration seems to be as common in marital-family therapy as in individual therapy. Also, therapist variables and patient-therapist interaction account for negative effects far more often than do patient factors alone.

5. Relationship skills of the therapist have a major impact on the outcome of marital and family treatment regardless of the clinician's theoretical persuasion.

SOME OTHER FORMS
OF CONTACT WITH FAMILIES

Child Abuse

Child abuse has taken a variety of forms ranging from crude to diabolical and from casual to lethal. Steele (1976) points out that families often provide violent environments. Statistics from the U.S. Federal Bureau of Investigation indicate that roughly only 25 percent of murders occur between strangers and that in roughly 3.5 percent of murders a parent kills a child. Keeping in mind that most child abuse does not result in death and that sometimes no charges may be brought even when it does, the rates of serious physical abuse may be large indeed. Gathering accurate statistics on prevalence is naturally difficult.

We can distinguish assault and battery, abuse due to neglect, willful torture, and sexual abuse. The abusive family gives signals of the ongoing process, which Ounstead and Lynch (1976) refer to as open warnings that abuse is occurring. Where major tragedies occur, social networks usually fail to recognize them as abuse and miss a long series of open warnings. Psychologically minded professionals are rarely stationed in the medical facilities to which the grossly injured child is brought, but their role in detection, treatment, and prevention of child abuse can be considerable.

Those who work with children must remain open to the possibility of abuse, but they must not engage in witch hunts or force facts to fit hypotheses. Many families will seek psychological help, during which the presence of abuse may become known. Psychologists must be intimately familiar with the provisions of the state law regarding the reporting of abuse. Reports may be mandatory; reporting may or may not waive confidentiality and privilege statutes. Clearly it may be desirable to inform clients at the outset about the law and the obligations it imposes. This issue is a complicated one.

It is difficult to generalize about child-abusing families. Neglect seems most likely in situations where poverty or immaturity exist. Assault and battery types of abuse occur over a rather wide range of family types. A mother's boyfriends may abuse her children in attempts to secure their place or their control. Sexual abuse may be found in the widest range of social levels, not infrequently occurring in families whose members seem to be pillars of the community. The forces allowing or prompting sexual abuse seem to be rather different from those prompting assault or neglect.

The prevention of child abuse is now receiving some political attention and public funding. Research in one special area, that of *bonding* between mothers and infants and fathers and infants, shows promise. Researchers are investigating the possibility that persons at the birth event, especially the mother, may be especially open to an "imprinted" attachment to the neonate. The basic rationale of the bonding researchers is that a mother well bonded to her infant is less likely to experience the infant as an object of anger, hatred, and abuse. If the findings hold up in further validational studies, the core notion has the potential for being a preventive measure that is easily applied and not particularly controversial. There is also some research (Clarke & Clarke, 1976; Thomas, 1981) indicating that early experience is *not* as controlling as some theorists have held. Perhaps, however, what the bonding investigators are finding is that the intensive and immediate postnatal experience changes mothers and thus the child's environment is changed for the better.

Termination of Rights

In the United States and many other countries, there are legal efforts to raise the standards for a child's home environment. Children are no longer seen as the chattels of their biologic parents, and although those parents have broad rights with respect to those children, society requires that parents must not subject children to abuse and neglect. In what seems to be an increasing number of cases, psychologically underdeveloped parents with a history of abusing or neglecting their child continue to respond to the child with competitive or desperately vengeful responses. In such cases courts of law face a solemn dilemma. If they act too hastily to terminate the rights of the parent, family structures may be needlessly broken; if they act too slowly, a child may die or else suffer gross physical or psychological impairment.

As the structure and the stability of families become even more varied and as casual reproduction becomes more common among young people whose physical, psychological, and economic immaturity make effective parenting almost impossible, the problem of who is fit to parent whom promises to become more and more vexing. The questions that a court is forced to examine are almost impossible to answer, such as "Does the parent have the capacity to become a good parent in the foreseeable future?" or "What is this parent's motivation to learn rudimentary parenting skills or to plan for the child's welfare?" They challenge psychologists and others to predict the future from quite limited data. The field needs specialists who will expand knowledge of assessment and prediction in such situations and who will extend the repertoire of methods needed to train reluctant or unwilling persons not to exploit children and to provide some minimal stability for them.

We need to know more about the effect on a child of having parental rights terminated. Conventional wisdom suggests that the event is traumatic; children removed from home to residential treatment centers usually show some form of bonding to their parents, often treasuring "memories" of wonderful love from the parent, memories that may be pure fantasy. One of the few follow-up studies done on children taken from their parents, however, showed them to be doing quite well in their new placements and to be showing few signs of missing their former homes (Schetky, Angell, Morrison, & Sack, 1979). Possibly when conditions have been terrible for a child, once he or she is sure that the parent will not return to accuse him or her of disloyalty or to take vengeance, the child is free to enter a new situation.

Parent Training

Studies of children's problems clearly show the number of children needing some kind of mental health service is beyond the capacity of a one-on-one professional system. The situation promises to become even worse as so many persons enter parenthood without the resources needed for adequate parenting. During the 1970s a variety of approaches to parent training or parent education has sprung up. The common feature among them remains their attempt to improve the skills of the parents and thus the life of the family and the psychological nurturance and socialization of the child or children involved.

All forms of family therapy have involved parent training, with mixed results. The early hope that parent training would make everybody an effective parent has been dashed, but more specific, outcome-oriented programs seem to have produced rather impressive, cost-effective results—for instance, parents of retarded children have been helped to care for the children at home rather than to institutionalize them.

CRITIQUE

How adequate are family and couple interventions conceptually? From a small beginning since Ackerman's observation in 1958 that a person seeking help was often the emissary of a sick family, assessment and therapy of families has taken a giant step. The area has progressed from virtually no family concepts at all to where the family is viewed as a living system in its own right by several competing schools of thought. The several approaches available emphasize different aspects or qualities in their view of family, and each has a core of ardent supporters.

But reflect momentarily on what theorists must face when they conceptualize families and couples. Besides the constant stream of highly complex behavior and the individuality of the component members, each of these small-group systems responds in some way to the sociopolitical context. Each has a developmental course of some type, too. And worse, those added factors interact; parents brought up in the 1960s appear to handle their family quite differently from parents brought up in the 1940s. In short, although there has been much progress in conceptualizing couples and families, there is still a far way to go.

How practical are the interventions?   This topic simply has to be filling an important need if we are to judge by the number of marriage counselors and family therapists in the United States. They occur in the private, the nonprofit, and the public sectors. They occur in institutions related to mental health, to religion, and to delinquency, to name only three. It appears almost certain that in the American and many other societies we will continue to form and to dissolve families in great numbers and that we will have ever greater percentages of children being raised in stepparent and single-parent situations. The miseries associated with instability, loss, and dissolution would seem to guarantee that working with families will carry a high demand for some time.

Students of prevention and public health have a solid argument when they point out, though, that either preventing the easily forecast miseries or dealing with them in a cohort or group basis would be far more practical than relying on individual clinical or counseling services. In developing practical procedures the prevailing environment for joining and separating couples needs great attention, including premarital counseling and alternatives to the adversarial procedures in the U.S. legal system. Regarding the latter, the move toward the use of mediation by lawyers working with psychologists and others seems promising. The lawyer and counselor work with the separating couple together to arrive at agreements about property and the sharing of the children; so rather than by fighting these settlements out in often nasty court battles, the couple arrives at some mutually agreed upon plan.

How effective and worthwhile is the approach empirically and socially?   Despite the great apparent need and the enthusiasm for family services, effectiveness remains elusive. The problem of criteria makes overall effectiveness difficult to measure. If, for example, a warring couple with a miserable child say they want to stay together and seek family therapy and if after several sessions they divorce, with the result that the child is happier, was that a failure or a success? Making the picture more mixed up, authorities disagree about the effect of divorce on children.

BOX 11-2   *MEDIATION IN DIVORCE AND CUSTODY DISPUTES*

Mediation offers an alternative to the usual adversarial process. Battling divorce and custody settlements out in court has major drawbacks: Court is generally a win or lose situation, one which pulls spouses into the roles of contesting enemies. Almost unavoidably, children become spoils to be won or allies to be courted. Unintended wounds and enmities result, and often at great financial cost. Mediation offers a process through which a couple may reach a voluntary mutual agreement.

Voluntary mediation, where people seek help in reaching an agreement, may be broad in its scope. *Mandatory* mediation, where people are required to try to agree before using adversarial processes, may be restricted to the topic of child custody, as in California. Both voluntary and mandatory mediation clients are able to reach mutual agreements in perhaps 75 percent of cases.

What do mediators do? Models differ, but mediation is clearly not family therapy. Mediators try to create a process within which clients work out their own self-determination. That process requires new cognitive and emotional sets. Mediators orient their clients, facilitate on-target communication, and explore and manage without stifling conflict. They continually look for areas of overlapping interest and common problems and try to broaden the range of available alternatives. They help the parties through problem solving and solution finding toward a mutual agreement (Haynes, 1981). Mediation agreements can be designed to anticipate long-term changes, such as child development or emancipation.

Many types of professionals become mediators, including psychologists and lawyers. Preliminary findings suggest that special training is necessary and supervised experience very desirable. The field is awash in ethical questions. Some have to do with departing from the guarantees of the adversarial system, and others with the values, vulnerabilities, biases, or hidden alliances of the mediators themselves. The opportunities for practice, research, and positive contribution to families appear exciting.

The type and direction of family therapy remains much influenced by setting. In some religious counseling centers, divorce cannot be an option. In some secular ones, marriage as a phenomenon may hold relatively little value. Empirical criteria are hard to establish, and family therapy appears to be governed more by local social, professional, and religious values than by invariant or objective criteria. For these reasons little research has appeared to date.

Whereas Samoan families have been said—in jest—to include Mom, Pop, the children, and the anthropologist, American families appear headed on a course where increasing numbers will have a family counselor of some type. Without undefined reasons to enter family therapy and with so many different goals for the therapy, we may find that routine struggles of families become a signal to enter the health care system or other providing network.

The social benefits of preventive or public health approaches are long over-due.

Nonetheless, despite all of these drawbacks, the fact that the movement attends to families and helps families to attend to themselves represents a positive social value. Even though the task may be difficult, promoting the well-being of relationships and families has intrinsic social worth.

SUMMARY

The importance of working with couples and families has increased greatly in the past decade. The fields of family therapy and couple therapy have produced several streams of inquiry, and more importantly, some real credibility for the idea that an individual's symptoms may be the signs of a dysfunctional family unit. Working with couples and families requires careful understanding of the current tasks and expectations of the family in society and of the problems that families commonly face.

Difficulties experienced by couples can be roughly grouped into sex, money, and in-laws—that is, intimacy, resource allocation, and emancipation. Assessment and couple therapy divides into the counseling and the learning or skills approaches, with increasing attention being given to the developmental maturation and evolution of couplehood.

Family therapy has experienced explosive growth so that it, rather than individual therapy for the presenting patient, may be the automatically assigned treatment. Goals and rationales for family therapy must be kept in clear focus. The structural approach has great prominence among the many schools of family therapy. In it the therapist joins the family and by investigating and understanding its structure and subsystems becomes able to encourage, promote, or even provoke change through carefully chosen activities such as escalating stress, assigning tasks, or exaggerating symptoms.

Another approach, behavioral family therapy, begins by assessing rates and sequences of particular target behaviors in members of the family and assessing the flow, direction, and quantity of reinforcers. Family therapy in the social learning model consists of teaching parents to be better observers of behavior and then to apply more consistently those consequences that will raise rates of desirable behavior.

Family therapies have produced some promising research, but each area has particular problems. Structural family therapy has difficulty making treatment uniform across therapists whereas behavioral family therapy, a model of data-based accuracy, appears to need broadened concepts for families of older children.

Psychologists working with couples and families must be aware of child abuse and of their legal responsibilities for required reports. Working with child abuse requires an understanding of developmental psychology, self-help groups, and legal processes. It needs a great deal more research than currently exists. Similarly the psychologist would seem to have much to contribute to the termination of rights process, but again, only when development and family processes are well understood and when legal processes give freedom for independent judgment. Finally, parent training has become popular. It ranges from teaching parents concrete skills to teaching them attitudes and mental sets. The diversity of approaches makes overall evaluation impossible, but some positive effects have been found.

RECOMMENDED READINGS

Gerson, M. J., & Barsky, M. For the new family therapist: Glossary of terms. *American Journal of Family Therapy*, 1979, 7, 15–20.

Family therapy attempts to shift the therapist's focus from a single, or identified, patient to the family as patient. That shift in focus has been attempted by a variety of family therapies, each of which have developed their own particular technical terms. Words such as *boundary*, *triangle*, or *restructuring* have acquired specific meaning in certain approaches to family therapy. The glossary explains many of these terms and relates them to their originators.

Gurman, A. S., & Kniskern, D. P. *Handbook of family therapy*. New York: Brunner/Mazel, 1981.

The Gurman-Kniskern handbook covers a wide range of topics in the family therapy area. Their chapters tend to deemphasize behavioral approaches to families but do include substantial coverage of parent training. Brodkin (1980), in a separate article, provides an analysis of family therapy over 25 years. He notes that it has moved through three phases: saving the individual by working with the family, fighting for the embattled family, to an era of ambiguity about separateness and togetherness.

Patterson, G. R. *Coercive family process*. Eugene, Oreg.: Castalia Publishing Co., 1982.

Patterson is a well-known researcher and clinician in work on family management and child rearing, especially in regard to out-of-control, antisocial, aggressive children. This book summarizes data from studies of 300 clinical cases and normal families to develop a theory of social aggression and recommendations for clinical applications.

Weiss, R. L., & Jacobson, N. S. Behavioral marital therapy as brief therapy. In S. H. Budman (Ed.), *Forms of brief therapy*. New York: Guilford, 1981, pp. 387–414.

Noting that what "is selected for change depends, in part, upon one's theory of human misery" (p. 388), Weiss and Jacobson present their view that problematic behaviors and thoughts are current adjustments in functioning. Their form of treatment, based on considerable research, focuses on the training of skills and the developing of competencies. There are four kinds of competencies: the ability to objectify or make reliable discriminations about marital behavior; the competency for support, understanding, and affection; the possession of problem-solving functions; and the ability to substitute behavior change tactics, such as negotiation and contracting, for aversive control.

Horne, A. M., & Ohlsen, M. M. (Eds.). *Family counseling and therapy.* Itasca, Ill.: Peacock, 1982.

Horne and Ohlsen provide a collection of fairly short presentations of all the major approaches to family therapy and counseling. For each there is a definition and history, a statement of principles, a case example, and an evaluation. The 14 chapters presenting different perspectives cover family systems therapy, structural family therapy, and Gestalt, transactional, person-centered (client-centered), rational-emotive, Adlerian/Dreikursian, and reality approaches.

Willis, D. (Ed.). Parent education and training. *Journal of Clinical Child Psychology,* 1981, *10,* 93–116.

Willis presents a collection of five articles which illustrate the development and diversity of parent training efforts. Topics include: using videotape modeling to reach larger numbers of parents, investigating differences in response due to socioeconomic factors (none was found), helping court-referred families communicate better, dealing with "smart-talk" and noncompliance, and helping abusive mothers manage constructively.

RESEARCH EXAMPLES

Barry, A. A research project on successful single parent families. *American Journal of Family Therapy,* 1979, *1,* 64–73.

Barry's work is important because it has been estimated that two out of every five children born during the 1970s will have spent at least part of their growing years in a single-parent household. This proportion may be higher in the 1980s and is particularly high in black families. Single-parent families have had to cope with a certain amount of social prejudice and the problem of having only one adult to carry all the day-to-day responsibilities. Although many researchers concentrate on how to help single parents and their children once they have had trouble, this study tries to lay a foundation for preventive work by establishing which variables are associated with successful single-parent families.

Twenty-five single-parent families volunteered to share positive family experiences; 20 percent were headed by males and 80 percent by females. The average parental age was 35; the sample involved 41 children with an age range of 1 to 21 years. Some 52 percent of the parents were college graduates, clearly reflecting the upper-middle-class nature of the sample. Families seemed to fall into four patterns: (1) Both parents shared the decision to separate and told the children together. The absent parent paid regular support and had frequent contact with children. (2) A strong sense of mutual cooperation existed between parents, and there was good positive contact with the children by the absent parent, but no regular support. (3) Little active collaboration between the parents, and the decision to separate was not mutual. No support was given, and the absent parent had limited, yet positive, contact with the children. (4) The absent parent played virtually no active part in the lives of the remaining members. Separation was always initiated by the custodial parent, and separation was often increased by physical distance because of the custodial parent's view that the absent parent was unable to make any positive contribution whatever.

Interview results suggest that successful adaptation requires conscious determination and effort and a period of time in which to learn and readjust. A large proportion of parents had chosen to work parttime and to endure the reduced standard of living in order to have more time with their children. On the other hand, the self-esteem and confidence coming from successful work appeared important.

Conclusions suggested that tasks of the adjustment period include recognizing the following: Major changes have taken place, time is needed to evaluate the changes, losses experienced need to be mourned; the new situation and opportunities must be realistically appraised; children must be understood and supported in their different ways of reacting; help should be sought if blockage occurs.

Tasks of the new family period involve clarifying the role of the absent parent, coping with financial and practical needs, readjusting parent and child roles to fit the new structure, establishing new personal goals, and setting up support networks to work toward positive family goals with positive parenting strategies.

Although Barry's work has a limited empirical base and a rather special sample, her approach has great potential for helping people anticipate and prepare for an increasingly widespread stress situation.

Fuhr, R. A., Moos, R. H., & Dishotsky, N. The use of family assessment and feedback in ongoing family therapy. *American Journal of Family Therapy,* **1981, 9, 24–36.**

The authors illustrate the use of a family assessment device to help the ongoing clinical processes. The Family Environment Scale (FES), completed by a family member, gives that member's view of family functioning on the ten subscales mentioned in the chapter. (Strictly speaking, this is an example of a case, rather than research; however, the FES is based on extensive research, and the reader is invited to imagine how a more exact study of its application to family therapy might take place.)

When several members fill out the scale, the therapist can learn how each rater views the family and what discrepancies in views exist among raters. An adolescent may, for example, see the family as much more controlling than does the father. Differences such as these can be conveyed by the therapist to the family and made a focus of the therapeutic work.

Fuhr et al. take the notion a step farther by asking family members to complete the scale for their ideal family, as well as for the real family. Contrast and comparison between real and ideal opens up the whole question of where each person supposes improvement lies. The paper illustrates one family in which parents found their ideal family quite congruent in some aspects and were able to take action for change in that direction.

The technique is an innovative application of an ecologically based device to measure views of real and ideal situations. The interest in differences between real and ideal has come largely from personality research and from the work of client-centered therapists in their measurements of shifts during therapy as clients improve. Results from the scale are used to focus therapy sessions and to help members set their own goals, approach problems, and give feedback about changes.

12 WORKING WITH GROUPS, ORGANIZATIONS, AND COMMUNITIES

Throughout this book we have made clear that psychology has become far broader than just "psyche-ology," the study of the individual. Psychologists have studied larger systems such as groups, organizations, and communities. In a general sense, of course, all larger systems are groups, but here we identify them separately and use the term *groups* to cover small groups of unrelated people.

We combine groups, organizations, and communities in a single chapter only because of space limitations. Each of the three areas has received a great deal of professional attention. General systems theory, which we discussed in Chapter 2, gives a useful way of seeing similarities in the three areas. It provides a useful way of making initial assessments, too. Armed with the list of subsystems (see Chapter 2), we can form a sound, if brief, impression by evaluating the status and functioning of each one. We might find out, for example, that a group's decider function has fallen into the hands of only one member, or that an organization's memory operates inadequately because records and policies are in disrepair, or that a community's perceptual and feedback processes need overhauling so that policy makers can hear the needs of a neglected group.

Although the general systems perspective allows us to study the common elements of groups, organizations, and communities, most work uses viewpoints or vocabulary unique to each area. In the following three sections, we will take up major contributions to groups, organizations, and communities in turn. Because the concept of prevention and the activity of consultation overlap the three areas, we will discuss them separately toward the end of the chapter.

GROUPS

Human beings are social, often gregarious creatures. Much of what we do or are relates to group action. Over a period of years each of us participates in many sorts of groups—for example, work crews, clubs, associations, fraternities and sororities, athletic teams, bands or orchestras, drama casts, or elected bodies. Most of us carry in our minds fond memories of some groups—formal ones or "our gang"—that influenced us deeply. It may be that what we gained from the group may have seemed embarrassing, hurtful, or at best not exactly fun at the time. We may also have recognized successive, predictable phases in groups to which we have belonged. It has been said that just as families have a predictable developmental cycle, every group forms, storms, norms, and adjourns. In the following sections we will look at these potent and somewhat predictable phenomena.

Group Therapy

Group therapy consists of a group of patients, usually numbering between five and ten, all with some presenting complaints of their own, meeting together on a regular basis to talk in special ways, usually with a leader present, and holding expectations of benefit. On what notions should the expectations of benefit rest? Yalom (1970, 1975), a widely respected authority on group therapy, suggests approaching the question, not through the terms therapists use or the complex rationales they express, but through an analysis of effects. He identifies several primary curative or helpful effects:

Instillation of hope: The group communicates hope or new possibilities to its members.

Universality: Members can be relieved of their feelings of uniqueness and isolation and given some sense of belonging and commonality of experience.

Imparting of information: New ideas and views can play a crucial role in reducing fear of the unknown and in laying a basis for new skills.

Altruism: "In therapy groups . . . patients receive through giving, not only as part of the reciprocal giving-receiving sequence but also from the intrinsic act of giving. Psychiatric patients beginning therapy are demoralized and possess a deep sense of having nothing of value to offer others. They have long considered themselves as burdens, and it is a refreshing, self-esteem-boosting experience to find that they can be of importance to others" (Yalom, 1975, p. 13).

The corrective recapitulation of the primary family group: Most patients enter group therapy having had unsatisfactory experiences in their families of origin. The group offers an opportunity for old patterns to reappear, be reenacted, and then be relived correctively or solved in more mature, less growth-blocking ways.

Developing socializing techniques: Groups provide the opportunity for members to recognize and replace harmful habits or to learn pleasant affiliative responses. Patients learn effective responses by watching and imitating models.

Interpersonal learning: Interpersonal learning involves a complex sequence beginning as a member's typical behavior is displayed in the social microcosm of the group. Next, through feedback or self-observation, the member begins to appreciate the nature of his or her behavior and its impact on others' opinions and feelings. This awareness allows the person to take responsibility and to risk trying new types of behavior. Each step requires, says Yalom (1975), specific facilitation by the therapist such as offering specific feedback, encouraging self-observation, clarifying the concept of responsibility, and encouraging risk taking.

Group cohesiveness: Instead of the patient-therapist relationship upon which most individual therapy rests, group therapy involves the patient in a three-part relationship, to the therapist, to the other individual group members, and to the group as a whole. Group cohesiveness can be regarded as the sum of all of those forces that work to keep a group member involved with the others. Yalom (1975) points out the power that groups may have in people's lives ("I couldn't face my group if I did that," "People in my group always hold those standards," and so on). He suggests that for many psychiatric patients who have simply never been a participating member of a group, the successful negotiation of a group experience may in itself be curative.

What are the major tasks of the group therapist? In repeating Yalom's major tasks, we must be careful to emphasize, as he does, the complexity and subtlety of the group therapy enterprise. We can only encapsulate the major directions and landmarks and cannot convey a good sense of the moment-to-moment experience of the group therapist. First, the *norms of the group must be set.* The therapist may do that through orientation or structuring of expectancies in the beginning and continues to do it through shaping, reinforcement, and personal modeling. What types of norms should be fostered? General norms require that patients will be self-monitoring and hold that self-disclosure is positive, procedures for safety and dignity will be observed, the group is important, and group members are agents of help for one another.

The second and third tasks of the therapist overlap or interact. The therapist must *provide a clear focus on the here and now* and must *illuminate the processes* taking place in the group. The focus on the here and now means that the group rarely discusses events in the outside life of the members—certainly immediate events *in* the meeting take precedence. The leader's task is to focus members' energy on their relationships with one another and to comment on the group process. In process commentary the therapist discusses in depth on here-and-now behavior and on the nature of the immediately current relationship between people. The comments refer not to the content of the communication, but to the implications of that communication about the nature of the relationship between the communicating parties. For example, Yalom (1975) describes the following:

> [Two group members] had a sexual affair which eventually came to light in the group. The other members reacted in various ways, but none so condemning nor so vehemently as Diana, a forty-five-year-old nouveau moralist, who criticized them both for breaking group rules—Tim, for being "too intelligent to act like such a fool," Marjorie for "her irresponsible disregard for her husband and child," and the "Lucifer therapist" who just "sat there and let it happen." The therapist eventually pointed out that in her formidable moralistic broadside some individuals had been obliterated, that the Marjorie and Tim with all their struggles and doubts and fears whom Diana had known for so long had suddenly been replaced by faceless one dimensional stereotypes. Furthermore, the therapist was the only one to recall the reasons for seeking therapy which Diana had expressed at the first group meeting: namely that she needed help in dealing with her rage toward a nineteen-year-old, sexually awakening daughter, who was in the midst of a search for her identity and autonomy! From here it was but a short step for the group and then for Diana herself to enter the experiential world of her daughter and to understand with great clarity the nature of the struggle between mother and daughter. (pp. 130–131)

Through norms, the general here-and-now focus, and process commentary, Yalom sets the group therapist the task of guiding the patient to accept and incorporate one, several, or all of these notions:

> Only I can change the world I have created for myself.
> There is no danger in change.
> To attain what I really want, I must change.
> I can change; I am potent.

Figure 12-1   Group therapy. (Ken Karp)

In considering the group as a whole, Yalom's final task for the group therapist is to make mass group process comments. Occasionally a group will come up against an event that stalls its progress and causes it simply to "mill around," or it may swerve toward antitherapeutic norms. In such cases mass group process commentary should be used to overcome the obstacles preventing progress—for example, "Two meetings ago John said he had herpes.* Nobody has even mentioned it since—but the group has begun to spend its time discussing what's wrong with the group and how members want to leave it. Anyone see a connection?"

Group therapy furnishes tools, methods, and forces not available in individual psychotherapy. There are, of course, other ways of conceptualizing the therapeutic elements and the therapist's tasks, but however we think about them, group phenomena have great importance in psychology. Yalom's particular analysis appears powerful because, although it shows the uniqueness of group experience, it links it well to personality theory and social psychology.

Encounter groups and the encounter group movement have already been discussed in Chapter 10. Because of their primary emphasis on human potential and growth, that discussion might well have occurred here following group therapy, from which encounter borrows heavily, and preceding

---

*A sexually transmitted disease currently uncurable.

the T-groups (training groups) of organizational psychology, to be discussed in the organization section.

Psychodrama and Role Playing

Psychodrama is another social approach to treatment. Its father is generally considered to be J. L. Moreno. His *Stegreiftheater*—literally the theater of (speaking from) the stirrup, or theater of spontaneity—sprang from his reaction against the psychoanalytic movement, dominant in Vienna at that time.

Moreno became convinced of the therapeutic importance of acting out personality problems on the stage when he observed changes in people as a result of their spontaneous performances. Over the years he contributed a number of ideas including the beginnings of sociometrics. Although he was a pioneer in the development of group psychotherapy, he is best known for his work with psychodrama.

Psychodrama takes place upon a stage, often a specially designed one, in front of an audience. The chief participants are the protagonist (the client), the director (the chief therapist), the auxiliary egos (assistant therapists or other clients), and the group making up the audience. The therapist director gets the scene going by asking the client to act out a scene spontaneously. Auxiliary egos take parts that will support the action and help bring out the problems and conflicts of the client. The techniques for developing the production are many and varied (Moreno, 1959). The director encourages the client to achieve catharsis in order to be liberated from his or her problems. The goal is to produce a spontaneous, creative person. One of the interesting byproducts of psychodrama is its importance to the client-audience.

Role playing, perhaps psychodrama's first cousin, is less formal than psychodrama. With its great flexibility, role playing may be used as an adjunct to therapy or as the major vehicle for change or problem solving. Its distinguishing feature is that roles are assigned and played out. The source of the roles may be historical—for example, a group therapy patient may be invited to play out a typical problem she had with her father. They may be contemporary—for example, children may play out disagreements they have with each other. Finally, they can be prospective—for example, clients may prepare for future events that may be stressful. Role playing may be done in a wide variety of settings because its purposes are straightforward and its techniques do not require psychologists or psychiatrists as leaders. Role playing has two primary goals: first, to help people learn to *take role*—that is, figuratively to try on someone else's shoes or to see the world through someone else's eyes; and second, to be a vehicle through which people can *experiment with roles* that are otherwise inaccessible or develop new skills that they might otherwise have no chance to try. George Kelly (1955) encouraged clients to try out roles in real life in what he called *fixed-role therapy*.

The concept of *role taking* occupies a prominent place in the thinking of many social psychologists. Some have used it as a cornerstone of personality development. They view many forms of delinquency and criminality as failures of role taking. The golden rule—do unto others as you would have others do unto you—a pillar of Western civilization, is really an exhortation to take the role of others. Children especially seem to role play as a natural part of their development and show special interest in interventions involving role playing. Furness (1976) has written a valuable book showing teachers and others how to guide children toward constructive solutions and empathic feelings in a number of poignant situations that may easily "go wrong." "We don't like to sit by Johnny . . . he smells," "Why is Lisa always so hungry in the morning?" and similar situations can become, through the vehicle of role playing, opportunities for learning and empathy rather than opportunities for name calling and alienation.

As a final illustration of the flexibility and power of role playing and its beneficial side effects, Furness (1982) randomly took eight behavior problem children from a list of 16 offered by a grade school. The eight Ss were each asked to select a role model ("pick a person who's doing real well in school, someone you'd like to have in our project"). The eight Ss and eight role models were then designated as the project, "Growing with Dramatics." Their task was to learn short segments of plays, some published and some especially written, to perform for the school and parents at the end of the term. Role assignments were clinically matched to the subject. For example, the shy, depressed boy was assigned the role of leading and asserting; the angry, impulsive girl, the role of teaching others problem-solving techniques and self-controls. To date, students' ability to learn lines, use equipment, and make the project a success has surprised skeptics. Professionals attending pilot performances have misidentified target Ss and role model children. Preliminary checklist ratings before and after the project show improvement, although they reflect only a part of the project's impact. Besides the advantage of avoiding labels, there is real economy in treating the children in a group rather than referring them individually for therapy. Additionally social changes that have occurred appear encouraging. There has been a broadening of the children's friendship networks. Target children and role model children have visited in each other's homes. Target parents have had positive involvement with the school, and project parents have gotten to know each and have worked together to help the project.

Self-Help Groups, Crisis Groups

In past years if people were asked to name self-help groups for those suffering from a serious disorder, the task would have been difficult. Probably only one —Alcoholics Anonymous (AA)—would have occurred to most people. Today self-help groups of many descriptions occupy a major place in the lives of

Americans. AA has companion groups for spouses, for teenagers, and for young children. Other groups, frequently carrying "Anonymous" in their titles, offer services for drug abusers, the obese, child abusers, those involved in sexual offenses in the family, those with problems of mental illness—the list is endless.

And what do the groups provide? In general, each of them offers a constructive reframing of the problem, sometimes in the form of a creed, a set of 12 steps, or a statement of belief. Most groups provide ways to unmask excuses or self-deception, a process which often a fellow sufferer can manage more effectively than can a professional. The groups frequently provide acceptance by a cross-section of the wider community. They usually offer contacts—"Call us if you get into trouble"—or even outreach. They have little or no cost and for the lost or floundering offer a meaning for life or a way of becoming organized. In a short time a new member can feel the vitality of being able to help someone worse off.

Although professionals sometimes look askance at self-help groups because of the quasi-religious nature of some, they deserve our deepest respect. One-to-one therapies or even therapy groups may have better research and perhaps higher social acceptability, but in terms of the numbers served and the practical durable nature of the help, self-help groups are a powerful force indeed. In recent years many psychologists have realized their value and have come to understand them not as competitors in treating people but as valuable community resources with unique capabilities.

ORGANIZATIONS

An *organization* is a group with a continuing purpose. To attain the purpose, organizations usually have a good deal of structure, both in terms of people— officers, rules, bylaws, division of labor—and in terms of physical setting— an address and property which add to its permanence. Organizations concern psychology for several reasons. For one thing they create the working environment of importance for clients. One special type of organization— the school—has unique powers to gather together and to influence the young. Also, of course, many psychologists work in or head organizations and influencing or helping organizations has become a task of high importance for them. Psychologists use different bodies of knowledge to play different roles in organizations. Four of the most important are being a consultant, a trainer, a manager, or a program evaluator. After a brief mention of consulting (to be expanded later in the chapter), we will look at industrial-organizational psychological work, and then we will discuss management. Program evaluation will be discussed in the next chapter.

As consultants, clinical or counseling psychologists respond to the requests of schools or treatment organizations such as hospitals, foster homes, residential centers, and halfway houses. Consultants using a mental health consultation format help consultees see what from their past processes and structures is interfering with present problem-solving behavior. Consultants apply knowledge from developmental, social, and clinical psychology. They analyze the systems that they are trying to help. Because consultation concerns not only organizations, but groups and communities as well, we have placed its discussion at the end of the chapter.

Overview
of Industrial-Organizational
Psychology

In learning to appreciate the nature of consultation and training, it will be useful to look at the work of a related professional field—industrial-organizational (I-O) psychology. The clinician serving as a consultant or a trainer in a mental health organization or school will find many parallels with the work of an I-O psychologist. It is also true that many clinicians in the course of their careers have become I-O psychologists. Since private and public organizations and bureaucracies are pervasive in modern societies, knowlege of I-O work will be useful to human service workers in general.

The industrial-organizational psychologist responds to the concerns of businesses and industries by applying findings from systems research, personnel selection, motivation, group dynamics, and other areas of psychological knowledge. Industrial-organizational psychology differs in many ways from clinical, counseling, or community psychology. The purpose of the latter three is ultimately to help individuals, often individuals who have come to someone's attention because of a troublesome problem or symptom. The major focus of industrial-organizational psychologists, by contrast, is to improve corporate functioning. To harken back to general systems terms, whereas clinical and counseling psychologists usually focus on individual, group, or family systems, the I-O psychologist focuses more on the organizational system. I-O psychologists are consultants to (or perhaps staff members of) large corporations and are only very indirectly involved in helping individuals with personal problems.

In an important recent development industrial-organizational psychologists, like their counterparts in clinical psychology, have realized that assessment is best conducted by tasks as close to reality as possible. Bray (1982; Bray, Campbell, & Grant, 1974) and others have developed assessment centers, where managers can be assessed on a variety of carefully chosen and representative managerial and administrative tasks. Research to date has been generally favorable to the assessment center method, but the technique tends to be practical only in large corporations.

But what do I-O psychologists do? Let's imagine that Sally and John Armstrong are having dinner with Peter and May Hargreaves. Conversation uncovers Armstrong's interest in cooking and Sally's discovery that her invention ("my kitchen widget") saves time and gives good results in the kitchen. The Hargreaves have been seriously playing around with their home computer, and they think of several ways a computer might help. Both the Armstrongs and the Hargreaves seem certain of a market for widgets, and in minutes a new company is born. The first family of industrial-organizational tasks of AH, Inc. involves *job analysis, job classification, and personnel selection:* how to describe and classify jobs to be performed and how to select workers to perform them. Dr. Bennett, the I-O psychologist retained by AH, Inc., shares with the partners what he knows about the factors that predict how well particular kinds of persons will work out in particular roles. He explains the importance of using only tests that have been clearly shown to select better workers—that is, are criterion related. He discusses a variety of tests and measures with the partners, helps them to design forms, and coaches them in job-related interviewing.

AH, Inc. gets off to a fine start. It begins to expand somewhat and acquires new machinery to make Widget II. By this time it seems clear that none of the four partners can any longer serve as shop supervisor, and that means appointing one. Alice Gage, the senior employee, is the obvious choice for the position but can she handle the supervisory aspects of the job since she is, after all, younger than several other employees? Dr. Bennett is called in to plan and supervise the supervisor's *development* and *training*. Learning new equipment is relatively straightforward—some safety films, demonstrations by the manufacturers' representatives, assisted practice and learning of policies about the machinery. But should Gage be given a pep talk and turned loose—or sent away to managers' training for three months at company expense? What new skills does she need, and how can she most quickly and easily acquire them? Dr. Bennett designs an appropriate program.

As time passes, AH, Inc. appears to be doing well. The four partners decide to take a much-needed vacation, their first in 2½ years, but when they get back, the atmosphere in the plant seems to have changed. People have lost the pride or excitement they once had. Griping, complaining, excuse making—even threats to quit—seem commonplace. The partners are angry and a bit frightened. Again they call Dr. Bennett. He helps the partners to understand *attitudes* and *motivation*, as they have been studied by I-O psychologists for years. Although they have no panaceas, I-O psychologists have a good idea of which aspects of a work situation are likely to lead to low morale and disaffection and which are likely to have a positive effect. Dr. Bennett plans a survey to assess worker opinions and attitudes. His findings lead him to recommend ways in which the employeees, now so many more than at the beginning, can feel some of the same direct involvement in the corporation's destiny as had the founding employees a couple of years before.

Dr. Bennett's last round of consultation to AH, Inc. comes after an accountant confronted the partners with the need for a more complete and detailed corporate financial structure. No longer, he said, could they afford the simpler methods appropriate to tiny organizations. They decide to have a full-scale corporate review in which Dr. Bennett participates. He examines the ways in which leadership and supervision are conducted and makes recommendations to increase the degree of worker participation in decision making. He examines the prevailing organizational structure and the flow of communications and information within the organization. He recommends that the organization become more goal centered and also that fewer details are referred to the partners for approval. Finally, he makes recommendations about ways in which conflicts can be minimized and resolved.

We should note that in real life, Dr. Bennett would have anticipated several of the problems faced by AH, Inc. and also that, as in real life, consultees sometimes resist action until virtually forced into it.

A major technique of organizational psychology is the T-group (for *training group;* see also Chapter 10). These unstructured but intensive group experiences in Mann's (1978) words

> provide participants with an opportunity to learn about the impressions they created on others in a group setting, as opposed to the impressions they thought they were creating, as well as to learn about the psychological processes of group functioning (Bradford, Gibb, & Benne, 1964). Central to this learning process is the concept that group members are "defensive" about the revelation of their true feelings to others in the group, and, as a consequence, the process of communicating real meanings to each other becomes distorted. (p. 120)

T-groups have been the most commonly used means of improving communications and organizational functioning. Some of their original purpose has been blurred by an excessive focus on here-and-now experience rather than on results and by a focus on feelings as an endpoint rather than as a way to facilitate thinking as was the original intent, but they still constitute a major tool of the I-O psychologist. One important offshoot of the T-group movement has been the encounter group movement discussed in Chapter 10.

One serious criticism of the method even in its best form is that it may not fit in with the power structure of industrial organizations. A democratic or pseudodemocratic sensitivity group can be an anomaly in an organization. Numerous studies using the method within organizations and between groups in the community have produced mixed but predominantly favorable findings. However, they show that unless participants work in an environment supportive of the changes that have occurred, these changes tend to evaporate once training is over.

There are several competing perspectives and major figures in industrial-organizational psychology. It has its own doctoral training programs, its own division in APA, and a professional literature quite separate from that of the clinical-counseling-community area. Because of its contributions to human well-being in the work place and its secure status in the private industrial sector, its potential appears exciting, and bridges between I-O psychology and human service work are important.

The Psychologist as Manager

The truism that psychologists are taught psychology; nurses, nursing; social workers, social work; and so on should prompt us to recognize that managers, just like other professionals, need to be taught management. The manager's role demands skills usually quite outside the repertoire of most human service professionals. An inability to assume managerial responsibilities will, in many cases, prevent a professional from exerting maximal influence over the course of events in an organization, an influence often sorely needed because clinicians are in a good position to understand clients' needs and to advocate for them.

Clinical and community psychologists and other human service professionals who want to become managers face a difficult task. They need a broad range of knowledge and skills—for instance, those appropriate to running a small department in a hospital or university, or perhaps an agency somewhere in the community. Industrial-organizational psychology tends to be narrower and specialized, usually dealing with large manufacturing entities, not with small groups of human service co-workers. The neophyte manager also needs the basics—basic vocabulary, basic expectations, and elementary managerial tools. Specific training is needed. (One may, of course, try to become a manager with on-the-job training. The danger is that in the heat of the workplace, one only learns better and better responses to crises but little about their prevention.)

Several continuing education workshops have been developed to address the problem. We will outline a workshop developed by one of us (Taplin) and presented in the United States and Canada. In its introduction the workshop stresses that many new skills (such as accounting, personnel law, and planning) are required for successful management. The fledgling manager must be familiar enough with these skills to understand their contributions and to ensure that they are properly provided. Students are also cautioned to see their psychological skills as both potential assets and potential liabilities. For example, psychotherapeutic responses by a manager toward a disgruntled employee can be disastrous, but sensitivity to underlying themes in a group meeting can be a real asset.

The first major section teaches psychologists to think of their organization or section as a living system with its own goals and processes. General systems concepts (mentioned earlier in this chapter) help psychologists to focus on goals and purposiveness and on the condition of the subsystems of their organization.

The second major section reviews the typical content of managerial responsibilities. Although some have more, most managers find that their

BOX 12-1 *BRIEF APPRAISAL OF A SMALL MENTAL HEALTH CENTER*

The systems concepts in Chapter 2 (see Figure 2–2 and Box 2–1) can be used to inventory subsystems in an organization. Here are a psychologist's abbreviated notes after visiting a small mental health center with productivity and morale problems.

Decider

Centers on executive director, omitting staff and board. Generally reactive and blame oriented. Not proactive, planful, or goal oriented. Any effort to clarify is suspected by staff, director, or board.

Boundaries

Nothing immediately alarming, though director seems to mix his personal boundaries and the organization's in potentially dangerous ways.

Perceptual and Feedback Functions

No internal information system; no outcome data or even follow-up effort. No regular efforts to keep in touch with the surrounding mental health network.

Input, Central Processes, Output

Seems to be seeing a broader range of clients than it is equipped for. Supervision minimal but legal, though methods appear traditional and costly. Some staff believe that clients have to be cured rather than helped to function in their community.

Memory

Insufficient use of policy ("too bureaucratic") with the result that they use hours solving the same problems time after time. In the absence of reports or reviews of organizational attainment, memory is oral not written, and differs for staff, directors, and board.

Formal and Informal structure

Even the formal structure isn't too well defined. Informal structure looks to be a pyramid with director's secretary near the top.

Linkages

Director is a member of the county agency directors' group, also of United Way Executives, but seldom attends meetings. Not much linkage with citizens' groups, planning bodies, university psychology department, school of social work, etc.

---

responsibilities are a subset of outside political forces, outside fiscal forces, public relations, personnel, training, professional operations, information management, and budget, fiscal, contracts, supply, and property planning. Managers must be able to define their particular scope of responsibilities exactly.

What do managers actually do? The third section expands on the five classic managerial activities (plan, organize, direct, control, and innovate) and offers a modified group—plan, organize, facilitate, regulate and stimulate, and innovate—more appropriate for working with professionals. Common techniques for all these areas are taught. Planning involves clarifying and testing goals, as well as developing forecasts and responses. Specific planning, such as for work force or projects, must be undertaken for short, intermediate, and long-range periods. Decision making is perhaps the major activity in directing. Janis and Mann (1977) have made important contributions to decision making, going beyond the traditional comparison of gains and losses to consider the types and degrees of psychological conflict in the decision process.

Organizing and facilitating involve building coherence among goals, functions, and structures. A popular maxim, "form follows function," expresses the idea that structures should be designed to achieve specific results. Participants in the workshop learn to write job descriptions which link together ultimately to achieve a section's goals.

Monitoring might be another term for controlling or regulating. A manager, much like a flight engineer, must look at a set of indicators (usually reports, conferences, and conversations, rather than dials and gauges) to learn the condition of various essential operating components. Whereas the aircraft manufacturer supplies the dials and gauges, often managers must design their own indicators, asking, "What do I really need to know to be certain of our condition and progress?" When funds in the public and private sectors become less available, innovating or stimulating acquires added importance. It involves degrees of risks and requires good judgment.

The fourth section of the workshop includes several topics. Responses from workshop participants indicate some of the hazards of being a psychologist-manager: a tendency to give short shrift to planning and to controlling-regulating functions; a reluctance to build sufficient structure in an organization; a tendency to underestimate the importance of unfamiliar but vital areas such as personnel, law, and accounting; and, finally, the risk of using the wrong skill—for example, a psychologist who gives a disgruntled employee nonpossessive warmth, reflection of feeling, or psychodynamic interpretations when evaluations, policies, due processes, and decisions are needed can be made to appear not just inept but downright incompetent by the employee's attorney.

Organizational climates must be monitored because meeting goals and maintaining a positive internal climate are the two key indicators of managerial functioning. Moos (1974) and Mahler (1973) present different methods for measuring organizational climate. Finally, being a manager has aspects of stress and loneliness. Typically a manager stands between forces outside and inside the organization—a person at the boundaries—a marginal person. The manager must have a support network and a well-designed plan for coping with crises.

Although short courses such as the one described here cannot suddenly turn a psychologist into a competent manager, they do furnish basic vocabulary and rudimentary skills. As the helping professions mature, one aim should be to prepare their students more effectively for managerial opportunities.

COMMUNITY

Although community is certainly at a higher level on the hierarchy of systems than is individual personality, concern for community issues has been present since the emergence of clinical psychology. John Dewey, in 1899, spoke on "Psychology and Social Practice" in his presidential address to the American Psychological Association. Freud's book *Civilization and Its Discontents* was published in 1930. Lewin's work with community systems was done in the 1940s. A now-famous Boston Conference (Bennett et al., 1966) sparked enough energy so that a new Division of Community Psychology was organized within APA. Since then journals and training programs have elaborated special methods and concepts, and community psychology is now a distinctive subspeciality within psychology.

It is not easy to define community psychology. To some extent it overlaps with social work and with other professions striving to improve communities. The distinction between *community psychology* and *community mental health* is far from clear. The principal hallmarks of community psychologists are their use of *psychological* knowledge (as contrasted to, say, knowledge about economics, housing, transportation, or employment) and their dedication to empirical methods for measuring effectiveness or outcome. In these respects they are like clinical psychologists.

Sometimes psychologists in private practice are said to be "in the community." Although their offices are indeed in the community, they generally function as extensions of the medical referral and payment network and are thus quite different in function and in philosophy from community psychologists.

The Meaning of Community

There are various ways of conceptualizing what a community is. One is to emphasize *common interests and strivings* and the security and support that members provide for one another. Another is to emphasize *sociogeographical factors*, the common locality in which a group of people live and interact with one another. A third way of conceptualizing community is in terms of *communicating networks* of people, wherever they live. A fourth kind of conceptualization emphasizes *organizational structure and interaction.* We may define *community* as *a locality recognized as having a separate identity by most of the people in it and nearby, having comprehensive services and provisions to meet most human needs, and consisting of a loosely organized set of groups and organizations.* Figure 12–2 shows the human care organizations often contacted over the life cycle.

Figure 12-2   "Community clock" of subsystems contacted over the life cycle. (From Sundberg, Tyler, & Taplin, 1973, p. 442. Copyright © 1973 by Prentice-Hall and used by permission)

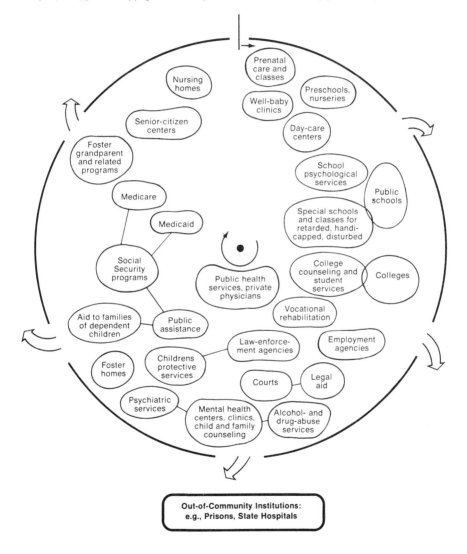

Community Subsystems

We may view a community as another living system and go over in our minds what constitutes the boundary, the memory, the deciders, and the other common components. Remembering the standard subsystems from the model and being able to identify them in an actual community gives us a good way of becoming familiar with a community's basic structure.

However, the community proves to be far more complex than the simplified model suggests. Several levels of government affect it and with differing degrees of authority. Administrative entities crisscross and overlap. Helping subsystems are often designed without clear goals in mind. They all too often compete with one another or compete for desirable clients.

We often assume a careful matching of person in need and helping subsystem. In practice, however, elements of happenstance, even bias and unfairness, can enter in. People receive classifying labels that reflect probably more the subsystem into which they fell than it does their own needs. The following example, less farfetched than it seems, gives some of the flavor:

Thirteen-year-old Amos Green isn't doing well in school—even in his inner-city school, where standards are not high. One day Amos, a bit sleepless because of a prolonged conflict with his mother's boyfriend, threatens his teacher with physical violence. What to do?

Alternative future 1. Amos's teacher has been having a fairly good day otherwise. She recalls his likable moments and some of his strengths. She remembers an in-service training session, relating delinquency to poor reading ability. Amos reads very poorly. He is referred for testing, classified as "learning disabled" and entered into a special class. He becomes an "LD child"—a label which qualifies him for the extra resources and special teaching which the school system believes will help him to overcome his disability.

Alternative future 2. The teacher is not amused but not panicked either. After consultation with the principal and a call to the mother, Amos is suspended for the rest of the week. His mother's anger and distress results in a call to the local child welfare office. "He's getting uncontrollable, just like his dad," she says. "I'll sign anything; put him in a foster home." Next day Amos is an "open case" in the child welfare subsystem, which believes Amos will be helped by the foster placement and periodic contacts with his caseworker.

Alternative future 3. Amos is suspended. His mother believes he'll return to school, but next day Amos is picked up by the police for a minor infraction. At the Juvenile Hall the intake worker calls in the psychologist to see a contrite-looking young man who is earnestly saying he's sorry and talking nervously about trying to become somebody in life. Counseling is agreed to because Amos seems so well motivated. Amos now carries a DSM III diagnosis and is "in treatment" in the mental health system, which believes that if a deep, meaningful relationship is provided, his impulses will become better contained by his defenses.

Alternative future 4. Amos is referred to Juvenile Court. Once at the court, things go badly. Amos's abusive language gets worse. He is hard to control. He kicks a couple of the staff members; so nobody advocates dropping charges. In the preliminary hearing his fate is suddenly sealed when he calls the judge a dumb broad and advises that she copulate with herself. Amos becomes a "delinquent" in the juvenile justice subsystem, which believes that restraint and structure will socialize him.

Although Amos is a fictitious person, the subsystems operate at least as haphazardly in many communities, competing, overlapping, and taking people that they like and leaving the others. A central concern for community psychology, then, besides the design of good subsystems and intelligent patterns of subsystems, must be matching the personal need situation with subsystem capability. In Amos's case the problem was choosing among simultaneous alternatives. The Community Clock (Figure 12–2) illustrates the importance of sequential access to a community's services because as people age, grow, or develop, new relations to community components must be made and old ones dropped.

Community Psychology

What force presses psychologists toward community psychology? Clearly there is no single impetus. First, many psychologists are dissatisfied with some of their traditional functions. The effectiveness of psychotherapy is still questioned in many quarters, and there are serious problems of its cost and access. Many forms of traditional assessment, especially projective techniques, no longer seem as worthwhile as they once did, and, of course, one-to-one approaches can never meet the growing need. Mental health resources are not distributed equitably. Several studies (e.g., Ryan, 1969) have shown that mental health resources congregate where the bright, young, intelligent, and verbal live. Psychological services in many countries are not very available to many sectors of society—the aged, children, minority groups, and the chronically mentally ill. The poor, generally, do not receive the same kinds of treatment as do the rich.

Several epidemiologic studies (e.g., Leighton, 1956; Srole et al., 1962) have found a higher-than-expected prevalence of mental disorder in some groups of people. Such findings indicate, first, the overwhelming need and, second, the problem of getting a high percentage of sufferers to come forward for treatment. Many psychologists recall the discoveries and triumphs of public health approaches to medicine—triumphs which have made modern society possible. They press for a parallel in psychology and psychiatry, a reaching of the masses not with treatment, but with preventive strategies; not relying on a doctor-patient relationship for a cure, but on interrupting a malevolent cycle or arming people with protective skills so they may better surmount life's crises.

Such challenges provide reasons for community psychology's emergence and also for the shape it is taking. It emphasizes prevention, skill acquisition, early detection, and the spread of effect through the use of nonprofessionals, volunteers, and community networks. More abstractly Zax and Specter (1974) define community psychology as ". . . an approach to human behavior problems that emphasizes contributions made to the development of these problems by environmental forces as well as the potential contributions to be made toward their alleviation by the use of these forces" (p. 459).

Figure 12-3 Some communities present enormous problems. (A.T.&T. Photo Center)

Figure 12-4 Some communities present broad opportunities and advantages.

The community mental health approach. After an earlier start in Northern Europe, community mental health in the United States began by federal action when, in 1963, President Kennedy proposed the construction and staffing of community centers for the psychiatrically disturbed. Although many such centers were funded nationwide, they have not been as successful as was initially hoped in bringing new standards of accessibility and new forms of service to groups typically not served. In particular the chronically mentally ill and children have often not benefited. The system of federal funding and control satisfied almost no one and sowed the seeds of the demise of the Community Mental Health Center Act and the rise of the Mental Health Systems Act—a "back to the states" reform—in the early 1980s. Although the network of community mental health centers achieved few startling successes, the community mental health ideology bolstered such important concepts as prevention and early detection, positive mental health, and consultation. Prevention and consultation will be discussed later.

The organizational approach. Earlier in the chapter we discussed the basics of the organizational approach—an underlying belief in the growth potential of people and in sensitivity of T-groups as vehicles to elicit or facilitate that growth. This approach is used as the centerpiece in some approaches to community psychology—the analysis and development of key community agencies.

The social action approach. According to Roman and Schmais (1972; cited in Mann, 1978), social action approaches of the 1960s stemmed from the need for comprehensive efforts to deal with deep-rooted and interrelated social problems, the recognition that the sources of these problems lay in the social structure, and the awareness that existing services and facilities were both unresponsive and inadequate in dealing with widespread need. It was hoped that the development of competence for community action through the organization and involvement of residents would be an important factor in devising effective solutions.

We are familiar with many social action efforts at the federal level—the Community Action Program, VISTA, the Economic Opportunity Act, and special programs such as Harlem Youth Opportunities Unlimited (HARYOU), to name only a few. But if we extend our thinking from federal to local level, we see that pioneer social workers in the settlement house movement used the approach around the beginning of the century.

Community psychologists of the social action stripe view housing, transportation, employment, even literacy as important issues in promoting successful individual adaptive behavior. However, quite severe political problems crop up (e.g., the widespread objections to government-sponsored "social engineering"), with the result that social action advocates, even more than community mental health advocates, saw their political stars wane, if not set, in the 1970s.

BOX 12-2 *THE COMMUNITY AND PSYCHOPATHOLOGY:*
THE MAGNITUDE OF PROBLEMS

Communities and nations must be concerned with the amount and nature of mental illness because they affect productivity, need for services, and quality of life in many ways. Epidemiology is the study of the distribution and determinants of diseases and disorders and is one concern of community psychology. In the following quotation, the Dohrenwends, eminent community researchers and epidemiologists, and their colleagues (Dohrenwend, Dohrenwend, Gould, Link, Neugebauer, & Wunsch-Hitzig, 1980, pp. 150–152) provide a picture of the enormous mental health problem in the United States:

The term "prevalence" in the following summary refers to the number of cases found in existence during a brief study period somewhere between a point in time and a year. Consider first the main results for children. On the basis of the evidence available, we hypothesize as follows:

That the true prevalence of clinical maladaptation among school children in a representative sample of U.S. communities is unlikely to average less than 12 percent and is likely to vary according to age, social class, ethnic group, and geographic region. Studies providing the relevant information indicate that the large majority of these maladjusted children were not receiving treatment.

We hypothesize that in a representative sample of U.S. communities, the true prevalence of psychiatric disorders with no known organic basis for adults below age 60–65 would be:

An overall rate for the aggregated functional disorders of between 16 and 25 percent.

Between 0.6 and 3.0 percent for schizophrenia.

About 0.3 percent for affective psychosis.

Between 8.0 and 15.0 percent for neurosis.

About 7.0 percent for personality disorder.

For the elderly over age 60, we hypothesize on the basis of available evidence that rates of psychiatric disorders are as follows:

An aggregated overall rate of functional and organic psychiatric disorders of 18.0 to 24.5 percent.

Organic psychoses, 3.5 to 5.5 percent.

Functional psychoses, 3.5 percent.

Neuroses, 6.0 to 10.5 percent.

Personality disorders, 5.0 percent.

In addition to clinical cases of psychiatric disorder, we hypothesize that

About 13 percent of the population on the average in a representative sample of U.S. communities would show severe psychological and somatic distress that was not accompanied by clinical psychiatric disorder.

Whether accompanied by diagnosable psychiatric disorder as it is in some persons, or without the presence of such disorder as in others, we think that Frank's concept of "demoralization" is the best description of this type of distress (*Persuasion and Healing*, 1973).

Considering all demoralized persons, those with and those without psychiatric disorders, we estimate the rate of demoralization at about 25 percent at any given time.

As with children, there are likely to be sharp differences in rates of psychiatric disorders among adults from different social backgrounds. On the basis of the evidence, we hypothesize that if a representative sample of U.S. communities were studied, sharp differences would be found in rates of various types of disorders for males by contrast with females, and for higher versus lower social classes.

Rates of neurosis and of affective psychosis are likely to be considered higher among women.
Rates of personality disorder are likely to be consistently higher among men.
Rates of overall functional psychiatric disorder, and the subtypes, schizophrenia and personality disorder, are likely to be consistently highest in the lowest social class.
Rates of demoralization are likely to be consistently higher in women than in men and consistently higher in lower than in higher social classes.

With regard to the treatment of identified cases among adults in the general population we hypothesize that only about a quarter of those with clinically significant functional disorders have ever received treatment from mental health professionals.
Even for the most severe disorders such as schizophrenia and other psychoses, large minorities, perhaps 20% for schizophrenia and 40% for all psychoses, have never received treatment from mental health professionals.

From B. P. Dohrenwend et al. *Mental illness in the United States*, pp. 150–152. Copyright © 1980 by Praeger Publishers. Reprinted by permission of Praeger Publishers.

The ecological model.   The ecological model predates the popularization of the term by several decades. Noted psychologist Kurt Lewin asserted that behavior is a function of person and environment. In the 1950s and 1960s the research group of Barker, Wright, Schoggen, and co-workers studied behavior in natural surroundings and developed the concept of *behavior setting.* They presented detailed analysis of the types of settings and their frequency of change in towns in the United States and in England and used the term *ecological psychology* (Barker, 1965; Barker & Associates, 1978).

James G. Kelly (1968) formulated four principles to guide the ecological analysis of community settings: *interdependence* of living units within the ecosystem; *cycling of resources*, analogous to food chains in the animal world, using new resources for changing requirements; *adaptation*, recognizing how the environment shapes adaptations; and *succession*, recognizing the instability of community orders and forms and the way in which they will be replaced by newer orders and forms. Well-known psychologist Uri Bronfen-brenner (1979) also regards the ecological approach as essential for understanding development and has formulated a long set of propositions and hypotheses. The theoretical development is becoming impressive, but the several different approaches need integration.

The concepts of *networks* and *support systems* can also be seen as an applied psychoecology. The subtitle for *networks* might be "working with a person's community" or "creating minicommunities." The networks, or support systems, of individuals consist of nodes and linkages; size, density, and clustering are components of network structure. Baker and Kelly (1980) point out the importance of definitions and instructions to research respondents. A map of a network of acquaintances will have vastly more people in it than will a map of the network of people with whom we could live for three months. *Support*, a particularly important function of the network, has the following components, according to Baker and Kelly:

> *Cognitive guidance.* Instruction or advice that will increase or augment our skills.
>
> *Feedback or reinforcement.* Knowledge of how we are doing or how we are perceived.
>
> *Emotional support, spiritual support.* People with whom affect can be openly experienced and shared.
>
> *Socialization.* Somebody with whom to do constructive or happy things; somebody with whom to talk.
>
> *Tangible support.* Somebody from whom to borrow a cup of sugar or a few nails to finish a project.
>
> *Reciprocity.* The opportunity to give back. Without such opportunity, the support may be treatment, or just patronage.

Baker and Kelly are careful to point out that each of the six components has the potential for negative, as well as positive, impact—for example, a socialization opportunity that provides ridicule or a cognitive guidance opportunity that increases confusion may be isolating rather than supportive. The Baker-Kelly analysis provides community psychologists with a practical way to inventory or design effective support networks for people. If, as they suspect, inadequate or incomplete support networks lead to dependence on institutions, the analysis and design of support networks will be an important factor in the readaptation to the community of people who have been released from institutions. Rueveni (1979), Collins and Pancoast (1977), and Caplan and Killilea (1976) have made helpful suggestions about creating, maintaining, and revitalizing such support networks.

Disasters in the Community

Community psychologists and other professionals have begun to study how to help in communities suffering from a large-scale disaster. After a disaster people seem to go through some predictable phases. For the first week or two after the event, people seem to be in the *heroic phase*. They engage in impressive actions to save lives and minimize losses. There is a clear sense of altruism and shared community. From perhaps one week to three to six months, the *honeymoon phase* involves political visits and a strong sense of shared experience with other victims, especially in reconstruction work such as the clearing of debris or reestablishing homes. A climate of anticipating help from outside officials builds up. Next, the *disillusionment phase* sets in, from perhaps two months to a year. The breaking up of the spirit of togetherness is painful. Delays, failures, or disappointments with official aid become the focus for anger, resentment, and bitterness. The final phase, *reconstruction*, sees the end of looking back and the willingness of individuals once again to pursue their separate lives with independence and self-reliance. (The parallels with the phases of culture shock when a person moves to another land are striking.)

The following simple summary makes important divisions among disaster-related problems. First, there are problems in living. There may be interference with primary needs, such as food, clothing, shelter, or basic health needs, and with secondary needs, such as transportation, employment, income, and freedom of movement. The second category is adjustment reactions, which can be divided into early reactions (such as shock, panic, and confusion) and longer-range affective syndromes (such as maladaptive denial, anxiety, depression, survivor guilt, irritability, and frustration). The third and most serious category, mental health problems and illnesses, can

Figure 12-5 Flooding after the eruption of Mt. St. Helens. (Copyright © 1982 by Ancil Nance and used by permission)

also be divided into two groupings. Exacerbation of domestic conflicts may involve spouse abuse and child abuse, and exacerbation of preexisting chronic conditions may lead to the reappearance of, say, schizophrenia, manic depression, or alcoholism. (Many of these same problems occur as sequelae to unemployment—for instance, following the closure of a factory or mill; see Liem & Rayman, 1982; Weeks & Drengacz, 1982.)

Some tentative principles of intervention have emerged. Mental health workers are taught to regard the disturbance as transitory and to emphasize that things will become restored. Workers should avoid, as much as possible, labeling people and creating a more long-lasting problem. It is helpful to design new patterns of help which fit the community. They should find existing networks of nontraditional providers of service and train mental health line staff to use them. Finally, the workers should plan for the mental health of the mental health personnel—that is, anticipate their need for support and respite as they work with the grieving or the maimed.

Questions such as "What are the long-term effects of community disasters?" or "Who is at highest risk in the event of disaster?" are just beginning to be explored systematically. It appears that high levels of stress and high vulnerability before the disaster make people more prone to poor outcome, whereas good psychological adjustment and an effective social support network reduce the likelihood of poor outcomes. Bromet's (1980) work following the Three Mile Island nuclear power plant disaster is a good example of postdisaster research. It is summarized at the end of the chapter.

PREVENTION AND CONSULTATION

Prevention (the idea that psychopathology can and should be prevented) and *consultation* (the process or activity of consulting as a way of spreading the effect of psychological knowledge) play a central role in working with groups, organizations, and communities. For both concepts, human service professionals have developed voluminous literatures, liberally sprinkled with technical terms. Readers should remember that prevention and consultation can be done *by* an individual, group, or organization *to* an individual, group, or organization and should be careful to clarify the particulars of each instance.

Prevention

On the surface prevention seems like a straightforward idea, and certainly a good one. Although it may be good—may, in fact, be the only idea that makes any sense, given the plight of our populations—the notion is anything but straightforward. First, three types of prevention (after Caplan, 1964) are usually recognized: *Primary prevention* attempts to reduce the incidence of mental disorders of all types in the community. *Secondary prevention* attempts to reduce the duration or lighten the course of disorders already begun. *Tertiary prevention* attempts to reduce impairment that may result from a disorder.

The great challenge lies in primary prevention (along with early iden-

BOX 12–3   *STRESS INOCULATION TRAINING*

Novaco (1977) presents a program for helping law enforcement officers cope with the stresses of their jobs by giving them specific skills to cope with stress—stress inoculation training. His table summarizes an important approach.

Examples of Anger Management Self-Statements Rehearsed in Stress-Inoculation Training.

Preparing for a provocation

This could be a rough situation, but I know how to deal with it. I can work out a plan to handle this. Easy does it. Remember, stick to the issues and don't take it personally. There won't be any need for an argument. I know what to do.

Impact and confrontation

As long as I keep my cool, *I'm* in control of the situation. You don't need to prove yourself. Don't make more out of this than you have to. There is no point in getting mad. Think of what you have to do. Look for the positives and don't jump to conclusions.

Coping with arousal

Muscles are getting tight. Relax and slow things down. Time to take a deep breath. Let's take the issue point by point. My anger is a signal of what I need to do. Time for problem solving. He probably wants me to get angry, but I'm going to deal with it constructively.

Subsequent reflection

a.   *Conflict unresolved*
Forget about the aggravation. Thinking about it only makes you upset.
Try to shake it off. Don't let it interfere with your job.
Remember relaxation. It's a lot better than anger.
Don't take it personally. It's probably not so serious.

b.   *Conflict resolved*
I handled that one pretty well. That's doing a good job!
I could have gotten more upset than it was worth.
My pride can get me into trouble, but I'm doing better at this all the time.
I actually got through that without getting angry.

From R. W. Novaco, A stress inoculation approach to anger management in the training of law enforcement officers. *American Journal of Community Psychology*, 1977, 5, 327–346. Copyright © 1977 by Plenum Publishing Corporation and used by permission.

tification in the secondary category). Clearly for effective prevention we must know the course of the disorder we aim to treat so the cause can be removed or blocked. Or we can discover the characteristics of immune or resistant populations and help others to adopt similar conditions.

The etiology of mental disease or disorder now appears so complex that interrupting supposed psychogenic causation is scarcely warranted as a strategy. Rutter (1979b) and other workers on the problem of vulnerability have made a promising start by showing that psychological problems relate more to the number and severity of predisposing factors and stressors than to particular single psychic traumas. Progress in prevention has been exemplary with some physical problems where a single factor or mechanism appears accountable. For example, lead poisoning and tertiary syphilis have generally yielded to effective public health measures.

Promoting competence as a way to optimize human development and avoid mental disorder has great appeal, but we must prove that added competence either interrupts a pathogen or makes people resistant or immune. Our brief discussion here can merely present the challenge. Mental health work badly needs demonstrably good preventive programs to make an impact on both the vast number of sufferers and on those who allocate funds. Bloom (1979) documents several good beginnings that are both practical and conceptual.

Psychologist George Albee deserves special mention for making prevention and positive social action more visible nationally. With his co-workers at the University of Vermont and with help from the Waters Foundation, Albee has promoted the annual Vermont Conferences on Primary Prevention. The printed volumes of the proceedings comprise some of the best thinking and research on prevention. The first volume (Albee & Joffe, 1977) gives an especially thorough introduction to conceptual issues, whereas later ones explore particular issues in depth. For a briefer summary the short section on primary prevention in Kiesler, Cummings, and VandenBos (1979) is clear and well balanced.

Consultation

The early leader in the community mental health movement, Gerald Caplan (1963), brought consultation to prominence as a mental health activity. Some people in the movement had glimpsed the possibility of a general improvement in psychological health for masses of people. It seemed that consultation might spread or multiply the effect, and thus it was much studied. Initially because Caplan came from a background of one-to-one psychiatric treatment, the major methods centered on intrapsychic phenomena, what we have called *individual systems*. The consultant's job was to unravel the consultee's presentation of a problem—typically a teacher's problems with a pupil—by identifying a lack of objectivity that might be present when a child reawakens or resymbolizes past conflicts or unresolved issues.

Quite understandably consultees now want more from their consultants than only a gentle exploration of such *theme interference* as Caplan (1963) called it. Important as such sensitivity is, consultants must additionally possess real expertise in the area of the problem. Where treatment or educational programs are concerned, for instance, consultants must be able to make vital distinctions between physical, psychological, family, or organizational issues. The decline of resources plus consultees' desire to find somebody to *do* something—not somebody with whom to talk about it—has bolstered the shift from mental health consultation to more specific content-oriented or problem-oriented consultation.

The term *consultation* has acquired a variety of meanings because of different practices and differing theoretical views (Swenson, 1974). In attempting to create a universal framework encompassing all consultation, Dworkin and Dworkin (1975) present ten ways in which consultation differs:

1. implied or explicit definition of consultation
2. self-perception of the consultant
3. target population
4. motivation of the client system
5. mode of entry of the consultant into the system
6. goal of consultation
7. role of the consultant in problem diagnosis
8. techniques employed by the consultant
9. when and how consultation is terminated
10. how consultation is evaluated

Consultation is a complicated activity requiring great subtlety. In advising large organizations about their program or their internal functioning, the consultant will face the problems of competing subsystems, posing such questions as "How can I be approachable by childcare workers, yet not have management feel I'm a tool of the workers?" Finally, the successful consultant must realize that termination of consultation, not client dependency, represents the criterion of success. Even the rather abrupt termination of consultation without effusive thanks *may* be a sign of consultee growth and independence, a job well done.

Whether the psychologist-consultant offers insights about interpersonal situations, knowledge about diagnosis and treatment, or knowledge about organizational systems and worker motivation, consultation offers a potent method for extending the impact of psychological knowledge.

CRITIQUE

Our decision to discuss groups, organizations, and communities in one chapter was made not just because of limited space, but because the book resembles psychology in general in giving more emphasis to individuals rather than to the larger systems. Bringing the three topics together has obviously given us a heterogeneous chapter, and one difficult to critique as a unit.

How adequate are these topics conceptually? The overall conceptual adequacy rests on accepting groups, organizations, and communities as living systems with similar arrays of subsystems. As Chapter 2 suggested, that view has a good deal of support. Within the three areas we have considered many specific topic areas, each one necessarily quite briefly. Had space permitted, some variability in conceptual adequacy would have become more obvious. Group therapy has conceptual strength, as do role playing and psychodrama. Much from industrial-organizational psychology has both conceptual clarity and empirical validation, although the T-group efforts have not been without their critics. As we noted, several basically different conceptual perspectives compete for working with communities. The most dominant, the community mental health perspective, has been in many ways the most conventional and least conceptually clear of the group, whereas of the others, the ecological approach appears to merit more notice than it has received.

How practical are these topics? Without hesitation we must say that work with groups, organizations, and communities is potentially intensely practical. The welcome prospect of being able to change an entire group or to alter a whole organization or segment of a community may be one of the major forces maintaining interest in these areas, each of which have produced some worthwhile and practical results. The practical nature particularly of I-O and community work may be due in part to the fact that funding sources tend to insist on a high degree of relevance and to eliminate work obviously not practical.

How effective and worthwhile are these topics empirically and socially? Group approaches to intervention have features not found in individual therapies—that is, the social contact and social skills features, which are worthwhile, even indispensable, in daily living. Group approaches often involve some cost savings, but unfortunately patients are often assigned to groups because of those savings, rather than because of the special contributions groups have for their participants.

Psychological work in private industries and organizations often must attain standards of effectiveness and worth in the eyes of corporate officers, or it cannot thrive. Mainly it has succeeded in doing so. Work with human services agencies in communities, which is under the more open scrutiny of the taxpaying public, often rates mixed reviews as to effectiveness and worth. The public's view of what it wishes to support undergoes considerable fluctuation, both because of political forces and because of large economic shifts. Community programs often have difficulty in showing effectiveness, and even when they can, several constituencies may indicate an absence of support. Community psychology has not only not sold the public on its worth, but it also faces considerable opposition to such intervention. Some American conservative groups fear public planning and organized community development. They often believe instead that "proper basic neighborly values," "pioneer spirit," or other qualities may be harmed by community intervention. We should note in fairness that work with individuals has similarly based detractions but far less, because few oppose service for the profoundly disturbed and because many conservative and fundamentalist groups have begun their own individual psychological services. Those who work in clinical-community relations and in community development need to be attuned to the wide spectrum of attitudes in their localities.

SUMMARY

Psychologists have become concerned with human behavior in groups, in organizations, and in communities. Each of these three can be understood as a living system having similar essential subsystems. Assessment and interventions can be undertaken by considering the functioning or condition of each subsystem.

Group process, an essential part of our lives, has been used in several ways for positive therapeutic effects. In group therapy, for example, the group may instill hope, let people see how normal they are, give opportunity to become important to others, and have many other profoundly positive influences. Most of these effects are different from the effects of individual psychotherapy, so that group therapy should not be seen as psychotherapy's poor cousin. Effective therapeutic groups require careful leadership.

Psychodrama and role playing have roots in social approaches to treatment. In psychodrama, players take the parts of several egos to represent and play out internal conflicts. Role playing emphasizes trying on new roles and thus experiencing one's self and the world differently. Many self-help groups provide support, guidance, and structure for persons with a variety of problems. Self-help groups deserve respect and study because of their considerable positive influence in people's lives.

Organizations are enduring groups with purposes and usually a division of roles. Clinical and counseling psychology has a good deal to offer treatment organizations through consultation. Similarly industrial-organizational psychologists work with business and industry to apply findings from research in job classification, attitudes, and motivation and in T-groups, unstructured but intensive group experiences.

Psychologists are increasingly invited to manage small mental health and human service organizations, opportunities for which they have no training and for which much industrial-organizational psychology is too specialized. They need skills to see the organization as a living system with its own goals, an understanding of managerial responsibilities and the ability to use clinical skills only when appropriate.

Community has been defined in many ways—by locality, by communication patterns, or as networks which satisfy basic needs. Different community resources serve at different parts of the life cycle. Community subsystems define problems differently and sometimes overlap, compete, or eject clients. Community psychologists note the overwhelming psychological needs of large segments of the population shown by epidemiology studies. They argue that community treatment, support systems, consultation, prevention, and early intervention must replace costly one-to-one treatment. The community mental health movement was an effort to have multidisciplinary treatment take place in a community rather than in institutions. Although not overwhelmingly successful, it has been more prevalent than have organizational, social action, and ecological approaches. Consultation and prevention feature prominently in nearly all community work.

Prevention, a great hope in recent years, suffers from the unclear etiology of most mental and social disorders and from difficulty in generating politically powerful data. As mental health services fall back toward treating the more florid and more chronic, primary prevention has lost ground to secondary and tertiary prevention. Consultation has a wide variety of forms, styles, and goals. One major division is between those consultants who help or facilitate the consultee's efforts and those who bring new information or guidance for the consultee. Consultation, which appeared to be a wave of the future some years ago, continues to be useful, particularly in schools.

RECOMMENDED READINGS

Mannino, F. V., MacLennon, B. W., & Shore, M. F. *The practice of mental health consultation.* DHEW publication (ADM) 74–112. Washington, D.C.: U.S. Government Printing Office, 1975.

   The authors give a good overview of mental health consultation with chapters on scope and on effecting change through consultation. They then provide a series of examples of consultation programs—to juvenile police, schools, alternative services to young people, media, and early childcare. Their third section focuses on training mental health consultants and troubleshooting consultation problems. The book finishes with an extensive reference guide to the consultation literature presented by topic.

Fine, L. J. Psychodrama. In R. J. Corsini (Ed.), *Current psychotherapies* (2nd ed.). Itasca, Ill.: Peacock, 1979, pp. 428–459.

   In one of his books Corsini (1981, p. 333) states, "It is my belief that of all methods of psychotherapy, none is either more logically correct or more therapeutically effective than psychodrama." In this chapter Fine presents a good overview—the history, basic concepts, techniques, and a case example. The reader may also want to read Adams-Webber's "Fixed-Role Therapy" (1981), describing the approach developed by George Kelly.

Yalom, I. D. *The theory and practice of group psychotherapy* (2nd ed.). New York: Basic Books, 1975.

Yalom's work covers aspects of group therapy and encounter groups. It is particularly strong because it looks at effects of group process and at therapist behaviors rather than taking a theoretically doctrinaire viewpoint. We have summarized several of Yalom's points.

Faucheau, C., Amado, G., & Laurent, A. Organizational development and change. *Annual Review of Psychology*, 1982, *33*, 343–370.

This review is particularly interesting because (1) it expands the idea of organizational development to the broader notion of quality of working life, and (2) it goes well beyond North America in looking at organizational innovations. Since work occupies a large percentage of the waking time and the psychological concerns of adults, it is important for those who work in clinical-community settings to be familiar with the problems and processes of improving work experience. Ideas of industrial democracy from northern Europe and "familialism" or social participation and protection in Japan are important considerations for organizational developments in other places in the world. Certainly one of the most important organizations for clinicians to understand is the school. With an ecological orientation Gump (1980) reviews research in "The School as a Social Situation," covering aspects of the physical setting, the social climate, and evaluation of changes such as those accompanying desegregation of the races in the United States. Beer (1980) presents a systems view of organizational development and a number of case studies.

Bloom, B. L. *Community mental health: A general introduction.* Monterey, Calif.: Brooks/Cole, 1983.

Bloom presents the history of the community mental health movement and the American policies and legislation that promoted the development of centers in the 1960s and 1970s. He discusses at some length prevention, consultation, crisis intervention, and assessment of community needs. Levine (1981) has an excellent book on the history and politics in community mental health. For a review of community mental health services in the United States focusing on social networks, self-help movements, citizen participation, and impacts of organizational variables, see Gonzales, Hays, Bond, and Kelly (1983). People with high school or baccalaureate degrees and others having a good knowledge and rapport with indigenous community groups are frequently involved in community programs as paraprofessionals; see books by Kahn (1981) and Alley, Blanton, and Feldman (1979). Weisenfeld and Weis (1979) present a study of hairdressers as informal caregivers in the community, and Dooley (1980) discusses the screening of paratherapists and the research needs. Muñoz, Snowden, and Kelly (1979) cover the designing and conducting of research in community settings. Roosens (1979) recounts one of the most interesting stories about community care of chronic mental patients; for 700 years the citizens of Gheel, Belgium, have been taking such patients into their homes and accepting them as they live in the community.

Russell, J. A., & Ward, L. M. Environmental psychology. *Annual Review of Psychology*, 1982, *33*, 651–688.

Those interested in clinical psychology and the helping professions have a great deal to learn about the physical environment—the places in which people live and plan to carry out their lives. There is considerable evidence in this *Annual Review* chapter of the interaction between *where* a person is and *what* she or he does. In addition the images that people have of situations influences important decisions. Some aspects of environmental psychology that should concern clinicians interested in organizations and communities include the design and interior arrangements of mental hospitals and clinics, the relation of crowding to behavioral problems, the relation between social

climate and physical layouts, the stimulating or calming characteristics of various environments, and the effects of size and placement of landmarks and other physical
features on sense of orientation and identification with a community. There are many
interesting assessment possibilities, as illustrated in the following: "Assessing Children's
Psychological Environments: Issues, Methods and Some Data from Five Contemporary
Instruments" by Sines and Zimmerman (1981), "Nature and Assessment of Behavior
Settings" by Wicker (1981), and "Environmental Dispositions" by McKechnie (1978).

Argyris, C., & Schön, D. A. *Organizational learning: A theory of action perspective.* Reading, Mass.: Addison-Wesley, 1978.
    This book represents an extension of the theory-of-practice perspective (see these
authors' book summarized at the end of Chap. 9) to the complicated problem of bringing about changes in the theory governing the actions of organizations such as corporations or educational institutions. The theory-in-use governing the actions of an organization and internalized by all of its members consists of norms, assumptions, and
strategies. The consultant as an outside observer can bring to light aspects of the total
pattern of which the members are unaware and thus set in motion communication processes that can enable them to change it.

Cowen. E. L. (Ed.). Special issue: Research in primary prevention in mental health.
American Journal of Community Psychology, 1982, *10,* 239–367.
    Persons looking for a selection of solid primary prevention studies will find this
special issue of great importance. It contains nine studies selected by a review panel,
each one dealing with people at risk and attempting "to build competencies in people
that will avert maladjustment and/or to intervene with the vulnerable to stay a menac-
ing tide" (p. 243). The research covers a variety of age, ethnic, and income groups and
displays an array of methods for preventive work, such as skill development, use of mass
media, environmental change, harnessing of social supports, and reinforcing prosocial
behaviors.

RESEARCH EXAMPLES

Coyne, J. C., & Fabricatore, J. M. Group psychotherapy in a corrections facility: A
case study of individual and institutional change. *Professional Psychology,* 1979,
10, 8–14.
    Changing institutions is difficult. Myriad forces work hard to maintain the status
quo—often successfully—and many who attempt to change institutions find themselves the objects of considerable anger. Thus case histories of institutional change are
important to study. In this article the authors describe the transition of a community
corrections center in north central Florida from a traditional group therapy focus to
more of a therapeutic community emphasizing member responsibility.
    The authors describe the history and constraints of the setting. The project did
not begin as an effort to promote institutional change. The weekly two-hour group
therapy session with 11 to 15 participants was scheduled to run for eight months. The
first significant issue raised in the group concerned trust. Exploration of the trust issue
led initially to frank mutual exchanges and renegotiation of relationships among
prisoners. The group soon shifted, however, to focus on prisoner-staff and prisoner-
institution relationships. It undertook role playing of the predicament of a zealous new
black guard. Out of this work came a great deal of direct hostility toward the guard, yet

also a real empathy for his predicament by many of the black prisoners who had suffered most.

The group decided to ask to meet with the lieutenant supervising the guard in question. The session with the lieutenant included the predictable hostility but significantly included some prisoners attempting to divert the hostility and shield the lieutenant.

From this opening, meetings began to focus on prisoners' taking responsibility for each other's behavior, including infractions of center rules. Camp administration responded positively, ultimately announcing an improvement in the terms for weekend passes. That change and others were put into effect without negative incidents.

This case study contains elements important in consultation for institutional change. There are no road maps. The quest is one of seizing serendipity and of pursuing various leads. In this case the chain is obvious from a post-hoc perspective but could not have been obvious from a prospective view. The authors are careful to acknowledge that their success here might not generalize to other institutions, but their careful exploratory posture and willingness to continue follow-up on openings and successes gives a useful example of organizational change agents at work. This is not an account of exact, quantitative research, but it is a useful report of empirical experience.

Gutkin, T. B. Teacher perceptions of consultation services provided by school psychologists. *Professional Psychology*, 1980, *11*, 637–642.

For years psychologists and other human service professionals have had differing reasons for believing that consultation was a worthwhile and effective activity. Indeed some writers have suggested that teachers may have little choice but to welcome a consultant, no matter what their feelings about the effectiveness of the consultation activity. In this study Gutkin has attempted to ascertain teachers' perceptions of school psychology consultation.

The subjects consisted of the teaching staffs of 12 midwest schools—2 parochial, 2 rural public, 7 moderately urban, and 1 heavily urban—for a total number of teachers of 173. Each consultant worked in a school for two half days per week for a period of 14 weeks. The consultants—12 advanced school psychology graduate students —operated as teacher resources and only rarely worked directly with referred students.

The core consulting process consisted primarily of defining each problem in behavioral terms, analyzing it with an emphasis on observable classroom behavior and on extrapersonal causes of student dysfunction, brainstorming alternative solutions, choosing the most appropriate solutions, implementing the chosen solution, and evaluating the impact of intervention.

At the conclusion of the 14-week period, all teachers were asked to fill out a questionnaire indicating their reactions to the consultation approach. Some 70 percent of the questionnaires were returned.

Analysis showed that teachers reacted very positively to the consultation. Teachers indicated that, in general, they found consultation services to be more effective than the traditional testing role of the school psychologist, although some teachers expressed a need for both services. Findings indicated that school psychology consultation services seem to have broad positive appeal for teachers working in a broad range of school environments; teachers appeared to believe that it was important for them to be involved in the development of remedial plans for their students and that it was important to work along with the consultant in the development of treatment strategies.

Gutkin believes that the findings provide support for consultation theorists who have argued that the consultation process results in professional growth for the consultee and is thus a viable mechanism for the prevention of psychological and educational dysfunction.

Hirsch, B. J. Natural support systems and coping with major life changes. *American Journal of Community Psychology*, 1980, 8, 159–172.

A natural support system is often considered to be an important buffer against debilitating collapse when life crises occur. In this exploratory study Hirsch's subjects were 20 recently widowed university students and 14 mature women who had returned to college. He obtained information on several categories of support, including a list of people significantly interacting with them, a daily log of interactions, and a report of the density of their support system (i.e., the relative number of close relationships, or cliques, existing within their whole support network). He also collected several measures of mental health symptoms and moods and the number of recent life changes. To supplement the questionnaire and test data, he also conducted interviews.

Findings from the study confirmed the buffer hypothesis—that is, helpful support did correlate with good adaptation under stress. Of the five forms of support—socializing, social praise or criticisms, tangible assistance, emotional support, and cognitive guidance—the last one, which involved giving information or explaining something, was most helpful for these women, most related to mental health symptoms and mood. Socializing with friends was most related to self-esteem. Another finding was that having many different connections for social support, not having a high density (all one's friends in one basket), was associated with better support and mental health. Hirsch discusses the need for developing ways to promote better adaptation to life crises through improved social networks suggested by this study. For further elaboration of procedures for research on networks, see Hirsch (1979).

Rutter, M., Maugham, B., Mortimore, P., & Ouston, J. *Fifteen thousand hours: Secondary schools and their effects on children.* Cambridge, Mass.: Harvard University Press, 1979.

In a major study of British secondary schools, the authors examine the environment and the influences provided by 12 inner London secondary schools. Their study builds on previous large-scale work done by Rutter and others and attempts to specify which differences between schools affect students in what ways.

Three types of measures were used: *intake* variables, referring to what the children were like when admitted to the schools, *process* variables dealing with the social organization of the schools and the types of environments for learning which they provided, and *outcome* variables reflecting the performance of the school through the attachments and behaviors of the children who went there.

Intake measures were a quantified verbal reasoning measure at age ten, children's scores on a behavioral measure completed by teachers, and parental occupation. Outcome measures were children's behavior in school, their attendance, their success on standardized examinations, their employment after school, and their delinquency records. The process, or ecological, variables included aspects of the geographical area, demography of the student group taken by each school, parental choices, and several variables dealing with processes within the schools themselves.

The main conclusions of the study include the following: (1) Schools differed markedly in the behavior and attainment shown by their pupils. (2) Although schools differed markedly in their proportion of behaviorally difficult or low achieving children, those differences did not wholly account for observed variations. Marked school influences remained and clearly suggested that some schools did better than others. (3) In general, better schools did better on most variables—that is, forms of success seemed closely connected. (4) Differences in outcome were *not* due to size of school, age of buildings, or available space, nor were they due to differences in type of administrative status or organization. (5) Differences *were* related to qualities of the social climate such as degree of academic emphases, teacher preparedness and professionalism, the availability of incentives and rewards, good conditions for pupils, and the extent to which pupils were able to take responsibility. (6) Some outcome factors were outside staff control. Examination (that is, academic) success tended to be better in schools with a substantial nucleus of at least average-ability children. Delinquency rates were higher in schools taking a large proportion of the least intellectually able. (7) Process variables seemed to interact—that is, where a school had a clear identity, sense of purpose, sense of cohesiveness, and so on, it did clearly better.

The total pattern of the findings, say the authors, makes it highly probable that school processes have a causal effect on pupil outcome; in particular, qualities of the school as a social institution appear powerful.

This major project deserves careful study. Its findings that children benefit from attending schools that set good standards, where teachers model good behavior, where praise and responsibility are readily available, and where lessons are well conducted is neither surprising nor new. But factors which the investigators found to be irrelevant do require notice—a modern, convenient physical plant, favorable pupil-teacher ratio, firm discipline, and parental involvement. The study suggests that with a consistent identity as a purposeful, helpful social institution, the school can be a substantial force for positive outcome in the lives of its students even in very disadvantaged areas. Rutter's book *Changing Youth in a Changing Society* (1979a), analyzing many studies of adolescent development and delinquency, will also be of interest.

Bromet, E. *Three Mile Island: Mental health findings.* Pittsburgh: Western Psychiatric Institute, 1980.

The study by Bromet and associates is somewhat of a landmark among studies of its type. She reports on the mental health of three groups of people believed to be vulnerable—mothers of preschool children, nuclear power plant workers, and community mental health system clients. They were interviewed at nine months and at one year after the Three Mile Island (TMI) nuclear accident. The study provides comparison groups from the vicinity of another nuclear facility.

This investigation of the stress associated with the disaster had greater methodological power than had previous studies: a longitudinal design, comparison groups, and the use of standardized instruments for assessing mental health. Social support measures were also assessed so that social support as a protector or buffer variable could be studied. A substantial sample size was involved at Time 1 (T1): at Three Mile Island, 328 mothers, 189 workers, and 177 mental health clients, and at the comparison site, 133 mothers, 143 workers, and 70 mental health clients. Attrition at T2 averaged only 10.5 percent.

In the first interview at T1, interviewers recorded background information, social supports, current symptomatology, current job stress, mental health in the past year, and measures of stress. At T2, interviewers recorded current symptomatology, lifetime mental health, and current job stress.

Results indicated that TMI mothers were very likely to experience clinical episodes of depression and anxiety during the year after the accident. TMI mothers also reported more subclinical symptoms of anxiety and depression than did contrast mothers. TMI mothers who were most symptom prone had a prior psychiatric history, lived within five miles of the plant, or had less adequate social support from friends and relatives. Being pregnant at the time of the accident was also a clear risk factor.

There tended to be small differences in mental health between TMI and contrast workers. In both areas workers with greater social support were less symptomatic and felt more rewarded by their jobs. Among mental health clients those who perceived the accident as dangerous and felt living near a nuclear facility was unsafe had higher anxiety scores. TMI and contrast clients did not show significantly different symptom levels.

Bromet's work is an important step in tying together the perspectives of epidemiology, crisis, and social support. Disasters are particularly important for community psychology, since they offer unusual opportunities for help and change. Though seldom predictable they occur often enough to merit considerable attention—floods, fires, earthquakes, riots, certain wartime events, and so on. The eruption of Mt. St. Helens in May 1980 provided one such emergency. One study (Leik, Leik, Ekker & Gifford, 1982) on the basis of interviews with more than 100 households indicated considerable stress but little increased mental health service; the researchers recommended provisions for emergency expansion of services.

PART IV

THE PLACE OF CLINICAL WORK IN LARGER CONTEXTS

The last two chapters ask questions about the worth and directions of clinical psychology. A responsible profession must continually evaluate the effectiveness of its activities and attempt to improve on the store of knowledge for clinical practice. Evaluation and research are the keys to accountability, and ultimately these are dependent on assumptions about values, social justice, and the nature of society. A responsible profession also attempts continually to improve the education and training of its aspiring students and its experienced members. A profession gives attention to ethical standards and to the many ethical questions that arise in the course of the work of clinicians. The developments of the future are likely to raise even more ethical questions and more career paths in the human services. There are many conflicting influences within clinical psychology and between clinical psychology and other professions. Finally at the end of the book we speculate about the future and the possibilities it holds for clinical psychology and society.

13 BEING ACCOUNTABLE:
Evaluation, Research,
and the Furtherance
of Knowledge

In previous chapters we focused on the various system levels at which assessment and intervention occur. Now we will examine important aspects of clinical psychology that cut across all of those levels—the psychological concerns for doing evaluation and research. Now the clinician steps back from direct involvement with clients and communities and asks, "Do these programs work?" "What do we know about these services and their underlying principles?" "How can we improve our understanding of the human problems and possibilities with which we deal?" With such questions psychologists show their accountability for their work and their field.

Accountability means that clinicians examine with critical rigor how a program operates so that they can explain or account for the processes and outcomes of the program. To whom is the clinician accountable? The fully accountable person keeps many relevant people in mind—the clients in the program (the consumers), the organization in which the program is embedded, the outside funding agency if there is one, the taxpayers or private contributors, the profession, and the general body of knowledge to which the program contributes. Thus "being accountable" means not just that we evaluate the practicality, costs, and benefits of a program but also that we do research to push forward our understanding of clinical work in general. The clinician is concerned not only with the sensible improvement of programs but also with the theoretical improvement of the field. Evaluation and research are thus not cut-and-dried maneuvers but creative explorations of basic concerns for mental health and the general enhancement of individuals and communities. Evaluation is to be done in ways that serve the underlying purpose of the clinical professions—that is, to help humanize an organizational society.

Typically a distinction is made between evaluation and other research. Program evaluation (evaluation, for short) is rapidly developing into an interdisciplinary profession with its own special techniques and principles (Schulberg & Perloff, 1979). In organizations it is necessarily closely tied to decision making and requires that the evaluator know something about budgeting, planning, management, and organizational development. Social scientists from any field, as well as specialists in business, government, and education, might be involved in program evaluation. In the United States strong impetus for evaluation came during the 1960s when many of the Great Society programs, such as Headstart, began. For many years federal rules required that a small percentage of grants for services be set aside for evaluation. Terms such as *cost-benefit analysis, program planning budgeting systems, policy analysis, systems analysis, management information systems,* and *program planning* came into professional use. Psychology has been in the evaluation movement because of its traditional emphasis on research with people, the research designs developed by psychologists, its professional ethical commitments, and the many psychological assessment techniques

used in evaluating programs. Psychologists have been among the most prominent leaders in developing program evaluation.

At this point we should note that the terms *evaluation, research,* and
assessment overlap a great deal. *Research* covers a broader area than the
others, actually including evaluation within its scope, and encompasses any
kind of quantitative study of a problem. *Evaluation* basically refers to a practical problem or program. One definition is as follows: "Evaluation is the
process of ascertaining the decision areas of concern, selecting appropriate information, and collecting and analyzing information in order to report summary data useful to decision makers in selecting among alternatives" (Alkin,
1972, p. 207). The emphasis on purposes in this definition reminds one of
earlier discussions of assessment—a reflection of the closeness between direct
clinical assessment and program evaluation. The difference is in the units of
concern. Evaluation attends to the larger organizations and the programs
within them. Assessment techniques for individuals may be used in evaluation, but only to ascertain outcomes or large processes of the organization.
Research of any sort includes the wide array of units of focus. Research, as we
have noted, is broader and may deal with theoretical questions, explorations
and descriptions of events of interest, and improvement of methods that may
be unrelated to immediate program needs. There is no need to belabor the
fine differences; it is sufficient to say that the furtherance of the field of
knowledge underlying clinical psychology, as well as the practical evaluation
of programs, is the responsibility of clinicians.

In this chapter we will first look at the "larger picture" of evaluation of
programs and then at the "smaller picture" of much relevance to clinical
psychology—namely, research on psychotherapy and counseling—which has
occupied a great deal of psychologists' time and effort. We will also look at
the general problem of increasing the knowledge base in clinical psychology,
and finally we will discuss a number of criticisms of evaluation and research.

PROGRAM EVALUATION

Properly used, program evaluation functions in the feedback component of
human helping systems. It keeps the organization on target, steadily improving its impact and moving in significant directions. The task of evaluation is
to monitor the operations and effects of a system in such a way that programs
(or subsystems) are accelerated, decelerated, or changed. Figure 13–1 illustrates a typical program evaluation model. At the center are a series of
events in the program about which assumptions and hypotheses are made in
aiming at program objectives. Evaluation looks at the events, evaluates their
relationships and attainments, and feeds back the information to management, which in turn allocates resources that affect the program. For instance,

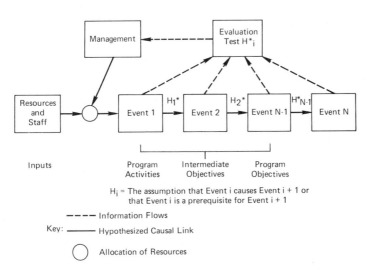

Figure 13-1 Model of program evaluation and feedback in an organization.
(Reprinted from Leonard Rutman, *Evaluation Research Methods: A Basic Guide*,
p. 46. Copyright © 1977 by Sage Publications, Inc., with permission of the
publisher.)

a new program for combating vandalism and fire setting is set up in the run-down section of a city making use of the resources and staff of a community agency. One event may be the institution of a teenage community cleanup and beautification effort with a series of events, such as recruitment in high schools, cooperative planning sessions, and work on selected vacant lots. Other parts of the program may involve the establishment of street watches during critical hours. The program is based on a set of hypotheses, one being that vandalism is primarily from local youngsters having nothing better to do; it is presumed that if many of them can be recruited for the beautification program, they will change attitudes, become proud of their communities, and will prevent other youngsters from vandalizing. Measures of attitudes, hours worked, and records of fires and vandalism can be used to feed back information to management for continuing and improving the program.

Unfortunately in reality few human service organizations do much systematic evaluation, and even among those that do, evaluation efforts are only small parts of a complex interweaving of political considerations, personal preferences, budgetary limitations, and external forces that modulate the activities of the sociotechnical systems of the modern world. We will return to these "real world" problems from time to time in this chapter and especially in the critique.

A fundamental question before the decision is made to evaluate a program is simply whether the agency is willing or able to keep records—records of client characteristics, records of the activities of the program, and records of outcome and follow-up information. Unless records are kept, there can be only impressionistic evaluation, which is often fallible and subject to bias. One of the first concerns for a program evaluator is to find out what kind of information is now available, what kinds of record keeping the agency will initiate, and how long the records may be maintained.

Process Evaluation

Starting with the basic record keeping, there are two major directions that evaluation can take: process and outcome. *Process evaluation* asks questions and gathers data about the ongoing activities and nature of a program with little direct concern about overall effectiveness. Who uses the program or is served by it? What proportion of time do staff members spend on direct client contact, on record keeping, on community consultation, and so on? How are decisions made about various kinds of problems? Evaluators obtain data for process studies by analyzing records, interviewing staff members and clients, asking staff members to keep activity diaries, and various other means.

Spielberger, Piacente, and Hobfall (1976) give an illustration of a process evaluation in a university counseling center. The goals of the study were to obtain data on performance and costs to use in developing the program. The evaluators used intensive interviews with all people connected with the center—staff members, practicum students, and paraprofessionals. Each person reported time spent on all activities. The evaluators also classified all operations of the counseling center in a set of programs. Despite the emphasis of the center on innovative crisis and walk-in programs, the study showed that individual counseling took more staff time than did any other program. Dollar cost per client was very high for individual counseling and much less for behavior therapy and group counseling. The results also pointed to the high costs of administrative meetings. As a result the center reviewed its operations and looked for ways of making more use of group and behavioral treatment and of delegating administrative activities to lower-paid staff.

Outcome Evaluation

Outcome evaluation involves the study of the effectiveness of a program in achieving its stated goals at the end of the process or of the comparison of the results of two or more programs. Ideally the research design should provide for random assignment of clients to treatment and comparison groups, assessments before and after intervention, and a follow-up survey some time after the termination of client contact with the program. Since for ethical and humanitarian reasons an experimenter can seldom assign suffering people to no treatment or to a treatment thought to be poorer than others, it is unusual to have truly random assignment. Also people making referrals to an agency tend to be upset when they do not know if a client is to receive treatment or what kind will be offered.

BOX 13-1 PATIENT RECORDS

Professionals must keep adequate records of their dealings with patients. Emergencies, transfers, review committees, and courts of law all are reasons to have clear records, not to mention that clear recording procedures can be a help in conceptualizing and dealing with problems. Although there is no standard way in which records must be kept, the work of Weed (1968, 1969) has had wide influence in medicine and psychiatry.

Psychologists in medical settings are most likely to run across derivatives or developments of Weed's Problem Oriented Record System (PORS). Obviously related to a medical model or pathology orientation, the PORS has some shortcomings when used with learning, development, or ecological views. Nonetheless, the PORS requires disciplined steps and systematic followthrough, a most positive aid to the clinical enterprise.

Broadly, the PORS has four main sections.

Data base. Data base contains essential background such as chief complaint, present illness, psychosocial history, family history and medical data, mental status exam, psychological testing, etc.

Problem list. Problems are numbered. The number is constant throughout the record so that the problem list is in effect an index. A problem list for a 22-year-old hospitalized woman might be: (1) Schizophrenia, (a) inappropriate affect, (b) loose associations, (c) delusions of grandeur, (d) excessive religious talk; (2) refusal to take medications; (3) has no job; (4) has no place to live; and (5) leaves hospital without permission (added later).

Plans. The plans are a statement of strategy: How will each problem be worked up or understood? What are the objectives of treatment, the criteria for their attainment? What types of treatment are proposed? What is the patient to be told?

Followup. The well known "SOAP notes" fall into this section: After each session or treatment, each problem should have a note setting down the *s*ubjective or symptomatic data, the *o*bjective or clinician's data, the *a*ssessment of progress or status, and the *p*lan for the next tactical move in treatment. Followup may also contain flow sheets summarizing medication usage.

Psychologists might well continue to develop record keeping systems congenial to the several common perspectives while retaining Weed's lead toward accountability in clinical thinking and recording.

As Spielberger et al. (1976) point out, outcome studies can provide useful information for practical service purposes, such as assignment of clients to available programs. Knowledge about the overall effectiveness of a program should also contribute to decisions about its funding and continuation. Process studies are important in clarifying what actually happens within the program. If a program turns out to be very effective and people wish to duplicate it, a study of the actual operations provides important

descriptive information and identifies problem areas. Thus program evaluation often includes both process and outcome studies.

Formative and Summative Evaluation

A somewhat similar distinction is that between formative and summative
evaluation (Scriven, 1967). *Summative evaluation* is the same as the outcome
approach just mentioned, its aim being to judge the ultimate utility of a program. *Formative evaluation*, like process evaluation, focuses on the operations of the program, but it has a stronger mission, that of providing feedback
as the program goes along so that programs can be altered to attain their goals
more closely. Thus formative evaluation requires *ongoing* monitoring of effectiveness. As the name suggests, it helps form or shape the program. (Continuous behavioral analysis in some kinds of therapy may be used as formative
evaluation for personal system interventions.) There are numerous ways
whereby formative evaluation may function. Certainly the evaluator must
work with the agency to develop a clear specification of goals. Then in
monitoring the program the evaluator must ascertain whether the planned
activities are actually carried out, and if so, how. Formative evaluators aim
to identify program effects, both the attainment of stated objectives and the
unforeseen side effects. Very commonly the researchers obtain data directly
from clients, asking them about the program and its effects. Demographic
data about age, sex, and ethnic composition of clientele also help in describing who uses the program and finding out who benefits and who does not.
Evaluators need to have several sources for judging benefits of a program.
Even consumer feedback may not be positively correlated with good
results—for instance, convicted child abusers are often furious about a treatment program that the judge has required them to take. Sometimes formative
evaluators ask staff members to keep problem-oriented records, which are
coded and put into computers. These, for example, can provide a running
record of the nature of patients passing through a hospital. Formative
research does not attempt to evaluate the ultimate worth of the whole program as summative research does, and it tends to use much subjective judgment, but a formative strategy can be very important in the *development* of a
program. Rutman has summarized the differences: "The emphasis in formative research is on discovery, while effectiveness evaluations are essentially
concerned with verification." (1977, p. 63).

Steps in Developing an Evaluation Study

There are a number of concepts and principles relating to evaluation which
can be arranged roughly in the order in which they must be considered.
(These largely follow the presentation in Rutman, 1977.) First, the evaluator

must *consider evaluability*—that is, he or she must analyze the decision-making system to see if the program is sufficiently clear, if goals can be articulated, and if management, staff, and clientele are interested and cooperative enough so that evaluation efforts are feasible and potentially useful. If these conditions look favorable, the evaluator must carefully *determine the purposes of the evaluation*. In addition to overt purposes, one needs to be alert to covert intentions of management or staff, such as that of using the study to "whitewash" program failures or to destroy or postpone an unwanted program. Then the evaluator will need to arrange to *articulate the program*—that is, to identify the subprograms or program components. For instance, in a legal aid clinic the program would include informing potential clients, providing legal advice, referring them to appropriate agencies, educating consumers, and representing clients in court. Each of these components will be tested in the process of evaluation. Another important step is to *specify the goals and anticipated effects*. The evaluator must look at not only the goals stated by the management and staff but also other possible consequences. The problem is often to make sure goals are specific, such as increased earnings, improved grades in school, or number of favorable judgments in court; otherwise, they are difficult to measure accurately. In addition to outcomes (or outputs), the evaluator needs to *specify antecedent variables* (inputs), those factors that provide the context and constraints on the program. She or he looks for descriptive characteristics of the organization and the community as they impinge on the program, the social class of clients, the general climate of the organization, and the nature of the problems that clients bring to the service. The evaluator must also *specify intervening variables* (throughput)—training provided staff in handling problems in the program and hypothesized links between different components or activities in the program. Examination of program documents and interviews with staff and community members will help with all of these steps. All of these activities help to determine what to measure.

Now the evaluator needs to *determine how to measure* and to consider the issues surrounding measurements to be used in the evaluation. First, the evaluator must select valid ways of measuring the variables developed from the analysis. For example, clients' social class may be one of the antecedent variables, but there are several ways to assess social class, and a justified choice must be made. Likewise, the evaluator must choose well the indicators of desired outcome, such as increased income, more community participation, greater self-confidence, or less hospitalization. As we have noted in the earlier assessment chapter, these *criteria* of effectiveness are crucial; many studies have floundered on the criterion problem. The choice of criteria is a complex issue. Consider the difference between a conservative and a liberal political climate; an arch-conservative administrator might want to prove a program just gets people off the tax rolls, whereas an arch-liberal would be interested in the happiness and social contribution of the clients. The evaluator must also consider the reliability and validity of all measures. Clinical, social, and community psychologists have developed many tests, attitude scales, and other measures that may be used in evaluations.

After all of these steps, the evaluator must *develop the research design.* The intent is to allow dependable inferences about the relation of the program to the effects. As mentioned earlier, good experimental design in summative evaluation requires pre- and posttesting with groups selected by random assignment. Randomness is important in true experiments to meet statistical assumptions of independence—that is, to guarantee that measured and unknown variables are distributed without bias in both groups. There are many administrative and ethical problems preventing random assignment in many situations, and for these Cook and Campbell (1976) prescribe quasi-experimental designs. There are two major problems to consider, pointed out by Campbell in his classic article on evaluation, entitled "Reforms as Experiments" (1969). *Internal validity* addresses the question: Can we infer that the program produced the measurable effects? The only way to contend with this question is to examine as carefully as possible what might have been causes for the results other than the program itself. In a school situation did the children in the experimental program have a different socioeconomic status from the ones in the comparison program? Were they influenced by the heightened attention given them in the experimental program? Did some children dropping out of the program affect the results? Were there statistical artifacts, such as regression toward the mean (the tendency, if measures are repeated, for extreme ones to move closer to the average)? One particular problem is the *placebo effect.* Discovered first with drug studies, it refers to the psychological effects of thinking one is receiving treatment. If a patient *believes* he or she is receiving a powerful drug, even if it is an inert substance or a sugar pill, the effects can still be great, and the patient's condition may improve. Campbell recounts a long list of possibilities to consider in identifying the plausible alternative explanations; the evaluator must think of these possibilities ahead of time and rule out as many as possible.

External validity refers to the generalizability of findings across settings, people, and times. To avoid problems the subjects should be as representative as possible of the population to which one is generalizing. The experiment itself would be conducted in a natural way in a typical setting, so that it would be feasible to install the same program elsewhere. If the experiment is repeated with several different groups and settings, the results become more convincing. Of course, the design of the study must also involve careful planning and consultation about the manipulation and analysis of data. Because many variables are often involved in outcome studies, multivariate analysis is often necessary (Spector, 1981)—that is, statistical procedures for finding the contribution of all the prominent features of a program to several different measures of outcome.

The final step in the full evaluation sequence, after the study is carried out and the results are favorable, is to provide for the *utilization and dissemination of the findings*. Unfortunately evaluators are frequently disappointed by the small impact produced by their hard work. An important reason for this low utilization is the failure to involve management and planning groups in setting up the study. To avoid this problem, evaluators should consider from the beginning how the results will be integrated in the organization or disseminated to other places. Using key decision makers to help plan and interpret the study is also essential. When the program is connected with legislation and political pressures of various kinds, the problem of articulating the evaluation processes and outcomes becomes more complex. When a political administration changes, rules and funding for a project may be changed in mid-course, or those who enthusiastically started the program are now gone. Other problems have to do with resistance to change by organizations—both professional and nonprofessional. Particularly delicate are findings that could imply loss of jobs, hiring less expensive people to replace professionals, and changes in professional responsibilities, or "turf." Legislators and administrators are also often bombarded with different sets of statistics and may choose only those which "prove" a preestablished position.

There is a great variety in the extensiveness and quality of evaluation efforts. Any particular evaluation study may not be concerned with the full range of steps outlined here. Each of the steps could itself be the focus of a study—for instance, research on the reliability and validity of a criterion of outcome or on the dissemination of the findings. What is called *evaluation* in

Figure 13-2
Presentation of report to a planning committee. (A.T.&T. Co. Photo Center)

the "real world" also varies a great deal in the formality of the research design. Some of it can hardly be called *research*. For instance, the first administrators of the Peace Corps volunteer program relied heavily on the reports of journalists who went to the foreign settings and investigated the opinions of volunteers and American and host country staff members about the successes and failures of the projects. Leaders of many short programs, such as workshops, simply ask the participants to fill out a form in which they express their attitudes toward the experience. The usual methods of evaluating the teaching of college instructors seldom go beyond obtaining the opinions of students and colleagues, although the performance of students before and after the course might be more appropriate and relevant to instructional goals. Evaluation goes on constantly, but it seldom is carried on with the systematic care suggested in the sequence of steps presented in the previous section. Of course, for many purposes such a formal and expensive operation is not necessary; simple opinions are sufficient.

Despite the importance of evaluating the huge programs that spend millions of dollars on education, health, crime control, and other human services and problems, it is very difficult to find an outstanding example of well-applied outcome research procedures such as those just outlined. Governmental and private organizations are very ambivalent about being evaluated and seldom allow enough funding to hire and train the personnel needed for an effective study of programs and their implications for policy change. In an earlier chapter we briefly mentioned studies of the federally supported Headstart programs. The results of the studies evaluating that important form of educational supplementation for three- and four-year-olds in low-income families are somewhat conflicting (Bronfenbrenner, 1975; Rivlin, 1978). Studies involving younger children and infants have reported more impressive findings (see the summary of the study by Ramey & Haskins, 1981, at the end of this chapter).

Kiesler (1980, 1982) presents excellent discussions of how psychologists might contribute to mental health policy development. He particularly calls attention to the question of deinstitutionalization of mental patients. He shows that this policy, which has been in effect in the United States for over two decades, has been sabotaged by other governmental programs, such as Medicaid which provides payment only for hospitalization and certain restricted services. Analyzing research studies, Kiesler also demonstrates that typical alternative care is more effective and less expensive than hospitalization. Thus he shows that evaluations must consider the larger system and the competition and inconsistencies among programs.

An interesting illustration of a special kind of outcome is provided by Kiesler (1980), a summary of the work of Cummings and his colleagues (Cummings, 1977; Cummings & Follette, 1968; Kiesler, Cummings, & VandenBos, 1979) at the Kaiser-Permanente hospitals in California. (These operate under prepaid health care funding rather than a fee-for-service system—a difference which probably has implications for the generalizability of the results.) These studies show the usefulness of thinking of the *marginal utility* of psychological services—that is, the effect of adding counseling and therapy to an existing health care system. It is estimated that well over 50 percent of the health problems for which people see a family doctor are predominantly psychological, and in a high proportion of these cases the patients are given inappropriate care through drugs, needless operations, and other somatic treatments. Cummings and his group developed baseline data on patients coming to the Kaiser-Permanente services. They found that people under emotional stress were extremely high users of the medical services, and that as part of a study some of these people were being shunted into brief psychotherapy. The researchers found that one psychotherapy session could reduce medical utilization by 50 percent over a period of five years. Two to eight psychotherapy sessions reduced use of expensive medical services by 75 percent. Kiesler reports other studies with similar findings. The implications for national health policy, if such studies hold up, are staggering, since the cost of medical care is enormous (Kiesler, Cummings, & VandenBos, 1979; Rosen & Wiens, 1979).

RESEARCH ON THERAPY AND COUNSELING

Because the problems of mental illness and behavioral disorders affect a high proportion of the population, produce enormous amounts of suffering, impair productivity, and are costly in private and public funds, the search for ways to alleviate such problems has led to much research. Estimates of serious psychological disturbance in the general population range from 10 to 20 percent in the United States, about the same as in Great Britain (Kiesler, 1980). Considering general health and mental health problems, Kiesler (1980) estimates that up to 100 million people in the United States are receiving inappropriate treatment for problems largely psychological in nature, and Dohrenwend et al. (1980) show that a significant proportion of the seriously disturbed are never seen by the mental health system.

Concentrating on therapy and counseling and not on the larger system, many questions of evaluation and research arise. All of the concerns of sampling and research design mentioned earlier are applicable. The *placebo effect* is particularly important. We know that people respond psychologically to attention and interest, that belief in efficacy of a procedure is an important influence in psychological reactions, and that many people are suggestible (cf. Frank, 1973); therefore, the results from a particular therapy approach may simply be a result of attention, beliefs, and suggestion rather than the "active ingredient" of the therapy itself. Many studies use untreated control groups, but some, allowing for the placebo effect, use groups that receive some other kind of treatment or at least some kind of attention rather than untreated controls.

Criterion Problem

The *criterion problem* is another complicated aspect of evaluation studies. We have already mentioned some of the sociopolitical problems in connection with the general steps in evaluation studies. For therapy studies, Lichtenstein (1980) points out, there are three basic concerns for evaluators: empirical effectiveness, practical costs and benefits, and quality of the theory. Here we will be mainly concerned with the first—outcomes of therapy. Looking at outcomes, there are several possible criteria we might use. Strupp and Hadley (1977) point out that the criteria fall in three categories according to their sources: (1) self-reports by clients or patients concerning improvement; (2) indicators of improvement in clients' relationships to others and to society, such as getting along with one's family, maintaining a job, and keeping out of prison; and (3) judgments by experts, especially the therapists, who may use special tests, such as the MMPI or behavioral records, as a basis for their conclusions. These three kinds of indicators of improvement or deterioration are not necessarily correlated with one another; in many treatment evaluations we must pay attention to changes in all three domains.

Variables in Therapy

We also need to note the variety of supplementary variables that enter into a study of treatment effectiveness. In addition to criterion (or dependent) variables, there are a larger number of possible predictors (or independent) variables, such as characteristics of clients, which can vary along many dimensions. The situations from which clients come and to which they go vary in many ways. Clinical interventions only cover a small part of a client's time (often one hour per week); what happens during the other 167 hours in the week is also important. The personal characteristics of therapists or counselors also vary a great deal, as do the methods of therapy used. Some psychologists have identified approximately 250 different kinds of psychotherapy (Corsini, 1981; Herink, 1980). Parloff (1980, pp. 289–290) reduces these to 17 general types (psychoanalytic, psychodynamic, humanistic, associative conditioning, contingent reinforcement, social learning, cognitive, relaxation, expressive-cathartic, directive, activity, crisis intervention, multiple-person, environmental modalities, and three combined modalities). Parloff (1980) figures that if we applied the standards of the U.S. Food and Drug Administration to therapy research, requiring at least one independently replicated study, we would have to have 13,600 studies of all the therapies with different kinds of cases, and the cost would be around $20 billion! Obviously psychotherapy outcome research has a long way to go, even if we can reduce drastically the number of categories of clients, situations, therapists, and methods.

There have, however, been a large number of studies of psychotherapy, behavior therapy, and counseling. Smith, Glass, and Miller (1980), in an extensive search of the literature, found over 400 studies. There have been many reviews of psychotherapy research, and it is, of course, not possible to summarize them all nor to go into detail on individual studies. Certain aspects of these reviews show us where the major conflicts have been and what the current state of outcome research is.

Major Analyses of Therapy Outcome Research

Probably the most quoted and most challenging review ever published is that of Eysenck (1952). This famous British psychologist compared the results of two studies of untreated neurotics with the results of 24 studies of neurotics who received psychotherapy. The untreated groups were hospitalized neurotics and patients making claims for insurance. In both studies two-thirds of the patients were rated as "recovered" or "considerably improved" within a year or two. This figure provides the baseline for spontaneous remission of symptoms without psychotherapy. For the other 24 studies Eysenck placed the subjects in categories such as "cured or much improved," "improved," or "not improved or left treatment." He concluded that only 44 percent of the patients treated by psychoanalysis improved; 64 percent of those having eclectic treatment improved. The obvious conclusion, that psychotherapy was useless, was a devastating condemnation, especially of the Freudian variety. Needless to say there was much anger and consternation in the psychological and psychiatric community as a result, and many criticisms of Eysenck's methods were mounted. It was pointed out that Eysenck used his own judgment in categorizing the therapy case results and that the "control group" showing spontaneous remissions might have had considerable informal psychotherapy from general physicians and hospital staff members. But the challenge was a powerful one that still troubles defenders of psychotherapy.

A number of early reviews after Eysenck's showed similar figures indicating that two-thirds of the patients recovered without psychotherapy. For instance, those surveying therapy with children (Barrett, Hampe, & Miller, 1978; Levitt, 1971) have reported about two-thirds improved. One book (Strupp, Hadley, & Gomes-Schwartz, 1977) investigated 48 research studies reporting that there were possible negative effects on clients receiving psychotherapy. They conducted a survey of the opinions of psychotherapists about such damaging effects. Mentioned by therapists were such things as exacerbation of symptoms, overdependency on the therapist, and disillusionment with therapy or the therapist. In the studies using various indicators (such as patient's or therapist's ratings or test results), the percentages of clients or patients showing deterioration varied a great deal, and many studies had serious flaws. In the one judged to be free from shortcomings, from 3 to 6 percent of the outpatients suffering neurotic difficulties and personality disorders who were treated by experienced therapists showed negative effects; these rates are similar to those for untreated cases waiting for treatment. The authors make the point that deterioration and negative effects do occur, and we know very little about the causes.

In the many years since the Eysenck review, many more studies have been done, some of them with more adequate control groups and criteria. Researchers and reviewers now see the problem as much more complex than it was originally thought to be. In general, a more positive impression seems to be emerging. Bergin and Lambert (1978) concluded in the second edition of the *Handbook of Psychotherapy and Behavior Change* that recent outcome data were more than modestly positive and that "findings generally yielded clearly positive results when compared with no-treatment, wait-list, and placebo or pseudotherapies . . . we believe that a major contributor to these newer findings is that more experienced and competent therapists have been used in recent studies" (p. 180).

In a massive *meta-analysis* of psychotherapy research, Smith and her colleagues (Smith & Glass, 1977; Smith, Glass, & Miller, 1980) coded the details of over 400 outcome studies and used statistics that transformed results to a common scale. They attended to problems of classification of therapies, clients, and other characteristics in their extensive coding system. Averaged across 475 controlled studies, the difference in the means between groups receiving psychotherapy of any type and the untreated control groups was 0.85 standard deviation units (Smith et al., 1980, p. 85). They interpret this figure to mean that the average person who receives therapy is better off at the end of it than are 80 percent of the persons who do not. They also found little evidence for negative effects. Smith and her colleagues note that the result of nine months of reading instruction in elementary school is only .67 standard deviation units—considerably less than the effects of psychotherapy. Their general conclusion is as follows (Smith et al., 1980, p. 183): "Psychotherapy is beneficial, consistently so and in many different ways. Its benefits are on a par with other expensive and ambitious interventions, such as schooling and medicine. The benefits of psychotherapy are not permanent, but then little is." In a later rigorous reanalysis of the data, Landman and Dawes (1982) also reached a positive conclusion about the efficacy of psychotherapy.

Smith et al. (1980) addressed several other interesting questions, such as "Are some forms of therapy better than others?" Although some of their analyses suggest that cognitive and cognitive-behavioral therapies have the largest effects and that particular kinds of therapy work better than others with particular kinds of problems (e.g., behavioral approaches with phobias and anxiety), they come to the general conclusion that the "different types of psychotherapy (verbal or behavioral, psychodynamic, client-centered, or systematic desensitization) do not produce different types or degrees of benefit" (p. 184). It is interesting, however, that they do not embrace eclecticism as a result but say that "although all therapies are equally effective, one must choose only one to learn and practice. . . . Pluralism is the more intelligent alternative to eclecticism. Pluralism in psychotherapy is not the mixing of orthodoxies within a therapy hour, but rather the tolerance and nurture of alternatives at a higher level. . . . Pluralism means that each school of psychotherapy should be allowed to train its next generation of practitioners, conduct its research, and advance itself as a profession" (p. 185). They also conclude from their research findings that differences in how psychotherapy is conducted (whether by experienced or novice therapists, individually or in groups, or for long or short periods) makes very little difference in benefits. Their research, it should be noted, does not address the problems of comparative costs to patients and therapists.

Another interesting part of this extensive investigation was the question: How effective is psychotherapy in comparison with drug therapy for psychological problems? The interpretations of the complete data on over 400 studies are complex, but the conclusion Smith et al. reach is that psychotherapy is about equal with drug therapy even in treating the very serious psychological disorders, and together the pharmacological and psychological approaches produce greater benefits than either one alone, but only slightly more.

Undoubtedly there will be many more outcome research studies and reviews in the future. In this complicated task of comparing studies, almost any finding can be interpreted in different ways. For instance, in their reanalysis of the Smith et al. data, Landman and Dawes (1982) found flaws in the research design, procedures, and statistics of many studies. They found, for instance, many studies that did not randomize the experimental and control groups properly. They also found that it was important to categorize target problems, which Smith et al. did not do; a larger proportion of studies showed positive results with circumscribed problems, such as simple phobias and anxieties than with more serious syndromes, as might be expected. Any number of other questions remain about the efficacy of psychotherapy and counseling. For instance, we need to know a lot more about the special problems involved in working with clients from different backgrounds; there have been very few studies of effectiveness in cross-cultural and cross-ethnic situations (Sundberg, 1981) and with people from disadvantaged and low-income backgrounds (Lorion, 1978).

Although most of the research has focused on outcomes, there is a considerable body of research on psychotherapeutic processes. A good many interesting questions arise with process research: How do verbalizations change from beginning to end in therapy? What kinds of client reactions follow therapist interpretations or other activities? How do different orientations to therapy affect the various processes of therapy? How might we analyze behavioral sequence in observations of therapy? We will not take the space here to recount process research or the work on characteristics of therapists and clients. Interested readers will find many references in books on therapy and overviews and reviews, such as to be found in Garfield and Bergin (1978).

THE FURTHERANCE
OF CLINICAL KNOWLEDGE

An aim of this book has been to present the state of knowledge in clinical psychology to students who will probably use this knowledge in their future work with people in a variety of roles and situations. We hope that some of those readers will be contributing to the expansion of that shared store of tested knowledge; we are sure that all, if they are to keep up with their fields of chosen effort, will be continuing to learn throughout their lives. How does one add to personal knowledge and to general knowledge?

Personal Learning

The personal need for knowledge—the continuing need to learn more about human conditions—is a condition of living in today's world. The next chapter will discuss a bit about the world trends and the career paths of clinical psychologists and other human service workers. Let us note here that personal knowledge for work with other people comes not just from books but to a large extent from experience. *Experiential learning* is acquired in three primary ways: through personal therapy or therapylike experiences, through organized training, and through field learning. Just as in learning about tests it is helpful to take the test oneself to understand the client's viewpoint, it is useful to participate in personal counseling or therapy or group procedures. The human service worker not only may develop insight into one's own dynamics but also may enlarge the "intuitive" or quick, empathic understanding important in the lively interaction with clients. Organized experiential training for work with people often involves workshops devoted to the skills of assessment, therapy, communications, and teamwork. It may also involve role playing in simulations of decision making in organizations or communities. People interested in continued learning about work with human beings also seek field experience. Field learning, through practica, internships, and other direct interactions with people in helping situations, is going to be much more effective if it is combined with opportunities to relate practical experiences to concepts, principles, and relevant research; this process is sometimes called *theory-practice integration*. Field learning and field instruction also need a great deal of conceptualization and research development (Keeton et al., 1976; Sundberg, 1969). The general consensus is that field learning, in contrast with academic classroom and library learning, involves strong personal feelings and immediate tests of personal ability to solve real problems and make decisions. One learns "with the gut and the heart, as well as with the head."

Some students have reported enormous emotional learning from such experiences as living for a week in a mental hospital or in homes of poor people, working as an aide in a hospital, accompanying a police officer on a beat, spending a day in a wheelchair like a handicapped person, making home visits in a ghetto with a social worker (e.g., Weitz, 1972). Others have developed personal knowledge of minority groups and other important potential clients through reading literature about them and attending ethnic festivals and music presentations. There are many means by which one can improve one's understanding of the world in which the people live. Of course, just how best to learn empathy and "folk wisdom" is an elusive educational goal, subject itself to evaluation questions.

These personal experiences develop one kind of knowledge of social reality. It seems reasonable to expect that personal experiences in participant observation of relevant human problems and problem solving are the most effective, for clinical psychology in practice is more an art than a science. Another kind of knowledge is the more formally developed information obtained through theory and research. Clinical psychology is fortunate in many ways that it straddles the basic science of psychology and the applied world of human problems and possibilities. Its concern is to keep each side in touch with the other so that the scientists' "construction of social reality" is not lost in the clouds of impractical and officious theory.

The Contexts of Discovery and Justification

Many years ago the philosopher Reichenbach (1938) pointed out an important distinction in the development of knowledge. The furtherance of research and theory depends not only on the "hard" side of science—the operational definitions, the exact designs that control extraneous variance, the careful methods, and testing of hypotheses—but also on the "soft" side—the creative insights, leaps of the imagination, an interest in playing with problems. Reichenbach called one the *context of justification* and the other the *context of discovery*.

The study of creativity is full of examples of important scientific events that arose from such a leap in imagination. Kekulé's grasp of the chemical structure of benzine popped into his head as he sat in a chair dozing; he dreamed of snakes dancing around and circling by grabbing each other's tails, and suddenly he saw the benzine ring. Fleming discovered penicillin serendipitously when he found a mold that had killed bacteria in a culture dish that had accidentally been left out overnight. No doubt the insights of many psychologists have come by accident or in periods of imaginative reverie, when old mental sets were broken allowing a reconstruction of ideas or images. Afterwards, of course, these insights must be checked against the facts, and the context of verification or justification comes into play. Knowledge is gained by oscillation between speculation and skepticism.

One of the special possibilities for clinical psychology to contribute to the advancement of science lies in the attention that clinicians give to individuals. Certainly Freud's intensive study of cases was part of the reason he was able to develop the theory and methods of psychoanalysis. Piaget also founded his theories to a large extent on his clinical observations of the thinking of children, especially his own. Behavioral therapy has gained enormously from its attention to single cases and from the monitoring of changes in stimuli and responses in individuals. The interest in the methodology and development of theories about the individual person and the surrounding situation is very promising and important: For example, several articles and books have been written about research with N = 1 (e.g., Davidson & Costello, 1969; Kazdin, 1982) and about Goal Attainment Scaling (Smith, 1981)—a procedure which can be used to see how well therapy meets the goals of the individual client. The way is open for the clinician to design ways to modify and improve his or her treatment strategies, thus becoming a true scientist-practitioner. Somewhat similar techniques could be applied to larger systems than the personal one—to families, organizations, and communities.

The development and change in the world of knowledge is subject to fads and influences from the *Zeitgeist*. There is a context around clinical psychology that encourages behaviorism at one time, cognitivism at another, and interest in unconscious motivation at another. Sometimes the opposition between various camps—psychoanalysis versus behaviorism, humanism versus empiricism—contributes to lively investigation and learning, but sometimes the conflicts between theorists lead to wasting valuable time and energy in profitless argument and controversy, time that might otherwise be used to promote new conceptual syntheses and new research directions.

Kuhn (1970) popularized the word *paradigm* as a label for such scientific convictions and showed how paradigm shifts lead to scientific revolutions. He defines paradigm as the set of *exemplars*, or problems, that researchers recognize and students are taught to deal with. From this vantage point we can see that human nature is such a rich and complex mixture that it is only natural that different groups of psychologists should have chosen different exemplars as building blocks in their systems. Psychoanalysts are not really working on the same problems that behaviorists are. The predominance of measurement, statistics, and experimental design in the exemplars that graduate students encounter in their training has been producing a particular kind of research worker. As we have been adding new exemplars to their programs from field experience, computer technology, and observations of whole ecological systems, we may now be producing a new kind of psychologist. Many observers see signs of a real scientific revolution in psychology.

CRITIQUE

How good is the conceptual framework for evaluation and research?   The furtherance of organized and generalized knowledge requires theoretical conceptions. The basis of conclusions about evaluation and other research is some conception about cause and effect. Real-life, complex systems are highly interactive, and the simple cause-and-effect assumptions used in highly controlled laboratory situations do not work in the field. A more complex theory of interaction and scientific development is needed (Maruyama, 1978).

The noted ecological psychologist Roger Barker (1965) found that it is easy to study frustration in children in a laboratory—you simply take away their toys—but in the natural situation of everyday life you may wait a long time before frustration accidentally occurs, and when it does, one situation may be very different from another. To improve knowledge we need to work back and forth between laboratory and field. Nearly all clinical research until recently has taken place under relatively controlled conditions—laboratories, clinics, and classrooms—but the behaviors and experiences we wish to affect take place in the hurly-burly, almost random life in the community. Theories relating to daily life are much needed.

Clinical research requires a confluence of theories about personality, organizations, psychometrics, and many other topics as well as principles growing out of practical experience. These various sources of ideas and principles need to be interwoven into *theories of practice.* Most of our present approaches involve either theories of personality or, as in much behavioral work, simply a set of techniques and low-level principles. For improving research in therapy and other applications, we need to develop more organized models of actions and principles at a middle level between direct clinical application and abstract theory. Despite all of our theorizing and research on psychotherapy we still know very little about the effective features or elements in that practice. Furthermore, although a great deal of psychological service is not psychotherapy but case management or custodial care, we have accumulated very little confirmed knowledge about the environments for care or for daily living in the community. When we come to the practice of prevention, we have even less of a theory of practice.

One competency that clinical researchers or evaluators should have if they hope to contribute to theory is the ability to come up with *plausible rival hypotheses* in designing studies and explaining findings. The more they can take several possibilities into consideration, the more likely it is that the findings will hold up to scrutiny. A good researcher investigates all conditions that might contribute to an outcome. After a study is finished, she or he explores again all the possible factors that might explain the findings.

How practical is evaluation and research?   Kurt Lewin said there is nothing as practical as a good theory. A well-designed research project taking account of different rival hypotheses can lead to many applications in practice and policy. However, the attitude of many administrators and many working clinicians is less than favorable toward research and evaluation. They often see such efforts as taking time and money away from direct services to clients and patients. In a "zero-sum" situation in which limited agency funds are available for allocation to direct service, evaluation, or other uses, the agency has to set priorities. Administrators must ask whether the agency should attend to short-range immediate problems only or whether it will set aside some funds to see if its programs are working well and how they might be improved. Some federal grants in the United States stipulate that a certain percentage (often only 1 or 2 percent) be put into evaluation.

There is surprisingly little evaluation of evaluation. In their review of the field Glass and Ellett (1980) say, "Evaluation, of the contemporary professional type, is done largely out of faith. Considering that the interest and commitment to evaluation is widespread, it is surprising how little solid evidence of its value can be found" (p. 225). One indicator of value would be whether results are used or not. They report two studies showing that program evaluations for the American federal government, although favored by officials, had questionable impact on legislation or management and seem to have been used selectively to lend rationality to modes of decision making that were essentially political. Studies of evaluation research that was carefully built into the organizational decision-making structure might produce other results.

The practicality of general clinical research, other than evaluation, is also a problem that is seldom investigated although often asserted. There have been many illustrations of the value of natural science research, including the research on pharmaceuticals. Because of the complexity of social science research problems, it is more difficult to show the connections between findings and usage. The Kiesler article (1980) mentioned earlier pointed to implications for policy from findings that brief psychotherapy saved on usage of medical services. Many articles in the *American Psychologist* or the *Journal of Social Issues* report studies that have implications for public policy. Both decision makers and social scientists view mental health research as important, although they differ somewhat in beliefs about its usage and the influence of politics (Weiss & Weiss, 1981).

Another area where research findings should be used is in the daily activities of clinicians themselves. Again there seems to be little research on this. One relevant area is how clinical psychologists use studies of the validity of tests. A number of people have noticed (Reynolds, 1979; Wade & Baker, 1977) that there is far from a one-to-one correspondence between the usage of a test and the amount of research on it or its judged psychometric quality. Clinicians tend to keep on using the projective techniques and other assessment procedures with which they are familiar; they see most research as not relevant to their particular clinical situation. If it could be clearly proved, however, that new methods work better for their clinical cases and if the cost of retraining were not too high, it is likely that most professional psychologists would change their procedures. If they did not, there would be reasons to raise questions about ethical responsibility for maintaining competence.

What is the social worth of evaluation and research?   To some extent we have already been discussing the answers to this question as we talked about the influence of research on policies. There are some other points that need to be made. For instance, if the decision makers were completely accountable, evaluation and research might get more support. Many bureaucrats and ordinary workers are resistant to evaluation, fearful that their inadequacies may be revealed, worried about "rocking the boat," and reluctant to make the extra effort that self-examination requires. Sometimes this resistance arises from evaluators' lack of appreciation of the different needs and values of evaluators and administrators; the development of a good working relationship is important. Evaluators often do not appreciate the stresses and constraints that decision makers and budget directors are under.

Work in mental health could benefit from comparisons across nations and societies. In many cultures there is no organized, fee-for-service psychotherapy. Human problems of living and of dealing with deviance are handled in many different ways by different societies (Triandis & Draguns, 1980). Few systematic efforts have been made to evaluate the whole enterprise of psychotherapy in various kinds of societies—traditional and modern.

Another question that can be raised about evaluation is whether it contributes to social justice. The assumptions that lie behind the choice of goals, of data to collect, and of interpretation of findings leave room for biases against certain groups. Indeed, as mentioned earlier, there is danger that some people use evaluation only to kill some programs or to make someone look good. Evaluation almost always is concerned with decisions about the allocation of resources and privileges among people. Although evaluation, which does, after all, incorporate *value* in its name, cannot be value-neutral, good evaluation can be fair; the evaluator needs to look for plausible rival explanations, for different ways of interpreting the results, and point out alternative implications.

In general, the choice of research topics and the ways in which clinicians choose to further the knowledge base of their field present problems of values. The balance between long-range goals and short-range needs is one

BOX 13-2 *MASS ASPECTS OF ACCOUNTABILITY*

Who is accountable for the masses of people who are unserved or underserved by mental health facilities? How should these sufferers be viewed by a nation's leaders and citizens? Who should be offered treatment at government expense? These are questions which may be applied to epidemiological findings given below—conclusions based on extensive research (Dohrenwend et al., 1980, p. 147):

Our exploration of the relationship between true and treated rates of psychological disorder in the true prevalence studies has led us to the following findings:

Large proportions, perhaps 75 percent, of individuals suffering from either a clinical psychological disorder or a significant degree of psychological distress have never been in treatment.

For the more severe psychotic disorders large proportions, perhaps as many as 45 percent of the cases, have never received treatment from a mental health professional.

Even for schizophrenia it seems that a large minority, perhaps 20 percent, have never been in contact with a mental health professional.

There is a tendency for women, given an equal level of distress, to seek treatment more frequently than men.

People living in urban areas are more likely to receive treatment than people in rural areas.

Separated and divorced persons are more likely to seek treatment, given an equal level of distress, than are married persons or widows.

Younger persons suffering from distress are more likely than older persons to have been in treatment.

While persons in the lower social classes are more likely to suffer from psychological distress they are less likely to have been in treatment with a mental health professional.

aspect of the large social problem of allocating resources and setting priorities. At one time in human history, decision makers allocated great resources to the building of pyramids for the glory of pharaohs, and at another time communities built cathedrals for the glory of their god. Today enormous public resources go into military armaments, and large amounts of private resources go into alcohol and drugs. When one considers the total efforts of a society, where do psychological services and their means of improvement fit on the priority list? The next chapter will touch on such questions, as we look to the future.

SUMMARY

In this chapter we have raised questions about how the clinical enterprise and individual clinicians may show their responsibility for improving their practices. Being accountable refers not only to the concern for determining the effectiveness and the costs of services but also to the advancement of the base of confirmed knowledge in the profession and science. Program evaluation is a growing field of endeavor that includes the study of both processes and outcomes of interventions. *Formative evaluation* involves monitoring the ongoing program and providing feedback to effect improvements. *Summative evaluation* is another name for outcome studies. The steps in evaluation include considering the evaluability of the program, determining its purposes, articulating the program, specifying the goals and anticipated effects and the antecedent and intervening variables, deciding on how to measure predictors and criteria, developing a research design that considers internal and external validity questions and problems such as the placebo effect, and providing for the utilization and dissemination of the findings.

Research on therapy and counseling was reviewed. We noted the importance of considering the criterion of effectiveness from several different standpoints—from that of (1) the client, (2) society and significant people in contact with the client, and (3) experts, particularly the therapists. Improvement from one viewpoint does not necessarily go along with improvement from another. We noted the complexity of the variables affecting therapeutic outcome. Major reviews of many studies suggest that therapy is effective but that with some possible exceptions, one psychotherapeutic approach seems not to be more beneficial than another.

In considering the advancement of the body of knowledge of clinical psychology, we looked at the personal experiential learning of clinicians and considered it to be a very important (although little researched) component. The general body of clinical knowledge and the theories of practice are advanced by two processes: one in the context of discovery (the gaining of insights and hypotheses) and one in the context of justification (the careful checking of the hypotheses). We noted that there are basic paradigms or assumptions about the nature of human beings and the world that occasionally shift and generate new ways of thinking and research. In the critique section we noted the importance of studying problems of clinical relevance, not just in the clinic and laboratory, but also in the field of daily behavior. We also noted the value of looking for plausible rival hypotheses in setting up and drawing conclusions from research. We concluded that evaluation itself needs evaluation and that political factors often need to be recognized as major influences in the use of evaluation and its findings. In the end we raised questions about the contribution of evaluation and research endeavors to social justice.

RECOMMENDED READINGS

Fischer, J. **Does anything work?** *Journal of Social Service Research*, 1978, *1*, 215–244.
    This article is a review of outcome research in social work, psychotherapy, corrections, psychiatric hospital services, and education. Fischer concludes pessimistically that professions operate with little empirical evidence to justify their efforts. He recom-

mends that human service professionals rid themselves of the "rescue fantasy" that they can help everyone, that they recognize their responsibility to changing social conditions, that some clients have "incurable" disorders, that calculated costs be used to determine programs if one approach is not clearly better than another, and that they adopt a more empirical model (especially a behavioral one) for training and practice. Marshall (1980) raises a relevant question in his article "Psychotherapy Works, But for Whom?"

Perloff, R., & Perloff, E. (Eds.). Special issue: Evaluation of psychological service delivery programs. *Professional Psychology*, 1977, 8(4), 377–673.

The Perloffs outline the current state of knowledge about evaluation in this special issue of *Professional Psychology* (November 1977). They make the point that evaluation has two roots: One in the humanitarian traditions of our culture and the other in the consumer movement. The following articles expand on many topics including issues such as efficiency versus justice and quality of life indicators. The APA book by Kiesler, Cummings, and VandenBos (1979) incorporates many ideas, such as the benefits of short-term psychotherapy for members of a prepaid medical plan. One paper on factors affecting utilization of evaluative findings concludes that evaluation findings have had relatively little impact on mental health program policy and examines contributing characteristics of the research itself, of the participants, of the organization, and of the communication channels through which results are communicated.

The *Annual Review* chapter by Glass and Ellett (1980) and the book *Toward Reform of Program Evaluation* by Cronbach et al. (1980) are good supplements. Bloom and Fischer (1982) in *Evaluating Practice: Guidelines for the Accountable Professions* give many helpful aids to the practitioner and show how to do a self-study of effectiveness. A. Smith (1981) reviews the development of procedures for evaluating individual cases as well as programs by Goal Attainment Scaling. The two volumes of the *Handbook of Evaluation Research* by Guttentag and Struening (1975) provide a rich source of methods and examples of evaluation.

Garfield, S. L., & Bergin, A. E. (Eds.). *Handbook of psychotherapy and behavior change* (2nd ed.). New York: John Wiley, 1978.

This book is a major resource and reference for those who are interested in psychotherapy. It covers general topics such as experimental designs, outcome research, effects of client, therapist, and process variables, as well as more specific areas such as drug therapy, child therapy, and marital counseling.

Kendall, P. C., & Butcher, J. N. (Eds.). *Handbook of research methods in clinical psychology*. New York: John Wiley, 1982.

This book is a good resource for answering questions about research problems and design in the field. Kazdin's book (1980) emphasizes evaluation of treatment, the need for multiple assessment methods, and replication designs with individuals. An important kind of research in clinical work is that involved in studying one person. The book edited by Kratochwill (1978) entitled *Single Subject Research* tells of the problems and possibilities for studying change in one person. Chasson (1979) is also helpful.

Fisher, J. D., Nadler, A., & Whitcher-Alagna, S. Recipient reactions to aid. *Psychological Bulletin*, 1982, 91, 27–54.

Sometimes in the helping professions, we assume that helping others is always desirable. What is seen as help in the short run, however, may not be help in the long run. Dependency and resentment may be the outcomes. This article is a comprehensive review of research and theory about reactions to help. The authors conclude that the best model for predicting reactions to aid involves considering the threat to self-esteem.

In evaluating helping programs it seems wise to consider how assistance might be more damaging than supportive.

Brickman, Rabinowitz, Karuza, Coates, Cohn, and Kidder (1982) look at helping from another angle—ways in which people are held responsible for problems and solutions. They raise questions about how various types of problems are most effectively viewed and propose relevant models.

Austin, J. H. *Chase, chance, and creativity: The lucky art of novelty.* **New York: Columbia University Press, 1978.**

Here a research neurologist presents his personal ideas and observations about the true nature of research, especially the chance factors that are seized and used by the alert and knowledgeable scientist and the contribution of ideas that come in "off moments." He starts out with a quotation: "What scientists do has never been the subject of a scientific . . . inquiry. It is no use looking to scientific 'papers,' for they not merely conceal but actively misrepresent the reasoning that goes into the work they describe" (p. xi). Child (1973) considers some of the "softer" sides of research including the context of discovery and creativity in *Humanistic Psychology and the Research Tradition.* For a review of research in the field see the *Annual Review* chapter by Barron and Harrington (1981) entitled "Creativity, Intelligence and Personality." Bringing together the enterprise of scientific inquiry with a systems orientation is the book by Churchman (1979), *The Systems Approach and Its Enemies.*

RESEARCH EXAMPLES

Saslow, M. *FIG-Waiver continuum of care project for the elderly. Final project report.* **Salem, Oreg.: Department of Human Resources, December 1981.**

The FIG-Waiver project was a demonstration project directed toward improved care for the elderly. It was carried out in a five-county area of southwestern Oregon. These counties are similar enough in geography, economic conditions, and demography so that results of different treatments can be compared. (Two of the counties are so sparsely populated that they were combined for the purposes of this research. There were thus four treatment groups.)

The independent variables were two changes in procedures used in providing service to the elderly. The first change, FIG (Flexible Intergovernmental Grant), consisted of taking necessary steps to *coordinate* the resources, plans, procedures, and record forms of the several community agencies active in this area. The second change, Waiver, was to obtain a waiver of the Medicaid regulations that prohibit the use of Medicaid funds for services other than nursing homes and thus permit the use of such funds for home services such as housekeepers and home-delivered meals. The research design called for the FIG change in one of the four groups, the Waiver change in another, both FIG and Waiver in a third, and no change at all in the fourth.

The dependent variables were of two kinds: direct and indirect. The direct variables, which are all that we will report in this summary, were measures of the frequency and cost of institutional and home services under the four treatment conditions, taken from quarterly reports of the participating agencies. The indirect variables concerned a variety of quantitative and qualitative changes in the service delivery systems of the agencies.

During Phase 1 of the project, contacts with agency personnel were made, forms were standardized, assessment instruments were designed and tested, and computer programs for processing data were worked out. The experiment itself began on January

1, 1980, and the final report was issued in December 1981. The researchers set up several hypotheses about what the figures would show, the most basic of which was that in the experimental counties the use of nursing homes would decrease and the use of home services increase. They also hoped to discover which of the two policy changes produced the greater effect. The data show clear support for the FIG policy change, but not for Waiver. In the county with the FIG change only, the quarterly ratio of nursing home caseload to community-based caseload declined from 3.08 to 2.28 over the period from the beginning of 1979 to the middle of 1981. In the county with both FIG and Waiver, the decline was from 2.60 to 1.90. In the Waiver-only group, the initially high ratio of 3.95 actually increased to 5.76. There was some decline in the ratio in the control group and in the state as a whole during the period, but it was smaller than in the FIG groups. In attempting to account for the anomalous Waiver results, the investigators noted that this two-county group had a substantially higher number of nursing facility beds for its population than did the other counties and thus there might have been pressure to utilize them. The major conclusion drawn from this and a large number of other kinds of data analysis was that coordination of community services can keep significantly more elderly persons functioning in their own homes. Promoting independence in the elderly is more a matter of organizational than of financial arrangements. The recommendations from this report were subsequently adopted as general practice for the state.

Ramey, C. T., & Haskins, R. The modification of intelligence through early experience. *Intelligence*, 1981, 5, 5–19.
   Infants judged to be at risk for subnormal intellectual growth on the basis of mothers' IQ and a number of social factors such as income and intactness of family, were assigned at random to an experimental (N = 27) or a control group (N = 25) very soon after birth. Both groups received nutritional supplements and pediatric care, but the experimental group also participated in a daycare program at 6 to 12 weeks of age. Appropriate tests were given at 6 months, 9 months, 12 months, 18 months, 24 months, and 36 months.
   The experimental group scored significantly higher than did the control group at all testing periods, and the difference increased with time. At the last round the average IQ for the controls was 81, similar to their mothers'. The experimental group averaged 95, in comparison with their mothers' average of 83. This report built on the authors' earlier work (Haskins, Finklestein & Stedman, 1978). Heber, in a series of studies, has also shown improvements from very early interventions with children and parents (Heber & Garber, 1973).*

Evans, R. I., Rozelle, R. M., Maxwell, S. E., Raines, B. E., Dill, C. A., Guthrie, T. J., Henderson, A. H., & Hill, P. C. Social modeling films to deter smoking in adolescents: Results of a three-year field investigation. *Journal of Applied Psychology*, 1981, 66, 399–414.
   This study is a large and well-designed one for evaluating the effects of a smoking prevention program and thus is relevant to the preceding chapters covering health psychology and prevention as well as this chapter. Richard Evans and his colleagues at the University of Houston had carried out a series of studies including extensive interviews with young adolescent students about smoking. On the basis of these they concluded that peer pressure, parents' modeling of smoking, and mass media frequently override the belief that smoking is dangerous. In addition they pointed out that many antismoking programs depend on a long-time perspective, focusing excessively on

---

*Questions have been raised about adequacy and accuracy of Heber's research (Herrnstein, 1982).

future dangers rather than immediate effects. Evans and his colleagues designed a social learning and persuasive communication program for young people to overcome these problems. They developed a set of films and posters using student narrators and actors showing immediate physiological effects from carbon monoxide that accompanies smoking; a method of detecting nicotine in the saliva; social pressures from peers, parents, and ads favoring smoking; and situations in which students successfully resist pressures to smoke.

Evans and colleagues worked in 13 junior high schools in Houston, presenting the films and setting up posters in physical education classes of selected representative schools, keeping some schools for a control group. Altogether there were 1,300 to 3,300 students involved at various times over three years during first presentations and follow-ups in the seventh, eighth, and ninth grades. The dependent variables were a questionnaire on current smoking behavior, future smoking intentions, information about smoking and its effects and with some, the saliva test for nicotine. The experimental and control groups were split into several different treatments and follow-up procedures.

The general results of this quasi-experimental design were encouraging for the interventions aimed at prevention. At the end of the eighth and ninth grades, the experimental subjects smoked less frequently and intended to smoke less than did the control subjects. Also amount of knowledge gained from the films was significantly related to smoking intentions and behaviors. Reading this study and the authors' comments would be useful for obtaining ideas about design of evaluative research. For a short review of research on smoking prevention in adolescence, see the U.S. Surgeon General's report (U.S. Department of Health and Human Services, 1982).

Sloane, R. B., Staples, F. R., Cristol, A. H., Yorkston, N. J., & Whipple, K. *Psychotherapy versus behavior therapy.* **Cambridge, Mass.: Harvard University Press, 1975.**

This well-designed study was done in the outpatient clinic of a university hospital. Patients came with a variety of symptoms such as anxiety, lack of ability to perform work or social activities, unwanted habits such as drinking, and bodily complaints such as ulcers. Students made up about half of the sample. Severely disturbed people were excluded, as were people who demanded drugs or some other kind of therapy other than psychotherapy. Of 126 people interviewed, 94 were accepted for the study. The subjects were randomly assigned to a four-month wait-list control group or to one of two treatment groups—psychotherapy emphasizing insight (with a psychoanalytic basis) or behavior therapy. In the assessment work-up, patients were given several tests, including the MMPI. An assessor other than the therapist interviewed the patient at the beginning and made ratings. Informants (usually family members) were also interviewed. After four months the same assessor interviewed the patient again, avoiding discussion of the therapy, and made ratings again. The two principal measures of change were the assessor's rating of severity of symptoms chosen initially by the patient as targets of treatment and ratings from a structured interview of adjustment in various spheres of life.

The results were that at four months all three groups had improved significantly as to severity of target symptoms, but both treatment groups were significantly better than was the wait-list group. Improvement differences on the target symptoms were not different between those participating in psychotherapy and those in behavior therapy. However, behavior therapy patients showed significantly more improvement in the area of work and social adjustment. At the time of a one-year follow-up, improvement was maintained in most patients. After a two-year period a reduced number of patients were again interviewed; again both symptomatic and adjustment measures and MMPI scales showed increased improvement or maintenance of the earlier level.

There is a great deal more information in this extensive report, which readers might want to investigate, including findings about process variables. The study is one of many in recent years showing that therapy in general "works" and is not due just to spontaneous recovery or a placebo effect. The authors conclude that behavior therapy is at least as effective and perhaps more effective than psychotherapy for moderately severe neuroses and personality disorders typically seen in an outpatient clinic. They also conclude that the patient-therapist relationship is a critical factor in success in both forms of therapy.

14 THE LARGER QUESTIONS:

Issues for Professionals, Society, and the Future

Throughout this book we have aimed to present the fundamental concepts and activities of clinical psychology as a knowledge base for students considering any one of the human services as a strong possibility for their life's work. The purpose of this final chapter is to place the profession in context— to examine the larger picture of clinical psychology as an example of a developing profession in a changing environment. We are particularly interested in identifying the issues that concern the field and society and that students will likely face in the future.

CLINICAL CAREERS

As children and adolescents develop their interests in the world of work, they usually start out with a variety of broad possibilities and gradually narrow and focus on a general direction, within which there are still many possibilities. For instance, a young woman who has her heart set on work helping sick people could end up as a social worker, a psychologist, a physician, a medical technician, a nurse's aide, a dentist, a paramedic working in an ambulance, a health educator, or even an undertaker. If she has the motivation and ability to become a social worker, psychologist, or physician, there is again within each a range of possible specialties she might pursue.

Mental health professions fall within the much broader field of human services, which have been defined as follows:

> Human services . . . comprise an intricate variety of programs and services which communities require for their own social health; for the expression of the essential humanity of interpersonal and social relations; and possibly, to avoid a breakdown in the civil order. . . . This complex range . . . includes at the very minimum the provision of income guarantees, of child welfare services, of mental health, and other health services, and of personal counseling and guidance. (Anderson, Frieden, & Murphy, 1977, p. 6)

Human services may include provisions for public welfare, housing for low-income people, rehabilitation, daycare for children, medical care, juvenile and adult corrections, human rights, senior services, alcohol and drug abuse, employment and training services, education, and so on. All of these activities as well as many others may eventually be related to clinical or mental health problems, as we have seen earlier in this book, so it is not surprising that the knowledge base of clinical psychology must be very broad and be of value to a great variety of people.

The Mental Health Professions

Within the mental health occupations the four primary professions are psychiatry, clinical and counseling psychology, psychiatric nursing, and social work. There are a host of other vocations, such as occupational therapy, pastoral counseling, and special education, that are closely related to mental health. There are also a variety of paraprofessionals, usually trained at the baccalaureate or associate of arts degree level, who work with mental patients and mental problems, as well as psychiatric aides and others who help in mental hospitals and clinics. Each of these mental health workers requires training at a different level with a variety of job descriptions; these lead to a variety of salaries, prestige levels, and duties within the whole mental health delivery system. Among these workers some might object strongly to the label *mental health*, and as can be inferred from this book, we would not be comfortable with it either. The field does not deal just with "the mind" or with medical aspects that might be implied by the word *health*. However, the term is so enshrined in daily usage and in administrative and legal language that we will continue to use it for this broad array of activities having to do with problem solving about abnormal behavior and enhancing the sociopsychological quality of life.

Because the overlap in activities among mental health workers is very great—they all practice some form of counseling or psychotherapy and assessment, for instance—one might expect that it would be easy to move from one occupation to the other or for paraprofessionals to move up the ladder to become social workers or psychiatrists, but such is not the case. There are many barriers to upward mobility on a *career ladder* and to sideways mobility into related lines of work. A *career lattice* for the several mental health occupations, allowing for ready movement across as well as up and down in the professional fields, is far from realization. For instance, a person who has started as a psychiatric paraprofessional would probably have to stop working entirely in order to go through medical school and several years of additional training in order to become a psychiatrist, even though nearly all of the detailed learning about physical diseases and broken bones would have little relevance to the daily activities of a psychiatrist. Some people have recommended that the four core mental health professions be melded into a fifth profession, psychotherapy (Henry, Sims, & Spray, 1971).

Becoming a Psychologist

Those who choose to go into professional clinical psychology in the United States typically obtain a doctoral degree, including a year of full-time supervised internship in a clinical facility. In graduate studies the standards of the American Psychological Association (APA Committee on Accreditation, 1980) require the following: (1) basic psychology courses in statistics and research, history and systems, scientific and professional ethics, biological bases of behavior, cognitive-affective bases of behavior, social bases of behavior, and individual behavior, (2) courses in assessment and intervention theory and methods, and (3) supervised practice for the personal development of

BOX 14-1 *WHAT CLINICAL PSYCHOLOGISTS DO—IN ONE BIG FELL SWOOP*

CLINICAL PSYCHOLOGISTS,
usually doctorates in psychology with several years of experience,
working within a sociocultural milieu
including a sponsoring organization,
confront
problems of psychobiological and psychosocial distress and behavioral
disorder
with the goals
of maintaining and enhancing the function of persons,
singly and collectively,
through
occupying a variety of occupational roles in a variety of settings,
acting within a conceptual framework related to behavioral science,
and performing the tasks of
designing improvement plans,
through appraisal of clients and situations,
thereby providing realistic and constructive *image building* and
decision making,
implementing improvement programs
through communication and effective cooperation with clients and
their significant surroundings, and
use of such skills as psychotherapy, behavior modification, and consultation,
and
evaluating program effectiveness,
meanwhile contributing to
the *managing, teaching, and training* of others
and
the *furtherance of knowledge of the human condition.*

From this excruciating sentence, we can summarize the varied roles of clinical
psychologists as follows:

1. *Assessor* for the gathering, organizing, evaluating, and transmitting of
   information about persons and situations, including image making.
2. *Designer* of therapy and other improvement programs.
3. *Intervener—therapist* on an individual and small-group level.
4. *Consultant—facilitator* of organizational and community processes.
5. *Administrator* of programs—planning, organizing, and reviewing.
6. *Teacher-facilitator* for conceptual and socioemotional growth.
7. *Evaluator* of programs.
8. *Knowledge developer* and researcher.

From Sundberg, Tyler, & Taplin, 1973, pp. 475–476.

clinical skills and knowledge. Among other requirements for APA approval of clinical programs is an emphasis on knowledge and experience in cultural and individual differences. In addition to university training and the internship, the psychologist who wishes to be legally certified or licensed in an American state or Canadian province must usually have at least another year of supervised experience and must pass written and oral examinations covering knowledge of psychology, competencies in clinical work, and ethical standards. In addition to provincial or state licensing, there is also national recognition through examinations by the American Board of Professional Psychology after five years of experience. The requirements for a doctorate in counseling psychology are very similar. Counseling and clinical psychologists overlap a great deal in the kind of work they do, as has been noted in some earlier chapters. Counseling psychologists need to know relatively more about vocational and educational procedures and problems, and clinical psychologists need to know relatively more about abnormal behavior, but after a few years beyond the doctorate, it is often difficult to distinguish the two.

At the master's level there are quite a few clinical positions available, particularly in public clinics, hospitals, and centers in the United States, and some states license practitioners at the master's level. However, nearly all psychologists doing private practice in the United States, independent of state or federal institutions, have a Ph.D. or its equivalent. One study (Anderson, Parenté, & Gordon, 1981) of predictions by mental health professionals suggested that master's programs will continue to be important, but that for permission to do private practice, certification at the doctoral level will be necessary in all of the core professions. In many other countries—e.g., Australia (Montgomery & Sundberg, 1977)—the master's or even the bachelor's degree is the usual level at which a person is called a psychologist and is hired for mental health services, but in most American states only doctorates with licenses may use the title.

Aside from the training and experience, there are many other characteristics to be considered in choosing to be a clinical or counseling psychologist. Of course, the psychologist must be interested in working with people. She or he needs to have a capacity for being both empathic and realistic in interactions, for conceiving of not only the individual client in the office but also the family and other systems involving the person, for coping with institutions and organizational relationships, and for understanding and respecting oneself. One of the dangers of mental health work is that of *burnout*—a feeling of tedium and hopelessness about work with difficult cases and situations day after day (Pines, Aronson, & Kafry, 1981). Clinicians must know how to set limits on their professional involvement, to find interesting aspects to it as their jobs develop over time, and to develop a support system. Phares (1979) particularly advises clinicians to have a tolerance for ambiguity —for getting along without clear answers to difficult problems—and for flexibility in meeting the changing conditions of the future. A persistent interest

BOX 14-2 *APPLYING FOR GRADUATE WORK IN CLINICAL PSYCHOLOGY*

Many undergraduate students and some with masters degrees think about applying to doctoral programs in clinical psychology. Most deadlines for application are early February but others are even earlier; so the graduating senior has to be getting information at the start of the fall term before graduating. Many people apply to 5, 10, or more different universities. There are over 100 clinical doctoral programs in the United States that are approved by the APA and over 25 doctoral programs in counseling psychology. These programs vary a great deal in emphasis on research and professional practice, in expectations about number of courses, in financial support offered, and in the nature of the faculty members. The annual APA publication *Graduate Study in Psychology* will give considerable information to a prospective applicant—the kinds of degrees offered, the requirements for application including the test results such as those from the Graduate Record Examination that are to be submitted—but the thoughtful student will want to know a lot more. It can be helpful to talk with professors in one's own department and write for information.

Most psychology departments can be of considerable assistance. If possible, it is helpful to visit the department to get a feel for its academic atmosphere, the nature of other graduate students and faculty members and the facilities. Some students look ahead to choose places where they would like to remain in professional work. For the application itself, in addition to forms to fill out, transcripts of courses taken and test results, departments will want a statement of personal interests and plans, and at least three letters of reference. Some departments require interviews and personality tests. Departments will have committees (sometimes including graduate students) reviewing all the materials and rating them. In this highly competitive situation in which perhaps five admissions are granted for 200 applicants, several aspects of the application will be important, varying with the values of the program. Certainly grades will be important, but also evidence of research interests and capabilities, evidence of clinical experience, and special background, such as minority status, will be considered. It is hard to predict whether one will be accepted or not, but by the middle of April, you will know.

in learning new things about psychology helps to keep a clinician professionally alive. This learning may occur through continued education or through research. Although a large number of clinical practitioners do little research, psychologists who are members of the APA clinical division publish a median number of five articles according to a survey (Norcross & Prochaska, 1982), and most actively participate in professional organizations. It is possible to see a clinical career as a very creative one, in which one is dealing with the most intimate and important personal and social challenges (Sundberg et al., 1973). As society changes and economic cycles for support of psychological services come and go, the flexible, creative psychologist will find many opportunities. Because of the wide usefulness of knowledge and skills in clinical psychology, she or he need not be limited to work in the "mental health industry."

PROFESSIONAL ETHICS
AND STANDARDS

One of the most important hallmarks of a profession is its establishment and enforcement of a code of ethics. Psychology can be justly proud of its history of ethical concern. In the 1950s the American Psychological Association took an empirical approach to the development of ethical standards. The association collected hundreds of examples of good, bad, and questionable cases of ethical behavior; through an extensive process of categorizing and summarizing the examples, the association arrived at a set of ethical principles. Subsequently these have been revised several times, based on the experience of the ethics committee of the APA and the proposals from committees set up to formulate standards in special areas such as research or encounter groups. The 1981 *Ethical Principles* is a distillation from this extended process. The preamble to the document is as follows:

> Psychologists respect the dignity and worth of the individual and strive for the preservation and protection of fundamental human rights. They are committed to increasing knowledge of human behavior and of people's understanding of themselves and others and to the utilization of such knowledge for the promotion of human welfare. While pursuing these objectives, they make every effort to protect the welfare of those who seek their services and of the research participants that may be the object of the study. They use their skills only for purposes consistent with these values and do not knowingly permit their misuse by others. While demanding for themselves freedom of inquiry and communication, psychologists accept the responsibility this freedom requires: competence, objectivity in the application of skills, and concern for the best interests of clients, colleagues, students, research participants, and society (APA, 1981a, p. 633)

The *Ethical Principles* then presents ten topics, with more specialized statements of ethical behavior and attitudes, including such issues as confidentiality, professional relationships, public statements, and consumer welfare. To illustrate these in more detail, here are a few questions and answers based on statements in the *Principles:*

> What should a psychologist do if research findings might touch on social policy or might be interpreted so as to adversely affect blacks, Hispanics, women or other social groups? The psychologist, according to ethical guidelines, should be particularly careful to present the limitations of the data, to minimize the possibility of misuse, and acknowledge the possibility of alternative hypotheses and explanations.
> What should a psychologist do, in planning for work with age groups or low-

income people with whom he or she has had no experience? The psychologist should obtain training, experience, and counsel to make sure that he or she provides competent services and establishes adequate relationships.

If another professional, not on the staff of the agency to which the client is coming, asks for information about a client, what should the psychologist do? He or she should obtain the written consent of the client (or the client's legal representative, in the case of children or people who are legally incompetent) to give the information to the third party. (There are certain legal exceptions, for instance, if someone is clearly in danger.) Information about clients or consultations should be discussed only for professional purposes, and reports should present only information that is relevant to those purposes.

Does an ethical psychologist have sexual intimacies with clients or engage in sexual harassment of clients, students, or employees? No.

Does a client have a right to an explanation about the nature and purposes of tests being taken? Yes, unless a contrary agreement has been made in advance.

When state or institutional rules or practices are in conflict with psychological standards and ethical principles, what should a psychologist do? The psychologist should make known his or her commitment to those principles and standards and work toward a resolution of the conflict, and toward procedures more beneficial to the public interest.

These carefully developed guidelines would apply not only to psychologists, but with some modification of details to all other human service work. As agencies use more paraprofessionals, it is important to train them to understand ethical guidelines and think through ethical problems that arise in their working situations (Pilcher & Sundberg, 1981).

The American Psychological Association has also developed a number of statements of standards in other areas of professional functioning. For instance, there are guidelines for the proper development and usage of tests (APA, 1974), which are revised from time to time. In the four most common specialties of professional psychological work—clinical psychology, counseling psychology, school psychology, and industrial-organizational psychology—the association provides approved guidelines for such matters as maintaining competence, responsiveness to service consumers, the rights of clients, and the accountability of the psychologist (APA Committee on Professional Standards, 1981).

The professional organization is concerned, then, with setting up models for high-quality performance by psychologists. The main mechanisms for attaining such desirable objectives are to educate and monitor the training institutions and to deal with complaints about violations of principles. The APA organizes inspections of training programs every five years. APA approval is highly desired by training programs and internship sites, since federal and state monies as well as academic and professional recognition and prestige may rest upon such approval. All state psychological organizations and the national organization also have ethics committees to which clients, fellow professionals, and the public in general may address inquiries and complaints for investigation.

PROFESSIONAL ISSUES

As with any vocation, there are a diversity of opinions about how well clinical psychology is doing, how it relates to other professions, and where it should be going. Problems may arise within the profession or between the profession and outside organizations and groups.

Interprofessional Rivalry and Cooperation

Some of the most troublesome problems relate to the overlapping of the boundaries of different professional specialties. There is conflict as well as confusion in the total picture of the professions in mental health. The sharpest and most persistent struggle has been between psychology and medicine, especially psychiatry. Psychiatrists—that is, physicians who specialize in the treatment of mental illness—naturally view themselves as highly qualified for this role. They have the legal right to prescribe the drugs widely used in treating mental patients. Historically they have headed the teams, made the final decisions, set the policies, and received the highest salaries. But increasingly during the decades since World War II psychologists have been challenging this leadership. Many, perhaps most, of the problems that people bring to mental health clinics do not really seem to be "illnesses" at all, but are problems of living and of choice among alternative goals, life styles, and views of self and the world. They are primarily difficulties that have arisen over the course of the individual's development through the learning processes that psychologists have been studying for years, or they are behavior patterns generated by particular social settings and circumstances. Psychologists and even some psychiatrists contend that much of medical training is irrelevant in such cases and that the professional worker best equipped to deal with them is the one with the most extensive and intensive psychological knowledge. The reader will recall from Chapters 2, 3, and 4 that there are several orientations other than the curative or pathological. Psychologists are trained not only in that perspective, which is the primary one in the training of psychiatrists, but also in the learning, developmental, and ecological viewpoints. In this continuing power struggle over the decades, psychologists have gained the right to act as therapists, to practice independently, and to act as administrators of hospital wards, agencies, and programs. The shape of clinical psychology today is partly determined by this continuing dynamic interplay in the mental health systems.

Psychologists in their turn are being challenged by specialists in other disciplines, such as social work, nursing, marriage counseling, pastoral counseling and education, and by the paraprofessionals mentioned earlier. There are those who think that the differentiation into separate professions, each with its own standards, organizations, and skills, has outlived its usefulness. Should the top position in a community mental health clinic with its prestige and high salary, for example, go to either a psychiatrist with a medical degree or a psychologist with a Ph.D. if there is on the staff a dedicated nurse or social worker whose helping skills, knowledge of the community, and administrative competence are greater than those of any other member of the staff? Should insurance payments for mental health services be channeled only to professionals with designated degrees, or should they be available to the paraprofessionals who clients think have been most helpful? Such questions are currently producing a ferment in clinical psychology that anyone who hopes to understand it must recognize. Many mental health professionals believe that in the United States a national health insurance plan will eventually include coverage for services of all core mental health paraprofessionals (Anderson et al., 1981).

Before leaving the topic of interprofessional relations, we should also note that there is much cooperation in addition to rivalry. The mental health professions share common needs for public support and legislation for mental health. They work well together in daily interaction in many settings and support and supplement each other's efforts.

Intraprofessional Diversity

Under the broad umbrella of psychology, there are many special interests. Although probably less than half of the psychologists in the United States and Canada belong to the American Psychological Association, that association is a good reflection of the issues and interests that divide the field. In the early 1980s there were over 40 divisions within the approximately 50,000-member APA, including divisions on the teaching of psychology, experimental psychology, psychology and the arts, adult development and aging, psychological hypnosis, and psychology and the law. Among the largest is the division of clinical psychology, many of whose members also belong to the counseling, community, and private practice divisions. The major polarity within the organization is between theoretical-experimental psychologists, who are usually in academic settings, and the applied psychologists, especially the clinical ones, most of whom work in nonacademic settings such as veterans' hospitals, government, the military, industry, or private practice. The experimental-academic psychologists are concerned with promoting theory and research and are seldom enthusiastic about issues of licensing, malpractice insurance, and national mental health provisions. These do interest clinicians. From the founding of the APA in 1892 until the last half of this century, academic psychologists were dominant. For a few years in the 1930s and early 1940s, applied psychologists formed a separate association. In 1959 some experimental psychologists split off to form the Psychonomic Society. In the 1960s and 1970s professional psychologists became increasingly influential. The APA is still struggling to develop an organization that will accommodate both factions. Such factionalism is not unusual in professional organizations, but in many that split has been formalized. For instance, engineering is separate from physics and chemistry, and medicine from biology. Social work and public administration are forms of applied social science, separate from such parent disciplines as sociology and political science. Psychology, at the national level and in universities, has tried to keep the theory-and-research-oriented people as closely connected as possible with the applied or practice-oriented people. A lively conversation between the two aspects of the field is likely to be productive of both better theory and better service than a formal split would be, but the strains are continual and they show up in many ways—struggles over organizational structure, over how APA dues should be spent, over what publications to support, and over how to lobby legislatures and Congress. Within university departments there are often struggles over appointments of new faculty members and standards for training and research. The decreasing governmental support for research in the early 1980s and the declining numbers of college-age students, together with the increase in psychologists in private practice, suggests that the applied wing will continue its expansion and organizational clout.

Training Models and Issues

One important focus of this theoretical-applied tension in psychology is on the training of clinical psychologists. The APA, as mentioned in Chapter 1, has confronted these issues in a series of national meetings. The first and most influential was at Boulder, Colorado, which produced the *Boulder model—* the *scientist-practitioner* concept of the clinical psychologist. Most of the 100-plus APA-approved clinical programs endorse this model, although they vary a great deal in the details for implementing it. They emphasize knowledge of basic psychological theory and performance of research along with clinical training and practical experience. However, many practicing clinical psychologists came to view the research and theoretical requirements of the Boulder model as excessive or unnecessary for performing services in private practice or other applied settings. They began to clamor for more training emphasis on procedures and principles that are useful and practical for clinical work. Relevancy was the cry of the 1960s in the halls of academe! Meanwhile the demand for admissions to clinical programs was growing. Psychology courses are among the most popular undergraduate selections in the United States, and many students want to go on to graduate work. It has not been unusual for the number of applicants to be 30 or 40 times larger than the number of admissions into clinical doctoral programs in universities.

In the 1970s some clinical psychologists began to set up professional training programs in which the emphasis shifted toward practical applications. In such programs research, if it was required at all, is carried out on practical rather than theoretical topics, and less rigorous mastery of statistics and research design is required. Some grant the Psy.D. (Doctor of Psychology) degree rather than the Ph.D. Some of these programs (Fox, Barclay, & Rodgers, 1982; Peterson, 1976; Peterson & Baron, 1975) have been carefully developed and are located in highly regarded universities. Other programs are more questionable, many of them with no university affiliation at all. Some of the freestanding (nonuniversity) professional programs are concerned about maintaining standards, and a few are approved by the APA, but others are little more than diploma mills, where willingness to pay thousands of dollars for tuition is enough to guarantee a Ph.D. or Psy.D. degree. Programs not affiliated with a university are likely to be highly dependent on tuition and on parttime volunteer help from private practitioners and are thus subject to problems of maintaining quality and continuity. It has been estimated that in the near future the programs using the practitioner model will be turning out more graduates with doctoral degrees than will those using the scientist-professional model (Watson, Caddy, Johnson, & Rimm, 1981). It remains to be seen whether the professional schools will evolve in a reputable and socially useful direction or whether clinical psychology will degenerate into such a mixed-up, ragtag collection of practitioners that the public will lose respect for the field.

In any case many issues confront the continuing development of clinical psychology, as well as other human service professions. The directions of the development will depend heavily both on internal forces within the field and on external social forces, especially the amount and kind of economic support available for mental health efforts. We have mainly been concerned here with happenings in clinical psychology in North America. Other countries are in various stages of professionalization of psychotherapy and clinical psychology (Fichter & Wittchen, 1980); most of them have no legislation governing the profession. The number of psychologists in many developing countries is so low that they have little impact on the population in general. How other cultures and societies should develop in general is an interesting topic for speculation, and the place of the helping professions in that development may take different forms in different places.

SOCIETAL ISSUES

Every nation and every culture varies somewhat from others, and the issues about mental health and human services will be related to the laws, politics, institutions, beliefs, and family life styles of the particular region. For instance, Torrey (1972) and Frank (1974) have demonstrated that medicine men and witch doctors may be very successful *within* their own cultures—as successful as psychiatrists and psychologists are within their Western cultures. The forms of psychotherapy in Japan (Reynolds, 1980) fit the needs and expectations of distressed people there for gentle confrontation of social obligations, for withdrawal and meditation, and for reintegration into the family and society. No doubt the strong family orientation and the preference for cooperation rather than competition existing in Mexico should lead to a different use of clinical psychology than is common in the United States (Diaz-Guerrero, 1977). We mention all of these points to emphasize that our following analysis of societal issues in the United States needs to be recognized as somewhat culture-bound; readers in other societies and subcultures must do their own analyses of issues most relevant to their locales.

The Helpers, the Helped, and the Unhelped

In any society the general question is "Who helps whom and how?" In North America since World War II there has been tremendous growth in the "psychological industry"—in testing, in psychotherapy and counseling, in encounter and self-exploration groups, and in consultation. Probably this growth stems from general affluence, more recognition and acceptance of psychological explanations of human problems, the increase in family breakdown and divorce, a general malaise (sometimes called the "Age of Anxiety" or the "Age of Depression"), and probably the societal emphasis on individualism and competition whereby the person who has problems keeping up with others is likely to blame himself or herself and to lose self-esteem.

But who gets psychological help? The evidence from many studies (e.g., Hollingshead & Redlich, 1958; Lorion, 1978; Ryan, 1969) is that those who receive psychotherapy are mainly those who are most promising and most liked by the dominant white, middle-class therapists—what Schofield (1964) has called the *YAVIS clients* (Young, Attractive, Verbal, Intelligent, and Successful). These people have the money for private therapists and the time to participate in therapy financed by insurance or other means. The people who do not receive much psychotherapeutic attention are what might be called *QUOID clients* (Quiet, Ugly, Old, Institutionalized, and Different culturally) (Sundberg, 1981). These are usually from low-income backgrounds. Typically in public clinics and mental hospitals they are given only drugs and short visits with professionals; yet there is considerable evidence (Lorion, 1978) that with a proper approach, many low-income people are as interested in and responsive to psychotherapy as are other clients.

There are significant problems in working with many of the mentally ill —especially the chronically mentally ill and those from nonmainstream cultures. Many trained mental health workers do not want to live and work in the ghetto or remote rural areas. Many do not speak the language or understand the culture of Hispanics or Indo-Chinese refugees. People who work with chronic patients often experience professional "burnout" and turn to other work. It has become quite apparent that governmental policies in training and in support for service programs might be used to meet these service needs. In the past most psychiatrists and many psychologists trained at great public expense have turned to private practice, where the majority of their clients are of the YAVIS type. Will it be possible to change interests of students and the reward systems in training and subsequent service, so that more professionals will help more of the QUOID kind of people? This question needs to be discussed and tested experimentally.

Who helps people with their psychological needs? Within the core mental health professions, we have already discussed some issues. There are also issues concerning the proper position and authority of these core professions, and about professionalism in general. Illich (1976; Illich et al., 1977) is the most vitriolic attacker of professionalism (of all sorts, including medicine, education, and law). He portrays stereotypical professionals as persons who set themselves up as highly trained authorities with monopolistic control over certain knowledge (and in the case of physicians, over drugs and surgery), encouraging dependency and extracting disproportionate fees from a partially helpless populace. Illich advocates the deprofessionalization of society and encourages people to take education and health into their own hands as much as possible.

"Natural Helping" and Alternative Helpers

In the 1970s and 1980s there was considerable growth of alternatives to professional treatment. The value of native helpers among Chicanos and other groups has been recognized. The paraprofessional movement can be seen as a way to broaden the base of help giving and to move away from professional dominance. Paraprofessionals have been valued in programs for minority groups and women, who are in short supply among the professionals. A wide variety of programs utilize paraprofessionals such as homemakers trained for working with mental patients or college students working in mental hospitals or nursing homes. Durlak (1979) concluded from a review that the clinical outcomes from paraprofessionals equaled or exceeded those of professionals.

Natural (sometimes called *alternative*) helpers often provide support systems in times of stress. Gottlieb and Schroter (1978) classify these into three kinds: *self-help* groups, such as Alcoholics Anonymous; *community care givers*, that is, nonmental health professionals, such as teachers, the clergy, or people offering personal services, like bartenders and hair dressers (cf. Weisenfeld & Weis, 1979); and *social intimates*, that is, close friends and family members. Many community psychologists are concerned with improving social support groups that occur naturally in the community. Some people advocate programs of *empowerment* for groups that are downtrodden and poor; the basic hypothesis is that lack of control of one's destiny and an accompanying sense of alienation or anger about the rest of society is destructive of mental health. One of the most important ways to empower people is to get them into respected and interesting jobs. This is why many people are very concerned about the low levels of employment among black youth in ghettoes and other places. In addition to the danger of riots, crime, and social unrest, *demoralization* among the unemployed and others is often seen as a general cause of mental disorder (Dohrenwend et al., 1980; Frank, 1974). Those who are concerned about prevention and about long-term community epidemiology of mental disorders need to consider issues of policy and planning in the light of psychological principles.

Fiscal Issues

Another set of problems concerns the lack of agreement between what forward-looking psychologists see as promising future directions for the professions and what policy makers see as a desirable way of paying for the service. Increasingly U.S. social policies have favored what is called *third-party reimbursement*, which in medicine has become the preferred system. The patient goes to the doctor to be diagnosed and treated, and his or her insurance company pays some or all of the bill. Many, perhaps most, psychological difficulties do not fit neatly into this mold. There is often no clear diagnosis, especially at the outset, and the individual's family, school, friends, and community may require the psychologist's attention more urgently than does the individual patient. Furthermore, the importance of *prevention* of psychological problems, especially those of children, has been increasingly recognized, as has been discussed in Chapter 12. A psychologist on a salary in a community-supported clinic may set priorities, choosing to spend some time dealing with undesirable situations in order to prevent pathology rather than to devote all of it to changing pathological behavior of individuals who have already suffered from these situations, but it is difficult or impossible to pay for such preventive efforts under insurance reimbursement. Moves in the early 1980s to focus the efforts of the National Institute of Mental Health and the states' mental health machinery only on those already chronically mentally ill also work against early detection and prevention of disorders.

We have repeatedly called attention to the operation of organized systems calling for intervention at different levels in different cases. We are also convinced of the importance of prevention in the fight against psychological difficulties, but we recognize that there must be changes in prevailing social institutions if such efforts are to succeed and that such changes do not come quickly or easily. A young psychologist, even though she or he considers the "medical model" inadequate as a framework for dealing with the complexities of human maladjustment, must still make a living. Some uneasy compromises are being reached in a situation that has inherent tensions and potential instabilities.

There are other patterns of service and reimbursement in existence, such as the Health Maintenance Organization (HMO), to which people make regular payments in exchange for medical and psychological care. A large number of psychologists work in salaried positions in programs such as county, state, and federal clinics and hospitals, where people receive regular care free or for a minimal general payment. The possibility of a comprehensive National Health Service repeatedly comes up in Congress. Many other countries, especially those of northern Europe, have had free or inexpensive public health services including mental health services for many years. Psychologists and others in the human services need to be sensitive to the larger context in which they work and the broad societal needs for mental health that go beyond the fee-for-service possibilities.

THE FUTURE?

Chapter 1 mentioned that the period since 1960 has been one of doubts and reorientations and that there is a sense of unease as we approach the end of the century—the second millenium. In a rapidly changing world in which new technological developments are reported every week, in which all life could be easily destroyed by nuclear war, and in which problems of population, energy, pollution, and food supplies loom large, the future of clinical psychology seems only a small part of a dynamic puzzle that may turn out to form a most horrible or most beautiful picture. The growing multidisciplinary field of *future studies* (Cornish, 1977; Fowles, 1978) offers some intriguing possibilities. No one can predict the future with any sense of accuracy. The futurist Toffler (1970) quotes the ironic Chinese proverb "To prophesy is extremely difficult—especially with respect to the future" (p. 5). Yet there are many benefits to be gained from looking at future possibilities. Out of this can come a clarification of our values and goals and an awareness of steps we might take to forestall undesirable consequences or to promote creative efforts to enhance quality of life. Thus a vision of the future can be a motivating force for actions today. Certainly some of the great religious teachings upholding possible ways for people to live together and some of the literary views of utopias and dystopias have given people goals and food for thought and have led to decisions about courses of action.

Forecasting

Some kinds of future thinking may be quite concrete. For instance, we already know the populations of various countries and the age distributions. We can project trends of growth within a certain range of error. We know about how many children will be starting school next year or college ten years from now. These people are already alive, and barring a catastrophe or a large change in immigration policies we can project the numbers quite accurately. We know that the percentage of Americans over 65 has risen from 4 percent in 1900 to 11 percent in 1980 and will be 13 percent by 2000 and nearly 20 percent by 2030 (Schweiker, 1981). America and much of the industrialized world will be graying, a forecast suggesting many consequences in store for clinical and counseling psychology—problems of retirement, adjustment to loss and dying, effects of failing memory and strength, the community mental health aspects of living alone or in nursing homes. Future studies make use of such demographic projections.

Another quite concrete element in future projections is provided by technological developments already in existence but not yet put into application. The potentials of computers and communication satellites were recognized decades before they were fully applied. The future studies specialist can obtain expert judgments from people who are knowledgeable about an area and can combine them to come up with considered "guesstimates" about the likelihood of any number of future events. There are a few such projections or estimates specific to the field of mental health. One psychiatrist, Maxmen (1976), has listed a number of events based on his reading of various futurology sources, for instance:

> By 1990: Chemical cure for schizophrenia.
> Wide use of tests in children that will reliably predict their developing some major mental illness in adulthood.
> Wide use of computers to prescribe medications.

Figure 14-1 Computer literacy is a requirement for the future—a schoolroom in North America. (Ken Karp)

By 1995:	General availability of computers to conduct psychotherapy.
	Frequent use of conference videophones for group psychotherapy.
	General availability of physical and chemical means to modify some forms of criminal behavior.
	Virtual elimination of state mental hospitals.
	First human clone.
By 2000:	Wide availability of computers that "learn" from experience.
	Moderate chemical control of senility.
	Periodic polling of public on health care issues, by computer.
By 2010:	Wide use of interactive television for psychotherapy, greatly diminishing need for out-patient clinics.
	Wide use of artificial insemination to produce genetically superior offspring.
	Reliable tests available to predict interpersonal skills of medics, which are used as admission criteria.
By 2015:	Demonstration of man-machine symbiosis, enabling people to extend their intelligence by direct electromechanical interaction between brain and computer.
	Use of drugs or altered prenatal conditions to raise IQ of normal individuals by 10 to 20 points.
	Average U.S. life expectancy 95 years old, with commensurate prolongation of vigor. (pp. 276–282)

Forecasts and predictions are, of course, speculative. It is doubtful that people in 1950 could have predicted the many developments in psychology by 1980—e.g., the behavioral movement, the Peace Corps and astronaut selection programs, the deinstitutionalization of mental hospital patients.

The Complexity of Future Forces

Clinical psychology will develop in the future in response to two major kinds of forces: the internal ones arising within the profession and the external ones arising from the surrounding society. We have already discussed many of the internal issues—the concern over who shall do the training of psychologists, whether it be universities or free-standing professional schools, the problems of getting psychologists to work with certain kinds of cases (the QUOID people), the power struggles between experimental and applied branches of psychology. The internal influences are great, but the external influences seem much greater. The dramatic downturn brought on in 1981 by the Reagan administration in federal funding of training, research, and services by the National Institute of Mental Health and of the social science part of the National Science Foundation was an illustration of how dependent the psychological research and training is on national politics, as was the reverse upswing in funding provided by the Kennedy-Johnson administration in the 1960s. Even larger external influences are depicted by Figure 14–2; these were derived by writings on long-range trends over the last hundred years (Sundberg & Thurber, 1980).

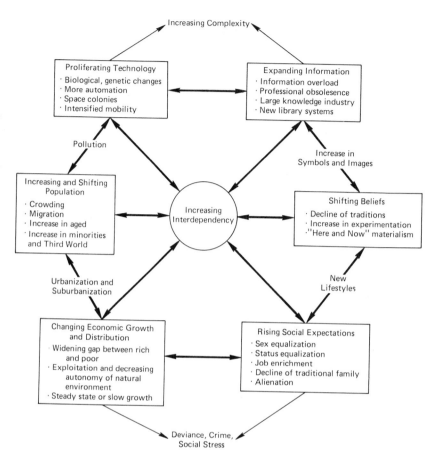

Figure 14-2   Frequently mentioned forces of the future and examples. (Reprinted with permission from *International Journal of Intercultural Relations*, 4. N. Sundberg & C. Thurber, World trends and future prospects for the development of human resources. Copyright © 1980, Pergamon Press, Ltd.

Figure 14–2 shows on the left side some of the "harder" facts and factors of the future—those in technology, demographics, and economics. On the right side are some of the "softer" developments—informational expansion, shifting beliefs, and social expectations. All of these are interconnected and provide a *Zeitgeist* of rapid change and turbulence. One of the great challenges for theorists and statisticians is how to deal with the complex interactive causality involved here—the *heterogenistics* as Maruyama calls it—and the discontinuous transformations that may occur (Maruyama, 1963, 1978). With any of these six areas of likely future trends, a large number of implications for clinical psychology and mental health work in general can be derived. The projections can become so complex that it is difficult to untangle them and see the resulting picture, but with expert estimates, specified assumptions, and computer assistance, such projected futures can be outlined or approximated.

As a final exercise in future gazing, we have developed a set of scenarios written from the year 2000 about clinical psychology and related mental health activities:

Scenario A: An Optimistic Look Ahead

By the year 2000 the population of the planet Earth has reached the six billion predicted by the United Nations several decades earlier; this amount is a tremendous increase from the less than one billion in 1800 and the less than two billion in 1900. However, several factors have made this number seem less of a problem. Research by biologists has created long-acting birth control vaccinations which are easily used in mass programs because the materials simply increase certain natural body processes; alternative birth control medication can be taken as natural foods. The formerly opposed religious organizations now endorse them. Also the Soviet Union and the United States are jointly sponsoring a set of "space colonies" to orbit the Earth, and psychologists are helping to select people from many countries to live in experimental societies; it is anticipated that by the year 2025, ten million people will be living on the moon or in these various colonies and that the results of the experiments in new sociotechnical systems and different life styles will lead to redesigning many communities on Earth. The trend on Earth is also toward small, optimum-sized, decentralized social units and communities; these have been shown to cut down on crime and promote better family and group relations.

Through research and development projects social scientists, working with technicians, have produced many innovations in mass media and education—interactive procedures whereby people can exchange information on many topics immediately. The problem of information overload has been attacked by developing programs for values clarification and exercises in priority setting on personal and community levels, used routinely in school, college, and postgraduate education, as well as community meetings. Future studies and research on social indicators have been well funded in the late 1980s and 1990s. The commonality and differences among various philosophies and religions is widely known and accepted. Commentators in mass media frequently analyze the value assumptions underlying political decisions and project, through computerized technology, the concrete future outcomes of policy decisions under consideration. The diversity of opinions and life styles has increased in the last part of the twentieth century, and there have been strong efforts to encourage diversity, including traditional ways of life, and to preserve cultures that once were in danger of extinction.

It is also widely accepted now, based on social science research, that it is economically as well as socially better to have a much more equal distribution of wealth than was common in the previous centuries. As part of the "voluntary equality" movement, it has been customary for people to share their wealth with others (although they still complain about taxes) and to volunteer for community and foreign projects promoting self-help in less developed areas. The work force is now drastically altered by the widespread use of robotics in menial factory tasks, and everybody has more leisure. The standard work week is 30 hours. Social scientists and recreation specialists are working with communities to develop many ingenious ways for people to make meaningful use of their time and to sort out their values and priorities for the 24 hours of the day (which is still the accepted amount of time allotted to each person!). Children have opportunities to participate in training for prosocial and proactive behavior, programs that have been shown to prevent later behavioral disorders and interpersonal problems. It is customary for young people to give two years of national service after high school; they may choose among the military services or many projects meeting community and public needs either in their home country or in some other part of the world. Many people now start partial retirement at age 55 but may continue to work if they wish until late in life. The average length of life in countries with modern public health and advanced antipollution programs is now 85.

In the field of mental health there have been many fortunate developments. Geneticists have discovered ways of detecting schizophrenia-prone people at various levels of risk for their offspring; genetic counseling and postnatal training have drastically cut the incidence of schizophrenia and manic-depressive psychoses and will, it is estimated, nearly eliminate schizophrenia by the year 2025, except among the older chronically mentally ill. Even the chronic psychotics and the severely retarded have benefited a great deal from the research and training programs instituted in the last two decades of the twentieth century. Building on behavioral and cognitive (information-processing) assessment procedures started in the 1970s and 1980s, psychologists and other mental health workers have produced extensive training programs to develop potentials of the chronically mentally ill for contributing to society and maintaining independent or partially independent lives. The aim is as much "normalization" as possible, but communities have extended their acceptance of nonharmful abnormality so that people showing unusual behavior are more readily valued for whatever they can contribute to society. The small neighborhood units now common in cities also allow for more care, protection, and education of people who need special attention, including children.

Another mental health problem seems on the way to solution—substance abuse. Through educational programs in the schools and effective mass media efforts, the number of young people taking up destructive drug habits has fallen to half of what it was in 1980. Some biological discoveries have aided by identifying genetic characteristics that put some people at risk for alcoholism; research workers have developed pharmaceuticals that counter that tendency. Other new drugs provide experience-enhancement that is psychologically more rewarding but not as destructive as heroin, and these are being increasingly used. Psychological research shows that new programs of leisure-time activities, especially for adolescents and retirees, have helped to solve many social problems. Demonstrating and evaluating such programs and monitoring social problems by means of national and local indicators of crime, mental disorders, and level of alienation, boredom, and depression have facilitated the acceptance of plans for preventing difficulties. Much has been accomplished, but much remains to be done, of course.

Scenario B: A Pessimistic View

Looking back from the year 2000, this observer sees many things that went wrong and led to the mental health mess that we are in today. Fortunately the Earth still carries its load of humanity, although it has been much distorted by overpopulation (now about 6 billion) and by sporadic radioactive "outbreaks," the results of terrorist activity and of accidents. Certain sections of the globe have become unusable; sections that, like Bikini atoll earlier, have too much radioactive residue to support human beings or other complex forms of life. The amount of food-producing area on land and sea has thus diminished at the same time that soil erosion, pollution, and urbanization has taken more land out of production. The collapse predicted in *Limits to Growth* (Meadows et al., 1972) has not yet come, but it appears that the computerized projections of population, pollution, food production, and energy were not far wrong. However, let us set aside the great problems of the physical environment and population and look at the current status of mental health.

What we were calling "the age of anxiety" in the 1950s, "the age of depression" in the early 1980s, along with the "me-ism" and other discouraging human characteristics in that general period, was only the beginning of a very unfortunate trend. The severe unemployment growing out of industrial automation and robotics, the influx of poor people and refugees into the United States and other affluent and relatively open countries, and the unwise economic policies of the last two decades have produced great discontent; many riots have been put down with police force; and many people have experienced much boredom, alienation, and escape through drugs and alcohol. Crime has continued to rise, and many affluent people have moved from separate suburban houses into fortified centers, thus restricting their freedom of movement, even during the day. Inequality in the distribution of wealth has increased dramatically since 1981, and general alienation among both rich and poor has decreased the support for mental health services. "Look out for yourself" is the slogan. Both the left and the right have condemned mental

Figure 14-3 Over half the world is poor and in less developed countries—a schoolroom in Bangladesh. (John Isaac, United Nations)

health professionals—the left for elitism and ineffectiveness; the right for their cost to taxpayers and the need to exert strong control over deviants. However, some parts of the social sciences and applied psychology have profited. Psychiatrists, psychologists, nurses, and social workers who are willing to work in the large "warehouses" for criminals and political malcontents are getting jobs. In the last two decades the major support for research has been in the military. In general, mental illness has come to mean social opposition to those in power and has been used quite effectively to justify social control. Otherwise mental health is not much talked about, since it is so closely tied to political dissent. Large proportions of the population are permanently on tranquilizers and other psychotropic drugs. The old medical model popular earlier in the century has come back in full force reinforced by many genetic and biomedical developments. The weakening of the social, cultural, and psychological approaches to treatment is partly a result of a dramatic downturn in research support in the early 1980s. Those psychologists trained in the 1970s and 1980s who have found work are with private industry, mainly in personnel selection and bioengineering, or in the large government institutions for the "mentally ill" already noted. There is still considerable mental retardation, especially because of the upswing in alcohol fetal syndrome and other genetic and birth defects due to the large amount of substance abuse and to the demise of services for pregnant women and early childcare programs. Custodial care has again become the main way of dealing with retardation, because it is cheaper than other programs; there are rumors of "euthanasia" in some institutions.

Scenario C: An Intermediate Scenario

Looking back from the year 2000, one sees a mixed picture of the recent decades. The predicted dire warnings about severe energy and food shortages have not proven true because of new technological developments, but the dangers are not over. The population of the Earth is now about 6 billion and that of the United States 310 million. The proportion of "Anglos" has declined as the number of Hispanics and nonwhites has increased, because of differences in birth rates and immigration. Hispanics are now the largest minority, and nearly every mental health clinic must employ Spanish-speaking clinicians. Among the many service occupations, those most closely related to mental health have grown at about the same rate as the others. In the public employment sector, the relative number of psychologists and other human service workers is somewhat larger than it was two decades ago; the conservative U.S. governments in the 1980s did not expand services or continue training programs as had previous administrations. The recent swing back to a liberal government has not resulted in much change yet.

The most notable changes in the mental health area have been in some of the details of service delivery, particularly as it has profited from technology. A nationwide system of record keeping has resulted in new methods for protecting privacy and from the accelerated concern for keeping track of people with criminal records or potentialities. Despite fears by many, this national system was inaugurated in the late 1980s, and only minor problems have appeared. In psychological assessment there are now computerized "multiphasic" procedures that combine a great deal of life history, physical, psychometric, and observational data and provide the complex diagnoses used in DSM V, as well as personality descriptions and predictions of performance in response to various kinds of drugs, environments, and psychotherapies. The complexity of the new psychotherapy systems developed in the third quarter of the twentieth century have been reduced to four major varieties: cognitive learning, motoric action, affect change, or socioenvironmental management. Among these four there are still swings in popularity and research attention; the most effective approaches combine all four. Some advances in preventive work have come through improved genetic understanding and through monitoring and pinpointing populations at risk for the major psychoses, but little has been done to affect the rate of alcoholism or drug abuse or to prevent crime by youth. Unemployment is still high (about 10 percent) in the United States. The relative numbers of delinquents and criminals have declined as the population bulge of the post–World War II baby boom reached middle age. Looking toward 2025 there seem to be no great breakthroughs in mental health ahead, although technology continues to improve the speed of data manipulation and the biological understanding of physical functioning. In basic research the psychologists in information processing have used computer analogy of human mental functioning to discover many useful details, but now the pendulum has swung from behavioral and cognitive approaches to genetic, biological, and physiological inquiry, with particular attention to emotional states; this swing seems to be partly a result of decisions of the federal government in the early 1980s to restrict research support for the social sciences. The general picture of the future beyond 2000 in the human services and mental health is neither highly positive nor highly negative; the basic issues remain, and human nature is much the same as it has been for a hundred thousand years. Short of a catastrophe, people will muddle through, and psychologists will continue to help them muddle.

Final Comment

These are three speculations about the future. There are many other possibilities in the complex interaction of many variables and assumptions. As research technology and theories of future studies develop, forecasts will be better, and analyses of values and assumptions will be clearer. Undoubtedly such scenarios are already limited by the time in which they are written and by our knowledge and values. Readers are encouraged to try their own scenarios from the vantage point of their positions and times.

We are ending this book on a mystery—the future. This is appropriate in many ways. Clinical psychology should be questioning and imagining possible alternatives. As David Loye, a futurist and psychologist says, our relation to the future is two-sided; it involves not only forecasting, but intervention—not only being a seer, but being a visionary, explicating an ideal on which decisions now might be based. He says, "We do know . . . that in small but vital ways the future is chosen" (Loye, 1978, p. 150). Loye and prominent futurists such as Michael (1973), another psychologist, and Toffler (1970, 1980) advocate that society become foreknowing, that it develop future-responsive learning and that social mechanisms such as future assemblies, the monitoring of social indicators, and forecasting systems be established. Clinical psychology, along with other applied sciences that have humanitarian aims, has much to contribute to future-related understanding. Although any future projections and speculations such as the scenarios in this chapter are bound to reflect the times in which they are written and thus to seem outdated later, it is in the process of trying to puzzle out such possibilities that we learn.

We will end this book with two quotations by people who have thought a great deal about the future. One raises a pessimistic question. The second

Figure 14-4 A perspective of earth. (NASA)

recognizes the likelihood of many problems but calls for optimism about the potentialities of humankind.

> There is a question in the air, more sensed than seen, like the invisible approach of a distant storm, a question that I would hesitate to ask aloud did I not believe it existed unvoiced in the minds of many: "Is there hope for man?" (Heilbroner, 1974, p. 13)

> The dangers and difficulties of the present time are very great. Nevertheless, the only unforgiveable sin is despair, for that will justify itself. Man is very far from having exhausted the potential of his extraordinary nervous system. The troubles of the 20th century are not unlike those of adolescence—rapid growth beyond the ability of organizations to manage, uncontrollable emotion, and a desperate search for identity. Out of adolescence, however, comes maturity in which physical growth with all its attendant difficulties comes to an end, but in which growth continues in knowledge, in spirit, in community, and in love; it is to this that we look forward as a human race. This goal, once seen with our eyes, will draw our faltering feet toward it. (Boulding, 1973, p. 21)

SUMMARY

In this chapter we have been concerned with the profession of clinical psychology and its relation to society as it evolves into the future. We noted that the body of knowledge called *clinical psychology* serves a larger audience than just clinical psychologists; it is relevant to all the human services. The four core mental health professions are psychiatry, psychiatric nursing, social work, and clinical (and counseling) psychology. These professions overlap a great deal in their activities, but there is no easy way to move from one to the other on a career lattice. The educational level for most people who call themselves clinical psychologists in the United States is the doctorate; state licensing bodies usually require that degree plus two years of supervised experience.

We examined the purposes and problems of professional ethics and noted the extensive work of the American Psychological Association in setting up and reviewing standards. The APA also monitors clinical programs that ask for APA approval.

There are a number of professional issues, some interprofessional and some intraprofessional. Psychologists have had a long struggle for achieving some measure of independence and equality with psychiatrists particularly. Psychologists are also being challenged from specialists in other fields such as social work and marriage counseling. Within the field of psychology there are many divisions and interest groups, with clinical psychology being one of the largest. Tensions often appear—essentially between general experimental and applied psychologists, including clinicians. There are also conflicts over training philosophies in clinical psychology, especially between the scientist-practitioner model (the Boulder model) and the more recent professional schools and programs. Clinical psychology in countries outside North America and parts of Europe is generally less developed and other forms of service may appear there.

We discussed several larger issues about the place of helping services within society. We noted that each culture has its own accepted way of helping with disorders of behavior. Witch doctors may be as successful within their own cultures as psychologists and psychiatrists are within theirs. The psychological industry—assessment, therapy, and research—has grown very rapidly in North America, but it is quite evident that professionals are not yet serving the majority who need assistance. The poor, the elderly, minority groups, and rural citizens in the United States are particularly not well served by the professional service agencies. There have been some attacks on professionalism, and some people strongly advocate turning toward "natural helpers" and self-help. Others point to the importance of societal factors in setting up the conditions for poor adjustment by providing the climate for demoralization and helplessness.

How should mental health services be paid for? In many countries of Europe and elsewhere, people are entitled to free or low-cost health and mental health services, but in the United States there has never been a universal health insurance program. The differences between fee-for-service payments and prepaid health care arrangements are of interest. It is much easier to work on prevention with prepaid plans.

In looking toward the future, we noted that quantitative projections can be made from demographic trends and other extrapolations from data. Also studies can use experts' judgments to forecast the future. However, the influences on the future are complex and interdependent and include proliferating technology, increasing and shifting population, changing economic growth patterns and distribution patterns, expanding information, shifting beliefs, and rising social expectations. We presented three scenarios: an optimistic one, a pessimistic one, and a third possibility. The future holds possibilities for catastrophes, but there is also reason to believe in the potentialities of humankind for creative problem solving.

RECOMMENDED READINGS

American Psychological Association. Ethical principles of psychologists. *American Psychologist*, 1981, *36*, 633–638.

This official statement of ethical principles, presented briefly in the text of this chapter, is worth careful study in its entirety. Each of the ten principles is enunciated briefly, then clarified and illustrated. The *American Psychologist* and *Professional Psychology* occasionally have articles devoted to explaining principles and illustrating with cases. For example, an article by London and Bray (1980) examines ethical issues in personnel testing. Another article by Baldick (1980) presents some research on ethical discriminations among psychologists in training. One APA report (Monahan, 1980) discusses ethical dilemmas of psychologists working in police, court, and correctional settings. A special issue of *Professional Psychology* (Claiborn, Stricker, & Bent, 1982) explores the developments of peer review as a means of assuring quality of psychological service.

Norcross, J. C., & Prochaska, J. O. A national survey of clinical psychologists: Characteristics and activities. *Clinical Psychologist*, 1982, *35*(2), 1–8.

This is the first of several articles reporting on a survey of clinical psychologists in the United States. It is based on returns from almost 500 members of the clinical division of the APA. These are experienced psychologists for the most part, and the picture is of the work and backgrounds of clinicians over a decade after the obtaining of the doctorate. They spend over a third of their time, on the average, in psychotherapy and 12 to 13 percent of their time each in assessment, administration, and teaching. The predominant theoretical orientation is eclectic. Some trends among younger people are discerned, and comparisons are made with earlier surveys. Walker (1981a), in a chapter on "Continuing Professional Development," examines career satisfaction, burnout, and continuing education of clinical psychologists. For a further consideration of the life of a clinician, see "Competing Role Demands of Therapists' Professional and Marital Lives" by Racusin, Abramowitz, and Herrera (1981), an interesting analysis of the problems of two different kinds of intimacies. For a research study of some future features of mental health professions, see Anderson, Parenté, and Gordon (1981). Among other predictions they indicate that competency-based examinations are likely and that requirements for certification will increase.

Kiesler, C. A. Mental health policy as a field of inquiry for psychology. *American Psychologist*, 1980, *35*, 1066–1080.

This former executive secretary of the APA calls on his experience with Congress and federal agencies to outline the possible use to which psychological research and expertise might be put in formulating needed legislation and administrative decision making. In a later article (Kiesler, 1982) he applies this concern for research usage to the problem of hospitalizing mental patients and shows that alternative care is better. For an extensive history and discussion of issues, see Mechanic's *Mental Health and Social Policy* (1980). Levine (1981) also gives a good account of the history and problems of community centers and the 1980 report of the President's commission in his *History and Politics of Community Mental Health*. Kiesler, Cummings, and Vanden-Bos (1979) have edited a book of relevance to national health insurance, an important consideration for American mental health policy. Kaswan (1981) argues that current mental health policies are wrong and should be replaced by innovations that promote less centralized and technologized processes.

Fichter, M. M., & Wittchen, H. U. Clinical psychology and psychotherapy: A survey of the present state of professionalization in 23 countries. *American Psychologist*, 1980, *35*, 16–25.

These two German psychologists obtained information largely from North American and European countries on the requirements for people to be officially recognized as psychologists. Most countries do not require the doctorate, and many do not have methods for licensing or registering psychologists. Many other parts of the world view the problem of mental illness and the need for care much differently than does the industrialized West. For one such different view, see "The Conception of Man in Mao Tse-tung Thought" by David Ho (1978).

Williams, T. A., & Johnson, J. H. (Eds.). *Mental health in the 21st century*. Lexington, Mass.: Lexington Books, 1979.

This selection of projections and speculations edited by a psychiatrist and a psychologist suggests, among other things, that computers will be much used in diagnosis and treatment, that disorders will be treated with more finely targeted chemotherapy and psychotherapy, and that clients will be able to communicate wherever they are with their therapists or monitoring computers. Harman's *An Incomplete Guide to the Future* (1979) provides a humanistic discussion of the transformation many believe the world is going through as it moves into a transindustrial era. Loye (1978) discusses a systematic way of forecasting the future based on convergence of attitudes. Keniston (1968) provides a fantasy about how mental health professionals might be perverted into becoming instruments of dictatorial social control. Resnick (1976) provides a light-hearted prognostication for mental health in the next century. The *Handbook of Futures Research* (Fowles, 1978) is a resource for finding considerable information about the methods and theories of futurists. A former APA president, Cummings (1982), forecasts a great growth in health psychology, attention to behavioral genetics, research-developed brief therapies, and more detailed, exacting testing; he forecasts clinical psychology as generic education for people in a wide spectrum of endeavors.

REFERENCES

ACKERMAN, N. W. *Psychodynamics of family life: Diagnosis and treatment of family relationships.* New York: Basic Books, 1958.

ADAMS, H. E., DOSTER, J. A., & CALHOUN, K. S. A psychologically based system of response classification. In A. R. Ciminero, K. S. Calhoun, & H. E. Adams (Eds.), *Handbook of behavioral assessment.* New York: John Wiley, 1977.

ADAMS, K. M. In search of Luria's battery: A false start. *Journal of Consulting and Clinical Psychology,* 1980, *48,* 511–516.

ADAMS-WEBBER, J. R. Fixed role therapy. In R. J. Corsini (Ed.), *Handbook of innovative psychotherapies.* New York: Wiley-Interscience, 1981.

ADINOLFI, A. A. Relevance of person perception research to clinical psychology. *Journal of Consulting and Clinical Psychology,* 1971, *37,* 167–176.

ADLER, A. Individual psychology. In C. Murchison (Ed.), *Psychologies of 1930.* Worcester, Mass.: Clark University Press, 1930.

ADLER, A. *What life should mean to you.* New York: Capricorn, 1958.

AFFLECK, D. C., & STRIDER, F. D. Contribution of psychological reports to patient management. *Journal of Consulting and Clinical Psychology,* 1971, *37,* 177–179.

ALBEE, G. W., & JOFFE, J. M. (Eds.). *Primary prevention of psychopathology* (Vol. 1): *The issues.* Hanover, N.H.: University of New England Press, 1977.

ALKIN, R. C. Evaluation theory development. In C. H. Weiss (Ed.), *Evaluating action programs: Readings in social action and evaluation.* Boston: Allyn & Bacon, 1972.

ALLEY, S. R., BLANTON, J., & FELDMAN, R. E. (Eds.). *Paraprofessionals in mental health: Theory and practice.* New York: Human Sciences Press, 1979.

ALLPORT, G. W. *Letters from Jenny.* New York: Harcourt Brace Jovanovich, 1965.

American Psychiatric Association. *Diagnostic and statistical manual of mental disorders* (3rd ed.). Washington, D.C.: American Psychiatric Association, 1980.

American Psychological Association. *Standards for educational and psychological tests.* Washington, D.C.: American Psychological Association, 1974.

American Psychological Association. Ethical principles of psychologists. *American Psychologist*, 1981, *36*, 633–638. (a)

American Psychological Association. Special issue: Testing: Concepts, policy, practice and research. *American Psychologist*, 1981, *36*, 997–1189. (b)

American Psychological Association Committee on Accreditation. *Accreditation handbook*. Washington, D.C.: American Psychological Association, 1980.

American Psychological Association Committee on Professional Standards. Specialty guidelines for the delivery of services. *American Psychologist*, 1981, *36*, 639–685.

ANASTASI, A. *Psychological testing* (5th ed.). New York: Macmillan, 1982.

ANDERSON, J. K., PARENTE, F. J., & GORDON, C. A forecast of the future for the mental health profession. *American Psychologist*, 1981, *36*, 848–855.

ANDERSON, R. E., & CARTER, I. *Human behavior in the social environment: A social systems approach* (2nd ed.). New York: Aldine, 1978.

ANDERSON, R. L. Mental retardation. In R. H. Woody (Ed.), *Encyclopedia of clinical assessment* (Vol. 2). San Francisco: Jossey-Bass, 1980.

ANDERSON, W. F., FRIEDEN, B. J., & MURPHY, M. J. (Eds.). *Managing human services*. Washington, D. C.: International City Management Assn., 1977.

ANNIS, L. V., & PERRY, D. F. Self-disclosure modeling in same-sex and mixed-sex unsupervised groups. *Journal of Counseling Psychology*, 1977, *24*, 370–372.

APONTE, H. The anatomy of a therapist. In P. Papp (Ed.), *Family therapy: Full length case studies*. New York: Gardner Press, 1977.

APPLETON, W. S. Third psychoactive drug usage guide. *Diseases of the Nervous System*, 1976, *37*, 39–51.

ARKES, H. R. Impediments to accurate clinical judgment and possible ways to minimize their impact. *Journal of Consulting and Clinical Psychology*, 1981, *49*, 323–330.

ARLOW, J. A. Psychoanalysis. In R. J. Corsini (Ed.), *Current psychotherapies* (2nd ed.). Itasca, Ill.: Peacock, 1979.

ASHTON, S. G., & GOLDBERG, L. R. In response to Jackson's challenge: The comparative validity of personality scales constructed by the external (empirical) strategy and scales developed intuitively by experts, novices and laymen. *Journal of Research in Personality*, 1973, *7*, 1–20.

AUSTIN, J. H. *Chase, chance and creativity: The lucky art of novelty*. New York: Columbia University Press, 1978.

BAKER, L., & KELLY, J. G. Components of support systems. Paper presented at the Fall Symposium of the Morrison Center for Youth and Family Services. Portland, Oreg., 1980.

BALDICK, T. L. Ethical discrimination ability of intern psychologists: A function of training in ethics. *Professional Psychology*, 1980, *11*, 276–282.

BANDLER, R., GRINDER, J., & SATIR, V. *Changing with families*. Palo Alto, Calif.: Science & Behavior Books, 1976.

BANDURA, A. *Principles of behavior modification*. New York: Holt, Rinehart & Winston, 1969.

BANDURA, A. Behavior theories and models of man. *American Psychologist*, 1974, *29*, 859–869.

BANDURA, A. Self efficacy: Toward a unifying theory of behavioral change. *Psychological Review*, 1977, *84*, 191–215.

BANDURA, A. Self-efficacy mechanism in human agency. *American Psychologist*, 1982, *37*, 122–147.

BARKER, R. G. Explorations in ecological psychology. *American Psychologist*, 1965, *20*, 1–35.

BARKER, R. G., & ASSOCIATES. *Habitats, environments, and human behavior*. San Francisco: Jossey-Bass, 1978.

BARLOW, D. H. (Ed.). *Behavioral assessment of adult disorders*. New York: Guilford Press, 1981.

BARNES, M., & BERKE, J. *Mary Barnes, two accounts of a journey through madness*. New York: Harcourt Brace Jovanovich, 1971.

BARRETT, C. L., HAMPE, I. E., & MILLER, L. Research on psychotherapy with children. In S. L. Garfield & A. E. Bergin (Eds.), *Handbook of psychotherapy and behavior change: An empirical analysis* (2nd ed.). New York: John Wiley, 1978.

BARRON, F., & HARRINGTON, D. M. Creativity, intelligence and personality. *Annual Review of Psychology*, 1981, *32*, 439–476.

BARRY, A. A research project on successful single parent families. *American Journal of Family Therapy*, 1979, *7*, 64–73.

BARTLETT, F. C. *Remembering*. Cambridge, England: Cambridge University Press, 1932.

BASS, B. M. The leaderless group discussion. *Psychological Bulletin*, 1954, *51*, 465–492.

BEBOUT, J., & GORDON, B. The value of encounter. In L. N. Solomon & B. Berzon (Eds.), *New perspectives on encounter groups*. San Francisco: Jossey-Bass, 1972.

BECK, A. T. *Depression: Clinical and theoretical aspects*. New York: Hoeber, 1967. (Republished as *Depression: Causes and treatments*. Philadelphia: University of Pennsylvania Press, 1973.)

BECK, A. T. *Cognitive therapy and the emotional disorders*. New York: International Universities Press, 1976.

BECK, A. T., RUSH, A. J., SHAW, B. F., & EMERY, G. *Cognitive therapy of depression*. New York: Guilford Press, 1979.

BEER, M. *Organization change and development: A systems view*. Santa Monica, Calif.: Goodyear, 1980.

BELL, A. P., WEINBERG, M. S., & HAMMERSMITH, S. K. *Sexual preference: Its development in men and women*. Bloomington: Indiana University Press, 1981.

BELL, N. W., & VOGEL, E. F. *A modern introduction to the family* (Rev. ed.). New York: Free Press, 1968.

BELLACK, A. S., & HERSEN, M. *Introduction to clinical psychology*. New York: Oxford Press, 1980.

BENJAMIN, A. *The helping interview*. Boston: Houghton Mifflin, 1969.

BENNETT, C. C., ANDERSON, L. S., COOPER, S., HASSOL, L., KLEIN, D. C., & ROSENBLUM, G. *Community psychology: A report of the Boston conference on the education of psychologists for community mental health*. Boston: Boston University, 1966.

BERGER, N. S. Beyond testing: A decision-making system for providing school psychological consultation. *Professional Psychology*, 1979, *10*, 273–277.

BERGIN, A. E. The evaluation of therapeutic outcomes. In A. E. Bergin & S. L. Garfield (Eds.), *Handbook of psychotherapy and behavior change*. New York: John Wiley, 1971.

BERGIN, A. E., & LAMBERT, M. J. The evaluation of therapeutic outcomes. In S. L. Garfield & A. E. Bergin (Eds.), *Handbook of psychotherapy and behavior change: An empirical analysis* (2nd ed.). New York: John Wiley, 1978.

BERNE, E. *Transactional analysis in psychotherapy*. New York: Grove Press, 1961.

BERNSTEIN, D. A., & NIETZEL, M. T. *Introduction to clinical psychology*. New York: McGraw-Hill, 1980.

BERTALANFFY, L. VON. *General systems theory: Foundations, development, applications*. New York: Braziller, 1968.

BIGLER, E. D., & EHRFURTH, J. W. The continued inappropriate singular use of the Bender Visual Motor Gestalt Test. *Professional Psychology*, 1981, *12*, 562–569.

BINGHAM, W.V.D., & MOORE, B. V. *How to interview*. New York: Harper & Row, 1924.

BINSTOCK, R. H., & SHANAS, E. (Eds.). *Handbook of aging and the social sciences.* New York: Van Nostrand Reinhold, 1976.

BIRREN, J. E., & SCHAIE, W. K. (Eds.). *Handbook of the psychology of aging.* New York: Van Nostrand Reinhold, 1977.

BLOCK, J. *The Q-sort method in personality assessment and psychiatric research.* Springfield, Ill.: Chas. C Thomas, 1961.

BLOOM, B. L. Prevention of mental disorders: Recent advances in theory and practice. *Community Mental Health Journal,* 1979, *15,* 179–191.

BLOOM, B. L. *Community mental health: A general introduction* (2nd ed.). Monterey, Calif.: Brooks/Cole, 1983.

BLOOM, M., & FISCHER, J. *Evaluating practice: Guidelines for the accountable professional.* Englewood Cliffs, N.J.: Prentice-Hall, 1982.

BODIN, A. M. Conjoint family assessment: An evolving field. In P. McReynolds (Ed.), *Advances in psychological assessment* (Vol. 1). Palo Alto, Calif.: Science & Behavior Books, 1968.

BOULDING, K. E. Towards a 21st century politics. *Span,* 1973, *14,* 16–21.

BOWERS, K. S. The relevance of hypnosis for cognitive-behavioral therapy. *Clinical Psychology Review,* 1982, *2,* 67–78.

BRADFORD, L., GIBB, J., & BENNE, K. (Eds.). *T-group theory and laboratory method.* New York: John Wiley, 1964.

BRADY, J. P. Concluding remarks. In R. B. Williams, Jr., & W. D. Gentry (Eds.), *Behavioral approaches to medical treatment.* Cambridge, Mass.: Ballinger, 1977.

BRAY, D. W. The assessment center and the study of lives. *American Psychologist,* 1982, *37,* 180–189.

BRAY, D. W., CAMPBELL R., & GRANT, D. *Formative years in business: A long term AT&T study of managerial lives.* New York: John Wiley, 1974.

BREUER, J., & FREUD, S. *Studies on hysteria.* New York: Basic Books, 1957.

BRICKMAN, P., RABINOWITZ, V. C., KARUZA, P., COATES, D., COHN, E., & KIDDER, L. Models of helping and coping. *American Psychologist,* 1982, *37,* 368–384.

BRODKIN, A. M. Family therapy: The making of a mental health movement. *American Journal of Orthopsychiatry,* 1980, *50,* 4–17.

BROMET, E. *Three Mile Island: Mental health findings.* Pittsburgh: Western Psychiatric Institute, 1980. (Also available from Disaster and Emergency Mental Health Section, NIMH, 5600 Fishers Lane, Rockville, Md. 20852.)

BRONFENBRENNER, U. Is early intervention effective? In M. Guttentag & E. L. Struening (Eds.), *Handbook of evaluation research* (Vol. 2). Beverly Hills, Calif.: Sage Publications, Inc., 1975.

BRONFENBRENNER, U. *The ecology of human development: Experiments by nature and design.* Cambridge, Mass.: Harvard University Press, 1979.

BROWN, W. R., & McGUIRE, J. M. Current psychological assessment practices. *Professional Psychology,* 1976, *7,* 475–484.

BRUCH, H. *Learning psychotherapy.* Cambridge, Mass.: Harvard University Press, 1974.

BRUHN, A. R., & LAST, J. Earliest childhood memories: Four theoretical perspectives. *Journal of Personality Assessment,* 1982, *46,* 119–127.

BRUHN, A. R., & SCHIFFMAN, H. Invalid assumptions and methodological difficulties in early memory research. *Journal of Personality Assessment,* 1982, *46,* 265–267.

BRUNSWICK, E. *Systematic and representative design of psychological experiments with results in physical and social perception.* Berkeley: University of California Press, 1947.

BUDMAN, S. H., & WERTLIEB, D. (Eds.). Psychologists in health care settings. *Professional Psychology,* 1979, *10,* 397–644.

BURNS, D. D., & BECK, A. T. Cognitive behavior modification of mood disorders. In J. P. Foreyt & D. Rathjen (Eds.), *Cognitive behavior therapy: Research and application*. New York: Plenum, 1978.

BUROS, O. K. (Ed.). *The seventh mental measurements yearbook* (Vols. 1 & 2). Highland Park, N.J.: Gryphon Press, 1972.

BUROS, O. K. (Ed.). *The eighth mental measurements yearbook* (Vols. 1 & 2). Highland Park, N.J.: Gryphon Press, 1978.

BUTTENWEISER, P. *Free association*. Boston: Little, Brown, 1981.

BYRD, E. A study of validity and constancy of choice in a sociometric test. *Sociometry*, 1951, *14*, 175–181.

CAIRNS, R. B. *Social development: The origins and plasticity of interchanges*. San Francisco: W. H. Freeman & Company Publishers, 1979.

CAMPBELL, D. P. A counseling evaluation with a "better" control group. *Journal of Counseling Psychology*, 1963, *10*, 334–339.

CAMPBELL, D. P. The Strong Vocational Interest Blank: 1927–1967. In P. McReynolds (Ed.), *Advances in psychological assessment* (Vol. 1). Palo Alto, Calif.: Science & Behavior Books, 1968.

CAMPBELL, D. P. *Manual for the Strong-Campbell Interest Inventory* (Rev. ed.). Stanford, Calif.: Stanford University Press, 1977.

CAMPBELL, D. T. Reforms as experiments. *American Psychologist*, 1969, *24*, 409–429.

CAPLAN, G. Types of mental health consultation. *American Journal of Orthopsychiatry*, 1963, *33*, 470–481.

CAPLAN, G. *Principles of preventive psychiatry*. New York: Basic Books, 1964.

CAPLAN, G., & KILLILEA, M. (Eds.). *Support systems and mutual help: Multidisciplinary exploration*. New York: Grune & Stratton, 1976.

CARR, A. C., & GOLDSTEIN, E. G. Approaches to the diagnosis of borderline conditions by use of psychological tests. *Journal of Personality Assessment*, 1981, *45*, 563–574.

CARTER, E. A., & McGOLDRICK, M. (Eds.). *The family life cycle*. New York: Academic Press, 1979.

CATTELL, R. B., EBER, H. W., & TATSUOKA, M. M. *Handbook for the sixteen personality factor questionnaire*. Champaign, Ill.: Institute for Personality and Ability Testing, 1970.

CAUTELA, J. Covert processes and behavior modification. *Journal of Nervous and Mental Disease*, 1973, *157*, 27–35.

CHAIKIN, A. L., DERLEGA, V. J., & MILLER, S. J. Effects of room environment on self-disclosure in a counseling analogue. *Journal of Counseling Psychology*, 1976, *23*, 479–481.

CHAPMAN, L. J., & CHAPMAN, J. P. Genesis of popular but erroneous psychodiagnostic observations. *Journal of Abnormal Psychology*, 1967, *72*, 193–204.

CHASSAN, J. B. *Research design in clinical psychology and psychiatry* (2nd ed.). New York: Irvington, 1979.

CHELUNE, G. J. Nature and assessment of self-disclosing behavior. In P. McReynolds (Ed.), *Advances in psychological assessment* (Vol. 4). San Francisco: Jossey-Bass, 1978.

CHESNEY, M. A., & SHELTON, J. L. A comparison of muscle relaxation and electromyogram biofeedback treatments for muscle contraction headache. *Journal of Behavior Therapy and Experimental Psychiatry*, 1976, *7*, 221–225.

CHILD, I. L. *Humanistic psychology and the research tradition: Their several virtues*. New York: John Wiley, 1973.

CHIN, R., & O'BRIEN, G. General intersystem theory: The model and a case practitioner application. In A. Sheldon, F. Baker, & C. McLaughlin (Eds.), *Systems and medical care*. Cambridge, Mass.: M.I.T. Press, 1970.

CHUN, K. T., COBB, S., & FRENCH, J.R.P., JR. *Measures for psychological assessment: A guide to 3000 original sources and their applications.* Ann Arbor, Mich.: Institute of Social Research, 1975.

CHURCHMAN, C. W. *The systems approach and its enemies.* New York: Basic Books, 1979.

CIMINERO, A. R., CALHOUN, K. S., & ADAMS, H. E. (Eds.). *Handbook of behavioral assessment.* New York: John Wiley, 1977.

CLAIBORN, W. L., STRICKER, G., & BENT, R. J. Special issue: Peer review and quality assurance. *Professional Psychology*, 1982, *13*, 4–164.

CLARK, T. L., & TAULBEE, E. S. A comprehensive and indexed bibliography of the Interpersonal Check List. *Journal of Personality Assessment*, 1981, *45*, 505–525.

CLARKE, A. M., & CLARKE A.D.B. *Early experience: Myth and evidence.* New York: Free Press, 1976.

COHEN, S., & McKAY, G. Social support, stress and the buffering hypothesis: A theoretical analysis. In A. Baum, J. E. Singer, & S. E. Taylor (Eds.), *Handbook of psychology and health* (Vol. 4). Hillsdale, N.J.: Lawrence Erlbaum Associates, 1983.

COLLINS, A., & PANCOAST, D. *Natural helping networks.* Washington, D.C.: National Association of Social Workers, 1977.

COMREY, A. L., BACKER, T. E., & GLASER, E. M. *A sourcebook for mental health measures.* Los Angeles: Human Interaction Research Institute, 1973.

CONDIOTTE, M. M., & LICHTENSTEIN, E. Self-efficacy and relapse in smoking cessation programs. *Journal of Consulting and Clinical Psychology*, 1981, *49*, 648–658.

CONE, J. D., & HAWKINS, R. P. *Behavioral assessment: New directions in clinical psychology.* New York: Brunner/Mazel, 1977.

CONLEY, J. J. An MMPI typology of male alcoholics: Admission, discharge and outcome comparisons. *Journal of Personality Assessment*, 1981, *45*, 33–39.

COOK, T. D., & CAMPBELL, D. T. The design and conduct of quasi-experiments and true experiments in field settings. In M. D. Dunnette (Ed.), *Handbook of industrial and organizational psychology.* Chicago: Rand McNally, 1976.

CORNISH, E. *The study of the future.* Washington, D.C.: World Future Society, 1977.

CORSINI, R. J. (Ed.). *Current personality theories.* Itasca, Ill.: Peacock, 1977.

CORSINI, R. J. (Ed.). *Current psychotherapies* (2nd ed.). Itasca, Ill.: Peacock, 1979.

CORSINI, R. J. (Ed.). *Handbook of innovative psychotherapies.* New York: John Wiley, 1981.

COWEN, E. (Ed.). Special issue on primary prevention. *American Journal of Community Psychology*, 1982, *10*, 239–367.

COX, D. J., FREUNDLICH, A., & MEYER, R. Differential effectiveness of electromylographic feedback, verbal relaxation instructions and medication placebo. *Journal of Consulting and Clinical Psychology*, 1975, *43*, 892–898.

COX, F. M., ERLICH, J. L., ROTHMAN, J., & TROPMAN, J. E. (Eds.). *Strategies of community organization.* Itasca, Ill.: Peacock, 1970.

COYNE, J. C., & FABRICATORE, J. M. Group psychotherapy in a corrections facility: A case study of individual and institutional change. *Professional Psychology*, 1979, *10*, 8–14.

CRADDICK, R. A. Sharing oneself in the assessment procedure. *Professional Psychology*, 1975, *6*, 279–282.

CRAIK, K. H. The assessment of places. In P. McReynolds (Ed.), *Advances in psychological assessment* (Vol. 2). Palo Alto, Calif.: Science & Behavior Books, 1971.

CRONBACH, L. J. *Essentials of psychological testing* (2nd ed.). New York: Harper & Row, 1960.

CRONBACH, L. J. *Essentials of psychological testing* (3rd ed.). New York: Harper & Row, 1970.

CRONBACH, L. J. Five decades of public controversy over mental testing. *American Psychologist*, 1975, *30*, 1–14.

CRONBACH, L. J., *Toward reform of program evaluation: Aims, methods and institutional arrangements*. San Francisco: Jossey-Bass, 1980.

CRONBACH, L. J., & GLESER, G. C. *Psychological tests and personnel decisions* (2nd ed.). Urbana: University of Illinois Press, 1965.

CRONBACH, L. J., & MEEHL, P. E. *Construct validity in psychological tests*. *Psychological Bulletin*, 1955, *52*, 281–302.

CROW, W. J. The effect of training upon accuracy and variability in interpersonal perception. *Journal of Abnormal and Social Psychology*, 1957, *55*, 355–359.

CUMMINGS, N. A. Prolonged (ideal) versus short-term (realistic) psychotherapy. *Professional Psychology*, 1977, *8*, 491–501.

CUMMINGS, N. A. The future of clinical psychology in the United States. Address to the First Joint Chinese-American Conference on Psychology, Beijing, China, August 1982.

CUMMINGS, N. A., & FOLLETTE, W. T. Psychiatric services and medical utilization in a prepaid health plan setting: Part II. *Medical Care*, 1968, *6*, 31–41.

CUMMINGS, N. A., & VANDENBOS, G. R. The twenty years of Kaiser-Permanente experience with psychotherapy and medical utilization: Implications for national health policy and national health insurance. *Health Policy Quarterly*, 1981, *1*, 159–175.

DAHLSTROM, W. G., WELSH, G. S., & DAHLSTROM, L. E. *An MMPI handbook, Clinical interpretation*, (Vol. 1, Rev. ed.). Minneapolis: University of Minnesota Press, 1972.

DAHLSTROM, W. G., WELSH, G. S., & DAHLSTROM, L. E. *An MMPI handbook, Research developments and applications* (Vol. 2, Rev. ed.). Minneapolis: University of Minnesota Press, 1975.

DANA, R. H., & LEECH, S. Existential assessment. *Journal of Personality Assessment*, 1974, *38*, 428–435.

DANET, B. N. Prediction of mental illness in college students on the basis of nonpsychiatric MMPI profiles. *Journal of Consulting and Clinical Psychology*, 1965, *29*, 577–580.

DASON, P., & HERON, A. Cross-cultural tests of Piaget's theory. In H.C. Triandis & A. Heron (Eds.), *Handbook of cross-cultural psychology: Developmental psychology* (Vol. 4). Boston: Allyn & Bacon, 1981.

DAVIDSON, P. W., & COSTELLO, C. G. (Eds.). *N = 1: Experimental studies of single cases*. New York: Van Nostrand Reinhold, 1969.

DAWES, R. M. The robust beauty of improper linear models in decision making. *American Psychologist*, 1979, *34*, 571–582.

DEWITT, K. N. The effectiveness of family therapy. *Archives of General Psychiatry*, 1978, *35*, 549–561.

DIAZ-GUERRERO, R. A Mexican psychology. *American Psychologist*, 1977, *32*, 934–944.

DIGMAN, J. M., & TAKEMOTO-CHOCK, N. K. Factors in the natural language of personality: Re-analysis, comparison, and interpretation of six major studies. *Multivariate Behavioral Research*, 1981, *16*, 149–170.

DINARDO, P. H., & RAYMOND, J. N. Locus of control and attention during meditation. *Journal of Consulting and Clinical Psychology*, 1979, *47*, 1136–1137.

DOHRENWEND, B. P., DOHRENWEND, B. S., GOULD, M. S., LINK, B., NEUGEBAUER, R., & WUNSCH-HITZIG, R. *Mental illness in the United States: Epidemiological estimates*. New York: Praeger, 1980.

DOOLEY, D. Screening of paratherapists: Empirical status and research directions. *Professional Psychology*, 1980, *11*, 242–251.

DURLAK, J. A. Comparative effectiveness of paraprofessionals and professional helpers. *Psychological Bulletin*, 1979, *86*, 80–92.

DWORKIN, A. L., & DWORKIN, E. P. A conceptual overview of selected consultation models. *American Journal of Community Psychology*, 1975, *3*, 151–159.

EDELWICH, J. (with A. BRODSKY). *Burn-out: Stages of disillusionment in the helping professions.* New York: Human Sciences Press, 1980.

EGAN, G., & COWAN, M. *People in systems: A model for development in the human-service professions and education.* Monterey, Calif.: Brooks/Cole, 1979.

ELLIS, A. *Reason and emotion in psychotherapy.* New York: Lyle Stuart, 1962.

ELLIS, A. *The essence of rational psychotherapy: A comprehensive approach to treatment.* New York: Institute for Rational Living, 1970.

ELLIS, A. Rational-emotive therapy. In R.J. Corsini (Ed.), *Current psychotherapies.* Itasca, Ill.: Peacock, 1979.

ELSTEIN, A. S., SHULMAN, L. S., & SPRAFKA, S. A. *Medical problem solving: An analysis of clinical reasoning.* Cambridge, Mass.: Harvard University Press, 1978.

EMERY, F. E. (Ed.). *Systems thinking.* Harmondsworth, England: Penguin, 1969.

ENDICOTT, T., & SPITZER, R. A. A diagnostic interview. The Schedule for Affective Disorders and Schizophrenia. *Archives of General Psychiatry*, 1978, *35*, 837–844.

ERIKSON, E. H. *Childhood and society.* New York: W. W. Norton & Co., Inc., 1950.

ERIKSON, E. H. *Childhood and society* (2nd ed.). New York: W. W. Norton & Co., Inc., 1963.

ESCALONA, S. Intervention programs for children at psychiatric risk: The contribution of child psychology and developmental theory. In E. J. Anthony & C. Koupernik (Eds.), *The child in his family: Children at psychiatric risk.* New York: John Wiley, 1974.

ESHBAUGH, D. M., TOSI, D. J., & HOYT, C. Some personality patterns and dimensions of male alcoholics: A multivariate description. *Journal of Personality Assessment*, 1978, *42*, 409–417.

ESTROFF, S. E. Psychiatric deinstitutionalization: A sociocultural analysis. *Journal of Social Issues*, 1981, *37*, 116–132.

EVANS, R. I., ROZELLE, R. M., MAXWELL, S. E., RAINES, B. E., DILL, C. A., GUTHRIE, T. J., HENDERSON, A. H., & HILL, P. C. Social modeling films to deter smoking in adolescents: Results of a three-year field investigation. *Journal of Applied Psychology*, 1981, *66*, 399–414.

EXNER, J. E. *The Rorschach: A comprehensive system.* New York: John Wiley, 1974.

EYSENCK, H. J. The effects of psychotherapy: An evaluation. *Journal of Consulting Psychology*, 1952, *16*, 319–324.

EYSENCK, H. J. (Ed.) *Experiments in behavior therapy.* Elmsford, N.Y.: Pergamon Press, 1964.

FALK, J. D. Understanding children's art, a review of the literature. *Journal of Personality Assessment*, 1981, *45*, 465–472.

FAUCHEAU, C., AMADO, G., & LAURENT, A. Organizational development and change. *Annual Review of Psychology*, 1982, *33*, 343–370.

FEE, A. F., ELKINS, G. R., & BOYD, L. Testing and counseling psychologists: Current practices and implications for training. *Journal of Personality Assessment*, 1982, *46*, 116–118.

FELTON, B. J., & SHINN, M. Ideology and practice of deinstitutionalization. *Journal of Social Issues*, 1981, *37*, 158–172.

FERGUSON, M. *The Aquarian conspiracy: Personal and social transformation in the 1980's.* Los Angeles: J. P. Thatcher, 1980.

FERSTER, C., NURNBERGER, J. I., & LEVITT, E. B. The control of eating. *Journal of Mathetics*, 1962, *1*, 87–109.

FEUERSTEIN, R. *The dynamic assessment of retarded performance: Learning Potential Assessment Device: Theory, instruments, techniques.* Baltimore: University Park Press, 1979.

FICHTER, M. M., & WITTCHEN, H. U. Clinical psychology and psychotherapy: A survey of the present state of professionalization in 23 countries. *American Psychologist*, 1980, *35*, 16–25.

FILSKOV, S. B., & BOLL, T. J. (Eds.). *Handbook of clinical neuropsychology.* New York: John Wiley, 1981.

FINE, L. J. Psychodrama. In R. J. Corsini (Ed.), *Current psychotherapies* (2nd ed.). Itasca, Ill.: Peacock, 1979.

FINKELSTEIN, P., WENEGRET, B., & YALOM, I. Large group awareness training. *Annual Review of Psychology*, 1982, *33*, 515–540.

FISCHER, J. Does anything work? *Journal of Social Service Research*, 1978, *1*, 215–244.

FISHER, J. D., NADLER, A., & WHITCHER-ALAGNA, S. Recipient reactions to aid. *Psychological Bulletin*, 1982, *91*, 27–54.

FISKE, D. W. *Measuring the concepts of personality.* Chicago: Aldine, 1971.

FLAVELL, J. H. *The developmental psychology of Jean Piaget.* Princeton, N.J.: Van Nostrand, 1963.

FLAVELL, J. H. *Cognitive development.* Englewood Cliffs, N.J.: Prentice-Hall, 1977.

FORER, B. R. The fallacy of personal validation: A classroom demonstration of gullibility. *Journal of Abnormal and Social Psychology*, 1949, *44*, 118–123.

FOREST, J., & SICZ, G. A review of the Personal Orientation Dimensions Inventory. *Journal of Personality Assessment*, 1981, *45*, 433–435.

FORGUS, R., & SHULMAN, B. *Personality: A cognitive view.* Englewood Cliffs, N.J.: Prentice-Hall, 1979.

FOWLES, J. (Ed.). *Handbook of futures research.* Westport, Conn.: Greenwood Press, 1978.

FOX, R. E., BARCLAY, A. G., & RODGERS, D. A. The foundations of professional psychology. *American Psychologist*, 1982, *37*, 306–313.

FRALEIGH, P. W. *The person-action-context perspective for developmental intervention: A case study of career planning with two intimate male partners.* Paper presented at the symposium "Eclectic intervention: In theory and in practice," Western Psychological Association, Honolulu, May 1980.

FRANK, G. H. *Psychiatric diagnosis: A review of research.* Oxford, England: Pergamon Press, 1975.

FRANK, J. D. *Persuasion and healing: A comparative study of psychotherapy.* Baltimore: Johns Hopkins University Press, 1973.

FRANK, J. D. *Persuasion and healing* (Rev. ed.). New York: Schocken, 1974.

FRANK, J. D. Nature and functions of belief systems. Humanism and transcendental religion. *American Psychologist*, 1977, *32*, 555–559.

FREUD, S. *Collected papers* (4 vol.). London: Hogarth Press, 1924.

FROMM, E., & SHOR, R. E. (Eds.). *Hypnosis: Developments in research and new perspectives* (2nd ed.). New York: Aldine, 1979.

FUHR, R. A., MOSS, R. H., & DISHOTSKY, N. The use of family assessment and feedback in ongoing family therapy. *American Journal of Family Therapy*, 1981, *9*, 24–36.

FURNESS, P. *Growing with dramatics: Findings and mental health implications.* Unpublished manuscript, Morrison Center, Portland, Oreg., 1982.

FURNESS, P. R. *Role playing in the elementary school.* New York: Hart, 1976.

GALASSI, J. P., FRIERSON, H. T., & SHARER, R. Behavior of high, moderate and low test anxious students during an actual test situation. *Journal of Consulting and Clinical Psychology,* 1981, *49,* 51–62.

GARFIELD, S. L. Psychotherapy: A 40 year appraisal. *American Psychologist,* 1981, *36,* 174–183.

GARFIELD, S. L. Editorial: The 75th anniversary of the first issue of *The Psychological Clinic. Journal of Consulting and Clinical Psychology,* 1982, *50,* 167–170.

GARFIELD, S. L., & BERGIN, A. E. (Eds.). *Handbook of psychotherapy and behavior change: An empirical analysis* (2nd ed.). New York: John Wiley, 1978.

GARMEZY, N. The experimental study of children vulnerable to psychopathology. In A. Davids (Ed.), *Child personality and psychopathology* (Vol. 2). New York: John Wiley, 1975.

GAUDRY, E., & SPIELBERGER, C. D. *Anxiety and educational achievement.* New York: John Wiley, 1974.

GENDLIN, E. T. *Focusing.* New York: Everest House, 1978.

GENDLIN, E. T. Experiential psychotherapy. In R. J. Corsini (Ed.), *Current psychotherapies.* Itasca, Ill.: Peacock, 1979.

GERSON, M. J., & BARSKY, M. For the new family therapist: Glossary of terms. *American Journal of Family Therapy,* 1979, *7,* 15–20.

GILMORE, S. K. *The counselor-in-training.* Englewood Cliffs, N.J.: Prentice-Hall, 1973.

GILMORE, S. K. A comprehensive theory for eclectic intervention. *International Journal of Advising and Counseling,* 1980, *3,* 185–210.

GLASS, G. V., & ELLETT, F. S. Evaluation research. *Annual Review of Psychology,* 1980, *31,* 211–228.

GOH, D. S., TESLOW, C. J., & FULLER, G. B. The practice of psychological assessment among school psychologists. *Professional Psychology,* 1981, *12,* 696–706.

GOLDBERG, L. R. The effectiveness of clinicians' judgements: The diagnosis of organic brain damage from the Bender Gestalt test. *Journal of Consulting Psychology,* 1959, *23,* 25–33.

GOLDBERG, L. R. Simple models or simple processes? Some research on clinical judgements. *American Psychologist,* 1968, *23,* 483–496.

GOLDBERG, L. R. Man versus model of man: A rationale, plus some evidence, for a method of improving on clinical inferences. *Psychological Bulletin, 1970, 73,* 422–432.

GOLDBERG, L. R. From ace to zombie: Some explorations in the language of personality. In C. D. Spielberger & J. N. Butcher (Eds.), *Advances in personality assessment* (Vol. 1). Hillsdale, N.J.: Lawrence Erlbaum Associates, 1982.

GOLDBERG, L. R. Objective diagnostic tests and measures. *Annual Review of Psychology,* 1974, *25,* 343–366.

GOLDBERG, P. A review of sentence completion methods in personality assessment. *Journal of Projective techniques and Personality Assessment,* 1965, *29,* 12–45.

GOLDEN, C. J. *Clinical interpretation of the objective psychological tests.* New York: Grune & Stratton, 1979.

GOLDEN, C. J. The Luria-Nebraska Neuropsychological Battery: Theory and research. In P. McReynolds (Ed.), *Advances in psychological assessment* (Vol. 5). San Francisco: Jossey-Bass, 1981.

GOLDEN, C. J., KANE, R., SWEET, J., MOSES, J. A., CARDELLINO, J. P., TEMPLETON, R., VICENTE, P., & GRABER, B. Relationship of the Halstead-Reitan Neuropsychological Battery to the Luria-Nebraska Neuropsychological Battery. *Journal of Consulting and Clinical Psychology,* 1981, *49,* 410–417.

GOLDEN, C. J., MOSES, J. A., FISHBURNE, F. J., ENGUM, E., LEWIS, G. P., WISNIEWSKI, A. M., CONLEY, F. K., & BERG, R. A. Cross-validation of the Luria-Nebraska Neuropsychological Battery for the presence, lateralization, and localization of brain damage. *Journal of Consulting and Clinical Psychology*, 1981, *49*, 491–507.

GOLDEN, M. Some effects of combining psychological tests on clinical inferences. *Journal of Consulting Psychology*, 1964, *28*, 440–446.

GOLDING, S. G., & RORER, L. Illusory correlation and subjective judgement. *Journal of Abnormal Psychology*, 1972, *80*, 249–260.

GOLDMAN, B. A., & BUSCH, J. C. (Eds.). *Directory of unpublished experimental measures* (Vol. 2). New York: Human Sciences Press, 1978.

GOLDSTEIN, K. M., & BLACKMAN, S. Assessment of cognitive style. In P. McReynolds (Ed.), *Advances in psychological assessment* (Vol. 4). San Francisco: Jossey-Bass, 1978.

GONZALES, L. R., HAYS, R. B., BOND, M. A., & KELLY, J. G. Community mental health. In M. Hersen, A. E. Kazdin, & A. S. Bellack (Eds.), *The clinical psychology handbook*. Elmsford, N.Y.: Pergamon, 1983.

GORDON, E. W., & TERRELL, M. D. The changed social context of testing. *American Psychologist*, 1981, *36*, 1167–1171.

GOODENOUGH, F. L. *Mental testing*. New York: Holt, Rinehart & Winston, 1949.

GOODSTEIN, L. O., & RUSSELL, S. W. Self-disclosure: A comparative study of reports by self and others. *Journal of Counseling Psychology*, 1977, *24*, 365–369.

GOTTLIEB, B. H., & RIGER, S. Social intervention in the community: Three professional roles. *Professional Psychology*, 1972, *3*, 231–240.

GOTTLIEB, B. H., & SCHROTER, C. Collaboration and resource exchange between professionals and natural support systems. *Professional Psychology*, 1978, *9*, 614–622.

GOUGH, H. G. An interpreter's syllabus for the California Psychological Inventory. In P. McReynolds (Ed.), *Advances in psychological assessment* (Vol. I). Palo Alto, Calif.: Science & Behavior Books, 1968.

GOUGH, H. G. A cluster analysis of Home Index status items. *Psychological Reports*, 1971, *28*, 923–929.

GREEN, B. Body therapies. In R. J. Corsini (Ed.), *Handbook of innovative psychotherapies*. New York: John Wiley, 1981.

GREEN, C. J. The diagnostic accuracy and utility of MMPI and MCMI computer interpretive reports. *Journal of Personality Assessment*, 1982, *46*, 359–365.

GRINDER, J., & BANDLER, R. *Trance-formations: Neuro-linguistic programming and the structure of hypnosis*. Moab, Ut.: Real People Press, 1981.

GUMP, P. V. The school as a social situation. *Annual Review of Psychology*, 1980, *31*, 553–582.

GURMAN, A. S., & KNISKERN, D. P. Research on marital and family therapy: Progress, perspective and prospect. In S. Garfield & A. Bergin (Eds.), *Handbook of psychotherapy and behavior change* (2nd ed.). New York: John Wiley, 1978.

GURMAN, A. S., & KNISKERN, D. P. *Handbook of family therapy*. New York: Brunner/Mazel, 1981.

GUSTAITIS, R. *Turning on*. New York: Macmillan, 1969.

GUTKIN, T. B. Teacher perceptions of consultation services provided by school psychologists. *Professional Psychology*, 1980, *11*, 637–642.

GUTTENTAG, M., & STRUENING, E. L. (Eds.). *Handbook of evaluation research* (Vol. 2). Beverly Hills, Calif.: Sage Publications, Inc., 1975. (For Vol. 1, See Struening & Guttentag, 1975).

GYNTHER, M. Ethnicity and personality: An update. In J. N. Butcher (Ed.), *New developments in the use of the MMPI*. Minneapolis: University of Minnesota Press, 1979.

HALEY, J. *Problem solving therapy*. San Francisco: Jossey-Bass, 1976.

HALL, C. S., & LINDZEY, G. *Theories of personality* (3rd ed.). New York: John Wiley, 1978.

HAMPDEN-TURNER, C. *Maps of the mind*. New York: Macmillan, 1981.

HARDER, D. W., GIFT, T. E., STRAUSS, J. S., RITZLER, B. A., & KOKES, R. F. Life events and two-year outcome in schizophrenia. *Journal of Consulting and Clinical Psychology*, 1981, 49, 619–625.

HARMAN, W. W. *An incomplete guide to the future*. New York: W. W. Norton & Co., Inc., 1979.

HARTMANN, H. *Essays on ego psychology: Selected problems in psychoanalytic theory*. New York: International Universities Press, 1964.

HASE, H. D., & GOLDBERG, L. R. The comparative validity of different strategies of deriving personality inventory scales. *Psychological Bulletin*, 1967, 67, 231–248.

HASKINS, R., FINKELSTEIN, N. W., & STEDMAN, D. J. Infant stimulation programs and their effects. *Pediatric Annals*, 1978, 7, 123–144.

HATHAWAY, S. R., & MEEHL, P. E. *An atlas for the clinical use of the MMPI*. Minneapolis: University of Minnesota Press, 1951.

HAYNES, J. *Divorce mediation*. New York: Springer, 1981.

HAYWOOD, H. C., FILLER, J. W., SHIFMAN, M. A., & CHATELANAT, G. Behavioral assessment in mental retardation. In P. McReynolds (Ed.), *Advances in psychological assessment* (Vol. 3). San Francisco: Jossey-Bass, 1975.

HEBER, F. R., & GARBER, H. The Milwaukee project: A study of the use of family intervention to prevent cultural-familial mental retardation. In B. Z. Friedlander, G. M. Sterritt, & G. E. Kerk (Eds.), *Exceptional infant* (Vol. 3). New York: Brunner/Mazel, 1973.

HEILBRONER, R. L. *An inquiry into the human prospect*. New York: W. W. Norton & Co., Inc., 1974.

HELLER, K. Laboratory interview research as analogue to treatment. In A. E. Bergin & S. L. Garfield (Eds.), *Handbook of psychotherapy and behavior change*. New York: John Wiley, 1971.

HELLER, K. Interview structure and interviewer style in initial interviews. In A. W. Siegman & B. Pope (Eds.), *Studies in dyadic communication*. New York: Pergamon Press, 1977.

HELLER, K. The effects of social support: Prevention and treatment implications. In A. P. Goldstein & F. H. Kaufos (Eds.), *Maximizing treatment gains*. New York: Academic Press, 1979.

HELLER, K., DAVIS, J. D., & MYERS, R. A. The effects of interviewer style in a standardized interview. *Journal of Consulting Psychology*, 1966, 30, 501–508.

HENRY, W. E., SIMS, J. H., & SPRAY, S. L. *The fifth profession*. San Francisco: Jossey-Bass, 1971.

HERINK, R. (Ed.). *The psychotherapy handbook: The A to Z guide to more than 250 different therapies in use today*. New York: New American Library, 1980.

HERRNSTEIN, R. J. IQ testing and the media. *Atlantic Monthly*, 1982, 250 (2), 68–74.

HERSEN, M., & BELLACK, A. S. (Eds.). *Behavioral assessment: A practical handbook*. Oxford, England: Pergamon Press, 1976.

HERSEN, M., & BELLACK, A. S. (Eds.). *Behavioral assessment: A practical handbook*. (2nd ed.). Elmsford, N.Y.: Pergamon Press, 1981.

HIGLEN, P. S., & GILLIS, S. F. Effects of situational factors, sex, and attitude on affective self-disclosure and anxiety. *Journal of Counseling Psychology*, 1978, 25, 270–276.

HILGARD, E. R. Hypnosis. *Annual Review of Psychology*, 1975, *26*, 45–64.

HIRSCH, B. J. Psychological dimensions of social networks: A multimethod analysis. *American Journal of Community Psychology*, 1979, 7, 239–262.

HIRSCH, B. J. Natural support systems and coping with major life changes. *American Journal of Community Psychology*, 1980, 8, 159–172.

HO, D.Y.F. The conception of man in Mao Tse-tung thought. *Psychiatry*, 1978, *41*, 391–402.

HOBBS, N. (Ed.). *Issues in the classification of children* (Vols. I & II). San Francisco: Jossey-Bass, 1975.

HOFFMAN, H., LOPER, R., & KAMMEIER, M. Identifying future alcoholics with MMPI alcoholism scales. *Quarterly Journal of Studies on Alcohol*, 1974, *35*, 490–498.

HOFFMAN-GRAFF, M. A. Interviewer use of positive and negative self-disclosure and interviewer-subject sex pairing. *Journal of Counseling Psychology*, 1977, *24*, 173–177.

HOLLAND, J. C., MAGOON, T. M., & SPOKANE, A. R. Counseling psychology: Career interventions, research, and theory. *Annual Review of Psychology*, 1981, *32*, 279–305.

HOLLINGSHEAD, A. B., & REDLICH, F. C. *Social class and mental illness: A community study*. New York: John Wiley, 1958.

HOLMEN, M. G. et al. *An assessment program for OCS applicants* (HumRRo Tech. Rep. 26). Alexandria, Va.: Human Resources Research Organization, 1956.

HOLMES, T. H., & RAHE, R. H. The Social Readjustment Rating Scale. *Journal of Psychosomatic Research*, 1967, *11*, 213–218.

HOLT, R. R. On reading Freud. In C. L. Rothgeb (Ed.), *Abstracts of the standard edition of the complete psychological works of Sigmund Freud*. New York: Jason Aronson, 1973

HOLT, R. R. *Methods in clinical psychology: Prediction and research* (Vol. 2). New York: Plenum, 1978.

HOLTZMAN, W. H. New developments in Holtzman Inkblot Technique. In P. McReynolds (Ed.), *Advances in psychological assessment* (Vol. 3). San Francisco: Jossey-Bass, 1975.

HOOVER, T. O. The hand test: Fifteen years later. *Journal of Personality Assessment*, 1978, *42*, 128–138.

HORNE, A. M., & OHLSEN, M. M. (Eds.). *Family counseling and therapy*. Itasca, Ill.: Peacock, 1982.

HOROWITZ, M. J. A study of clinicians' judgements from projective test protocols. *Journal of Consulting Psychology*, 1962, *26*, 251–256.

HUTCHINGS, B., & MEDNICK, S. Registered criminality in the adoptive and biological parents of registered male criminal adoptees. In R. Fieve, D. Rosenthal, & H. Brill (Eds.), *Genetic research in psychiatry*. Baltimore: John Hopkins University Press, 1975.

ILLICH, I. *Medical nemesis*. New York: Pantheon, 1976.

ILLICH, I., ZOLA, I. K., McKNIGHT, J., CAPLAN, J., & SHAIKEN, H. *Disabling professions*. London: Marion Boyars, 1977.

IRVIN, L. K., & HALPERN, A. S. A process model of diagnostic assessment. In G. T. Ballamy, G. O'Conner, & O. Karan (Eds.), *Vocational rehabilitation of severely handicapped persons*. Baltimore: University Park Press, 1979.

JACKSON, D. N. Interpreter's guide to the Jackson Personality Inventory. In P. McReynolds (Ed.), *Advances in psychological assessment* (Vol. 4). San Francisco: Jossey-Bass, 1978.

JACOBSON, N. S., & MOORE, D. Spouses as observers of the events in their relationship. *Journal of Consulting and Clinical Psychology*, 1981, *49*, 269–277.

JAMES, W. *Principles of psychology* (Vol. I). New York: Holt, Rinehart & Winston, 1890. (Reprinted Cambridge, Mass.: Harvard University Press, 1981.)

JANIS, I. L., & MANN, L. *Decision making: A psychological analysis of conflict, choice and commitment.* New York: Free Press, 1977.

JENSEN, A. R. Raising the IQ: The Ramey and Haskins study. *Intelligence*, 1981, *5*, 29–40.

JOHNSON, S. M., & BOLSTAD, O. D. Methodological issues in naturalistic observation: Some problems and solutions for field research. In L. A. Hamerlynck, L. C. Handy, & E. J. Mash (Eds.), *Behavior change: Methodology, concepts and practice.* Champaign, Ill.: Research Press, 1973.

JOHNSON, S. M., & BOLSTAD, O. D. Reactivity to home observation: A comparison of audio recorded behavior with observers present or absent. *Journal of Applied Behavioral Analysis*, 1975, *8*, 181–187.

JONES, K., SMITH, D., STREISSGUTH, A., & MYRIANTHOUPOULOUS, N. Outcome in off-spring of chronic alcoholic women. *Lancet*, 1974, *1*, 1076.

JONES, K., SMITH, D., ULLELAND, C., & STREISSGUTH, A. Pattern of malformation in offspring of chronic alcoholic mothers. *Lancet*, 1973, *1*, 1267.

JONES, L. K. *Occ-U-Sort.* Monterey, Calif.: Publishers Test Service, 1981.

JONES, M. C. Personality correlates and antecedents of drinking patterns in adult males. *Journal of Consulting and Clinical Psychology*, 1968, *32*, 2–12.

JONES, M. C., BAYLEY, N., MACFARLANE, J. W., & HONZIK, M. P. (Eds.). *The course of human development.* Waltham, Mass.: Xerox, 1971.

JONES, R. R., REID, J. B., & PATTERSON, G. R. Naturalistic observation in clinical assessment. In P. McReynolds (Ed.), *Advances in psychological assessment* (Vol. 3). San Francisco: Jossey-Bass, 1975.

KAHN, M. W. *Basic methods for mental health practitioners.* Cambridge, Mass.: Winthrop, 1981.

KANFER, F. H., & GOLDSTEIN, A. P. (Eds.). *Helping people change.* New York: Pergamon Press, 1975.

KANNER, L. Autistic disturbances of affective contact. *Nervous Child*, 1943, *2*, 217–250.

KAPLAN, B. (Ed.). *The inner world of mental illness.* New York: Harper & Row Pub., Inc., 1964.

KAPLAN, R. M., & SACCUZZO, D. P. *Psychological testing: Principles, applications and issues.* Monterey, Calif.: Brooks/Cole, 1982.

KARSON, S., & O'DELL, J. W. *A guide to the clinical use of the 16PF.* Champaign, Ill.: Institute of Personality and Ability Testing, 1976.

KASAMATSU, A., & HIRAI, T. An electrographic study of the Zen meditation (Zazen). *Psychologia*, 1969, *12*, 205–225.

KASWAN, J. Manifest and latent functions of psychological services. *American Psychologist*, 1981, *36*, 290–299.

KAZDIN, A. E. *Behavior modification in applied settings.* Homewood, Ill.: Dorsey Press, 1975.

KAZDIN, A. E. *The token economy.* New York: Plenum, 1977.

KAZDIN, A. E. *Research design in clinical psychology.* New York: Harper & Row, 1980.

KAZDIN, A. E. Single-case experimental designs. In P. C. Kendall & J. N. Butcher (Eds.), *Handbook of research methods in clinical psychology.* New York: John Wiley, 1982.

KEETON, M. T. *Experiential learning: Rationale, characteristics, and assessment.* San Francisco: Jossey-Bass, 1976.

KELLY, E. L. Clinical psychology—1960: A report of survey findings. *Newsletter, Division of Clinical Psychology of the APA*, 1961, *14*, 1–11.

KELLY, E. L., & FISKE, D. W. *The prediction of performance in clinical psychology.* Ann Arbor: University of Michigan Press, 1951.

KELLY, G. A. *The psychology of personal constructs* (Vol. 1). *A theory of personality* (Vol. 2). *Clinical diagnosis and therapy.* New York: W. W. Norton & Co., Inc., 1955.

KELLY, G. A. The theory and technique of assessment. *Annual Review of Psychology,* 1958, 9, 325–352.

KELLY, J. G. Towards an ecological conception of preventive interventions. In J. W. Carter (Ed.), *Research contributions from psychology to community mental health.* New York: Behavioral Publications, 1968.

KELLY, L. Evaluation of the interview as a selection technique. In *Proceedings of the 1953 Invitational Conference on Testing Problems.* Princeton, N.J.: Educational Testing Service, 1954.

KENDALL, P. C., & BRASWELL, L. On cognitive-behavioral assessment: Model, measures and madness. In C. D. Spielberger & J. N. Butcher (Eds.), *Advances in personality assessment* (Vol. 1). Hillsdale, N.J.: Lawrence Erlbaum Associates, 1982.

KENDALL, P. C., & BUTCHER, J. N. (Eds.). *Handbook of research methods in clinical psychology.* New York: John Wiley, 1982.

KENDALL, P. C., & NORTON-FORD, J. D. *Clinical psychology: Scientific and professional dimensions.* New York: John Wiley, 1982.

KENDALL, R. E., PICHOT, P., & VON CRANACH, M. Diagnostic criteria of English, French, and German psychiatrists. *Psychological Medicine,* 1974, 4, 187–195.

KENISTON, K. How community mental health stamped out the riots (1968–78). *Trans-Action,* 1968, 5, 21–30.

KIESLER, C. A. Mental health policy as a field of inquiry for psychology. *American Psychologist,* 1980, 35, 1066–1080.

KIESLER, C. A. Mental hospitals and alternative care: Noninstitutionalization as potential public policy for mental patients. *American Psychologist,* 1982, 37, 349–360.

KIESLER, C. A., CUMMINGS, N. A., & VANDENBOS, G. R. *Psychology and national health insurance: A sourcebook.* Washington, D.C.: American Psychological Association, 1979.

KLEINMUNTZ, B. Clinical information processing by computer. In T. M. Newcomb (Ed.), *New directions in psychology* (Vol. 4). New York: Holt, Rinehart & Winston, 1970.

KLEINMUNTZ, B. *Personality and psychological assessment.* New York: St. Martin's Press, 1982.

KLOPFER, W. G. Integration of projective techniques in the clinical case study. In A. I. Rabin (Ed.), *Assessment with projective techniques: A concise introduction.* New York: Springer, 1981.

KLOPFER, W. G. Writing psychological reports. In C. E. Walker (Ed.), *Handbook of clinical psychology: Theory, research and practice.* Homewood, Ill.: Dow Jones-Irwin, 1982.

KNOWLES, J. H. The responsibility of the individual. In J. H. Knowles (Ed.), *Doing better and feeling worse: Health in the United States.* New York: W. W. Norton & Co., Inc., 1977.

KOHLBERG, L. Development of moral character and moral ideology. In M. L. Hoffman & L. W. Hoffman (Eds.), *Review of child development research* (Vol. 1). New York: Russell Sage Foundation, 1964.

KOLB, J. E., & GUNDERSON, J. G. Diagnosing borderline patients with a semistructured interview. *Archives of General Psychiatry,* 1980, 37, 37–41.

KORCHIN, S. J. *Modern clinical psychology.* New York: Basic Books, 1976.

KORCHIN, S. J., & SCHULDBERG, D. The future of clinical assessment. *American Psychologist*, 1981, *36*, 1147–1158.

KOSTLAN, A. A method for the empirical study of psychodiagnosis. *Journal of Consulting Psychology*, 1954, *18*, 83–88.

KRANZLER, G. *You can change how you feel: A rational-emotive approach.* Eugene, Oreg.: Kranzler, 1974.

KRASNER, L., & ULLMANN, L. P. *Behavior influence and personality: The social matrix of human action.* New York: Holt, Rinehart & Winston, 1973.

KRATOCHWILL, T. R. (Ed.). *Single subject research: Strategies for evaluating change.* New York: Academic Press, 1978.

KRUMBOLTZ, J. D., BECKER-HAVEN, J. F., & BURNETT, K. F. Counseling psychology. *Annual Review of Psychology*, 1979, *30*, 555–602.

KRUMBOLTZ, J. D., & THORESEN, C. E. (Eds.). *Behavioral counseling: Cases and techniques.* New York: Holt, Rinehart & Winston, 1969.

KRUMBOLTZ, J. D., & THORESEN, C. E. (Eds.). *Counseling methods.* New York: Holt, Rinehart & Winston, 1976.

KUHN, T. S. *The structure of scientific revolutions* (2nd ed.). Chicago: University of Chicago Press, 1970.

KURTZ, R. M., & GARFIELD, S. L. Illusory correlation: A further exploration of Chapman's paradigm. *Journal of Consulting and Clinical Psychology*, 1978, *46*, 1009–1015.

LACHAR, D., BUTKUS, M., & HRYHORCZUK, L. Objective personality assessment of children: An exploratory study of the Personality Inventory for Children (PIC) in a psychiatric setting. *Journal of Personality Assessment*, 1978, *42*, 529–537.

LACHAR, D., & WIRT, R. D. A data-based analysis of the psychometric performance of the Personality Inventory for Children (PIC): An alternative to the Achenbach review. *Journal of Personality Assessment*, 1981, *45*, 614–616.

LADD, C. E. Record-keeping and research in psychiatric and psychological clinics. *Journal of Counseling Psychology*, 1967, *14*, 361–367.

LAH, M. I., & ROTTER, J. B. Changing college student norms on the Rotter Incomplete Sentences Blank. *Journal of Consulting and Clinical Psychology*, 1981, *49*, 985.

LANDFIELD, A. W., & LEITNER, L. M. *Personal construct psychology: Psychotherapy and personality.* New York: John Wiley, 1980.

LANDMAN, J. T., & DAWES, R. M. Psychotherapy outcome: Smith and Glass' conclusions stand up under scrutiny. *American Psychologist*, 1982, *37*, 504–516.

LASZLO, E. *The systems view of the world.* New York: Braziller, 1972.

LAZAR, I., HUBBELL, V. R., MURRAY, H., ROSCH, M., & ROYCE, J. *The persistence of preschool effects: A long-term follow-up of fourteen infant and preschool experiments* (Final report for grant #18–76–07843). Ithaca, N.Y.: Cornell University, Community Service Laboratory, 1977.

LAZARUS, A. A. *Behavior therapy and beyond.* New York: McGraw-Hill, 1971.

LAZARUS, A. A. Multimodal behavior therapy: Treating the "BASIC ID." *The Journal of Nervous and Mental Disease*, 1973, *156*, 404–411.

LAZARUS, A. A. *Multimodal behavior therapy.* New York: Springer, 1976.

LEARY, T. F. *The interpersonal diagnosis of personality.* New York: Ronald, 1957.

LEDERER, W. J., & JACKSON, D. D. *Mirages of marriage.* New York: W. W. Norton & Co., Inc. 1968.

LEIGHTON, D. C. Distribution of psychiatric symptoms in a small town. *American Journal of Psychiatry*, 1956, *112*, 716–723.

LEIK, R. K., LEIK, S. A., EKKER, K., & GIFFORD, G. A. *Under the threat of Mt. St. Helens: A study of chronic family stress.* Washington, D.C.: Federal Emergency Management Agency, 1982.

LERNER, B. Representative democracy, "men of zeal" and testing legislation. *American Psychologist*, 1981, *3*, 270–275.

LEVENBERG, S. B., & WAGNER, M. K. Smoking cessation: Long-term irrelevance of mode of treatment. *Journal of Behavior Therapy and Experimental Psychiatry*, 1976, *7*, 93–95.

LEVENSON, A. J. *Basic psychopharmacology*, New York: Springer, 1981.

LEVINE, E., & FRANCO, J. N. A reassessment of self-disclosure patterns among Anglo-Americans and Hispanics. *Journal of Counseling Psychology*, 1981, *28*, 522–524.

LEVINE, M. *The history and politics of community mental health.* New York: Oxford University Press, 1981.

LEVINE, M., & LEVINE, A. *A social history of helping services.* New York: Appleton-Century-Crofts, 1970.

LEVINSON, D. J. (with C. N. DARROW, E. B. KLEIN, M. H. LEVINSON, & B. McKEE). *The seasons of a man's life.* New York: Knopf, 1978.

LEVITT, E. E. Research on psychotherapy with children. In A. E. Bergin & S. L. Garfield, (Eds.), *Handbook of psychotherapy and behavior change.* New York: John Wiley, 1971.

LEVY, L. H. *Psychological interpretation.* New York: Holt, Rinehart & Winston, 1963.

LEVY, M. R., & FOX, H. M. Psychological testing is alive and well. *Professional Psychology*, 1975, *6*, 420–424.

LEWINSOHN, P. M., & AMENSON, C. S. Some relations between pleasant and unpleasant mood-related events and depression. *Journal of Abnormal Psychology*, 1978, *87*, 644–654.

LEWINSOHN, P. M., & LEE, W.M.L. Assessment of affective disorders. In D. Barlow (Ed.), *Behavioral assessment of adult disorders.* New York: Guilford, 1981.

LEWINSOHN, P. M., MUÑOZ, R. F., YOUNGREN, M. A., & ZEISS, A. M. *Control your depression.* Englewood Cliffs, N.J.: Prentice-Hall, 1978.

LEWINSOHN, P. M., & TALKINGTON, J. Studies on the measurement of unpleasant events and relations with depression. *Applied Psychological Measurement*, 1979, *3*, 83–101.

LEZAK, M. D. *Neuropsychological assessment.* New York: Oxford University Press, 1976 (2nd ed., 1983).

LICHTENSTEIN, E. *Psychotherapy: Approaches and applications.* Monterey, Calif.: Brooks/Cole, 1980.

LIEBERMAN, M. A., YALOM, I. D., & MILES, M. B. Impact on participants. In L. N. Solomon & B. Berzon (Eds.), *New perspectives on encounter groups.* San Francisco: Jossey-Bass, 1972.

LIEBERMAN, M. A., YALOM, I. D., & MILES, M. B. *Encounter groups: First facts.* New York: Basic Books, 1973.

LIEM, R., & RAYMAN, P. Health and social costs of unemployment: Research and policy considerations. *American Psychologist*, 1982, *37*, 1116–1123.

LINDEMANN, J. E. (Ed.). *Psychological and behavioral aspects of physical disability: A manual for health practitioners.* New York: Plenum, 1981.

LINDZEY, G. *Projective techniques and cross-cultural research.* New York: Appleton-Century-Crofts, 1961.

LINDZEY, G., & BYRNE, D. Measurements of social choice and interpersonal attractiveness. In G. Lindzey & E. Aronson (Eds.), *The handbook of social psychology* (Vol. II) (2nd ed.). Reading, Mass.: Addison-Wesley, 1968.

LINDZEY, G., LOEHLIN, J., MANOSEVITZ, M., & THIESSEN, O. Behavioral genetics. *Annual Review of Psychology*, 1971, *22*, 39–94.

LITT, C. J. Children's attachment to transitional objects: A study of two pediatric populations. *American Journal of Orthopsychiatry*, 1981, *51*, 131–139.

LITTLE, B. R. *Personal projects: A rationale and method for investigation.* Unpublished manuscript, Department of Psychology, Carleton University, Ottawa, 1977.

LITTLE, K. B., & SHNEIDMAN, E. S. Congruencies among interpretations of psychological test and anamnestic data. *Psychological Monographs*, 1959, *73*,(6, Whole No. 476).

LOBITZ, W. C., & LOBITZ, G. K. Clinical assessments in the treatment of sexual dysfunction. In J. LoPiccolo & L. LoPiccolo (Eds.), *Handbook of sex therapy.* New York: Plenum, 1978.

LOEVINGER, J., WESSLER, R., & REDMORE, C. *Measuring ego development: Construction and use of a sentence completion test* (Vol. 1). *Scoring manual for women and girls* (Vol. 2). San Francisco: Jossey-Bass, 1970.

LONDON, M., & BRAY, D. W. Ethical issues in testing and evaluation for personnel decisions. *American Psychologist*, 1980, *35*, 890–901.

LOPICCOLO, J. The treatment of sexual dysfunction. In J. LoPiccolo & L. LoPiccolo (Eds.), *Handbook of sex therapy.* New York: Plenum, 1978.

LOPICCOLO, J., & STEGER, J. The sexual interaction inventory: A new instrument for assessment of sexual dysfunction. *Archives of Sexual Behavior*, 1974, *3*, 585–595.

LORBER, R. *Parental tracking of childhood behavior as a function of family stress.* Doctoral dissertation, University of Oregon, 1981.

LORION, R. P. Research on psychotherapy and behavior change with the disadvantaged: Past, present and future directions. In S. L. Garfield & A. E. Bergin (Eds.), *Handbook of psychotherapy and behavior change: An empirical analysis* (2nd ed.). New York: John Wiley, 1978.

LORR, M. Dimensions and categories for assessment of psychotics. In P. McReynolds (Ed.), *Advances in psychological assessment* (Vol. 2). Palo Alto, Calif.: Science & Behavior Books, 1971.

LOTHSTEIN, L. M., & JONES, P. Discriminating violent individuals by means of psychological tests. *Journal of Personality Assessment*, 1978, *42*, 237–243.

LOWEN, A. *Bioenergetics.* New York: Penguin, 1975. (a)

LOWEN, A. *Love and orgasm.* New York: Collier, 1975. (b)

LOYE, D. *The knowable future: A psychology of forecasting and prophecy.* New York: John Wiley, 1978.

LUBIN, B., WALLIS, R. R., & PAINE, C. Patterns of psychological test usage in the United States: 1935–1969. *Professional Psychology*, 1971, *2*, 70–74.

LUBORSKY, L. L., & SPENCE, D. P. Quantitative research on psychoanalytic therapy. In S. L. Garfield & A. E. Bergin (Eds.), *Handbook of psychotherapy and behavioral change: An empirical analysis.* New York: John Wiley, 1978.

LURIA, A. R. *The working brain.* New York: Basic Books, 1973.

LURIA, A. R. *Higher cortical functions in man* (2nd ed.). New York: Basic Books, 1980.

LYKKEN, D. T. Psychology and the lie detector industry. *American Psychologist*, 1974, *29*, 725–739.

LYKKEN, D. T. *A tremor in the blood: Uses and abuses of the lie detector.* New York: McGraw-Hill, 1981.

MACANDREW, C. The differentiation of male alcoholic outpatients from nonalcoholic psychiatric patients by means of the MMPI. *Quarterly Journal of Studies on Alcohol*, 1965, *26*, 238–246.

MACKINNON, D. W. *Human assessment: Perspective and context for current practice.* Paper presented at the American Psychological Association meetings, Chicago, 1975.

MACPHILLAMY, D. J., & LEWINSOHN, P. M. The Pleasant Events Schedule: Studies on reliability, validity and scale intercorrelation. *Journal of Consulting and Clinical Psychology*, 1982, *50*, 363–380.

MAHLER, W. R. *Diagnostic studies.* Reading, Mass.: Addison-Wesley, 1973.

MAHONEY, M. J., & ARNKOFF, D. Cognitive and self-control therapies. In S. L. Garfield & A. E. Bergin (Eds.), *Handbook of psychotherapy and behavior change* (2nd ed.). New York: John Wiley, 1978.

MAHRER, A. R. *Experiencing: A humanistic theory of psychology and psychiatry.* New York: Brunner/Mazel, 1978.

MALONEY, M. P., & WARD, M. P. *Psychological assessment: A conceptual approach.* New York: Oxford University Press, 1976.

MANN, P. A. *Community psychology: Concepts and applications.* New York: Free Press, 1978.

MANNINO, F. V., MACLENNON, B. W., & SHORE, M. F. *The practice of mental health consultation* (DHEW publication [ADM] 74-112). Washington, D.C.: U.S. Government Printing Office, 1975.

MARKS, P. A., SEEMAN, W., & HALLER, D. L. *The actuarial use of the MMPI with adolescents and adults.* Baltimore: Williams & Wilkins, 1974.

MARSELLA, A. J. Depressive experience and disorder across cultures. In H. C. Triandis & J. G. Draguns (Eds.), *Handbook of cross-cultural psychology: Psychopathology* (Vol. 6). Boston: Allyn & Bacon, 1980.

MARSHALL, E. Psychotherapy works, but for whom? *Science,* 1980, *207,* 506-508.

MARUYAMA, M. The second cybernetics: Deviation-amplifying mutual causal processes. *American Scientist,* 1963, *51,* 164-179.

MARUYAMA, M. Heterogenistics and morphogenetics: Toward a new concept of the scientific. *Theory and Society,* 1978, *5,* 75-96.

MASH, E. J., & TERDAL, L. G. (Eds.). *Behavioral assessment of childhood disorders.* New York: Guilford, 1981.

MASLING, J. The influence of situational and interpersonal variables in projective testing. *Psychological Bulletin,* 1960, *57,* 65-85.

MASLOW, A. H. *Toward a psychology of being* (2nd ed.). New York: Van Nostrand Reinhold, 1968.

MASLOW, A. H. *The farther reaches of human nature.* New York: Viking, 1971.

MASTERPASQUA, F. Toward a synergism of developmental and community psychology. *American Psychologist,* 1981, *36,* 782-786.

MASTERS, W., & JOHNSON, V. *Human sexual inadequacy.* Boston: Little, Brown, 1970.

MASTERSON, S. The adjective checklist technique: A review and critique. In P. McReynolds (Ed.), *Advances in psychological assessment* (Vol. 3). San Francisco: Jossey-Bass, 1975.

MATARAZZO, J. D. *Wechsler's measurement and appraisal of adult intelligence* (5th ed.). Baltimore: Williams and Wilkins, 1972.

MATARAZZO, J. D. The interview: Its reliability and validity in psychiatric diagnosis. In B. B. Wolman (Ed.), *Clinical diagnosis of mental disorders: A handbook.* New York: Plenum, 1978.

MATARAZZO, J. D. Behavioral health and behavioral medicine: Frontiers for a new health psychology. *American Psychologist,* 1980, *35,* 807-817.

MATARAZZO, J. D. Behavioral health's challenge to academic, scientific and professional psychology. *American Psychologist,* 1982, *37,* 1-14.

MATARAZZO, J. D., & WIENS, A. N. *The interview: Research on its anatomy and structure.* Chicago: Aldine, 1972.

MAXMEN, J. *The post-physician era: Medicine in the 21st century.* New York: John Wiley, 1976.

MAYS, D. T., & FRANKS, C. M. Getting worse: Psychotherapy or no treatment—the jury should still be out. *Professional Psychology,* 1980, *11,* 78-92.

McCARTHY, P. R., & BETZ, N. E. Differential effects of self-disclosing versus self-involving counselor statements. *Journal of Counseling Psychology,* 1978, *25,* 251-256.

McCAULLEY, M. H. Jung's theory of psychological types and the Myers-Briggs Type Indicator. In P. McReynolds (Ed.), *Advances in psychological assessment* (Vol. 5). San Francisco: Jossey-Bass, 1981.

McKECHNIE, G. E. Environmental dispositions: Concepts and measures. In P. McReynolds (Ed.), *Advances in psychological assessment* (Vol. 4). San Francisco: Jossey-Bass, 1978.

McLEMORE, C. W., & BENJAMIN, L. S. Whatever happened to interpersonal diagnosis? A psychosocial alternative to DSM-III. *American Psychologist*, 1979, *34*, 17–34.

McNEIL, E. B. *The quiet furies: Man and disorder.* Englewood Cliffs, N.J.: Prentice-Hall, 1967.

McREYNOLDS, P. (Ed.). *Advances in psychological assessment* (Vol. 1). Palo Alto, Calif.: Science & Behavior Books, 1968.

McREYNOLDS, P. (Ed.). *Advances in psychological assessment* (Vol. 2). Palo Alto, Calif.: Science & Behavior Books, 1971.

McREYNOLDS, P. (Ed.). *Advances in psychological assessment* (Vol. 3). San Francisco: Jossey-Bass, 1975.

McREYNOLDS, P. (Ed.). *Advances in psychological assessment* (Vol. 4). San Francisco: Jossey-Bass, 1978.

McREYNOLDS, P. (Ed.). *Advances in psychological assessment* (Vol. 5). San Francisco: Jossey-Bass, 1981.

MEADOR, B. D., & ROGERS, C. R. Person-centered therapy. In R. J. Corsini (Ed.), *Current psychotherapies* (2nd ed.). Itasca, Ill.: Peacock, 1979.

MEADOWS, M. E. Assessment of college counseling: A follow-up study. *Journal of Counseling Psychology*, 1975, *22*, 463–470.

MEADOWS, D. H., MEADOWS, D. L., RANDERS, J., & BEHRENS, W. W. *The limits to growth: A report for the Club of Rome's project on the predicament of mankind.* New York: Signet, 1972.

MECHANIC, D. *Mental health and social policy* (2nd ed.). Englewood Cliffs, N.J.: Prentice-Hall, 1980.

MEEHL, P. E. *Clinical versus statistical prediction.* Minneapolis: University of Minnesota Press, 1954.

MEEHL, P. E. Wanted—a good cookbook. *American Psychologist*, 1956, *11*, 263–272.

MEEHL, P. E. A comparison of clinicians with five statistical methods of identifying psychotic MMPI profiles. *Journal of Counseling Psychology*, 1959, *6*, 102–109.

MEEHL, P. E. The cognitive activity of the clinician. *American Psychologist*, 1960, *15*, 19–27.

MEEHL, P. E. *Psychodiagnosis: Selected papers.* Minneapolis: University of Minnesota Press, 1973.

MEEHL, P. E., & ROSEN, A. Antecedent probability and the efficiency of psychometric signs, patterns, or cutting scores. *Psychological Bulletin*, 1955, *52*, 194–216.

MEICHENBAUM, D. *Cognitive-behavior modification: An integrative approach.* New York: Plenum, 1977.

MELZAK, R. The McGill Pain Questionnaire: Major properties and scoring methods. *Pain*, 1975, *1*, 277–299.

MERCER, J. R. *System of Multicultural Pluralistic Assessment (SOMPA): Technical Manual.* New York: Psychological Corp., 1979.

MERCER, J. R. & LEWIS, J. F. *System of Multicultural Pluralistic Assessment (SOMPA).* New York: Psychological Corp., 1978.

MERLUZZI, T. V., GLASS, C. R., & GENEST, R. (Eds.). *Cognitive assessment.* New York: Guilford Press, 1981.

MICHAEL, D. N. *On learning to plan—and planning to learn.* San Francisco: Jossey-Bass, 1973.

MIKAWA, J. K. Evaluation in community mental health. In P. McReynolds (Ed.), *Advances in psychological assessment* (Vol. 3). San Francisco: Jossey-Bass, 1975.

MILLER, G. H., GALANTER, E., & PRIBRAM., K. N. *Plans and the structure of behavior.* New York: Holt, Rinehart & Winston, 1960.

MILLER, J. G. *Living systems.* New York: McGraw-Hill, 1978.

MILLER, J. G., & MILLER, J. L. Systems science: An emerging interdisciplinary field. *The Center Magazine*, 1981, *14*, 44–55.

MILLER, L. S., BERGSTROM, D. A., CROSS, H. J., & GRUBE, J. W. Opinions and use of the DSM system by practicing psychologists. *Professional Psychology*, 1981, *12*, 385–391.

MILLER, N. E. Biofeedback and visceral learning. *Annual Review of Psychology*, 1978, *29*, 373–404.

MILLON, T. *Millon Clinical Multiaxial Inventory: Manual.* Minneapolis: NCS Interpretive Scoring Systems, 1977.

MILLON, T., GREEN, C., & MEAGHER, R. (Eds.). *Handbook of clinical health psychology.* New York: Plenum, 1982.

MINUCHIN, S. *Families and family therapy.* Cambridge, Mass.: Harvard University Press, 1974.

MINUCHIN, S., & FISHMAN, H. C. *Family therapy techniques.* Cambridge, Mass.: Harvard University Press, 1981.

MINUCHIN, S., ROSMAN, B., & BAKER, L. *Psychosomatic families: Anorexia nervosa in context.* Cambridge, Mass.: Harvard University Press, 1978.

MISCHEL, W. *Personality and assessment.* New York: John Wiley, 1968.

MISCHEL, W. Toward a cognitive social learning reconceptualization of personality. *Psychological Review*, 1973, *80*, 252–283.

MISCHEL, W. On the interface of cognition and personality: Beyond the person situation debate. *American Psychologist*, 1979, *34*, 740–754.

MONAHAN, J. (Ed.). *Who is the client? The ethics of psychological intervention in the criminal justice system.* Washington, D.C.: American Psychological Assn., 1980.

MONTGOMERY, R. B., & SUNDBERG, N. D. Current and alternative training models in clinical psychology. *Australian Psychologist*, 1977, *12*, 95–102.

MOORE, G. H., BOBBITT, W. E., & WILDMAN, R. W. Psychiatric impressions of psychological reports. *Journal of Clinical Psychology*, 1968, *24*, 373–376.

MOOS, R. *The social climate scales: An overview.* Palo Alto, Calif.: Consulting Psychologists Press, 1974.

MOOS, R. H. Assessment and impact of social climate. In P. McReynolds (Ed.), *Advances in psychological assessment* (Vol. 3). San Francisco: Jossey-Bass, 1975.

MOOS, R. H., & FUHR, R. The clinical use of social-ecological concepts: The case of an adolescent girl. *American Journal of Orthopsychiatry*, 1982, *52*, 111–122.

MORENO, J. L. Psychodrama. In S. Arieti (Ed.), *American handbook of psychiatry* (Vol. 2). New York: Basic Books, 1959.

MORGANSTERN, K. P., & TEVLIN, H. E. Behavioral interviewing. In M. Hersen & A. S. Bellack (Eds.), *Behavioral assessment: A practical handbook* (2nd ed.). New York: Pergamon Press, 1981.

MOSAK, H. H. Adlerian psychotherapy. In R. J. Corsini (Ed.), *Current Psychotherapies* (2nd ed.). Itasca, Ill.: Peacock, 1979.

MOWRER, O. H. (Ed.). *Morality and mental health.* Chicago: Rand McNally, 1967.

MUKTANANDA, P. *Meditate.* Albany, N.Y.: State University of New York Press, 1980.

MULLER, C. The overmedicated society. *Science*, 1972, *176*, 488.

MUNFORD, P. R., REARDON, D., LIBERMAN, R. P., & ALLEN, L. Behavioral treatment of hysterical coughing and mutism: A case study. *Journal of Consulting and Clinical Psychology*, 1976, *44*, 1008–1014.

MUÑOZ, R. F., SNOWDEN, L. R., & KELLY, J. G. (Eds.). *Social and psychological research in community settings: Designing and conducting programs for social and personal well-being.* San Francisco: Jossey-Bass, 1979.

MURRAY, E. J., & JACOBSON, L. F. Cognition and learning in traditional and behavioral therapy. In S. Garfield & A. Bergin (Eds.), *Handbook of psychotherapy and behavior change*. New York: John Wiley, 1978.

MURRAY, H. A. *Explorations in personality*. New York: Oxford, 1938.

MURSTEIN, B. I. *Love, sex and marriage through the ages*. New York: Springer, 1974.

NATHAN, P. E. Alcoholism. In H. Leitenberg (Ed.), *Handbook of behavior modification and behavior therapy*. Englewood Cliffs, N.J.: Prentice-Hall, 1976.

NAY, W. R. *Multimethod clinical assessment*. New York: Gardner Press, 1979.

NIDICH, S., SEEMAN, W., & DRESHIN, T. Influence of transcendental meditation: A replication. *Journal of Counseling Psychology*, 1973, *20*, 565–566.

NIETZEL, M. T., & BERNSTEIN, D. A. The effects of instructionally-mediated demand upon the behavioral assessment of assertiveness. *Journal of Consulting and Clinical Psychology*, 1976. *44*, 500.

NISBETT, R., & ROSS, L. *Human inference: Strategies and shortcomings of social judgement*. Englewood Cliffs, N.J.: Prentice-Hall, 1980.

NOPPE, L. D. Creative thinking. In R. H. Woody (Ed.), *Encyclopedia of clinical assessment* (Vol. 2). San Francisco: Jossey-Bass, 1980.

NORCROSS, J. C., & PROCHASKA, J. O. A national survey of clinical psychologists: Characteristics and activities. *Clinical Psychologist*, 1982, *35*(2), 1–8.

NORMAN, W. T. Toward an adequate taxonomy of personality attributes: Replicated factor structure in peer nomination personality ratings. *Journal of Abnormal and Social Psychology*, 1963, *66*, 574–583.

NOVACO, R. W. A stress inoculation approach to anger management in the training of law enforcement officers. *American Journal of Community Psychology*, 1977, *5*, 327–346.

OFFICE OF STRATEGIC SERVICES STAFF. *Assessment of men*. New York: Holt, Rinehart & Winston, 1948.

OTTO, H. A. (Ed.). *Human potentialities: The challenge and the promise*. St. Louis: Warren Green, 1968.

OUNSTEAD, C., & LYNCH, M. A. Family pathology as seen in England. In R. E. Helfer & C. A. Kempe (Eds.), *Child abuse and neglect*. Cambridge, Mass.: Ballinger, 1976.

OWENS, W. A., & SCHOENFELDT, L. F. Toward a classification of persons. *Journal of Applied Psychology Monographs*, 1979, *65*, 568–607.

PALMER, J., & McGUIRE, F. L. The use of unobtrusive measures in mental health research. *Journal of Consulting and Clinical Psychology*, 1973, *40*, 431–436.

PALYS, T. S., & LITTLE, B. R. Perceived life satisfaction and the organization of personal project systems. *Journal of Personality and Social Psychology* (in press).

PANKRATZ, L. D. A review of the Munchausen syndrome. *Clinical Psychology Review*, 1981, *1*, 65–78.

PANKRATZ, L. D., & TAPLIN, J. R. Issues in psychological assessment. In J. R. McNamara & A. C. Barclay (Eds.), *Critical issues in professional psychology*. New York: Praeger, 1982.

PAPP, P. (Ed.). *Family therapy: Full length case studies*. New York: Gardner Press, 1977.

PARLOFF, M. B. Psychotherapy and research: An anaclitic depression. *Psychiatry*, 1980, *43*, 279–293.

PARLOFF, M. B., WASKOW, I. E., & WOLFE, B. E. Research on client variables in psychotherapy. In S. L. Garfield & A. E. Bergin (Eds.), *Handbook of psychotherapy and behavior change: An empirical analysis* (2nd ed.). New York: John Wiley, 1978.

PATTERSON, G. R. *Families: Application of social learning to family life*. Champaign, Ill.: Research Press, 1971.

PATTERSON, G. R. Naturalistic observation in clinical assessment. *Journal of Abnormal Child Psychology*, 1977, 5, 309–322.

PATTERSON, G. R. *Coercive family process*. Eugene, Oreg.: Castalia Publishing Co., 1982.

PATTERSON, G. R., & GULLION, E. *Living with children* (Rev. ed.). Champaign, Ill.: Research Press, 1971.

PAUL, G. L. Insight *vs* desensitization in psychotherapy two years after termination. *Journal of Consulting Psychology*, 1967, *13*, 333–348.

PEARCE, J. W., LeBow, M. D., & ORCHARD, J. Role of spouse involvement in the behavioral treatment of overweight women. *Journal of Consulting and Clinical Psychology*, 1981, *49*, 236–244.

PERLOFF, R., & PERLOFF, E. (Eds.). Special issue: Evaluation of psychological service delivery programs. *Professional Psychology*, 1977, *8*, 377–673.

PERLS, F. S. *The Gestalt approach and eye witness to therapy*. Palo Alto: Science and Behavior Books, 1977.

PETERSON, D. R. *The clinical study of social behavior*. New York: Appleton-Century-Crofts, 1968.

PETERSON, D. R. Need for the doctor of psychology degree in professional psychology. *American Psychologist*, 1976, *31*, 792–798.

PETERSON, D. R., & BARON, A., JR. Status of the Illinois doctor of psychology program, 1974. *Professional Psychology*, 1975, *6*, 88–95.

PETZELT, J. T., & CRADDICK, R. Present meaning of assessment in psychology. *Professional Psychology*, 1978, *9*, 587–591.

PHARES, E. J. *Clinical psychology: Concepts, methods, and profession*. Homewood, Ill.: Dorsey Press, 1979.

PIAGET, J. *The origins of intelligence in children*. New York: International Universities Press, 1952.

PIAGET, J. *Structuralism*. New York: Basic Books, 1970.

PIKOFF, A. Biofeedback: A resource directory and outline of the literature. *Professional Psychology*, 1981, *12*, 261–270.

PILCHER, A. J., & SUNDBERG, N. D. Proposed ethical guidelines for work in the human services. *Australian Child and Family Welfare Quarterly*, 1981, *6*, 3–7.

PINES, A. M., ARONSON, E., & KAFRY, D. *Burnout: From tedium to personal growth*. New York: Free Press, 1981.

PLOMIN, R., DeFRIES, J. C., & McCLEARN, G. E. *Behavioral genetics: A primer*. San Francisco: Jossey-Bass, 1980.

POLSTER, E., & POLSTER, M. *Gestalt therapy integrated: Contours of theory and practice*. New York: Brunner/Mazel, 1973.

POPE, B. *The mental health interview: Research and application*. New York: Pergamon, 1979.

POTKAY, C. R. The role of personal history data in clinical judgement: A selective focus. *Journal of Personality Assessment*, 1973, 37, 203–213.

PRIGOGINE, I. *From being to becoming: Time and complexity in the physical science*. San Francisco: W. H. Freeman & Company Publishers, 1980.

RABKIN, L. Y. (Ed.). *Psychopathology and literature*. New York: Harper & Row, 1966.

RACUSIN, G. R., ABRAMOWITZ, S. I., & HERRERA, H. R. Competing role demands of therapists' professional and marital lives. *Clinical Psychology Review*, 1981, *1*, 103–118.

RAMEY, C. T., & HASKINS, R. The modification of intelligence through early experience. *Intelligence*, 1981, 5, 5–19.

REICH, W. *The function of the orgasm*. New York: Farrar, Straus, & Giroux, 1970.

REICH, W. *Character analysis*. New York: Farrar, Straus, & Giroux, 1971.

REICHENBACH, H. *Experience and prediction: An analysis of the foundations and the structure of knowledge.* Chicago: University of Chicago Press, 1938.

REISMAN, J. M. *A history of clinical psychology.* New York: Irvington, 1976.

REISMAN, J. M. History and current trends in clinical psychology. In C. E. Walker(Ed.), *Clinical practice of psychology: A guide to mental health professionals.* New York: Pergamon Press, 1981.

REITAN, R. M., & DAVISON, L. A. *Clinical neuropsychology: Current status and applications.* New York: Winston/Wiley, 1974.

RESNICK, E. V. Mental health care in America: 2076. *Hospital and Community Psychiatry,* 1976, *27,* 519–521.

REYNOLDS, D. K. *The quiet therapies: Japanese pathways to personal growth.* Honolulu: University of Hawaii Press, 1980.

REYNOLDS, W. M. Psychological tests; Clinical usage versus psychometric quality. *Professional Psychology,* 1979, *10,* 324–329.

RIGLER, D. A monument to longitudinal research (Review of Jones, Bayley, MacFarlane, & Honzik). *Contemporary Psychology,* 1973, *18,* 316–317.

RIMLAND, B. Infantile autism: Status and research. In A. Davids (Ed.), *Child personality and psychopathology.* New York: John Wiley, 1974.

RIVLIN, A. *Childcare and preschool: Options for federal support.* Washington, D.C.: Congressional Budget Office, U.S. Government Printing Office, 1978.

ROBINS, L. N. *Deviant children grown up.* Baltimore: Williams & Wilkins, 1966.

ROBINSON, E. A., & EYBERG, S. M. The dyadic parent-child interaction coding system: Standardization and validation. *Journal of Consulting and Clinical Psychology,* 1981, *49,* 245–250.

ROGERS, C. R. *Counseling and psychotherapy.* Boston: Houghton Mifflin, 1942.

ROGERS, C. R. Persons or science? A philosophical question. *American Psychologist,* 1955, *10,* 267–278.

ROGERS, C. R. *A way of being.* Boston: Houghton Miffin, 1980.

ROMAN, M., & SCHMAIS, A. Consumer participation and control: A conceptual overview. In H. H. Barten & L. Bellak (Eds.), *Progress in community mental health* (Vol.2). New York: Grune & Stratton, 1972.

ROOSENS, E. *Mental patients in town life: Gheel-Europe's first therapeutic community.* Beverly Hills, Calif.: Sage Publications, Inc., 1979.

ROSE, D., & BITTER, E. J. The Palo Alto Destructive Content Scale as a predictor of physical assaultiveness in men. *Journal of Personality Assessment,* 1980, *44,* 228–233.

ROSEN, J. C., & WIENS, A. N. Changes in medical problems and use of medical services following psychological intervention. *American Psychologist,* 1979, *34,* 420–431.

ROSENHAN, D. L. On being sane in insane places. *Science,* 1973, *180,* 250–258.

ROSENTHAL, D. *Genetic theory and abnormal behavior.* New York: McGraw-Hill, 1970.

ROSS, A. O. *Psychological disorders of children: A behavioral approach to theory, research and therapy* (2nd ed.).New York: McGraw-Hill, 1980.

ROTTER, J. B. Generalized expectancies for internal versus external control of reinforcement. *Psychological Monographs,* 1966, *80*(1, Whole No. 609).

RUDESTAM, K. E. *Experiential groups in theory and practice.* Monterey, Calif.: Brooks/Cole, 1982.

RUEVENI, U. *Networking families in crisis.* New York: Human Sciences Press, 1979.

RUSSELL, J. A., & WARD, L. M. Environmental psychology. *Annual Review of Psychology,* 1982, *33,* 651–688.

RUTMAN, L. (Ed.). *Evaluation research methods: A basic guide.* Beverly Hills, Calif.: Sage Publications, Inc., 1977.

RUTTER, M. *Changing youth in a changing society: Patterns of adolescent development and disorder.* London: Nuffield Provincial Hospitals Trust, 1979. (a)

RUTTER, M. Protective factors in children's responses to stress and disadvantage. In M. W. Kent & J. E. Rolf (Eds.), *Primary prevention of psychopathology* (Vol. 3). Hanover, N.H.: University of New England Press, 1979. (b)

RUTTER, M., MAUGHAM, B., MORTIMORE, P., & OUSTON, J. *Fifteen thousand hours: Secondary schools and their effects on children.* Cambridge, Mass.: Harvard University Press, 1979.

RUTTER, M., & SCHOPLER, E. (Eds.). *Autism; A reappraisal of concepts and treatment.* New York: Plenum, 1978.

RYAN, W. *Distress in the city: Essays on the design and administration of urban mental health services.* Cleveland: Case Western Reserve, 1969.

SAGER, C. J. *Marriage contracts and couple therapy.* New York: Brunner/Mazel, 1976.

SALZINGER, S., ANTROBUS, J., & GLICK, S. (Eds.). *The ecosystem of the "sick" child: Implications for classification and intervention for disturbed and mentally retarded children.* New York: Academic Press, 1980.

SAMELSON, F. J. B. Watson's Little Albert, Cyril Burt's twins and the need for a critical science. *American Psychologist*, 1980, 35, 619–625.

SANTOSTEFANO, S. *A biodevelopmental approach to clinical child psychology.* New York: John Wiley, 1978.

SARASON, I. G. Test anxiety and the intellectual performance of college students. *Journal of Educational Psychology*, 1961, 52, 201–206.

SARASON, I. G. The Test Anxiety Scale: Concept and research. In C. D. Spielberger & I. G. Sarason (Eds.), *Stress and anxiety* (Vol. 5). Washington, D.C.: Hemisphere, 1978.

SARBIN, T. R. A contribution to the study of actuarial and individual methods of prediction. *American Journal of Sociology*, 1943, 48, 593–602.

SARBIN, T. R., TAFT, R., & BAILEY, D. E. *Clinical inference and cognitive theory.* New York: Holt, Rinehart & Winston, 1960.

SARGENT, H. D., & MAYMAN, M. Clinical psychology. In S. Arieti (Ed.), *American handbook of psychiatry* (Vol. 2). New York: Basic Books, 1959.

SASLOW, M. *FIG-Waiver continuum of care project for the elderly. Final project report.* Salem, Oreg.: Department of Human Resources, December 1981.

SATTLER, J. M. Racial "experimenter effects" in experimentation, testing, interviewing and psychotherapy. *Psychological Bulletin*, 1970, 73, 137–160.

SATTLER, J. M., AVILA, V., HOUSTON, W. B., & TONEY, D. H. Performance of bilingual Mexican-American children on Spanish and English versions of the Peabody Picture Vocabulary Test. *Journal of Consulting and Clinical Psychology*, 1980, 48, 782–784.

SATTLER, J. M., & GWYNNE, J. White examiners generally do not impede the intelligence test performance of black children: To debunk a myth. *Journal of Consulting and Clinical Psychology*, 1982, 50, 196–208.

SATTLER, J. M., & THEYE, F. Procedural, situational, and interpersonal variables in individual intelligence testing. *Psychological Bulletin*, 1967, 68, 347–360.

SAWYER, J. Measurement *and* prediction, clinical *and* statistical. *Psychological Bulletin*, 1966, 66, 178–200.

SCHAEFER, C. E., & MILLMAN, H. L. *Therapies for children: A handbook for effective treatment of problem behaviors.* San Francisco: Jossey-Bass, 1977.

SCHETKY, D. H., ANGELL, R. H., MORRISON, C. V., & SACK, W. H. Parents who fail: A study of 51 cases of termination of parental rights. *Journal of the American Academy of Child Psychiatry*, 1979, 18, 366–383.

SCHOFIELD, W. *Psychotherapy: The purchase of friendship.* Englewood Cliffs, N.J.: Prentice-Hall, 1964.

SCHULBERG, H. C., & PERLOFF, R. Academia and the training of human service delivery program evaluators. *American Psychologist*, 1979, *34*, 247–254.

SCHWEIKER, R. S. Reagan attuned to problems of aging. *Eugene Register-Guard*, Dec. 4, 1981, p. 11A. (From the *Washington Post*).

SCRIVEN, M. *The methodology of evaluation* (AERA Monograph Series on Curriculum Evaluation No. 1). Skokie, Ill.: Rand McNally, 1967.

SECHREST, L. Incremental validity: A recommendation. *Educational and Psychological Measurement*, 1963, *23*, 153–158.

SELYE, H. *The stress of life*. New York: McGraw-Hill, 1956.

SELYE, H. *Stress without distress*. Philadelphia: Lippincott, 1974.

SHAKOW, D. *Clinical psychology as science and profession—a forty year odyssey*. Chicago: Aldine, 1969.

SHAKOW, D. Clinical psychology seen some 50 years later. *American Psychologist*, 1978, *33*, 148–158.

SHAPIRO, D. H. *Meditation: Self-regulation strategy and altered state of consciousness: A scientific/personal exploration*. New York: Aldine, 1980.

SHEEHY, G. *Passages*. New York: Dutton, 1976.

SHURE, M. B., & SPIVACK, G. *Problem-solving techniques in child-rearing*. San Francisco: Jossey-Bass, 1978.

SHURE, M. B., & SPIVACK, G. Interpersonal problem-solving in young children: A cognitive approach to prevention. *American Journal of Community Psychology*, 1982, *10*, 341–356.

SIMON, H. A. *The sciences of the artificial* (2nd ed.). Cambridge, Mass.: M.I.T. Press, 1981.

SINES, J. O., & ZIMMERMAN, M. Assessing children's psychological environments: Issues, methods, and some data from five contemporary instruments. *Clinical Psychology Review*, 1981, *1*, 387–414.

SKINNER, B. F. *Walden two*. New York: Macmillan, 1948.

SLOANE, R. B., STAPLES, F. R., CRISTOL, A. H., YORKSTON, N. J., & WHIPPLE, K. *Psychotherapy versus behavior therapy*. Cambridge, Mass.: Harvard University Press, 1975.

SMELSER, N. J., & ERIKSON, E. H. *Themes of work and love in adulthood*. Cambridge, Mass.: Harvard University Press, 1980.

SMITH, A. Goal Attainment Scaling: A method for evaluating the outcome of mental health treatment. In P. McReynolds (Ed.), *Advances in psychological assessment* (Vol. 5). San Francisco: Jossey-Bass, 1981.

SMITH, D. W. *Recognizable patterns of human malformation; Genetic, embryologic and clinical aspects* (2nd ed.). Philadelphia: Saunders, 1978.

SMITH, K. Observations on Morita therapy and culture-specific interpretations. *Journal of Transpersonal Psychology*, 1981, *13*, 59–69.

SMITH, M. L., & GLASS, G. V. Meta-analysis of psychotherapy outcome studies. *American Psychologist*, 1977, *32*, 752–760.

SMITH, M. L., GLASS, G. V., & MILLER, T. I. *The benefits of psychotherapy*. Baltimore: Johns Hopkins University Press, 1980.

SMITH, P. B. Controlled studies of the outcome of sensitivity training. *Psychological Bulletin*, 1975, *82*, 597–622.

SMYTH, R., & REZNIKOFF, M. Attitudes of psychiatrists toward the usefulness of psychodiagnostic reports. *Professional Psychology*, 1971, *2*, 283–288.

SNYDER, C. R., & NEWBURG, C. L. The Barnum effect in a group setting. *Journal of Personality Assessment*, 1981, *45*, 622–629.

SNYDER, C. R., SHENKEL, R. J., & LOWERY, C. R. Acceptance of personality interpretations: The "Barnum Effect" and beyond. *Journal of Consulting and Clinical Psychology*, 1977, *45*, 104–114.

SNYDER, M., & WHITE, P. Testing hypotheses about other people: Strategies of verification and falsification. *Personality and Social Psychology Bulletin*, 1981, 7, 39–43.

SOLOMON, L. N., & BERZON, B. (Eds.). *New perspectives on encounter groups*. San Francisco: Jossey-Bass, 1972.

SPECTOR, P. E. Multivariate data analysis for outcome studies. *American Journal of Community Psychology*, 1981, 9, 45–54.

SPEISMAN, J. C. Depth of interpretation and verbal resistance in psychotherapy. *Journal of Consulting Psychology*, 1959, 23, 93–99.

SPIELBERGER, C. D. *Understanding stress and anxiety*. New York: Harper & Row, 1979.

SPIELBERGER, C. D., & BUTCHER, J. N. (Eds.). *Advances in personality assessment* (Vol. 1). Hillsdale, N.J.: Lawrence Erlbaum Associates, 1982.

SPIELBERGER, C. D., JACOBS, G. A., RUSSELL, S., & CRANE, R. S. Assessment of anger: The State-Trait Anger Scale. In J. N. Butcher & C. D. Spielberger (Eds.), *Advances in personality assessment*, Vol. 2. Hillsdale, N.J.: Lawrence Erlbaum Associates, 1982.

SPIELBERGER, C. D., PIACENTE, B. S., & HOBFOLL, S. E. Program evaluation in community psychology. *American Journal of Community Psychology*, 1976, 4, 393–404.

SPIELBERGER, C. D., VAGG, P. R., BARKER, L. R., DONHAM, G. W., & WESTBERRY, L. G. Factor structure of the State-Trait Anxiety Inventory. In I. G. Sarason & C. D. Spielberger (Eds.), *Stress and anxiety*, Vol. 7. New York: Hemisphere, 1980.

SPIERS, P. A. Have they come to praise Luria or to bury him? The Luria-Nebraska Battery controversy. *Journal of Consulting and Clinical Psychology*, 1981, 49, 331–341.

SPITZER, R. L., & ENDICOTT, T. Research diagnostic criteria: Rationale and reliability. *Archives of General Psychiatry*, 1978, 35, 773–782.

SPIVACK, G., PLATT, J. J., & SHURE, M. B. *The problem solving approach to adjustment*. San Francisco: Jossey-Bass, 1976.

SPIVACK, G., & SHURE, M. *Social adjustment of young children: A cognitive approach to solving real life problems*. San Francisco: Jossey-Bass, 1974.

SPRINGER, S. P., & DEUTSCH, P. *Left brain, right brain*. San Francisco: W. H. Freeman & Company Publishers, 1981.

SROLE, L., & FISCHER, A. K. (Eds.). *Mental health in the metropolis: The Midtown Manhattan study* (Revised and enlarged edition). New York: New York University Press, 1978.

SROLE, L., LANGER, T. S., MICHAEL, S. T., OPLER, M. K., & RENNIE, T. A. *Mental health in the metropolis* (Vol. 1). New York: McGraw-Hill, 1962.

STEELE, B. F. Experience with an interdisciplinary concept. In R. E. Helfer & C. H. Kempe (Eds.), *Child abuse and neglect*. Cambridge, Mass.: Ballinger, 1976.

STERNBACH, R. A. *Pain patients: Traits and treatment*. New York: Academic Press, 1974.

STERNBACH, R. A., & TIMMERMANS, G. Personality changes associated with reduction of pain. *Pain*, 1975, 1, 177–181.

STOKES, J., CHILDS, L., & FUEHRER, A. Gender and sex roles as predictors of self-disclosure. *Journal of Counseling Psychology*, 1981, 28, 510–514.

STONE, G. C., COHEN, F., & ADLER, N. E. *Health psychology—A handbook: Theories, applications, and challenges of a psychological approach to the health care system*. San Francisco: Jossey-Bass, 1979.

STRUENING, E. L., & GUTTENTAG, M. (Eds.). *Handbook of evaluation research* (Vol. 1). Beverly Hills, Calif.: Sage Publications, Inc., 1975.

STRUPP, H. H. Psychotherapy, research and practice: An overview. In S. Garfield & A. Bergin (Eds.), *Handbook of psychotherapy and behavior change* (2nd ed.). New York: John Wiley, 1978.

Strupp, H. H., & Hadley, S. W. A tripartite model of mental health and therapeutic outcomes: With special reference to negative effects of psychotherapy. *American Psychologist*, 1977, *32*, 187–196.

Strupp, H. H., Hadley, S. W., & Gomes-Schwartz, B. *Psychotherapy for better or worse: The problem of negative effects*. New York: Jason Aronson, 1977.

Stuart, R. B. Behavioral control of overeating. *Behavior Research and Therapy*, 1967, *5*, 357–365.

Stuart, R. B. Operant interpersonal treatment of marital discord. In C. J. Sager & H. S. Kaplan (Eds.), *Progress in group and family therapy*. New York: Brunner/Mazel, 1972.

Sundberg, N. D. The acceptability of "fake" versus "bona fide" personality test interpretations. *Journal of Abnormal and Social Psychology*, 1955, *50*, 145–147.

Sundberg, N. D. Toward systematic learning in natural settings. In W. Sheppard (Ed.), *Proceedings of the conference on instructional innovations in undergraduate education*. Eugene: University of Oregon, 1969.

Sundberg, N. D. *Assessment of persons*. Englewood Cliffs, N.J.: Prentice-Hall, 1977.

Sundberg, N. D. Cross-cultural counseling and psychotherapy: A research overview. In A. J. Marsella & P. B. Pedersen (Eds.), *Cross-cultural counseling and psychotherapy*. New York: Pergamon Press, 1981.

Sundberg, N. D., & Gonzales, L. R. Cross-cultural and cross-ethnic assessment: Overview and issues. In P. McReynolds (Ed.), *Advances in psychological assessment* (Vol. 5). San Francisco: Jossey-Bass, 1981.

Sundberg, N. D., Snowden, L. R., & Reynolds, W. M. Toward assessment of personal competence and competence in life situations. *Annual Review of Psychology*, 1978, *29*, 179–222.

Sundberg, N. D., & Thurber, C. E. World trends and future propects for the development of human resources. *International Journal of Intercultural Relations*, 1980, *4*, 245–274.

Sundberg, N. D., & Tyler, L. E. *Clinical psychology: An introduction to research and practice*. New York: Appleton-Century-Crofts, 1962.

Sundberg, N. D., Tyler, L. E., & Taplin, J. R. *Clinical psychology: Expanding horizons*. Englewood Cliffs, N.J.: Prentice-Hall, 1973.

Svanum, S., & Dallas, C. L. Alcoholic MMPI types and their relationship to patient characteristics, polydrug abuse, and abstinence following. *Journal of Personality Assessment*, 1981, *45*, 278–287.

Swenson, C. H. Empirical evaluations of human figure drawings. *Psychological Bulletin*, 1968, *70*, 20–44.

Swenson, C. H. The process of psychological consultation, a symposium. *Professional Psychology*, 1974, *5*, 287–306.

Szucko, J. J., & Kleinmuntz, B. Statistical *vs* clinical lie detection. *American Psychologist*, 1981, *36*, 488–496.

Tallent, N. *Psychological report writing* (2nd ed.). Englewood Cliffs, N.J.: Prentice-Hall, 1983.

Taplin, J. R. Implications of general systems theory for assessment and intervention. *Professional Psychology*, 1980, *11*, 722–727

Tart, C. T. (Ed.). *Transpersonal psychologies*. New York: Harper & Row, 1975.

Tasto, D. L., Hickson, R., & Rubin, S. E. Scaled profile analysis of Fear Survey Schedule factors. *Behavior Therapy*, 1971, *2*, 543–549.

Thomas, A. Current trends in developmental theory. *American Journal of Orthopsychiatry*, 1981, *51*, 580–609.

Thompson, C. *Psychoanalysis: Evolution and development*. New York: Evergreen, 1957. (Originally published, 1950.)

THORESEN, C. E., & ANTON, J. L. Intensive experimental research in counseling. *Journal of Counseling Psychology*, 1974, *21*, 553–559.

THORESEN, C. E., & COATES, T. J. What does it mean to be a behavior therapist? *Counseling Psychologist*, 1978, *7*, 3–20.

TOFFLER, A. *Future shock*. New York: Bantam, 1970.

TOFFLER, A. *The third wave*. New York: Morrow, 1980.

TORREY, E. F. *The mind game: Witchdoctors and psychiatrists*. New York: Emerson Hall, 1972.

TOWNES, B. D., TRUPIN, E. W., MARTIN, D. C., & GOLDSTEIN, D. Neuropsychological correlates of academic success among elementary school children. *Journal of Consulting and Clinical Psychology*, 1980, *48*, 675–684.

TRIANDIS, H. C., & DRAGUNS, J. G. (Eds.). *Handbook of cross-cultural psychology* (Vol. 6). *Psychopathology*. Boston: Allyn & Bacon, 1980.

TRUAX, C. B., & CARKHUFF, R. R. The experimental manipulation of therapeutic conditions. *Journal of Consulting Psychology*, 1965, *29*, 119–124.

TRUAX, C. B., & MITCHELL, K. M. Research on certain therapist interpersonal skills in relation to process and outcome. In A. E. Bergin & S. L. Garfield (Eds.), *Handbook of psychotherapy and behavior change: An empirical analysis*. New York: John Wiley, 1971.

TYLER, L. E. *The work of the counselor* (3rd ed.). Englewood Cliffs, N.J.: Prentice-Hall, 1969.

TYLER, L. E. *Individuality: Human possibilities and personal choice in the psychological development of men and women*. San Francisco: Jossey-Bass, 1978.

TYLER, L. E., SUNDBERG, N. D., ROHILA, P. K., & GREENE, M. M. Patterns of choices in Dutch, American, and Indian adolescents. *Journal of Counseling Psychology*, 1968, *15*, 522–529.

ULLMANN, L. P., & KRASNER, L. *A psychological approach to abnormal behavior* (2nd ed.). Englewood Cliffs, N.J.: Prentice-Hall, 1975.

U.S. DEPARTMENT OF HEALTH AND HUMAN SERVICES. *The health consequences of smoking. Cancer: A report of the surgeon general* (DHHS No. 82–50179). Washington, D.C.: U.S. Government Printing Office, 1982.

VAILLANT, G. E. *Adaptation to life*. Boston: Little, Brown, 1977.

VERNON, P. E. The validation of civil service selection board procedures. *Occupational Psychology*, 1950, *24*, 75–95.

WADE, T. C., & BAKER, T. B. Opinions and the use of psychological tests. *American Psychologist*, 1977, *32*, 874–882.

WADE, T. C., BAKER, T. B., MORTON, T. L., & BAKER, L. J. The status of psychological testing in clinical psychology: Relationships between test use and professional activities and orientations. *Journal of Personality Assessment*, 1978, *42*, 1–10.

WALKER, C. E. (Ed.). *Clinical practice of psychology: A guide for mental health professionals*. New York: Pergamon Press, 1981.

WALLACE, R. K., & BENSON, H. The physiology of meditation. *Scientific American*, 1972, *226*(2), 84–91.

WALSH, K. W. *Neuropsychology: A clinical approach*. Edinburgh: Churchill Livingston, 1978.

WALSH, R. N. Meditation. In R. J. Corsini (Ed.), *Handbook of innovative psychotherapies*. New York: John Wiley, 1981.

WALSH, R. N., & VAUGHAN, F. (Eds.). *Beyond ego: Transpersonal dimensions in psychology*. Los Angeles: Tarcher, 1980.

WAMPOLD, B. E., CASAS, J. M., & ATKINSON, D. R. Ethnic bias in counseling: An information processing approach. *Journal of Counseling Psychology*, 1981, *28*, 498–503.

WATSON, J. B., & RAYNOR, R. Conditional emotional reactions. *Journal of Experimental Psychology*, 1920, *3*, 1–14.

WATSON, N., CADDY, G. R., JOHNSON, J. H., & RIMM, D. C. Standards in the education of professional psychologists. *American Psychologist*, 1981, *36*, 514–519.

WEARY, G., & MIRELS, H. L. *Integrations of clinical and social psychology.* New York: Oxford University Press, 1982.

WEBB, E. J., CAMPBELL, D. T., SCHWARTZ, R. D., SECHREST, L., & GROVE, J. B. *Nonreactive measures in the social sciences* (2nd ed.). Boston: Houghton Mifflin, 1981.

WEED, L. L. Medical records that guide and teach. *New England Journal of Medicine*, 1968, *278*, 593–600, 652–657.

WEED, L. L. *Medical records, medical education and patient care.* Cleveland: Case Western Reserve University Press, 1969.

WEEKS, E. C., & DRENGACZ, S. The noneconomic impact of community economic shock. *Journal of Health and Human Resource Administration*, 1982, *4*, 303–318.

WEISS, J. A., & WEISS, C. H. Social scientists and decision makers look at the usefulness of mental health research. *American Psychologist*, 1981, *36*, 837–847.

WEISS, R. L., & JACOBSON, N. S. Behavioral marital therapy as brief therapy. In S. H. Budman (Ed.), *Forms of brief therapy.* New York: Guilford Press, 1981.

WEISS, R. L., & MARGOLIN, G. Assessment of marital conflict and accord. In A. R. Ciminero, K. S. Calhoun, & H. E. Adams (Eds.), *Handbook of behavioral assessment.* New York: John Wiley, 1977.

WEISSBERG, R. P., GESTEN, E. L., RAPKIN, B. D., COWEN, E. L., DAVIDSON, E., FLORES DE APODACA, R., & McKIM, B. J. The evaluation of a social-problem-solving training program for suburban and inner city third grade children. *Journal of Consulting and Clinical Psychology*, 1981, *49*, 251–261.

WEITZ, W. A. Experiencing the role of a hospitalized psychiatric patient: A professional's view from the other side. *Professional Psychology*, 1972, *3*, 151–154.

WENDER, P. H., & KLEIN, D. F. *Mind, mood and medicine: A guide to the new biopsychiatry.* New York: Farrar, Straus & Giroux, 1981.

WENDER, P., ROSENTHAL, D., RAINER, J., GREENHILL, L., & SARLIN, M. Schizophrenics' adopting parents: Psychiatric status. *Archives of General Psychiatry*, 1977, *34*, 777–784.

WEXLER, D. B. Token and taboo: Behavior modification, token economies and the law. *California Law Review*, 1973, *61*, 81–109. (Summarized in *Mental Health Digest*, 1973, *5*, 27–34.)

WHITMER, G. E. From hospitals to jails: The fate of California's deinstitutionalized mentally ill. *American Journal of Orthopsychiatry*, 1980, *50*, 65–75.

WICKER, A. W. Nature and assessment of behavior settings: Recent contributions from the ecological perspective. In P. McReynolds (Ed.), *Advances in psychological assessment* (Vol. 5). San Francisco: Jossey-Bass, 1981.

WIDIGER, T. A. Psychological tests and the borderline diagnosis. *Journal of personality Assessment*, 1982, *46*, 227–238.

WIENER-LEVY, D., & EXNER, J. E. The Rorschach comprehensive system: An overview. In P. McReynolds (Ed.), *Advances in psychological assessment* (Vol. 5). San Francisco: Jossey-Bass, 1981.

WIENS, A. N. The assessment interview. In I. B. Weiner (Ed.), *Clinical methods in psychology.* New York: John Wiley, 1976.

WIESENFELD, A. R., & WEIS, M. M. Hairdressers and helping: Influencing the behavior of informal caregivers. *Professional Psychology*, 1979, *10*, 786–792.

WIGGINS, J. S. *Personality and prediction: Principles of personality assessment.* Reading, Mass.: Addison-Wesley, 1973.

WIGGINS, J. S. Clinical and statistical prediction: Where are we and where do we go from here? *Clinical Psychology Review*, 1981, *1*, 3–18.

WILLIAMS, T. A., & JOHNSON, J. H. (Eds.). *Mental health in the 21st century*. Lexington, Mass.: Lexington Books, 1979.

WILLS, T. A. Perceptions of clients by professional helpers. *Psychological Bulletin*, 1978, *85*, 968–1000.

WILLIS, D. (Ed.). Parent education and training. *Journal of Clinical Child Psychology*, 1981, *10*, 93–116.

WILSON, E. O. *On human nature*. Cambridge, Mass.: Harvard University Press, 1978.

WIRT, R. D., & LACHAR, D. The Personality Inventory for Children: Development and clinical applications. In P. McReynolds (Ed.), *Advances in psychological assessment* (Vol. 5). San Francisco: Jossey-Bass, 1981.

WITKIN, H., MEDNICK, S., SCHULSINGER, F., BAKKESTROM, E., CHRISTIANSEN, K., GOODENOUGH, D., HIRSCHHORN, K., LUNDSTEEN, C., OWEN, D., PHILIP, J., RUBIN, D., & STOCKING, M. Criminality in XYY and XXY men. *Science*, 1976, *193*, 547–555.

WITKIN, H. A., & GOODENOUGH, D. R. *Cognitive styles: Essence and origins*. New York: International Universities Press, 1981.

WOLFE, L. The question of surrogates in sex therapy. In J. LoPiccolo & L. LoPiccolo (Eds.), *Handbook of sex therapy*. New York: Plenum, 1978.

WOLMAN, B. B. (Ed.). *Clinical diagnosis of mental disorders: A handbook*. New York: Plenum, 1978.

WOLMAN, B. B., & STRICKER, G. (Eds.). *Handbook of developmental psychology*. Englewood Cliffs, N.J.: Prentice-Hall, 1982.

WOLPE, J. *Psychotherapy by reciprocal inhibition*. Stanford, Calif.: Stanford University Press, 1958.

WOLPE, J. *The practice of behavior therapy*. New York: Pergamon Press, 1969.

WOLPE, J., & LANG, P. J. A fear survey schedule for use in behavior therapy. *Behavior Research and Therapy*, 1964, *2*, 17–34.

WOLPE, J., & LANG, P. J. *Fear Survey Schedule*. San Diego, Calif.: Educational and Industrial Testing Service, 1969.

WOODY, R. H. (Ed.). *Encyclopedia of clinical assessment* (Vols. 1 & 2). San Francisco: Jossey-Bass, 1980.

YALOM, I. D. *The theory and practice of group psychotherapy*. New York: Basic Books, 1970.

YALOM, I. D. *The theory and practice of group psychotherapy* (2nd ed.). New York: Basic Books, 1975.

YARMEY, A. D. *The psychology of eyewitness testimony*. New York: Free Press, 1979.

YATES, A. J. *Behavior therapy*. New York: John Wiley, 1970.

YOUNG, J. Z. *Programs of the brain*. Oxford: Oxford University Press, 1978.

ZAX, M., & SPECTER, G. A. *An introduction to community psychology*. New York: John Wiley, 1974.

ZIGLER, E. A plea to end the use of the patterning treatment for retarded children. *American Journal of Orthopsychiatry*, 1981, *51*, 388–390.

Name Index

Subject Index